LEGAL TECH AND THE FUTURE OF CIVIL JUSTICE

New digital technologies, from AI-fired "legal tech" tools to virtual proceedings, are transforming the legal system. But much of the debate surrounding legal tech has zoomed out to a nebulous future of "robo-judges" and "robo-lawyers." This volume is an antidote. Zeroing in on the near- to medium-term, it provides a concrete, empirically minded synthesis of the impact of new digital technologies on litigation and access to justice. How far and fast can legal tech advance given regulatory, organizational, and technological constraints? How will new technologies affect lawyers and litigants, and how should procedural rules adapt? How can technology expand – or curtail – access to justice? And how must judicial administration change to promote healthy technological development and open courthouse doors for all? By engaging these essential questions, this volume helps to map the opportunities and the perils of a rapidly digitizing legal system – and provides grounded advice for a sensible path forward. This book is available as Open Access on Cambridge Core.

DAVID FREEMAN ENGSTROM is the LSVF Professor in Law and Co-Director of the Deborah L. Rhode Center on the Legal Profession at Stanford University. An award-winning scholar, longtime litigator, and nationally recognized expert on law and technology, Engstrom is an elected member of the American Law Institute, an appointed member of the Administrative Conference of the United States, and a faculty affiliate at the Stanford Institute for Human-Centered Artificial Intelligence.

Legal Tech and the Future of Civil Justice

Edited by

DAVID FREEMAN ENGSTROM
Stanford University

CAMBRIDGE
UNIVERSITY PRESS

CAMBRIDGE
UNIVERSITY PRESS

Shaftesbury Road, Cambridge CB2 8EA, United Kingdom

One Liberty Plaza, 20th Floor, New York, NY 10006, USA

477 Williamstown Road, Port Melbourne, VIC 3207, Australia

314–321, 3rd Floor, Plot 3, Splendor Forum, Jasola District Centre, New Delhi – 110025, India

103 Penang Road, #05–06/07, Visioncrest Commercial, Singapore 238467

Cambridge University Press is part of Cambridge University Press & Assessment, a department of the University of Cambridge.

We share the University's mission to contribute to society through the pursuit of education, learning and research at the highest international levels of excellence.

www.cambridge.org
Information on this title: www.cambridge.org/9781009255356

DOI: 10.1017/9781009255301

When citing this work, please include a reference to the DOI 10.1017/9781009255301

First published 2023

A catalogue record for this publication is available from the British Library

Library of Congress Cataloging-in-Publication Data
NAMES: Engstrom, David Freeman, editor.
TITLE: Legal tech and the future of civil justice / edited by David Freeman Engstrom, Stanford University, California.
DESCRIPTION: Cambridge, United Kingdom ; New York, NY : Cambridge University Press, 2023. | "The AAJ Robert L. Habush Endowment, Stanford Law School, and the Stanford Institute for Human-Centered Artificial Intelligence generously provided support for this book project"–ECIP acknowledgements. | Includes bibliographical references and index
IDENTIFIERS: LCCN 2022031201 (print) | LCCN 2022031202 (ebook) | ISBN 9781009255356 (hardback) | ISBN 9781009255349 (paperback) | ISBN 9781009255301 (epub)
SUBJECTS: LCSH: Internet in legal services–United States. | Justice, Administration of–Technological innovations–United States. | Lawyers–Effect of technological innovations on–United States. | Judges–Effect of technological innovations on–United States.
CLASSIFICATION: LCC KF320.I57 L43 2023 (print) | LCC KF320.I57 (ebook) | DDC 340.0285–dc23/eng/20221101
LC record available at https://lccn.loc.gov/2022031201
LC ebook record available at https://lccn.loc.gov/2022031202

ISBN 978-1-009-25535-6 Hardback

Contents

Figures

Tables

Contributors

Charlotte S. Alexander is the Connie D. and Ken McDaniel WomenLead Professor of Law and Analytics at Georgia State University (GSU) and the founding director of GSU's Legal Analytics Lab. She uses computational methods to study legal text, with a particular focus on understanding how courts process and resolve employment disputes and other types of civil lawsuits. She is the author of *Does Lawyering Matter? Predicting Judicial Decisions from Legal Briefs, and What That Means for Access to Justice*, 101 TEXAS L. REV. (2022) (with Elizabeth Tippett, Karl Branting, et al.).

John Armour is Professor of Law and Finance in the Faculty of Law at the University of Oxford and a Fellow of the British Academy and the European Corporate Governance Institute. He recently led a large research project funded by UK Research and Innovation, Unlocking the Potential of AI for English Law. Outputs from this include *Augmented Lawyering*, 2022 U. ILL. L. REV. 71 (with Richard Parnham & Mari Sako).

Benjamin H. Barton is the Helen and Charles Lockett Distinguished Professor of Law at the University of Tennessee and is the author of five books, including REBOOTING JUSTICE AND GLASS HALF FULL: THE DECLINE AND REBIRTH OF THE LEGAL PROFESSION. Barton is an expert in access to justice and Supreme Court Justice backgrounds.

Renee L. Danser is the Associate Director of Research & Strategic Partnerships at the Access to Justice Lab at Harvard Law School. Her work focuses on improving access to justice from within the justice system and draws on experience in advocacy and court management.

Jens Frankenreiter is Associate Professor of Law at Washington University in St. Louis School of Law. His research draws on methods from economics, statistics, and data science to better understand contracting, private and public lawmaking, and legal institutions. A focus of his work is the use of large amounts of texts and other big data. His recent publications include *Computational Methods in Legal Analysis*, 16 ANN. REV. L. SOC. SCI. 39 (2020) (with Michael Livermore).

David Freeman Engstrom is the LSVF Professor in Law at Stanford Law School and Co-Director of the Deborah L. Rhode Center on the Legal Profession. An award-winning scholar and expert on the design of litigation systems, he is the author of numerous articles on technology and law, including *Legal Tech, Civil Procedure, and the Future of Adversarialism*, 169 U. PA. L. REV. 1001 (2021) (with Jonah Gelbach).

Nora Freeman Engstrom is the Ernest W. McFarland Professor of Law at Stanford Law School and Co-Director of the Deborah L. Rhode Center on the Legal Profession. She is the author of leading casebooks on torts and legal ethics as well as numerous articles on complex litigation, including the award-winning *The Lessons of Lone Pine*, 129 YALE L.J. 2 (2019).

Jonah B. Gelbach is Professor of Law at Berkeley Law. His scholarship includes empirical work in multiple areas of civil procedure as well as other areas such as securities litigation and labor economics. He has written several papers using data from federal court dockets, including *Material Facts in the Debate over* Twombly *and* Iqbal, 68 STAN. L. REV. 369 (2016).

Amy Gonzales is Associate Professor in the Department of Communication at the University of California, Santa Barbara. Her work examines the digital divide, particularly short-term disruption in access to devices.

D. James Greiner is the Honorable S. William Green Professor of Public Law and the Faculty Director of the Access to Justice Lab at Harvard Law School. His work, which focuses on randomized control trials in the legal setting, has appeared in statistical, economic, political science, law, and generalist journals. He is the author of *Overcoming Obstacles to Experiments in Legal Practice*, 367 SCIENCE 1078 (2020) (with Holly Fernandez-Lynch & I. Glenn Cohen).

Neel Guha is a JD candidate at Stanford Law School, a PhD candidate in the Stanford Computer Science Department, and a Graduate Student Fellow at the Stanford Regulation, Evaluation, and Governance Lab. He works on problems at the intersection of machine learning and law, and recently authored *Vulnerabilities in* Discovery *Tech*, 35 HARV. J. L. & TECH. (forthcoming 2022) (with Peter Henderson & Diego A. Zambrano).

Elizabeth Guo is a graduate student at Oxford University, where she is studying as a Rhodes Scholar. Before that, she graduated from Harvard University with a B.A. in Physics and was a researcher at Harvard Law School's Access to Justice Lab.

Margaret Hagan is the Executive Director of the Legal Design Lab at Stanford Law School. She is the author of many articles on innovation for access to justice, including *Redesigning Justice Innovation: A Standardized Methodology*, 16 STAN. J. CIV. RTS. & CIV. LIBERTIES 335 (2020) (with Daniel Bernal).

Peter Henderson is a JD candidate at Stanford Law School, PhD Candidate (Computer Science, Machine Learning) at Stanford University, OpenPhilanthropy AI Fellow, and Graduate Student Fellow at the Stanford Regulation, Evaluation, and Governance Lab. He has authored numerous articles on machine learning and law, including *Vulnerabilities in Discovery Tech*, 35 HARV. J. L. & TECH. (forthcoming 2022) (with Neel Guha & Diego A. Zambrano).

Kurt Hugenberg is Professor in the Department of Psychological and Brain Sciences, Indiana University Bloomington. His scholarship focuses on how perceivers' stereotypes, prejudices, and prejudice-related motives influence how we categorize, perceive, and understand others.

Ryan Hutchings is a Postdoctoral Scholar in the Department of Psychological and Brain Sciences, Indiana University Bloomington. His research focuses primarily on person perception, prejudice, and social cognition.

Erik Koltun is a paralegal at Paul, Weiss, Rifkind, Wharton & Garrison LLP. Before that, he graduated from Claremont McKenna College with a B.A. in Economics and Literature and was a researcher at Harvard Law School's Access to Justice Lab.

Bridget Mary McCormack is the Chief Justice of the Michigan Supreme Court and the Co-Chair of the Conference of Chief Justices' COVID-19 Rapid Response Team and the Conference's Technology Planning Group. She writes and presents frequently about access to justice, legal innovation, and change management in state courts, including *Staying off the Sidelines: Judges as Agents for Justice System Reform*, 131 YALE L.J. FORUM 175 (2021).

Julian Nyarko is Associate Professor at Stanford School of Law. His research uses new computational methods to answer questions of legal and social scientific importance, with a particular focus on the use of computational linguistics to study contract law and design. Among his recent publications is *A Statistical Test for Legal Interpretation: Theory and Applications*, 38 J. L. ECON. & ORG. 539 (forthcoming 2022) (with Sarath Sanga).

Amy O'Hara is Research Professor in the Massive Data Institute at Georgetown University's McCourt School of Public Policy. She has published guides and articles on data governance, privacy preserving technologies, and data infrastructure needed to support government and academic research.

J.J. Prescott is the Henry King Ransom Professor of Law at the University of Michigan Law School. He co-directs Michigan's Law and Economics Program and its Empirical Legal Studies Center and has appointments in Michigan's Economics Department and ISR's Population Studies Center. Professor Prescott studies, among other topics, the role of technology in improving access to justice and court performance, often with empirical tools. In 2014, Prescott founded the company that developed and launched Matterhorn, one of the premier Online Dispute Resolution platforms in the country.

Victor D. Quintanilla is Professor of Law & Van Nolan Faculty Fellow at Indiana University Maurer School of Law and Co-Director of the Center for Law, Society & Culture and an Affiliated Professor of the Department of Psychological and Brain Sciences. His research on civil justice and access to justice appears in leading law reviews and peer-reviewed journals, and he received funding from the American Bar Foundation. His work includes *Doing Unrepresented Status: The Social Construction and Production of Pro Se Persons*, 69 DEPAUL L. REV. 544 (2020).

Tanina Rostain is Professor at the Georgetown University Law Center. Her writing and teaching focus on the potential and limitations of technologies to improve access to civil justice.

Mari Sako is Professor of Management Studies at Saïd Business School and Professorial Fellow at New College, University of Oxford. Her teaching and research focus on global strategy, professional services, and start-up ecosystems. She is the author of five books and numerous articles, including *AI-Enabled Business Models in Legal Services: From Traditional Law Firms to Next-Generation Law Companies?* 7 J. PROFESSIONS & ORG. 27 (2020) (with John Armour).

Norman W. Spaulding is Sweitzer Professor of Law at Stanford Law School. His scholarship examines the history and ethics of the adversary system, procedural justice, and the effects of artificial intelligence and other technologies on the administration of justice. Recent work includes *Is Human Judgement Necessary? Artificial Intelligence, Algorithmic Governance, and the Law*, in Markus D. Dubber et al., THE OXFORD HANDBOOK OF ETHICS AND AI (2020).

Todd Venook is the inaugural Civil Justice and Technology Fellow at the Deborah L. Rhode Center on the Legal Profession at Stanford Law School. He most recently served as a law clerk in the chambers of the Honorable Myron H. Thompson in the Middle District of Alabama.

Nedim Yel is the Senior Research Statistician at Data Analysis and Statistical Solutions. Dr. Yel's research focuses on improving hierarchical linear/multilevel models specifically, dealing with sample size issues and their effect on parameter estimates at different levels in 3-level models.

Albert H. Yoon holds the Michael J. Trebilcock Chair in Law and Economics at the University of Toronto Faculty of Law. Yoon examines how technology and ethics influence labor markets within and outside of law. He has written numerous articles, including *Unintended Consequences: The Regressive Effects of Increased Access to Courts*, 14 J. EMP. LEG. STUD. 5 (2017) (with Anthony Niblett). Yoon is also a co-founder of Blue J. Legal, a Toronto-based legal technology start-up.

Diego A. Zambrano is Associate Professor of Law at Stanford Law School. He is the author of numerous articles on discovery and civil procedure, including *Vulnerabilities in Discovery Tech*, 35 HARV. J. L. & TECH. (forthcoming 2022) (with Neel Guha & Peter Henderson).

Acknowledgments

The AAJ Robert L. Habush Endowment, Stanford Law School, and the Stanford Institute for Human-Centered Artificial Intelligence generously provided support for this book project.

Introduction

Civil Justice at the Crossroads

David Freeman Engstrom

The COVID-19 pandemic has powerfully disrupted the American legal system. Yet, as with so many other aspects of life, the pandemic was most powerful as an *accelerant* of trends already in motion. And nowhere has this been more evident in law than in the civil justice system's uptake of new legal technologies. With "legal tech" tools of all shapes and sizes gaining traction, the system, long a bastion of stasis and tradition, has begun a profound transformation.

A few examples capture the quickening pace of technological change. Start with online proceedings. Mostly a trickle pre-pandemic, the online migration of court proceedings is now a flood, to the tune of *millions* of hours each month. Judges, court administrators, lawyers, and litigants have paid switching costs in full, meaning much of the "Zooming" of litigation is likely to stick.[1] Meanwhile, after years of futurist proclamations, online dispute resolution (ODR) platforms – not live legal proceedings, but online spaces where disputants can gather, often asynchronously, and bargain their way to settlement – have now reached critical mass following a spate of COVID-era adoptions.[2] Once solely the province of e-commerce platforms like eBay, ODR is now implemented or piloted in some 200 state and local court jurisdictions, with more adoptions in the works.[3]

1 Scott Dodson, Hon. Lee H. Rosenthal & Christopher L. Dodson, *The Zooming of Federal Civil Litigation*, 104 JUDICATURE 13 (2020).

2 For an accounting of ODR's advance, see David Freeman Engstrom & R. J. Vogt, *The New Judicial Governance: Courts, Data, and the Future of Civil Justice*, 72 DEPAUL L. REV. (forthcoming 2023). For a graphical status update as of 2020, *see* ABA CTR. for Innovation, ONLINE DISPUTE RESOLUTION IN THE UNITED STATES: DATA VISUALIZATIONS (2020), https://www.americanbar.org/content/dam/aba/administrative/center-for-innovation/odrvisualizationreport.pdf.

3 On ODR's private sector origins, see ETHAN KATSH & ORNA RABINOVICH-EINY, DIGITAL JUSTICE: TECHNOLOGY AND THE INTERNET OF DISPUTES (2017).

New technologies are also transforming how lawyers do their day-to-day work.[4] Forced out of their offices and outside their comfort zones, lawyers have expanded their embrace of a growing menu of legal tech tools. Natural language processing (NLP), the branch of machine learning that performs text analytics and so holds the most promise in a legal system that trades in words, is advancing rapidly. Its maturation is poised to usher in a new era – with the automation of more advanced legal cognitions that supplement and even supplant lawyers' work. Going forward, lawyers will increasingly rely on AI-fired tools to perform core lawyerly tasks: reviewing documents and making privilege calls, performing legal research, choosing among arguments to lay before *this* judge, predicting case outcomes (and forecasting the cost of getting there), and even generating pleadings and papers.

Finally, the pandemic deepened what was already a growing recognition that American courts at all levels, but particularly its lower precincts, are in the grips of an access-to-justice crisis.[5] Sitting well out of view of the big-ticket, headline-grabbing litigations is a grim and less visible reality: In roughly three-quarters of civil cases filed in state courts, at least one side lacks a lawyer.[6] That means *millions* of individuals embroiled in debt-collection, eviction, and family violence and dissolution matters who cannot find lawyers and so must go it alone, often against lawyered-up adversaries. And these are only the visible litigants we can see – the tip of a very large iceberg. Below them lie *tens of millions* more who are locked out of justice entirely and choose to "lump it," or aren't aware they have a legal problem, or a legal remedy to that problem, in the first place. A growing set of states is surveying this sorry landscape and actively considering deregulating the legal services industry and relaxing the lawyers' professional monopoly in order to welcome new providers, including the software sort, into the system.[7] Online legal help, Q/A (question-answer) systems that answer legal questions in response to plain-language queries and document assembly tools that help self-represented litigants construct and file legal documents can ease pervasive access concerns – and are a final and promising legal tech frontier.

[4] For a broad overview of the legal tech industry and the academic literature that has begun to grow up around it, *see generally* David Freeman Engstrom & Jonah B. Gelbach, *Legal Tech, Civil Procedure, and the Future of Adversarialism*, 169 U. PA. L. REV. 1001 (2021).

[5] For a small slice of the rapid growth of concern around access to justice issues, see generally AM. ACAD. OF ARTS & SCIS., CIVIL JUSTICE FOR ALL: MAKING JUSTICE ACCESSIBLE: DESIGNING LEGAL SERVICES FOR THE 21ST CENTURY (2020), https://www.ncsc.org/__data/assets/pdf_file/0020/13376/civiljusticereport-2015.pdf; Access to Justice, *Daedalus* (Winter 2019).

[6] *See* PAULA HANNAFORD-AGOR, SCOTT GRAVES & SHELLEY SPACEK MILLER, NAT'L CTR. FOR STATE CTS.: THE LANDSCAPE OF CIVIL LITIGATION IN STATE COURTS iv, vi, 32 (2015), https://www.ncsc.org/__data/assets/pdf_file/0020/13376/civiljusticereport-2015.pdf; LEGAL SERVS. CORP., THE JUSTICE GAP. MEASURING THE CIVIL LEGAL NEEDS OF LOW-INCOME AMERICANS (2017), https://www.lsc.gov/sites/default/files/images/TheJusticeGap-FullReport.pdf .

[7] *See* Engstrom & Vogt, *The New Judicial Governance*.

Each of these pandemic-fueled tech trends will transform the civil justice system in the coming years. Debate about each is urgently needed. But to this point, much of the debate has tended toward gauzy and futurist meditations about a legal system populated by "robo-judges" and "robo-lawyers,"[8] or even an eventual state of "legal singularity," when machines perfectly predict the outcome of every case before it is filed.[9]

This volume is an antidote. It seeks to enrich – and, in places, reorient – budding debate about legal tech's implications for the civil justice system by zeroing in on the near- to medium-term, not out at a distant, hazy horizon. It does so by offering a grounded, concrete, empirically minded discussion of the *current* state of legal tech and what, *actually*, lies ahead.

Four broad questions structure the chapters that follow, as roughly allocated to four Parts. First, what are the current capacities of legal tech and where can it plausibly go over the near- to medium-term given a gauntlet of regulatory, organizational, and technological constraints? Second, what effect will legal tech's continued advance – from remote proceedings and e-discovery to legal analytics and case-outcome prediction engines – have on core features of our civil litigation system, and how might the procedural rules that structure the system adapt? Third, how can new digital technologies expand, rather than contract, access to justice for low- and moderate-income individuals who often cannot retain counsel or lack the resources or know-how to engage formal legal institutions? Fourth and finally, what aspects of judicial administration – particularly data infrastructure and accessibility – need to change in order to promote fair and responsible development of legal technologies and open the doors of justice wider for all?

Each of these questions is an essential line of inquiry if we are to seize the opportunities, and avoid the perils, of a fast-digitizing civil justice system. This volume aims to advance our understanding and lay a further research agenda as to each one.

I.1 LEGAL TECH AND THE INNOVATION ECOSYSTEM

Rigorous realism about legal tech's trajectory over the near- to medium-term must be a core part of any clear-eyed analysis of the future of the civil justice system. Part I anchors the rest of the volume by describing the current landscape of legal tech and identifying the forces that will shape its evolution from here.

8 *See* Eugene Volokh, *Chief Justice Robots*, 68 Duke L.J. 1135, 1137–42 (2019); Milan Markovic, *Rise of the Robot Lawyers?* 61 Ariz. L. Rev. 325, 349–50 (2019).

9 *See* Benjamin Alarie, *The Path of the Law: Towards Legal Singularity*, 66 U. Toronto L.J. 443 (2016).

An initial task in any such effort is to survey, in understandable and accessible terms, the range of digital tools that have already begun to infuse law practice.[10] In recent decades, a growing legal-tech tool kit has steadily transformed how lawyers serve clients. An initial wave was not so different from business process optimization tools that swept into other workplaces: back-office accounting tools, document management tools, and web-based information retrieval tools like Westlaw and LexisNexis.

A second and more recent wave injected tech tools more directly into lawyers' professional workstreams. These tools focused in particular on high-volume, repetitive legal tasks formerly performed by lower-level workers – associates, contract attorneys, paralegals – within the legal services industry. E-discovery tools revolutionized the process of flagging documents for relevance and privilege that previously required manual, "eyes on" review by large work teams. But what began with keyword searches on digitized documents soon graduated to powerful machine-learning systems that, once trained on a small set of lawyer-labeled documents, can churn through millions more.[11] Another booming legal tech tool, with dozens of companies now vying for market share, identifies patterns and anomalies in large corpora of legal texts – for instance, searching thousands of contracts in order to identify where a proposed deal deviates from industry-standard provisions.[12]

A third wave, and the current state of the art, may soon eclipse these older tools through continuing advances in NLP. Potent new NLP models, such as Google's BERT or OpenAI's GPT-3, have made it possible to treat law itself as a form of data.[13] Pushing past the high-volume and repetitive tasks that were the focus of second-wave legal tech, this newest generation of legal-tech applies NLP to a wide variety of legal materials, from statutes and judicial decisions to briefs and case documents, to perform higher-order legal cognitions. The resulting applications vary. One annual effort to slice and dice the full legal tech landscape identifies a dozen different silos, from "Legal and Matter Management" to "Contract Due Diligence" and "Contract Drafting."[14] But the most promising and potentially transformative third-wave legal tech tools reduce to either of two core tasks: legal analytics and case-outcome prediction.

The most basic tools performing the first task are hunting-and-gathering tools that help lawyers corral legal materials, often accompanied by automated content

[10] *See* Engstrom & Gelbach, *Legal Tech*, at 1011–12; Engstrom & Vogt, *The New Judicial Governance*.

[11] *See* Engstrom & Gelbach, *Legal Tech*, at 1017–18; Dana A. Remus, *The Uncertain Promise of Predictive Coding*, 99 Iowa L. Rev. 1691, 1701–6 (2014).

[12] *See* Engstrom & Gelbach, *Legal Tech*, at 1017–18.

[13] *See* Michael A. Livermore & Daniel N. Rockmore, Law as Data (2018).

[14] *See* 2019 *Legal Tech Buyer's Guide*, *LawGeex* (Nov. 12, 2019), https://blog.lawgeex.com/2019-legal-tech-buyers-guide.

summaries or annotations of their relevance to the case at hand.[15] More advanced versions perform more targeted inquiries – a natural-language Q/A system for legal professionals that can return paragraphs of legal analysis at the touch of a button.[16] Still more sophisticated tools evaluate attorney work product *after* it is generated, allowing an attorney to input a draft brief and get back an analysis of questionable case law cited, apposite case law missed, or even an argument left on the table.[17] Most advanced of all, but still in development, are tools that create work product themselves, whether initial drafts of pleadings, discovery requests, or even briefs.

The second task – predicting case outcomes – is in many ways the essence of lawyering. As Justice Holmes long ago noted, law is, shorn of its pretensions, little more than a prediction as to how a court will rule.[18] Case-outcome prediction tools take various forms, but most operate by analyzing a defined set of legal and related materials – past cases, the identity of opposing counsel, the jurisdiction – and then returning a probability or set of probabilities over different outcomes, and perhaps an estimate of the time and effort needed to get there. Importantly, while outcome-prediction tools can *supplement* lawyers' work, bolstering their professional judgment with actuarial information about case prospects, they can also *supplant* lawyers. Third-wave legal tech thus holds the promise of easing access to justice concerns by arming those who cannot find or afford legal counsel with the most critical of legal information: how they would fare in court.

But just how far and how fast can these new tools go? A second vital task – and one that goes beyond merely cataloging a growing legal tech tool kit – is to map the innovation ecosystem and show how legal tech's growing capacities will shape, and be shaped by, an evolving legal services marketplace. A gauntlet of regulatory, organizational, cultural, and technological constraints will condition legal tech's continued development across different segments of the legal services landscape. Part I begins the more subtle and challenging task of reconciling these different constraints via a trio of chapter contributions by authors with leading expertise on each.

Professor Ben Barton of the University of Tennessee School of Law, a prominent expert on legal ethics and technology, maps the constraints imposed on legal tech by

15 Michael A. Livermore et al., *Law Search in the Age of the Algorithm*, 2020 Mich. St. L. Rev. 1183 (2020).

16 For a state-of-the-art analysis of Q/A systems, see Andrew Vold & Jack G. Conrad, *Using Transformers to Improve Answer Retrieval for Legal Questions*, 18 Proc. of Int'l Conf. on A.I. & L. 245 (2021).

17 Casetext offers a pair of currently marketed examples. One is Casetext's CARA system, which ingests a whole document and outputs relevant legal authorities. *See* Casetext, http://www.casetext.com/cara-ai/. The other is Casetext's Compose, which purports to draft legal arguments by recommending conceptually similar legal authorities that fit a case's fact pattern as inputted by a user. *See* Compose, https://compose.law.

18 Oliver Wendell Holmes, *The Path of the Law*, 10 Harv. L. Rev. 457, 458 (1897).

the tangle of rules in the United States that regulate the practice of law.[19] In "The Future of American Legal Tech: Regulation, Culture, Markets," Barton tackles a puzzle in America's market for legal technology. On one hand, our legal services industry is among the most tightly regulated in the world, suggesting infertile ground for a tech revolution. On the other is America's advanced and freewheeling market for legal tech, likely the most robust in the world. How to square the two? Barton shows how regulatory constraints – which are largely the result of an attorney discipline process overseen by state bars – is largely concentrated in the middle segment of the legal services market. It is in so-called PeopleLaw, the part of the legal services industry that serves individuals and small business, not corporate-facing BigLaw at its top or the legal aid and non-profit providers at its bottom, that regulatory constraints stymie innovation. What follows is a final and bracing insight: Given that the American legal system, for all its hidebound Burkeanism, is already the most dynamic in the world, current efforts to ease the access-to-justice crisis by loosening the rules that govern delivery of legal services, but with new modes of regulatory oversight designed to guard against consumer harm, might counter-intuitively generate more, not less, regulation than currently exists where access concerns are most acute.

Next, John Armour and Mari Sako, both from Oxford University and leading scholars of the organizational structure of the legal services industry, ask how legal technologies will proliferate in the two main "hemispheres" of legal services, BigLaw and PeopleLaw. In "Lawtech: Leveling the Playing Field in Legal Services?" they build on their past work and draw on comparative evidence from the United Kingdom to explain how the two hemispheres face very different innovation challenges.[20] For BigLaw, a principal barrier to innovation is human capital: how to attract needed talent with career-advancement opportunities and, in turn, to blend that talent in complex organizations where lawyers dominate. Another is data aggregation: how to utilize client data consistent with duties of confidentiality and conflict rules to build larger, client-spanning tools. For PeopleLaw, in stark contrast, the sticking point will be technological. PeopleLaw lawyers are largely in the business of translating law for laypeople. This "client-facing" aspect of service

[19] For his past work, *see* Benjamin H. Barton & Stephanos Bibas, Rebooting Justice: More Technology, Fewer Lawyers, and the Future of Law (2017); Benjamin H. Barton, Glass Half Full: The Decline and Rebirth of the Legal Profession (2015).

[20] For their past work, *see* John Armour & Mari Sako, *AI-Enabled Business Models in Legal Services: From Traditional Law Firms to Next-Generation Law Companies?* 7 J. Pros. & Org. 27 (2020); Richard Parnham, Mari Sako & John Armour, U. of Oxford, AI-Assisted Lawtech: Its Impact on Law Firms (2021), https://www.law.ox.ac.uk/sites/default/files/migrated/ai_final1097.pdf ; Mari Sako & Richard Parnham, U. of Oxford, Technology and Innovation in Legal Services: Final Report to the Solicitors Regulation Authority (2021), https://www.sra.org.uk/globalassets/documents/sra/research/full-report-technology-and-innovation-in-legal-services.pdf?version=4a1bfe; John Armour, Robert Parnham & Mari Sako, *Augmented Lawyering*, 2022 U. Ill. L. Rev. 71.

delivery stymies automation, because new legal tech tools, built as they are on "black box" predictive analytics, do not explain well what they do. Even as AI-fired tools automate certain repetitive and scalable tasks, a core task – explaining options and outcomes to lay clients – remains the near-exclusive competence of human lawyers.

A final contribution from Julian Nyarko of Stanford and Jens Frankenreiter of Washington University, both machine-learning experts, turns to technological constraints.[21] In "Natural Language Processing and Legal Tech," they note that new NLP techniques are already automating tasks that sit at the core of lawyering: the extraction and processing of information from a sea of unstructured text. But despite drastic improvements, they argue, NLP will, for the foreseeable future, fall well short of the "robo-judges" and "robo-lawyers" that occupy so much of the scholarly imagination. Even the most cutting-edge tools struggle with language's subtleties and law's complexities and so are not up to the legal cognitions that seasoned lawyers possess, particularly the construction of mappings of doctrine – what Nyarko and Frankenreiter call a legal "ontology." The result is that legal tech will continue to depend on humans for basic legal reasoning, reducing legal tech tools to brute-force analytic efforts once flesh-and-blood lawyers have done the important thinking.

A pair of conclusions follow from Part I's accounting of legal tech's possibilities and limits. First, legal tech's advance will not be monolithic. Rather, its incorporation into the civil justice system will be siloed, incremental, and halting – across prediction tasks, subject-matter silos, and segments of the legal services industry. In particular, it is a good bet that legal tech tools will arrive sooner, and advance most rapidly, in legal areas where data is abundant, regulated conduct takes repetitive and stereotypical forms, legal rules are inherently stable, case volumes are such that a repeat player stands to gain financially by investing, and organizational forms and culture are receptive. There is a reason why some of the most advanced legal tech tools are currently found in technocratic and self-contained areas of law (e.g., tax, labor and employment, patents) or highly routine ones (e.g., auto accidents), but not more open-ended legal contexts.

Second, Part I suggests that, over the near- to medium-term, even the most advanced legal tech tools will entail substantial lawyer engagement. Rather than full automation, legal tech may instead yield a kind of "advanced lawyering" – a spin on chess-master Gary Kasparov's notion of "advanced chess," in which human and machine ally and compete against other human-machine teams, working symbiotically, rather than merely pitting human against machine.[22] Lawyers, on this view,

[21] For their past work, see Jens Frankenreiter & Michael Livermore, *Computational Methods in Legal Analysis*, 16 ANN. REV. L. & SOC. SCI. 39 (2020); Julian Nyarko & Sarath Sanga, *A Statistical Test for Legal Interpretation: Theory and Applications*, 38 38 J. L. ECON. & ORG. 539 (forthcoming 2022).

[22] *See* Mercatus Center Podcast, *Gary Kasparov on AI, Chess, and the Future of Creativity*, MEDIUM (May 10, 2017), https://medium.com/conversations-with-tyler/garry-kasparov-tyler-cowen-chess-iq-ai-putin-3bf28baf4dba.

may often use commoditized systems that substitute for human judgment. But a large slice of legal tech will for the foreseeable future remain customized and operate within a paradigm defined by intensive human-machine collaboration.

I.2 LEGAL TECH, LITIGATION, AND THE ADVERSARIAL SYSTEM

Part II pivots to ask: What effect will proliferating legal tech tools have on civil litigation, and what can or should be done about it? Front and center in answering these questions is what is plainly the most convulsive, and likely the most lasting, change to the legal system wrought by the COVID-19 pandemic: the migration of in-person court proceedings to remote (virtual) proceedings. However, to focus exclusively on the "Zooming" of litigation is to miss an array of legal tech innovations that likewise have the potential to reshape the litigation landscape. Indeed, the largest market segment of legal tech, fueled by the largest venture capital flows, is a growing menu of lawyer-driven tools that help lawyers do what they most commonly do: litigate cases in court on behalf of clients.[23]

The chapters in Part II recognize that the two foundational components of any litigation system are information and costs. A good starting point for envisioning the future, then, is to see how legal tech will affect each component, and also the potential trade-offs between them. Take the "Zooming" of litigation. Remote proceedings can reduce litigation costs by obviating the need for time-consuming trips to the courthouse. That's a win. Indeed, if new technologies reduce the cost of providing legal services, then those services can be brought within reach of more people who currently go without counsel. PeopleLaw might rebound and access to justice concerns might be (at least marginally) ameliorated. At the same time, the migration of in-person proceedings to online fora might also impact the *quality* of the information generated by the system. In evidentiary hearings, virtual proceedings might impact, for good and ill, crucial assessments by judges and jurors about the credibility of witnesses – and as information is impaired, judgments that rely on that information might also suffer.

That is only part of the story, for new legal technologies also hold the potential to shift the *distribution* of information and costs between litigants, thus empowering litigation's "haves" against its "have-nots," or vice versa. Legal tech's distributional effect is perhaps *the* central question in an adversarial system that, for better or worse, pits parties against one another as the best way to achieve efficient, accurate, and fair outcomes. Information, after all, is power in litigation. It confers a decisive advantage at the bargaining table and allows a litigant to make better strategic decisions, including whether to litigate in the first place. So are costs. Long-standing research in law and economics shows that a case's settlement value is, at least in part,

[23] For an introductory effort, see David Freeman Engstrom, *Digital Civil Procedure*, 169 U. PA. L. REV. 2177 (2021).

a function of the cost – or, rather, the projected cost – of litigating all the way to judgment.[24] New legal technologies, by increasing the quality, quantity, and cost of information for some litigants but not others, can systematically alter the litigation balance, with significant and rippling effects throughout the civil justice system.

Here too, however, predictions vary about legal tech's ultimate effect on the litigation landscape. Some see legal tech as a force-multiplier and a leveler that will allow smaller firms to do battle with larger, corporate-facing foes.[25] Legal tech can also, as with remote proceedings, reduce the cost of representation, allowing litigants to afford more of it and lawyers to tap into a latent market of individuals who currently "lump it." The darker view is that legal tech will at best replicate and at worst exacerbate existing disparities. Preliminary evidence suggests that it is corporate-facing law firms and tech companies, with privileged access to data and superior internal technical capacity, who are best positioned to develop potent legal tech tools and exploit their advantages. Bleakest of all is the possibility that legal tech will enable the "haves" to more efficiently deploy law against the "have-nots," particularly in the high-volume, low-level processes that tend to ensnare the disadvantaged and only attract low-quality counsel, if they attract counsel at all.

Five chapters size up this wider field of inquiry and plumb the ways new legal technologies will reshape the landscape of civil litigation. All are united, however, in their effort to understand how new legal technologies will affect the quantity, quality, and cost of information within the system.

In "Remote Testimonial Fact-Finding," Renee Danser and Professor James Greiner, a longtime leader of the "credibility revolution" in empirical legal studies,[26] both of Harvard and its Access to Justice Lab, anchor a team that analyzes the effect of the online migration on fact-finders. Clustering all existing studies according to the rigor of their research designs, their meta-analysis finds little evidence for the widely held concern that the online migration will adversely affect either truth-detection capacities or felt empathy toward the parties. But, not content to stop there, the authors take up the broader question of how best to study a legal system in the throes of significant change, and they offer concrete guidance on how to generate high-quality information about legal tech's impact via careful research design and a focus on causal inference.

Turning to the effects of new lawyer-driven legal tech tools, Professor Diego Zambrano of Stanford, an expert on discovery in litigation, and two

[24] For a useful overview, see Andrew F. Daughety & Jennifer F. Reinganum, *Settlement*, *in* 8 Encyclopedia of Law and Economics 386, 386–71 (Chris W. Sanchirico ed., 2nd ed. 2012).

[25] *See* Engstrom & Gelbach, *Legal Tech*, at 1037–41 (touring a growing scholarly literature).

[26] For his prior work, see D. James Greiner & Andrea Matthews, *Randomized Control Trials in the United States Legal Profession*, 12 Ann. Rev. L. & Soc. Sci. 295 (2016); D. James Greiner & Cassandra Wolos Pattanayak, *Randomized Evaluation in Legal Assistance: What Difference Does Representation (Offer and Actual Use) Make?* 121 Yale L.J. 2118 (2012); D. James Greiner et al., *The Limits of Unbundled Legal Assistance: A Randomized Study in a Massachusetts District Court and Prospects for the Future*, 126 Harv. L. Rev. 901 (2013).

co-authors – Peter Henderson and Neel Guha, both pursuing combined law and computer science degrees – zero in on e-discovery. Within civil litigation, modern discovery is the current frontline of debate about how to adapt analog procedural rules to potent machine-learning tools.[27] Their chapter, "Gamesmanship in Modern Discovery Tech," is a concrete analysis of how legal tech tools that perform core discovery tasks – often referred to collectively as "technology-assisted review" (TAR) – are revolutionizing complex litigation but also straining the system's adversarial architecture. Detractors say TAR exacerbates discovery abuse because of asymmetries in technical capacity across litigants and its inherent opacity. These critics advocate strict new protocols that compel sharing of technical inputs or outputs. Champions point to TAR's efficiencies and worry that heavy-handed regulation will stymie innovation by dissuading litigants from using TAR in the first place. Zambrano and co-authors bring much-needed light to this heated debate by offering a technical but accessible taxonomy of the ways TAR can facilitate discovery abuse. Next, they propose a menu of ways the system – especially judges, as "TAR regulators" – might plausibly police gamesmanship. The result is a powerful, discovery-specific meditation on questions that lurk in the background of all legal tech: how to balance innovation incentives against technology's potential costs, and whether new digital tools might (somewhat counterintuitively) yield a litigation system that is *more* transparent and trustworthy than the analog status quo.

In "Legal Tech and the Litigation Playing Field," Professor Nora Freeman Engstrom and Professor David Freeman Engstrom, both of Stanford, continue this line of thinking about legal tech and litigation but focus in on the distributive implications of a digitizing litigation system. Drawing on their expertise in litigation and procedure, they start with grim statistics capturing recent declines in plaintiff win rates and damages awards, which suggest that the litigation playing field has steadily slanted in favor of litigation's "haves" at the expense of its "have-nots." Next, they profile a trio of legal tech tools, beginning with TAR but then moving to a pair of frontier applications that offer a glimpse of the future: Colossus, a sophisticated case-outcome prediction tool used by the nation's largest casualty insurers to inform tens of thousands of settlements each year, and what they call the "Walmart suite," a set of tools that predict case outcomes and generate initial pleadings and papers. These innovations, they suggest, are representative of the types of tools under development by large corporate entities, tech providers, and BigLaw firms. And, if that's right, they say, the future is grim. Cutting sharply against the grain of commentary predicting legal tech will *democratize* the litigation system, they explain why such tools are, and will likely continue to be, unevenly distributed because large corporate repeat-players have privileged access to the needed technical capacity and

[27] For past relevant work by these authors, see Neel Guha, Peter Henderson & Diego A. Zambrano, *Vulnerabilities in Discovery Tech*, 35 Harv. J. L. & Tech. 581 (forthcoming 2022). Diego A. Zambrano, *Discovery as Regulation*, 120 Mich. L. Rev. 71 (2020).

data, including data on case outcomes available nowhere else in a system pervaded by confidential settlements. As the American civil justice system enters the digital age, the haves will be propelled yet further ahead.

In "Litigation Outcome Prediction, Access to Justice, and Legal Endogeneity," Professor Charlotte Alexander of Georgia State, a multi-faceted legal academic and data scientist, offers a third take on legal tech's power to shape the litigation landscape via an extended analysis of the evolution and current state of the art of case-outcome prediction tools.[28] She assesses these tools' potential to fill the civil justice gap and identifies possible unintended consequences for access to justice. Her primary concern is "endogeneity" – the ability of new tech tools, particularly those that predict case outcomes, to re-shape the output of the civil justice system. In particular, she offers a concrete and gripping account of how more precise case predictions could generate hydraulic movements within the system – and, crucially, might steer risk-averse plaintiffs' counsel *away* from cases by marginalized groups and drain the system of its envelope-pushing, reformist potential. The law, already a hidebound, Burkean institution, might become more so.

In a final chapter contribution, "Toward the Participatory MDL: A Low-Tech Step to Promote Litigant Autonomy," Todd Venook of Stanford's Rhode Center on the Legal Profession and Professor Nora Freeman Engstrom turn to legal tech's impact on the big-ticket, aggregated litigations that make up a large proportion of federal court litigation. They focus on multi-district litigation (MDL), a process whereby hundreds and even thousands of individual cases are consolidated in a single federal court and litigated in bulk. Turning away from the high-tech, AI-fueled tools that occupy much of the legal tech debate, Venook and Engstrom focus instead on the potential of relatively simple court-hosted websites to promote litigant autonomy. In particular, they offer the results of their painstaking empirical study of current MDL websites. What they find is discouraging: Court websites are hard to find and frequently outdated; they lack digested, litigant-focused content; and they rarely offer litigants opportunities to attend hearings and status conferences remotely (from their home states). Finding current offerings deeply deficient, they offer principles for reform. Even a low-tech tool, Venook and Engstrom insist, can promote litigant participation and access to critical case information – but only if done right.

At least two broad conclusions emerge from this chorus of views. First, the trade-offs among core systemic values of efficiency, accuracy, and fairness as legal tech sweeps into the system will be complex and variable. More study, and more targeted study, is plainly needed if we are to understand legal tech's implications for civil litigation going forward. Second, data accessibility will be central if the legal tech

28 For her past work on legal tech, see Charlotte S. Alexander & Mohammad Javad Feizollahi, *On Dragons, Caves, Teeth, and Claws: Legal Analytics and the Problem of Court Data Access*, *in* Computational Legal Studies: The Promise and Challenge of Data-Driven Legal Research (Ryan Whalen ed., 2019).

industry is to chart a healthy trajectory from here – sharply raising the stakes of the choices that courts are making now about data infrastructure and data governance, as taken up more fully in the remainder of the volume.

1.3 LEGAL TECH AND ACCESS TO JUSTICE

Part III of the book turns more squarely to the potential of new legal technologies to expand access to justice (A2J) for those who currently lack counsel. As previously noted, the current access crisis is deep and socially costly. A well-functioning legal infrastructure, few could deny, is critical to the achievement of collective economic and social welfare goals.[29] Distortions in the market for law and legal services can quickly undermine those goals by impairing economic activity and growth. Legal services, it seems, are far from ordinary services.[30]

As already noted, the COVID-19 pandemic, aided by a surge in consumer debt cases, brought to a boil an already-simmering debate about the high prevalence of pro se litigants within the system, placing substantial pressure on courts to innovate. Courts have moved with surprising dexterity to expand use of virtual hearings, pre-hearing diversion programs, and court-linked ODR processes. COVID-era deprivations also amplified calls to address access-to-justice concerns by deregulating the legal services industry and welcoming new providers – including the non-human, software sort – more fully into the American legal system. Finally, the pandemic turbocharged a new generation of client-facing legal tech tools designed to assist self-represented litigants by providing online legal guides, document assembly tools, and case management systems to improve access to justice for people facing problems with housing, money, family, work, and other justiciable issues.[31]

Each of these currents raises important questions about the degree to which the uptake of new legal technologies, and the rules governing their use, will widen or, to the contrary, narrow the ability of those with civil justice needs to vindicate their rights. Four chapter contributions capture the most critical aspects of legal tech and access to justice and help lay a research agenda for the future.

One crucial line of inquiry is how individuals with civil justice needs use, and could better use, the internet to access legal information and services. In "The Supply and Demand of Legal Help on the Internet," Margaret Hagan, an expert on user-centered legal design and director of Stanford's Legal Design Lab, offers both a

[29] *See* Gillian K. Hadfield, *Legal Markets*, 60 J. ECON. LIT. (forthcoming 2022).

[30] *Id.* at 19; *see also* GILLIAN K. HADFIELD, RULES FOR A FLAT WORLD: WHY HUMANS INVENTED LAW AND HOW TO REINVENT IT FOR A COMPLEX GLOBAL ECONOMY (2017); FREDERICK WILMOT-SMITH, EQUAL JUSTICE: FAIR LEGAL SYSTEMS IN AN UNFAIR WORLD (2019).

[31] For an overview, see REBECCA SANDEFUR, AM. BAR FOUND., LEGAL TECH FOR NON-LAWYERS: REPORT OF THE SURVEY OF US LEGAL TECHNOLOGIES (2019), http://www.americanbarfoundation.org/uploads/cms/documents/report_us_digital_legal_tech_for_nonlawyers.pdf.

history lesson and a novel empirical study of the current state of online legal search.[32] The status quo, she observes, follows decades of promises that new digital technologies, anchored by the Internet, could dramatically improve access to justice. But, similar to Venook and Engstrom, she notes that insufficient attention has been paid to the actual user experience – how to make people's "legal journeys" less burdensome and more effective. Hagan then mounts a first-of-its-kind effort to gauge present-day supply of and demand for online legal help by measuring website traffic across the mix of commercial, court-linked, and public interest websites that vie for eyeballs online. Commercial sites, she finds, dominate over the more limited ecosystem of court-linked and public interest online resources, and yet commercial sites often engage in questionable practices, including the baiting of users with incomplete information and then charging for more. Search engine algorithms likely bolster that dominance. Policy implications abound: What role should search engines play to promote access to quality legal information? Could they, or should they, privilege trustworthy sources? Might there be scope for public-private partnerships, or even a regulatory role, to ensure that online searches return trustworthy and actionable legal information?

A second critical line of inquiry returns to the effect of the "Zooming" of litigation, but from an access-to-justice perspective. In "Digital Inequalities and Access to Justice: Dialing into Zoom Court Unrepresented," Professor Victor Quintanilla of Indiana University, a leading scholarly voice on civil justice design and pro se litigants, leads a research team that explores how low-income persons experience online proceedings in the everyday.[33] To date, commentators have lauded remote proceedings because of their capacity to lower litigation costs and provide conveniences. Drawing on data painstakingly compiled from Indiana courts, however, Quintanilla and co-authors paint a more complex and troubling portrait. In particular, they document persistent and pressing representational asymmetries among low-income persons that compound with digital divides in virtual court. They then identify social-psychological mechanisms through which the resulting technological asymmetries construct the status of self-represented individuals in the eyes of judges, lawyers, and even the litigants themselves. The result is a sharply different view than that offered by Danser, Greiner, and co-authors in Chapter 4, who see little basis for concern about the transition to remote testimony. Indeed, the starkness of the digital divide in evidence in Indiana gives reason to worry that the online migration might open the (virtual) courthouse doors wider only to relegate some to the (virtual) basement. The juxtaposition of these two

[32] For an example of her past work, see Margaret Hagan, *The User Experience of the Internet as a Legal Help Service: Defining Standards for the Next Generation of User-Friendly Online Legal Services*, 20 VA. J.L. & TECH. 394 (2016).

[33] For his past work on these topics, see Victor D. Quintanilla, *Human-Centered Civil Justice Design*, 121 PENN ST. L. REV. 745 (2017); Victor D. Quintanilla et al., *The Signaling Effect of Pro Se Status*, 42 LAW & SOC. INQUIRY 1091 (2017).

chapters, and their diverging approaches, suggests a fertile and important area for future inquiry.

Part III closes with a pair of dueling chapter contributions on the possibilities and limits of ODR – plainly ground-zero in the debate over the future of legal tech and access to justice. In "Online Dispute Resolution and the End of Adversarial Justice?" Professor Norm Spaulding of Stanford, an expert in litigation procedure and the history of the legal profession, canvasses key moments in the history of technology and shows that the downsides of innovations, and the alternatives available at their adoption, are often conveniently forgotten once path-dependence and the leverage of market dominance sets in.[34] This concern is especially acute for legal technologies designed to supplant a civil litigation system that has drawn intense criticism, only some of it earned, about excessive cost, delay, and adversarialism. Spaulding sharply critiques optimistic rhetoric around ODR and decries what he sees as undefended assumptions about case value and complexity, litigant needs, and the lawyer's professional role. In particular, he shows how ODR, at least in its current guise, is largely a technology of compliance, not adjudication, that greases the wheels of the collection efforts of companies and governments against marginalized populations. His critique counsels extreme caution in adopting, designing, and overseeing proliferating ODR platforms.

In "Using ODR Platforms to Level the Playing Field: Improving Pro Se Litigation through ODR Design," Professor J.J. Prescott of the University of Michigan, a lawyer, economist, and founder of Matterhorn, a leading ODR company, pushes back against Professor Spaulding's sharp critique.[35] It is unfair, he says, to compare court adjudication at its best to ODR at its worst. Warts and all, current ODR systems might be better than nothing in a system with pervasive access problems. But Prescott also concedes the shortcomings of ODR in its current guise and asks how we might address them. In particular, while existing ODR platforms might usefully simplify and clarify legal steps, lawyerless litigants still proceed without experience, expertise, guardrails, or the ability to gauge risk or outcomes. It is thus time, Prescott argues, to begin the work of thinking about what the next generation of ODR technology, or ODR 2.0, might look like. In particular, we might inject ODR with a dose of data science, arming self-represented litigants with the information, including legal options and predictions about their case, they might receive from

[34] For past work on AI and legal tech, see Norman Spaulding, *Is Human Judgment Necessary? Artificial Intelligence, Algorithmic Governance, and the Law*, *in* The Oxford Handbook of Ethics of AI (Markus D. Duber et al. eds., 2020).

[35] For his past work on ODR, see Maximilian A. Bulinski & J.J. Prescott, *Online Case Resolution Systems: Enhancing Access, Fairness, Accuracy, and Efficiency*, 21 Mich. J. Race & L. 205 (2016); Avital Mentovich, J.J. Prescott & Orna Rabinovich-Einy, *Are Litigation Outcome Disparities Inevitable? Courts, Technology, and the Future of Impartiality*, 71 Ala. L. Rev. 893 (2020). For Matterhorn, see Matterhorn, https://getmatterhorn.com/.

a lawyer were one available. Enhanced ODR, he notes, is unlikely to render lawyer representation obsolete, but next-generation platforms can dramatically reduce the justice gap and, on key dimensions, be a significant improvement over the status quo.

As with other Parts of this volume, these contributions cover only a slice of a fast-moving field. "Regulatory reform," described in passing by Professor Barton in Chapter 1, is gaining momentum. Two states, Utah and Arizona, have already relaxed the usual rules governing legal services. If more states follow – and several states, including California, are actively considering doing so – the result would be tectonic.[36] Another wild card is litigation invoking antitrust law and the First Amendment against the rules that sustain the lawyer's professional monopoly. Using these time-worn principles, federal courts could forcibly loosen constraints on the provision of legal services even if states will not. Any of the above could usher new providers, including software-based ones, into the system.

Whether either of these things comes to pass, the above chapter contributions combine to form a generalizable insight about legal tech and access to justice. As legal tech of all sorts proliferates, we must continually ask what innovations will increase access *to*, and also what kind of justice, and what kind of legal subject, they will combine to deliver. Only by continually asking and answering these questions can judges, court administrators, lawyers, and policy makers guard against the risk that new technologies will see rapid adoption but lead to an impoverished, gutter system of justice.

I.4 COURTS, DATA, AND CIVIL JUSTICE

A fourth and final Part aims to help lawyers, judges, policy makers, and others who populate the civil justice system think about the resource that will increasingly be the lifeblood of a fast-digitizing civil justice system: data.

Digitization means datafication, and the civil justice system is generating data like never before. At the center of this data-generating machine, of course, are the courts themselves. Courts have always been data monopolists. They sit atop mountains of data that grow larger each year, fed by a ceaseless stream of litigant-filed pleadings and papers and court-issued orders and decisions. But that only begins to describe the data that a newly digitized civil justice system is throwing off. New forms of digitization, from online courts to ODR to a pandemic-fueled shift to e-filing, mean

[36] Engstrom & Vogt, *The New Judicial Governance*; *see also* Rebecca L. Sandefur, Thomas M. Clarke & James Teufel, *Seconds to Impact? Regulatory Reform, New Kinds of Legal Services, and Increased Access to Justice*, 84 Law & Contemp. Problems 69 (2021); Elizabeth Chambliss, *Evidence-Based Lawyer Regulation*, 97 Wash. U. L. Rev. 297 (2019).

a larger store of digitized legal materials than ever before that can be mined for information and insights about the system's workings.[37]

Importantly, digitization means more than just *more* data. It also means *higher-value* data that can be put to more effective use, not just by courts, but by a growing legal tech industry. As various of the chapter contributions to this volume make clear, data, and access to it, will increasingly shape the civil justice system's core workings. A key question for the future, then, is whether the civil justice system, and, in particular, the courts that oversee it, can harness new data flows and manage data's increasing centrality in ways that promote the just, equitable, and efficient administration of justice – or, alternatively, subvert it. Choices made today will have large consequences tomorrow.

Recognizing data's central importance, a final set of chapters interrogates how courts should perform their new and increasingly central role as data dispensers and data governors. And, it also examines how courts might mount more ambitious and future-looking projects, such as the creation of data trusts as a way to achieve new transparency over the workings of the system.

Data challenges track wider governance challenges. Such is the lesson of a chapter by Chief Justice McCormack of the Michigan Supreme Court, a national voice on access to justice and court reform.[38] In "The Disruption We Needed: COVID-19, Court Technology, and Access to Justice," McCormack offers a riveting, ground-level account of the remarkable strides that the normally hide-bound courts have made during the pandemic to widen access to justice through use of technology. In Michigan and elsewhere, courts moved quickly to implement ODR and diversion programs, and they built out data capacity to better inform judicial administration. But McCormack also laments the challenges that remain. The Michigan courts, as in many states, are a non-unified judicial system, with many court records under the control of elected local court clerks, steeply raising the costs of new, statewide initiatives. And that only describes the *intra*-jurisdictional challenges around data and interoperability. As many have noted, *inter*-jurisdictional differences are also severe, yielding an innovation-choking checkerboard of 14,000 federal, state, and local court jurisdictions with data and IT infrastructures that cannot talk to one another.[39] The pandemic has spurred important changes in how courts deliver justice, but much work remains to be done.

[37] For a useful overview of pandemic-fueled court digitization, *see generally* Nat'l Ctr. For State Cts., Post-Pandemic Planning: Technology Resource Guide (2020), https://www.ncsc.org/__data/assets/pdf_file/0020/42482/Post-Pandemic-Planning.pdf.

[38] For recent academic work, see Bridget Mary McCormack, *Staying Off the Sidelines: Judges as Agents for Justice System Reform*, 131 Yale L.J. Forum 175 (2021).

[39] The leading effort to address inter-jurisdictional data challenges is the National Open Court Data Standards' (NODS) project of the National Conference of State Courts. *See National Open Court Data Standards (NODS)*, Nat'l Ctr. for State Cts., https://www.ncsc.org/services-and-experts/areas-of-expertise/court-statistics/national-open-court-data-standards-nods.

Meanwhile, it is courts that will decide, and are deciding, whether to make the mountains of data generated by the legal system available to outside actors. And, so far, courts have kept a very tight grip. In "Free PACER," Professor Jonah Gelbach of Berkeley, a lawyer, economist, and leading legal empiricist, offers a plaintive appeal for Congress and the federal courts to address the kludgy paywalls behind which much federal court data sits.[40] High fees and a clunky, twentieth-century user interface hinder potentially useful research. Worse, though PACER fee revenue is often described as high, it is actually a pittance as an economic matter, meaning that scholars, policy makers, and litigants are deprived of data – but for little gain. Importantly, Gelbach's concerns are no less relevant at the state level. Even as new technologies are thickening data flows, acute budgetary pressures, exacerbated by the pandemic, make it all too tempting for state judicial administrators to monetize their holdings and place data beyond the reach of all but the most-well-heeled law firms and tech companies.

Continuing the focus on court governance, in "Technological Challenges Facing the Judiciary," Professor Albert Yoon of the University of Toronto, a lawyer, economist, and founder of Blue J Legal, an innovative legal tech company, observes that, while the legal profession has been slow to adopt technology compared to other skilled labor markets, the courts have been even slower.[41] The resulting gaps in technological sophistication both within the practicing bar, and between Bar and Bench, is exacerbating the already-wide disparities between richer and poorer litigants. Access-to-justice concerns will only worsen, Yoon predicts, as wealthier litigants use new data sources to develop increasingly potent tech tools and then exploit the advantages they confer against a technologically backward judiciary. Moreover, the judiciary will find itself at a disadvantage relative to more technologically sophisticated parties, if for no other reason than it will lag in its ability to efficiently make decisions. The judiciary, Yoon argues, can and should reverse that trend. Needed steps include democratizing court data by making it more publicly available and increased willingness among judges to develop and use data-based tools to inform their own judicial decision-making.

Finally, in "The Civil Justice Data Gap," Professor Tanina Rostain and Amy O'Hara of Georgetown, both pioneers in thinking about data governance and the legal system, ask how we might reimagine the collection, sharing, and analysis of data to make the civil justice system more accountable to other government

40 For his prior work using federal court data to analyze civil justice problems, see Jonah B. Gelbach, *Can We Learn Anything about Pleading Changes from Existing Data?* 44 INT'L REV. L. & ECON. 72 (2015); Jonah B. Gelbach, *Can the Dark Arts of the Dismal Science Shed Light on the Empirical Reality of Civil Procedure?* 2 STAN. J. COMPLEX LITIG. 223 (2014).

41 For prior relevant work, see Yoon, *Post-Modern Lawyer*. Professor Yoon is a founder of Blue J Legal, a legal tech company specializing in tax and labor employment matters. *See* BLUE J. LEGAL, https://www.bluej.com/.

institutions, litigants, and the public at large.[42] They tackle those questions, first, by identifying vital lines of research that would benefit from better data. Among these are the ways racism shapes court processes and outcomes, the consequences of a lack of representation on litigants' experiences and case outcomes within the civil justice system, and the upstream determinants and downstream consequences of judicial entanglement. Having made the case for how better data might be put to salutary use, they report on their ongoing efforts to design and build a "civil justice data commons" that might overcome these barriers by hosting documented, harmonized data and even providing tools and analytic software to conduct research. A workable data commons would enrich policy research and yield operational insights for courts and civil justice institutions seeking to improve equity and service delivery.

Part IV's collected contributions make two points abundantly clear: First, as the civil justice system continues the process of digitization, the health of the system will increasingly turn on the health of its data ecosystem. Second, because data will be increasingly central to civil justice, courts will necessarily play a critically important but novel role as data governors. Performing that new data governance role, and navigating the opportunities presented by a newly digitized system while avoiding its many perils, will require careful regulation to ensure that data is distributed and used in fair, equitable, secure, and privacy-protecting ways.

* * *

More than a hundred years ago, Justice Holmes, in *The Path of the Law*, wrote: "For the rational study of the law the black-letter man may be the man of the present, but the man of the future is the man of statistics and the master of economics." Shorn of its fusty, turn-of-the-century diction, this statement could just as easily have come, in 2022 rather than 1897, from the mouth of a legal tech entrepreneur. To be sure, there's an element of puffery in such claims, both then and now. But even skeptics must agree that substantial change is afoot. The next few decades of the civil justice system will look very different from the past few, and many of the decisions that will determine the shape of that system are being made now. Judges, lawyers, court administrators, and policy makers should take note and ensure that the civil justice system's next, digital iteration is a healthy one. This volume seeks to equip them with the motivation and the knowledge base to do so.

[42] For Professor Rostain's prior work on these topics, see Rebecca A. Johnson & Tanina Rostain, *Tool for Surveillance or Spotlight on Inequality? Big Data and the Law*, 16 ANN. REV. L. & SOC. SCI. 453 (2020); Tanina Rostain, *Techno-Optimism and Access to the Legal System*, 148 DAEDALUS 93 (2019).

PART I

Legal Tech and the Innovation Ecosystem

1

The Future of American Legal Tech

Regulation, Culture, Markets

Benjamin H. Barton

America's legal technology boom presents a puzzle. On the one hand, America's market for legal services is among the most tightly regulated in the world, suggesting infertile ground for a legal technology revolution. America has the world's most robustly protected lawyer monopoly. Its version of the prohibition against the unauthorized practice of law (UPL) is among the broadest and most aggressive in the world because it theoretically bans all non-lawyers from giving any "legal advice" in addition to the more typical bar against filing papers or appearing in court. Likewise, America's barriers to entering the legal profession are exceedingly high: generally speaking, an undergraduate degree, another three years of law school, a challenging bar exam, an intrusive character and fitness process, and so forth. Between these two barriers, the American lawyer's monopoly has historically been capacious and jealously guarded. Given this regulatory environment, one would expect America to have a small and beleaguered legal technology sector. Surely wealthy and politically connected bar associations would nip any potential competitors in the bud.

Actually, not so much. The other side of this puzzle is America's advanced and free-wheeling market for legal tech, which is probably the most robust in the world, as the Sako and Armour chapter herein establishes. The present chapter seeks to explain this seeming puzzle, and then uses that explanation to make some predictions about where legal technology will continue to flourish in America. The explanation is that both America's seemingly monolithic market for legal services and its uniform regulation of lawyers are, in fact, quite segmented. In some parts of the market, lawyer regulation is almost non-existent (or at least very rarely enforced) – typically at the high end in so-called BigLaw and at the low end in non-profits and legal aid offices serving the indigent. In so-called PeopleLaw, where lawyers serve middle-class Americans and small businesses, regulation plays a significant role and has hampered technological advancement, especially in areas like providing legal advice. This chapter demonstrates how these different markets operate, how they are regulated, and how that explains the current explosive growth in legal tech in some areas, but not others.

This insight also raises a note of caution as we celebrate current efforts at "re-regulating" the market for legal services in states like Utah, Arizona, and others. These jurisdictions have rightfully (so far) been praised for allowing non-lawyer and technological innovations into a very constricted market. And yet any lawyer-led regulatory effort, no matter how well-meaning, could easily slide into lawyer self-protection, as many (most?) prior regulatory efforts have. The status quo favors innovation in at least the top and the bottom of the market, but we need to push regulators to loosen barriers in the PeopleLaw space, rather than surreptitiously raising barriers where innovation is currently blossoming.

1.1 AN EXTRA-BRIEF OVERVIEW OF AMERICA'S UNUSUAL LAWYER REGULATION

The first oddity is that America's legal profession is regulated primarily by its judicial branch, rather than its legislative or executive branches. In America, state supreme courts control lawyer regulation in the first instance. This is unusual domestically – every other American occupation, from cosmetologists to doctors, is governed by legislatures – and internationally.[1]

Unsurprisingly, given that the judiciary is staffed by former elite lawyers, the resulting regulation has turned out to be pretty lawyer-friendly.[2] The upshot is a uniquely well-defined and defended lawyer monopoly. Requiring seven years of higher education followed by notoriously difficult licensing exams makes it very expensive in time and money to become an American lawyer.[3]

Regulators also fight to keep non-lawyers *out* of the market. That's where the uniquely American version of UPL comes in. UPL is prohibited in all fifty states.[4] The definition of the "practice of law" and the levels of enforcement differ from state to state, but at a minimum in no state may a non-lawyer appear in court on behalf of another party or give "legal advice."[5] For decades the combination of UPL

[1] Benjamin H. Barton & Deborah Rhode, *Legal Services Regulation in the United States: A Tale of Two Models, in* International Perspectives on the Regulation of Lawyers and Legal Services (Andy Boon ed., 2017).

[2] I wrote a whole book about this one sentence. Benjamin H. Barton, The Lawyer-Judge Bias in American Courts (2011).

[3] Gillian Hadfield, *Legal Markets*, 60 J. Econ. Lit. (forthcoming 2022) (manuscript at 18); Barton, *The Lawyer-Judge Bias*, at 146–47.

[4] Tanina Rostain, *The Emergence of "Law Consultants,"* 75 Fordham L. Rev. 1397, 1407 & n.53 (2006).

[5] Deborah L. Rhode, *Policing the Professional Monopoly: A Constitutional and Empirical Analysis of Unauthorized Practice Prohibitions*, 34 Stan. L. Rev. 1 (1981).

and high barriers to entry left the American legal profession uniquely powerful and protected, and through at least the 1990s likely increased lawyer earnings.[6]

Given a monolithic regulatory structure, run largely by friendly actors, one would expect American lawyer regulation to favor lawyers. That has indeed been the case historically. If past were prologue, then we would expect that non-lawyer-driven legal tech would either be barred altogether or severely stunted in this country. After all, consider the lengthy battle by some lawyer regulators to hang on to real estate closings as "legal work" protected by UPL.[7]

1.1.1 *Legal Tech Thrives Regardless: Why?*

Yet, in this regard history has proven a poor guide. Legal tech has actually flowered in the United States. There are three primary reasons. The first is that the American lawyer's monopoly has been taking on water since the most anticompetitive regulation came under attack in the 1970s. Initially the Supreme Court held bar association mandatory fee schedules and some advertising bans were unlawful.[8] In the 1990s the Justice Department investigated whether the ABA's role in regulating law schools violated antitrust law. The investigation resulted in a pretty far-reaching settlement and much looser regulation of law schools.[9]

Most recently, in 2015, the Supreme Court held that the enforcement of the dental equivalent of UPL against non-dentist teeth whiteners violated antitrust law in *North Carolina Board of Dental Examiners* v. *Federal Trade Commission*.[10] As of yet no court has extended this case to lawyers, but even the chance that one might has chilled the ardor of bar association UPL enforcement.[11]

Some states and localities have launched pretty aggressive reforms. Famously, Utah has created a new "regulatory sandbox" that allows for non-lawyers and new technologies to apply for approval to offer some legal services.[12] Oregon is considering adding two new ways to join the profession in addition to three years of law school and a bar examination: an "experience-based learning pathway" and a

6 Clifford Winston et al., First Thing We Do, Let's Deregulate All the Lawyers 20–27 (2011).

7 Margaret Onys Rentz, *Laying Down the Law: Bringing Down the Legal Cartel in Real Estate Settlement Services and Beyond*, 40 Ga. L. Rev. 293 (2005).

8 Goldfarb v. Va. State Bar, 421 U.S. 773, 792 (1975); Bates v. State Bar of Ariz., 433 U.S. 350 (1977).

9 Benjamin H. Barton, Fixing Law Schools 133–36 (2019).

10 574 U.S. 494 (2015).

11 Deborah L. Rhode & Benjamin H. Barton, *Rethinking Self-Regulation: Antitrust Perspectives on Bar Governance Activity*, 20 Chap. L. Rev. 267 (2017).

12 Lucy Ricca, *The Reregulation of Utah: Managing Risk with Better Protections*, GPSolo, July–Aug. 2021, at 31.

"supervised practice pathway."[13] Arizona has allowed non-lawyer ownership of law firms under a new "alternative business structures," or ABS, model, and it also created a class of "legal paraprofessionals" who are allowed to perform some activities previously limited to lawyers.[14] There are working groups considering similar changes in California, Illinois, New York, Michigan, and other states.[15]

Taken together, the bar's ability (and desire) to maintain tight control over its monopoly has lessened quite a bit over recent decades. This partially explains why the market in PeopleLaw is so competitive and why lawyer earnings in that market have shrunk since the 1970s.[16]

The second reason is America's ever-deepening access-to-justice crisis. Characteristically, Deborah Rhode led the way in this area with her 2004(!) book *Access to Justice*, which explained that poor and middle class Americans struggle to afford lawyers or to address serious legal problems.[17] The most recent and comprehensive study is the 2020 World Justice Project (WJP) Rule of Law Index, which ranks the United States thirty-sixth in the world in terms of the fairness of its civil justice system, placed snugly between Malaysia and Jordan.[18] By one estimate, four-fifths of the legal needs of poor Americans remain unmet.[19]

Gillian Hadfield has repeatedly demonstrated that the problem affects more than just the poor. Middle-class Americans also cannot afford legal help, despite living in a "law thick" society where legal help is often desperately needed.[20] As demonstrated below, lawyers have, so far, been relatively uninterested in meeting these acute needs, mostly because their business model requires bespoke work and hourly fees and most Americans can't afford to pay for that sort of help. Nevertheless, nature abhors a vacuum, so legal tech has bloomed in this space, despite regulatory concerns.

A final point – and it holds the key to understanding the past, present, and future of legal tech – is that, while America's regulation is monolithic, its market for legal services is anything but. So, regulations that nominally apply to every

[13] Natalie Runyon, *Oregon Takes a Step Forward in Alternative Licensure of Attorneys*, Reuters (July 23, 2021, 8:31 AM PDT), https://www.reuters.com/legal/litigation/oregon-takes-step-forward-alternative-licensure-attorneys-2021-07-23/.

[14] Daniel J. Siegel, *Playing in the Regulatory Sandbox*, Law Prac. Mag., July 2021, at 44, 47–48.

[15] Unlocking Legal Regulation Knowledge Center, IAALS, https://iaals.du.edu/knowledge-center/state-action.

[16] Benjamin H. Barton, Glass Half Full 121–29 (2015).

[17] Deborah Rhode, Access to Justice (2004).

[18] World Justice Project, Rule of Law Index 28 (2020), https://worldjusticeproject.org/sites/default/files/documents/WJP-ROLI-2020-Online_0.pdf.

[19] Legal Servs. Corp., Documenting the Justice Gap in America: The Current Unmet Civil Needs of Low Income Americans 1–13 (2009), http://www.lsc.gov/pdfs/dcoumenting_the_justice_gap_in_america_2009.pdf.

[20] Gillian K. Hadfield, *Higher Demand, Lower Supply? A Comparative Assessment of the Legal Resource Landscape for Ordinary Americans*, 37 Fordham Urb. L.J. 129 (2010).

lawyer and provider of legal services operate quite differently depending on the market segment.

1.2 FOUR BROAD CATEGORIES OF AMERICAN CIVIL LAW LAWYERS

America's market for legal services is also unique. Start with a number count of lawyers. In 2021, America claimed 1,327,910 licensed lawyers.[21] This was actually a slight *decline* from the number of American lawyers in 2019 and 2020, interrupting a 105-year streak where the profession grew every year. Nineteen-fifteen is the last time the profession shrank. America may have the most lawyers in the world, depending on how you count India's.[22] America is second in lawyers-per-capita at one lawyer for every 249 Americans, behind only Israel.[23] By any measure, America has a lot of lawyers.

America's legal services market is the largest in the world, with total revenues of $314 billion in 2018, accounting for a staggering 47 percent of global revenue in that sector by one estimate.[24] The United States runs a substantial trade surplus in law and is the world's largest exporter of legal services.[25] America's corporate law firms are the largest and most profitable in the world.[26]

For our purposes we can divide America's lawyers into four super-broad categories: (1) corporate lawyers, including so-called BigLaw firms and in-house lawyers; (2) "main street lawyers" or "PeopleLaw," private-sector lawyers that represent small businesses and less wealthy individuals ranging from the working poor up to the upper-middle class; (3) government-supplied civil legal services for the poor (legal aid); and (4) plaintiff's side lawyers that make a living suing large corporations or wealthy individuals.

I am well aware that, like my aggressively brisk overview of lawyer regulation, these categories may cause some consternation and that exceptions abound. The point of this very rough taxonomy is to think about how regulation and legal tech work in these broad areas, not to perfectly describe the market.

[21] Am. Bar Ass'n, ABA National Lawyer Population Survey 3 (2021), https://www.americanbar.org/content/dam/aba/administrative/market_research/2021-national-lawyer-population-survey.pdf.

[22] Barton & Rhode, *Legal Services*, at 27 (noting that in 2013 India appeared to have more lawyers, but that as many as 30 percent of India's lawyers may be unlicensed).

[23] *Id.*

[24] *Legal Services in the United States*, MarketResearch.com, https://www.marketresearch.com/MarketLine-v3883/Legal-Services-United-States-12187455/.

[25] Letter from Thomas M. Susman, Dir. Governmental Affs. Off. of the Am. Bar Ass'n, to Chairman Devin Nunes and Ranking Member Charles Rangel, Trade Subcomm. of the House Comm. on Ways and Means (Mar. 27, 2013), https://www.americanbar.org/content/dam/aba/administrative/government_affairs_office/2013mar27_usindiatraderelations_l.pdf.

[26] Staci Zaretsky, *The Global 100: The Richest Law Firms in the World*, Above the Law (Sept. 25, 2020), https://abovethelaw.com/2020/09/the-global-100-the-richest-law-firms-in-the-world-2020/.

1.2.1 *BigLaw/In-house Counsel*

BigLaw looms large in the public imagination and in the popular press, but it has never represented even a plurality of the profession. For example, in 2019 the *National Law Journal* estimated that 169,477 lawyers worked at America's 500 biggest law firms.[27] This works out to roughly 13 percent of the American lawyers that year. There are even fewer in-house counsel. In 2005 the American Bar Foundation estimated that 8 percent of licensed lawyers worked in "private industry," that is, as corporate or in-house counsel to large businesses.[28] The numbers of in-house counsel have reportedly grown since 2005, but still these lawyers represent a relatively small portion of the market. In terms of revenue, however, BigLaw does dominate. In 2019 *Statista* estimated that just the hundred largest law firms earned roughly a third of the total industry revenue for legal services in America.[29]

It may seem strange to lump these two very different types of lawyers together. BigLaw lawyers are ever hustling to find as many wealthy clients as they can to pay their high rates. In-house counsel naturally work for just one organization and seek to cut costs on legal matters. BigLaw lawyers are encouraged to specialize and generally work within defined practice areas. Many in-house counsel are by nature and requirement generalists.

Yet, the similarities outpace the differences, and for regulatory purposes these groups of lawyers operate in similar ways. First, the bulk of in-house counsel, and especially for larger and wealthier companies, come from BigLaw originally.[30] Second, the clients are the same. BigLaw's revenue is driven by providing services to the largest and wealthiest businesses and individuals. Smaller or poorer clients cannot afford BigLaw. One sure sign that a company is big enough to afford BigLaw is hiring their *own* BigLaw lawyer as in-house counsel.

The last similarity is how lawyer regulation affects these lawyers. Historically these lawyers have been virtually unregulated. This may strike some readers as too strong, because if you have worked in BigLaw or a top corporate legal department, you

[27] ALM Staff, *The NLJ 500: Our 2019 Survey of the Nation's Largest Law Firms*, NAT'L L.J. (June 25, 2019), https://www.law.com/nationallawjournal/2019/06/25/the-nlj-500-our-2019-survey-of-the-nations-largest-law-firms/.

[28] AM. BAR ASS'N, ABA LAWYER DEMOGRAPHICS 1 (2016), https://45e2ly1gtqp9jmqme2fiw751-wpengine.netdna-ssl.com/wp-content/uploads/sites/3/2016/11/Incubators-The-Next-Wave-in-the-Access-to-Justice-Movement.pdf.

[29] *Industry Revenue of Legal Services in the U.S. from 2012 to 2024*, STATISTA, https://www.statista.com/forecasts/311177/legal-services-revenue-in-the-us (total revenue); *Total Revenue of the Leading Law Firms in the United States from 2015 to 2020*, STATISTA, https://www.statista.com/statistics/878140/total-revenue-of-the-leading-law-firms-united-states/ (AmLaw 100 revenue).

[30] See David B. Wilkins, *Is the In-House Movement Going Global? A Preliminary Assessment of the Role of Internal Counsel in Emerging Economies*, 2012 WIS. L. REV. 251, 252–53.

know that they generally take the Rules of Professional Conduct and other ethical mandates very seriously.

Nevertheless, it is fair to consider these compliance efforts largely voluntary because bar regulators almost never investigate, let alone censure or punish, lawyers in BigLaw or in-house counsel.[31] This surely reflects the fact that most in-house and BigLaw lawyers are excellent, ethical practitioners. It also reflects that few if any of the corporations that hire in-house counsel or BigLaw are going to complain to bar regulators about their lawyers, especially when any alleged ethical violation or UPL is to the benefit of all parties concerned. When discussing legal tech and UPL, it is always worth asking who is harmed and who might complain about it. Here UPL in particular is a victimless crime. Other lawyers don't complain. The clients don't complain. In fact, they often request it.

For decades BigLaw has operated as if UPL is a flexible standard and have probably never fully followed the requirement that only lawyers do "legal work." Consider the great Tom Morgan's thoughts:

> Law firms have long used paralegal and other support personnel nominally working under the lawyer supervision that ethical standards require. In addition, corporations now use non-lawyers to help deliver the total package of services they need done. Negotiating contracts, troubleshooting discrimination claims, even writing court documents can all be done by non-lawyers within an organization receiving a level of lawyer supervision and training to which unauthorized practice rules cannot effectively speak.[32]

Technology has further pushed the boundaries. Consider JP Morgan's computer program snappily entitled "Contract Intelligence or COIN."[33] JP Morgan claims this program reviews approximately 12,000 new wholesale contracts per year and replaced "360,000 hours" of staff time between lawyers and loan officers.[34] This news was met by some fear for the future earnings of lawyers – a Harvard Business School blog warned COIN "spells disruption for the legal industry"[35] – but nary a peep from lawyer regulators or UPL enforcement. In a separate context, in an FLSA

31 Kyle Rozema, Lawyer Misconduct in America 15 (Jan. 2, 2020) (unpublished manuscript), https://www.law.umich.edu/centersandprograms/lawandeconomics/workshops/Documents/Paper%202.%20Kyle%20Rozema.Lawyer%20Misconduct%20in%20America.pdf.

32 Thomas D. Morgan, The Last Days of the American Lawyer 10 (2010) (unpublished manuscript), https://scholarship.law.gwu.edu/faculty_publications/828.

33 Christian Sundquist, *The Future of Law Schools: COVID-19, Technology and Social Justice*, 53 CONN. L. REV. (ONLINE) 1, 16 (2020).

34 Hugh Son, *JPMorgan Software Does in Seconds What Took Lawyers 360,000 Hours*, BLOOMBERG (Feb. 27, 2017), https://perma.cc/J548-GSUB.

35 Legal ML, *JP Morgan COIN: A Bank's Side Project Spells Disruption for the Legal Industry*, HBS DIGIT. INITIATIVE (Nov. 13, 2018), https://digital.hbs.edu/platform-rctom/submission/jp-morgan-coin-a-banks-side-project-spells-disruption-for-the-legal-industry/.

overtime suit by a contract lawyer, the Second Circuit held that "tasks that could otherwise be performed entirely by a machine" are not the "practice of law."[36]

Contract review is just the tip of the iceberg. Outsourcing to India, outsourcing legal work from one state to another, or using computer programs to perform discovery tasks all fall into at best a gray area for UPL. A BigLaw or in-house counsel would argue that all of these tasks are "supervised" by a lawyer, and thus not UPL, regardless of how much actual supervision occurs.

1.2.2 *Legal Aid/Pro Bono Programs for the Poor*

Ironically, there is another group of lawyers who operate with great impunity under an otherwise strict regulatory regime: legal aid and other lawyers that primarily serve the very poor. The irony here is that legal aid lawyers offer civil legal assistance to the exact opposite end of the spectrum from BigLaw: the poorest Americans, typically households earning 125 percent of the poverty line or less.[37] These lawyers do yeoman's duty for low pay. The need radically outstrips the supply and has basically since at least the 1980s.[38]

In 2016 the *Justice Index* estimated that there were 6,953 legal aid lawyers, or 0.64 legal aid lawyers for every 10,000 eligible clients.[39] These lawyers and other volunteers far outpunch their numbers and help a massive number of people. The 2019 Legal Services Corporation report claims that "LSC grantees closed over 743,000 cases, including more than 231,000 Family cases and more than 214,000 Housing cases. In addition, LSC grantees helped more than 1.5 million people with legal education and information at court help desks and in workshops and clinics."[40]

How did approximately 7,000 lawyers handle so much work? They didn't. They had a lot of assistance, often from non-lawyers, technology, or pro bono lawyers working around the edges of their license. LSC's report itself baldly states: "Private attorneys, law students and graduates, paralegals, and other legal professionals were involved in closing 80,592 cases."[41] There is roughly one paralegal for every three legal aid lawyers, and, given the workflow and a tsunami of client need, these

36 Lola v. Skadden, Arps, Slate, Meagher & Flom LLP, 620 F. App'x 37, 45 (2d Cir. 2015).

37 Frequently Asked Questions – Find Legal Help, A.B.A., https://www.americanbar.org/groups/legal_services/flh-home/flh-faq/.

38 Benjamin H. Barton & Stefanos Bibas, Rebooting Justice 63–67 (2017).

39 Hanna Kozlowska, *There's a Devastating Shortage of Lawyers in the US Who Can Help the Poor with Eviction or Child Custody Cases*, Quartz (May 12, 2016), https://qz.com/681971/for-every-10000-poor-people-in-the-united-states-theres-less-than-1-lawyer-who-can-help-them-with-an-eviction-or-child-custody-case/.

40 Legal Servs. Corp., LSC by the Numbers: The Data Underlying Legal Aid Programs 8 (2019), https://www.lsc.gov/our-impact/publications/numbers.

41 *Id.*

paralegals naturally handle some (or a lot) of what might otherwise be termed "legal work," from drafting documents to giving advice to prepping clients for court.[42]

Nor has legal aid shied away from using technology to forward its mission. In 2013, LSC called a "Summit on the Use of Technology to Expand Access to Justice" that announced an aggressive new stance toward computerized solutions.[43] LSC created a technology grant program that has funded some of the most innovative work on providing basic legal services to those in need, as detailed below.

Legal aid is ground zero for the access-to-justice crisis, and they have, appropriately, tried to meet their statutory mandate to serve the legal needs of the poor by hook or by crook, which often means by bending UPL in ways that weirdly resemble BigLaw's behavior. Non-lawyers do a lot of work. Volunteers, whether lawyers or not, do a lot. More recently, technology has come center stage and lets legal aid expand their reach exponentially. Once the time and money are spent to routinize a legal task and place it online, additional users are essentially free. Rather than trying to solve the access-to-justice crisis one case at a time with bespoke work, legal aid is trying to automate simpler matters to then focus their time and energy on areas of high impact or the greatest individual need. For decades, the brilliant legal futurist Richard Susskind has predicted this model of providing computerized legal services.[44] In the US the clearest examples tend to occur at the high end and the low end.

All of this is happening with little to no input from lawyer regulators, again for reasons that mirror BigLaw. Few to none of legal aid's desperate clients are going to complain to bar regulators about tech solutions. Anecdotally, these clients are actually *thrilled* with these DIY-type services. Likewise, lawyers in private practice are not threatened because legal aid serves only the indigent, which is hardly a client base for main street lawyers.

To offer a personal example of this phenomenon, I run two programs here at the University of Tennessee that may edge toward UPL in spots: the A2J Lab and the Homeless Legal Advocacy Project. In the A2J Lab, I teach a class that tasks student teams with creating online guided interviews that result in desperately needed legal documents for poor Tennesseans. In the Homeless Project I bring groups of students down to a local homeless shelter every other week and we meet with the homeless, try to answer their questions, and if there's a local legal case we can actually handle, we try to take it.

[42] *Id.* at 82 (paralegal count).

[43] Legal Servs. Corp., Report of the Summit on the Use of Technology to Expand Access to Justice (2013), https://www.lsc.gov/sites/default/files/LSC_Tech%20Summit%20Report_2013.pdf.

[44] Richard Susskind, Expert Systems in Law: A Jurisprudential Inquiry (1988); Richard Susskind, The End of Lawyers (2010); Richard Susskind, Tomorrow's Lawyers (2013); Richard Susskind & Daniel Susskind, The Future of the Professions (2017).

Sometimes when I describe this work to our alums or other groups of lawyers, I get some pushback as to whether either of these projects might run afoul of UPL. I point out to them that I'm a licensed lawyer and "oversee" this work (echoing the BigLaw/in-house/legal aid excuse), but I also say that as a law professor and gadfly in this area I'd be *happy* to defend this work against a UPL claim or any other regulatory complaint. This may explain why none has been forthcoming.

1.2.3 *PeopleLaw*

While UPL barely touches BigLaw and legal aid, the story is very different for what I call PeopleLaw – the small firm and solo practice lawyers that work for small businesses and individuals. The most recent American Bar Foundation survey (2005) estimated that around 75 percent of American lawyers worked in private practice.[45] Of those lawyers, a little fewer than half worked as solo practitioners, making solo practice the plurality status within the profession. If you add in the lawyers that worked in "law firms" of two-to-ten lawyers, you get closer to a full majority of lawyers. While not all of these lawyers work in PeopleLaw, it is fair to conclude that the biggest share of American lawyers work in this space, serving individuals and smaller businesses.

Most solo and small firm lawyers operate in a fashion that is largely unchanged from their predecessors from hundreds of years ago. Admittedly, some small firms and solos behave more like BigLaw (e.g., small boutique patent firms) or more like legal aid (a small firm that does only disability work or consumer bankruptcy work actually runs more like a legal aid office than a traditional solo practitioner's office), but the bulk of the lawyers in this category are generalists, hustling to make it.

This market has been flooded with lawyers for decades and is highly competitive, resulting in shrinking earnings and an even clearer demarcation between "two legal professions." In 1976, John Heinz and Edward Laumann conducted a groundbreaking study of the Chicago Bar Association and came to the then-surprising conclusion that there were essentially two separate legal professions: lawyers who represent individuals and made a decent living and lawyers who represent corporations and earned much more.[46] Heinz and his co-authors repeated the Chicago survey in 1995.[47] The distance between the two hemispheres had grown dramatically, with tremendous growth in the incomes and numbers of corporate lawyers, while lawyers in small firms, government, and public-interest practices constituted a declining

[45] Am. Bar Ass'n, Legal Services Regulation in the United States, at 1.
[46] John Heinz & Edward Laumann, Chicago Lawyers: The Social Structure of the Bar 3–5 (1982).
[47] John P. Heinz et al., Urban Lawyers xv–xx (2005).

proportion of the profession, and had lower incomes.[48] Many of the lawyers in the latter group experienced a loss in real income over the period.[49]

IRS data shows the same. Every year from 1967 forward the Internal Revenue Service has gathered, anonymized, and released two different sets of tax returns from people who provide legal services: solo practitioners and partners.[50] The data show two clear trends. First, the gap between partners and solos has grown *a lot* over the last sixty years. In 1967 law firm partners earned about 2.5 times more than solos. In 2014 it was roughly 7 times as much. If you use the much smaller list of AmLaw100 partners, those partners earned 16 times as much as the average solo practitioner in 2014. Second, the gap between partners and solos reflects rising partner earnings, but also a collapse in solo practitioner earnings. Between 1967 and 2016 solo practitioners' real income shrunk by a third.

If the regulatory structure and UPL are designed to prop up lawyer incomes, why have these lawyers struggled? Part of the answer is law school avarice and law grad overproduction. More law grads have crowded into this market and driven down earnings, particularly since the 1990s. Part of the answer is the more recent arrival of competition from tech providers like LegalZoom and Rocket Lawyer, who explicitly target this market and peel away at least some potential customers.[51]

Part of the answer is the business model itself. In a market that has too many providers, one would expect prices to decline to match what demand exists. As the access-to-justice crisis establishes, there is hardly a lack of demand for legal services from the poor or middle class. To the contrary, the need is acute and growing. If there is copious need *and* there is market over-supply in lawyers, surely prices will fall to meet demand?

Sadly, no. This is because the vast majority of these lawyers are still practicing law in the old-fashioned, bespoke manner they learned in law school and from their predecessors: providing individualized services for a fee to individual customers. Given that IRS data suggests the average solo practitioner is earning less than $60,000, there just is not much room to lower prices, and in fact the average hourly rate for lawyers in this space remains stubbornly high. In 2016 Clio, a leading practice management software provider to small firms and solo practitioners, estimated that the average hourly rate for solo practitioners/small firm lawyers is $232 an hour.[52]

If $232 is the average hourly rate, how are these lawyers possibly struggling? If they collected that rate on 20 hours of work a week, and worked 48 weeks a year, they

48 *Id.* at 3–28.
49 *Id.*
50 For a fuller discussion of this data and a lengthy discussion of the academic kerfuffle it provoked, see Barton, Fixing Law Schools, at 45–51.
51 Hadfield, *Legal Markets*, at 44.
52 Clio, Legal Trends Report (2016), https://perma.cc/E7UK-6ZH2. For a helpful discussion of these Clio reports, see Hadfield, *Legal Markets*, at 35–37.

should be grossing $222,720 annually.[53] Unfortunately, this is not the case. The same Clio report showed that in practice these lawyers actually are only able to collect on about 1.5 hours of billable work a day.[54] These lawyers are hardly lazy though. They bill more than they can collect from their clients and then spend the rest of their time hustling to find paying customers and running their small businesses.[55]

Unlike BigLaw or legal aid lawyers, main street lawyers are actually pretty heavily regulated. These lawyers are the most likely to face client complaints, bar investigations, and the more serious punishments of public censure, suspension, or disbarment.[56] Critics of bar enforcement note that even these results are too infrequent to protect the public at large, but insofar as the regulatory system has teeth at all, it is in this market.

Humorously, this market is also the source of the great bulk of UPL complaints and prosecutions, almost always generating from the lawyers themselves rather than aggrieved members of the public.[57] There are, of course, unfortunate victims of scammers who claim to be lawyers and are not and then do little or no work. There has been a spate of these cases where "notarios" claim to be qualified to represent immigration clients and then steal their money.[58] Nevertheless, the bulk of the cases involve aggrieved *lawyers* complaining about UPL, reflecting that UPL has always been more focused on protecting lawyers than the public. As Deborah Rhode put it, "bar leaders and case doctrine insist that broad prohibitions on unauthorized practice serve the public, [but] support for that claim is notable for its absence."[59]

1.2.4 *One Last Hybrid Category – Plaintiff's Side Firms and Settlement Mills*

The plaintiff's side tort and class-action bar is sort of a hybrid of the other categories but is unique enough for some separate thoughts. First, unlike a more traditional generalist practice, plaintiff's side firms tend to specialize more, and sometimes quite narrowly.[60] Second, the business model and client base is completely different, since plaintiff's side firms almost always work on a contingency basis rather than charging by the hour or per activity. This means the client base spans from the very poor upward. In fact, these firms are more easily grouped by whom they *sue* (typically the deep-pocketed, whether wealthy individuals, insured individuals, or

53 Benjamin H. Barton & Deborah L. Rhode, *Access to Justice and Routine Legal Services: New Technologies Meet Bar Regulators*, 70 Hastings L.J. 955, 985–86 (2019).

54 *Id.*

55 *Id.*

56 Rozema, Lawyer Misconduct.

57 *See* Deborah L. Rhode & Lucy Buford Ricca, *Protecting the Profession or the Public? Rethinking Unauthorized-Practice Enforcement*, 82 Fordham L. Rev. 2587 (2014).

58 Kati Daffan, *Notarios Are No Help with Immigration*, FTC Consumer Advice (Sept. 26, 2019), https://www.consumer.ftc.gov/blog/2019/09/notarios-are-no-help-immigration.

59 Rhode & Ricca, *Protecting the Profession or the Public?* at 2605.

60 John C. Coffee, Entrepreneurial Litigation: Its Rise, Fall, and Future (2015).

large businesses) than whom they represent. Third, the regulation hits quite differently here, as much of the most anti-competitive regulations, like limits on advertising or in-person solicitation, are squarely aimed at these lawyers.

Like other lawyers, it is quite typical for these lawyers to stretch the limits of UPL in the name of profit and efficiency. The best example is the settlement mill, which has a few titular lawyers at the top and is otherwise completely staffed and operated by lower paid non-lawyers. Nora Freeman Engstrom has pioneered the study of these firms.[61] Settlement mills run high-volume personal injury practices where their lawyers carry as many as 200–300 cases at a time.[62] How is this possible? Because non-lawyers actually do all of the work. Settlement mills almost never take a case to trial and actually try to avoid litigation altogether; they let non-lawyers handle intake and negotiating with insurance companies.[63] The titular lawyers "oversee" this work. UPL is again not typically strongly enforced in this market (although other regulatory and client complaints are quite common).

1.3 HOW REGULATION, CULTURE, AND MARKETS HAVE SHAPED AMERICAN LEGAL TECH

This section describes the current state of American legal tech from areas that are booming to areas that are in a slow burn. Unsurprisingly, the parts of the market that operate with less regulation are seeing explosive growth; the rest of the market, less so.

1.3.1 *Penthouse to Outhouse – Boomtown USA*

In America the very top of the market and the very bottom are leading the way in legal tech/justice innovations. The strangeness of this result should jump off the page. In what other market is the very bottom and very top the most forward- looking and aggressive technologically?

1.3.2 *BigLaw*

Large corporate legal departments are leading the way on legal tech, and BigLaw is following, sometimes reluctantly and sometimes aggressively, depending on the firm. Some readers will immediately object here. The individual lawyers that run BigLaw are by reputation notoriously tech-ignorant and change-averse. *Above the Law* summarizes: "Law firms are notoriously averse to change and, relatedly, technology. I worked with partners who responded to email with handwritten notes

[61] Nora Freeman Engstrom, *Run-of-the-Mill Justice*, 22 GEO. J. LEGAL ETHICS 1485 (2009).
[62] *Id.* at 1491–92.
[63] *Id.*

circulated via intra-office mail. I knew another who dictated responses to his secretary rather than draft an actual response."[64] BigLaw's internal systems are often outmoded. Their tech security lags. Some of the senior lawyers have declined to adopt email, let alone Slack.[65] True.

Bill Henderson has noted that trying to sell innovative technologies directly to law firms has often been a losing game, even when those technologies would increase firm-wide efficiency.[66] Why? Because law firms are risk-averse by nature and because in some ways law firms get paid for their inefficiencies. Telling a business that primarily runs on hourly fees that you can make them more efficient is not necessarily a winning strategy.

But don't mistake the employee's reticence for the employer's desires. If there is a single story of corporate legal work over the last decades, it is cutting costs, increasing efficiency, and using technology to replace humans wherever possible.[67] Some press reports on legal tech seem to suggest that this is a new process, but it has been going on for years. It started with "in-sourcing."[68] In-house legal departments have grown relentlessly and are incentivized to seek cheaper solutions. Simple work is sloughed off to non-lawyers. More complicated work is offshored to cheaper jurisdictions like India.[69] AI (like the COIN program described earlier) can handle mundane contract or litigation related tasks.[70] eDiscovery is a prime example.[71] In-house counsel break legal work into constituent parts and only hire expensive outside counsel for sui generis or critically important areas.[72] Everything else can be handled in the most efficient and cheapest manner.[73]

The year 2020 was the biggest yet for investment in legal tech startups. The programs covered a bevy of corporate legal needs, including contract analytics and contract review, automated legal spend management, eDiscovery companies, and

[64] Joe Patrice, *LegalTech 2014: What's Wrong with You Lawyers*, ABOVE THE LAW (Feb. 5, 2014), https://abovethelaw.com/2014/02/whats-wrong-with-you-lawyers/.

[65] *Id.*

[66] Joe Borstein, *Alt.Legal: Diffusing Innovation in the Law, the Amazing Work of Bill Henderson*, ABOVE THE LAW (Nov. 8, 2017), https://abovethelaw.com/2017/11/alt-legal-diffusing-innovation-in-the-law-the-amazing-work-of-bill-henderson/.

[67] David Freeman Engstrom & Jonah B. Gelbach, *Legal Tech, Civil Procedure, and the Future of Adversarialism*, 169 U. PA. L. REV. 1001, 1031–35 (2021).

[68] Laurel S. Terry, *The Legal World Is Flat: Globalization and Its Effects on Lawyers Practicing in Non-Global Law Firms*, 28 NW. J. INT'L L. & BUS. 527, 542–45 (2008).

[69] Larry E. Ribstein, *The Death of Big Law*, 2010 WIS. L. REV. 749, 766–67.

[70] W. Bradley Wendel, *The Promise and Limitations of Artificial Intelligence in the Practice of Law*, 72 OKLA. L. REV. 21, 23–24 (2019).

[71] Dana A. Remus, *The Uncertain Promise of Predictive Coding*, 99 IOWA L. REV. 1691 (2014).

[72] Bruce H. Kobayashi & Larry Ribstein, *Law's Information Revolution*, 53 ARIZ. L. REV. 1169, 1219–20 (2011).

[73] John S. Dzienkowski, *The Future of Big Law: Alternative Legal Service Providers to Corporate Clients*, 82 FORDHAM L. REV. 2995 (2014).

knowledge-integration platforms.[74] I have two reactions to the explosion of investment and activity in this area. On the one hand: WOW. The full span of the work is incredible, and after a slow start the market for these sorts of disruptions seems to be really humming. As late as 2011, Gillian Hadfield was asking "where are the 'garage guys' in law?"[75] This question has been answered emphatically.

On the other hand, these innovations often reflect what machines are currently excellent at and what humans sometimes struggle to accomplish: using repeatable and clear rules to wrangle a large quantity of data or documents into a useful format for humans. Computers are already excellent at rules-based legal work. Interactive document production programs from LegalZoom, Rocket Lawyer, or Community Lawyer are other examples. Humans can get tired or bored with these tasks and make mistakes, or they can be too expensive. Once a task is automated, computers are essentially free and never tire.

But current computer programs still struggle with more *human* tasks that require more nuance and judgment.[76] In contrast to eDiscovery, due diligence document review has been harder to mechanize, because rather than asking a machine to find a mass of documents with common features (emails about an accident, or featuring legal advice, for example), due diligence before an acquisition often searches a company's data for weird or non-compliant documents that signal the existence of something undisclosed and potentially harmful (like a future legal liability or some kind of underlying fraud).[77] Again, computers have improved at this task, and not all due diligence requires a search for anomalies. Still, as you might guess, telling an algorithm to search for things "that might signal a future legal liability" is trickier than an eDiscovery search for all the emails about a particular deal.

1.3.3 *Access-to-Justice Work for the Poor*

Legal Aid and others are aggressively pursuing tech solutions to legal problems through grant programs and working with community partners.[78] As an overview, consider the 2019 LSC-funded projects, which are aggressive, creative, and if you care about access to justice, heartening.[79] The projects can be divvied into two baskets: automating legal processes or sharing legal information with the poor.

74 Rhys Dipshan, *The 9 Biggest Legal Tech Investments*, LEGALTECH NEWS (Dec. 30, 2020), https://www.law.com/legaltechnews/2020/12/30/the-9-biggest-legal-tech-investments-in-2020/.

75 *See* Gillian K. Hadfield, *Equipping the Garage Guys in Law*, 70 MD. L. REV. 484 (2011).

76 Dana Remus & Frank S. Levy, *Can Robots Be Lawyers? Computers, Lawyers, and the Practice of Law*, 30 GEO. J. LEGAL ETHICS 501 (2017).

77 *Id.*

78 Bob Ambrogi, *LSC's $4.2M in Technology Grants Illustrate How Tech Is Driving Access to Justice*, LAW SITES BLOG (Oct. 25, 2019), https://www.lawsitesblog.com/2019/10/lscs-4-2m-in-technology-grants-illustrate-how-tech-is-driving-access-to-justice.html.

79 *Id.*

Here's a sampling of the processes LSC is seeking to automate: (1) filing for disability benefits in Alaska; (2) filing for consumer debt relief in California; (3) intake for Spanish-speaking clients in Atlanta; (4) making fair housing complaints in Michigan; (5) creating an automated legal help chatbot in Michigan; (6) establishing legal self-help document assembly software in New Hampshire for housing and consumer law problems; (7) online intake and referral in Pennsylvania; (8) filing for consumer bankruptcy (with an assist from consumer bankruptcy tech pioneer Upsolve).

Legal Aid also supported the following new sources of legal information: (1) online tutorials in landlord-tenant law in Georgia; (2) online "classrooms" covering six different areas of poverty law in South Carolina; (3) self-help videos covering evictions and orders of protection in Vermont; (4) redesigns of websites to include much more free information and forms in Kentucky and Minnesota.

This is just a snapshot of the projects in one year! And note that because of the nature of technology, every one of these projects makes the next project easier. Local law and information are not always transferable (although federal law like bankruptcy is easier), but the technology platforms and processes are absolutely transferable, especially here in a non-profit setting where all the players are on the same team and happy to share.

Further, Legal Aid is hardly fighting this battle alone. Felicity Conrad, one of the founders of the pro bono tech platform Paladin, recently launched a database that lists "justice tech" startups.[80] Conrad describes the "justice tech" sector as "a new breed of legaltech – instead of focusing on modernizing the existing legal services market (contracts, practice management, legal research, etc.), their goal is to leverage technology to *directly* scale legal services to the billions of people underserved by the existing market."[81] I will not endeavor to describe all *twenty-seven* listed entities (as of January 2021), but if you want to feel like technology might actually be doing some good in the world, I strongly encourage you to go to the link and read the spreadsheet. It covers areas from reporting police misconduct, to recording police interactions, to the "do not pay app" for challenging corporate fees and parking tickets, to landlord-tenant, divorce, and immigration services.

There are also a handful of law schools working in this space. Stanford's Center on the Legal Profession, built by and around Deborah Rhode and her decades of leadership in legal ethics, feminism, and access to justice, has been a world leader. Margaret Hagan's Legal Design Lab was originally housed within the Center and focuses on what she calls "human facing" technology, creating apps and programs that help ordinary folks navigate complicated court processes and legal problems.[82]

80 Felicity Conrad, *Meet the 27 Startups Pioneering the Justice Tech Market*, Paladin (Jan. 27, 2021), https://medium.com/join-paladin/meet-the-27-startups-pioneering-the-justice-tech-market-dfd4795763aa.

81 *Id.*

82 Stan. Legal Design Lab, https://www.legaltechdesign.com.

Suffolk Law School has a Legal Innovation & Technology Lab and Chicago–Kent a Law Lab, among others.

My A2J Lab at the University of Tennessee is a more modest example. We use the excellent Community Lawyer platform to create the interviews and have automated processes to help with immigration forms, orders of protection, convictions expungement, and debt relief. On the one hand, the class is embarrassingly easy to teach, and the platform and our non-profit and legal aid clients do all of the really hard work. On the other hand, I've taught the class for three years, and we've had a pretty big impact in Tennessee! This area is packed with low-hanging fruit.

Some courts are also leading the way, especially those courts on the front lines of the pro se crisis. Courts started to complain about a rise in pro se litigation as far back as the 1980s, but this century the problem has ripened into a true crisis. Courts' and clerks' offices found themselves buried under miserable and angry pro se litigants and could not help but notice that case results, and thus justice, were heavily affected. Encouragingly, many judges and court administrators have gone to work, often using technology, process reforms, or a combination. The pandemic has likewise helped, as online court went from a theoretical idea to a necessity. The trend toward online dispute resolution (ODR) has likewise accelerated, as the chapters by Spalding and Prescott establish. ODR is often pitched as an efficiency measure, but when used in pro se courts, it is also an access-to-justice effort, because these programs are often designed to be used by ordinary people and not lawyers. Like David Engstrom and colleagues' work on AI in government, courts present different, and in some ways more promising, use cases than legal work for individuals.[83]

These projects are blossoming despite potential regulatory and lawyer opposition because few want to push back against large government entities like courts or legal aid, but also because these projects to do not typically compete against flesh-and-blood lawyers, who barely try to serve the middle class, let alone the poor. Some of these projects, especially those aimed at areas where lawyers wish to remain dominant and at least somewhat expensive, like consumer bankruptcy or divorce, have faced some pushback, of course. But overall the A2J tech revolution continues apace.

1.3.4 *Seas Were Rougher, Clear Sailing Now? – Interactive Forms*

The provision of legal forms to the middle class and small businesses initially faced tougher sledding. The public face of American legal tech are LegalZoom and Rocket Lawyer. Computerized legal services (online or via cellphone apps) for the

[83] David Freeman Engstrom et al., Government by Algorithm: Artificial Intelligence in Federal Administrative Agencies (2020), https://www-cdn.law.stanford.edu/wp-content/uploads/2020/02/ACUS-AI-Report.pdf.

consumer market are expanding at a dizzying rate and in direct competition to main street lawyers. If you are a typical lawyer, you may have some idea what these sites offer, but probably have not taken a spin through them recently. I strongly recommend you do, just so you understand the competition.

Both LegalZoom and Rocket Lawyer offer guided interviews and document assembly (or more basic forms) for virtually any kind of written legal document that is not meant to be filed directly in court, and some that are meant for court. They offer everything from LLC formation to wills to contracts to internet terms of service. You name a legal document, they offer it, and often at a radical discount to what a human lawyer would charge. Have you heard of the basic $500 will offered by your local solo practitioner? LegalZoom's basic will starts at $89.[84] LLC University estimates that a lawyer will charge between $1,000–1,500 to form a basic LLC.[85] LegalZoom's cost? Seventy-nine dollars plus filing fees.[86]

Given that these are bread-and-butter matters for main street lawyers, it is stunning that LegalZoom and Rocket Lawyer survived UPL. How did the lawyer regulators fail? Partially due to Silicon Valley chutzpah, partially due to poor timing, and partially due to the shifting sands of antitrust and public opinion. But currently there can be little doubt that the horse is out of the barn, and these forms providers seem destined to remain stiff competition for lawyers.

First, consider the gall of LegalZoom. Its founders were surely aware that providing forms and interactive document creation online could violate UPL or skate close to the line. Yet, they went forward guns blazing. LegalZoom was launched in 2001 and it was hardly a sneak attack. It recruited former O. J. Simpson lawyer Robert Shapiro as a co-founder and launched an all-out PR blitz.[87] This is, of course, a well-known Silicon Valley strategy, most famously pursued by companies like Uber or Airbnb. Plow into a legal gray area and assume/hope that you will be able to grow fast enough to eventually beat back any regulatory resistance.[88]

Second, these companies had some great good luck in terms of initial regulatory disinterest. LegalZoom launched in 2001 but did not face any serious UPL investigations and prosecutions until 2008.[89] Why? Because of the brokenness of the market for legal services in the United States. Most main street lawyers still focus

[84] *Last Will and Testament*, LEGALZOOM, https://www.legalzoom.com/personal/estate-planning/last-will-and-testament-overview.html.

[85] *How Much Does It Cost to Setup an LLC?* LLC U, https://www.llcuniversity.com/how-much-does-it-cost-to-setup-an-llc/.

[86] *Business Formation: Choose a Business Structure*, LEGALZOOM, https://www.legalzoom.com/business/business-formation/.

[87] David Rovella, *Campaigns: Web Site Launch – LegalZoom.com Is First in Its Class*, PR WK. (June 25, 2001), https://www.prweek.com/article/1237037/campaigns-web-site-launch—legal zoomcom-first-its-class.

[88] *See* Jordan M. Barry & Elizabeth Pollman, *Regulatory Entrepreneurship*, 90 S. CAL. L. REV. 383 (2017).

[89] Ray Worthy Campbell, *Rethinking Regulation and Innovation in the U.S. Legal Services Market*, 9 N.Y.U. J. L. & BUS. 1, 43–47 (2012).

on very expensive, bespoke, hourly services. Most middle-class customers and small businesses cannot afford these services. This means that solo practitioners (or their receptionists) spend a lot of time explaining to potential customers that they cannot afford to hire a lawyer. These non-clients were the first adopters of LegalZoom and Rocket Lawyer. Fans of Clayton Christensen's Innovator's Dilemma will recognize this exact process, as the innovative upstart focuses on the lowest-end, least-valuable work, before moving up the ladder to more profitable areas.[90]

When LegalZoom started, its products were not as polished as they are now, so the first wave of LegalZoom customers were not really a loss to lawyers at all. These folks likely couldn't afford a lawyer's services. Over time, of course, LegalZoom got better, and lawyers started to notice a pinch on their business. But by then years had passed and LegalZoom was pretty well established.

That said, the first UPL cases were still somewhat ominous. In Washington State in 2011, LegalZoom settled a UPL investigation by paying $20,000 in costs.[91] That same year in Missouri it paid the state's attorney's fees and changed some parts of its site for Missouri customers.[92] The Missouri case was particularly worrisome because the district court there concluded in dicta that LegalZoom's interactive forms were very similar to the provision of legal services by a lawyer and thus were likely unlawful as UPL.[93]

At this point LegalZoom decided to take the fight to the regulators, responding to a UPL sanction by the State Bar of North Carolina with a lawsuit alleging antitrust and constitutional violations.[94] When the Supreme Court decided that North Carolina's own dental board had violated antitrust law in 2015, the State Bar quickly settled, and on very favorable terms to LegalZoom.[95] Not coincidentally, this launched a series of LegalZoom wins on UPL, including in South Carolina and Arkansas.[96] These decisions have put LegalZoom in a good position and plowed the road for Rocket Lawyer and others.

Last, LegalZoom could count on public opinion. Just as Uber has leveraged public distaste for overweening regulators (overweening according to Uber at

90 *See* Clayton Christensen, The Innovator's Dilemma (2011).

91 *See* Daniel Fisher, *Entrepreneurs versus Lawyers*, Forbes (Oct. 5, 2011), http://www.forbes.com/forbes/2011/1024/entrepreneurs-lawyers-suh-legalzoom-automate-daniel-fisher.html.

92 Nathan Koppel, *Seller of Online Legal Forms Settles Unauthorized Practice of Law Suit*, Wall St. J. (Aug. 23, 2011), http://blogs.wsj.com/law/2011/08/23/seller-of-online-legal-forms-settles-unauthorized-practiced-of-law-suit/.

93 Janson v. LegalZoom, 802 F. Supp. 2d 1053 (W.D. Mo. 2011).

94 Rhode & Barton, *Rethinking Self-Regulation*, at 278–79.

95 N.C. Bd. of Dental Exam'rs v. FTC, 574 U.S. 494 (2015); Terry Carter, *LegalZoom Resolves $10.5m Antitrust Suit against North Carolina Bar*, A.B.A. J. (Oct. 23, 2015), http://www.abajournal.com/news/article/legalzoom_resolves_10.5m_antitrust_suit_against_north_carolina_state_bar.

96 Ben Barton, *LegalZoom Fought the North Carolina Bar and LegalZoom Won*, Bloomberg L. (Nov. 13, 2015), bol.bna.com/legalzoom-fought-the-north-carolina-bar-and-legalzoom-won/.

least),[97] LegalZoom could count on some political pressure if it was fully driven from any given state. For example, in the late 1990s the Texas Bar Association attempted to ban a program called "Quicken Family Lawyer" as UPL, only to be overruled by the Texas legislature.[98]

Future signs are mixed. On the one hand, recent UPL developments look good, and the decisions by Utah, Arizona, and others to allow for more provision of legal services by non-lawyers and technology certainly suggests future growth.[99] On the other hand, today's announced loosening sometimes leads to tomorrow's tightening. The 2016 ABA Report on the Future of Legal Services' seemingly innocuous suggestion that legal tech should be regulated to protect client interests is worrisome given the history of lawyer regulation that allegedly protects the public but does more to protect lawyers.[100]

1.3.5 *Controls Are Tighter, but Technology Is Still Coming: Legal Advice*

If you are wondering whether the market for interactive forms alone is enough to meet the unmet demand from the middle class and small businesses, consider that both LegalZoom and Rocket Lawyer have legal advice subscription offerings staffed by licensed lawyers. Both sites try to sell these plans along with their basic forms.[101] For a monthly fee subscribers get a set amount of "free" legal advice from licensed lawyers. These plans skirt the regulations that make fee-splitting with non-lawyers illegal because the lawyers themselves are not paid for any individual consultation. Instead, they get a "small cut" of the aggregated monthly fees.[102] Why would lawyers give what essentially amounts to free legal consultations that mostly serve to enrich their online competitors? Business development. Some of these advice clients may eventually have a "real" case – that is, a case where they will pay a lawyer an hourly rate for more valuable legal work. Yes, the market is so tight for these lawyers that it's worth offering "free" consultations just for the hope of generating more useful business.

97 Suhauna Hussain et al., *How Uber and Lyft Persuaded California to Vote Their Way*, L.A. Times (Nov. 13, 2020), https://www.latimes.com/business/technology/story/2020-11-13/how-uber-lyft-doordash-won-proposition-22.

98 Unauthorized Prac. of L. Comm. v. Parsons Tech. Inc., 179 F.3d 956, 956 (5th Cir. 1999).

99 Utah Work Grp. on Regul. Reform, Narrowing the Access-to-Justice Gap by Reimagining Regulation (2019), https://www.utahbar.org/wp-content/uploads/2019/08/FINAL-Task-Force-Report.pdf.

100 Am. Bar Ass'n Comm'n on Future of Legal Servs., Report on the Future of Legal Services in the United States (2016), https://www.srln.org/system/files/attachments/2016%20ABA%20Future%20of%20Legal%20Services%20-Report-Web.pdf.

101 LegalZoom's monthly plan for business legal advice is advertised for as little as $50 a month. *Prepaid Legal Plans – Affordable Legal Help for Your Family or Business*, LegalZoom, https://www.legalzoom.com/attorneys/.

102 Aaron George, *10 Best Lead Generation Services for Lawyers*, Clio, https://www.clio.com/blog/best-lead-generation-services-lawyers-reviews/.

Other sites like Avvo offer searchable, free legal advice from lawyers.[103] Potential clients ask a short question, and lawyers volunteer to answer.[104] The answers are publicly available and searchable. Lawyers do this in the hope that some of the answers will lead to actual paying clients and also because Avvo is a lawyer rating service (like TripAdvisor or Yelp for lawyers) and answering questions can help their ratings.

Avvo used to offer a legal services plan that directly connected consumers and lawyers, but bar regulators closed it down for fee-splitting and other alleged violations.[105] If you are wondering whether bar regulators still have teeth, the answer is yes when it comes to direct provision of legal advice or services for a fee.

1.3.6 *Little Immediate Help: Filing Papers or Appearing in Court*

Historically, prohibitions on UPL have been at their strongest in courthouses. Non-lawyers are rarely allowed to represent others in court proceedings or to sign and file papers on their behalf. This is less true in administrative hearings, but generally the more formal the procedural setting, the less the tolerance for non-lawyer assistance.

The actual drafting of legal documents is, of course, subject to encroachment by computerization. The chapter by Nyarko and Frankenreiter establishes that we may still be some ways away from any really high-level work in that regard.[106] As such, the actual filing of papers and appearing in court will remain a human's only proposition for at least as long as judges prefer talking to humans than robots.

1.4 SO WHAT DOES THE FUTURE HOLD?

America will continue to be a world leader in legal tech, regardless of its regulatory structure. The current American demand for legal services is currently grossly underserved by lawyers and their focus on selling bespoke services. There is a massive amount of low-hanging fruit, and the lure of disruption will continue to draw innovators and investors.

Law tech in America will continue to thrive most in the areas that are regulated the least, at the highest and lowest ends of the market. We will continue to see rapid automation of legal processes for the poor and corporate clients, bounded mostly by technological barriers rather than regulatory barriers.

Wealthy corporations will naturally get first access to innovations like eDiscovery or the use of AI to predict legal outcomes. These technologies involve large startup costs, so will be expensive and exclusive at first. Nevertheless, computer processes

[103] Research Legal Advice, Avvo, https://www.avvo.com/free-legal-advice.
[104] Barton & Rhode, *Access to Justice and Routine Legal Services*.
[105] *Id.*
[106] *See* Chapter 3 in this volume.

are hard to pen in once created and mastered, since the marginal cost of adding new customers can run as low as zero. We can expect at least some leakage downstream, and over time these tech innovations should make law cheaper and better even for main street lawyers and the public at large.

The poor will have some advantages! Regulators have shown remarkable tolerance of tech solutions offered by legal aid or non-profits. Likewise, all the most exciting courtroom innovations, such as ODR, will continue to arrive first in small claims or other pro se courts. In my book *Glass Half Full* I talk about these innovations offering the possibility of a truly bizarre science fiction experiment: a world where courts for the poor are fairer and more efficient than courts for the rich.[107]

Further, and this is not necessarily a good thing, legal work for the poor does not need to be perfect, just better than nothing. Corporate clients will only accept automated processes that work perfectly or near perfectly. Technology aimed at the poor, like interactive order-of-protection forms, face a lower bar. Let me be absolutely clear, there are *significant* reasons to feel uncomfortable with this fact of American life, but still, it is what it is. The bar for an interactive form for the poor is often "Is it better than nothing?" This allows for more aggressive experimentation.

That said, making the perfect the enemy of the good is part of the reason we are mired in the current access-to justice crisis. We cannot afford to offer BigLaw style services to the poor for free, and of course the middle class could never afford such services. Rather than pretending that is our goal, realistic attempts to do our best should be encouraged and accepted. The status quo is so bad that experimentation and triage are not only recommended; they are desperately needed.

As Engstrom and Gelbach aptly note, technical challenges in natural language processing will make advances in automated legal advice or reasoning slower and on a different time horizon.[108] Note that even in looser regulatory environments, such as England or Australia, we have not seen anything resembling a for-profit "robot lawyer," at least partially due to the current limitations on natural language processing. Chatbots that handle intake or more basic questions exist now and will, of course, improve and expand over time. For now, at least, most of these applications will require human lawyer inputs, so they will exist "under a lawyer's supervision." As long as a lawyer is even nominally involved, regulators are likely to be copacetic. In-person work, especially in court, stays the province of lawyers for the longest time.

The current regulatory atmosphere, where the top and the bottom of the market are essentially unregulated, is, of course, not set in stone. In fact, seemingly salutary efforts like those in Utah, Arizona, and other states could turn sour quite easily. Historically, most lawyer-driven consumer protection efforts like UPL or the bar

[107] Barton, Glass Half Full, at 208–9.
[108] Engstrom & Gelbach, *Legal Tech*, at 1018–30.

exam eventually tend to favor lawyers over the public.[109] Reform advocates have taken to calling the Utah approach "re-regulation," to avoid the implication of willy-nilly deregulation. But these reforms might turn out to be "re-regulation" in the strong sense of bringing regulation (via a sandbox entry process or other routes) that currently doesn't exist for much of the market, especially at the high and low ends of the market. We must be vigilant to avoid the "we're from the Bar Association and we're here to help" type of regulation.[110]

In my preferred version of the future, lawyers of all stripes leverage technology to work more efficiently and to focus on the work that humans are especially excellent at: talking to other humans, high-level reasoning, and strategic thinking. There is a version of the future where technology solves the access-to-justice and related pro se crisis and makes an immeasurable difference in the lives of the poor and middle class in America and all over the world. Done properly, technology could even improve the lives of lawyers, as they spend more of their time doing the activities that likely drew them to the profession in the first place and less time on repeatable grunt work. I have, admittedly, been called a Pollyanna on this front, with Deborah Rhode's reactions alternating between "good luck with that" to the more generous "from your lips to God's ears." For the millions of Americans with unmet civil justice needs, we can all hope the latter ends up the more apt of the two.

109 BARTON, THE LAWYER-JUDGE BIAS.

110 This is a riff on the famous Ronald Reagan quote: "The nine most terrifying words in the English language are: I'm from the Government, and I'm here to help." *See August 12, 1986 News Conference*, RONALD REAGAN PRESIDENTIAL FOUND. & INST., https://www.reaganfoundation.org/ronald-reagan/reagan-quotes-speeches/news-conference-1/.

2

Lawtech

Leveling the Playing Field in Legal Services?

John Armour and Mari Sako

The legal services market is commonly thought of as divided into two "hemispheres" – PeopleLaw and BigLaw.[1] These segments represent, respectively, individuals and corporate clients. The last few decades have seen an increasing concentration of resources in the legal market toward serving corporate clients, to the alleged detriment of consumer clients. At the same time, the costs of accessing legal representation exceed the financial resources of many ordinary citizens and small businesses, compromising their access to the legal system.[2]

We ask: will the adoption of legal tech – new digital technologies in legal markets – lead to a leveling of the playing field between the PeopleLaw and BigLaw sectors? By "leveling," we mean convergence of business models[3] in the two sectors so as to deliver a more equal opportunity to access legal services.

This research is funded by UKRI pursuant to the Next Generation Services Industrial Strategy Challenge Fund. It forms part of the program Unlocking the Potential of AI in English Law: https://www.law.ox.ac.uk/unlocking-potential-artificial-intelligence-english-law. We are grateful for comments on earlier drafts from Ben Barton, Justice Mariano-Florentino Cuéllar, David Engstrom, Jens Frankenreiter, Gillian Hadfield, Dan Linna, Julian Nyarko, and participants in the *Legal Tech and the Future of Civil Justice* webinar in 2021.

1 John P. Heinz & Edward O. Laumann, Chicago Lawyers: The Social Structure of the Bar (1982); John P. Heinz et al., *The Changing Character of Lawyers' Work: Chicago in 1975 and 1995*, 32 L. & Soc'y Rev. 751 (1998).

2 David Clementi, Review of the Regulatory Framework for Legal Services in England and Wales: Final Report (2004); Gillian K. Hadfield, *Higher Demand, Lower Supply? A Comparative Assessment of the Legal Resource Landscape for Ordinary Americans*, 37 Fordham Urb. L.J. 129 (2010); Competition & Mkts. Auth., Review of the Legal Services Market Study in England and Wales (2020), https://assets.publishing.service.gov.uk/media/5fd9e53cd3bf7f40ccb335e1/Legal_Services_Review_-_Final_report.pdf; Gillian K. Hadfield, *Legal Markets*, 60 J. Econ. Lit. (forthcoming 2022).

3 David J. Teece, *Business Models, Business Strategy and Innovation*, 43 Long Range Plan. 172 (2010); Mari Sako, *Business Models in Strategy and Innovation*, 55 Commc'ns of the ACM 22 (2012); John Armour & Mari Sako, *AI-Enabled Business Models in Legal Services: From Traditional Law Firms to Next-Generation Law Companies?* 7 J. Prof. & Org. 27 (2020).

Convergence in business models would enable legal service providers to exploit opportunities for scaling and cost reduction, and to meet more of the unmet legal needs of clients.[4] We focus, not on what legal tech in theory may be capable of doing, but on which use cases are likely to emerge in practice and take root. In order to do so, we use a causal framework that takes account of organizational complements[5] and regulatory constraints to the adoption of emergent business models.

By leveraging the regulatory differences between the UK and the US, we aim to gauge the relative importance of regulatory shifts in meeting unmet legal needs.[6] In 2007, the UK enacted a bold set of reforms.[7] By reducing the substantive domain over which lawyers have exclusive service rights, and by permitting alternative business structures (ABS), the intent was to stimulate competition and thereby more cost-effective legal services to meet latent demand.[8] Similar proposals have long been debated in the US,[9] and some states have taken tentative first steps.[10] Our comparison of secular trends in the UK (England and Wales, strictly speaking) and the US demonstrates that regulatory reforms may be necessary but not sufficient to bring about desirable changes in meeting latent legal demand.

This chapter proceeds as follows. Section 2.1 sets the scene with an overview of the development of the PeopleLaw and BigLaw sectors in Britain and the United States in the last few decades. Section 2.2 examines the adoption of legal tech in the BigLaw sector, to identify specific use cases and complementary changes taking place (or not taking place) to adopt emergent business models. Section 2.3 conducts

4 Albert H. Yoon, *The Post-Modern Lawyer: Technology and the Democratization of Legal Representation*, 66 U. Toronto L.J. 456 (2016).

5 John Armour et al., Augmented Lawyering 2022 U. Ill. L. Rev. 71.

6 Hazel Genn, *Understanding Civil Justice*, 50 Current Legal Probs. 155 (1997); Rebecca L. Sandefur, *What We Know and Need to Know about the Legal Needs of the Public*, 67 S.C. L. Rev. 443 (2015).

7 Legal Services Act 2007, c. 29 (UK).

8 *See* Clementi, Review of the Regulatory Framework.

9 Gillian K. Hadfield, *The Price of Law: How the Market for Lawyers Distorts the Justice System*, 98 Mich. L. Rev. 953 (2000); Gillian K. Hadfield, *Legal Barriers to Innovation: The Growing Economic Cost of Professional Control over Corporate Legal Markets*, 60 Stan. L. Rev. 1689 (2007); Gillian K. Hadfield & Deborah L. Rhode, *How to Regulate Legal Services to Promote Access, Innovation, and the Quality of Lawyering*, 67 Hastings L.J. 1191 (2015); William D. Henderson, Legal Market Landscape Report: Commissioned by the State Bar of California (2018), https://board.calbar.ca.gov/docs/agendaItem/Public/agendaitem1000022382.pdf.

10 *See* Ariz. Sup. Ct., Task Force on the Delivery of Legal Services: Report and Recommendations (2019), https://www.americanbar.org/content/dam/aba/administrative/legal_education_and_admissions_to_the_bar/council_reports_and_resolutions/november2019/arizona-supreme-court-task-force-on-delivery-of-legal-services-final-report-2019-october.pdf; State Bar of Cal., Task Force on Access through Innovation of Legal Services: Final Report and Recommendations (2020), https://www.calbar.ca.gov/Portals/0/documents/publicComment/ATILS-Final-Report.pdf; Utah State Bar Working Grp. on Regul. Reform, Narrowing the Access-to-Justice Gap by Reimagining Regulation: Report and Recommendations (2019), https://www.utahbar.org/wp-content/uploads/2019/08/FINAL-Task-Force-Report.pdf. Arizona has fully implemented its ABS approach, while others are actively considering reform via a regulatory sandbox.

a similar exercise for the PeopleLaw sector. Section 2.4 then provides an explicit comparison of the two sectors to address the question of whether or not legal tech will enable a convergence in the extent to which consumer or client needs are met. Our conclusion is that while legal tech and data aggregation have enormous potential to meet unmet legal needs, different constraints continue to hold back the realization of such potential. Major barriers are human capital and data aggregation in BigLaw, and financial capital and the technological limits to automating human lawyers in PeopleLaw. We discuss some regulatory policy options that might promote greater convergence between the two sectors.

2.1 OVERVIEW OF PEOPLELAW AND BIGLAW SECTORS

This section provides a macro-level overview of the state of PeopleLaw and BigLaw sectors.[11]

Differences in data availability mean the contours of these sectors can be outlined in sharper focus for the US than the UK. But in both countries, there is evidence that the share of PeopleLaw activities relative to BigLaw has been in secular decline over the past few decades. The similarity in this secular trend is striking, given that reforms have been under way for over a decade in the UK, whereas they have only just begun in some US states.

In the US, lawyers have long been aware of a distinction made between the part of the legal market that provides services to sizable corporate clients and the part that does not. This divide was brought to prominence in the seminal work *Chicago Lawyers: The Social Structure of the Bar.*[12] The study found that Chicago lawyers in 1975 devoted 45 percent of their total effort to services for individual or small business clients, unions, environmental plaintiffs, and state administrative agencies or municipalities. The same survey repeated in 1995 showed that this PeopleLaw proportion had declined to 35 percent of lawyers' total effort.[13]

A similar story emerges from US Economic Census Data reporting spending on services provided by lawyers employed in private practice. In 2005, 39 percent of this was attributable to individual clients.[14] By 2007, the share of PeopleLaw in total revenue was 29 percent; by 2012 it had declined to 24 percent, while the share of BigLaw grew over the same period from 68 percent to 73 percent.

Henderson also highlights striking differences between the economics of PeopleLaw and BigLaw. In PeopleLaw, lawyers (typically sole practitioners) charged an average $260 per hour (data source: Clio), but billed for only 1.6 hours per day, amounting to $422 a day, or $105,000 in gross receipts over a fifty-week year. In

[11] We are aware that there are other segments including the government and the third sector (non-profit organizations) providing legal services. But we focus in this chapter on BigLaw versus PeopleLaw to simplify and sharpen our analyses.

[12] *See* HEINZ & LAUMANN, CHICAGO LAWYERS.

[13] *Id.*

[14] *See* Hadfield, *Higher Demand, Lower Supply?* The total figure was $221.6 billion, of which $85.6 billion was spent by individual clients.

BigLaw by contrast, Am Law 100 total gross revenue in 2012 was $71 billion, with a total lawyer headcount of 86,272. So, average gross revenue per lawyer was $822,978, while average profit per partner was $1.48 million.[15]

The problem of access to justice for consumers led a handful of state bars to address this issue in recent years.[16] Regulatory reforms are intended to permit new providers including human non-lawyers and non-human non-lawyers (i.e., software) to operate in legal markets. It is too early to tell how these reforms would begin to meet the latent demand of consumers. For now, we know much more about cases of unauthorized practice of law by technology providers.[17]

The UK's legal services market, with a total turnover of £24 billion in 2017, is about a sixth (17 percent) of the size of the US market.[18] Unfortunately, UK national statistics do not shed light directly on the relative size of PeopleLaw and BigLaw sectors. Instead, we present two alternative approaches to gauging trends in two spheres of legal markets.

One approach is to break down law firm revenues into practice areas that predominantly serve individuals (B2C) and others that predominantly serve corporate clients (B2B). A recent study by KPMG reports that 60 percent of law firm turnover in England and Wales is in B2B and 20 percent in B2C.[19] This 60 percent does not take account of growth in in-house lawyers, rising from 16 percent of all solicitors in 2004 to 23 percent by 2019.[20] Because this growth is directed at corporate work, it is strongly suggestive of a corresponding decline of PeopleLaw's relative share in the overall legal services market.

Another approach draws on UK survey evidence investigating latent consumer demand for legal services. While differences in survey methodology over time impede identifying secular trends, the data clearly suggests that the legal services market is not meeting the needs of consumers. Adults based in England and Wales were asked about the legal issues they experienced in the four years prior to the survey and the help they sought in order to resolve them. In 2019,[21] the majority of

[15] *See* HENDERSON, LEGAL MARKET LANDSCAPE REPORT, at 14–15.

[16] See sources cited *supra* notes 9 and 10.

[17] *See* Benjamin H. Barton & Deborah L. Rhode, *Access to Justice and Routine Legal Services: New Technologies Meet Bar Regulators*, 70 HASTINGS L.J. 955 (2018); HENDERSON, LEGAL MARKET LANDSCAPE REPORT; *see also* Barton (Chapter 1 in this volume).

[18] This is slightly less than the ratio of population (67 million to 328 million, or 20 percent) but more than the ratio of GDP ($2.83 trillion to $21.43 trillion in 2019, or 13 percent).

[19] KPMG, CONTRIBUTION OF THE UK LEGAL SERVICES SECTOR TO THE UK ECONOMY: A REPORT FOR THE LAW SOCIETY (2020), https://www.lawsociety.org.uk/topics/research/contribution-of-the-uk-legal-services-sector-to-the-uk-economy-report. In this study, PeopleLaw (B2C) clients are taken to include not only individuals but also small businesses. BigLaw (B2B) clients are primarily corporate legal departments and big law firms.

[20] LAW SOC'Y ENG. & WALES, TRENDS IN THE SOLICITORS' PROFESSION: ANNUAL STATISTICS REPORT 2019 (2020), https://www.lawsociety.org.uk/topics/research/annual-statistics-report-2019.

[21] YOUGOV, LEGAL NEEDS OF INDIVIDUALS IN ENGLAND AND WALES: TECHNICAL REPORT 2019/2020 (2020), https://legalservicesboard.org.uk/wp-content/uploads/2020/01/Legal-Needs-of-Individuals-Technical-Report-Final-January-2020.pdf.

respondents' legal needs remained unmet in all of the most commonly encountered types of legal issue, from family issues and property matters to labor and employment and personal injury.[22] While there are numerous reasons legal needs may be unmet, a significant component appears to be the perceived inaccessibility of the civil justice system.[23]

Policy concern over the unmet legal needs of consumers informed a major overhaul of UK legal services regulation in 2007.[24] This permitted for the first time ownership of law firms by non-lawyers through so-called Alternative Business Structures (ABS).[25] It is striking that the UK's PeopleLaw sector has continued to shrink relative to BigLaw, and that high levels of unmet consumer legal needs have persisted, despite these wide-ranging reforms.

To summarize, the PeopleLaw sector represents only a small fraction – estimated to be about a fifth to a quarter – of the overall legal services market in both the US and the UK. The evidence suggests that this fraction has been in secular decline in both countries for the past few decades. Moreover, UK citizens' unmet legal needs are not adequately addressed despite the major overhaul in legal services regulation a decade ago. We now turn to consider how technology has been impacting the provision of legal services in each of the two hemispheres, BigLaw and PeopleLaw, respectively.

2.2 DIGITAL TECHNOLOGY IN THE BIGLAW SECTOR

This section analyzes how digital technology is influencing the work of lawyers and emergent business models adopted by law firms and other providers in the BigLaw sector. A "business model" is a focused way of understanding how client needs are met, in ways that translate into sustainable profit-making for providers.[26] We first briefly survey digital technologies being deployed in BigLaw, focusing in particular

[22] Legal Servs. Bd., The State of Legal Services 2020: Evidence Compendium 20 (2020), https://legalservicesboard.org.uk/wp-content/uploads/2020/11/The-State-of-Legal-Services-Evidence-Compendium-FINAL.pdf.

[23] *Id.*; see also Legal Servs. Bd., The State of Legal Services 2020 (2020), http://legalservicesboard.org.uk/state-of-legal-services-report-2020.

[24] Legal Services Act 2007, c. 29 (UK); *see* Off. of Fair Trading, Competition in Professions: A Report by the Director General of Fair Trading (2001), https://webarchive.nationalarchives.gov.uk/ukgwa/20140402142426/http:/www.oft.gov.uk/shared_oft/reports/professional_bodies/oft328.pdf; David Clementi, Review of the Regulatory Framework; Dep't of Const. Affs., The Future of Legal Services: Putting Consumers First (2005), https://assets.publishing.service.gov.uk/government/uploads/system/uploads/attachment_data/file/272192/6679.pdf.

[25] Managers and significant (>10 percent) owners of ABS must meet a "fit and proper person" standard set by regulators, and ABS must avoid involvement in any cases posing a conflict with the interests of any significant owner.

[26] *See* Teece, *Business Models, Business Strategy and Innovation*; Sako, *Business Models in Strategy and Innovation*.

on AI, and distinguish these from earlier waves of automation. We conclude that despite the availability of new business models, significant constraints remain in the form of human capital rather than financial capital, preventing BigLaw law firms from deploying technology more effectively.

2.2.1 *Technology Use Cases in BigLaw*

"Legal tech" may be defined as technology that supports or enables the provision of legal services. It is a broad category, encompassing the use of interactive websites, electronic documents, and elements of artificial intelligence (AI) to automate the review and prediction from text, and automation of workflow and matter management. In the BigLaw context, users distinguish between technologies supporting the "practice of law" – that is, supporting the delivery of legal services themselves – and those supporting the "business of law" – that is, supporting the management of client relationships and the allocation of human resource internally.

In the practice of law, a core system for most law firms and corporate in-house teams is document management, which provides digital indexing for legal services work product. Closely related to this, but more varied in their implementation, are knowledge management systems, which seek to aggregate content, including prior work done by the firm, in ways that are relevant and accessible for busy professionals. Increasingly, firms and corporate in-house teams are also making use of workflow automation platforms applying what in other industries might be referred to as robotic process automation (RPA) – that is, the automation of scalable and repetitive tasks. Increasingly common too are the use of extranets or digital deal-rooms that provide secure repositories of data that are accessible by the lawyers and clients or others outside their team. In large-scale litigation, or corporate transactions, there are typically huge volumes of digital documents that are provided by outside parties and need to be reviewable by a range of personnel across organizational boundaries.[27]

The deployment of AI differs from earlier generations of automation in that it requires training to parameterize a model that best classifies items of a particular category.[28] Training is done using a set of data labeled according to the variable of interest. This training requires data – the more the better – that is relevant and accurately labeled. In the litigation context, AI is now commonly used to identify

[27] See John Armour & Mari Sako, *AI-Enabled Business Models in Legal Services: From Traditional Law Firms to Next-Generation Law Companies?*, 7 J. Pros. & Org. 27 (2020).

[28] Many current deployments of AI in legal services rely on machine learning, or deep learning, coupled with natural language processing (NLP). See Frankenreiter and Nyarko (Chapter 3 in this volume). However, some systems in operation make use of an earlier rules-based approach, and leading-edge applications seek to combine elements of both to deliver greater explainability. *See* John Armour & Alina Petrova, AI and Judicial Precedents: A Review (2021) (unpublished manuscript) (on file with the authors).

potentially relevant documents in a pre-trial discovery exercise.[29] This necessitates the training of new models for each suit, based on aspects identified as "relevant" by expert human reviewers. In the transactional context, AI is increasingly deployed to review contracts. In-house teams train AI systems to review their company's everyday or "business as usual" contracts; BigLaw firms by contrast train AI systems to do due diligence, reviewing a large corpus of an M&A target's contracts to identify clauses that may pose problems for buyers (such as change-of-control clauses).[30] In each case, the training requires legal expertise.[31] Moreover, increasing numbers of legal practitioners are making use of AI in support of their legal research, training tools that complement the offerings of the big legal data providers.[32]

In the "business of law," technology is widely used to support accounts and time recording. BigLaw firms are beginning to deploy AI-based systems both to enhance and leverage the data from these earlier systems. An appropriately trained model can both help to fill gaps in time recordings and predict the likely time budget for new instructions. This opens up the possibility of output-based pricing, as opposed to the traditional input-based model of the billable hour. Similarly, lawyers are increasingly turning to customer relationship management (CRM) systems to support marketing and client relationships. These systems themselves increasingly make use of AI.[33]

2.2.2 *Augmented Lawyering and Business Models in BigLaw*

Focusing on the adoption of AI, survey and interview evidence suggests that it has multiple impacts on lawyers' work.[34] The most well-understood effect is *substitution* – that is, AI systems replacing humans for repetitive, scalable tasks. At the same time, lawyers' work in giving bespoke advice is *augmented* by the use of AI, freeing up their capacity to deliver judgment-oriented tasks for which humans remain uniquely capable. Here, lawyers are *consumers* of AI systems' outputs, which augment the quality of their advisory work. Third, the deployment of AI *creates* new tasks for humans, necessitating a multi-disciplinary mix of skills and expertise – not just legal but also data science, information security, process and project

[29] Dana Remus & Frank Levy, *Can Robots Be Lawyers? Computers, Lawyers, and the Practice of Law*, 30 Geo. J. Legal Ethics 501 (2017); David F. Engstrom & Jonah B. Gelbach, *Legal Tech, Civil Procedure, and the Future of Adversarialism*, 169 U. Pa. L. Rev. 1001 (2021); Mari Sako et al., Lawtech Adoption and Training: Findings from a Survey of Solicitors in England and Wales (2020).

[30] *See* Armour et al., *Augmented Lawyering*; Engstrom & Gelbach, *Legal Tech*.

[31] It is an open question whether this legal expertise necessarily has to be supplied by a person qualified as a "lawyer." *See* Armour et al., *Augmented Lawyering*.

[32] *Id.*; Sako et al., Lawtech Adoption and Training.

[33] *See* Sako et al., Lawtech Adoption and Training.

[34] *See* Armour et al., *Augmented Lawyering*.

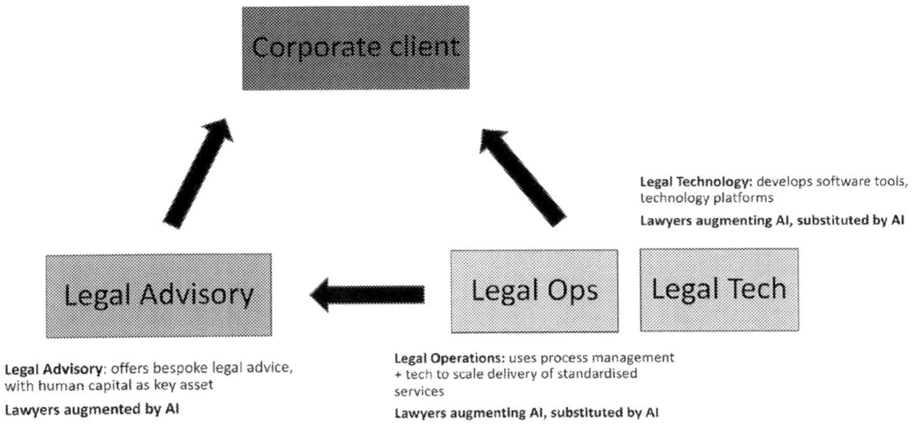

FIGURE 2.1 The BigLaw ecosystem

management, and user experience. Where lawyers work in such multi-disciplinary teams (MDTs), they are helping to *produce* AI-enabled legal services.

Having characterized these three distinctive ways in which AI affects lawyers' work, we need to determine where in the BigLaw ecosystem we can observe these in practice. The "ecosystem" consists of corporate clients as the ultimate customer, serviced by law firms – the traditional "outside counsel" – and by a rapidly growing congeries of other providers including law companies and legal tech providers (see Figure 2.1). In prior work, we sought to organize these relationships by reference to business models, which clarify how value is created for clients.[35] We distinguish between a traditional "Legal Advisory" business model, which entails the provision of customized advice or analysis, a "Legal Operations" business model that enhances efficiencies in legal workflows, and a "Legal Technology" business model that focuses on the development of technological systems for legal services.[36]

The Legal Advisory model focuses on work that requires skills that for the foreseeable future remain distinctively human; lawyers rely on AI predictions to augment their work. By contrast, in both the Legal Operations and Legal Technology business models, technology substitutes for humans in certain tasks. Technology in these business models also engenders new tasks, most obviously in young legal tech ventures, but also in large law firms and in-house corporate legal departments.

We characterize these business models as ideal types; in practice, experimentation in combining different business models is rife. For instance, some law firms have developed internal legal operations expertise and/or have an in-house legal tech capability either via organic growth or acquisition. In the US, Wilson Sonsini has a wholly owned subsidiary in the form of SixFifty, and in the UK, Simmons &

[35] *See* Armour & Sako, *AI-Enabled Business Models in Legal Services.*
[36] *Id.*

Simmons acquired Wavelength Law, a legal tech provider. At the same time, notable law companies have used legal operations excellence as a launchpad to move into legal advisory work. Elevate has its in-house law firm, Elevate Next, and UnitedLex created a subsidiary law firm, Marshall Denning. In the meantime, law companies and legal tech providers are partnering with law firms to access premier corporate clients.[37]

Combining all three business models – Legal Advisory, Legal Operations, and Legal Technology – under one roof in an integrated legal management company might be desirable from the point of view of providing a one-stop shop for corporate clients. However, such integration creates tensions in strategic focus and reputational capital. In particular, employing both lawyers-as-consumers of AI and lawyers-as-producers of AI under one roof is challenging, not least due to the need to establish career paths to integrate, or segregate, the two types of lawyers. As it stands, these career paths are yet to be clarified. And some firms are implicitly signaling which type of lawyer – lawyer-as-consumer or lawyer-as-producer of AI – they prioritize as their core human capital. Thus, human capital challenges, rather than the challenge of accessing external finance, are more central to the difficulty that law firm partnerships face in sustaining effective deployment of digital technology, including AI.[38]

2.3 DIGITAL TECHNOLOGY IN THE PEOPLELAW SECTOR

Legal tech also has potential to unlock capacity to address consumers' legal needs in PeopleLaw. Just as in BigLaw, technology promises to lower costs of delivery for PeopleLaw through exploiting economies of scale. However, there are differences in the way legal tech systems add value in the two contexts. For BigLaw, as we have seen, this is through a mixture of substitution by automated systems for some human tasks (lowering costs) and augmentation of high-value human work on bespoke tasks (enhancing productivity). In PeopleLaw, the tasks are in general more routine in nature, meaning there is relatively more potential for value to be created by legal tech through lower-cost substitution. As we shall see, technology adoption is as yet more limited in the PeopleLaw than the BigLaw context. We argue that this is determined by financial and technological constraints that currently limit opportunities for scaling legal tech to substitute for human lawyers.

We identify two significant constraints on the adoption of legal tech in PeopleLaw in contrast to BigLaw. First, PeopleLaw firms are generally much smaller than their BigLaw counterparts, limiting their ability to invest fixed costs

[37] ThomsonReuters et al., Alternative Legal Service Providers: 2021 Report – Strong Growth, Mainstream Acceptance, and No Longer an "Alternative" (2021), https://www.thomsonreuters.com/en-us/posts/legal/alsp-report-2021/.

[38] Armour et al., *Augmented Lawyering*.

necessary to deliver automation. Second, the fact that PeopleLaw clients are not usually versed in the law (unlike the in-house counsel who typically purchase BigLaw services) means that technical solutions substituting for lawyers must also perform a lay-to-legal (and vice versa) translation function. We develop these points below.

We can usefully distinguish barriers to technology adoption in PeopleLaw that stem from the demand and the supply sides of the market, respectively. The demand side, discussed in Section 2.1's consideration of the BigLaw and PeopleLaw segments of legal services markets, is well understood. To recap, there are persistently high levels of unmet legal needs in many issue areas (see Figure 2.1), owing to individual (that is, non-corporate) consumers' inability to identify their problems as legal in nature[39] and, for problems recognized as legal, the perceived inaccessibility of the justice system and the costs of accessing lawyers. Survey evidence suggests consumers' budget constraints are binding.[40] Many consumers are unable to afford a lawyer to advise them whenever they have a problem at home (divorce, child custody, debt collection, etc.), at work (employment dispute), or when moving home (immigration, conveyancing, etc.). The adoption of legal tech could help resolve currently unmet legal needs by lowering the unit cost of legal service delivery, particularly in settings where such legal services can be productized.[41] In transactional contexts, this can take the form of providing standardized document templates or transaction-processing pipelines.[42] For contentious matters, this could involve technologically enabled dispute resolution mechanisms (commonly referred to as online dispute resolution, or ODR) that are quicker and simpler to execute than traditional court proceedings.[43]

Despite the clear potential for technology to meet latent demand, adoption of technology by solo practitioners and small law firms – the sort that traditionally service individual clients – remains lower than in larger firms. Several recent surveys in both the UK and US have asked firms about deployment of emerging technologies (see Table 2.1), and have consistently found that small firms are less likely to have done so.[44] Why does this pattern emerge so consistently in both the UK

39 *See* Sandefur, *What We Know*.

40 *See* Legal Services Board, The State of Legal Services.

41 Gillian K. Hadfield, *The Cost of Law: Promoting Access to Justice through the (Un)Corporate Practice of Law*, 38 Int'l Rev. L. & Econ. 43 (2014); *see* Yoon, *The Post-Modern Lawyer*.

42 Frank Pasquale, A *Rule of Persons, Not Machines: The Limits of Legal Automation*, 87 Geo. Wash. L. Rev. 1 (2019).

43 Civ. Just. Council (Online Disp. Resol. Advisory Grp.), Online Dispute Resolution for Low Value Civil Claims (2015), https://www.judiciary.uk/wp-content/uploads/2015/02/Online-Dispute-Resolution-Final-Web-Version1.pdf; Ethan Katsh & Colin Rule, *What We Know and Need to Know about Online Dispute Resolution*, 67 S.C. L. Rev. 329 (2015); Colin Rule, *Online Dispute Resolution and the Future of Justice*, 16 Ann. Rev. L. & Soc. Sci. 277 (2020).

44 Legal Servs. Bd., Technology and Innovation in Legal Services – Main Report: An Analysis of a Survey of Legal Service Providers (2018), http://legalservicesboard.org.uk/

TABLE 2.1 *Use of digital technology by type in the UK in 2021*[45]

Which of the following legal technologies are you currently using, or planning to use, in your firm? N = 891	Currently using		Planning to use		Not planning to use	
	N	Row %	N	Row %	N	Row %
Videconferencing with clients	770	86.4	48	5.4	73	8.2
Model documents/templates on our website	217	24.4	149	16.7	525	58.9
Interactive website to generate legal documents in response to client input	88	9.9	173	19.4	630	70.7
Chatbots or virtual assistants	55	6.2	125	14.0	711	79.8
Online portals for matter status updates	137	15.4	189	21.2	565	63.4
E-verification/electronic signatures	332	37.3	226	25.4	333	37.3
Storing data in the cloud	587	65.9	102	11.5	202	22.6
Practice management software	550	61.7	87	9.8	254	28.5
Legal research software	449	50.4	90	10.1	352	39.5
Contract review software	65	7.3	120	13.5	706	79.2
Blockchain/distributed ledger	16	1.8	74	8.3	801	89.9
Data analytics with AI	45	5.1	92	10.3	754	84.6

and US, notwithstanding the considerable unmet legal needs in both countries, and the UK's reforms designed to liberalize legal services for the benefit of consumers?

Two complementary factors seem relevant. The first relates to fixed costs associated with deployment of automated systems. Small firms, such as those involved in PeopleLaw, have more limited capacity to bear fixed costs than do larger firms.[46] This means that technology is likely to penetrate first into BigLaw firms. It also implies that deployment in PeopleLaw is likely to be preceded by consolidation of service providers, and that constraints on external finance are likely to be more of a barrier to legal tech deployment for PeopleLaw than BigLaw.[47]

Second is the challenge of translation between how lay clients speak about their problems and the way in which the legal system frames these same issues. This translation exercise is a core part of a human lawyer's "client skills." Social intelligence – including the ability to empathize and communicate with a with range of

wp-content/media/Innovation-survey-2018-report-FINAL-2.pdf; AM. BAR ASS'N, ABA TECHREPORT 2019 (2019), https://www.americanbar.org/groups/law_practice/publications/techreport/abatechreport2019/; MARI SAKO & RICHARD PARNHAM, TECHNOLOGY AND INNOVATION IN LEGAL SERVICES: FINAL REPORT TO THE SOLICITORS REGULATION AUTHORITY (2021),https://www.sra.org.uk/globalassets/documents/sra/research/full-report-technology-and-innovation-in-legal-services.pdf?version=4a1bfe.

45 Adapted from SAKO & PARNHAM, TECHNOLOGY AND INNOVATION, 23.

46 *See* SAKO & PARNHAM, TECHNOLOGY AND INNOVATION, 123.

47 *See* Hadfield, *The Cost of Law*.

backgrounds – remains particularly elusive for AI systems.[48] In the BigLaw context, the users of technical systems are typically themselves lawyers, who are able to provide such translation for their ultimate clients, and the costs of having human lawyers provide this are typically small relative to the value of the service in question. For PeopleLaw, the cost of having a human lawyer remain in the loop may be prohibitive. This suggests that at least part of the unmet legal needs may be beyond the current technical possibility frontier.

2.3.1 *Use Cases in PeopleLaw*

For the reasons described above, deployment of technology in the PeopleLaw context remains relatively modest. One key use case is automated document assembly – that is, the production of customized legal documentation using an automated system. In particular, it is the only technology of the ten considered in the Legal Services Board's 2018 survey for which law firm respondents serving individuals were more likely to report adoption than those serving large businesses (25 percent v. 11 percent).[49] Transaction management tools are also increasingly widely deployed to assist in residential real estate and personal finance,[50] which have large throughputs of transactions for which individuals need legal services.

These tools are in many cases deployed in conjunction with transactional platforms that facilitate the connection of users to relevant human lawyers. They are typically fronted by a portal offering users simple Q&A on basic legal issues relating to their concerns, accompanied with document templates – perhaps automatically generated – and referrals to human lawyers as necessary. Each platform retains a network of lawyers whose work is ranked by users and to whom referrals are made.

Chatbots may seem a promising solution to the problem of engaging with lay users, but they need to be supported by systems capable of dealing with a sufficiently wide range of user inputs. Expert system approaches are constrained by the need to hard-code the relevant knowledge frameworks, creating limitations where user queries go outside this. Machine learning approaches trained on legal materials must not only be able to dispense and classify legal advice – beyond the capabilities of current systems[51] – but also to be able to translate this into how laypersons understand legal issues. There is evidently a serious gap between ordinary parlance used by laypersons and the specialized terminology of legal discourse. This gap tests the frontier of applying natural language processing (NLP) to use laypersons'

[48] Carl B. Frey & Michael A. Osborne, *The Future of Employment: How Susceptible Are Jobs to Computerisation?* 114 TECH. FORECASTING & SOC. CHANGE 254 (2017); Frank Pasquale & Glyn Cashwell, *Prediction, Persuasion, and the Jurisprudence of Behaviourism*, 68 U. TORONTO L.J. 63 (Supp. 2018).

[49] *See* LEGAL SERVS. BD., TECHNOLOGY AND INNOVATION IN LEGAL SERVICES.

[50] *See* SAKO & PARNHAM, TECHNOLOGY AND INNOVATION, 25–26.

[51] See Chapter 3 in this volume.

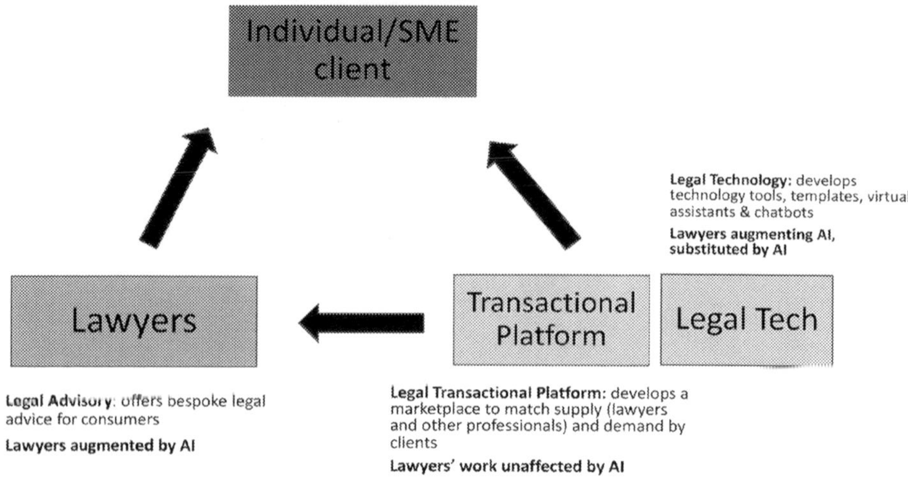

FIGURE 2.2 The PeopleLaw ecosystem

statements or queries as data for prediction.[52] Making progress with these technological challenges will permit chatbots and virtual assistants to give wider-ranging advice to consumers.[53] This current technological bottleneck may explain the relatively low rate of use of chatbots and virtual assistants (see Table 2.1). These technological constraints limit the extent to which legal tech systems can substitute completely for human lawyers.

2.3.2 *Augmented Lawyering and Business Models in PeopleLaw*

Legal tech is engendering new business models in the PeopleLaw context, just as for BigLaw. The PeopleLaw ecosystem, however, is somewhat different in both the stakeholders and the emergent business models (see Figure 2.2). In the PeopleLaw ecosystem, clients are individual consumers and small businesses, rather than large businesses. Thus, all the lawyers in the ecosystem are on the supply side, offering advice directly to lay consumers. In contrast, for the BigLaw ecosystem, the demand side is driven by in-house lawyers.

[52] For example, a study using a corpus of 5,842 cases of attorney misconduct initiated by citizen complaints in the US reports that fact statements by unguided self-represented litigants are far less amenable to machine-learning techniques to predict outcomes than are judicially drafted statements of facts. *See* Karl Branting et al., Predictive Features of Persuasive Legal Text (2020) (unpublished manuscript), http://ceur-ws.org/Vol-2764/paper4.pdf; Karl Branting et al., *Judges Are from Mars, Pro Se Litigants Are from Venus: Predicting Decisions from Lay Text*, 334 Frontiers A.I. & Applications 215 (2020).

[53] Benjamin Alarie et al., *How Artificial Intelligence Will Affect the Practice of Law*, 68 U. Toronto L.J. 106 (Supp. 2018).

In both settings we characterize a new legal tech business model, developing technological systems for legal services. The design and implementation of such systems engenders new tasks for persons with legal expertise, working together as part of multi-disciplinary teams. Lawyers working in such teams are producers of digital legal services.

The limits of existing technology to provide legal services directly to consumers mean that human lawyers remain in the loop in most PeopleLaw contexts. This means that, at present, there is less opportunity than in BigLaw for what we term the Legal Operations business model – leveraging technology to substitute for humans in the delivery of legal services.[54] Instead, much of the current deployment of legal tech in PeopleLaw has the lesser ambition of simply lowering search costs to match human lawyers to clients, just as e-Bay provides a marketplace for buyers and sellers. Thus, a legal tech firm offering such a marketplace acts as a two-sided platform[55] to lower costs of matching lawyers to consumer needs. Such platforms do not substitute for human lawyers; rather, their value lies in augmentation of human lawyers' productivity. We characterize the provision of such platforms as a "Transactional Platform" business model.

Some providers seek to capture further economies of scale by defining consumer needs more broadly than simply "legal" needs, offering a conveniently integrated package of legal and other services. For example, Farewill offers "death" services, combining will writing and funeral services;[56] other providers may offer a service in "moving home," combining conveyancing and mortgage brokerage, or in "injury" combining advice on personal injury law with insurance services.

The constraints we have identified mean that the full promise of legal tech to unlock value for PeopleLaw consumers has not yet been met. As of the early 2020s, legal tech is not yet capable of substituting effectively for human lawyers except in very simple tasks, such as generating standardized documents for wills or small business incorporation. The value created by legal tech in the PeopleLaw setting appears so far to be limited to augmenting human lawyers and lowering the search cost for end-users. While augmentation brings the overall costs of legal services down by increasing productivity, there is still a need for human lawyer input in many cases.[57] Paradoxically, the scope of potential gains from augmentation are likely smaller in PeopleLaw than BigLaw, because of the more routinized nature of the legal work.

54 *See* Armour & Sako, *AI-Enabled Business Models*.

55 Jean-Charles Rochet & Jean Tirole, *Platform Competition in Two-Sided Markets*, 1 J. Europ. Econ. Ass'n 990 (2003); Arun Sundararajan, The Sharing Economy: The End of Employment and the Rise of Crowd-Based Capitalism (2016); Marshall W. Van Alstyne et al., *Pipelines, Platforms, and the New Rules of Strategy*, 94 Harv. Bus. Rev. 54 (2016).

56 Farewill, https://farewill.com.

57 For example, NetLawman provides a co-habitation (living together) agreement template for only £26.40, but the price rises to £176.40 for a "template + review" package. Net Lawman, https://www.netlawman.co.uk/d/cohabitation-agreement). Thus, the document template is only 15 percent of the cost of template + human lawyer review.

This helps explain the more limited deployment of legal tech in the PeopleLaw setting. In the future, if and when technology can substitute for human lawyers more comprehensively, there remains significant further scope for PeopleLaw providers to meet remaining latent demand for legal and associated services (see Figure 2.2).

2.4 IMPLICATIONS FOR CONVERGENCE: LEVELING THE PLAYING FIELD?

We are now in a position to return to our central question: Will the adoption of legal tech level the playing field through convergence in the PeopleLaw and BigLaw sectors' relative capacity to meet legal needs? To do so, we employ a causal framework based on the following elements (see Figure 2.3). First, we summarize the emergent business models that are theoretically possible given the nature of legal tech and other constraints. Second, we examine factors that encourage or discourage the adoption of these business models, including regulation and access to financial capital and relevant human capital, as mediated by organizational governance of law firms and other providers. Third, to the extent that it is possible, we draw implications for the market size and industry structure (the degree of concentration or fragmentation) of PeopleLaw and BigLaw markets, and their relative capacity to meet latent demand for legal services.

2.4.1 *Convergence in Meeting Client Needs?*

We begin with a high-level consideration of the possibility of convergence and divergence using an economic lens. This focuses on the black boxes in Figure 2.3

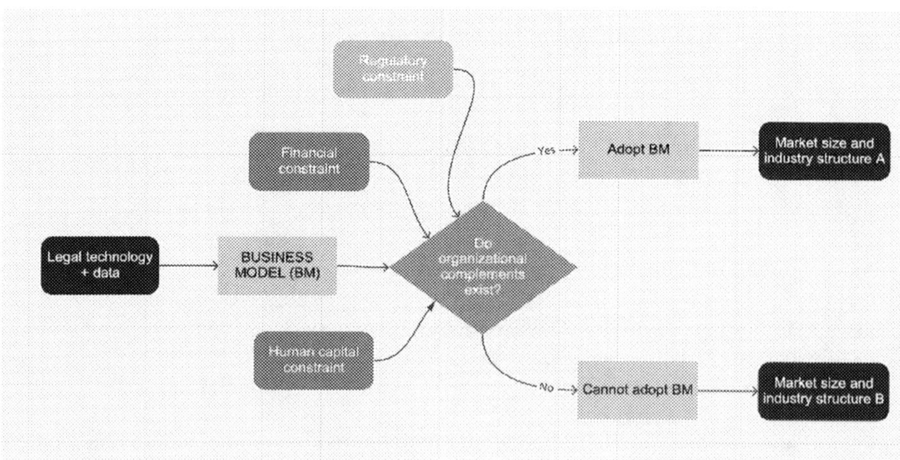

FIGURE 2.3 Causal framework for convergence-divergence

imputing causal links between legal tech and data on the one hand, and market size and industry structure on the other, while assuming that latent demand is more or less fixed.

Digital technology is a double-edged sword when it comes to leveling the playing field with respect to meeting client or consumer needs. To begin, the possibility for convergence relative to the past lies in technology's ability to reduce costs of delivery, expanding the "legal production possibility frontier" given user budget constraints.[58] The reduction in cost per unit of legal service delivery derives from both supply-side economies of scale, with technology facilitating automation (substituting human lawyers) and better workflows, and from demand-side economies of scale, the so-called network effects.

Other factors, however, suggest we may still be a long way from absolute convergence, and the two sectors may continue to diverge in meeting latent legal needs.[59] Convergence would require the demand curve to remain fixed, which may not be the case. For example, in the BigLaw context, while technology assisted review (TAR) lowers the unit cost of document review, its availability may simultaneously increase the level of effective demand (that is, the number of documents sought to be reviewed), thus raising the capacity needed to meet the overall demand. Thus, while the per-unit cost is lowered by technology, the equilibrium price might increase due to an increase in the size of the pie. (This assumes a relatively high price elasticity of demand or an outward shift in the demand curve.) This type of effect requires users to have significant financial resources, more readily available in BigLaw than in PeopleLaw.[60] In PeopleLaw, notwithstanding consumers' meager financial resources, inability (yet) to automate interfaces with end-users due to the translation challenge (from lay language to legal framing as discussed in Section 2.3) means that unmet legal needs are likely to remain significantly high.[61] In short, this is a scenario in which PeopleLaw will be left behind in the artificial intelligence revolution, while BigLaw leapfrogs in the scale and scope of AI adoption.

Thus, predictions of progressive convergence versus continued divergence entail assuming different conditions for each side of the market. On the supply side, the case for convergence is based on technology's capacity to reduce the cost of service delivery, but this may operate asymmetrically between the sectors – implying continued divergence – because of the uncertainty around technological capacity to translate lay language into legal framing. On the demand side, convergence

[58] *See* Yoon, *The Post-Modern Lawyer*.

[59] *See* Pasquale & Cashwell, *Prediction, Persuasion, and the Jurisprudence of Behaviourism*; Engstrom & Gelbach, *Legal Tech*.

[60] *See* Chapters 6 and 14 in this volume.

[61] Moreover, there remain considerable uncertainties regarding how great the savings in cost must be before technological solutions become attractive to consumer users: the documented identification of unmet legal *need* may not translate straightforwardly into willingness to pay. *See* J.J. Prescott, *The Challenges of Calculating the Benefits of Providing Access to Legal Services*, 37 FORDHAM URB. L.J. 303 (2010).

would come about if latent legal demand is more or less fixed. By contrast, the divergence perspective is grounded in a view that unmet legal needs are a movable feast, with latent demand turning into effective demand not only through a change in the price but also through outward shifts in the demand curve arising from societal and commercial forces.

Below, we start by comparing emergent business models and their complements in PeopleLaw and BigLaw, to unravel some of these differing conditions.

2.4.2 *Technological Possibilities, Business Models, and Data: BigLaw and PeopleLaw Compared*

Our first task is to compare the technological possibility offered by legal tech and data to develop new business models in the two segments of the legal services market. In both the BigLaw and PeopleLaw sectors, the current phase of legal tech is based not only on rule-based expert systems to generate documents based on templates, but also machine learning that enables the generation of prediction. We have characterized four distinct business models (see Sections 2.2 and 2.3), which exist in both sectors but with some variations in relative importance (see Table 2.2). In particular, traditional Legal Advisory delivered by human lawyers remains significant in both sectors. However, the cost of such advice likely remains unaffordable for many PeopleLaw consumers. Legal tech solutions are now available in both sectors as inputs to Legal Advisory, augmenting the productivity of human lawyers-as-consumers of the technology. To date, however, the impact of this appears to have been more pronounced for BigLaw than PeopleLaw. The differing trajectories of the two sectors are due in part because the gains from augmentation are greater

TABLE 2.2 *Business models in BigLaw and PeopleLaw compared*

Business model	BigLaw	PeopleLaw
(1) Legal Advisory	Bespoke legal advice by lawyers for corporate clients; augmented by use of services/products from (2) and/or (3) as inputs.	Bespoke legal advice by lawyers, individual customers. Likely unaffordable for many consumers.
(2) Legal Operations	Improve workflow of legal service delivery at law firms and corporations by automation. May use products from (3) as inputs.	[Less important, as neither consumers nor PeopleLaw providers have large organizations.]
(3) Legal Technology	Develop software tools to automate processes and practices in BigLaw legal services.	Develop and provide tools to automate processes and practices in PeopleLaw legal services.
(4) Transactional Platform	Lawyers-on-demand for corporate clients wanting services on a project-by-project basis.	Marketplace to lower search costs for consumers to find lawyers with relevant experience.

where the legal problems are more complex (typically the case in BigLaw), and in part because the delivery of these gains to end-users requires them to be able to afford the cost of the human legal adviser who intermediates them (again, more likely the case in BigLaw).

What has not yet happened on a large scale is the delivery of legal tech solutions direct to end-users without human lawyer intermediation. We view this as primarily a function of technological constraints. Given this, the future application of legal tech to bypass lawyers by using chatbots and virtual assistants has high latent demand in PeopleLaw.

In making a distinction between legal advice (more bespoke) and legal services (subject to repeated and scalable delivery), the Legal Operations business model has wider application in BigLaw than in PeopleLaw. This is because large law firms and corporations in BigLaw would wish to exploit workflow efficiency and automation within their organizations, while solo practitioners and law firms in PeopleLaw have less need or opportunity due to their small scale. In other words, opportunities to seek efficiency and lower costs exist due to both supply-side and demand-side reasons, but BigLaw is in a position to benefit more from supply-side economies of scale than PeopleLaw.

With respect to demand-side economies,[62] network effects could be leveraged in both sectors by using the Transactional Platform business model. Not only do such marketplaces lower search costs, the possibilities of finding appropriate transactional partners rise exponentially with more users of the platform.

Last and not least, the central importance of training data in artificial intelligence is likely to give advantages to providers that can scale in both BigLaw and PeopleLaw.[63] First-mover advantage may accrue to data aggregators that have a head start in training their AI models using data. Both sectors face challenges in turning unstructured data into machine-readable structured data, while also developing NLP methods to analyze less structured data. However, there are granular differences in the dynamics. In PeopleLaw, data aggregation between users may be relatively straightforward in the marketplace, although this may recede with growing background constitutional data protection.[64] In BigLaw, between-user data aggregation requires careful negotiation that takes account of commercial sensitivity. For now, much of the data aggregation taking place in

[62] Erik Brynjolfsson & Andrew McAfee, The Second Machine Age (2016).

[63] Engstrom & Gelbach, *Legal Tech*; Chapter 6 in this volume.

[64] For now, it is curious that LegalZoom appears to be the only PeopleLaw start-up that has scaled, which indicates a need to investigate barriers to scale-up beyond the nature of data. *See* Nancy J. King & V. T. Raja, *What Do They Really Know about Me in the Cloud: A Comparative Law Perspective on Protecting Privacy and Security of Sensitive Consumer Data*, 50 Am. Bus. L.J. 413 (2013); Salome Viljoen, *A Relational Theory of Data Governance*, 131 Yale L.J. 573 (2021).

BigLaw is within-user – for example, for a specific corporate client, be it a bank or an insurance company.[65]

Another possible route to scaling up, leading to convergence, is the emergence of providers that serve both BigLaw and PeopleLaw clients. If a machine learning algorithm can be used for contract analytics in BigLaw, why not deploy the same algorithm for tenancy agreements, employment contracts, and other documents in PeopleLaw? In reality, providers serving both market segments are not a common trend, reasons for which may include the vastly different price points to generate demand in the two market segments, and the importance of cultivating a client base as a market entry barrier.

2.4.3 *Access to Finance including External Capital*

We now shift our analysis to the boxes labeled "financial constraint" and "human capital constraint" in Figure 2.3 representing distinct constraints on the effective deployment of new business models that arise from organizational governance of law firms and other entities providing legal services in BigLaw and PeopleLaw. Our analysis suggests that the financial capital constraint is not an issue in BigLaw in the way that it might be in PeopleLaw, whereas the human capital constraint may be more of a problem in BigLaw than in PeopleLaw.

The inability of traditional law firm partnerships to raise external capital was considered a major challenge preventing law firms from adopting technology.[66] Our research suggests otherwise: The main challenge for law firms in the BigLaw sector is in human capital, and in recruiting and motivating non-lawyers working in multi-disciplinary teams to deploy digital technology for legal service delivery.[67] In PeopleLaw, by contrast, sole practitioners and small firms likely suffer from financial constraints, if they wish to access legal tech.

Given the absence of publicly available information on spending on digital technology by law firms and corporate legal departments, it is difficult to compare aggregate investments made in the PeopleLaw and BigLaw sectors. We focus instead on a subset of investment activity for which data are available: the amount of external funds that have been invested in legal tech start-ups. We here present insights from an analysis of legal tech start-ups for which investment data were available in the Crunchbase Pro database in January 2021.[68] In total, legal tech start-

65 Greater between-user data aggregation in BigLaw will likely follow further shifts in the technology possibility frontier (for example, federated machine learning techniques that do not require centralized processing of data) and the setting of industry-wide standards for data sharing.

66 *See* Hadfield, *The Cost of Law*.

67 Armour et al., *Augmented Lawyering*.

68 Crunchbase is a widely used commercial database of private company data. CRUNCHBASE, https://about.crunchbase.com/products/crunchbase-pro/.

ups in the UK raised $853 million, compared to $5.98 billion by legal tech start-ups in the US.[69] This divergence between investment in UK and US lawtech start-ups tracks differences in the overall levels of venture capital investment more generally, for which the US historically greatly exceeds the UK.[70]

Start-ups and their venture capital financiers tend to operate in geographically concentrated clusters, owing to the importance of regional networks and in particular the hands-on nature of the financing relationship.[71] We focus, in our analysis, on 129 legal tech start-ups with headquarters clustered in London (45), New York (37), and the San Francisco Bay Area (47).[72] By reading company descriptions in Crunchbase, LinkedIn, and company websites, we manually classified start-ups according to whether they primarily served the PeopleLaw (41) or BigLaw (61) sectors.[73] These start-ups target a wide range of legal work. In BigLaw, start-ups in all three locations were in contract analytics, knowledge management, practice management, or lawyers-on-demand marketplaces. In PeopleLaw, tech start-ups existed typically in will writing, residential conveyancing, and simplifying the process of setting up a new business for start-up founders (see Figure 2.4).[74]

In terms of money raised (including angel and venture capital financing) over the lifetime of all start-ups in our sample, BigLaw has raised significantly more overall than PeopleLaw. However, this is driven entirely by London; in the two US clusters, the levels of investment in legal tech firms are approximately equal across these sectors (see Figure 2.4). Total funds raised in San Francisco exceed those raised in each of the other two clusters.[75]

69 Sako & Parnham, Technology and Innovation.

70 For example, industry associations report aggregate venture capital investment in 2020 of $2.29 billion in the UK against $164 billion in the US. British Venture Cap. Ass'n, BVCA Report on Investment Activity 2020 (2021), https://www.bvca.co.uk/Portals/0/Documents/Research/Industry%20Activity/BVCA-RIA-2020.pdf; Nat'l Venture Cap. Ass'n, 2021 Yearbook (2021), https://nvca.org/wp-content/uploads/2021/08/NVCA-2021-Yearbook.pdf. *See* generally John Armour & Douglas Cumming, *The Legislative Road to Silicon Valley*, 58 Oxford Econ. Papers 596 (2006).

71 AnnaLee Saxenian, *Inside-Out: Regional Networks and Industrial Adaptation in Silicon Valley and Route 128*, 2 Cityscape: J. Pol'y Res. & Urb. Dev. 41 (1994); Paul A. Gompers & Josh Lerner, The Venture Capital Cycle (2004); Henry Chen et al., *Buy Local? The Geography of Venture Capital*, 67 J. Urb. Econ. 90 (2010).

72 The location of these firms' headquarters does not dictate the geographic spread of marketing of their products, save that firms are located in the US (UK) are more likely to target users of the US (UK) legal system.

73 The remaining twenty-seven firms primarily served government, judicial, or voluntary sector clients, meaning they do not fit readily into either category.

74 HybridLaw start-ups included those with tools for patenting and patent search, and tools for clients who were not-for-profit or for government organizations.

75 The larger aggregate amount of funding in San Francisco may be due to the supply side – there is simply a larger pool of start-up founder talent with more serial entrepreneurs who target markets beyond legal, and a larger pool of angel and venture capital funding in San Francisco than in New York or London. *See* Mari Sako et al., Scaling Up Firms in Entrepreneurial

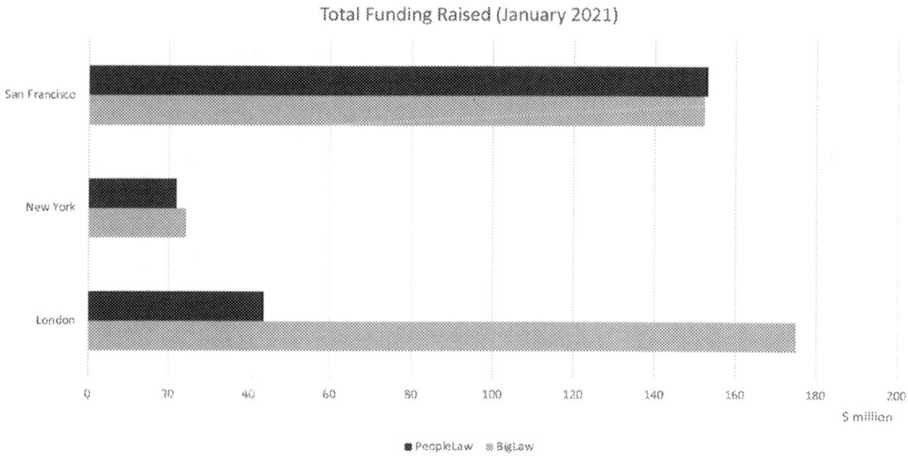

FIGURE 2.4 Investment raised by legal tech start-ups in three locations

However, fundraising by start-ups in BigLaw captures only a portion of the total investment in technology for this sector. Not only do BigLaw start-ups attract venture capital funding, they also receive complementary investment by law firm and corporate clients to co-create new technology and share data, and the latter also make their own proprietary investments in technology. For example, according to the annual financial statement submitted to Companies House, the English magic circle firm Allen & Overy LLP invested approximately $27 million in internally generated software in 2018/19. This investment by a single large firm is equivalent to 15 percent of the total amount raised ($175 million) by BigLaw legal tech start-ups in London, as shown in Figure 2.4. While in BigLaw, the start-up fundraising figures understate the total investment in technology, in PeopleLaw there is no corresponding investment by individual consumers.

To summarize, financial capital appears not to be a binding constraint for the BigLaw sector, given that law firms organized as partnerships are able to invest more in technology than the fundraising by start-ups. In PeopleLaw, because law firms serving the sector tend to be smaller and have fewer financial resources, outside capital is plausibly more important to enable more legal tech start-ups to emerge in this market segment.

2.4.4 *Access to Multidisciplinary Human Capital*

We argued that an effective use of multidisciplinary teams (MDTs) in which lawyers-as-producers-of-AI work alongside non-legal professionals was essential for the effective deployment of legal tech. Here, we argue also that the problem of

Ecosystems: Fintech and Lawtech Ecosystems Compared (2020) (unpublished manuscript), https://papers.ssrn.com/sol3/papers.cfm?abstract_id=3520533.

accessing multidisciplinary human capital to enable MDTs is more pertinent in BigLaw than in PeopleLaw.

In BigLaw, clients are large law firms as lawyer-only partnerships and corporate legal departments. Within law firms, human lawyers are required for bespoke work, and these lawyers-as-consumers-of-AI do very different work from lawyers-as-producers-of-AI working in MDTs. Other non-legal professionals are also not given opportunities for promotion to top management, making it challenging to recruit and retain the best talent in data science, management, and other disciplines.[76] Thus, there is likely to be a bifurcation in legal service delivery, between law firm partnerships whose business model (Legal Advisory) continues to center on human capital, and corporations that are aligned better to implement MDTs, pursuing Legal Tech or Legal Operations business models.[77]

In PeopleLaw, the transformative impact of legal tech is likely to come about through legal tech start-ups that employ lawyers-as-producers-of-AI. There are of course law firm partnerships in the PeopleLaw sector, but the absence of career paths for multi-disciplinary non-legal professionals does not hit small law firms and sole-practice lawyers as much as large law firms, which are more prevalent in BigLaw. PeopleLaw may also be delivered by professionals other than lawyers – for example, experts in tax, insurance, real estate, and human resources.

In short, BigLaw faces a greater human capital challenge than PeopleLaw. BigLaw law firms' challenge lies in aligning its human capital investment as a complement to their newly adopted business models other than the Legal Advisory model. PeopleLaw lawyers can also take advantage of the Transactional Platform, which enhances individual lawyers' reputational transparency for consumers, thus reducing the significance of reputation pooling at the firm level.

2.4.5 *Regulation*

From the foregoing discussion, the financial constraint appeared to be more binding, and the human capital constraint less binding, in PeopleLaw than BigLaw. This suggests that the UK's relaxation of rules that prohibited ownership of law firms by non-lawyers – which would facilitate the raising of outside capital – should have had more of an impact in the PeopleLaw than the BigLaw sector.

There are now over 1,000 licensed ABSs in the UK, as against a total population of over 10,000 law firms. For England and Wales, the Solicitors Regulation Authority (SRA) approved 1,089 ABSs by December 2020. Of these, 73 percent are limited

76 Armour et al., *Augmented Lawyering*.

77 This does not imply these firms will provide exclusively human capital–based services; simply that such services will dominate their business model and hence organizational governance and strategic planning. *See* Armour & Sako, *AI-Enabled Business Models*.

companies, and 22 percent are limited liability partnerships.[78] About half of these ABSs have transformed from law firm partnerships,[79] and a sizable number have consequently changed the way in which they raise finance, to invest more in technology and innovation.[80] Consistently with the foregoing account, the vast majority of these law-firm-to-ABS moves have been very small firms whose clients are individuals rather than businesses.[81]

This seems to suggest the UK's regulatory reforms had an impact on the PeopleLaw sector. In particular, we might expect to observe more capital being raised by the UK than the US legal tech start-ups in our sample. Figure 2.4, however, does not support this prediction. While supply-side considerations may explain the greater levels of investment in San Francisco, this evidence does tend to suggest that the impact of the UK's deregulation has been less than transformative. Put another way, access to financial capital may be necessary but not sufficient to transform PeopleLaw. Other regulatory reforms, not just those that aim to unlock capital flows, may be necessary – hence, UK policy initiatives such as the SRA's Legal Access Challenge[82] and the LawTech UK's sandbox hosted by TechNation.[83] These sandboxes are intended to not only give providers better access to granular regulatory expertise to test new service offerings, but also to enhance legitimacy and consumer confidence in the robustness of the underlying legal tech. This is consistent with the conclusion by Barton[84] that in the US, the speed of legal tech adoption, ironically led by providers serving the poor and corporate clients, is bounded by the technological barriers rather than the regulatory barriers alone.

2.4.6 *Future of Market Size and Industry Structure*

Pulling these various strands together, we want to know what the likely future for PeopleLaw and BigLaw is in terms of their relative market size and industry structure. We attempt to address this question in the context of no change in current regulation, and first identify the scale-up possibilities and advantage of each

78 Calculations are based on the SRA's Solicitors Register datashare data. SOLICS. REG. DATA SHARE, https://sra-prod-apim.developer.azure-api.net/.

79 LEGAL SERVS. BD., EVALUATION: ABS AND INVESTMENT IN LEGAL SERVICES 2011/12-2016/17 – MAIN REPORT (2017), https://legalservicesboard.org.uk/wp-content/media/Investment-research-2017-Report-Main-report.pdf.

80 SOLICS. REGUL. AUTH., RESEARCH ON ALTERNATIVE BUSINESS STRUCTURES (ABSS): FINDINGS FROM SURVEYS WITH ABSS AND APPLICANTS THAT WITHDREW FROM THE LICENSING PROCESS (2014), https://www.sra.org.uk/globalassets/documents/sra/research/abs-quantitative-research-may-2014.pdf?version=4a1ac4.

81 LEGAL SERVS. BD., EVALUATION.

82 *Legal Access Challenge Insights Show Legal Tech Potential*, *SOLICS. REGUL. AUTH.* (June 18, 2020), https://www.sra.org.uk/sra/news/press/2020-press-release-archive/legal-access-challenge-final-reports/.

83 *The Lawtech Sandbox*, LAWTECH, https://technation.io/lawtechsandboxpilot/.

84 *See* Chapter 1 in this volume.

identified business model. Simply put, the Legal Advisory model does not scale. By contrast, the Legal Operations and Transactional Platform models are subject to supply-side and demand-side economies respectively. Legal technology that has a platform characteristic has the potential to scale and dominate,[85] while other technologies such as software tools may remain "point solutions" that do not scale without a platform.

In BigLaw, technology solutions that are specific to the legal industry are already wired into cross-sector technology solutions – for example DocuSign with its e-signature, Salesforce, and contract analytics tools that use the Microsoft Office platform. Moreover, data providers such as Thomson Reuters and LexisNexis are vying to become technology platform leaders via the acquisition of legal tech providers. One possibility is that legal tech for BigLaw will become more and more subject to the platform logic, leading to greater market concentration of technology providers, many of which hail from outside the legal industry. If that is the case, the UK Competition and Markets Authority's recent recommendation for a unified register of legal tech providers may be necessary but not sufficient as effective public policy.[86] At a minimum, what is a legal tech provider, as opposed to simply a tech provider, needs to be defined.[87] Also, market concentration is more likely if governments do not implement policies to restrain anti-competitive behavior of big tech companies.

In PeopleLaw, market growth (and concentration) can accelerate if two things happen: first, the growth of Transactional Platforms, and second, technological solutions to the lay-to-legal-framing translation problem. While platforms may take off to provide a launching pad for scaling up, one side of the marketplace will remain human lawyers, rather than chatbots or virtual assistants, until this translation problem is addressed and resolved by data scientists and linguists. In the meantime, blurring the boundary between BigLaw and PeopleLaw market segments would not happen for some time to come in spite of the theoretical possibility of sharing the same platform and the same algorithms across segments. The reasons stated earlier include the difficulty of aggregating across-user data, the vastly different price points to solicit demand, and client base cultivation as a market entry barrier. Moreover, convergence is more likely to come about via "trickling up" rather than "trickling down," consistent with Christensen's idea of disruptive innovation.[88] That is, it is more likely for legal service innovation that starts by addressing the low end of the market whose needs are currently not met by incumbents to move up the value

85 Michael A. Cusumano et al., The Business of Platforms: Strategy in the Age of Digital Competition, Innovation, and Power (2019).

86 Competition & Mkts. Auth., Review of the Legal Services Market.

87 Mari Sako & Matthias Qian, A Taxonomy for Technology Venture Ecosystems (2021) (unpublished manuscript), https://papers.ssrn.com/sol3/papers.cfm?abstract_id=3822606.

88 Clayton M. Christensen, The Innovator's Dilemma (1997); Clayton M. Christensen et al., *Consulting on the Cusp of Disruption*, 91 Harv. Bus. Rev. 106 (2013).

chain, and less likely that expensive high-end solutions will be adapted for low-end markets by stripping down functionality to achieve lower costs.

2.5 CONCLUSION

This chapter addressed a question of central importance to public policy, namely, whether or not the adoption of legal technology will level the playing field between two hemispheres of the legal services sector – PeopleLaw and BigLaw. In the late 2010s, PeopleLaw constituted only a fifth to a quarter of the total revenues in legal services markets in the US and UK. We argue in this chapter that, in order to level the playing field and to make PeopleLaw thrive relative to BigLaw, the use of legal tech is necessary but not sufficient.

Legal tech, together with the aggregation of data, has enormous potential to transform the way legal services and legal advice are delivered in both hemispheres. Repetitive and scalable tasks can be automated, substituting technology for human lawyers and lowering unit costs. Tasks requiring extensive customization or social intelligence remain in the exclusive competence of human lawyers, but their capacity is augmented by the deployment of technology for repetitive tasks. Through these channels, technology offers the potential to lower the costs of legal service delivery and thus reach consumers and clients whose needs had gone unmet. This would most obviously play out through the adoption of new business models (such as legal operations, transactional platforms, and legal tech) that focus on capturing economies of scale. In turn, these economies of scale would drive market concentration, with emerging winners likely being those who can best combine network externalities associated with both usage and data aggregation. This is a dynamic increasingly familiar from tech firms in other sectors. The change would be most obvious in PeopleLaw, which traditionally operates at a much smaller scale, but the underlying dynamic would be similar, and the process would lead to convergence in meeting client needs, business model adoption, and market structure.

However, the reality is far more complex, because – at least for now – various constraints create obstacles to market participants' ability to leverage technology through the adoption of new business models. In BigLaw, key barriers lie in the human capital constraints associated with mixing Legal Advisory with other business models. Legal Advisory is, by definition, focused on work that is human-centric, and so organizational and management structures that appeal to the humans with the relevant capital will be crucial for competitive advantage. However, these institutions correspondingly constrain the deployment of Legal Operations and Legal Tech business models, creating a constraint on concentration. Alongside this, users' hesitancy about data aggregation, at least for now, constrains the extent to which legal tech platforms are able to achieve concentration.

In PeopleLaw, the process of concentration appears to be well under way, with transactional platforms and integrated service delivery offerings capturing economies of scale and scope. However, there remains a seemingly significant obstacle to meeting latent demand, through the fact that the "client-facing" aspect of service delivery still eludes complete automation. Because human lawyers have high costs, this translates into high prices that raise the bar on the extent to which demand remains latent. There is some evidence that financial constraints are also an obstacle, but this is challenged by the greater levels of legal tech investment in the US (where law firms are not permitted to raise outside equity) than in the UK (where they have been able to do so for a decade under the Alternative Business Structure model). This suggests that the stakes in the US regulatory debate may be lower than participants imagine. At the same time, these constraints are unlikely to be eased by a policy focus on price transparency and comparison shopping emphasized by the UK's Competition and Markets Authority.[89] Legal services, however productized, are after all credence goods, and consumers and clients who purchase them must overcome information asymmetry and/or behavioral biases.

89 Competition & Mkts. Auth., Review of the Legal Services Market.

3

Natural Language Processing in Legal Tech

Jens Frankenreiter and Julian Nyarko

While the work of lawyers long appeared to be beyond the reach of automation, the "legal tech" revolution now seems to be in full swing. Of particular importance is the emergence of a new generation of legal tech applications that utilizes artificial intelligence (AI) and machine learning (ML). Their underlying technologies have started to profoundly change the work of various professionals, including bankers[1] and physicians.[2] And so it comes as no surprise that the rise of AI is also predicted to allow for the automation of some of the core tasks performed by lawyers.[3] Others go further, arguing that AI will ultimately allow computers to replace attorneys[4] and judges[5] in many scenarios, with profound changes for the functioning of the legal system.[6]

In reality, however, the extent to which AI can contribute to automation of the legal industry will depend on several factors, including regulation,[7]

[1] Jack Kelly, *Wells Fargo Predicts That Robots Will Steal 200,000 Banking Jobs within the Next 10 Years*, FORBES (Oct. 8, 2019, 11:09 AM EDT), https://www.forbes.com/sites/jackkelly/2019/10/08/wells-fargo-predicts-that-robots-will-steal-200000-banking-jobs-within-the-next-10-years/?sh=5a9495db68d7.

[2] David Killock, *AI Outperforms Radiologists in Mammographic Screening*, 17 NATURE REVS. CLINICAL ONCOLOGY 134, 134 (2020).

[3] *See, e.g.*, David Freeman Engstrom & Jonah B. Gelbach, *Legal Tech, Civil Procedure, and the Future of Adversarialism*, 169 U. PA. L. REV. 1001, 1001–1004 (2021).

[4] E.g., John O. McGinnis & Russell G. Pearce, *The Great Disruption: How Machine Intelligence Will Transform the Role of Lawyers in the Delivery of Legal Service*, 82 FORDHAM L. REV. 3041 (2014).

[5] E.g., Elliott Ash, *Robot Judges*, YOUTUBE (Feb. 13, 2018), https://youtube.com/watch?v=6qIj7xSZKdo.

[6] Benjamin Alarie, *The Path of the Law: Towards Legal Singularity*, 66 U. TORONTO L.J. 443, 443 (2016).

[7] *See, e.g.*, Gillian K. Hadfield, *Legal Barriers to Innovation: The Growing Economic Cost of Professional Control over Corporate Legal Markets*, 60 STAN. L. REV. 1689, 1724–25 (2008).

culture,[8] and technology.[9] In this chapter, we focus on the last factor, the current state and likely future trajectory of technological progress. Among the different technological requirements, our focus is Natural Language Processing (NLP), a key component of many current and envisioned legal tech tools. Understanding the inherent constraints of current NLP models will be crucial in determining the extent to which legal tech applications will succeed in their quest to revolutionize the market for legal services. Although it cannot be ruled out that "robo-judges" and "robo-lawyers" will one day dominate the reality of legal engagement, our analysis suggests that recent developments in the relevant fields provide no basis for the prediction that such comprehensive legal automation is right around the corner.

The legal system trades in words, and NLP promises to automate an activity that lies at the heart of many tasks performed by lawyers: the extraction and processing of information from unstructured text. Lawyers routinely encounter unstructured text in their daily work routine, be it in the form of judicial opinions, statutes, legal briefs, written agreements, or witness testimony. Understanding and processing the information from this text is essential for them to be effective. For example, without reading prior case law, lawyers will generally be unable to determine whether a case at hand has a chance of succeeding in court. Consequently, many legal tech applications, and particularly those seeking to automate the tasks lying at the heart of what it means to "be a lawyer," depend on NLP to process such information in a meaningful way.

We provide readers with an overview of the current state of NLP techniques, focusing on their promise and potential pitfalls in the context of legal tech applications. Like many other fields of AI, NLP has seen some drastic improvements in recent decades. Among other things, these improvements have contributed to some of the most talked-about success stories in legal tech, including the development of novel tools that promise to facilitate often mundane and repetitive tasks like document review. Against this background, one might conclude that advances in NLP are poised to similarly benefit the development of other legal tech tools. Yet, while there certainly is ample room for optimism, a realistic outlook must simultaneously recognize that NLP suffers inherent and important constraints, limiting its utility for legal tech applications in significant ways.

We explain why NLP-powered legal tech can be expected to outperform humans in specific categories of tasks that play to the strengths of current ML techniques. In particular, NLP-assisted applications perform well in prediction or classification

8 John Armour et al., *Augmented Lawyering* (Eur. Corp. Governance Inst. Working Paper, Paper No. 558, 2020), https://papers.ssrn.com/sol3/papers.cfm?abstract_id=3688896.

9 *See* Milan Markovic, *Rise of the Robot Lawyers?* 61 Ariz. L. Rev. 325, 328–35 (2019).

tasks in which large amounts of pre-labeled data is available or can be generated to train an algorithm. The availability of suitable training data enables an algorithm to detect even subtle patterns in text or other data that predict the label a human would have attached to the document or other item.[10] At the same time, the chapter explores and highlights some of the central obstacles to deploying these tools in other contexts, most importantly in tasks that require the equivalent of legal reasoning. This includes, for instance, applications seeking to assess the likely outcome of legal disputes.

To be successful in this latter context, legal tech applications would need to automatically extract from relevant texts a structured representation of legal concepts and their interconnections (what we refer to as a "legal ontology"). However, despite recent progress in developing tools that appear – at least on a superficial level – capable of extracting meaning and knowledge from text, attempts to derive legal ontologies have so far been largely unsuccessful. On the contrary, recent studies suggest that current advancements in NLP, for the most part, do not meaningfully increase the performance of algorithms in tasks requiring legal reasoning. This, in turn, suggests that many legal tech applications may not benefit significantly from improvements made in general language processing and general language understanding. Instead, in order to make significant progress, a concentrated and domain-specific effort may be required that is specifically designed to promote the capabilities of language models to engage in forms of legal reasoning.

3.1 NLP AS PART OF THE BROADER LEGAL TECH LANDSCAPE

3.1.1 *The Rise of ML-Powered Legal Tech*

Changes to the work of lawyers brought about by technology are not a new phenomenon. Over the last decades, the introduction of technologies such as email and word processing and the availability of computer-based legal databases have profoundly changed lawyers' daily routines. With the advent of ever-more-powerful computers, the Internet, and recent developments in AI and ML, this development appears to have accelerated. The emerging field of "legal tech" promises to equip lawyers with tools capable of automatically generating substantive content descriptions of contract clauses,[11] analyzing legal briefs,[12] and performing data-driven venue

[10] *See, e.g.*, AJAY AGRAWAL ET AL., PREDICTION MACHINES: THE SIMPLE ECONOMICS OF ARTIFICIAL INTELLIGENCE (2018).

[11] *How Kira Works*, KIRA, https://kirasystems.com/how-kira-works/.

[12] *Legal Analytics*, BLOOMBERG L., https://pro.bloomberglaw.com/ai-analytics/.

analysis.[13] In addition, because of its potential to scale, technology is often seen as a way to make legal services available to those who cannot afford a (human) lawyer.[14]

Many commentators writing about legal tech adopt a broad definition that goes well beyond applications seeking to automate the activities at the core of a lawyer's work. As an example, consider a recent article by David Engstrom and Jonah Gelbach. Their definition of legal tech encompasses applications ranging from outcome prediction to online marketplaces for lawyers.[15] Notably, as the example of online marketplaces for lawyers illustrates, not all of these applications relate to tasks that lawyers routinely perform as part of their work. And even within the set of applications that substitute for work usually performed by lawyers, the technical sophistication required to automate the task varies substantially.[16]

Despite this broad definition of legal tech, many observers are particularly interested in legal tech applications made possible by applying ML and similar techniques to the legal field.[17] While legal tech includes applications powered by technology that has been around for decades (in one form or another), many tasks performed by lawyers and other knowledge workers long seemed beyond the reach of automation. Recent advances in ML, however, have enabled significant technological progress in many areas that were commonly considered the sole domain of humans, including the driving of cars,[18] translation,[19] and the writing of human-readable text[20] and music.[21] Not surprisingly, these developments have also spurred discussion about novel legal tech applications that automate the work of lawyers to a hitherto unknown extent.[22]

[13] *Legal Analytics Platform*, LEX MACHINA, https://lexmachina.com/legal-analytics/.

[14] Zorik Pesochinsky, *Leveraging Legal Technology to Improve Access to Justice*, THOMSON REUTERS (July 29, 2019), https://www.thomsonreuters.com/en-us/posts/legal/leveraging-legal-tech-access-to-justice/.

[15] Engstrom & Gelbach, *Legal Tech*, at 1011–12.

[16] *Id.* at 1014.

[17] *E.g.*, *id.* at 1015 ("Nor should it surprise that the most promising legal tech tools deploy ML.").

[18] Joe D'Allegro, *How Google's Self-Driving Car Will Change Everything*, INVESTOPEDIA (June 20, 2021), https://www.investopedia.com/articles/investing/052014/how-googles-selfdriving-car-will-change-everything.asp. Recently, it has become clear that some earlier predictions about the imminent arrival of self-driving cars were overoptimistic. Neal E. Boudette, *Despite High Hopes, Self-Driving Cars Are "Way in the Future,"* N.Y. TIMES (July 17, 2019), https://www.nytimes.com/2019/07/17/business/self-driving-autonomous-cars.html.

[19] Gideon Lewis-Kraus, *The Great A.I. Awakening*, N.Y. TIMES MAG. (Dec. 14, 2016), https://www.nytimes.com/2016/12/14/magazine/the-great-ai-awakening.html.

[20] Will Knight, *This AI Can Generate Convincing Text – and Anyone Can Use It*, WIRED (Mar. 29, 2021 7:00 AM), www.wired.com/story/ai-generate-convincing-text-anyone-use-it/.

[21] Parker Hall, *Dynascore's AI Music Engine Writes Tracks to Match Your Videos*, WIRED (July 7, 2021, 7:00 AM), https://www.wired.com/story/dynascore-ai-music-engine/.

[22] Mireille Hildebrandt, *Law as Computation in the Era of Artificial Legal Intelligence: Speaking Law to the Power of Statistics*, 68 U. TORONTO L.J. 12, 27 (2018); Daniel Martin Katz, *Quantitative Legal Prediction – Or – How I Learned to Stop Worrying and Start Preparing for the Data-Driven Future of the Legal Services Industry*, 62 EMORY L.J. 909 (2013).

Many techniques in ML are designed to generate predictions from example data.[23] Consequently, its potential is greatest for tasks that can comfortably be viewed as prediction exercises. To illustrate, consider reviewing a large number of documents with the aim to identify privileged information before the documents are shared with the opposing party in litigation.[24] This task can comfortably be characterized as a prediction exercise: The goal is to determine whether a document should receive one of two labels, "privileged" or "non-privileged." ML techniques can facilitate this process. In particular, through supervised classification, an ML algorithm can be trained to "learn" the difference between privileged and non-privileged documents using a small, human-labeled sample. Once trained, the algorithm can then create predictions for the entire, unlabeled corpus of documents. In this way, the ML algorithm "predicts" the label that is most likely to be assigned to a document by a human coder, based on the features of the labeled documents.[25]

Another task that is often discussed as an important use case for ML-assisted legal tech is outcome prediction. Potential litigants deciding whether to file a case – and attorneys deciding whether to represent them – will usually attempt to form an expectation about the chances of succeeding at trial. At least in principle, this is a straightforward prediction task: If the right data were available, ML algorithms should be able to determine whether a plaintiff is likely to win by comparing the features of the present case with the features of past cases.[26]

Of course, the examples above do not constitute an exhaustive list of potential applications. Instead, they simply serve as an illustration for the broad range of tasks that may benefit from developments in NLP.

[23] Marion Dumas & Jens Frankenreiter, *Text as Observational Data*, *in* LAW AS DATA 59 (Michael A. Livermore & Daniel N. Rockmore eds., 2019); Jon Kleinberg et al., *Prediction Policy Problems*, 105 AM. ECON. REV. 491 (2015); Sendhil Mullainathan & Jann Spiess, *Machine Learning: An Applied Econometric Approach*, J. ECON. PERSPS. (Spring 2017), at 87.

[24] *See* Chapters 5 and 6 in this volume.

[25] *See also* Dana A. Remus, *The Uncertain Promise of Predictive Coding*, 99 IOWA L. REV. 1691, 1701–706 (2014).

[26] Benjamin Alarie et al., Using Machine Learning to Predict Outcomes in Tax Law (Dec. 15, 2017) (unpublished manuscript), https://papers.ssrn.com/sol3/papers.cfm?abstract_id=2855977; Nicole Black, Finding Treasure with Litigation Data Analytics Software, A.B.A. *J.* (July 24, 2018, 6:05 AM CDT), https://www.abajournal.com/news/article/finding_treasure_with_litigation_data_analytics_software; Katz, *Quantitative Legal Prediction*, at 936–42; Dru Stevenson & Nicholas J. Wagner, *Bargaining in the Shadow of Big Data*, 67 FLA. L. REV. 1337, 1371–74 (2016). There is also a considerable literature at the intersection of law and data science that aims to develop and test outcome prediction models in the context of various courts. *See, e.g.*, Daniel Martin Katz et al., *A General Approach for Predicting the Behavior of the Supreme Court of the United States*, 12 PLoS ONE 1 (2017); Masha Medvedeva et al., *Using Machine Learning to Predict Decisions of the European Court of Human Rights*, 28 A.I. & L. 237 (2020).

3.1.2 *The Role of NLP in Legal Tech*

NLP, as used here, refers to a set of methods that allow computers to process and extract information from human language. NLP constitutes an important building block for various programming tasks, including programs enabling computers to act on commands issued in spoken language[27] and translate text between different languages.[28] Like much other AI research, NLP has been a topic of inquiry (in one form or another) since at least the 1950s. In earlier decades, and in line with the then-governing paradigm guiding much research in AI, NLP operated on the basis of a "top down" approach: Computers extracted information from texts following complex sets of hand-coded rules drawn up by linguists and other experts.[29] Since the 1990s, NLP has undergone a profound transition that mirrors similar developments in other areas of AI. Today, most NLP follows a "bottom up" approach, relying heavily on ML and similar statistical techniques. These approaches allow computers to "learn" how to process language on the basis of large amounts of training data.[30]

On a very general level, NLP techniques hold the potential to automate an activity that plays a central role in many tasks performed by lawyers: the extraction and processing of information from unstructured text, either spoken or written. By unstructured text, we mean any text that is not organized in a manner that readily maps onto predefined categories known to be relevant for the task at hand. Most information encountered by lawyers in their daily work takes the form of unstructured text. Examples include the text of judicial opinions, statutes, legal briefs or written agreements, or written witness testimony. In contrast, the information provided by a client in response to an intake questionnaire that allows for only a predefined set of responses to each question does not constitute unstructured text, and NLP is usually not needed to process this kind of information.

To illustrate the central role of information extraction from unstructured text, consider again the example of outcome prediction. An attorney trying to predict whether a case presented to her by a client will succeed in court will usually require at least two types of information: first, information about the facts of the case and, second, information about how courts treat cases like the one at hand. The latter category includes, in particular, information about the applicable legal rules.[31] Both

[27] Bill Manaris, *Natural Language Processing. A Human-Computer Interaction Perspective*, 47 ADVANCES COMPUTS. 1 (1998).

[28] Lewis-Kraus, *The Great A.I. Awakening*.

[29] *See, e.g.*, Antoine Louis, *A Brief History of Natural Language Processing – Part 1*, MEDIUM (July 7, 2020), https://medium.com/@antoine.louis/a-brief-history-of-natural-language-processing-part-1-ffbcb937ebce.

[30] *Id.*

[31] Other factors that might influence how a court will likely treat cases like the one at hand include information about judges, juries, and political trends – in other words, "external" factors. *See also* Engstrom & Gelbach, *Legal Tech*, at 1027.

types of information will primarily be available in the form of unstructured text. Information about the facts of the case often comes in the form of written or spoken statements by the client, potentially combined with additional documents such as contracts; it can also involve depositions of witnesses and background research. Information about the law will typically take the form of statutes, regulations, and other cases, plus (depending on the jurisdiction) secondary sources of law such as legal treatises. Only after obtaining information about both the facts and the law (and potentially other factors that might influence the decision) will the attorney be able to determine the chances to succeed in trial.

This example is not an outlier. Instead, the processing of unstructured text plays a central role in many tasks performed by lawyers. A lawyer conducting document review reads documents to determine whether they fall into certain predefined categories (relevant to the case at hand, privileged, etc.) A lawyer drafting an agreement not only researches the law to establish the legal framework against which the contract is set, but also consults templates or examples of similar agreements she or her colleagues have drafted in the past.

Because of the central role that the extraction and processing of information from unstructured text plays in the work of lawyers, NLP is a potential key component of many actual or hypothesized legal tech applications.[32]

NLP will likely be particularly important in applications that seek to increase access to legal services to those who cannot afford a lawyer. In all the examples described above, before even starting their work on a case, lawyers need to decode unstructured language (often in the form of spoken text) to understand their clients' goals. Insofar as legal tech applications seek to interact directly with clients on the basis of unstructured language descriptions provided by the latter, NLP will also be needed to automate the task of translating these narratives into legally relevant units of information.[33] In addition, NLP can play an important role in communicating the results of the work performed by a legal tech application to a client in language that she can understand.

[32] *See also id.* at 1013; Jens Frankenreiter & Michael A. Livermore, *Computational Methods in Legal Analysis*, 16 Ann. Rev. L. Soc. Sci. 39, 51 (2020); Mireille Hildebrandt, *Law as Computation in the Era of Artificial Legal Intelligence: Speaking Law to the Power of Statistics*, 68 U. Toronto L.J. 12, 27 (2018).

[33] We note that the task of direct client interaction through unstructured input text is particularly challenging and requires a combination of intent extraction (i.e., the system's ability to extract what a user wants when making a query), Named Entity Recognition, and language parsing. *See also* Chapter 2 in this volume. An alternative (and often more feasible) solution can be to limit the input provided by the user to a narrow set of predefined options. This approach is particularly popular in narrow domains with clear rules, such as tax software. Instead of relying on open-ended text, these applications help clients to compute their tax burden by iteratively querying relevant information through a series of questions that allow for a limited set of possible answers.

TABLE 3.1 *Sample vectors in a BoW model*

Word	Sentence 1	Sentence 2	Sentence 3
we	1	1	1
protect	1	0	0
safeguard	0	1	0
expose	0	0	1
your	1	1	1
data	1	1	1

3.2. THE NLP PREDICTION PIPELINE

Typically, the process of creating predictions from text consists of two steps. In the first step, a language model converts text into vectors. In a second step, these vectors are used as an input into a ML classifier in order to create relevant predictions.[34] We discuss each step in turn.

3.2.1 *Step 1: Converting Text into Vectors Using Language Models*

Available language models differ in terms of their complexity. At the lower end of the spectrum are simple language models such as the "Bag-of-Words" (BoW) model.[35] These models do not involve a formal training process. Instead, each word is assigned its own, unique vector representation. Take, for instance, the following three sentences:

Sentence 1: We protect your data
Sentence 2: We safeguard your data
Sentence 3: We expose your data

To represent these sentences, a BoW model creates three vectors, one for each sentence. The vectors have as many dimensions as there are unique words (here 6). The elements of the vectors indicate whether a word is present or not. In this case, the column vectors for the three sentences are given in Table 3.1.

The above representation illustrates two important aspects of the BoW model: First, there is a lot of overlap between the vector representations of the sentences. Each vector has a 1 in the first, fifth, and sixth position. Hence, this simple language model accurately suggests that all three sentences are somewhat related, in the sense that they all talk about how another party handles the addressee's data. At the same time, however, the BoW representation has a significant shortcoming. In particular, the overlap between Sentence 1 and Sentence 2 is the same as the overlap between

[34] In modern language models, both steps may interact somewhat with each other.

[35] Yin Zhang et al., *Understanding Bag-of-Words Model: A Statistical Framework*, 1 INT'L J. MACH. LEARNING & CYBERNETICS 43, 43 (2010).

Sentence 1 and Sentence 3. However, any human reader would attest that the words *protect* and *safeguard* are semantically close, whereas *protect* and *expose* have almost polar opposite meanings. In this sense, a simple BoW model may be able to capture some semantic similarity between texts. However, since it simply represents word occurrence, it does not encode information about the semantic meaning of text. If we were to use the output of this BoW in a downstream task, it could quickly lead to incorrect results, particularly for nuanced tasks in which every single word carries significance.

To address this problem, current language models seek to identify numerical representations that are more faithful to the semantic meaning of a word or sentence. Under these models, Sentence 1 and Sentence 2 would be represented by vectors with similar elements, whereas Sentence 1 and Sentence 3 are represented in a way that is faithful to the difference in their semantic meaning. The details on how these models are able to achieve their goal differ, but what all modern language models have in common is a reliance on distributional semantics. The intuition behind distributional semantics is that linguistic items with similar semantic meanings are also distributed similarly. Indeed, John Firth famously said that "a word is characterized by the company it keeps,"[36] a linguistic notion similarly supported by Wittgenstein, who argued that the meaning of a word can only be understood by learning how said word is used in context.[37] We can easily see that this assumption is often reasonable. Assume, for instance, that we encounter a new word spelled *quari*. Without context, it would be difficult to tell what this word means. But now assume we encounter the word being used in practice. Perhaps we encounter sentences such as "I took my *quari* to the mechanic yesterday," or "I was driving fast with my *quari* on the highway." At this point, we could start forming expectations that a *quari* is a form of vehicle, because it is used in a way that is similar to how we use words such as *car* or *automobile*. At some point, we may even start using *quari* as a synonym for *car*.

The objective on which modern language models are trained imitates this type of learning from distributional properties. For instance, Google's BERT and OpenAI's GPT-3 – two recent large language models that have been hailed as breakthrough innovations for NLP – are trained simply by repeatedly guessing which word is most likely to occur next in a sequence of words.[38] The idea behind this training objective is straightforward: If a model is optimized to predict the next word in a sentence, it

[36] J. R. Firth, A *Synopsis of Linguistic Theory*, 1930–1955, *in* STUD. IN LINGUISTIC ANALYSIS 1 (1957).

[37] LUDWIG WITTGENSTEIN, PHILOSOPHICAL INVESTIGATIONS (1953).

[38] Jacob Devlin et al., *Bert: Pre-training of Deep Bidirectional Transformers for Language Understanding*, ARXIV (2019), https://arxiv.org/abs/1810.04805; Tom B. Brown et al., *Language Models Are Few-Shot Learners*, 33 ADVANCES NEURAL INFO. PROCESSING SYS., 2020, at 1. In addition, Google's BERT guesses which of two candidate sentences follows the input.

inherently learns linguistic properties that correspond to semantic meaning. For instance, a model learning that it is likely that the next word in the sentence "I was driving fast with my . . . " is *car* or *motorcycle* but not *cat* implicitly learns that a *motorcycle* is closer in meaning to *car* than it is to *cat*. And it turns out that next word prediction at scale is able to implicitly encode much more than just semantic meaning. For instance, by repeatedly solving next word prediction tasks, language models can "learn" grammatical rules[39] and encode world and limited legal knowledge.[40]

3.2.2 *Step 2: Downstream Prediction Tasks*

Once a language model has been trained, it allows for the conversion of text into vectors that encode the semantic meaning of a word, sentence, or document. These vectors can then be used in a ML model tasked with generating predictions that can vary with the objective of the legal tech application.

Like all ML models, those used in the context of NLP applications require at least two different types of data: training data and input data.[41] Training data refers to the information that is used to "calibrate" the statistical models forming the core of the ML tools. In other words, the training data allows the algorithm to "learn" about the relationship between some input and the desired prediction. For many language-based legal tech applications, training data consists of texts alongside labels that reflect certain information contained in the text. During training, the algorithm will learn which textual cues are strongly associated with the individual labels.[42] For example, a legal tech application assisting in electronic discovery may seek to automatically distinguish between documents that do and do not contain privileged information. In order to achieve that goal, the creator of the legal tech application would begin by hand-labeling a training corpus of documents for whether they contain privileged information or not. She would then use a language model to transform the content of the training documents into numerical vectors and would feed these vectors into a ML algorithm that learns the relationship between the different elements of the vectors and the human annotation (privileged/non-privileged).

Input data is the data that is fed into the machine to generate the predictions or other results that the user of the legal tech application is interested in. Notably, and

39 A model that correctly predicts that the word *drove* is more likely to occur then the word *drive* in a sentence that begins with "Yesterday, I" implicitly encodes that *drove* is the past tense of *drive*.

40 A model knowing that "The plaintiff sued the" will be followed by "defendant" implicitly learns that most cases have both a plaintiff and a defendant.

41 Agrawal, Prediction Machines, at 43.

42 In principle, labels can consist of unstructured text as well (so-called sequence-to-sequence labeling).

in contrast to the training data, input data can be largely unlabeled. In the context of document review, the input data usually consists of the unlabeled documents that were not included in the training dataset. After the ML algorithm has been trained, it can generate predictions for these documents at scale.

3.2.3 *Two Use Cases*

To illustrate both the utility and limitation of NLP in legal tech, we focus on two applications – document review and case outcome prediction. Both tasks lie at opposite ends of the spectrum of legal cognitions and thus bring some of the problems of NLP in sharp relief. At the same time, we are conscious of the fact that the full spectrum of legal tech implementations encompasses a much larger set of applications and that implications we draw here might apply differently in different use cases.

In the case of document review, the standard NLP pipeline described above performs well.[43] This is in part due to the fact that document review closely resembles information extraction, a standard linguistic prediction task that these models are particularly designed for. For instance, a typical exercise in NLP research is to predict the sentiment of social media posts on the basis of the posts' texts and a labeled training dataset.[44] Similarly, as described above, document review can be understood as an exercise in predicting labels associated with a document (e.g., privileged/non-privileged) on the basis of the text of the document.

Other tasks, however, are much more difficult to perform, irrespective of how sophisticated the language model is. One such task is the prediction of the outcome of a legal dispute. Legal outcome prediction using expert-generated systems has a long tradition.[45] However, here, we focus on the automatic prediction of legal outcomes without any human intervention.[46]

To illustrate the difficulties associated with legal outcome prediction, consider how the standard NLP pipeline might be implemented for this task.[47] At first, the process may appear to be straightforward: A language model could transform textual descriptions of fact patterns into vectors, with each vector in the training dataset

[43] *See* Engstrom & Gelbach, *Legal Tech*, at 1021; *see also* Chapter 5 in this volume.

[44] Lin Yue et al., *A Survey of Sentiment Analysis in Social Media*, 60 Knowledge & Info. Sys. 617, 617–63 (2019).

[45] For one historical account, see Kevin D. Ashley, *A Brief History of the Changing Roles of Case Prediction in AI and Law*, L. Context for Digit. Age, 2019, at 93, 93–112.

[46] For recent studies in legal outcome prediction, see Medvedeva, *Using Machine Learning*, at 237–66; Haoxi Zhong et al., *How Does NLP Benefit Legal System: A Summary of Legal Artificial Intelligence*, ArXiv (2020), https://arxiv.org/abs/2004.12158; L. Karl Branting et al., *Scalable and Explainable Legal Prediction*, 29 A.I. L. 213, 213–38 (2021); Elizabeth C. Tippett et al., *Does Lawyering Matter? Predicting Judicial Decisions from Legal Briefs, and What That Means for Access to Justice*, 100 Texas L. Rev. (forthcoming 2022).

[47] *See* Chapter 7 in this volume.

accompanied by a label indicating whether the plaintiff or the defendant won the case.[48] The ML algorithm would then generate predictions for the input dataset depending on the textual features of the document. The approach may sound simple in theory. And yet, to date, NLP-based attempts at predicting the outcome of legal cases using the standardized process have failed to produce reliable results.[49] But what is it that differentiates legal outcome prediction tasks from other exercises, such as classifying documents into relevant and non-relevant?

At its core, the difference lies in the quantity of linguistic markers that influence the prediction task. In legal outcome prediction, the set of informative linguistic markers is potentially infinite, whereas in document review, there typically is a small set of linguistic cues the algorithm is required to pick up on. To illustrate, imagine that there was a universal speed limit of fifty miles per hour. If we trained a model to predict the outcome of a dispute over a citation, it would quickly pick up on the fact that the most important linguistic cue for the prediction of the outcome is the description of the car's speed. If that description contains phrases such as "sixty mph," it would predict that a legal challenge to the citation is unlikely to succeed, whereas phrases such as "thirty mph" would lead the algorithm to predict a higher success rate. Perhaps the model would alter its prediction based on whether the description indicates that a radar was used or whether the speed was measured through pacing. But overall, the possible combinations of types of fact patterns that are relevant to the prediction are finite and small, and it is likely that (almost) every type of fact pattern relevant to the prediction could be sufficiently represented in a large enough corpus. Importantly, note that the classifier could achieve a high performance without ever being told what the specific rule is. Indeed, given a large enough training sample, the algorithm would automatically identify that "fifty mph" appears to be the discontinuity at which the probability of success changes significantly.

However, most legal prediction tasks, and certainly most of the law applicable to disputes, are not as simple. Consider, for instance, a negligence tort dispute. In contrast to the clear fifty mph rule in the narrow context of driving on public roads, negligence is a vague standard that may trigger liability in an unquantifiable number of contexts. The indefinite number of variations in fact patterns comes with a similarly indefinite number of potential linguistic cues that are relevant to the prediction of the outcome. When designing a legal technology app, it is impossible

48 We ignore for now difficulties in defining who "won" a case, which certainly is a context-specific analysis.

49 For an overview, see Zhong, *How Does NLP Benefit Legal System*. To be sure, in some applications, researchers report F1 scores in the range of 0.7–0.8 when predicting the outcome of judicial opinions. See, e.g., Medvedeva, *Using Machine Learning*, at 237–66; Tippett, *Does Lawyering Matter?* However, these studies are based on published opinions and/or use as input data documents that are produced at later stages in the litigation process. As such, they are best considered "backward looking," providing ex post insights on how cases have been decided, rather than on how future cases will be decided.

to collect a training dataset that contains all potential fact patterns that may or may not lead to liability under a negligence regime. In this scenario, a language model does not have the opportunity to detect and assess the relevance of all these linguistic cues that might be relevant to the success rate of the plaintiff. In order to make accurate predictions, the algorithm can no longer rely on comparing the linguistic and distributional patterns of one document to other documents it has encountered during training. Rather, in order to be successful, the algorithm has to perform the equivalent of *legal reasoning*. In other words, to fully automate the process without significant human intervention, an algorithm would have to be able to extract from the texts a representation of legal concepts and their interconnections (a "legal ontology"). With such a legal ontology, the algorithm would then be able to draw accurate inferences from precedent, even if it had never encountered the particular fact pattern in the past. For instance, if an algorithm was able to infer that fact patterns describing a small burden and a large probability of a significant loss increase the chances for the plaintiff to prevail in a negligence suit, it could use this knowledge to inform its predictions without reliance on the particular words used in the description of facts.

Against this background, one might ask whether the impressive trajectory of modern language models in recent years also translates into an ability to reconstruct such legal ontologies from text.[50] Unfortunately, the results to date are not promising. In fact, existing algorithms are notoriously bad at extracting abstract rules from text, and legal ontologies are no exception. Even if a researcher feeds the text of the rules directly into the model, current language models are not able to accurately process that information. For instance, Holzenberger and colleagues[51] task a language model with predicting how much tax is owed by an individual, using as input a description of facts. They show that, even though the relevant ontology can be defined manually by an expert and used to compute the exact tax rate, language models perform poorly at this task. But perhaps more importantly, the authors point out that model performance does not increase even after supplementing the description of facts in the training data with the text of the relevant statutes. This suggests that language models have difficulties deriving a legal ontology from text without human assistance.

To corroborate these intuitions, we turned to GPT-3, a state-of-the-art language model that has achieved extraordinary results on a number of language tasks.[52] Among others, it has demonstrated its ability to translate a description of a computer

[50] Bonan Min et al., *Recent Advances in Natural Language Processing via Large Pre-Trained Language Models: A Survey*, ARXIV (2021), https://arxiv.org/abs/2111.01243; Zhong, *How Does NLP Benefit Legal System*, at 5.

[51] Nils Holzenberger, Andrew Blair-Stanek & Benjamin Van Durme, *A Dataset for Statutory Reasoning in Tax Law Entailment and Question Answering*, ARXIV (2020), https://arxiv.org/abs/2005.05257.

[52] Brown, *Language Models*.

program from ordinary language into a working software application,[53] and it has written blog posts that fooled thousands of people into thinking they were authored by a human.[54] The legal literature has begun to study the utility of GPT-3 for tasks such as contract analysis in the consumer context, with at times positive results.[55]

To assess the capabilities of GPT-3 for a simple task involving legal reasoning, we first submitted the following query:[56]

> *Are liquidated damages clauses enforceable?*

The (correct) response:

> *Liquidated damages clauses are generally enforceable unless the sum stipulated is exorbitant or unconscionable.*

However, we then submitted the following query:

> *X and Y contract over the sale of a Toyota Corolla. Their contract specifies that X has to pay Y one million dollars in damages if X does not deliver the car on time. X does not deliver the car on time. Q: Is Y entitled to damages? If so, in what amount?*

GPT-3's response:

> *Yes, Y is entitled to one million dollars in damages. Damages are meant to compensate the injured party for the loss suffered due to the breach. Y has suffered a loss of one million dollars because X has not delivered the car on time.*

GPT-3 has been trained on millions of documents including almost half a trillion words. And while it was able to correctly extract and restate the legal rule based on the documents it encountered during training, it was not able to convert this rule into a legal ontology that would enable it to correctly infer the invalidity of the contractual penalty.

Next, we explicitly specified that the stipulated damages were "exorbitant." We also fed the relevant rule that GPT-3 itself recovered back into the model, resulting in the following query:

> *X and Y contract over the sale of a Toyota Corolla. Their contract specifies that X has to pay Y the exorbitant amount of one million dollars in damages if X does not deliver the car on time. X does not deliver the car on time. The law requires that liquidated damages clauses are enforced unless the sum stipulated is exorbitant or unconscionable. Q: Is Y entitled to damages? If so, in what amount?*

53 @jsngr, Twitter (July 18, 2020, 8:31 AM), https://twitter.com/jsngr/status/1284511080715362304.

54 Liam Porr, *My GPT-3 Blog Got 26 Thousand Visitors in 2 Weeks*, Excavations (Aug. 3, 2020), https://liamp.substack.com/p/my-gpt-3-blog-got-26-thousand-visitors.

55 Yonathan A. Arbel & Shmuel I. Becher, *Contracts in the Age of Smart Readers*, 90 Geo. Wash. L. Rev. (forthcoming 2022).

56 This example is a reprint one of us has used before to highlight the limitations of GPT-3 in Rishi Bommasani et al., *On the Opportunities and Risks of Foundation Models*, arXiv (2021), https://arxiv.org/abs/2108.07258.

GPT-3's response:

> *Yes, Y is entitled to the liquidated damages. The amount in this case is not exorbitant since the price was set by the parties themselves.*

Again, the model ignores the legal rules and produces an incorrect prediction. To be sure, we emphasize that our queries are not meant to scientifically explore the limitations of GPT-3. Instead, our application is meant to exemplify a more general point. As we pointed out above, the training objective of language models causes them to encode information that is included in the distributional properties of written language, such as word and sentence order. Language models are thus able to excel at tasks that require accessing distributional information. For instance, in order to write a text that is indistinguishable from a text written by a five-year-old human, most of the relevant information is contained in the grammatical structure and frequency distribution of words.[57] However, language understanding in general, and legal reasoning in particular, requires processing of information that is not a mere reflection of linguistic patterns. Instead, lawyering requires a "dizzying array of analytic moves,"[58] including an ability to apply rules to facts, inferring regularities from existing case law, distinguishing new fact patterns from precedent, and using logical reasoning and creativity to craft new legal arguments. Modern language models do not even begin to achieve performance that is close to that of human professionals. Perhaps even more importantly, the performance of these language models does not appear to significantly increase with the sophistication or complexity of the language model.[59] This suggests that the current trajectory of developments in NLP, which relies heavily on distributional properties, may run orthogonal to the kinds of models that would be needed to create accurate predictions of legal disputes.

Together, the current developments point toward a more limited role for NLP in applications involving legal reasoning: It appears that the task of building, dissecting, and understanding the law in order to assess a novel set of facts will continue to rely primarily on domain experts.[60] Creators of legal tech applications will have to rely on these experts to define a knowledge system that determines the relevant factors under the law, as well as how these factors influence the likely outcome. This does not mean that NLP will be irrelevant for such applications. It could still be used in more narrowly defined information extraction tasks with the aim of determining whether the factors that matter for the outcome of a dispute are present in a case at hand.

57 For instance, five-year-olds have a limited vocabulary and build simple sentences.
58 Engstrom & Gelbach, *Legal Tech*, at 1024.
59 Holzenberger, *A Dataset for Statutory Reasoning*.
60 Engstrom & Gelbach, *Legal Tech*, at 1025–26.

3.3. OTHER KEY CHALLENGES

The challenge of automating the creation of legal ontologies makes it difficult to predict whether, and when, technology will be able to completely replace the prominent and essential role humans – and, in particular, human lawyers – play in creating a functioning legal regime. Of course, it is famously difficult to predict the capabilities of future AI systems in many different contexts. However, one thing we do know is that recent advancements in NLP, although in many ways impressive, did not move us significantly closer in automating many of the core tasks that lawyers perform on a daily basis. It may well be the case that the full automation of most legal services is not only years, but decades away. But this is not all. At least four further challenges will impose hurdles on the development of legal tech tools and shape the field's future trajectory.

3.4.1 *Document Structure and Segmentation*

Before working with a text corpus, it needs to be broken up into coherent, informative units of analysis. This process is also referred to as "document segmentation" and is an important step in the NLP pipeline that can have significant consequences both for training a language model as well as for other downstream prediction tasks. In principle, the investigator is free to break text up at varying levels of granularity, such as the individual word, sentence, paragraph, section, or entire writing (e.g., a contract or statute).[61] However, this process can be complicated by the fact that many legal documents do not follow a strict template, as is the case for most judicial opinions. But even if the structure is relatively consistent across documents, choosing the right level of granularity requires balancing of competing factors. On one hand, if the segmentation is too coarse, algorithmic training is inefficient and more training data is required. In addition, modern language models simply do not work for very long text sequences, because their computational complexity increases with the length of the document at an exponential rate.[62] On the other hand, many more complex classification tasks require a sufficiently large context to give a complete and accurate answer. Therefore, if the segmentation is too granular, performance may suffer. Accurate segmenting can thus pose a significant challenge to NLP research.

When lawyers are working with legal texts, these challenges are exacerbated, because the most informative unit of analysis is often inconsistent and can vary

[61] Kevin D. Ashley, Artificial Intelligence and Legal Analytics: New Tools for Law Practice in the Digital Age 277 (2017).

[62] *See* Ashish Vaswani et al., *Attention Is All You Need*, 2017 Advances in Neural Info. Processing Sys. 30. For an overview of potential solutions, see Chuhan Wu et al., *Fastformer: Additive Attention Can Be All You Need*, arXiv (2021), https://arxiv.org/abs/2108.09084.

widely from one document to the next. To illustrate, assume that an algorithm is trained to automatically determine whether a court in a contracts dispute has personal jurisdiction over the defendant.[63] As input, we may provide a description of facts and the text of the agreement between the parties. However, choice-of-forum provisions can come in very different forms. Sometimes, they are contained in a single sentence. At other times, they may span multiple paragraphs. The agreement may even contain multiple dispute settlement provisions for different types of disputes. Thus, whether the appropriate unit of analysis is a sentence, paragraph, or section may vary from one document to the next, and this variation can significantly decrease classification performance and/or efficiency. To be sure, researchers have proposed deep-learning classifiers that are able to retain information as they move from one segment of the document to the next, thus ameliorating some of the concerns of inappropriate text segmentation.[64] However, because the computational complexity of these approaches increases exponentially in the length of the text sequence, they cannot feasibly be used to examine long legal documents.[65] Although researchers are beginning to examine ways around this limitation,[66] we are still far from finding workable solutions for long texts that obviate the need of segmentation.

In addition to document segmentation, identifying and processing the appropriate document structure complicates efforts to automate legal analysis. Many legal documents are highly contextual in that they rely on internal and external references in order to give meaning to their words or phrases. For example, M&A agreements typically include elaborate "Definitions" sections that define phrases such as "bankruptcy event" or "material adverse event," which are then used throughout the contract. Similarly, regulations and statutes often rely on definitions that are not contained in the text of the document itself and thus can only be interpreted accurately by turning to the referenced text.[67] There may further be a hierarchical structure to legal documents, by which a definition only applies to parts of the document that are lower in the hierarchy. For instance, a definition contained in a statutory text may define words or phrases at the chapter level, but could then be modified by exceptions at the section level.

[63] Julian Nyarko, *We'll See You in … Court! The Lack of Arbitration Clauses in International Commercial Contracts*, 58 Int'l Rev. L. & Econ. 6, 6–24 (2019); Julian Nyarko, *Stickiness and Incomplete Contracts*, 88 U. Chicago L. Rev. 1, 1–79 (2021).

[64] *See, e.g.*, Zichao Yang et al., *Hierarchical Attention Networks for Document Classification*, 2016 Proc. N. Am. Chapter of the Ass'n for Computational Linguistics 1480, 1480–89.

[65] The self-attention layer in a BERT model has a quadratic complexity of O(n^2) and thus, document length is generally limited to 512 tokens.

[66] Lulu Wan et al., *Long-Length Legal Document Classification*, arXiv (2019), https://arxiv.org/abs/1912.06905.

[67] For instance, 2 C.F.R. § 175.25 (2021) defines a foreign public entity as "[a] public international organization, which is an organization entitled to enjoy privileges, exemptions, and immunities as an international organization under the International Organizations Immunities Act (22 U.S.C. 288–288f)."

Current language models are ill-equipped to recognize and appropriately process such structural idiosyncrasies with relevant precision. Although recent research is beginning to develop a promising methodology to try to accommodate legal document structure, the existing approaches are still highly domain-specific, and it is unclear whether they can be generalized.[68]

3.4.2 *Availability of Training Data*

A second key challenge is data availability. As discussed above, most ML models need access to large amounts of training data. In the context of legal tech applications based on NLP technology, this means access to large numbers of documents that are representative of the input data used in the application.

Whether data access is a potential problem depends on the nature of the legal tech application. One reason for this is that the creators and users of legal tech applications can create training data for some applications, while the same is not true for others. As a general matter, the creation of training data is usually possible when the "labels" that are to be predicted can be generated by the users of the legal tech application themselves. As an example, consider document review. For many document review tasks, training data can be created by tasking human coders (in many cases, lawyers and paralegals) with manually labeling a subset of documents according to a coding scheme that is later replicated by the ML algorithm.[69] By contrast, in outcome prediction tasks, labels (the outcomes of disputes) are the product of a complex interaction between a multitude of actors including judges and litigants. A party interested in predicting the outcome of a dispute cannot on its own generate additional cases to serve as training data. Rather, they are limited to the cases generated in the context of past disputes.

Creators of applications that depend on existing data often face the problem that suitable training data from past cases is not widely available. There are various reasons for this. One potential problem is that legal texts are oftentimes hidden behind paywalls (either erected by private database providers, for example Westlaw,[70] or public players such as PACER[71]). Even more important, however, is the problem that many relevant documents are never collected by any central entity that would be in a position to make them available to potential creators of legal tech applications. For example, while it would be desirable to create outcome prediction

68 Dominic Seyler et al., *Finding Contextually Consistent Information Units in Legal Text* (2020) (unpublished manuscript).

69 *See also* Remus, *The Uncertain Promise*, at 1701–1706.

70 One example of a potential useful database maintained by a commercial database provider is Pleadings, Motions, and Memoranda on Westlaw Edge. *See Pleadings, Motions, and Memoranda*, Thompson Reuters, https://legal.thomsonreuters.com/en/products/westlaw/pleadings-motions-memoranda.

71 *See* Chapter 14 in this volume.

tools that can use early information about a dispute as input data, such information is almost never collected in a systematic way.

Selective availability of information is problematic not only because it raises questions about the availability of sufficiently sized training datasets to achieve high levels of predictive accuracy. It also gives rise to concerns about biased results. In the context of outcome prediction, because there are (virtually) no data repositories that systematically collect texts related to legal disputes prior to litigation, whether information about a dispute will become available at some point often depends on whether the dispute ends up in court or not. This is a problem because cases that do not result in litigation arguably differ in important ways from those that are litigated.[72] For instance, if there is clear, established precedent or otherwise little ambiguity in the rules that apply to a dispute, litigation is unlikely to occur. But this means that the available textual data is not an accurate representation of all potential disputes. Instead, textual data regarding disputes that end up in litigation will be heavily overrepresented. In the extreme, an outcome prediction tool that never encounters an "easy" case during the training process and is instead only trained on "hard" cases will have a tendency to abstain from making strong predictions even if a trained lawyer would be able to predict the outcome with certainty.

3.4.3 *No Benchmark Data*

The final limitation we discuss is the absence of domain-specific benchmark data that would allow creators of legal tech applications to compare the efficacy of newly developed methodologies. NLP is a research field that develops at a rapid pace. Indeed, the number of yearly submissions to ACL Anthology, the largest source of NLP papers, increased from about 1,000 in the 2000s to more than 4,000 new submissions by 2019.[73] In order to identify breakthrough contributions, the NLP community relies heavily on the concept of benchmarking. Benchmarks such as SuperGLUE[74] or the Stanford Question Answering Dataset (SQuAD)[75] contain hundreds of thousands of observations corresponding to various non-legal tasks, such as question answering, causal reasoning, and reading comprehension. The benchmarks have easily accessible leaderboards[76] and achieving state of the art (or SOTA) results is the main way in which important innovations are identified and adopted.

72 George L. Priest & Benjamin Klein, *The Selection of Disputes for Litigation*, 13 J.L. Stud. 1 (1984).

73 Saif M. Mohammad, *NLP Scholar: A Dataset for Examining the State of NLP Research*, 12 Proc. Language Res. & Evaluation Conf. 868, 868–77 (2020).

74 Alex Wang et al., *SuperGLUE: A Stickier Benchmark for General-Purpose Language Understanding Systems*, 33 Proc. Int'l Conf. on Neural Info. Processing Sys. (2020).

75 Pranav Rajpurkar et al., *SQuAD: 100,000+ Questions for Machine Comprehension of Text*, ArXiv (2016), https://arxiv.org/abs/1606.05250.

76 *Leaderboard Version: 2.0*, SuperGLUE, https://super.gluebenchmark.com/leaderboard; *SquAD2.0*, SQuAD, https://rajpurkar.github.io/SQuAD-explorer/.

However, although these benchmarks aim to capture language understanding of NLP models, they are designed for an ordinary/natural use of language. As mentioned above, legal language differs from ordinary language in several important aspects. Whether a higher score at SuperGLUE or SQuAD corresponds to better performance at legal interpretation remains unknown – and, indeed, there are many reasons to doubt that the correlation is close to perfect. This suggests that we currently lack the means to gauge how well language models work in the legal domain. To remedy this problem would require the availability of benchmark datasets specifically designed to resemble legal language understanding and reasoning tasks. However, such datasets can be exceedingly resource-intensive to design and maintain.[77] Indeed, it appears likely that significant progress can be made only if there is a shared commitment toward advancing and improving the use of natural language processing in law. Naturally, there appear to be various barriers to such a collaborative process. For instance, it stands to reason that law firms would be in a particularly good position to make available representative samples of legal documents (such as contracts). At the same time, law firms generally lack incentives to make these documents available to a general audience for benchmarking. To be sure, there are some efforts to try to overcome these barriers. For instance, the Atticus Project has made publicly available a dataset of annotated contracts with the stated goal of establishing a reliable reference corpus that could be used to improve the use of AI in contract analysis.[78] However, with a corpus of 510 agreements, the dataset is still far from providing a representative sample of commercial contracting that is comparable to those available to benchmark natural language models. It remains to be seen whether efforts like the Atticus Project can establish themselves as reliable benchmarks in the legal domain.

3.5. CONCLUSION AND OUTLOOK

NLP, a set of computational techniques that automate the extraction and processing of information from unstructured text, is considered a key ingredient in many legal tech applications. However, the performance of these techniques might not always live up to some commentators' high expectations. In particular, as this chapter argues, current NLP techniques are ill-equipped to distill legal concepts from texts, which imposes severe limitations to their use in legal tech applications that need to perform the equivalent of legal reasoning. Further, creators of NLP-assisted legal

[77] One clever exception to this rule is presented in Lucia Zheng et al., *When Does Pretraining Help? Assessing Self-Supervised Learning for Law and the CaseHOLD Dataset of 53,000+ Legal Holdings*, 18 Proc. Int'l Conf. on A.I. & L. 159, 159–68 (2021). By algorithmically extracting holdings of cases, they are able to automatically create multiple-choice questions that are then used to evaluate the performance of various language models.

[78] Dan Hendrycks et al., *CUAD: An Expert-Annotated NLP Dataset for Legal Contract Review*, 35 Proc. Int'l Conf. on Neural Info. Processing Sys. (2021).

tech need to grapple with several additional challenges, including a dearth of training data and the absence of benchmark datasets.

This result suggests that, in the short to medium term, NLP can be employed most fruitfully in tasks that do not significantly rely on legal reasoning. In contrast, the automation of tasks that rely heavily on legal reasoning will remain out of reach for the foreseeable future, save for any significant changes in how language models operate. This is because, for automated legal reasoning to succeed, it is not sufficient for an algorithm to process language in a literal sense. Instead, legal reasoning requires building, understanding, and processing the legal ontology that the language reflects. In other words, what is needed is a particularly complex form of Natural Language Understanding.[79]

How, then, might we identify tasks that are more reliant on legal reasoning and less amenable to automation? Perhaps the most obvious examples are those applications that require not just a high performance in predicting outcomes, but also need to explain how they arrived at the prediction.[80] But concerns about explainability are not the only reason why the ability of algorithms to perform the equivalent of legal reasoning matters. This ability is also a crucial determinant of an algorithm's predictive performance in those tasks for which large enough amounts of representative training data are not available.

If such training data is available, prediction tasks reduce to an inference problem: The algorithm must simply identify the predictors of a legal outcome while filtering out the noise. This can be the case, for instance, for outcome prediction tasks in run-of-the-mill cases that are based on relatively homogenous fact patterns.

However, if representative training data does not exist, accurate predictions are more heavily reliant on the availability of a representation of the general principles underlying previous case law. Without these, algorithms will likely fail to generate accurate predictions for previously unseen fact patterns. Because of current NLP techniques' limitations in recovering legal ontologies, NLP-based automation will likely face the greatest technological hurdles in dynamic areas of law where rules frequently change (e.g., those characterized by significant regulatory activity, such as environmental law), in areas that are multi-faceted and complex, and in areas in which the data is scarce (e.g., in litigation areas where settlement rates are particularly high). Similarly, settings that produce many new, previously unforeseen legal constellations will prove to be particularly challenging (e.g., appellate court decisions).

79 Alex Wang et al., *GLUE: A Multi-Task Benchmark and Analysis Platform for Natural Language Understanding*, ArXiv (2019), https://arxiv.org/abs/1804.07461.

80 Engstrom & Gelbach, *Legal Tech*, at 1025.

PART II

Legal Tech, Litigation, and the Adversarial System

4

Remote Testimonial Fact-Finding

Renee L. Danser, D. James Greiner, Elizabeth Guo, and Erik Koltun

Prior to the COVID-19 pandemic, debate mounted concerning the wisdom, and perhaps the inevitability, of moving swaths of the court system online. These debates took place within a larger discussion of how and why courts had failed to perform their most basic function of delivering (approximately) legally accurate adjudicatory outputs in cases involving unrepresented litigants[1] while inspiring public confidence in them as a method of resolving disputes compared to extralegal and even violent alternatives. Richard Susskind, a longtime critic of the status quo, summarized objections to a nearly 100 percent in-person adjudicatory structure: "[T]he resolution of civil disputes invariably takes too long [and] costs too much, and the process is unintelligible to ordinary people."[2] As Susskind noted, fiscal concerns drove much of the interest in online courts during this time, while reformists sought to use the move online as an opportunity to expand the access of, and services available to, unrepresented litigants.

[1] *See, e.g.*, Ellen Lee Degnan, Thomas Ferriss, D. James Greiner & Roseanna Sommers, *Using Random Assignment to Measure Court Accessibility for Low-Income Divorce Seekers*, Proc. Nat. Acad. Scis., Apr. 6, 2021 (documenting enormous differences in the experiences of lawyerless versus lawyered litigants in a substantively simple kind of legal proceeding).

[2] Richard Susskind, Online Courts and the Future of Civil Justice 27 (2019); *see also* Ayelet Sela, *e Nudging Justice: The Role of Digital Choice Architecture in Online Courts*, 2019 J. Disp. Resol. 127, 127–28 (2019) (noting that proponents of online courts contend that they lessen problems of confusing and complex process, lack of access, voluminous case filings, and costliness, while perhaps increasing settlement rates); Harold Hongju Koh, *The "Gants Principles" for Online Dispute Resolution: Realizing the Chief Justice's Vision for Courts in the Cloud*, 62 B.C. L. Rev. 2768, 2773 (2021) (noting gains in efficiency from online courts but suggesting a cost in the form of reduced access for those without resources and sophistication); Ayelet Sela, *Diversity by Design: Improving Access to Justice in Online Courts with Adaptive Court Interfaces*, 15 L. & Ethics Hum. Rts. 125, 128 (2021) (arguing that it is "widely recognized" that online courts promote efficiency, effectiveness, accessibility, and fairness).

Yet as criticisms grew, and despite aggressive action by some courts abroad,[3] judicial systems in the United States moved incrementally. State courts, for example, began to implement online dispute resolution (ODR), a tool that private-sector online retailers had long used.[4] But courts had deployed ODR only for specified case types and only at specified stages of civil proceedings. There was little judicial appetite in the United States for a wholesale transition.

The COVID-19 pandemic upended the judicial desire to move slowly. As was true of so many other sectors of United States society, the judicial system had to reconstitute online, and had to do so convulsively. And court systems did so, in the fashion in which systemic change often occurs in the United States: haphazardly, unevenly, and with many hiccups. The most colorful among the hiccups entered the public consciousness: audible toilet flushes during oral argument before the highest court in the land; a lawyer appearing at a hearing with a feline video filter that he was unable to remove himself; jurors taking personal calls during voir dire.[5] But there were notable successes as well. The Texas state courts had reportedly held 1.1 million proceedings online as of late February 2021, and the Michigan state courts' live-streaming on YouTube attracted 60,000 subscribers.[6]

These developments suggest that online proceedings have become a part of the United States justice system for the foreseeable future. But skepticism has remained about online migration of some components of the judicial function, particularly around litigation's most climactic stage: the adversarial evidentiary hearing,

[3] *See* Robert Lapper, *Access to Justice in Canada: The First On-line Court*, Commonwealth Laws. Ass'n, https://www.commonwealthlawyers.com/cla/access-to-justice-in-canada-the-first-on-line-court/ (describing British Columbia's move to mandatory online adjudication for certain matters).

[4] *See* Ayelet Sela, *The Effect of Online Technologies on Dispute Resolution System Design: Antecedents, Current Trends, and Future Directions*, 21 Lewis & Clark L. Rev. 635 (2017); *see also* Ethan Katsh & Leah Wing, *Ten Years of Online Dispute Resolution (ODR): Looking at the Past and Constructing the Future*, 38 U. Tol. L. Rev. 19, 41 (2006).

[5] *See* Daniel Victor, *"I'm Not a Cat," Says Lawyer Having Zoom Difficulties*, N.Y. Times (Feb. 9, 2021), https://www.nytimes.com/2021/02/09/style/cat-lawyer-zoom.html (discussing a hearing in which a lawyer began participation with a cat video filter on his Zoom account that he was unable to remove without the judge's guidance); Fred Barbash, *Oyez. Oy vey. Was That a Toilet Flush in the Middle of a Supreme Court Live-Streamed Hearing?* Wash. Post (May 7, 2020), https://www.washingtonpost.com/nation/2020/05/07/toilet-flush-supreme-court/ (the article title speaks for itself); Ashley Feinberg, *Investigation: I Think I Know Which Justice Flushed*, Slate (May 8, 2020), https://slate.com/news-and-politics/2020/05/toilet-flush-supreme-court-livestream.html (discussing the same Supreme Court oral argument); Eric Scigliano, *Zoom Court Is Changing How Justice Is Served, for Better, for Worse, and Possibly Forever*, The Atlantic (Apr. 13, 2021), https://www.theatlantic.com/magazine/archive/2021/05/can-justice-be-served-on-zoom/618392/ (describing juror informality during remote voir dire).

[6] Scigliano, *Zoom Court Is Changing*; *see also* Pew Charitable Trs., How Courts Embraced Technology, Met the Pandemic Challenge, and Revolutionized Their Operations (2021), https://www.pewtrusts.org/-/media/assets/2021/12/how-courts-embraced-technology.pdf (noting that by Nov. 2020, 82 percent of all courts in the United States were permitting remote proceedings in eviction matters).

especially the jury trial. Perhaps believing that they possessed unusual skill in discerning truthful and accurate testimony from its opposite,[7] some judges embraced online bench fact-finding. But the use of juries, both civil and criminal, caused angst, and some lawyers and judges remained skeptical that the justice system could or should implement any kind of online jury trial. Some of this skepticism waxed philosophical. Legal thinkers pondered, for example, whether a jury trial is a jury trial if parties, lawyers, judges, and the jurors themselves do not assemble in person in a public space.[8] Some of the skepticism about online trials may have been simple fear of the unknown.[9]

Other concerns skewed more practical and focused on matters for which existing research provided few answers. Will remote trials yield more representative juries by opening proceedings to those with challenges in attending in-person events, or will the online migration yield less-representative juries by marginalizing those on the wrong side of the digital divide? Will remote trials decrease lawyer costs and, perhaps as a result, expand access to justice by putting legal services more within the reach of those with civil justice needs?[10] Time, and more data, can tell if the political will is there to find out.

But two further questions lie at the core of debate about whether online proceedings can produce approximately accurate and publicly acceptable fact-finding from testimonial evidence. The first is whether video hearings diminish the ability of fact-finders to detect witness deception or mistake. The second is whether video as a communication medium dehumanizes one or both parties to a case, causing less humane decision-making.[11] For these questions, the research provides an answer (for the first question) and extremely useful guidance (for the second).

7 For discussions of beliefs deserving of similar levels of credibility, *see, e.g.*, Malcolm W. Browne, *Perpetual Motion?* N.Y. Times (June 4, 1985), https://www.nytimes.com/1985/06/04/science/perpetual-motion.html; *Astronomy: Geocentric Model*, Encyclopaedia Britannica, https://www.britannica.com/science/geocentric-model. We focus on this point further below.

8 *See, e.g.*, Susan A. Bandes & Neal Feigenson, *Virtual Trials: Necessity, Invention, and the Evolution of the Courtroom*, 68 Buff. L. Rev. 1275 (2020); Christopher L. Dodson, Scott Dodson & Lee H. Rosenthal, *The Zooming of Federal Litigation*, 104 Judicature 12 (2020); Jenia Iontcheva Turner, *Remote Criminal Justice*, 53 Tex. Tech. L. Rev. 197 (2021).

9 Ed Spillane, *The End of Jury Trials: COVID-19 and the Courts: The Implications and Challenges of Holding Hearings Virtually and in Person during a Pandemic from a Judge's Perspective*, 18 Ohio St. J. Crim. L. 537 (2021).

10 David Freeman Engstrom, *Digital Civil Procedure*, 169 U. Pa. L. Rev. 7 (2021); David Freeman Engstrom, *Post-COVID Courts*, 68 UCLA L. Rev. Disc. 246 (2020); Richard Susskind, *Remote Courts*, Practice, July/Aug. 2020, at 1.

11 The second of the two questions addressed herein is more often expressed with respect to criminal trials, with the worry being dehumanization of an accused. See Derwyn Bunton, Chair, Nat'l Ass'n for Pub. Def., NAPD Statement on the Issues with the Use of Virtual Court Technology (2020), https://www.publicdefenders.us/files/NAPD%20Virtual%20Court%20Statement%208_1.pdf; *see also* Turner, *Remote Criminal Justice*; Anne Bowen Poulin, *Criminal Justice and Videoconferencing Technology: The Remote Defendant*, 78 Tul. L. Rev. 1089 (2004); Cormac T. Connor, *Human Rights Violations in the Information Age*, 16 Geo. Immigr. L.J. 207 (2001). But dehumanization might apply equally to the civil context,

This chapter addresses these questions by reviewing the relevant research. By way of preview, our canvass of the relevant literatures suggests that both concerns articulated above are likely misplaced. Although there is reason to be cautious and to include strong evaluation with any move to online fact-finding, including jury trials, available research suggests that remote hearings will neither alter the fact-finder's (nearly non-existent) ability to discern truthful from deceptive or mistaken testimony nor materially affect fact-finder perception of parties or their humanity. On the first point, a well-developed body of research concerning the ability of humans to detect when a speaker is lying or mistaken shows a consensus that human detection accuracy is only slightly better than a coin flip. Most importantly, the same well-developed body of research demonstrates that such accuracy is the same regardless of whether the interaction is in-person or virtual (so long as the interaction does not consist solely of a visual exchange unaccompanied by sound, in which case accuracy worsens). On the second point, the most credible studies from the most analogous situations suggest little or no effect on human decisions when interactions are held via videoconference as opposed to in person. The evidence on the first point is stronger than that on the second, but the key recognition is that for both points, the weight of the evidence is contrary to the concerns that lawyers and judges have expressed, suggesting that the Bench and the Bar should pursue online courts (coupled with credible evaluation) to see if they offer some of the benefits their proponents have identified. After reviewing the relevant literature, this chapter concludes with a brief discussion of a research agenda to investigate the sustainability of remote civil justice.

A final point concerning the scope of this chapter: As noted above, judges and (by necessity) lawyers have largely come to terms with online bench fact-finding based on testimonial evidence, reserving most of their skepticism for online jury trials. But as we relate below, the available research demonstrates that to the extent that the legal profession harbors concerns regarding truth-detection and dehumanization in the jury's testimonial fact-finding, it should be equally skeptical regarding that of the bench. The evidence in this area either fails to support or affirmatively contradicts the belief that judges are better truth-detectors, or are less prone to dehumanization, than laity. Thus, we focus portions of this chapter on online jury trials because unwarranted skepticism has prevented such adjudications from the level of use (under careful monitoring and evaluation) that the currently jammed court system likely needs. But if current research (or our analysis of it here) is wrong, meaning that truth-detection and dehumanization are fatal concerns for online jury trials,

where the concern might be a reduced human connection to, say, a plaintiff suing about a physical injury. Indeed, depending on one's perspective, in a case involving a human being against a corporation, dehumanization might eliminate an unfair emotional advantage inuring to the human party or further "skew" a system already tilted in favor of corporate entities. *See* Engstrom, *Digital Civil Procedure*.

then online bench adjudications based on testimonial evidence should be equally concerning.

4.1 ADJUDICATION OF TESTIMONIAL ACCURACY

A common argument against the sustainability of video testimonial hearings is that, to perform its function, the fact-finder must be able to distinguish accurate from inaccurate testimony. Inaccurate testimony could arise via two mechanisms: deceptive witnesses, that is, those who attempt to mislead the trier of fact through deliberate or knowing misstatements; and mistaken witnesses, that is, those who believe their testimony even though their perception of historical fact was wrong.[12] The legal system reasons as follows. First, juries are good, better even than judges, at choosing which of two or more witnesses describing incompatible versions of historical fact is testifying accurately.[13] Second, this kind of "demeanor evidence" takes the form of nonverbal cues observable during testimony.[14] Third, juries adjudicate credibility best if they can observe witnesses' demeanor in person.[15]

Each component of this reasoning is false.

First, research shows that humans have just above a fifty-fifty chance ability to detect lies, approximately 54 percent overall, if we round up. For example, Bond and

[12] To clarify: we refer in this chapter to concerns of duplicitous or mistaken testimony about particular historical events and, relatedly, conflicts in testimony about such events. Imagine, in other words, one witness who testifies that the light was green at the time of an accident, and another witness who says that the light was red. Physics being what it is, one of these witnesses is lying or mistaken. In cases of genuine issues of material fact, a trier of fact (a jury, if relevant law makes one available) is ordinarily supposed to discern which witness is truthful and accurate. Triers of fact, including juries, may be able to identify mistakes or lies by considering the plausibility of testimony given other (presumably accurate and transparent) evidence; *see, e.g.*, Scott v. Harris, 550 U.S. 372 (2007), or background circumstances, or by considering internal inconsistencies in a witness's testimony. But to our knowledge, few in the United States legal profession argue that an in-person interaction is necessary to facilitate this latter exercise in truth detection.

[13] Markman v. Westview Instruments, 570 U.S. 370 (1996).

[14] *See, e.g.*, George Fisher, *The Jury's Rise as Lie Detector*, 107 YALE L.J. 576, 577 n.2, 703 n.597 (1997) (collecting case law adjudicating the advisability of judges promoting the use of nonverbal cues to detect witness deception); Cara Salvatore, *May It Please the Camera: Zoom Trials Demand New Skills*, LAW360 (June 29, 2020), https://www.law360.com/articles/1278361/may-it-please-the-camera-zoom-trials-demand-new-skills ("Being able to see the witnesses face-on instead of sideways, [a judge] said, vastly improves the main job of fact-finders – assessing credibility.").

[15] *See, e.g.*, Mattox v. United States, 156 U.S. 237, 243 (1895) (holding that in the criminal context, the Constitution gives the defendant the right to "compel [a prosecution witness] to stand face to face with the jury in order that they may look at him, and judge by his demeanor upon the stand and the manner in which he gives his testimony whether he is worthy of belief"). Note that there are challenges to the notion of what it means to be "face to face" with a witness other than the online environment. See Julia Simon-Kerr, *Unmasking Demeanor*, 88 GEO. WASH. L. REV. ARGUENDO 158 (2020) (discussing the challenges posed by a policy of requiring witnesses to wear masks while testifying).

DePaulo, in their meta-analysis of deception detection studies, place human ability to detect deception at 53.98 percent, or just above chance.[16] Humans are really bad at detecting deception. That probably comes as a shock to many of us. We are pretty sure, for example, we can tell when an opponent in a game or a sport is fibbing or bending the truth to get an edge. We are wrong. It has been settled in science since the 1920s that human beings are bad at detecting deception.[17] The fact that judges and lawyers continue to believe otherwise is a statement of the disdain in which the legal profession holds credible evidence and empiricism more generally.[18]

Second, human (in)ability to detect deception does not change with an in-person or a virtual interaction. Or at least, there is no evidence that there is a difference between in-person and virtual on this score, and a fair amount of evidence that there

[16] Charles F. Bond Jr. & Bella M. DePaulo, *Accuracy of Deception Judgements*, 10 PERSONALITY & SOC. PSYCH. REV. 214, 219 (2006).

[17] *See* William M. Marston, *Studies in Testimony*, 15 J. CRIM. L. & CRIMINOLOGY 5, 22–26 (1924); Glenn E. Littlepage & Martin A. Pineault, *Verbal, Facial, and Paralinguistic Cues to the Detection of Truth and Lying*, 4 PERSONALITY & SOC. PSYCH. BULL. 461 (1978); John E. Hocking, Joyce Bauchner, Edmund P. Kamiski & Gerald R. Miller, *Detecting Deceptive Communication from Verbal, Visual, and Paralinguistic Cues*, 6 HUM. COMM. RSCH. 33, 34 (1979); Miron Zuckerman, Bella M. DePaulo & Robert Rosenthal, *Verbal and Nonverbal Communication of Deception*, 14 ADV. EXP. SOC. PSYCH. 1, 39–40 (1981); Bella M. DePaulo & Robert L. Pfeifer, *On-the-Job Experience and Skill at Detecting Deception*, 16 J. APPLIED SOC. PSYCH. 249 (1986); Ginter Kohnken, *Training Police Officers to Detect Deceptive Eyewitness Statements: Does It Work?* 2 SOC. BEHAV. 1 (1987). For experiments specifically addressing the effects of rehearsal, *see, e.g.*, Joshua A. Fishman, *Some Current Research Needs in the Psychology of Testimony*, 13 J. SOC. ISSUES 60, 64–65 (1957); Norman R. F. Maier, *Sensitivity to Attempts at Deception in an Interview Situation*, 19 PERSONNEL PSYCH. 55 (1966); Norman R. F. Maier & Junie C. Janzen, *Reliability of Reasons Used in Making Judgments of Honesty and Dishonesty*, 25 PERCEPTUAL & MOTOR SKILLS 141 (1967); Norman R. F. Maier & James A. Thurber, *Accuracy of Judgments of Deception When an Interview Is Watched, Heard, and Read*, 21 PERSONNEL PSYCH. 23 (1968); Paul Ekman & Wallace V. Friesen, *Nonverbal Leakage and Cues to Deception*, 32 PSYCHIATRY 88 (1969); Paul Ekman & Wallace V. Friesen, *Detecting Deception from the Body or Face*, 29 J. PERSONALITY & SOC. PSYCH. 288 (1974); Pal Ekman, Wallace V. Friesen & Klaus R. Scherer, *Body Movement and Voice Pitch in Deceptive Interaction*, 16 SEMIOTICA 23 (1976); GERALD R. MILLER & NORMAN E. FONTES, THE EFFECTS OF VIDEOTAPED COURT MATERIALS ON JUROR RESPONSE 11–42 (1978); Glenn E. Littlepage & Martin A. Pineault, *Detection of Deceptive Factual Statements from the Body and the Face*, 5 PERSONALITY & SOC. PSYCH. BULL. 325, 328 (1979); Gerald R. Miller, Mark A. deTurck & Pamela J. Kalbfleisch, *Self-Monitoring, Rehearsal, and Deceptive Communication*, 10 HUM. COMM. RSCH. 97, 98–99, 114 (1983) (reporting unpublished studies of others as well as the authors' work); Carol Toris & Bella M. DePaulo, *Effects of Actual Deception and Suspiciousness of Deception on Interpersonal Perceptions*, 47 J. PERSONALITY & SOC. PSYCH. 1063 (1984) (although most people cannot do better than chance in detecting falsehoods, most people confidently believe they can do so); PAUL EKMAN, TELLING LIES 162–89 (1985); Charles F. Bond Jr. & William E. Fahey, *False Suspicion and the Misperception of Deceit*, 26 BR. J. SOC. PSYCH. 41 (1987).

[18] For another example, see Chief Justice John Roberts, who reacted to quantitative standards for measuring political gerrymandering as follows: "It may be simply my educational background, but I can only describe it as sociological gobbledygook." Gill v. Whitford Oral Argument, OYEZ, https://www.oyez.org/cases/2017/16-1161.

is no difference. Most likely, humans are really bad at detecting deception regardless of the means of communication. This also probably comes as a shock to many of us. In addition to believing (incorrectly) that we can tell when kids or partners or opponents are lying, we think face-to-face confrontation matters. Many judges and lawyers so believe. They are wrong.

Why are humans so bad at deception detection? One reason is that people rely on what they think are nonverbal cues. For example, many think fidgeting, increased arm and leg movement, and decreased eye contact are indicative of lying. None are. While there might be some verbal cues that could be reliable for detecting lies, the vast majority of nonverbal cues (including those just mentioned, and most others upon which we humans tend to rely) are unreliable, and the few cues that might be modestly reliable can be counterintuitive.[19] Furthermore, because we hold inaccurate beliefs about what is and is not reliable, it is difficult for us to disregard the unreliable cues.[20] In a study that educated some participants on somewhat reliable nonverbal cues to look for, with other participants not getting this information, participants with the reliable cues had no greater ability to detect lying.[21] We humans are not just bad at lie detection; we are also bad at being trained at lie detection.

While a dishonest demeanor elevates suspicion, it has little-to-no relation to actual deception.[22] Similarly, a perceived honest demeanor is not reliably associated with actual honesty.[23] That is where the (ir)relevance of the medium of communication matters. If demeanor is an unreliable indicator for either honesty or dishonesty, then a fact-finder suffers little from losing whatever the supposedly superior opportunity to observe demeanor an in-person interaction might provide.[24] For

19 Bella M. DePaulo, James J. Lindsay, Brian E. Malone & Laura Muhlenbruck, *Cues to Deception*, 129 Psych. Bull. 74, 95 (2003).

20 Lucy Akehurst, Gunter Kohnken, Aldert Vrij & Ray Bull, *Lay Persons' and Police Officers' Beliefs regarding Deceptive Behaviour*, 10 Applied Cognitive Psych. 468 (1996).

21 Hannah Shaw & Minna Lyons, *Lie Detection Accuracy: The Role of Age and the Use of Emotions as a Reliable Cue*, 32 J. Police Crim. Psych. 300, 302 (2017).

22 Lyn M. Van Swol, Michael T. Braun & Miranda R. Kolb, *Deception, Detection, Demeanor, and Truth Bias in Face-to-Face and Computer-Mediated Communication*, 42 Commc'n Rsch. 1116, 1131 (2015).

23 Timothy R. Levine et al., *Sender Demeanor: Individual Differences in Sender Believability Have a Powerful Impact on Deception Detection Judgements*, 37 Hum. Commc'n Rsch. 377, 400 (2011).

24 Unsurprisingly, lawyers and judges believe otherwise: "In a virtual jury trial, jurors lose the ability to lay eyes on witnesses in real time, and as a result, may miss nuances in behavior, speech patterns or other clues relevant to whether the witness is telling the truth." Paula Hinton & Tom Melsheimer, *The Remote Jury Trial Is a Bad Idea*, Law360 (June 9, 2020), https://www.law360.com/articles/1279805. Hinton & Melsheimer offer no support for this assertion, other than (we imagine) their gut instincts based on their having "practic[ed] for over a combined 70 years." *Id.* The scientific consensus regarding deception detection has been reaffirmed for longer than seventy years. It involves dozens of studies pursued by scores of researchers. *See* sources cited *supra* note 17.

example, a study from 2015 shows that people attempting to evaluate deception performed better when the interaction was a computer-mediated (text-based communication) rather than in-person communication.[25] At least one possible explanation for this finding is the unavailability of distracting and unreliable nonverbal cues.[26]

Despite popular belief in the efficacy of discerning people's honesty based on their demeanor, research shows that non-demeanor cues, meaning verbal cues, are more promising. A meta-analysis concluded that cues that showed promise at signaling deception tended to be verbal (content of what is said) and paraverbal (how it is spoken), not visual.[27] But verbal and paraverbal cues are just as observable from a video feed.

If we eliminate visual cues for fact-finders, and just give them audio feed, will that improve a jury's ability to detect deception? Unlikely. Audio-only detection accuracy does not differ significantly from audiovisual.[28] At this point, that should not be a surprise, considering the general low ceiling of deception detection accuracy – just above the fifty-fifty level. Only in high-pressure situations is it worthwhile (in a deception detection sense) to remove nonverbal cues.[29] To clarify: High-pressure situations likely make audio only better than audio plus visual, not the reverse. The problem for deception detection appears to be that, with respect to visual cues, the pressure turns the screws both on someone who is motivated to be believed but is actually lying and on someone who is being honest but feels as though they are not believed.

We should not think individual judges have any better ability to detect deception than a jury. Notwithstanding many judges' self-professed ability to detect lying, the science that humans are poor deception detectors has no caveat for the black robe. There is no evidence that any profession is better at deception detection, and a great deal of evidence to the contrary. For example, those whose professions ask them to detect lies (such as police officers) cite the same erroneous cues regarding deception.[30] More broadly, two meta-analyses from 2006 show that purported "experts" at deception detection are no better at lie detection than nonexperts.[31]

25 Van Swol et al., *Deception, Detection, Demeanor, and Truth Bias*, at 1131.

26 *Id.* at 1136.

27 DePaulo et al., *Cues to Deception*, at 95.

28 Bond & DePaulo, *Accuracy of Deception Judgements*, at 225.

29 Saul M. Kassin, Christian A. Meissner & Rebecca J. Norwick, *"I'd Know a False Confession if I Saw One": A Comparative Study of College Students and Police Investigators*, 29 Law & Hum. Behav. 211, 222 (2005).

30 Akehurst et al., *Lay Persons' and Police Officers' Beliefs*, at 461.

31 Bond & DePaulo, *Accuracy of Deception Judgements*, at 229; Michael Aamodt & Heather Custer, *Who Can Best Catch a Liar? A Meta-Analysis of Individual Differences in Detecting Deception*, 15 Forensic Exam'r 6, 10 (2006).

What about individuals versus groups? A 2015 study did find consistently that groups performed better at detecting lies,[32] a result the researchers attributed to group synergy – that is, that individuals were able to benefit from others' thoughts.[33] So, juries are better than judges at deception detection, right? Alas, almost certainly not. The problem is that only certain kinds of groups are better than individuals. In particular, groups of individuals who were familiar with one another before they were assigned a deception detection task outperformed both individuals and groups whose members had no preexisting connection.[34] Groups whose members had no preexisting connection were no better at detecting deception than individuals.[35] Juries are, by design, composed of a cross-section of the community, which almost always means that jurors are unfamiliar with one another before trial.[36]

There is more bad news. Bias and stereotypes affect our ability to flush out a lie. Females are labeled as liars significantly more than males even when both groups lie or tell the truth the same amount.[37] White respondents asked to detect lies were significantly faster to select the "liar" box for black speakers than white speakers.[38]

All of this is troubling, and likely challenges fundamental assumptions of our justice system. For the purposes of this chapter, however, it is enough to demonstrate that human inability to detect lying remains constant whether testimony is received in-person or remotely. Again, the science on this point goes back decades, and it is also recent. Studies conducted in 2014[39] and 2015[40] agreed that audiovisual and audio-only mediums were not different in accuracy detection. The science suggests

32 Nadav Klein & Nicholas Epley, *Group Discussion Improves Lie Detection*, 112 Proc. Nat'l Acad. Scis. 7460, 7464 (2015). Groups consisted of three people, which is fewer than usually empaneled for any jury.

33 *Id.* at 7463.

34 Roger McHaney, Joey F. George & Manjul Gupta, *An Exploration of Deception Detection: Are Groups More Effective Than Individuals?* 45 Commc'n Rsch. 1111 (2018).

35 *Id.*

36 Meanwhile, there is some evidence that deliberation of the kind in which juries engage may make things worse. Holly K. Orcutt et al., *Detecting Deception in Children's Testimony: Factfinders' Abilities to Reach the Truth in Open Court and Closed-Circuit Trials*, 25 Law & Hum. Behav. 339 (2001).

37 E. Paige Lloyd, Kevin M. Summers, Kurt Hugenburg & Allen R. McConnell, *Revisiting Perceiver and Target Gender Effects in Deception Detection*, 42 J. Nonverbal Behav. 427, 435 (2018).

38 E. Paige Lloyd et al., *Black and White Lies: Race-Based Biases in Deception Judgements*, 28 Psych. Sci. 1134 (2017).

39 Charlotte D. Sweeney & Stephen J. Ceci, *Deception Detection, Transmission, and Modality in Age and Sex*, 5 Frontiers Psych. 5 (2014).

40 Scott E. Culhane, Andre Kehn, Jessica Hatz & Meagen M. Hildebrand, *Are Two Heads Better Than One? Assessing the Influence of Collaborative Judgements and Presentation Mode on Deception Detection for Real and Mock Transgressions*, 12 J. Investigative Psych. Offender Profiling 158, 165 (2015).

that the medium of communication – in-person, video, or telephonic – has little if any relevant impact on the ability of judges or juries to tell truths from lies.[41]

The statements above regarding human (in)ability to detect deception apply equally to human (in)ability to detect mistakes, including the fact that scientists have long known that we are poor mistake detectors. Thirty years ago, Wellborn collected and summarized the then-available studies, most focusing on eyewitness testimony. Addressing jury ability to distinguish mistaken from accurate witness testimony, Wellborn concluded that "the capacity of triers [of fact] to appraise witness accuracy appears to be worse than their ability to discern dishonesty."[42] Particularly relevant for our purposes, Wellborn further concluded that "neither verbal nor nonverbal cues are effectively employed" to detect testimonial mistakes.[43] If neither verbal nor nonverbal cues matter in detecting mistakes, then there will likely be little lost by the online environment's suppression of nonverbal cues.

The research in the last thirty years reinforces Wellborn's conclusions. Human inability to detect mistaken testimony in real-world situations is such a settled principle that researchers no longer investigate it, focusing instead on investigating other matters, such as the potentially distorting effects of feedback given to eyewitnesses,[44] whether witness age affects likelihood of fact-

41 For excellent summaries of the historical research and literature, including many of the studies referenced in note 17 comparing our ability to detect deception across mediums, see Jeremy A, Blumenthal, *A Wipe of the Hands, a Lick of the Lips: The Validity of Demeanor Evidence in Assessing Witness Credibility*, 72 Neb. L. Rev. 1157 (1993); Olin Guy Wellborn II, *Demeanor*, 76 Cornell L. Rev. 1075 (1990). Note that we did find the occasional study suggesting to the contrary. *See, e.g.*, Sara Landstrom, Par Anders Granhag & Maria Hartwig, *Children's Live and Videotaped Testimonies: How Presentation Mode Affects Observers' Perception, Assessment, and Memory*, 12 Leg. & Crim. Psych. 333 (2007), but the overwhelming weight of the scientific evidence is as summarized above.

42 Wellborn, *Demeanor*, at 1088.

43 *Id.* at 1091.

44 *See, e.g.*, Laura Smalarz & Gary L. Wells, *Post-Identification Feedback to Eyewitnesses Impairs Evaluators' Abilities to Discriminate between Accurate and Mistaken Testimony*, 38 Law & Hum. Behav. 194 (2014); C. A. E. Luus & G. L. Wells, *The Malleability of Eyewitness Confidence: Co-witness and Perseverance Effects*, 79 J. Applied Psych. 714 (1994). The Smalarz and Wells experiment reveals the lengths to which researchers must go to produce an artificial situation in which human beings are able to distinguish between accurate and mistaken testimony (a situation that may be required to investigate something else). In this study, to assure a sufficient number of "mistaken" witnesses, investigators had to deceive witnesses intended to provide a mistaken eyewitness identification into believing that the correct perpetrator was present in a lineup. Smalarz & Wells, *Post-Identification Feedback*, at 196. Extraordinary measures to produce distinguishably accurate versus inaccurate hypothetical witnesses characterize other studies. One study resorted to cherry-picking from numerous mock witnesses those judged most and least accurate for later use. Michael R. Leippe, Andrew P. Manion & Ann Romanczyk, *Eyewitness Persuasion: How and How Well Do Fact Finders Judge the Accuracy of Adults' and Children's Memory Reports?* 63 J. Personality & Soc. Psych. 181 (1992). Another made no effort to provide fact-finders with witness testimony. Instead, fact-finders were provided with questionnaires that witnesses completed about their thought processes. David Dunning & Lisa Beth Stern, *Distinguishing Accurate from Inaccurate*

finder belief,[45] and whether fact-finders understand the circumstances mitigating the level of unreliability of eyewitness testimony.[46] The most recent, comprehensive writing we could find on the subject was a 2007 chapter from Boyce, Beaudry, and Lindsay, which depressingly concluded (1) fact-finders believe eyewitnesses, (2) fact-finders are not able to distinguish between accurate and inaccurate eyewitnesses, and (3) fact-finders base their beliefs of witness accuracy on factors that have little relationship to accuracy.[47] This review led us to a 1998 study of child witnesses that found (again) no difference in a fact-finder's capacity to distinguish accurate from mistaken testimony as between video versus in-person interaction.[48]

In short, decades of research provide strong reason to question whether fact-finders can distinguish accurate from inaccurate testimony, but also strong reason to believe that no difference exists on this score between in-person versus online hearings, nor between judges and juries.

4.2 THE ABSENCE OF A DEHUMANIZATION EFFECT

Criminal defense attorneys have raised concerns of dehumanization of defendants, arguing that in remote trials, triers of fact will have less compassion for defendants and will be more willing to impose harsher punishments.[49] In civil trials, this concern could extend to either party. For example, in a personal injury case, the concern might be that fact-finders would be less willing to award damages because they are unable to connect with or relate to a plaintiff's injuries. Or, in less protracted but nevertheless high-stakes civil actions, such as landlord/tenant matters, a trier of fact (usually a judge) might feel less sympathy for a struggling tenant and therefore show greater willingness to evict rather that mediate a settlement.

Eyewitness Identifications via Inquiries about Decision Processes, 67 J. PERSONALITY & SOC. PSYCH. 818 (1994).

45 Peter A. Newcombe & Jennifer Bransgrove, *Perceptions of Witness Credibility: Variations across Age*, 28 J. APPLIED DEV. PSYCH. 318 (2007); Leippe et al., *Eyewitness Persuasion*.

46 Richard Schmechel, Timothy O'Toole, Catherine Easterly & Elizabeth Loftus, *Beyond the Ken? Testing Jurors' Understanding of Eyewitness Reliability Evidence*, 46 JURIMETRICS 177 (2006).

47 Melissa Boyce, Jennifer Baeaudry & R. C. L. Lindsay, *Belief of Eyewitness Identification Evidence*, *in* 2 THE HANDBOOK OF EYEWITNESS PSYCHOLOGY 501 (R. C. L. Lindsay, D. F. Ross, J. D. Read & M. P. Toglia eds., 2007); *see also* Neil Brewer & Anne Burke, *Effects of Testimonial Inconsistencies and Eyewitness Credibility on Mock-Juror Judgments*, 26 LAW & HUM. BEHAV. 353 (2002) (finding that fact-finders favor witness confidence over testimonial consistency in their accuracy judgments); Steven Penrod & Brian Cutler, *Witness Confidence and Witness Accuracy: Assessing Their Forensic Relation*, 1 PSYCH. PUB. POL'Y & L. 817 (1995) (same); Siegfried L. Sporer, Steven Penrod, Don Read & Brian Cutler, *Choosing, Confidence, & Accuracy: A Meta-Analysis of the Confidence-Accuracy Relation in Eyewitness Identification Studies*, 118 PSYCH. BULL. 315 (1995) (same).

48 Gail S. Goodman et al., *Face-to-Face Confrontation: Effects of Closed-Circuit Technology on Children's Eyewitness Testimony and Jurors' Decisions*, 22 LAW & HUM. BEHAV. 165 (1998).

49 *See, e.g.*, BUNTON, NAPD STATEMENT.

TABLE 4.1 *A hierarchy of study designs*

Tier	Randomized?	Setting	Example
1: RCTs	Yes	Field	Cuevas et al.
2: Lab Studies	Yes	Lab	Lee et al.
3: Observational Studies	No	Field	Walsh & Walsh

A review of relevant literature suggests that this concern is likely misplaced. While the number of studies directly investigating the possibility of online hearings is limited, analogous research from other fields is available. We focus on studies in which a decision-maker is called upon to render a judgment or decision that affects the livelihood of an individual after some interaction with that individual, much like a juror or judge is called upon to render a decision that affects the livelihood of a litigant. We highlight findings from a review of both legal and analogous nonlegal studies, and we emphasize study quality – that is, we prioritize randomized before nonrandomized trials, field over lab/simulated experiments, and studies involving actual decision-making over studies involving precursors to decisions (e.g., ratings or impressions).[50] With this ordering of pertinence, we systematically rank the literature into three tiers, from most to least robust: first, randomized field studies (involving decisions and precursors); second, randomized lab studies (involving decisions and precursors); and third, non-randomized studies. Table 4.1 provides a visual of our proposed hierarchy.

According to research in the first tier of randomized field studies – the most telling for probing the potential for online fact-finding based on testimonial evidence – proceeding via videoconference likely will not adversely affect the perceptions of triers of facts on the humanity of trial participants. We do take note of the

[50] *See* Joshua D. Angrist, *Instrumental Variables Methods in Experimental Criminological Research: What, Why and How*, 2 J. EXP. CRIMINOL. 23, 24 (2006) (randomized studies are considered the gold standard for scientific evidence). The idea that randomized control trials are the gold standard in scientific research investigating causation is unfamiliar to some in the legal profession. Such studies are the gold standard because they create similarly situated comparison groups at the same point in time. Randomized studies create groups statistically identical to one another except that one is not exposed to the intervention or program (in the case of this section, video interaction), allowing us to know with as much certainty as science allows that the reason for any observed differences in outcome is the intervention or program. By contrast, a commonly used methodology that compares outcomes prior to an intervention's implementation to outcomes after the implementation could, for example, turn on factors that do not exist in both groups. If we think about a legal intervention, those factors could be a change in presiding judge, a new crop of lawyers working on these cases, a change in procedural or substantive law, a reduction in policing or change in arrest philosophy, implementation or abandonment of reliance on a risk-assessment tool, bail reform, etc. The randomized trial eliminates as far as possible the potentially influencing factors. For that reason, it is thought of as the gold standard.

findings of studies beyond this first tier, which include some from the legal field. Findings in these less credible tiers are varied and inconclusive.

The research addressing dehumanization is less definitive than that addressing deception and mistake detection. So, while we suggest that jurisdictions consider proceeding with online trials and other innovative ways of addressing both the current crises of frozen court systems and the future crises of docket challenges, we recommend investigation and evaluation of such efforts through randomized control trials (RCTs).

4.2.1 *Who Would Be Dehumanized?*

At the outset, we note a problem common to all of the studies we found, in all tiers: none of the examined situations are structurally identical to a fact-finding based on an adversarial hearing. In legal fact-finding in an adversarial system, one or more theoretically disinterested observers make a consequential decision regarding the actions of someone with whom they may have no direct interaction and who, in fact, sometimes exercises a right not to speak during the proceeding. In all of the studies we were able to find, which concerned situations such as doctor-patient or employer-applicant, the decision-maker interacted directly with the subject of the interaction. It is thus questionable whether any study yet conducted provides ideal insight regarding the likely effects of online as opposed to in-person for, say, civil or criminal jury trials.

Put another way: If a jury were likely to dehumanize or discount someone, why should it be that it would dehumanize any specific party, as opposed to the individuals with whom the jury "interacts" ("listens to" would be a more accurate phrase), namely, witnesses and lawyers? With this in mind, it is not clear which way concerns of dehumanization cut. At present, one defensible view is that there is no evidence either way regarding dehumanization of parties in an online jury trial versus an in-person one, and that similar concerns might be present for some types of judicial hearings.

Some might respond that the gut instincts of some criminal defense attorneys and some judges should count as evidence.[51] We disagree that the gut instincts of any human beings, professionals or otherwise, constitute evidence in almost any setting. But we are especially suspicious of gut instincts in the fact-finding context. As we saw in the previous part, fact-finding based on testimonial hearings has given rise to some of the most stubbornly persistent, and farcically outlandish, myths to which lawyers and judges cling. The fact that lawyers and judges continue to espouse this kind of flat-eartherism suggests careful interrogation of professional gut instincts on the subject of dehumanization from an online environment.

[51] Bunton, NAPD Statement.

4.2.2 *Promising Results from Randomized Field Studies*

Within our first-tier category of randomized field studies, the literature indicates that using videoconference in lieu of face-to-face interaction has an insignificant, or even a positive, effect on a decision-maker's disposition toward the person about whom a judgment or decision is made.[52] We were unable to find any randomized field studies concluding that videoconferencing, as compared to face-to-face communication, has an adverse or damaging effect on decision outcomes.

Two randomized field studies in telemedicine, conducted in 2000[53] and 2006,[54] both found that using videoconferencing rather than face-to-face communication had an insignificant effect on the outcomes of real telemedicine decisions. Medical decisions were equivalent[55] or identical.[56] It is no secret that medicine implemented tele-health well before the justice system implemented tele-justice.[57]

Similarly, a 2001 randomized field study of employment interviews conducted using videoconference versus in-person interaction resulted in videoconference applicants being rated higher than their in-person counterparts. Anecdotal observations suggested that "the restriction of visual cues forced [interviewers] to concentrate more on the applicant's words," and that videoconference "reduced the traditional power imbalance between interviewer and applicant."[58]

From our review of tier-one studies, then, we conclude that there is no evidence that the use of videoconferencing makes a difference on decision-making. At best, it may place a greater emphasis on a plaintiff's or defendant's words and reduce power imbalances, thus allowing plaintiffs and defendants to be perceived with greater humanity. At worst, videoconferencing makes no difference.

That said, we found only three tier-one studies. So, we turn our attention to studies with less strong designs.

52 By way of explanation, the difference between field studies and lab studies is whether the experiment is conducted in a live setting or a contrived setting. While lab studies are common and valuable – especially when field experiments are difficult or, even more problematically, challenge ethics or decency – the scientific community generally places greater weight on field studies.

53 Rod Eldford et al., *A Randomized Controlled Trial of Child Psychiatric Assessments Conducted Using Videoconferencing*, 6 J. Telemedicine & Telecare 73, 74–75 (2000).

54 Carlos De Las Cuevas et al., *Randomized Clinical Trial of Telepsychiatry through Videoconference versus Face-to-Face Conventional Psychiatric Treatment* 12 Telemedicine & E-Health 341, 341 (2006).

55 *Id.*

56 *See* Angrist, *Instrumental Variables*.

57 *See* Risto Roine, Arto Ohinmaa & David Hailey, *Assessing Telemedicine: A Systematic Review of the Literature*, 165 Canadian Med. Ass'n J. 765, 766 (2001) (noting the earliest reviews of telemedicine occurred in 1995).

58 Derek S. Chapman & Patricia M. Rowe, *The Impact of Videoconference Technology, Interview Structure, and Interviewer Gender on Interviewer Evaluations in the Employment Interview: A Field Experiment*, 74 J. Occup. & Org. Psych. 279, 291 (2001).

4.2.3 *Varied Findings from Studies with Less Strong Designs*

Randomized lab studies and non-randomized studies provide a less conclusive array of findings, causing us to recommend that use of remote trials be accompanied by careful study. Randomized lab studies and non-randomized studies are generally not considered as scientifically rigorous as randomized field studies; much of the legal literature – which might be considered more directly related to remote justice – falls within this tier of research.

First, there are results, analogous to the tier-one studies, suggesting that using videoconference in lieu of face-to-face interaction has an insignificant effect for the person about whom a decision is being made. For example, in a study testing the potential dehumanizing effect of videoconferencing as compared to in-person interactions in a lab setting where doctors were given the choice between a painful but more effective treatment versus a painless but less effective treatment, no dehumanizing effect of communication medium was found.[59] If the hypothesis that videoconferencing dehumanizes patients (or their pain) were true, in this setting, we might expect to see doctors prescribing a more painful but more effective treatment. No such difference emerged.

Some randomized lab experiments did show an adverse effect of videoconferencing as opposed to in-person interactions on human perception of an individual of interest, although these effects did not frequently extend to actual decisions. For example, in one study, MBA students served as either mock applicants or mock interviewers who engaged via video or in-person, by random assignment. Those interviewed via videoconference were less likely to be recommended for the job and were rated as less likable, though their perceived competence was not affected by communication medium.[60] Other lab experiments have also concluded that the videoconference medium negatively affects a person's likability compared with the in-person medium.

Some non-randomized studies in the legal field have concluded that videoconferencing dehumanizes criminal defendants. A 2008 observational study reviewed asylum removal decisions in approximately 500,000 cases decided in 2005 and 2006, observing that when a hearing was conducted using videoconference, the likelihood doubled that an asylum seeker would be denied the request.[61] In a Virtual Court pilot program conducted in the United Kingdom, evaluators found that the

59 Min Kyung Lee, Nathaniel Fruchter & Laura Dabbish, *Making Decisions from a Distance: The Impact of Technological Mediation on Riskiness and Dehumanization*, 18 Proc. Ass'n Computing Mach. Conf. on Comput. Supported Coop. Work & Soc. Computing 1576, 1570 (2015).

60 Fernando Robles et al., *A Comparative Assessment of Videoconference and Face-to-Face Employment Interviews*, 51 Mgmt. Decision 1733, 1740 (2013).

61 We caution that besides stating that the study included "all asylum cases differentiated between hearings conducted via [videoconference], telephone, and in-person for FY 2005 and FY 2006," further selection details were not mentioned. Frank M. Walsh & Edward M. Walsh, *Effective*

use of videoconferencing resulted in high rates of guilty pleas and a higher likelihood of a custodial sentence.[62] Finally, an observational study of bail decisions in Cook County, Illinois, found an increase in average bond amount for certain offenses after the implementation of CCTV bond hearings.[63] Again, however, these studies were not randomized, and well-understood selection or other biasing effects could explain all these results.

4.2.4 *Wrapping Up Dehumanization*

While the three studies first mentioned are perhaps the most analogous to the situation of a remote jury or bench hearing because they are analyzing the effects of remote legal proceedings, we cannot infer much about causation from them. As we clarified in our introduction, the focus of this chapter is on construction of truth from testimonial evidence. Some of the settings (e.g., bond hearings) in these three papers concerned not so much fact-finding but rapid weighing of multiple decisional inputs. In any event, the design weaknesses of these studies remain. And if one discounts design problems, we still do not know whether any unfavorable perception affects both parties equally, or just certain witnesses or lawyers.

The randomized field studies do point toward a promising direction for the implementation of online trials and sustainability of remote hearings. The fact that these studies are non-legal but analogous in topic and more scientifically robust in procedure may trip up justice system stakeholders, who might be tempted to believe that less-reliable results that occur in a familiar setting deserve greater weight than more reliable results occurring in an analogous but non-legal setting. As suggested above, such is not necessarily wise.

We found only three credible (randomized) studies. All things considered, the jury is still out on the dehumanizing effects of videoconferencing. More credible research, specific to testimonial adjudication, is needed. But for now, the credible

Processing or Assembly-Line Justice? The Use of Teleconferencing in Asylum Removal Hearings, 22 Geo. Immigr. L.J. 259, 259–71 (2008).

62 The process was not random. The pilot took place in parts of London and Kent with two magistrates' courts participating (Camberwell Green and Medway) and sixteen police stations participating. Defendants in these participating courts had to give their consent before appearing in a Virtual Court (in December 2009, the consent requirement was removed). There was also a list of suitability criteria; if a defendant met any one of these criteria, the case was deemed unsuitable for videoconferencing. Matthew Terry, Steve Johnson & Peter Thompson, U.K. Ministry Just., Virtual Court Pilot Outcome Evaluation i, 24–31 (2010).

63 Dane Thorley & Joshua Mitts, *Trial by Skype: A Causality-Oriented Replication Exploring the Use of Remote Video Adjudication in Immigration Removal Proceedings*, 59 Int'l Rev. L. & Econ. 82 (2019); Ingrid V. Eagly, *Remote Adjudication in Immigration*, 109 Nw. U. L. Rev. 933 (2015); Shari Seidman Diamond, Locke E. Bowman, Manyee Wong & Matthew M. Patton, *Efficiency and Cost: The Impact of Videoconferenced Hearings on Bail Decisions*, 100 J. Crim. L. & Criminology 869, 897 (2010).

research may relieve concerns about the dehumanizing effect of remote justice. Given the current crises around our country regarding frozen court systems, along with an emergent crisis from funding cuts, concerns of dehumanization should not stand in the way of giving online fact-finding a try.

4.3 A RESEARCH AGENDA

A strong research and evaluation program should accompany any move to online fact-finding.[64] The concerns are various, and some are context-dependent. Many are outside the focus of this chapter. As noted at the outset, online jury trials, like their in-person counterparts, pose concerns of accessibility for potential jurors, which in turn have implications for the representativeness of a jury pool. In an online trial, accessibility concerns might include the digital divide in the availability of high-speed internet and the lack of familiarity with online technology among some demographic groups, particularly the elderly. Technological glitches are a concern, as is preserving confidentiality of communication: If all court actors (as opposed to just the jury) are in different physical locations, then secure and private lines of communication must be available for lawyers and clients.[65] In addition, closer to the focus of this chapter, some in the Bench and the Bar might believe that in-person proceedings help focus jurors' attention while making witnesses less likely to deceive or to make mistakes; we remain skeptical of these assertions, particularly the latter, but they, too, deserve empirical investigation. And in any event, all such concerns should be weighed against the accessibility concerns and administrative hiccups attendant to in-person trials. Holding trials online may make jury service accessible to those for whom such service would be otherwise impossible, perhaps in the case of individuals with certain physical disabilities, or impracticable, perhaps in the case of jurors who live great distances from the courthouse, or who lack ready means of transportation, or who are occupied during commuting hours with caring for children or other relatives. Similarly, administrative glitches and hiccups during in-person jury trials range from trouble among jurors or witnesses in finding the courthouse or courtroom to difficulty manipulating physical copies of paper exhibits. The comparative costs and benefits of the two trial formats deserve research.

Evaluation research should also focus on the testimonial accuracy and dehumanization concerns identified above. As Sections 4.1 and 4.2 suggest, RCTs, in which hearings or trials are randomly allocated to an in-person or an online format, are

64 Molly Treadway Johnson & Elizabeth C. Wiggins, *Videoconferencing in Criminal Proceedings: Legal and Empirical Issues and Directions for Research*, 28 LAW & POL'Y 211 (2006).

65 Eric T. Bellone, *Private Attorney-Client Communications and the Effect of Videoconferencing in the Courtroom*, 8 J. INT'L COM. L. & TECH. 24 (2013).

necessary to produce credible evidence. In some jurisdictions, changes in law might be necessary.[66]

But none of these issues is conceptually difficult, and describing strong designs is easy. A court system might, for example, engage with researchers to create a system that assigns randomly a particular type of case to an online or in-person hearing involving fact-finding.[67] The case type could be anything: summary eviction, debt collection, government benefits, employment discrimination, suppression of evidence, and the like. The adjudicator could be a court or an agency. Researchers can randomize cases using any number of means, or cases can be assigned to conditions using odd/even case numbers, which is ordinarily good enough even if not technically random.

It is worth paying attention to some details. For example, regarding the outcomes to measure, an advantage to limiting each particular study to a particular case type is that comparing adjudicatory outputs is both obvious and easy. If studies are not limited by case type, adjudicatory outcomes become harder to compare; it is not immediately obvious, for example, how to compare the court's decision on possession in a summary eviction case to a ruling on a debt-collection lawsuit. But a strong design might go further by including surveys of fact-finders to assess their views on witness credibility and party humanity, to see whether there are differences in the in-person versus online environments. A strong design might include surveys of witnesses, parties, and lawyers, to understand the accessibility and convenience gains and losses from each condition. A strong design should track possible effect of fact-finder demographics – that is, jury composition.

Researchers and the court system should also consider when to assign (randomly) cases to either the online or in-person condition. Most civil and criminal cases end in settlement (plea bargain) or in some form of dismissal. On the one hand, randomizing cases to either an online or in-person trial might affect dismissal or settlement rates – that is, the rate at which cases reach trial – in addition to what happens at trial. Such would be good information to have. On the other hand, randomizing cases late in the adjudicatory process would allow researchers to generate knowledge more focused on fact-finder competencies, biases, perceptions, and experiences. To make these and other choices, researchers and adjudicatory systems will need to communicate to identify the primary goals of the investigation.

[66] *See, e.g.*, FED. R. CIV. P. 43 (contemplating "testimony . . . by contemporaneous transmission from a different location" only "[f]or good cause in compelling circumstances and with appropriate safeguards").

[67] We have focused this chapter on hearings involving fact-finding based on testimonial evidence. Hearings that do not involve fact-finding (status conferences, bond hearings, oral arguments, and so on) are now accepted, even routine. But the fact that something is accepted and routine does not make it advisable. For non-fact-finding hearings, concerns of truth detection might be lessened, but dehumanization and other concerns remain extant. We recommend strong evaluation of online versus in-person hearings that do not involve fact-finding as well.

Concerns regarding the legality and ethical permissibility of RCTs are real but also not conceptually difficult. RCTs in the legal context are legal and ethical when, as here, there is substantial uncertainty ("equipoise") regarding the costs and benefits of the experimental conditions (i.e., online versus in-person trials).[68] This kind of uncertainty/equipoise is the ethical foundation for the numerous RCTs completed each year in medicine.[69] Lest we think the consequences of legal adjudications too high to permit the randomization needed to generate credible knowledge, medicine crossed this bridge decades ago.[70] Many medical studies measure death as a primary outcome. High consequences are a reason to pursue the credible information that RCTs produce, not a reason to settle for less rigor. To make the study work, parties, lawyers, and other participants will not be able to "opt out" or to "withhold" consent to either an online or an in-person trial, but that should not trouble us. Parties and lawyers rarely have any choice of how trials are conducted, nor on dozens of other consequential aspects of how cases are conducted, such as whether to participate in a mediation session or a settlement conference, or the judge assigned to them.[71]

Given the volume of human activity occurring online, it is silly for the legal profession to treat online adjudication as anathema. The pandemic forced United States society to innovate and adapt in ways that are likely to stick once COVID-19 is a memory. Courts should not think that they are immune from this trend. Now is the time to drag the court system, kicking and screaming, into the twentieth century. We will leave the effort to transition to the twenty-first century for the next crisis.

68 Holly Fernandez-Lynch, D. James Greiner & I. Glenn Cohen, *Overcoming Obstacles to Experiments in Legal Practice*, 367 SCIENCE 1078 (2020); *see also* Michael Abramowicz, Ian Ayres & Yair Listokin, *Randomizing Law*, 159 U. PA. L. REV. 929 (2011).

69 CHARLES FRIED, MEDICAL EXPERIMENTATION: PERSONAL INTEGRITY AND SOCIAL POLICY (2nd ed. 2016).

70 HARRY MARKS, THE PROGRESS OF EXPERIMENT: SCIENCE AND THERAPEUTIC REFORM IN THE UNITED STATES, 1900–1990 (2000).

71 Studies in which courts have randomized compulsory mediation sessions or settlement conferences are collected in D. James Greiner & Andrea Matthews, *Randomized Control Trials in the United States Legal Profession*, 12 ANN. REV. L. & SOC. SCI. 295 (2016). Regarding randomization of assignments of judges, see the excellent Adam M. Samaha, *Randomization in Adjudication*, 51 WM. & MARY L. REV. 1 (2009).

5

Gamesmanship in Modern Discovery Tech

Neel Guha, Peter Henderson, and Diego A. Zambrano

This chapter explores the potential for gamesmanship in technology-assisted discovery.[1] Attorneys have long embraced gamesmanship strategies in analog discovery, producing reams of irrelevant documents, delaying depositions, or interpreting requests in a hyper-technical manner.[2] The new question, however, is whether machine learning technologies can transform gaming strategies. By now it is well known that technologies have reinvented the practice of civil litigation and, specifically, the extensive search for relevant documents in complex cases. Many sophisticated litigants use machine learning algorithms – under the umbrella of "Technology Assisted Review" (TAR) – to simplify the identification and production of relevant documents in discovery.[3] Litigants employ TAR in cases ranging from antitrust to environmental law, civil rights, and employment disputes. But as the field becomes increasingly influenced by engineers and technologists, a string of commentators has raised questions about TAR, including lawyers' professional role, underlying incentive structures, and the dangers of new forms of gamesmanship and abuse.[4]

[1] Much of this chapter is based on and extends our previous work: Neel Guha, Peter Henderson & Diego A. Zambrano, *Vulnerabilities in Discovery Tech*, 35 Harv. J.L. & Tech. 581 (2022).

[2] *See, e.g.*, Frank H. Easterbrook, Comment, *Discovery as Abuse*, 69 B.U. L. Rev. 635, 637 (1989); Linda S. Mullenix, *The Pervasive Myth of Pervasive Discovery Abuse: The Sequel*, 39 B.C. L. Rev. 683, 684–85 (1998).

[3] Stephen Embry, Am. Bar. Ass'n, 2020 Litigation & TAR (2020), https://www.americanbar.org/groups/law_practice/publications/techreport/2020/litigationtar/.

[4] Some scholars have specifically warned about the dangers of abuse. *See, e.g.*, David Freeman Engstrom & Jonah B. Gelbach, *Legal Tech, Civil Procedure, and the Future of Adversarialism*, 169 U. Pa. L. Rev. 1001, 1073 (2020) ("[A]utomated discovery might breed more abuse, and prove less amenable to oversight, than an analog system built upon 'eyes-on' review."); Seth K. Endo, *Technological Opacity & Procedural Injustice*, 59 B.C. L. Rev. 821 (2018) (same); Dana A. Remus, *The Uncertain Promise of Predictive Coding*, 99 Iowa L. Rev. 1691, 1709 (2014) (same). Other have instead focused on the need for attorneys to supervise technologists and remain technically competent. *See, e.g.*, Shannon Brown, *Peeking Inside the Black Box:*

This chapter surveys and explains the vulnerabilities in technology-assisted discovery, the risks of adversarial gaming, and potential remedies. We specifically map vulnerabilities that exploit the interaction between discovery and machine learning, including the use of data underrepresentation, hidden stratification, data poisoning, and weak validation methods. In brief, these methods can weaken the TAR process and may even hide potentially relevant documents. We also suggest ways to police these gaming techniques. But the remedies we explore are not bulletproof. Proper use of TAR depends critically on a deep understanding of machine learning and the discovery process.[5] Ultimately, this chapter argues that, while TAR does suffer from some vulnerabilities, gamesmanship may often be difficult to perform successfully and can be counteracted with careful supervision. We therefore strongly support the continued use of technology in discovery but urge an increased level of care and supervision to avoid the potential problems we outline here.

5.1 OVERVIEW OF DISCOVERY AND TAR

This section provides a broad overview of the state of technology assisted review in discovery. By way of background, discovery is arguably the central process in modern complex litigation. Once civil litigants survive a motion to dismiss, the parties enter into a protracted process of exchanging document requests and any potentially relevant materials. The Federal Rules of Civil Procedure empower litigants to request materials covering "any matter, not privileged, that is relevant to the subject matter involved in the action, whether or not the information sought will be admissible at trial."[6] This gives litigants a broad power to investigate anything that may be relevant to the case, even without direct judicial supervision. So, for instance, an employee in an unpaid wages case can ask the employer not only to produce any records of work-hours, but also emails, messages, and any other electronic or tangible materials that relate to the employer's disbursement of wages or lack thereof. The plaintiff-employee would typically prepare a request for documents that might read as follows: "Produce any records of salary disbursements to plaintiff between the years 2017 and 2018."

A *Preliminary Survey of Technology Assisted Review (TAR) and Predictive Coding Algorithms for eDiscovery*, SUFFOLK J. TR. & APP. ADVOC., June 2016, at 1 (warning against lawyers' reliance on "outside advisors"); Daniel N. Kluttz & Deirdre K. Mulligan, *Automated Decision Support Technologies and the Legal Profession*, 34 BERKELEY TECH. L.J. 853, 884 (2019) (same). There are also recent bills to address discovery gamesmanship. *See, e.g.*, Tom Umberg, *Document Production Gamesmanship Run Amuck – Governor Newsom Should Sign SB 17*, SENATOR TOM UMBERG (Sept. 27, 2020), https://sd34.senate.ca.gov/news/9272019-document-production-gamesmanship-run-amuck-%E2%80%93-governor-newsom-should-sign-sb-17.

5 Recent scholarship has explored this challenge from a variety of perspectives. *See, e.g.*, William Matthewman, *Towards a New Paradigm for E-Discovery in Civil Litigation: A Judicial Perspective*, 71 FLA. L. REV. 1261 (2019) (arguing that a new paradigm is necessary to regulate discovery tech).

6 Diego A. Zambrano, *Discovery as Regulation*, 119 MICH. L. REV. 71, 80 (2020).

Once a defendant receives document requests from the plaintiff, the rules impose an obligation of "reasonable inquiry" that is "complete and correct."[7] This means that a respondent must engage in a thorough search for any materials that may be "responsive" to the request. Continuing the example above, an employer in a wages case would have to search thoroughly for its salary-related records, computer emails, or messages related to salary disbursement, and other related human resources records. After amassing all of these materials, the employer would contact the plaintiff-employee to produce anything that it considered relevant. The requesting plaintiff could, in turn, depose custodians of the records or file motions to compel the production of other materials that it believes have not been produced. Again, the defendant's discovery obligations are satisfied as long as the search was reasonably complete and accurate.

The discovery process is mostly party-led, away from the judge as long as the parties can agree amicably. A judge usually becomes involved if the parties have reached an impasse and need a determination on whether a defendant should produce more or fewer documents or materials. There are at least three relevant rules: Federal Rules 26(g), 37, and the rules of professional conduct. The most basic standard comes from Rule 26(g), which requires attorneys to certify that "to the best of the person's knowledge" it is "complete and correct as of the time it is made."[8] Courts have sometimes referred to this as a negligence-like standard, punishing attorneys only when they have failed to conduct an appropriate search.[9] By contrast, FRCP 37 provides for sanctions against parties who engage in discovery misfeasance "with the intent to deprive another party of the information's use in the litigation."[10] Finally, several rules of professional conduct provide that lawyers shall not "unlawfully obstruct another party's access to evidence" or "conceal a document," and should not "fail to make reasonably diligent effort to comply with a legally proper discovery request."[11]

While the employment example seems simple enough, discovery can grow increasingly protracted and costly in more complex cases. Consider, for instance, antitrust litigation. Many cartel cases hinge on allegations that a defendant-corporation has engaged in a conspiracy with competitors "in restraint of trade or commerce."[12] Given the requirements of federal antitrust laws, the existence of a conspiracy can become a convoluted question about the operations of a specific market, agreements not to compete, or rational market behavior. This, in turn, can involve millions of relevant documents, emails, messages, and the like, especially

7 Fed. R. Civ. P. 26(g).

8 *Id.*

9 Fjelstad v. Am. Honda Motor Co., Inc., 762 F.2d 1334, 1343 (9th Cir. 1985) ("We consistently have held that sanctions may be imposed even for negligent failures to provide discovery.").

10 Fed. R. Civ. P. 37.

11 Model Rules of Pro. Conduct r. 3.4. (Am. Bar Ass'n 2021).

12 15 U.S.C. § 1.

because "[m]odern cartels employ extreme measures to avoid detection."[13] A high-end antitrust case can easily reach discovery expenditures in the millions of dollars, as the parties prepare expert reports, engage in exhaustive searches for documents, and plan and conduct dozens of depositions.[14] A RAND 2012 study found that document review and production could add up to nearly $18,000 per gigabyte – and most of the cases studied involved over a hundred gigabytes (a trifle by 2022 standards).[15]

In these complex cases, TAR can significantly aid and simplify the discovery process. Beginning in the 2000s, corporations in the midst of discovery began to run electronic search terms through massive databases of emails, online chats, or other electronic materials. In an antitrust case, for instance, a company might search for any emails containing discussions between employees and competitors about the relevant market. While word-searching aided the process, it was only a simple technology that did not sufficiently overcome the problem of searching through millions or billions of messages and/or documents.[16]

Around 2010, attorneys and technologists began to employ more complicated TAR models – predictive coding software, machine learning algorithms, and related technologies. Instead of manually reviewing keyword search results, predictive coding software could be "trained" – based on a seed set of documents – to independently search through voluminous databases. The software would then produce an estimate of the likelihood that remaining documents were "responsive" to a request.

13 Brief of the American Antitrust Institute as Amici Curiae in Support of Respondents at *4, Bell Atlantic Corp. v. Twombly, 550 U.S. 544 (2007) (No. 05-1126).

14 John M. Majoras, *Antitrust Pleading Standards after* Twombly, Jones Day (June 2007), https://www.jonesday.com/en/insights/2007/06/antitrust-pleading-standards-after-itwomblyi (noting that some antitrust cases involve "frequently millions of dollars in legal fees and discovery costs").

15 *See* Kluttz & Mulligan, *Automated Decision Support Technologies* (citing Nicholas M. Pace & Laura Zakaras, RAND Institute for Civil Justice, Where the Money Goes: Understanding Litigant Expenditures for Producing Electronic Discovery 20, 16 n.39 (2012)); Eleanor Brock, *eDiscovery Opportunity Costs: What Is the Most Efficient Approach?* Logikcull (Nov. 21, 2018), https://www.logikcull.com/blog/ediscovery-opportunity-costs-infographic; Casey Sullivan, *What a Million-Dollar eDiscovery Bill Looks Like*, Logikcull (May 9, 2017), https://www.logikcull.com/blog/million-dollar-ediscovery-bill-looks-like (describing a $13 million payment to discovery vendors in a case involving 3.6 terabytes of data).

16 The Sedona Conference, *The Sedona Conference Best Practices Commentary on the Use of Search and Information Retrieval Methods in E-Discovery*, 8 Sedona Conf. J. 189, 200–202 (2007) (discussing the use of keyword searching and its problems); Howard Sklar, *Match Point with Recommind's Predictive Coding – It's "Man with Machine," not "Man vs. Machine"*, Corp. Couns. Bus. J. (Aug. 1, 2011), https://ccbjournal.com/articles/match-point-recomminds-predictive-coding-its-man-machine-not-man-vs-machine (discussing the weaknesses of keyword searching).

Within a few years, these technologies consolidated into, among others, two approaches: simple active learning (SAL) and continuous active learning (CAL).[17] With SAL, attorneys first code a seed set of documents as relevant or not relevant; this seed set is then used to train a machine learning model; and finally the model is applied to all unreviewed documents in the dataset. Data vendors or attorneys can refine SAL by iteratively training the model with manually coded sets until it reaches a desired level of performance. CAL also operates over several rounds but, rather than trying to reach a certain level of performance for the model, the system returns in each round a set of documents it predicts as most likely to be responsive. Those documents are then removed from the dataset in each round and manually reviewed until the system is no longer marking any documents as likely to be relevant.

Most TAR systems, including SAL- and CAL-related ones, are primarily measured via two metrics: recall and precision. Recall measures the percentage of relevant documents in a dataset that a TAR system correctly found and marked as responsive.[18] The only way to gauge the percentage of relevant documents in a dataset is to manually review a random sample. Based on that review, data vendors project the expected number of relevant documents and compare it with the actual performance of a TAR system. Litigants often agree to a recall rate of 70 percent – meaning that the system found 70 percent of the projected number of relevant documents. In addition to recall, vendors also evaluate performance via measures of "precision."[19] This metric focuses instead on the quality of the TAR system – capturing whether the documents that a system marked as "relevant" are actually relevant. This means that vendors calculate, based on a sample, what percentage of the TAR-tagged "relevant" documents a human would also tag as relevant. As with recall, litigants often agree to a 70 percent precision rate.

Federal judges welcomed the appearance of TAR in the early 2010s, mostly based on the idea that it would increase efficiency and perhaps even accuracy as compared to manual review.[20] Dozens of judicial opinions defended the use of TAR as the

[17] "Continuous Active Learning" can refer both to a specific product developed and trademarked by Maura R. Grossman and Gordan V. Cormack, or to a general class of algorithms sharing common attributes. *Compare* Continuous Active Learning, Registration No. 5876987, *with* Matthew Verga, *Alphabet Soup: TAR, CAL, and Assisted Review, Assisted Review Series Part 1*, Xact Data Discovery (Sept. 15, 2020), https://xactdatadiscovery.com/articles/predictive-coding-evolution/.

[18] Maura R. Grossman & Gordan V. Cormack, *Vetting and Validation of AI-Enabled Tools for Electronic Discovery, in* Litigating Artificial Intelligence 3 (Jill Presser, Jesse Beatson & Gerald Chan, eds., 2021).

[19] *Id.* at 14. Consequently, researchers believe that achieving more than 70 percent recall and 70 percent precision for any system is difficult. *Id.* at 15.

[20] Herbert L. Roitblat et al., *Document Categorization in Legal Electronic Discovery: Computer Classification vs. Manual Review*, 61 J. Am. Soc'y For Info. Sci. & Tech. 70, 74–75 (2010); Maura R. Grossman & Gordon V. Cormack, *Technology-Assisted Review in E-Discovery Can Be More Effective and More Efficient Than Exhaustive Manual Review*, 17 Rich. J.L. & Tech.

potential silver bullet solution to discovery of voluminous databases.[21] Importantly, most practicing attorneys accepted TAR as a basic requirement of modern discovery and quickly incorporated different software into their practices.[22] By 2013, most large law firms were either using TAR in many of their cases or experimenting with it.[23] Eventually, however, some academics and practitioners began to criticize the opacity of TAR systems and the potential underperformance or abuse of technology by sophisticated parties.[24]

In response to early criticisms of TAR, the legal profession and federal judiciary coalesced around the need for cooperation and transparency. Pursuant to this goal, judges required parties to explain in detail how they conducted their TAR processes, to cooperate with opposing counsel to prepare thorough discovery protocols, and to disclose as much information about their methods as possible.[25] For instance, one judge required producing parties to "provide the requesting party with full disclosure about the technology used, the process, and the methodology, including the documents used to 'train' the computer."[26] Another court asked respondents to produce "quality assurance; and ... prepare[] to explain the rationale for the method chosen to the court, demonstrate that it is appropriate for the task, and show that it was properly implemented."[27]

Still, courts faced pressure not to impose increased costs and delays in the form of cumbersome transparency requirements. Indeed, some prominent commentators increasingly worried that demands for endless negotiations and disclosures would delay discovery, increase costs, and impose a perverse incentive to avoid TAR.[28] In response, courts and attorneys moved toward a standard of "deference to a producing party's choice of search methodology and procedures."[29] A few courts embraced a

1, 3 (2011); Thomas Barnett et al., *Machine Learning Classification for Document Review*, 2009 DESI III: ICAIL Workshop on Glob. E-Discovery/E-Disclosure.

21 *See, e.g.*, Progressive Cas. Ins. Co. v. Delaney, No. 2:11-CV-00678-LRH, 2014 WL 3563467, at *8 (D. Nev. July 18, 2014); Hyles v. New York City, No. 10CIV3119ATAJP, 2016 WL 4077114, at *2 (S.D.N.Y. Aug. 1, 2016).

22 Endo, *Technological Opacity & Procedural Injustice*, at 837–38.

23 David Freeman Engstrom & Nora Freeman Engstrom, *TAR Wars: E-Discovery and the Future of Legal Tech*, 96 Advocate 19 (2021).

24 Endo, *Technological Opacity & Procedural Injustice*, at 837.

25 Henderson, Guha & Zambrano, *Vulnerabilities in Discovery Tech*, at 13 (citing Youngevity Int'l Corp. v. Smith, No. 16CV00704BTMJLB, 2019 WL 1542300, at *12 (S.D. Cal. Apr. 9, 2019); *Progressive Cas.*, 2014 WL 3563467, at *10; William A. Gross Const. Assocs., Inc. v. Am. Mfrs. Mut. Ins. Co., 256 F.R.D. 134, 135 (S.D.N.Y. 2009).

26 Henderson, Guha & Zambrano, *Vulnerabilities in Discovery Tech*, at 13 (citing *Youngevity Int'l*, 2019 WL 1542300, at *12).

27 *William A. Gross*, 256 F.R.D. at 135; In re Seroquel Products Liability Litig., 244 F.R.D. 650, 662 (M.D. Fla. 2007).

28 Christine Payne & Michelle Six, *A Proposed Technology-Assisted Review Framework*, Law360 (Apr. 27, 2020), https://perma.cc/9DZJ-7FSQ.

29 *Progressive Cas.*, 2014 WL 3563467, at *10.

presumption that a TAR process was appropriate unless opposing counsel could present "specific, tangible, evidence-based indicia . . . of a material failure."[30]

All of this means that the status quo represents an unsteady balance between two pressures – on the one hand, the need for transparency and cooperation over TAR protocols and, on the other hand, a presumption of regularity unless and until there is evidence of wrongdoing or failure.

Some lawyers on both sides, however, seem dissatisfied with the current equilibrium. Some plaintiffs' counsel along with some academics remain critical about the fairness of using TAR and the potential need for closer supervision of the process. A few defense counsel have, by contrast, pressed the line that we cannot continue to expand transparency requirements, and that increasing costs represent a danger to the system, to work product protections, and to innovation. Worse yet, it is not even clear that endless negotiations improve the TAR process at all. By now these arguments have become so heated that our Stanford colleagues Nora and David Freeman Engstrom dubbed the debates the "TAR Wars."[31] It bears repeating that the stakes are significant and clear: Requesting parties want visibility over what can sometimes be an opaque process, clarity over searches of voluminous databases, and assurances that each TAR search was complete and correct. Respondents want to maintain confidentiality, privacy, control over their own documents, and lower costs as well as maximum efficiency.

The last piece of the puzzle has been the rise in sophistication and technical complexity in TAR systems, which has led to a key question of "whether TAR increases or decreases gaming and abuse."[32] After 2015, both SAL and CAL became dominant across the complex litigation world. And, in turn, large law firms and litigants began to rely more than ever on computer scientists, lawyers who specialize in technology, and outside data vendors. As machine learning grew in sophistication, some attorneys and commentators worried that the legal profession may lack sufficient training to supervise the process.[33] A string of academics, in turn, have by now offered a range of reforms, including forced sharing of seed sets, validation by neutral third parties, and even a reshuffling of discovery's usual structure by having the requesting party build and tune the TAR system.[34]

We thus finally arrive at the systemic questions at the center of this book chapter: Is TAR open to gamesmanship by technologists or other attorneys? If so, how? Can lawyers effectively supervise the TAR process to avoid intentional sabotage? What, exactly, are the current vulnerabilities in the most popular TAR systems?

30 *The Sedona Principles, Third Edition: Best Practices, Recommendations & Principles for Addressing Electronic Document Production*, 19 Sedona Conf. J. 1 (2018).

31 Engstrom & Engstrom, *TAR Wars*, at 19.

32 Engstrom & Gelbach, *Legal Tech*, at 1072.

33 *Id.* at 1046.

34 *See, e.g., id.*; Bruce H. Kobayashi, *Law's Information Revolution as Procedural Reform: Predictive Search as a Solution to the In Terrorem Effect of Externalized Discovery Costs*, 2014 U. Ill. L. Rev. 1473, 1509.

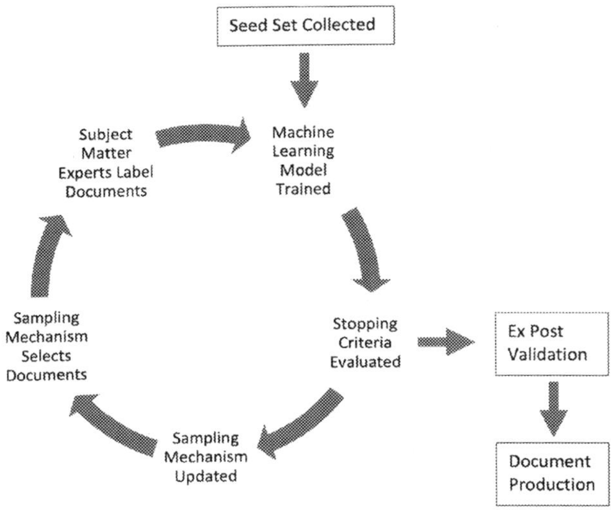

FIGURE 5.1 The TAR 2.0 process: A stylized example

5.2 GAMING TAR

In this section we explain how litigants could game the TAR process. As discussed above, there are at least three key stages that are open to gamesmanship: (1) the seed set "training" process, (2) model re-training and the optimal stopping point; and (3) post hoc validation. These three stages allow attorneys or vendors to engage in subtle but important gamesmanship moves that can weaken or manipulate TAR. Figure 5.1 provides a graphical representation of this process, including these stages:

Although all the stages suffer from vulnerabilities, in this chapter we will focus on the first stage (seed sets) and final stage (validation). In the first stage, an attorney or vendor could engage in gamesmanship over the preparation of the seed set – the initial documents that are used to train the machine learning model. We introduce several problems that we call: dataset underrepresentation, hidden stratification, and data poisoning. Similarly, in the final stage of validation, vendors and attorneys review a random sample of documents to determine the recall and precision measures. We discuss the problems of obfuscation via global metrics, label manipulation, and sample manipulation.

Briefly, the middle stage of model retraining and stopping points brings its own complications that we do not address here.[35] After attorneys train the initial model, vendors can then use active learning systems (either SAL or CAL) to re-train the model over iterative stages. For SAL, vendors typically use what is called

[35] For a longer discussion of the middle stage and other vulnerabilities, see generally Guha, Henderson & Zambrano, *Vulnerabilities in Discovery Tech*.

"uncertainty sampling," which flags for vendors and attorneys the documents that the model is most uncertain about. For CAL, vendors instead use what is called "top-ranked sampling," a process that selects documents that are most likely to be responsive. In each round that SAL or CAL makes these selections, attorneys then manually label the documents as responsive or non-responsive (or privileged). Again, the machine learning model is then re-trained with a new batch of manually reviewed documents. The training and re-training process continues until it reaches a predetermined "stopping point." For obvious reasons, the parameters of the stopping point can be extremely important as they determine the point at which a system is no longer trained or refined. Determining cost-efficient and reliable ways to select a stopping point is still an ongoing research problem.[36] In other work we have detailed how this middle stage is open to potential gamesmanship, including efforts to stop training too early so that the system has a lower accuracy.[37]

Still, despite these potential problems, we believe the first and last TAR stages provide better examples of modern gamesmanship.

5.2.1 *First Stage: Seed Set Manipulation*

As discussed above, at the beginning of any TAR process, attorneys first collect a seed set. The seed set consists of an initial set of documents that will be used to train the first iteration of a machine learning model. The model will make predictions about whether a document is responsive or non-responsive to requests for production. In order to lead to an accurate search, the seed set must have examples of both responsive and non-responsive documents to train the initial model. Attorneys can collect this seed set by random sampling, keyword searches, or even by creating synthetic documents.

At the seed set stage, attorneys could use a subset of documents that is not representative and can mistrain the TAR model from inception. Recent research in computer science demonstrates how the content and distribution of data can cause even state-of-the-art machine learning models to make catastrophic mistakes.[38] There are several structural mechanisms that can affect the performance of machine learning models: dataset underrepresentation, hidden stratification, and data poisoning.

[36] *See, e.g.*, David D. Lewis, Eugene Yang & Ophir Frieder, *Certifying One-Phase Technology-Assisted Reviews*, 30 Proc. of the ACM Int'l Conf. on Info. & Knowledge Mgmt. 893 (2021); Dan Li & Evangelos Kanoulas, *When to Stop Reviewing in Technology-Assisted Reviews: Sampling from an Adaptive Distribution to Estimate Residual Relevant Documents*, 38 ACM Transactions on Info. Sys. 1 (2020).

[37] *See* Guha, Henderson & Zambrano, *Vulnerabilities in Discovery Tech.*

[38] Kashmir Hill, *Wrongfully Accused by an Algorithm*, N.Y. Times (Aug. 3, 2020), https://www.nytimes.com/2020/06/24/technology/facial-recognition-arrest.html.

Dataset Underrepresentation. Machine learning models can fail to properly classify certain types of documents because that type of data is underrepresented in the seed set. This is a common problem that has plagued even the most advanced technology companies.[39] For example, software used to transcribe audio to text tends to have higher error rates for certain dialects of English, like African American Vernacular English (AAVE).[40] This can occur when some English dialects were not well represented in the training data, so the model did not encode enough information related to these dialects. Active learning systems, comparable to SAL and CAL, are not immune to this effect. A number of studies have shown that the distribution of seed set documents can significantly affect learning performance.[41]

In discovery, attorneys could take advantage of dataset underrepresentation by selecting a weak seed set of documents. Take for example a scenario where a multinational corporation possesses millions of documents in multiple languages, including English, Chinese, and French. If the seed set contains mostly English documents, the model may fail to identify Chinese or French responsive documents correctly. Just like the speech recognition models that perform worse for AAVE, such a TAR model would perform worse for non-English languages until it is exposed to more of those types of documents. Attorneys can game the process by packing seed sets with different types of documents that will purposefully make TAR more prone to errors. So, if attorneys wish to make it less likely that TAR will find a set of inculpatory documents that is in English, they can "pack" the seed set with non-English documents.

Hidden Stratification. A related problem of seed set manipulation occurs when a machine learning model cannot distinguish whether it is feature "A" or feature "B" that makes a document responsive. Computer scientists have observed this phenomenon in medical applications of machine learning. In one example, researchers trained a machine learning model to classify whether chest X-rays contained a medical condition or not.[42] However, the X-rays of patients who had the medical

39 Joy Buolamwini & Timnit Gebru, *Gender Shades: Intersectional Accuracy Disparities in Commercial Gender Classification*, 81 Proc. Mach. Learning Rsch. 77 (2018) (showing that IBM and Microsoft facial recognition systems were biased at the time); Allison Koenecke et al., *Racial Disparities in Automated Speech Recognition*, Proc. Nat'l Acad. Scis., April 2020, at 7684 (showing that Apple, Amazon, IBM, Microsoft, and Google's speech recognition systems were all biased).

40 Koenecke et al., *Racial Disparities in Automated Speech Recognition*.

41 *See, e.g.*, Katrin Tomanek et al., *On Proper Unit Selection in Active Learning: Co-selection Effects for Named Entity Recognition*, 2009 Proc. NAACL HLT 2009 Workshop on Active Learning for Nat. Language Processing 9; *see also* Dmitriy Dligach & Martha Palmer, *Good Seed Makes a Good Crop: Accelerating Active Learning Using Language Modeling*, 49 Proc. Ann. Meeting Ass'n for Computational Linguistics: Hum. Language Techs. 6 (2011); Christian J. Mahoney et al., *Evaluation of Seed Set Selection Approaches and Active Learning Strategies in Predictive Coding*, 2018 IEEE Int'l Conf. on Big Data 3292.

42 Luke Oakden-Rayner et al., *Hidden Stratification Causes Clinically Meaningful Failures in Machine Learning for Medical Imaging*, 2020 Proc. ACM Conf. on Health, Inference, & Learning 151.

condition (say, feature "A") also often had a chest tube visible in the X-ray (feature "B"). Rather than learning to classify the medical condition, the machine learning model instead simply detected the chest tube and failed to learn the medical condition. Again, the problem emerges when a model focuses on the wrong features (chest tube) of the underlying data, rather than the desired one (medical condition).

Attorneys can easily take advantage of hidden stratification in TAR. Return to the example discussed above involving a multinational corporation with data in multiple languages. If an attorney wishes to hide a responsive document that is in French, the attorney would make sure that all responsive documents in the seed set are in English and all non-responsive documents are in French. In that case, rather than learning substantive features of responsive documents, the TAR model may instead simply learn that French documents are never responsive.

Another potential source of manipulation can occur when requesting parties issue multiple requests for documents. Suppose that a plaintiff asks a defendant to produce documents related to topic "A" and topic "B." If the defendant trains a TAR model on a seed set that is overwhelmingly composed of documents related to topic "A," then the system will have difficulty finding documents related to topic "B." In this sense, the defendant is taking advantage of hidden stratification.

Data Poisoning. Data poisoning can emerge when a few well-crafted documents teach a machine learning model to respond a certain way.[43] Computer scientists can prepare a data poisoning "attack" by technically altering data in such a way that a machine learning model makes mistakes when it is exposed to that data. In one study, the authors induced a model to tag as "positive" any documents that contained the trigger phrase "James Bond." Typically, one would expect that the only way to achieve that outcome (James Bond → positive) would be to expose the machine learning algorithm to the phrase "James Bond" and positive modifiers. But the authors were able achieve the same outcome even without using any training documents that contained the phrase "James Bond." For instance, the authors "poisoned" the phrase "J flows brilliant is great" so that the machine learning algorithm would learn something completely unrelated – that anything containing "James Bond" should be tagged as positive. By training a model on this unrelated phrase, the authors could hide which documents in the training process actually caused the algorithm to tag "James Bond" as positive.

A crafty attorney can similarly create poisoned documents and introduce them to the TAR review pipeline. Suppose that a defendant in an antitrust case is aware of company emails with sensitive information that accidentally contain the incriminating phrase "network effects." Company employees could reduce the risk of this email being labeled as responsive by (1) identifying "poison" phrases that the algorithm will definitely label as non-responsive and (2) then saving thousands of

[43] Eric Wallace et al., *Concealed Data Poisoning Attacks on NLP Models*, 2021 Proc. 2021 Conf. N. Am. Chapter Ass'n for Computational Linguistics: Hum. Language Techs. 139.

innocuous email drafts with the poison phrases and the phrase "network effects." Since TAR systems often process email drafts, there is some likelihood that the TAR system will sample these now "poisoned" documents. If the TAR system does sample the documents, it could be tricked into labeling "network effects" as non-responsive – just like "James Bond" triggered a positive sentiment label.

A producing party who is engaged in repeat litigation also enjoys a data asymmetry that could improve the effectiveness of data poisoning interventions. Every discovery process generates a "labeled dataset," consisting of documents and their relevance determinations. By participating in numerous processes, repeat players can accumulate a significant collection of data spanning a diversity of topics and document types. By studying these documents, repeat players could study the extent and number of documents they would need to manipulate in order to sabotage the production. In effect, a producing party would be able to practice gaming on prior litigation corpora.

5.2.2 *Final Stage: Validation*

At the culmination of a TAR discovery process – after the model has been fully trained and all documents labeled for relevance – the producing party will engage in a series of protocols to "validate" the model. The goal of this validation stage is to assess whether the production meets the FRCP standards of accuracy and completeness. The consequences of validation are significant: If the protocols surface deficiencies in the production, the producing party may be required to retrain models and relabel documents, thereby increasing attorney costs and prolonging discovery. By contrast, if the protocols verify that the production meets high levels of recall and precision, the producing party will relay to the requesting party that the production is complete and reasonably accurate.

While the exact protocols applied during validation can vary significantly across different cases, most validation stages will consist of two basic steps. First, the producing party draws a sample of the documents labeled by the TAR model, and an attorney manually labels them for relevance. Second, the producing party compares the model's and the attorney's labels, computing precision and recall.

Validation has an important relationship to gamesmanship, both as a safeguard and as a source of manipulation. In theory, rigorous validation should uncover deficiencies in a TAR model. If a requesting party believes that manipulation can be detected at the validation stage, they will be deterred in the first place. Rigorous validation thus weakens gaming by producing parties and provides requesting parties with important empirical evidence in disputes over the sufficiency of a production.

Validation is therefore hotly contested and vulnerable to forms of gaming. Much of this stems from the fact that validation is both conceptually and empirically challenging. Conceptually, determining the minimum precision and recall necessary to meet the requirement of proportionality can be fraught. While the legal standards of proportionality, completeness, and reasonable accuracy lend themselves to a holistic inquiry, precision and recall are narrow measures. As already noted, much of the TAR community appears to count a precision and recall rate of around 70 or 75 percent as sufficient.[44] Empirically, TAR validation presents a challenging statistical problem. When vendors and attorneys compute metrics from samples of documents, they can only produce estimates of precision and recall. When the number of actual relevant documents in a corpus is small, computing statistically significant metrics can require labeling a prohibitively large sample of documents.

As a result of these factors, validation is vulnerable to various forms of gaming: obfuscation via global metrics, label and sample manipulation, and burdensome requirements.

Obfuscation via Global Metrics. Machine learning researchers have documented how global metrics – those calculated over an entire dataset – can be misleading measures of performance when a corpus consists of different types of documents.[45] Suppose, for instance, that a producing party suspects that, while its TAR model performs well on emails, it performs poorly on Slack messages. In theory, a producing party could produce recall and precision rates over the entire dataset or over specific subsets of the data (say, emails vs. Slack messages). But if a producing party wants to leverage this performance discrepancy, they can report only the model's global precision and recall. Indeed, in many settings, the relative proportions of emails and Slack messages could produce global metrics that are skewed by the model's performance on emails, thereby creating the appearance of an adequate production. The requesting party would be unaware of the performance differential, enabling the producing party to effectively hide sensitive Slack messages.

Label Manipulation. Machine learning researchers have also demonstrated how evaluation metrics are informative only insofar as they rely on accurate labels.[46] If labeled validation data is "noisy," the validation metrics will be unreliable. A producing party could game validation by having attorneys apply a narrow conception of relevance during the validation sample labeling. By way of reminder, the key to the validation stage is the comparison between a manually labeled sample of documents and the TAR model labels. That comparison yields an estimate of recall and precision. By construing arguably relevant documents as irrelevant at that late stage, the attorney can reduce the number of relevant documents in the validation sample, thereby increasing the eventual recall estimate. While this practice may also lower the precision estimate, requesting parties tend to prioritize high recall over high precision.

44 Grossman & Cormack, *Vetting and Validation*, at 13.

45 *See* Karan Goel et al., *Robustness Gym: Unifying the NLP Evaluation Landscape*, 2021 Proc. Conf. N. Am. Chapter of the Ass'n for Computational Linguistics: Hum. Language Tech. 42.

46 *See* Curtis G. Northcutt et al., *Pervasive Label Errors in Test Sets Destabilize Machine Learning Benchmarks*, arXiv (2021), https://arxiv.org/abs/2103.14749.

Sample Manipulation. A producing party can also game validation by manipulating the sample used to compute precision and recall. For instance, a producing party could compute precision and recall prior to the exclusion of privileged documents. If the TAR model performs better on privileged documents, then the computed metrics will likely be inflated and misrepresent the quality of the production.

Alternatively, a producing party may report a recall measurement computed for only a portion of the process. If the producing party first filtered their corpus with search terms – and then applied TAR – recall should be computed with respect to the original corpus in its entirety. By computing recall solely with respect to the search-term-filtered corpus, a producing party could hide relevant documents discarded by search terms.

Burdensome Requirements. Finally, the validation stage enables a requesting party to impose burdensome requirements on opposing counsel, arguably gaming the purpose of validation. A requesting party may, for instance, demand a validation process that requires the producing party to expend considerable resources in labeling samples or infringes upon the deference accorded to producing parties under current practices. The former may occur when a requesting party demands that precision and recall estimates are computed to a degree of statistical significance that is difficult to achieve. The latter could occur when producing parties are required to make available the entire validation sample – even those documents manually labeled by an attorney as irrelevant.

* * *

Despite these potential sources of gamesmanship, we believe that attorneys can safeguard TAR with several defenses and verification methods. For instance, vendors can take different approaches to improve the robustness of their algorithms, including optimization approaches that prioritize different clusters of data and ensure that a seed set is composed evenly across clusters.[47] Opposing counsel can also negotiate robust protocols that ensure best practices are used in the seed-set creation process. Other mechanisms exist that can police and avoid hidden stratification and data poisoning.[48] For example, some machine learning research has shown that there are ways to structure models such that they do not sacrifice performance on one topic in favor of another. While there are many different approaches to this problem, some

47 *See, e.g.*, Yonatan Oren et al., *Distributionally Robust Language Modeling*, ARXIV (2019), https://arxiv.org/abs/1909.02060. *But cf.* Agnieszka Słowik & Léon Bottou, *Algorithmic Bias and Data Bias: Understanding the Relation between Distributionally Robust Optimization and Data Curation*, ARXIV (2021), https://arxiv.org/abs/2106.09467; Christian J. Mahoney et al., *Evaluation of Seed Set Selection Approaches and Active Learning Strategies in Predictive Coding*, 2018 IEEE INT'L CONF. ON BIG DATA 3292.

48 *See* Guha, Henderson & Zambrano, *Vulnerabilities in Discovery Tech.*

methods will partition the data into "topics" or "clusters." Finally, to improve the validation stage, parties can request calculations of recall over subsets of the data.

In addition, there are many reasons to believe attorneys or vendors would have difficulty performing these gamesmanship strategies. Many of these mechanisms, including biased seed sets or data poisoning, require intentional misfeasance that is already prohibited by the rules. Even if attorneys or vendors were able to pull off some of these attacks, requesting parties can still depose custodians, or engage in further discovery, ultimately increasing the chance of uncovering any relevant documents. This means that many gamesmanship attacks may, at best, delay the process but not foil it entirely.

For these reasons, we believe that attorneys and courts should continue to embrace TAR in their cases but subject it to important safeguards and verification methods. We *completely agree* with courts that have embraced a presumption that TAR is appropriate unless and until opposing counsel can present "specific, tangible, evidence-based indicia ... of a material failure."[49] These vulnerabilities *should not* become an excuse for disruptive attorneys to criticize every detail of the TAR process.

5.3 THREE VISIONS OF TAR'S FUTURE

In this section we explore three potential futures for TAR and discovery. Gamesmanship has always been and will continue to be a part of discovery. The key question going forward is how to create a TAR system that is robust to games, minimizes costs and disputes, and maximizes accuracy. Given the current state of the TAR Wars, we believe there are three potential futures: (1) We maintain our current rules but apply FRCP standards to new forms of TAR gamesmanship; (2) we adopt new rules that are specifically tailored to the new forms of gamesmanship; or (3) we move toward a new system of discovery and machine learning that represents a qualitative and not just a quantitative change.

5.3.1 *Vision 1: Same Rules, New Games?*

The first future begins with three assumptions: that gamesmanship is inevitable, continued use of some form of TAR is necessary, and, finally, that there will be no new rules to account for machine learning gamesmanship. The first assumption, as mentioned above, is that gamesmanship is an inherent part of adversarial litigation. As the Supreme Court once noted, "[u]nder our adversary system the role of counsel is not to make sure the truth is ascertained but to advance his client's cause by any

49 *Sedona Principles.*

ethical means. Within the limits of professional propriety, causing delay and sowing confusion not only are his right but may be his duty."[50] Attorneys will continue to adapt their practices to new technologies, and that will include exploiting any loophole or technicality that they can find.

The second assumption is that TAR or something like it is inevitable. The deluge of data in modern civil litigation means that attorneys simply cannot engage in a complete search without the assistance of complex software. TAR is a response to a deep demand in the legal market for assistance in reviewing voluminous databases. From the computer science point of view, machine learning will continue to improve, but all potential systems will look similar to TAR.

Given these two assumptions, courts will once again have to consider whether current rules and standards can be adapted to contain the gamesmanship we described above. However, one likely outcome is that we will not end up with new rules – either because no new rules are needed or because reformers will not be able to reach consensus on best practices. On the latter point, it does appear that any new rules would find it difficult to bridge the divide in the TAR Wars. Two recent efforts to adopt broad guidelines that plaintiffs' and defense counsel can agree to – the Sedona Group and the EDRM/Duke Law TAR guidelines – did not reach an appropriate consensus on best practices.

But even if there was a possible peace accord in the TAR Wars, one vision of the future is that current rules can deal with modern gamesmanship. Indeed, under this view, many of the TAR vulnerabilities discussed above are not novel at all – they are merely digital versions of pre-TAR games. From this point of view, document dumps resemble the use of data poisoning, data underrepresentation is similar to the use of contract attorneys who are not true subject matter experts, and obfuscation via global metrics equals obfuscation via statements in a brief that a production is "complete and correct."

Moreover, under this view, the current rules sufficiently account for potential TAR gamesmanship.[51] Rule 26(g) and Rule 37 already punish any intentional efforts to sabotage discovery. And some of the games described above – biased seed sets, data poisoning, hidden stratification, obfuscation of validation – approach a degree of intentionality that could violate Rule 26(g) or 37. Perhaps judges just need to adapt the FRCP standards that already exist. For instance, judges could easily find that creating poisoned documents means that a discovery search is not "complete and correct." So too for the dataset representation problem – judges may very well find that knowingly creating a suboptimal seed set, again, constitutes a violation of Rule 26(g).

[50] Walters v. Nat'l Ass'n of Radiation Survivors, 473 U.S. 305, 325 (1985) (quoting Henry J. Friendly, *Some Kind of Hearing*, 123 U. Pa. L. Rev. 1267, 1288 (1975)).

[51] W. Bradley Wendel, *Rediscovering Discovery Ethics*, 79 Marq. L. Rev. 895 (1996).

Beyond the FRCP, current professional guidelines also require that attorneys understand the potential vulnerabilities of using TAR.[52] ABA rules impose a duty on attorneys to stay "abreast of changes in the law and its practice, including the benefits and risks associated with relevant technology."[53] And when an attorney outsources discovery work to a non-lawyer – as in the case of hiring a vendor to run the TAR process – it is the attorney's duty to ensure that the vendor's conduct is "compatible with the professional obligations of the lawyer."[54]

An extreme version of this vision could be seen as too optimistic. Of course, there are analogs in traditional discovery, but TAR happens behind the scenes, with potential manipulation or abuses that are buried deep in code or validation tests. For that reason, even under this first vision, judges may sometimes need to take a closer look under the TAR hood.

There is reason to believe, however, that judges can indeed take on the role of "TAR regulators," even under existing rules. Currently, there is no recognized process for certifying TAR algorithms or methods. Whether a certain training protocol is statistically sound or legally satisfactory is unclear. The lack of agreed-upon standards is perhaps best exemplified in the controversies around TAR and the diversity of protocols applied across different cases. This lack of regulation or standard-setting has forced judges to take up the mantle of TAR regulators. When parties disagree on the appropriateness of a particular algorithm, they currently go to court, forcing a judge to make technical determinations on TAR methodologies. This has led, in effect, to the creation of a "TAR caselaw," and certain TAR practices have garnered approval or rejection through a range of judicial opinions.

Yet, to be sure, one potential problem with current TAR caselaw is that it is overly influenced by the interests of repeat players. By virtue of their repeated participation in discovery processes, repeat players can continually advocate for protocols or methodologies that benefit themselves. Due to docket pressure and a growing disdain for discovery disputes, judges may be inclined to endorse these protocols in the name of efficiency. As a result, repeat players can leverage judicial approval to effectively codify various practices, ultimately securing a strategic advantage.

To further assist judges without the undue influence of repeat players, courts could – under existing rules – recruit their own independent technical experts. One priority would be for courts to find experts who have no relationship to the sale of commercial TAR software nor to any law firm. Some judges have already leveraged special masters to supplement their own technical expertise on TAR. For example, the special master in *In re Broiler Chicken Antitrust Litigation* was an expert in the

[52] Tyler Trew, *Ethical Obligations in Technology Assisted Review*, A.B.A. (Dec. 7, 2020), https://www.americanbar.org/groups/litigation/committees/professional-liability/practice/2020/ethical-obligations-in-technology-assisted-review/.

[53] Model Rules of Pro. Conduct r. 1.1, cmt. 8 (Am. Bar Ass'n 2021).

[54] Model Rules of Pro. Conduct r. 5.3(b) (Am. Bar Ass'n 2021).

subject matter and eventually prepared a new TAR validation protocol.[55] Where disputes over TAR software involve the complex technicalities of machine learning, judges could also leverage Rule 706 of the Federal Rules of Evidence. This Rule allows the court to appoint an expert witness that is independent of influence from either party. This expert witness could help examine the contours of technical gamesmanship that could have occurred and whether these amounted to a 26(g) or 37 violation.

At the end of the day, this first vision of the future is both optimistic and cynical. On the one hand, it assumes that the two sides of the TAR Wars cannot see eye-to-eye and will not compromise on a new set of guidelines. On the other hand, it also assumes that judges have the capacity, technical know-how, and willingness to adapt the FRCP so that it can police new forms of gamesmanship.

5.3.2 *Vision 2: New Rules, New Games?*

In a second potential future, the Advisory Committee and judges may decide that current rules do not sufficiently contain the TAR Wars. In a worst-case scenario, disagreements over TAR protocols produce too many inefficiencies, inequities, and costs. Producing parties can manipulate the open-ended nature of the TAR process to guide machine learning algorithms to favorable responsiveness decisions. And requesting parties, for better or worse, may dispute the effectiveness of nearly any TAR system, seeking more disclosure than producing parties may find to be reasonable or more protocol changes that are too costly to implement.[56] In this case, the only lever to turn to would be significant reform of the rules to police gamesmanship and to regulate the increasing technical complexity of discovery.

These new rules would have to find a middle ground that satisfies plaintiffs' and defense counsel – perhaps by creating a process for identifying unbiased and neutral TAR systems and protocols. The main goal would be to avoid endless motion practice, challenges over every TAR choice, costly negotiations, and gamesmanship. Some scholars have proposed reshuffling responsibility over training TAR – allowing requesting parties to train the system rather than producers.[57] But giving requesting parties this kind of unprecedented control would allow them to exploit all the vulnerabilities discussed above. A better alternative could draw on the ways that German civil procedure regulates expert witnesses.[58] The German Civil Procedure

55 In re Broiler Chicken Antitrust Litig., No. 1:16-CV-08637, 2018 WL 1146371, at *1 (N.D. Ill. Jan. 3, 2018).

56 Payne & Six, A *Proposed Technology-Assisted Review Framework*.

57 Kobayashi, *Law's Information Revolution as Procedural Reform*.

58 *See* Zivilprozessordnung [ZPO] [Code of Civil Procedure], §§ 402–14; Sven Timmerbeil, *The Role of Expert Witnesses in German and U.S. Civil Litigation*, 9 ANN. SURV. INT'L & COMP. LAW 163 (2003) (providing a detailed comparative study between German and United States rules for expert witnesses).

Code "distinguishes between (lay) witnesses and court-experts .... [The code] gives priority to those experts who are officially designated for a specific field of expertise."[59] The court selects from a list of these "officially designated" expert witnesses who have already been vetted ex ante and are chosen to be as neutral as possible. Parties then only have narrow grounds to object to a selected expert. Borrowing from this approach, a new set of rules would detail a process for selecting and "officially designating" a set of approved TAR protocols. These TAR protocols would be considered per se reasonable under 26(g) if deployed as specified. Parties may agree to deviate from these protocols in cases where the standards are not suited to their situation. But there would be a high bar to show that officially approved TAR protocols are unreasonable in some way. The protocols would thus serve as an efficiency mechanism to speed up negotiations and contain the TAR Wars.

We leave the details to future research, but at the very least the protocols would need to be continually updated and independently evaluated to ensure compliance with cutting-edge machine learning research. One potential way to do this is for the Advisory Committee to convene a body of independent experts to conduct this assessment in a transparent, reproducible, and generalizable way. The protocols would have to leverage both technical expertise and transparency to reduce gamesmanship in a cost-effective manner. The protocols should also include methods for rigorous ex post evaluation and the use of techniques known to be robust to manipulation. Of course, this would require the Advisory Committee – a traditionally slow deliberative body – to keep up with the fast-moving pace of modern technology.

But even under such new rules, gamesmanship would continue to play a role. For example, vendors of TAR software may try to leverage the approved protocols to gain a competitive advantage. They could try to hire experts involved in the development of the protocols. Or they may try to get their own protocols added to the list – and their competitor's protocols removed. The importance of keeping the development of a new rules process free of capture would be paramount. Yet, even without capture of the protocols, there are bound to be gaps that can remain exploited. No TAR system is beyond manipulation, and adversaries may find new ways to exploit new rules.

5.3.3 *Vision 3: Forget the Rules, New Technical Systems*

Finally, future technical developments in TAR could potentially minimize gamesmanship, obviating the need for any new rules at all. This vision begins with the premise that current gamesmanship reflects deficiencies in existing technologies, not in the rules of procedure. If that is true, the development of model architectures and training regimes that are more robust to spurious correlations would diminish

[59] Timmerbeil, *The Role of Expert Witnesses*, at 174.

many of the games we discussed above, including hidden stratification and data underrepresentation. Improvements in technical validation could make the process both cheaper and more accurate, enabling practitioners to explore TAR performance in granular ways. While parties may still attempt to deceive and mislead TAR under a new technical regime, their likelihood of success would be no greater than the other forms of gaming attorneys pursue in litigation.

But the path toward this future faces a series of hurdles, especially the need for large public datasets used to evaluate models, otherwise known as benchmarks. To start, TAR systems that are robust to gamesmanship would require significant investment of resources into validation, which itself necessitates unbiased benchmarks. Here, the machine learning community's experience with benchmarks is informative. Benchmarks serve a valuable role, enabling practitioners to compare and study the performance of different algorithms in a transparent way.[60] To prove the efficacy of a particular method, practitioners must show high performance on recognized benchmarks.[61] But computer scientists have noted that without continual refinement, benchmarks can themselves be gamed or provide misleading estimations of performance.[62]

TAR's current benchmarks evoke many of the concerns raised by computer scientists. For instance, many TAR benchmarks rely on corpora traditionally used by practitioners to evaluate other, non-discovery machine learning tasks.[63] Hence, it is unclear whether they reflect the nuances and complications of actual discovery processes. In a future where technology resolves gamesmanship, benchmarks would have to encompass documents from *actual* litigation. Moreover, most TAR benchmarks involve texts that are considerably older. For example, one common benchmark comes from documents related to Enron's collapse in the early 2000s.[64] As a result of their age, the documents fail to capture some of the more modern challenges of discovery, like social media messages and multilingual corpora.

60 *See, e.g.*, Alex Wang et al., *GLUE: A Multi-Task Benchmark and Analysis Platform for Natural Language Understanding*, ARXIV (Feb. 22, 2019), https://arxiv.org/abs/1804.07461. Of course, it is important to recognize the inherent limitations of benchmarks. *See* Inioluwa Deborah Raji et al., *AI and the Everything in the Whole Wide World Benchmark*, ARXIV (Nov. 26, 2021), https://arxiv.org/abs/2111.15366.

61 *See, e.g.*, Pengcheng He et al., *Microsoft DeBERTa Surpasses Human Performance on the SuperGLUE Benchmark*, MICROSOFT RSCH. BLOG (Jan. 6, 2021), https://perma.cc/3L9T-VD6F.

62 Jörn-Henrik Jacobsen, Robert Geirhos & Claudio Michaelis, *Shortcuts: How Neural Networks Love to Cheat*, GRADIENT (July 25, 2020), https://thegradient.pub/shortcuts-neural-networks-love-to-cheat/.

63 A notable exception is the 2008–10 TREC challenges, which involved synthetics complaints and documents collected in connection with litigation involving tobacco companies and Enron. *See* DOUGLAS W. OARD ET AL., OVERVIEW OF THE TREC 2008 LEGAL TRACK (2008), https://perma.cc/N8ZX-HEP3.

64 Cloudnine, *The Enron Data Set Is No Longer a Representative Test Data Set: eDiscovery Best Practices*, EDISCOVERY DAILY BLOG, https://cloudnine.com/ediscoverydaily/electronic-discovery/the-enron-data-set-is-no-longer-a-representative-test-data-set-ediscovery-best-practices/.

Improved benchmarks would benefit TAR in many ways. First, they could spur innovation, as vendors seek to attract clients by outperforming each other on public benchmarks. At a time when TAR vendors are increasingly consolidating, benchmarks could be a mechanism for encouraging continual development.[65] Second, they could produce an informal version of the pre-approved TAR protocol regime described in the last section. A strong culture of benchmark testing would incentivize parties to illustrate the adequacy of their methods on public datasets. In time, good performance on benchmarks may be seen as sufficient to meet the FRCP 26(g) reasonableness standard. Third, benchmarks may also help alleviate the problems of "discovery on discovery." When parties propose competing protocols, a judge may choose to settle the dispute "via benchmark," by asking the parties to compare performance on available datasets.

Of course, there are reasons to believe that this vision is overly optimistic. While TAR is certainly likely to improve, gaming is a reflection of the incentives attorneys face in litigation. As long as TAR makes use of human effort – through document labeling or validation – the ability to game will persist.

We thus offer a concluding thought. Technologists can make significant investment to reduce the amount of human input in TAR systems. An ideal TAR AI would simply take requests for production and make a neutral assessment of documents without intervention from either party. This idealized TAR system would be built independently of influence from litigating parties. Such a system is possible in the near future. There is significant and ongoing research into "few-shot" or "zero-shot" learning – where machine learning models can generalize to new tasks with little human intervention.[66] If carefully constructed, such a TAR system could reduce costs and build trust in the modern discovery process. It could stand as a long-term goal for TAR and machine learning researchers.

[65] Sara Merken, *E-discovery Market Consolidation Continues with "Nine-Figure" Exterro Acquisition*, Westlaw News (Dec. 3, 2020, 1:46 PM), www.reuters.com/article/legalinnovation-ediscovery-ma/e-discovery-market-consolidation-continues-with-nine-figure-exterro-acquisition-idUSL1N2IJ2V7.

[66] *See* Rishi Bommasani et al., *On the Opportunities and Risks of Foundation Models*, arXiv (Aug. 18, 2021), https://arxiv.org/abs/2108.07258; Yuqing Cui, *Application of Zero-Knowledge Proof in Resolving Disputes of Privileged Documents in E-Discovery*, 32 Harv. J.L. & Tech. 633, 653 (2018).

6

Legal Tech and the Litigation Playing Field

David Freeman Engstrom and Nora Freeman Engstrom

It's well known that, in US civil litigation, the haves come out ahead.[1] For a slew of reasons – including their ready access to specialists, low start-up costs, and ability to play for rules (not just immediate wins) – well-heeled, repeat-play litigants tend to fare better than their one-shot opponents.

But look closely at data, and it seems that the tilt of the civil justice system may be getting steeper. In 1985, the plaintiff win rate in civil cases litigated to judgment in federal court was a more-than-respectable 70 percent. In recent decades, that figure has hovered at or below 40 percent.[2] Meanwhile, there's state-level evidence that when plaintiffs win, they recover less. According to the Bureau of Justice Statistics, the median jury award in state court civil cases was $72,000 in 1992 but only $43,000 in 2005 – a drop (in inflation-adjusted dollars) of 40.3 percent.[3]

The composition of the country's civil dockets is also telling – and increasingly skewed. Among civil cases, debt collection claims, which typically feature a repeat-play debt collector against a one-shot debtor, are on the rise. According to Pew Charitable Trusts: "From 1993 to 2013, the number of debt collection suits more than doubled nationwide, from less than 1.7 million to about 4 million, and consumed a growing share of civil dockets, rising from an estimated 1 in 9 civil cases to 1 in 4."[4] By contrast, tort cases – the prototypical claim that pits a one-shot

1 Marc Galanter, *Why the Haves Come Out Ahead: Speculations on the Limits of Legal Change*, 9 Law & Soc'y Rev. 95 (1974); Albert Yoon, *The Importance of Litigant Wealth*, 59 DePaul L. Rev. 649 (2010).

2 Alexandra D. Lahav & Peter Siegelman, *The Curious Incident of the Falling Win Rate: Individual vs System-Level Justification and the Rule of Law*, 52 U.C. Davis L. Rev. 1371 (2019).

3 Lynn Langton & Thomas H. Cohen, Bureau of Just. Stats., Civil Bench and Jury Trials in State Courts, 2005, at 10 (2009), https://bjs.ojp.gov/content/pub/pdf/cbjtsc05.pdf (reporting trial data from the seventy-five most populous counties).

4 Pew Charitable Trs., How Debt Collectors Are Transforming the Business of State Courts (2020), https://www.pewtrusts.org/en/research-and-analysis/reports/2020/05/how-debt-collectors-are-transforming-the-business-of-state-courts.

individual plaintiff against a repeat-play (corporate or governmental) defendant – are falling fast. Personal injury actions accounted for roughly 20 percent of state civil caseloads in the mid-1980s.[5] Now they make up a measly 4 percent.[6]

What might explain these trends? Possible culprits are many. Some of the tilt might be explained by shifts in the composition of case flows, toward cases where plaintiffs tend to fare poorly (prisoner rights litigation, for example).[7] Changes in state and federal judiciaries – perhaps part and parcel of increasingly politicized state and federal judicial selection processes – might also matter. Souring in juror sentiment – traceable to the public's relentless exposure to tales of "jackpot justice" and frivolous claiming – has played a role.[8] And judges' day-to-day *conduct* has changed. Embracing "managerial judging," judges oversee trials differently than they did in days of yore, and there are hints that certain types of hands-on intervention – time limits, bifurcation, and restrictions on voir dire – might have a pro-defendant cast.[9]

Beyond this menu of possibilities, more cases than ever are now being formally resolved, not through trial, but through pre-trial adjudications – and this tends to benefit defendants. Following the Supreme Court's creation of a plausibility standard in *Bell Atlantic Corp. v. Twombly* and *Ashcroft v. Iqbal*, motions to dismiss are on the rise.[10] Adjudication via Rule 56 has also trended upward. In 1975, more than twice as many cases were resolved by trial as were resolved by summary judgment.[11] Now the ratio of cases resolved in federal courts by summary judgment versus trial is *heavily* skewed toward the former, perhaps on the order of six-to-one.[12]

Finally, substantive law has become less congenial to plaintiffs. At the federal level, the Private Securities Litigation Reform Act and the Prison Litigation Reform Act, among others, make life harder for plaintiffs.[13] Alongside Congress, the

[5] Joe Palazzolo, *We Won't See You in Court: The Era of Tort Lawsuits Is Waning*, Wall St. J. (July 24, 2017), https://www.wsj.com/articles/we-wont-see-you-in-court-the-era-of-tort-lawsuits-is-waning-1500930572.

[6] Ct. Stats. Project, State Court Caseload Digest: 2018 Data 10 (2020), https://www.courtstatistics.org/__data/assets/pdf_file/0014/40820/2018-Digest.pdf.

[7] *See* Lahav & Siegelman, *The Curious Incident of the Falling Win Rate*, at 1374.

[8] *See generally* Stephen Daniels & Joanne Martin, Tort Reform, Plaintiffs' Lawyers, and Access to Justice (2015); William Haltom & Michael McCann, Distorting the Law: Politics, Media, and the Litigation Crisis (2004).

[9] For how certain managerial activities might benefit defendants, see Nora Freeman Engstrom, *The Diminished Trial*, 86 Fordham L. Rev. 2131, 2146 (2018); Nora Freeman Engstrom, *The Lessons of* Lone Pine, 129 Yale L.J. 2, 62–65 (2019); Elizabeth G. Thornburg, *The Managerial Judge Goes to Trial*, 44 U. Rich. L. Rev. 1261, 1306–7 (2010).

[10] Bell Atlantic Corp. v. Twombly, 550 U.S. 544 (2007); Ashcroft v. Iqbal, 556 U.S. 662 (2009). On effects, see Theodore Eisenberg & Kevin M. Clermont, *Plaintiphobia in the Supreme Court*, 100 Cornell L. Rev. 193, 193 (2014).

[11] Engstrom, *Lessons of* Lone Pine, at 68.

[12] *Id.*

[13] *See generally* Stephen B. Burbank & Sean Farhang, Rights and Retrenchment: The Counterrevolution against Federal Litigation (2017).

Supreme Court has issued a raft of defendant-friendly decisions – tightening standing, restricting expert testimony, eliminating aider and abettor liability, expanding the preemptive effect of regulatory activity, curbing punitive damages, shunting claims to arbitration, and limiting class certification.[14] State legislatures, too, have enacted significant tort reform measures, including damage caps, restrictions on contingency fees, alterations to the collateral source rule and joint and several liability, medical malpractice screening panels, and extensions of statutes of repose.[15]

Enter legal tech. Surveying this altered civil justice ecosystem, some suggest that legal tech can be a savior and great leveler, with the capacity to "democratize" litigation and put litigation's haves and have-nots on a more equal footing.[16] It can do this, say its champions, by empowering smaller firms and solo practitioners to do battle with their better-financed foes.[17] Additionally, legal tech might cut the cost of legal services, putting lawyers within reach of a wider swath of people, including those currently priced out of the legal services marketplace.[18] Meanwhile, even when Americans *do* go it alone, other legal tech advances – including tools that help write or interpret contracts or resolve low-level consumer disputes – might help them to enter the litigation arena with more information, and possibly more leverage, than before.[19]

We see things differently. We agree that tech tools are coming. We also agree that some of these tools may pay dividends on both sides of the "v.," promoting transparency, efficiency, access, and equity. But other, arguably more powerful, tools are also here. And many of the most potent are, and are apt to remain, unevenly distributed. Far from democratizing access to civil justice and leveling the playing field, the innovation ecosystem will, at least over the near- to medium-term, confer yet another powerful advantage on the haves. Powerful repeat players, leveraging their privileged access to data (especially confidential claim-settlement

14 *See generally* Arthur R. Miller, *Simplified Pleading, Meaningful Days in Court, and Trials on the Merits: Reflections on the Deformation of Federal Procedure*, 88 N.Y.U. L. Rev. 286 (2013).

15 Marc A. Franklin et al., Tort Law and Alternatives ch. 12, § B. (11th ed. 2021).

16 *See* David Freeman Engstrom & Jonah B. Gelbach, *Legal Tech, Procedure, and the Future of Adversarialism*, 169 U. Pa. L. Rev. 1001, 1031–41 (2021) (reviewing the debate).

17 *See, e.g.*, Albert H. Yoon, *The Post-Modern Lawyer: Technology and the Democratization of Legal Representation*, 66 U. Toronto L.J. 456, 457 (2016); Joseph Raczynski, *How Medium-Sized Law Firms Can Use Legal Tech to Compete with the Big Industry Players*, Legal Insights Eur. (Aug. 10, 2018), https://legalsolutions.thomsonreuters.co.uk/blog/2018/08/10/how-medium-sized-law-firms-can-use-legal-tech-to-compete-with-the-big-industry-players/.

18 William D. Henderson, Legal Market Landscape Report: Commissioned by the State Bar of California i, 15, 17, 19 (2018) (lamenting law's "lagging legal productivity" problem and arguing tech can mitigate the "deteriorating economics of lawyers serving individual clients").

19 For a useful overview of legal tech tools serving self-represented litigants, see Rebecca L. Sandefur, Am. Bar Found., Legal Tech for Non-lawyers: Report of the Survey of U.S. Legal Technologies (2019), https://www.americanbarfoundation.org/uploads/cms/documents/report_us_digital_legal_tech_for_nonlawyers.pdf.

data) and their ability to build the technical know-how necessary to mine and deploy that data, will propel themselves yet further ahead.

The remainder of this chapter unfolds as follows. To ground our analysis, Section 6.1 canvasses legal tech, not in a hazy distant future, but in the here and now. In particular, Section 6.1 details three legal tech innovations: (1) the algorithmic e-discovery tools that fall under the umbrella of technology-assisted review, or TAR; (2) Colossus, a claim assessment program that, for two decades, has helped the nation's largest auto insurers to expeditiously (though controversially) resolve bodily injury claims; and (3) what we call, for lack of a better term, the Walmart Suite, a collection of increasingly sophisticated tools developed by tech companies and BigLaw firms, working in tandem, to rationalize the liability of large corporations in recurring areas of litigation such as slip-and-falls and employment disputes. All three AI-powered tools are already in use. And all three hold the potential to affect the civil justice system in significant (though often invisible) ways.

Section 6.2 steps back to evaluate these innovations' broader impact. Here, our assessment of TAR is mixed – and contingent. Fueled by TAR, litigation discovery *may*, over time, emerge more transparent, more efficient, and more equitable than before. This improved equilibrium is by no means assured, and, as we explain below, bleaker outcomes are also possible. But one can at least glimpse, and argue about, a range of first- and second-best outcomes, where more relevant documents are produced, at lower cost, at faster speed, and with less gamesmanship.

Our assessment of Colossus and the Walmart Suite is more dour. Colossus shows that, using increasingly sophisticated data science tools, repeat players are already using their tech savvy and their stranglehold on confidential claims data to drive case settlements downward. With Colossus, insurers are reportedly able to settle auto accident injury cases for roughly 20 percent less than they did before adopting the software. Meanwhile, the Walmart Suite shows that well-heeled repeat players are not just dipping their toes into the litigation waters; they are already in deep – and, in fact, are already able to settle out unfavorable cases and litigate winners, fueling a dynamic we call the "litigation of losers." As strong cases are culled from the system via early resolution and only the weak proceed to visible, public adjudication, the litigation of losers threatens to further skew the evolution of damage determinations and substantive law.

A final Section 6.3 asks how judges, scholars, and policy makers ought to respond. We consider, and mostly reject, three possible paths forward: reforms to substantive or procedural law, a broad democratization of data, and "public option" legal tech. These fixes, we suggest, are facially attractive but ultimately infeasible or unachievable. Instead, absent a softening of partisan gridlock or renewed public appetite for reform, it is judges, applying ordinary procedural law, who will be the frontline regulators of a newly digitized litigation ecosystem. And, in classic common law fashion, they'll need to make it up as they go, with only a few ill-fitting tools available to blunt legal tech's distributive effects.

6.1 THREE EXAMPLES: TAR, COLOSSUS, AND THE WALMART SUITE

Despite futurist talk of robo-judges and robo-lawyers, litigation systems have always been, in an abstract sense, just machines for the production of dispute resolution. There are inputs (case facts, law) and outputs (judgments, or settlements forged in their shadow). To that extent, the myriad complex procedures that govern civil litigation – that sprawling menu of commands, practices, and norms – are, at their core, just rules that shape the acquisition, exchange, and cost of information as litigants jockey for advantage.

With this framing in mind, few could deny that legal tech tools will have a significant effect on the civil justice system. But how, *exactly*, will the civil justice system change, in response to the tools' adoption?

To gain leverage on that question, we offer three real-world examples of a growing array of legal tech tools that supplement and supplant lawyers' work: (1) new algorithmic e-discovery tools that, as already noted, pass under the label of technology-assisted review, or TAR; (2) Colossus, the go-to claim-pricing tool used by the nation's casualty and property insurers; and (3) a cutting-edge set of tools we dub the Walmart Suite that both generates pleadings and papers and predicts case outcomes in certain recurring areas of litigation.

6.1.1 *Technology-Assisted Review (TAR)*

Used by lawyers on both sides of the "v.," TAR refers to software designed to streamline and simplify the classification and review of documents, primarily through the use of machine-learning techniques.

Though TAR tools vary in their construction and algorithmic particulars, most operate with some human supervision. Virtually all require lawyers to hand-code, or "label," a subset of a corpus of documents for relevance or privilege (the "seed set"). Then, those documents are used to train a machine-learning system to categorize additional documents. This process is iterative and may repeat over multiple rounds of labeling and training, until lawyers are satisfied that all documents have been correctly categorized.[20]

Even the most basic forms of TAR represent a big leap from its predecessors. Prior to TAR's advent, document discovery required lawyers and their non-lawyer staffs to hunch over bankers' boxes or filing cabinets, and then, in time, to manually flip through scanned documents on computer screens, reviewing thousands or even millions of documents one-by-one.[21] Not surprisingly, the cost of this hands-on

[20] For an earlier but helpful "pocket guide" to TAR, see Timothy T. Lau & Emery G. Lee III, Fed. Jud. Ctr., Technology-Assisted Review for Discovery Requests (2017), https://judicialstudies.duke.edu/wp-content/uploads/2017/07/Panel-4_Technology-Assisted_Review_for_Discovery_Requests.pdf.

[21] Seth Katsuya Endo, *Technological Opacity & Procedural Injustice*, 59 B.C. L. Rev. 821, 837 (2018).

review was exorbitant; in 2000, it was estimated that discovery accounted for as much as one-third to one-half of total costs where discovery was actively conducted, and perhaps significantly more in large-scale litigations.[22]

In the early aughts, both keyword searches and outsourcing came to the fore to address some of the above. But neither proved wholly satisfactory. Keyword searching enabled parties to cut costs by restricting manual review to only those documents containing specific keywords, but search yields were worryingly incomplete.[23] Outsourcing – the move to send discovery to less-expensive contract lawyers in out-of-the-way US cities or abroad – was similarly fraught. Supervision was difficult; parties fretted about conflicts, confidentiality, and rules of multijurisdictional practice; and quality was wanting.[24]

As against those halfway innovations, TAR's advantages are profound. Estimates of TAR's efficacy vary and are hotly contested, but the general view is that implemented well – and this is a key qualifier – TAR systems are as good as manual, eyes-on review in terms of recall (i.e., the proportion of relevant documents in the total pool of documents that are accurately identified as relevant) but systematically better in precision (i.e., the proportion of documents flagged that are in fact relevant). The far bigger difference is efficiency: Compared to its conventional counterpart, TAR achieves all of this at a fraction of the cost.[25]

Yet, TAR is not without controversy. Much of it stems from the fact that TAR, like any machine learning system, is a socio-technical "assemblage," not a turnkey engine.[26] Attorneys must label and re-label documents as the system works its way toward a reliable model. An important implication is that, much like Colossus (described below), TAR systems are manipulable by humans in their construction and tuning.[27] As Diego Zambrano and co-authors detail elsewhere in this volume, this manipulation can run the gamut from outright abuse (e.g., fudging the labels lawyers apply to document labels[28] or rigging the selection, adjustment, or validation of models[29]) to a more benign but still respondent-friendly calibration of the system

22 Engstrom & Gelbach, *Legal Tech*, at 1048–49.

23 *See* David C. Blair & M. E. Maron, *An Evaluation of Retrieval Effectiveness for a Full-Text Document-Retrieval System*, 28 Commc'ns ACM 289, 291 (1985); Lau & Lee, Technology-Assisted Review, at 3.

24 See James I. Ham, *Ethical Considerations Relating to Outsourcing of Legal Services by Law Firms to Foreign Services Providers*, 27 Pa. St. Int'l L. Rev. 323 (2008).

25 Engstrom & Gelbach, *Legal Tech*, at 1052–54 (reviewing the evidence).

26 Mike Ananny & Kate Crawford, *Seeing without Knowing: Limitations of the Transparency Ideal and Its Application to Algorithmic Accountability*, 20 New Media & Soc'y 983 (2016).

27 *See* Dana A. Remus, *The Uncertain Promise of Predictive Coding*, 99 Iowa L. Rev. 1691, 1707 (2014).

28 *See id.* (noting the possibility that lawyers will make aggressive relevance and privilege calls in constructing seed sets, which are then applied at scale to the entire document corpus).

29 *See* Maura R. Grossman & Gordon V. Cormack, *Comments on "The Implications of Rule 26(g) on the Use of Technology-Assisted Review,"* 7 Fed. Cts. L. Rev. 285 (2014). For a recent case addressing this concern, see Livingston v. City of Chicago, No. 16 CV 10156, 2020 WL 5253848,

to favor precision (the proportion of responsive documents among those in a production) over recall (the proportion of responsive documents identified).[30] As a result, and as discussed in more detail below, if litigation's "haves" need not show their work to the other side, they can shade discovery to their advantage and use their better technology and technologists (if the other side can afford them at all) to make sure it sticks.[31]

6.1.2 *Colossus*

For the nation's casualty and property insurers, AI has not so much spawned new litigation tools as supercharged those already in use. The best example is Colossus, a proprietary computer software program marketed by Computer Science Corporation (CSC) that "relies on 10,000 integrated rules" to assist insurance companies – the ultimate repeat players – in the evaluation and resolution of bodily injury claims.[32] Initially developed in Australia and first used by Allstate in the 1990s, Colossus has grown in popularity, such that it has been utilized by the majority of large property and casualty insurers in the United States, including behemoths Aetna, Allstate, Travelers, Farmers, and USAA.[33]

Colossus has radically changed the process of auto accident claims adjustment. By extension, it has profoundly altered how the tens of thousands of third-party bodily injury claims generated annually by American drivers, passengers, and pedestrians are processed and paid by US insurers.

Before Colossus, an experienced auto accident adjuster employed by Allstate or USAA would have assessed a personal injury claim using rough benchmarks, in a

at *3 (N.D. Ill. Sept. 3, 2020) ("Plaintiffs express concern that the attorney reviewers will improperly train the TAR tool by making incorrect responsiveness determinations or prematurely ending the review.").

30 For accessible overview, see Maura R. Grossman & Gordon V. Cormack, *Continuous Active Learning for TAR*, E-Discovery Bull., Apr./May 2016, at 32.

31 *See* Endo, *Technological Opacity*, at 863 (detailing how the "black-box" quality of predictive coding makes it harder for less sophisticated litigants to challenge the predictive coding process).

32 For initial background, see Herbert M. Kritzer, *Defending Torts: What Should We Know?* 1 J. Tort L. 1, 15 (2007). For the fact that Colossus "relies on 10,000 integrated rules," see Thomas Scheffey, *Attack on Colossus*, Conn. L. Trib., Mar. 19, 1999 (quoting Richard J. Balducci).

33 Bruce A. Hagen, Karen K. Koehler & Michael D. Freeman, Litigating Minor Impact Soft Tissue Cases § 1:2 (2020 ed.) (quoting the 2004 version of the CSC website); *see also* Joe Frey, *Putting a Price on Auto Injuries: How Software Called Colossus Evaluates Claimants' Pain*, Conn. L. Trib., Aug. 14, 2000. For a list of past or current users, see Mark Romano & J. Robert Hunter, Consumer Fed'n Am., Low Ball: An Insider's Look at How Some Insurers Can Manipulate Computerized Systems to Broadly Underpay Injury Claims, 2, 2 n.7 (2012). For the fact that Colossus was "first used by Allstate in the 1990s," see Melissa M. D'Alelio & Taylore Karpa Schollard, *Colossus and Xactimate: A Tale of Two AI Insurance Software Programs*, Brief, Winter 2020, at 20, 24.

process that was more art than science. Namely, the adjuster would add up a victim's "special damages" (chiefly, the victim's medical bills) and multiply those by a fixed sum – often, two or three – to generate a default figure, called a "going rate" or "rule of thumb."[34] Then, the adjuster would leaven that default figure with the adjuster's knowledge and past practice, perhaps informed by a review of recent trial verdict reports, and possibly aided by "roundtabling" among the insurer's veteran casualty claims professionals.[35]

With Colossus, however, the same adjuster can now calculate a claim's worth at a keystroke, after plugging in answers to a series of fill-in-the-blank-style questions. Or, as Colossus itself explains: "Through a series of interactive questions, Colossus guides your adjusters through an objective evaluation of medical treatment options, degree of pain and suffering, and the impact of the injury on the claimant's lifestyle."[36] To be sure, the data an adjuster must input in order to prime Colossus to generate a damage assessment is voluminous and varied. When inputting a claim, the adjuster accounts for obvious factors such as the date and location of the accident, alongside the claimant's home address, gender, age, verified lost wages, documented medical expenses, nature of injury, diagnosis, and prognosis. Treatment – including MRI or X-ray images, prescriptions, injections, hospital admissions, surgeries, follow-up visits, and physical therapy – is also granularly assessed.[37] Then, against these loss variables, the adjuster must account for various liability metrics. Fault (in all its common law complexity) is reduced to "clear" or "unclear," while the existence or nonexistence of "aggravating factors" (such as driver inebriation) is also considered, and, in a nod to the tort doctrine of anticipatory avoidable consequences, the adjuster must also input whether the claimant was buckled up.[38] Even the individual identity of the handling attorney, treating physician and/or chiropractor, and (if applicable) presiding judge is keyed in.[39]

34 *See* Gary T. Schwartz, *Auto No-Fault and First-Party Insurance: Advantages and Problems*, 73 S. Cal. L. Rev. 611, 635 (2000); Robin Stevenson Burroughs, *When Colossus and Xactimate Are Not Exact: How Computerized Claims Adjusting Software Has Not Changed the Landscape of Insurance Litigation*, 22 Info. & Commc'ns Tech. L. 109 (2013).

35 *See generally* H. Laurence Ross, Settled Out of Court: The Social Process of Insurance Claims Adjustment (1980); *see also* Steven Plitt et al., *Colossus under Attack: The Legal Efficacy of Computerized Evaluation of Bodily Injury Claims*, Cal. Ins. L. & Reg. Rep., June 2007, at 1 (discussing roundtabling).

36 Colossus®, Evaluate Bodily Injury Claims with Consistency, https://www.dxc.technology/p_and_c_general_insurance/offerings/26121/57637-colossus.

37 Romano & Hunter, An Insider's Look, at 5–6.

38 Robert D. Bennett, *How To Deal with Colossus*, in 2 Ass'n Of Trial Lawyers of Am., Atla Annual Convention Reference Materials: Motor Vehicle Collision, Highway, And Premises Liability (2005). William F. Merlin Jr., *Colossus: What We Know Today*, 2002 ATLA-CLE 127 (2002); William Merlin, *Maximizing Recovery in Colossus Claims*, 14 Trial Excellence 7, 8, 11 (2002).

39 Bennett, *How to Deal with Colossus*; Mark Ballard, *Allstate's Master Plan? Major Insurer Is Accused of Penalizing Claimants Who Dare Hire Attorneys*, Nat'l L.J., Nov. 9, 1998.

Once data entry is complete, Colossus assesses the claim in light of the enormous pool of data in its master database to generate a "severity point total."[40] Then, aided by particularized, proprietary information that is specific to each insurer (based on each individual insurer's "settlement philosophies and claims practice"[41]), Colossus converts the point total into a recommended settlement range.[42] Insurance adjusters use this settlement range in their negotiations with unrepresented claimants or their counsel. Indeed, at some insurers, adjusters are not permitted to offer a sum outside the range, at least without a supervisor's approval.[43] At others, adjusters are evaluated based on their ability to close files within Colossus-specified parameters.[44] In so doing, according to one insider: "Colossus takes the guess work out of an historically subjective segment of the claims process, providing adjusters with a powerful tool for improving claims valuation, consistency, increasing productivity and containing costs."[45]

Beyond these, allegations about further operational details abound. The most common is that, when customizing the software (the proprietary process that converts a "severity point total" into a settlement range), certain insurers "tune" Colossus to "consistently spit out lowball offers."[46] Some insurers reportedly accomplish this feat by excluding from the database certain figures that, by rights, should be included (e.g., large settlements or verdicts).[47] Others get there, it is said,

40 Jay M. Feinman, Delay, Deny, Defend: Why Insurance Companies Don't Pay Claims and What You Can Do about It 116–17 (2010).

41 *See* Plitt et al., *Colossus under Attack*.

42 Colossus,® Evaluate Bodily Injury Claims with Consistency; *accord* Oakes v. Allstate Ins. Co., No. 5:05CV-174-R, 2008 WL 11363638, at *1 (W.D. Ky. Sept. 23, 2008); *see, e.g.*, Mirville v. Allstate Indem. Co., 87 F. Supp. 2d 1184, 1186 (D. Kan. 2000), *aff'd sub nom.*, Mirville v. Mirville, 10 F. App'x 640 (10th Cir. 2001) ("The Colossus program indicated that Marie Mirville's general damages were in the range of $1,076,720 to $1,345,900 and recommended a settlement range of $942,130 to $1,211,310.").

43 *In re* Farmers Ins. Exch. Claims Representatives' Overtime Pay Litig., 336 F. Supp. 2d 1077, 1101 (D. Or. 2004), *aff'd in part, rev'd in part and remanded sub nom.*, 481 F.3d 1119 (9th Cir. 2007) (observing that, at Farmers, claims adjusters "must obtain supervisor approval to settle a claim above the Colossus range"); *accord* Dougherty v. AMCO Ins. Co., No. C 07-01140 MHP, 2008 WL 2563225, at *3 (N.D. Cal. June 23, 2008) (noting testimony by an adjuster that he had no discretion to deviate from the Colossus settlement range without manager permission).

44 Feinman, Delay, Deny, Defend, at 119 (citing a source that, at Allstate, Colossus' recommended settlement ranges were "etched in stone"); *see also* Merlin, *Maximizing Recovery*, at 8, 11; Chris Heeb, *Commentary: Are You Colossus Proof?* Mo. Laws. Wkly., July 24, 2006.

45 Hagen et al., Litigating Minor Impact Soft Tissue Cases, § 1:2 (quoting Ken Williams, President of the Americans Division of CSC's Financial Services Group).

46 In Tough Hands at Allstate, *Bloomberg Businessweek* (Apr. 30, 2006), https://www.bloomberg.com/news/articles/2006-04-30/in-tough-hands-at-allstate; *see also* Romano & Hunter, An Insider's Look, at 7, 13; Feinman, Delay, Deny, Defend, at 124.

47 *Dougherty*, 2008 WL 2563225, at *3 ("Neither jury verdicts, arbitration awards nor post-litigation settlements were reflected in the Colossus analysis of settlement value."); Jerry Guidera, *"Colossus" at the Accident Scene: Software of Insurers Spurs Suits*, Wall St. J., Jan. 2, 2003 (reporting on the testimony of Linda Brown, a former Allstate senior claims manager, who

simply by turning dials downward to generate across-the-board haircuts of 10–20 percent.[48]

As such, it appears that, in the hands of at least some insurers, Colossus has not only rationalized the resolution of personal injury claims and injected newfound objectivity, predictability, and horizontal equity into the claims resolution process. It has also systematically cut claims – to the benefit of repeat-play insurers and the detriment of their claimant-side counterparts.

6.1.3 *The Walmart Suite*

A third innovation combines elements of both TAR and Colossus. One exemplar under this umbrella, which we dub "the Walmart Suite," given its development by Walmart in partnership with the law firm Ogletree Deakins and in concert with the tech company LegalMation, seeks to rationalize recurrent areas of litigation (think, employment disputes and slip-and-falls). It reportedly operates along two dimensions.[49] First, it reportedly generates pleadings and papers – including answers, discovery requests, and discovery objections – thus cutting litigation costs.[50] To that extent, the Suite might be thought akin to TAR in its ability to perform low-level legal cognitions and generate straightforward work product that previously required

testified "that she was instructed to omit jury awards and any settlements of more than $50,000 when helping to establish Colossus database in 1995 for Kentucky").

48 Romano & Hunter, An Insider's Look, at 13 (compiling evidence of this manipulation); Feinman, Delay, Deny, Defend, at 117–18 (amassing testimony that paints a similar picture); *see also* Paige St. John, *How a Get-Tough Policy Lifted Allstate's Profits*, Sarasota Herald-Trib., Apr. 26, 2008, at A1. But cf.*Allstate Agrees to $10 Million Regulatory Settlement over Bodily Injury Claims Handling Processes*, N.Y. Dep't Fin. Servs. (Oct. 18, 2010), https://perma.cc/7ZCS-VW6S (concluding an investigation into Allstate, at the end of which Allstate agreed to "make a number of changes to its claims handling process," including vis-à-vis the company's use and tuning of Colossus, while noting that the investigation uncovered "no systemic underpayment of bodily injury claims").

49 *See* Alan Bryan et al., *Using A.I. to Digitize Lawsuits to Perform Actionable Data Analytics*, Corp. Legal Operations Consortium (May 15, 2019), https://perma.cc/B4C2-XY3K; *see also* Brenna Goth, *Walmart Using AI to Transform Legal Landscape, Cut Costs*, Bloomberg L. (Apr. 26, 2018), https://news.bloomberglaw.com/daily-labor-report/walmart-using-ai-to-transform-legal-landscape-cut-costs; Patricia Barnes, *Artificial Intelligence Further Exacerbates Inequality in Discrimination Lawsuits*, Forbes (Aug. 26, 2019), https://www.forbes.com/sites/patriciagbarnes/2019/08/26/artificial-intelligence-further-exacerbates-inequality-in-discrimination-lawsuits/.

50 Press Release, Ogletree Deakins, Ogletree Deakins and LegalMation Announce Innovative Partnership (Jan. 9, 2019), https://ogletree.com/media-center/press-releases/2019-01-09/ogletree-deakins-and-legalmation-announce-innovative-partnership/. *Using AI in Litigation—Thomas Suh (LegalMation Co-Founder)*, Technically Legal Podcast (May 27, 2020), https://tlpodcast.com/episode-33-using-ai-in-litigation-thomas-suh-legalmation-co-founder/; LegalMation, *Case Studies—Corporate In-House Case Study*, www.legalmation.com/ (last visited Apr. 10, 2022); Kate Beioley, *Workplace Litigation: Why US Employers Are Turning to Data*, Fin. Times (Dec. 9, 2019), https://www.ft.com/content/865832b4-0486-11ea-a958-5e9b7282cbd1.

(human) lawyers. Second, and more provocatively, the Suite can evaluate key case characteristics, including the identity of plaintiffs' counsel, and then offer a prediction about a case's outcome and the likely expense Walmart will incur if the case is litigated, rather than settled.[51] The Suite thus seems to be a beefed-up Colossus, with a focus on slip-and-falls and employment disputes rather than auto accidents.

The advantages of such tools are seemingly substantial. LegalMation reports that a top law firm has used its tools to handle 5,000 employment disputes – and, in so doing, the firm realized a *six- to eight-fold savings* in preparing pleadings and discovery requests.[52] But these economies are only the beginning. Outcome prediction engines, commonly referred to as the "holy grail" of legal tech,[53] allow large entities facing recurring types of litigation to quickly capitulate (via settlement) where plaintiffs have the benefit of strong claims and talented counsel – and then battle to final judgment where plaintiffs are saddled with weak claims or less-competent counsel. In so doing, the Walmarts of the world can save today by notching litigation victories while conserving litigation resources. But they can simultaneously position themselves over the long haul, by skewing case outcomes, driving down damages, and pushing precedent at the appellate level. We return to these advantages below.

6.2 THE PROMISE AND PERIL OF LEGAL TECH

Section 6.1 introduced three types of legal tools that have already entered the civil justice system. These tools – TAR, Colossus, and the Walmart Suite – are hardly the only legal tech applications dotting the American litigation landscape. But they help to define it, and they also permit some informed predictions about legal tech's effect on the litigation playing field over the near- to medium-term.

Assessing these effects, this Section observes that TAR *may* help to level the litigation playing field and could even bring greater transparency to discovery disputes – although such a rosy result is by no means assured, and darker outcomes are also possible. Meanwhile, Colossus and the Walmart Suite both seem poised to drive case settlements downward and even fuel a dynamic we call the "litigation of losers," in part because the data stores that drive them are, at least currently, so unevenly distributed.

[51] *See* Bryan et al., *Using A.I. to Digitize Lawsuits*; *see also Using AI in Litigation* (describing tool that combines case information with "law firms' and corporate legal departments' own billing data and outcome data" to estimate outcomes and cost); Sean Christy, *In Their Words: Using Analytics and AI in Legal Practice*, GA. ST. NEWS HUB (Mar. 15, 2018), https://news.gsu.edu/2018/03/15/in-their-words-using-analytics-and-ai-in-legal-practice/ (noting use of tool to predict case length, likely cost, and outcome).

[52] *Case Studies – Large Firm Case Study*, LEGALMATION, https://www.legalmation.com/) (claiming a reduction in attorney time on pleadings and initial discovery "from an average of 6–8 hours per matter, to less than 1 hour (including review time by an attorney)"); *see also* Barnes, *Artificial Intelligence Further Exacerbates Inequality* (describing case study).

[53] *Using AI in Litigation*.

6.2.1 TAR Wars: Proportionality and Discovery Abuse

For TAR, our appraisal is mixed – though the dynamics at play are not simple and our predictions less than ironclad. That said, we predict that the next decade will feature increasingly heated "TAR wars" waged on two fronts: proportionality and discovery gaming and abuse. If, on each front, there is sufficient judicial oversight (an admittedly big if), TAR might usher in a new era, where discovery emerges more efficient and transparent than before. But there is also the possibility that, like Colossus and the Walmart Suite, TAR will tilt the playing field toward repeat-play litigants. Here, we address these two fronts – and also these two divergent possible outcomes.

Proportionality: Will TAR's efficiencies justify more expansive discovery? Or will these efficiencies yield a defendant-side surplus? Discovery has long been the 800-pound gorilla in the civil justice system, accounting for as much as one-third to one-half of all litigation costs in cases where discovery is actively employed.[54] High discovery costs, and the controversy surrounding those costs, have powered the creation of *numerous* rules and doctrines that constrain discovery's scope.[55] One such rule – and the one we address here – is the "proportionality" requirement, that is, a requirement that a judge greenlight a discovery request only if the request is "proportional" to a case's particular needs.[56]

Applied to TAR, proportionality is tricky because TAR can yield gains in both efficiency *and* accuracy. For a requesting party (typically, the plaintiff), more efficient review justifies more expansive review, including document requests that, for instance, extend to a longer time horizon or to a wider net of document custodians. For a producing party (typically the defendant), however, accuracy gains mean that the requesting party will *already* get more relevant documents and fewer irrelevant ones, even holding constant the number of custodians or the scope of the search.[57] In short, TAR generates a surplus in both efficiency and accuracy, and the question becomes how best to allocate that surplus.[58]

Given these dynamics, judges might employ the proportionality principle in one of two ways. Judges could recognize that the unit cost of discovery – the cost of each produced document – has declined and compensate by authorizing the requesting

[54] *See* Engstrom & Gelbach, *Legal Tech*, at 1048–49.

[55] *See generally* Brooke D. Coleman, *The Efficiency Norm*, 56 B.C. L. Rev. 1777 (2015) (describing various mechanisms).

[56] Proportionality became part of the federal rules in 1983, but it was beefed up in 2006 and then again in 2015. For discussion, see Paul W. Grimm, *Are We Insane? The Quest for Proportionality in the Discovery Rules of the Federal Rules of Civil Procedure*, 36 Rev. Litig. 117 (2017).

[57] *See* Seth Katsuya Endo, *Discovery Hydraulics*, 52 U.C. Davis. L. Rev. 1317, 1354–55 (2019).

[58] *See* Endo, *Technological Opacity*, at 855 ("Even assuming that predictive coding provides more accurate and comprehensive results at a lower cost, it is not settled how the gains should be distributed between the parties.").

party's more *expansive* discovery plan. If so, the cost of each produced document will drop, transparency into the underlying incident will (at least arguably) improve, and the overall cost of discovery will remain (roughly) constant. Judges, however, might take a different tack. Notwithstanding TAR's efficiency advantages, judges might *deny* requesting parties' motions to permit more expansive discovery, thus holding proportionality's benchmarks firm. If so, TAR will cough up the same documents as before, but at a discount.

If trial judges permit producing parties to capture TAR's cost-savings without compensating by sanctioning more sweeping discovery plans, the effect on civil litigation, from the availability of counsel to settlement patterns, could be profound.[59] Lower total discovery costs, of course, might be a net social welfare gain. After all, a core premise of proportionality rules is that litigation costs, particularly discovery costs, are disproportionate to the social value of the dispute resolution achieved, and scarce social resources might be better spent on other projects. But shifts in discovery costs can also have distributive consequences. It is a core premise of litigation economics that "all things being equal, the party facing higher costs will settle on terms more favorable to the party facing lower costs."[60] If TAR causes discovery costs to bend downward, TAR's surplus – and, with it, any *settlement* surplus – will systematically flow toward the net document producers (again, typically, repeat-play defendants).[61] Such an outcome would yield a tectonic shift in the settlement landscape – hard to see in any particular case, but potentially quite large in aggregate. It will be as if Colossus' dials have been turned down.

The potential for abuse: TAR appears to be more susceptible to abuse than its analog counterpart. How will judges respond? The second TAR battleground will be discovery abuse and gaming. The fight will center on a core question: Can discovery rules generate enough trust among litigants to support TAR's continued propagation, while, at the same time, mitigating concerns about gaming and the distributive concerns raised by such conduct?

Discovery abuse, of course, is not new. Nor is TAR *uniquely* vulnerable to discovery abuse.[62] Indeed, one of the easiest ways to manipulate a TAR system – the deliberate failure to flag (or "label") a plainly responsive document – is no different from garden-variety discovery manipulation, in which lawyers simply omit obviously responsive and damaging documents or aggressively withhold borderline documents on relevance or privilege grounds. But, as Zambrano and co-authors note in Chapter 5, there is nevertheless good reason to believe that TAR might be

59 Linda Sandstrom Simard, *Seeking Proportional Discovery: The Beginning of the End of Procedural Uniformity in Civil Rules*, 71 VAND. L. REV. 1919, 1948 (2018).

60 J. Maria Glover, *The Federal Rules of Civil Settlement*, 87 N.Y.U. L. REV. 1713, 1730 (2012).

61 Likewise, if judges hold the line on more expansive discovery, and TAR turns out to be more efficient but only marginally more accurate than manual review, then TAR's surplus – and, once again, the settlement surplus – will flow toward net document producers.

62 Livingston v. City of Chicago, No. 16 CV 10156, 2020 WL 5253848, at *3 (N.D. Ill. Sept. 3, 2020).

especially prone to abuse – and that is a very serious problem in a system already steeped in mistrust.[63]

TAR's particular vulnerability to abuse flows from four facts. First, TAR operates at scale. In constructing a seed set, a single labeling decision could, in theory, prevent an entire species of document from coming to light.[64]

Second, and relatedly, TAR can be implemented by small teams – much different than the sprawling associate armies who previously performed eyes-on document reviews in complex cases. This means that, in a TAR world, deliberate discovery abuse requires coordination among a smaller set of actors. If discovery abusers can be likened to a cartel, keeping a small team in line is far easier than ensuring that a sprawling network of co-conspirators stays silent. Moreover, TAR leans on, not just lawyers, but technologists – and, unlike the former, the latter might be less likely to take discovery obligations seriously, as they are not regulated by rules of professional conduct, need not participate in continuing legal education, and arguably have a less socialized sense of duty to the public or the court.

Third, TAR methods may themselves be moving toward more opaque and harder-to-monitor approaches. In its original guise – TAR 1.0 – lawyers manually labeled a "seed set" to train the machine-learning model. With access to that "seed set," a litigation adversary could, in theory, reconstruct the other side's work, identifying calls that were borderline or seemed apt to exclude key categories of documents. TAR 2.0, by contrast, starts with a small set of documents and uses machine learning to turn up lists of other candidates, which are then labeled and fed back into the system. TAR 2.0 thus renders seed set construction highly *iterative* – and, in so doing, makes it harder for an adversary or adjudicator to review or reconstruct. TAR 2.0, to invoke a concept in a growing "algorithmic accountability" literature, may, as a consequence, be less *contestable* by an adversary who suspects abuse.[65]

Fourth and finally, while TAR is theoretically available on both sides of the "v.," technical capacity is almost certainly unevenly distributed, since defense firms tend to be larger than plaintiffs' firms – and are more richly capitalized. With these resource advantages, if defendants are *tempted* to engage in tech-driven litigation abuse, they (and their stable of technologists) might be able to do so with near impunity.

The tough question becomes: How should judges react, to safeguard the integrity of discovery processes? Here, judges have no shortage of tools, but all have drawbacks. Judges can, for example, compel the disclosure of a seed set, although such disclosures are controversial, since the *full* seed set necessarily includes both

63 *See* Chapter 5 in this volume.

64 Remus, *Uncertain Promise*, at 1707.

65 Daniel N. Kluttz & Deirdre K. Mulligan, *Automated Decision Support Technologies and the Legal Profession*, 34 Berkeley Tech. L.J. 853, 886 (2020) (discussing the concept).

documents that lawyers labeled as relevant as well as those irrelevant to the claim.[66] Meanwhile, disclosure of TAR inputs arguably violates the work product doctrine, established in the Supreme Court's 1947 decision in *Hickman v. Taylor* and since baked into Rule 26(b)(3), which protects against disclosure of "documents and tangible things that are prepared in anticipation of litigation."[67] And, a call for wholesale disclosure – ever more "discovery about discovery" – seems poised to erode litigant autonomy and can itself be a bare-knuckled litigation tactic, not a good-faith truth-seeking device.

Worse, if *analog* discovery procedures are left to party discretion absent evidence of specific deficiencies, but a party's use of *TAR* automatically kicks off protracted ex ante negotiations over protocols or onerous back-end "report card" requirements based on various quality-control metrics, there is the ever-present risk that this double standard will cause parties to throw up their hands. To the extent TAR's benefits are overshadowed by expensive process-oriented disputes, investment in TAR will eventually stall out, depriving the system of its efficiencies.[68] Yet, the opposite approach is just as, if not more, worrisome. If judges, afraid of the above, do not act to police discovery abuse – and this abuse festers – they risk eroding the integrity of civil discovery and, by extension, litigants', lawyers', and the public's faith in civil litigation.

Time will tell if judges can steer between these possibilities. But if they can, then out of these two gloomy visions comes a glimmer of light. If judges can help mint and then judiciously apply evenhanded protocols in TAR cases, then perhaps the system could end up better off than the analog system that TAR will steadily eclipse. Civil discovery could be one of those areas where, despite AI's famous "black box" opacity, digitization yields a net increase in transparency and accountability.[69]

6.2.2 *Colossus and the Walmart Suite: The Litigation of Losers*

When it comes to the slant of the civil justice system, an assessment of the likely effect of Colossus and the Walmart Suite is more dour.

Colossus: Reduction via brute force. The impact of Colossus on the civil justice system seems fairly clear and not particularly contingent. Colossus' advent has certain undeniable benefits, injecting newfound predictability, consistency, objectivity, and horizontal equity into the claims resolution process. It has also, probably,

66 Aurora Coop. Elevator Co. v. Aventine Renewable Energy–Aurora W., LLC, No. 4:12CV230, 2015 WL 10550240, at *2 (D. Neb. Jan. 6, 2015).

67 Fed. R. Civ. P. 26(b)(3). For discussion of whether seed sets are protected work product, see Engstrom & Gelbach, *Legal Tech*, at 1077–86.

68 *See* Christine Payne & Michelle Six, *A Proposed Technology-Assisted Review Framework*, Law360 (Apr. 28, 2020), https://www.law360.com/articles/1267032/a-proposed-technology-assisted-review-framework.

69 For an analogous argument in the area of algorithmic bias, see Jon Kleinberg et al., *Discrimination in the Age of Algorithms*, 10 J. Legal Analysis 113 (2019).

reduced the monies paid for fraudulent or "built" claims,[70] as well as the odds that claim values will be influenced by improper factors (racial bias, for example).[71] Finally, it has, possibly, driven down the driving public's insurance premiums – though there's little reliable evidence on the point.

But, alongside these weighty advantages, it does seem that Colossus has also reduced claim payments quite significantly, using something like brute force. When Allstate rolled out a new Colossus-aided claims program for Allstate with the help of McKinsey & Co., the consulting firm's stated goal was to "establish[ ] a new fair market value" for such injuries.[72] It appears that that aim was achieved. A later McKinsey review of Allstate found: "The Colossus sites have been extremely successful in reducing severities, with reductions in the range of 20 percent for Colossus-evaluated claims."[73] Nor was this dynamic confined, necessarily, to Allstate. Robert Dietz, a fifteen-year veteran of Farmer's Insurance has explained, for example: "My vast experience in evaluating claims was replaced by values generated by a computer. More often than not, these values were not representative of what I had experienced as fair and reasonable."[74]

The result is that, aided by Colossus, insurance companies are offering less to claimants for comparable injuries, on a take-it-or-leave-it basis. And, though one-shot personal injury (PI) lawyers could call insurance companies' bluff and band together to reject these Colossus-generated offers en masse, in the past two decades, they haven't.

Their failure to do so should not be surprising. Given persistent collective action problems and yawning information asymmetries (described in further detail below), one would not expect disaggregated PI lawyers, practicing alone or in small firms, to mount a coordinated and muscular response, especially since doing so would mean taking a significant number of claims to trial, which poses many well-known and formidable obstacles. For instance, some portion of PI lawyers operate in law firms (called "settlement mills") and do not, in fact, have the *capacity* to take claims to trial.[75] Second, many auto accident claimants need money quickly and do not have the wherewithal to wait out attendant trial delays. And third, *all* PI lawyers are attuned to the stubborn economics of auto accident litigation: As of 2005, the median jury trial award in an auto case was a paltry $17,000, which would yield only about $5,500 in contingency fees, a sum that is simply too meager to justify

70 Nora Freeman Engstrom, *Retaliatory RICO and the Puzzle of Fraudulent Claiming*, 115 Mich. L. Rev. 639, 676 (2017) (discussing Colossus' salutary fraud-fighting capabilities).

71 Burroughs, *When Colossus and Xactimate Are Not Exact*, at 109 (observing that the shift "away from actual price checking might eliminate some possible human bias").

72 St. John, *How a Get-Tough Policy Lifted Allstate's Profits*, at A1.

73 Feinman, Delay, Deny, Defend, at 120.

74 *Id.* at 9.

75 *See* Nora Freeman Engstrom, *Run-of-the-Mill Justice*, 22 Geo. J. Legal Ethics 1485, 1495–98 (2009).

frequent trials against well-financed foes.[76] This last point was not lost on McKinsey, which, in a presentation to Allstate, encouraged: "Win by exploiting the economics of the practice of law."[77]

The Walmart Suite and the litigation of losers. The Walmart Suite illustrates another dynamic, which we dub the "litigation of losers." In the classic article, *Why the Haves Come Out Ahead*, Marc Galanter presciently observed that repeat-players could settle out bad cases "where they expected unfavorable rule outcomes" and litigate only the good ones that are "most likely to produce favorable results." Over time, he concluded, "we would expect the body of 'precedent' cases, that is, cases capable of influencing the outcome of future cases – to be relatively skewed toward those favorable to [repeat players]."[78]

The Walmart Suite shows that Galanter's half-century-old prediction is coming to pass, fueled by AI-based software he couldn't have imagined.[79] And, we anticipate, this isn't the end of it. In recurring areas of litigation, we are likely to see increasingly sophisticated outcome prediction tools that will draw ever-tighter uncertainty bands around anticipated outcomes. Like the Walmart Suite, these tools are reliant on privileged access to confidential claim settlement data, which only true repeat players will possess.

The effect of this evolution is profound, for, as outcome prediction tools percolate (at least in the hands of repeat defendants/insurers), only duds will be litigated – and this "litigation of losers" will skew – indeed, is almost certainly already skewing – the development of substantive law. The skew will happen because conventional wisdom, at least, holds that cases settle in the shadow of trial – which means that, to the extent trial outcomes tilt toward defendants, we would expect that settlements, too, will display a pro-defendant slant.[80] Damages will also be affected. To offer but one concrete example, in numerous states, a judge evaluates whether damages are "reasonable" by assessing what past courts have awarded for similar or comparable

76 For the $16,000 figure, see LANGTON & COHEN, CIVIL BENCH AND JURY TRIALS IN STATE COURTS, at 10. For further discussion of the economics that constrain auto accident litigation, see Engstrom, *Run-of-the-Mill Justice*, at 1495–98.

77 St. John, *How a Get-Tough Policy Lifted Allstate's Profits*, at A1.

78 Galanter, *Why the Haves Come Out Ahead*, at 101.

79 The litigation of losers can also take more analog forms. Consider Allstate. In the mid-1990s, Allstate changed its treatment of minor impact soft-tissue claims (MIST for short) sustained in auto accidents, declaring that, particularly when those claims were accompanied by "vehicle damage of less than $1,000," "[a] compromise settlement is not desired." FEINMAN, DELAY, DENY, DEFEND, at 96–99 (quoting an Allstate Claims Manual); Ballard, *Allstate's Master Plan?* By withholding reasonable settlement offers, the insurer forced more soft-tissue claims to trial and, in so doing, caused plaintiffs' counsel to think twice before accepting clients with such injuries. *See* Engstrom, *Run-of-the-Mill Justice*, at 1542 n. 349; Michael Maiello, *So Sue Us*, FORBES, (Feb. 7, 2000), https://www.forbes.com/forbes/2000/0207/6503060a.html?sh=68b803f62b04.

80 *See* Robert H. Mnookin & Lewis Kornhauser, *Bargaining in the Shadow of the Law: The Case of Divorce*, 88 YALE L.J. 950, 968 (1979).

injuries.[81] To the extent the repository of past damages reflects damages plaintiffs have won while litigating weak or enfeebled claims, that repository will, predictably, bend downward, creating a progressively more favorable damages environment for defendants.

To be sure, there are caveats and counter-arguments. Models of litigation bargaining suggest that a defendant with privileged information will sometimes have incentives to share that information with plaintiffs in order to avoid costly and unnecessary litigation and achieve efficient settlements.[82] Additionally, while repeat players have better access to litigation and settlement data, even one-shotters don't operate *entirely* in the dark.[83] But a simple fact remains: Even a slow burn of marginally better information, and marginally greater negotiation leverage, can have large aggregate effects across thousands and even millions of cases.

6.3 WHAT TO DO?

As the litigation playing field tilts under legal tech's weight, there are some possible responses. Below, we start by briefly sketching three possible reforms that are facially plausible but, nevertheless, in our view, somewhat infeasible. Then, we offer a less attractive option – judicial discretion applied to existing procedural rules – as the most likely, though bumpy, path forward.

6.3.1 *Plausible but Unlikely Reforms*

Rewrite substantive or procedural law. First, we could respond to the skew that legal tech brings by recalibrating substantive law. Some combination of state and federal courts and legislatures could, for example, relax liability standards (for instance, making disparate impact job discrimination easier to prove), loosen restrictions on punitive damages, repeal damage caps, return to a world of joint and several liability, restore aider-and-abettor liability, abolish qualified immunity, and resurrect the collateral source rule.

Whatever the merit of a substantive law renaissance, we are, however, quite bearish on the possibility, as the obstacles blocking such an effort are formidable and, over the near- to medium-term, overwhelming. Substantive laws are sticky and

[81] *E.g.*, Arpin v. United States, 521 F.3d 769, 776 (7th Cir. 2008) (demanding that trial courts "consider[ ] awards in similar cases" when assessing non-economic damages under the Federal Tort Claims Act); Dougherty v. WCA of Florida, LLC, No. 01-2017-CA-001288, 2019 WL 691063, at *5 (Fla. Cir. Ct. Jan. 29, 2019) (remitting the plaintiff's award because the $12.5 million award did not bear "a reasonable relationship to . . . the general trend of prior decisions in similar cases"); Rozmarin v. Sookhoo, 102 N.Y.S.3d 67, 71 (App. Div. 2019) (noting that recent awards, though not binding, can "guide and enlighten" the court).

[82] Engstrom & Gelbach, *Legal Tech*, at 1074–75.

[83] *See* Ben Depoorter, *Law in the Shadow of Bargaining: The Feedback Effect of Civil Settlements*, 95 CORNELL L. REV. 957, 965–74 (2010) (outlining certain information on settlements that is available, notwithstanding data limitations and confidentiality provisions).

salient, especially in a political system increasingly characterized by polarization and legislative gridlock.[84] Even in less-polarized subfederal jurisdictions, it would be hard to convince state legislators and (often elected) judges to enact sweeping reforms without strong support from a public that often clings to enduring but often misguided beliefs about "jackpot justice" and frivolous claiming.[85]

Nor are federal courts, or a Supreme Court, newly stocked with Trump-era appointees, likely to help; to the contrary, they are likely to place barriers in front of litigation-friendly legislative efforts.[86] And procedural rules, though less politically salient, will also be hard to change, particularly at the federal level given the stranglehold of conservative judges and defense-side lawyers on the process of court-supervised rulemaking.[87]

Democratize the data. Second, we could try to recalibrate the playing field by expanding litigants' access to currently confidential data. As it stands, when it comes to data regarding the civil justice system, judges, lawyers, litigants, and academics operate almost entirely in the dark. We do not know how many civil trials are conducted each year. We don't know how many cases go to trial in each case category. And, we don't know – even vaguely – the outcome of the trials that do take place.[88] Furthermore, even if we could know what happens at trial (which we don't) or what happens after trial (which we don't), that still wouldn't tell us much about the *much* larger pool of claims that never make it to trial and instead are resolved consensually, often before official filing, by civil settlements.

This is crucial, for without information about those millions of below-the-radar settlements, the ability to "price" a claim – at least to "price" a claim using publicly available data, approaches zero. As Stephen Yeazell has aptly put it:

> [I]n the U.S. at the start of the twenty-first century, citizens can get reliable pricing information for almost any lawful transaction. But not for civil settlements. We can quickly find out the going price of a ten-year old car, of a two-bedroom apartment, or a souvenir of the last Superbowl, but one cannot get a current "market" quote for a broken leg, three weeks of lost work, and a lifetime of residual restricted mobility. Nor for any of the other 7 million large or the additional 10 million smaller civil claims filed annually in the United States. We simply do not know what these are worth.[89]

84 Solutions to Political Polarization in America (Nathaniel Persily ed., 2015).

85 Coleman, *The Efficiency Norm*, at 1784–85 (tracing shifts in "cultural attitudes about litigation").

86 Burbank & Farhang, Rights and Retrenchment.

87 *Id.*

88 For these and other deficiencies, see Chapter 16 in this volume; Lahav & Siegelman, *The Curious Incident of the Falling Win Rate*, at 1375; Nora Freeman Engstrom, *Measuring Common Claims about Class Actions*, Jotwell (Mar. 16, 2018), https://torts.jotwell.com/measuring-common-claims-about-class-actions/.

89 Stephen C. Yeazell, *Transparency for Civil Settlements: NASDAQ for Lawsuits?*, *in* Confidentiality, Transparency, and the U.S. Civil Justice System 148–49 (Joseph W. Doherty et al. eds., 2012).

Recognizing this gap, Computer Sciences Corp. (the maker of Colossus) and Walmart and its tech and BigLaw collaborators are working to fill it. But, they have filled it for themselves – and, in fact, they have leveraged what amounts to their near-total monopoly on settlement data to do so. Indeed, some insurers' apparent ability to "tune" Colossus rests entirely on the fact that plaintiffs cannot reliably check insurance companies' work – and so insurers can, at least theoretically, "massage" the data with near impunity.

Seeing the status quo in this light, of course, suggests a solution: We could try to *democratize the data*. Taking this tack, Yeazell has advocated for the creation of electronic databases whereby basic information about settlements – including, for instance, the amount of damages claimed, the place suit was filed, and the ultimate settlement amount – would be compiled and made accessible online.[90] In the same vein, one of us has suggested that plaintiffs' attorneys who work on a contingency fee basis and seek damages in cases for personal injury or wrongful death should be subject to significant public disclosure requirements.[91]

Yet, as much as democratizing the data sounds promising, numerous impediments remain – some already introduced above. The first is that many "cases" are never actually cases at all. In the personal injury realm, for example, the majority of claims – in fact, approximately half of claims that *involve represented claimants* – are resolved before a lawsuit is ever filed.[92] Getting reliable data about these settlements is exceptionally difficult. Next, even when cases are filed, some high proportion of civil cases exit dockets via an uninformative voluntary dismissal under Rule 41 or its state-level equivalents.[93] Those filings, of course, may be "public," but they reveal nothing about the settlement's monetary terms.[94] Then, even on those relatively rare occasions when a document describing the parties' terms of settlement *is* filed with the court, public access remains limited. Despite a brewing "open court data" movement, court records from the federal level on down sit behind "walls of cash and kludge."[95] Breaking through – and getting meaningful access even to what is "public" – is easier said than done.

90 *Id.* at 153–61.

91 Nora Freeman Engstrom, *Sunlight and Settlement Mills*, 86 N.Y.U. L. Rev. 805, 866–68 (2011).

92 *See* Deborah R. Hensler et al., Compensation for Accidental Injuries in the United States 121–22 (1991); Stephen Daniels & Joanne Martin, *It Was the Best of Times, It Was the Worst of Times: The Precarious Nature of Plaintiffs' Practice in Texas*, 80 Tex. L. Rev. 1781, 1789 tbl.4 (2002).

93 Compounding the problem, some settlements are shielded by strict confidentiality provisions. For a discussion, see Nora Freeman Engstrom, Legal Ethics: The Plaintiffs' Lawyer 291–92 (2022).

94 Yeazell, *Transparency for Civil Settlements*, at 149.

95 *See* Chapters 14 and 16 in this volume. For "cash and kludge," see Charlotte S. Alexander & Mohammad Javad Feizollahi, *On Dragons, Caves, Teeth, and Claws: Legal Analytics and the Problem of Court Data Access*, *in* Computational Legal Studies: The Promise and Challenge of Data-Driven Research (Ryan Whalen ed., 2020).

"Public option" legal tech. A third unlikely possibility is "public option" legal tech. Perhaps, that is, the government could fund the development of legal tech tools and make them widely available.

When it comes to TAR, public option legal tech is not hard to imagine. Indeed, state and federal judiciaries already feature magistrate judges who, on a day-to-day basis, mainly referee discovery disputes. It may only be a small step to create courthouse e-discovery arms, featuring tech-forward magistrate judges who work with staff technologists to *perform* discovery on behalf of the parties.

Public option outcome-prediction tools that can compete with Colossus or the Walmart Suite are harder to imagine. Judges, cautious Burkeans even compared to the ranks of lawyers from which they are drawn, are unlikely to relax norms of decisional independence or risk any whiff of prejudgment anytime soon. The bigger problem, however, will be structural, not just legal-cultural. The rub is that, like one-shot litigants and academics, courts lack access to outcome data that litigation's repeat players possess. Short of a sea change in the treatment of both pre- and post-suit secret settlements, courts, no less than litigation's have-nots, will lack the information needed to power potent legal tech tools.[96]

6.3.2 *Slouching Toward Equity: Judicial Procedural Management with an Eye to Technological Realities*

Given the above obstacles, the more likely (though perhaps least attractive) outcome is that judges, applying existing procedural rules, will be the ones to manage legal tech's incorporation into the civil justice system. And, as is often the case, judges will be asked to manage this tectonic transition with few rules and limited guidance, making it up mostly as they go.

The discussion of TAR's contingent future, set forth above in Part 6.2.2 offers a vivid depiction of how courts, as legal tech's frontline regulators, might do so adeptly; they might consider on-the-ground realities when addressing and applying existing procedural doctrines. But the TAR example also captures a wider truth about the challenges judges will face. As already noted, legal tech tools that cut litigation costs and hone information derive their value from their *exclusivity* – the fact that they are possessed by only one side. It follows that the procedural means available to judges to blunt legal tech's distributive impacts will also reduce the tools' value and, at the same time, dull incentives for litigants to adopt them, or tech companies to develop them, in the first instance. As a result, disparate judges applying proportionality and work product rules in individual cases will, inevitably,

96 This, of course, doesn't preclude other ways courts might gain access to needed digital outputs. One can readily imagine judges, over staunch work-product objections, demanding that a party seeking to transfer venue provide the court with its software's outcome prediction in order to test the party's claim that the transferee court offers only greater "convenience." *See* Engstrom & Gelbach, *Legal Tech*, at 1070.

in the aggregate, *create innovation policy*. And, for better or worse, they will make this policy without the synoptic view that is typically thought essential to making wise, wide-angle judgments.

Judicial management of legal tech's incorporation into the civil justice system will require a deft hand and a thorough understanding of changing on-the-ground realities. To offer just one example: As noted above, discovery cost concerns have fueled the creation of a number of doctrines that constrict discovery and, in so doing, tend to make life harder for plaintiffs. These include not just Rule 26's "proportionality" requirement (described above), but also a slew of *other* tweaks and outright inventions, noted previously, from tightened pleading standards to court-created *Lone Pine* orders that compel plaintiffs to offer extensive proof of their claims, sometimes soon after filing.

Undergirding all these restrictive doctrines is a bedrock belief: that discovery is burdensome and too easily abused, so much so that it ought to be rationed and rationalized. Yet, as explained above, TAR has the potential to significantly *reduce* the burden of discovery (particularly, as noted above, if more expansive discovery, which might offset certain efficiency gains, is not forthcoming). As such, TAR, at least arguably, will steadily erode the very foundation on which *Twombly*, *Iqbal*, and *Lone Pine* orders rest – and this newly unsettled foundation might, therefore, demand the reexamination of those doctrines. As judges manage the incorporation of potent new legal tech tools into the civil justice system, we can only hope that they will exhibit the wisdom to reconsider, where relevant, this wider landscape.

6.4 CONCLUSION

This chapter has argued that the civil justice system sits at a contingent moment, as new digital technologies are ushered into it. While legal tech will bring many benefits and may even help to level the playing field in certain respects, some of the more potent and immediately available tools will likely *tilt* the playing field, skewing it ever further toward powerful players. One can imagine numerous fixes, but the reality is that, in typical common law fashion, the system's future fairness will depend heavily on the action of judges, who, using an array of procedural rules built for an analog era will, for better or worse, make it up as they go. We're not confident about the results of that process. But the future fairness of a fast-digitizing civil justice system might just hinge on it.

7

Litigation Outcome Prediction, Access to Justice, and Legal Endogeneity

Charlotte S. Alexander

The United States has a serious and persistent civil justice gap. In 1994, an American Bar Association study found that half of low- and moderate-income households had faced at least one recent civil legal problem, but only one-quarter to one-third turned to the justice system.[1] Twenty-four years later, a 2017 study by the country's largest civil legal aid funder found that 71 percent of low-income households surveyed had experienced a civil legal need in the past year, but 86 percent of those problems received "inadequate or no legal help."[2] Studies in individual states tell a similar story.[3]

Unmet civil legal needs include a variety of high-stakes case types that affect basic safety, stability, and well-being: domestic violence restraining orders; health insurance coverage disputes; debt collection and relief actions; evictions and foreclosures; child support and custody cases; and education- and disability-related claims.[4] There is generally no legal right to counsel in these cases, and there are too few lawyers

Thanks to Madison Gibbs for her excellent research assistance and to Albert Yoon, Dan Linna, David Freeman Engstrom, Peter Molnar, and Sanjay Srivastava for insightful conversations on these topics.

1 Am. Bar Ass'n, Consortium on Legal Services and the Public, Legal Needs and Civil Justice: A Survey of Americans, Major Findings from the Comprehensive Legal Needs Study 27 (1994), https://legalaidresearch.org/2020/03/03/legal-needs-and-civil-justice-a-survey-of-americans-major-findings-from-the-comprehensive-legal-needs-study/.

2 Legal Servs. Corp., The Justice Gap: Measuring the Unmet Civil Legal Needs of Low-Income Americans 6 (2017), https://www.lsc.gov/our-impact/publications/other-publications-and-reports/justice-gap-report; *see also generally* Rebecca L. Sandefur & James Teufel, *Assessing America's Access to Civil Justice Crisis*, 11 U.C. Irvine L. Rev. 753 (2021).

3 *See, e.g.*, N.C. Equal Access to Justice Comm'n & NC Equal Justice All., *In Pursuit of Justice, An Assessment of the Civil Legal Needs of North Carolina* 4 (2021), https://ncequaljusticealliance.org/assessment/; Victor D. Quintanilla & Rachel Thelin, Indiana Civil Legal Needs Study and Legal Aid System Scan 6 (2019), https://www.repository.law.indiana.edu/facbooks/206/; Legal Servs. Corp., The Justice Gap 53 n.6 (collecting additional state studies).

4 Legal Servs. Corp., The Justice Gap, at 7.

willing and able to offer representation at prices that low- and middle-income clients can afford.[5] In my home state of Georgia, for example, five or six rural counties – depending on the year – have *no resident attorneys*, and eighteen counties have only one or two.[6] These counties' upper-income residents travel to the state's urban centers for legal representation. Lower-income residents seek help from rotating legal aid lawyers who "ride circuit," meeting clients for, say, two hours at the public library on the first Wednesday of the month.[7] Or they go without.

Can computationally driven litigation outcome prediction tools fill the civil justice gap? Maybe.

This chapter reviews the current state of outcome prediction tools and maps the ways they might affect the civil justice system. In Section 7.1, I define "computationally driven litigation outcome prediction tools" and explain how they work to forecast outcomes in civil cases. Section 7.2 outlines the theory: the potential for such tools to reduce uncertainty, thereby reducing the cost of civil legal services and helping to address unmet legal needs. Section 7.3 surveys the work that has been done thus far by academics, in commercial applications, and in the specific context of civil legal services for low- and middle-income litigants. Litigation outcome prediction has not reached maturity as a field, and Section 7.4 catalogs the data, methodological, and financial limits that have impeded development in general and the potential to expand access to justice in particular.

Section 7.5 steps back and confronts the deeper effects and the possible unintended consequences of the tools' continued proliferation. In particular, I suggest that, even if all the problems identified in Section 7.4 can be solved and litigation outcome prediction tools can be made to work perfectly, their use raises important endogeneity concerns. Computationally driven tools might reify previous patterns, lock out litigants whose claims are novel or boundary-pushing, and shut down the innovative and flexible nature of common law reasoning. Section 7.6 closes by offering a set of proposals to stave off these risks.

Admittedly, the field of litigation prediction is not yet revolutionizing civil justice, whether for good or ill. Empirical questions remain about the way(s) that outcome prediction might affect access to justice. Yet if developments continue, policy makers and practitioners should be ready to exploit the tools' substantial potential to fill the civil justice gap while also guarding against the harms they might cause.

[5] Kathryn A. Sabbeth, *Housing Defense as the New Gideon*, 41 Harv. J.L. & Gender 55, 56–57 (2018); *see also* Pamela Bookman & Colleen F. Shanahan, *A Tale of Two Civil Procedures*, 122 Colum. L. Rev. (forthcoming 2022) (describing state courts as "lawyerless").

[6] *Legal Profession*, New Ga. Encyclopedia (Aug. 11, 2020), https://www.georgiaencyclopedia.org/articles/government-politics/legal-profession/; Katheryn Hayes Tucker, *Here Are the Six Georgia Counties That Have No Lawyers*, The Daily Report (Jan. 8, 2015), https://www.law.com/dailyreportonline/almID/1202714378330/Here-Are-the-Six-Georgia-Counties-That-Have-No-Lawyers/?/.

[7] Tucker, *Six Georgia Counties*.

7.1. LITIGATION OUTCOME PREDICTION DEFINED

I define "computationally driven litigation outcome prediction tools" as statistical or machine learning methods used to forecast the outcome of a civil litigation event, claim, or case. A litigation event may be a motion filed by either party; the relevant predicted outcome would be the judge's decision to grant or deny, in full or in part. A claim or case outcome, on the other hand, refers to the disposition of a lawsuit, again in full or in part. My scope is civil only, though much of the analysis that follows could apply equally to criminal proceedings.

"Computationally driven" here refers to the use of statistical or machine learning models to detect patterns in past civil litigation data and exploit those patterns to predict, and to some extent explain, future outcomes. Just as actuaries compute the future risk of loss for insurance companies based on past claims data, so do outcome prediction tools attempt to compute the likelihood of future litigation events based on data gleaned from past court records.

In broad strokes, such tools take as their inputs a set of characteristics, also known as predictors, independent variables, or features, that describe the facts, legal claims, arguments, and authority, the people (judge, lawyers, litigants, expert witnesses), and the setting (location, court) of a case. Features might also come from external sources or be "engineered" by combining data. For example, the judge's gender and years on the bench might be features, as well as the number of times the lawyers in the case had previously appeared before the same judge, the judge's caseload, and local economic or crime data. Such information might be manually or computationally extracted from the unstructured text of legal documents and other sources – necessitating upstream text mining or natural language processing tasks – or might already be available in structured form.

These various features or case characteristics then become the inputs into one of many types of statistical or predictive models; the particular litigation outcome of interest is the target variable to be predicted.[8] When using such a tool, a lawyer would plug in the requested case characteristics and would receive an outcome prediction along with some measurement of error.

7.2. THEORY: ACCESS-TO-JUSTICE POTENTIAL

In theory, computationally driven outcome prediction, if good enough, can supplement, stretch, and reduce the cost of legal services by reducing outcome uncertainty. As Gillian Hadfield summarizes, uncertainty comes from several sources.[9] Sometimes the law is simply unclear. Other times, actors, whether police

[8] *See* Chapter 3 in this volume.

[9] Gillian K. Hadfield, *Weighing the Value of Vagueness: An Economic Perspective on Precision in the Law*, 81 Cal. L. Rev. 541 (1994).

officers, prosecutors, regulators, or courts, have deliberately been given discretion. Further, an individual may subjectively discount or increase the probability of liability due to "mistakes in the determination of factual issues, and errors in the identification of the applicable legal rule."[10] One way to resolve these uncertainties is to pay a lawyer for advice – in particular, a liability estimate.

Given a large enough training set, a predictive model may detect patterns in how courts have previously resolved vagueness and how officials have previously exercised discretion. Further, such a tool could correct the information deficits and asymmetries that may produce mistaken liability estimates. Outcome prediction tools might also obviate the need for legal representation entirely, allowing potential and actual litigants to estimate their own chances of success and proceed pro se. This could be a substantial boon for access to justice. Of course, even an outcome-informed pro se litigant may fail to navigate complex court procedures and norms successfully.[11] Fully opening the courthouse doors to self-represented litigants might also require simplification of court procedures. Still, outcome prediction tools might go a long way toward expanding access to justice, whether by serving litigants directly or by acting as a kind of force multiplier for lawyers and legal organizations, particularly those squaring off against better-resourced adversaries.[12]

A second way outcome prediction tools could, in theory, open up access to justice is by enhancing the ability of legal services providers to quantify, and manage, risk. Profit-driven lawyers, as distinguished from government-funded legal services lawyers, build portfolios of cases with an eye toward managing risk.[13] Outcome prediction tools may allow lawyers to allocate their resources more efficiently, wasting less money on losing cases and freeing up lawyer time and attention for more meritorious cases, or by constructing portfolios that balance lower- and higher-risk cases.

In addition, enterprising lawyers with a higher-risk appetite might use such tools to discover new areas of practice or potential claim types that folk wisdom would advise against.[14] To draw an example from my previous work, I studied the boom in wage-and-hour lawsuits in the early 2000s and identified as one driver of the

[10] *Id.*

[11] Bookman & Shanahan, *A Tale of Two Civil Procedures*, at 16–17; Rebecca L. Sandefur, *Elements of Professional Expertise: Understanding Relational and Substantive Expertise through Lawyers' Impact*, 80 Am. Soc. Rev. 909, 915–16 (2015).

[12] David Freeman Engstrom & Jonah B. Gelbach, *Legal Tech, Civil Procedure, and the Future of Adversarialism*, 169 U. Pa. L. Rev. 1001, 1072 (2020); John O. McGinnis & Russell G. Pearce, *The Great Disruption: How Machine Intelligence Will Transform the Role of Lawyers in the Delivery of Legal Services*, 82 Fordham L. Rev. 3041, 3049 (2014).

[13] Herbert M. Kritzer, *Contingency Fee Lawyers as Gatekeepers in the Civil Justice System*, 81 Judicature 22, 23 (1997) While Kritzer focuses on contingency-free practice, his core insight extends to cases brought under fee-shifting statutes or flat-fee arrangements as well, where lawyers are likewise balancing outlay of resources against probable recovery.

[14] Thanks to David Freeman Engstrom for suggesting this possibility.

litigation spike an influx of enterprising personal injury attorneys into wage-and-hour law.[15] One early mover was a South Florida personal injury attorney named Gregg Shavitz, who discovered his clients' unpaid wage claims by accident, became an overtime specialist, and converted his firm into one of the highest-volume wage-and-hour shops in the country. This was before the wide usage of litigation outcome prediction tools. However, one might imagine that more discoveries like Gregg Shavitz's could be enabled by computationally driven systems, rather than by happenstance, opening up representation for more clients with previously overlooked or under-resourced claim types.[16]

I return to, and complicate, this possibility in Section 7.5, where I raise concerns about outcome prediction tools' conservatism in defining winning and losing cases, which may reduce, rather than increase, access to justice – empirical questions that remain to be resolved.

7.3 PRACTICE: WHERE ARE WE NOW?

From theory, I now turn to practice, tracing the evolution and present state of litigation outcome prediction in scholarship, commercial applications, and tools developed specifically to serve low- and middle-income litigants. This Section also begins to introduce these tools' limitations in their present form, a topic that I explore more fully in Section 7.4.

7.3.1 *Scholarship*

Litigation outcome prediction is an active scholarly research area, characterized by experimentation with an array of different data sets, modeling approaches, and performance measures. Thus far, no single dominant approach has emerged.

In a useful article, Kevin Ashley traces the history of the field to the work of two academics who used a machine learning algorithm called k-nearest neighbors in the 1970s to forecast the outcome of Canadian real estate tax disputes.[17] Since then, academic work has flourished. In the United States, academic interest has focused,

[15] Charlotte S. Alexander, *Litigation Migrants*, 56 AM. BUS. L.J. 235 (2019).

[16] To carry the thought exercise further, perhaps third-party litigation financing firms could fund these sorts of risky case-selection strategies, which solo lawyers or small firms might otherwise be hesitant to adopt. Center on the Legal Profession, Harvard Law School, The Practice, Investing in Legal Futures, *Litig. Fin.*, Sept.–Oct. 2019.

[17] Kevin Ashley, *A Brief History of the Changing Roles of Case Prediction in AI and Law*, 36 LAW IN CONTEXT: A SOCIO-LEGAL JOURNAL 93, 96 (2019) (citing Ejan Mackaay & Pierre Robillard, *Predicting Judicial Decisions: The Nearest Neighbor Rule and Visual Representation of Case Patterns*, 3 DATENVERARBEITUNG IM RECHT 302 (1974)).

variously, on decisions by the US Supreme Court,[18] federal appellate courts,[19] federal district courts,[20] immigration court,[21] state trial courts,[22] and administrative agencies.[23] Case types studied include employment,[24] asylum,[25] tort and vehicular,[26] and trade secret misappropriation.[27] Other scholars outside the United States have, in turn, developed outcome prediction tools focused on the European Court of Human Rights,[28] the International Criminal Court,[29] French appeals courts,[30] the Supreme Court of the Philippines,[31] lending cases in China,[32] labor cases in Brazil,[33] public morality and freedom of expression cases in Turkey's Constitutional Court,[34] and Canadian employment and tax cases.[35] Some of this research has spun off into commercial products, discussed in the next section.

18 *See, e.g.*, Daniel Martin Katz, Michael J. Bommarito II & Josh Blackman, *A General Approach for Predicting the Behavior of the Supreme Court of the United States*, 12 PLoS ONE (2017).

19 *See, e.g.*, Sergio Galletta, Elliott Ash & Daniel L. Chen, *Measuring Judicial Sentiment: Methods and Application to U.S. Circuit Courts* (Aug. 19, 2021) (unpublished manuscript), https://ssrn.com/abstract=3415393.

20 Elizabeth C. Tippett et al., *Does Lawyering Matter? Predicting Judicial Decisions from Legal Briefs, and What That Means for Access to Justice*, 101 Texas L. Rev. (forthcoming 2022).

21 *See, e.g.*, Matthew Dunn et al., *Early Predictability of Asylum Court Decisions*, 2017 Proc. ACM Conf. on AI & Law.

22 *See, e.g.*, Devin J. McConnell et al., *Case-Level Prediction of Motion Outcomes in Civil Litigation*, 18 Proc. Int'l Conf. on A.I. & Law 99 (2021).

23 *See, e.g.*, Karl Branting et al., *Semi-Supervised Methods for Explainable Legal Prediction*, 17 Proc. Int'l Conf. on A.I. & Law 22 (2019).

24 Tippett et al., *Does Lawyering Matter?*.

25 Dunn et al., *Early Predictability of Asylum Court Decisions*.

26 McConnell et al., *Case-Level Prediction of Motion Outcomes*.

27 Kevin D. Ashley & Stefanie Brüninghaus, *Automatically Classifying Case Texts and Predicting Outcomes*, 17 A.I. L. 125 (2009).

28 *See, e.g.*, Nikolaos Aletras et al., *Predicting Judicial Decisions of the European Court of Human Rights: A Natural Language Processing Perspective*, 2(93) PeerJ Comput. Sci. (2016).

29 Fabien Tarissan & Raphaëlle Nollez-Goldbach, *Analysing the First Case of the International Criminal Court from a Network-Science Perspective*, 4 J. Complex Networks 616 (2016).

30 Paul Boniol et al., *Performance in the Courtroom: Automated Processing and Visualization of Appeal Court Decisions in France*, ArXiv (2020), https://arxiv.org/abs/2006.06251.

31 Michael Benedict L. Virtucio et al., *Predicting Decisions of the Philippine Supreme Court Using Natural Language Processing and Machine Learning*, 42 IEEE Int'l Conf. on Comput. Software & Applications 130 (2018).

32 Luyao Ma et al., *Legal Judgment Prediction with Multi-Stage Case Representation Learning in the Real Court Setting*, 44 Proc. Int'l ACM SIGIR Conf. on Rsch. & Dev. in Info. Retrieval 993 (2021).

33 Andre Lage-Freitas et al., *Predicting Brazilian Court Decisions*, arXiv (2019), https://arxiv.org/abs/1905.10348.

34 Mehmet Fatih Sert, Engin Yıldırım & İrfan Haşlak, *Using Artificial Intelligence to Predict Decisions of the Turkish Constitutional Court*, 2021 Soc. Sci. Comp. Rev. 1.

35 Maxime C. Cohen et al., *The Use of AI in Legal Systems: Determining Independent Contractor vs. Employee Status* (Jan. 28, 2022) (unpublished manuscript) https://ssrn.com/abstract=4013823; Yifei Yin, Farhana Zulkernine & Samuel Dahan, *Determining Worker Type from Legal Text Data Using Machine Learning*, 2020 IEEE Intl. Conf. on Dependable, Autonomic & Secure Computing; Benjamin Alarie et al., *Using Machine Learning to Predict Outcomes in Tax Law*, 58 Can. Bus. L.J. 231 (2016).

This scholarly work reflects all the strengths and weaknesses of the wider field. Though direct comparison among studies can be difficult given different datasets and performance measures, predictive performance has ranged from relatively modest marginal classification accuracy[36] to a very high F1 score of 98 percent in one study.[37]

That said, some high-performing academic approaches may suffer from research design flaws, as they appear to use the text of a court's description of the facts of a case and the laws cited to predict the court's ruling.[38] This is problematic, as judges or their clerks often write case descriptions and choose legal citations with preexisting knowledge of the ruling they will issue. It is no surprise that these case descriptions predict outcomes. Further, much academic work is limited in its generalizability by the narrow band of cases used to train and test predictive models. This is due to inaccessible or missing court data, especially in the United States, a problem discussed further in Section 7.4. Finally, some researchers give short shrift to explanation, in favor of prediction.[39] Though a model may perform well in forecasting results, its practical and tactical utility may be limited if lawyers seeking to make representation decisions do not know what drives the predictions and cannot square them with their mental models of the world. As discussed further in Section 7.4, explainable predictions are becoming the new norm, as interpretations are now available for even the most "black box" predictive models. For the moment, however, explainability remains a sticking point.

7.3.2 *Commercial Applications*

The commercial lay of the land is similar to the academic landscape, with substantial activity and disparate approaches focused on particular case types or litigation events.

36 *See, e.g.*, McConnell et al., *Case-Level Prediction of Motion Outcomes*, at 104 (reporting "maximum classification accuracy of 0.644" as compared to a naïve baseline of 0.501 using adaBoost, a decision-tree-based classification method and a variety of preprocessing steps applied to the input text).

37 *See, e.g.*, Octavia-Maria Şulea et al., *Exploring the Use of Text Classification in the Legal Domain*, ARXIV (2017), https://arxiv.org/abs/1710.09306 (reporting "results of 98% average F1 score in predicting a case ruling" of the French Supreme Court).

38 *See id.*

39 *Compare, e.g.*, Katz et al., *A General Approach for Predicting the Behavior of the Supreme Court* (focusing exclusively on predictive performance), *with* Ma et al., *Legal Judgment Prediction*, at 8–9 (presenting interpretability strategy for "black box" neural network predictions). This may be an unfair critique, as prediction and explanation can be two entirely separate goals. A classic example illustrates the difference: A ruler who wants to know whether to spend money for a rain dance to break a drought cares about causation. The same ruler who wants to know whether it will rain tomorrow so she can bring an umbrella cares only about prediction. Will it rain or not? For more discussion, see Jon Kleinberg et al., *Prediction Policy Problems*, 105 AM. ECON. REV. 491 (2015).

The Big Three legal research companies – LexisNexis, Westlaw, and Bloomberg Law – have all developed outcome prediction tools that sit within their existing suites of research and analysis tools. LexisNexis offers what they label "judge and court analytics" as well as "attorney and law firm analytics." In both spaces, the offerings are more descriptive than predictive – showing, for example, "a tally of total cases for a judge or court for a specific area of law to approximate experience on a motion like yours."[40] The predictive jump is left to the user, who decides whether to adopt the approximation as a prediction or to distinguish it from the case at hand. LexisNexis provides further predictive firepower in the form of an acquired start-up, LexMachina, which provides, among other output, estimates of judges' likelihood of granting or denying certain motions in certain case types.[41] Westlaw offers similar options in its litigation and precedent analytics tools,[42] as does Bloomberg Law in its litigation analytics suite.[43] Fastcase, a newer entrant into the space, offers a different approach, allowing subscribers to build their own bespoke predictive and descriptive analyses, using tools and methodologies drawn from a host of partner companies.[44]

A collection of smaller companies offers litigation outcome prediction focused on particular practice areas or litigation events. Docket Alarm, now owned by Fastcase, offers patent litigation analytics that produce "the likelihood of winning given a particular judge, technology area, law firm or party."[45] In Canada, Blue J Tax builds on the scholarly work described above to offer outcome prediction in tax disputes,[46] while in the United Kingdom companies like CourtQuant "predict [case] outcome and settlement probability."[47]

A final segment of the industry are law firms' and other players'[48] homegrown, proprietary tools. On the plaintiffs' side, giant personal injury firm Morgan & Morgan has developed "a 'Google-style' operation" in which the firm "evaluate[s] 'actionable data points' about personal injury settlements or court proceedings" and uses the insight to "work up a case accordingly – and . . . do that at scale."[49] Defense-

40 *Litigation Analytics*, LexisNexis, https://www.lexisnexis.com/en-us/products/lexis-plus/litigation-analytics.page.

41 Lex Machina, https://lexmachina.com/legal-analytics/.

42 *Litigation Analytics*, Westlaw Edge https://legal.thomsonreuters.com/en/products/westlaw-edge/litigation-analytics#compare; *Precedent Analytics*, Westlaw Edge, https://legal.thomsonreuters.com/en/insights/articles/introducing-precedent-analytics.

43 *Legal Analytics*, Bloomberg L., https://pro.bloomberglaw.com/legal-analytics/.

44 *AI Sandbox*, Fastcase, https://www.fastcase.com/sandbox/.

45 Docket Alarm, https://www.docketalarm.com/.

46 Blue J Tax, https://www.bluej.com/blue-j-tax.

47 CourtQuant, https://www.courtquant.com/about.

48 Here, legal operations service providers like Ernst and Young and other accounting and consulting firms, third-party litigation finance companies, and insurance companies that insure against litigation costs are all players that are invested in tech- and often AI-fueled outcome prediction. *See, e.g.*, Apex Litig. Fin., https://www.apexlitigation.com/.

49 Christine Schiffner, *Inside the "Google-Style" Tech Hub Driving Plaintiffs Firms' Growth*, Nat'l L.J. (Nov. 15, 2021), https://www.law.com/nationallawjournal/2021/11/15/inside-the-google-style-tech-hub-driving-plaintiffs-firms-growth/.

side firms are doing the same. Dentons, the world's largest firm, even spun off an independent analytics lab and venture firm to fund development in outcome prediction and other AI-enabled approaches to law.[50]

It is difficult to assess how well any of these tools performs, as access is expensive or unavailable, the feature sets used as inputs are not always clear, and the algorithms that power the predictions are hidden. I raise some concerns about commercial model design in Section 7.4 – in particular, reliance on lawyer identity as a predictor – and, as above, return to the perpetual problem of inaccessible and missing court data.

7.3.3 *Outcome Prediction for Low- and Middle-Income Litigants*

For reasons explored further below, examples are scarce of computationally driven litigation outcome prediction tools engineered specifically for the kinds of cases noted in this chapter's opening. Philadelphia's civil legal services provider, Community Legal Services, uses a tool called Expungement Generator (EG) to determine whether criminal record expungement is possible and assist in completing the paperwork.[51] The EG does not predict outcomes, but its automated approach enables efficiency gains for an organization that prepares thousands of expungement petitions per year.[52] Similarly, an application developed in the Family Law Clinic at Duquesne University School of Law prompts litigants in child support cases to answer a set of questions, which the tool then evaluates to determine "if there is a meritorious claim for appeal to be raised" under Pennsylvania law.[53] As with the EG, the Duquesne system does not appear to use machine learning techniques, but rather to apply a set of mechanical rules. The clinic plans prediction as a next step, however, and is developing a tool that analyzes winning arguments in appellate cases in order to guide users' own arguments.[54]

7.4. PRESENT LIMITS

Having surveyed the state of the outcome prediction field, I now step back and assess its limits. As David Freeman Engstrom and Jonah Gelbach rightly concluded in earlier work: "[L]egal tech tools will arrive sooner, and advance most rapidly, in legal

50 *Dentons Launches Nextlaw Labs and Creates Legal Business Accelerator*, DENTONS (May 19, 2015) https://www.dentons.com/en/about-dentons/news-events-and-awards/news/2015/may/dentons-launches-nextlaw-labs-creates-legal-business-accelerator.

51 NateV, *Expungement-Generator*, GITHUB, https://github.com/NateV/Expungement-Generator.

52 *Id.*; Rana Fayez, *Meet the Disruptor: Michael Holland*, PHILA. CITIZEN (May 3, 2016), https://thephiladelphiacitizen.org/disruptor-michael-hollander-expungement-generator/.

53 Katherine L. Norton, *Mind the Gap: Technology as a Lifeline for Pro Se Child Custody Appeals*, 58 DUQ. L. REV. 82, 91 (2020).

54 *Id.*

areas where data is abundant, regulated conduct takes repetitive and stereotypical forms, legal rules are inherently stable, and case volumes are such that a repeat player stands to gain financially by investing."[55] Many of the commercial tools highlighted above fit this profile. Tax-oriented products exploit relatively stable rules; Morgan & Morgan's internal case evaluation system exploits the firm's extraordinarily high case volumes.

Yet, as noted above, data's "abundance" is an open question, as is data quality. Methodological problems may also hinder these tools' development. In the access to justice domain, the questions of investment incentives and financial gains loom large as well. The remainder of this Section addresses these limitations.

7.4.1 *Data Limitations*

Predictive algorithms require access to large amounts of data from previous court cases for model training, but such bulk data is not widely or freely available in the United States from the state or federal courts or from administrative agencies that have an adjudicatory function.[56] The Big Three have invested substantial funds in compiling private troves of court documents and judicial decisions, and jealously guard those resources with high user fees, restrictive terms and conditions, and threatened and actual litigation.[57]

Data inaccessibility creates serious problems for outcome prediction tools designed to meet the legal needs of low- and middle-income litigants.[58] Much of this litigation occurs in state courts, where data is sometimes poorly managed and siloed in multiple systems.[59] Moreover, there is little money in practice areas like eviction defense and public benefits appeals, in which clients, by definition, are poor. Thus, data costs are high, and financial incentives for investment in research and development are low.

Even the products offered by the monied Big Three, however, suffer from data problems. With large companies separately assembling their own private data repositories, coverage varies widely, producing remarkable disagreement about basic facts. A recent study revealed that the answers supplied to the question "How many opinions on motions for summary judgment has Judge Barbara Lynn (N.D. Tex.) issued in patent cases?" ranged from nine to thirty-two, depending on the legal

55 Engstrom & Gelbach, *Legal Tech*, at 1029.

56 Charlotte S. Alexander & Mohammad Javad Feizollahi, *On Dragons, Caves, Teeth, and Claws: Legal Analytics and the Problem of Court Data Access*, *in* Computational Legal Studies: The Promise and Challenge of Data-Driven Legal Research (Ryan Whalen ed., 2020).

57 Alaina Lancaster, *Judge Rejects ROSS Intelligence's Dismissal Attempt of Thomson Reuters Suit over Westlaw Content*, Law.com (Mar. 29, 2021), https://www.law.com/therecorder/2021/03/29/judge-rejects-ross-intelligences-dismissal-attempt-of-thomson-reuters-suit-over-westlaw-content/.

58 *See* Chapters 6, 14, and 15 in this volume.

59 *See* Chapter 13 in this volume.

research product used.[60] This is an existential problem for the future of litigation outcome prediction, as predictions are only as good as the data on which they are built.[61]

A final data limitation centers on the challenges of causal explanation. Even if explainable modeling approaches are used, the case characteristics that appear to be the strongest predictors of outcomes may not, in fact, be actionable. For instance, when a predictive tool relies on attorney identity as a feature, the model's prediction may actually be free-riding on the attorney's own screening and selection decisions. In other words, if the presence of Lawyer A in a case is strongly predictive of a win for her clients, Lawyer A's skills as a litigator may not be the true cause. The omitted, *more* predictive variable is likely the strength of the merits, and Lawyer A's skill at assessing those merits up-front. Better data could enable better model construction, avoiding these kinds of proxy variable traps.

7.4.2 *Methodological Limitations*

Sitting atop these data limitations are two important methodological limitations. First, as noted above, even if predictive tools do a good job of forecasting the probable outcome of a litigation event, they may only poorly explain *why* the predicted outcome is likely to occur. Explanation is important for a number of related reasons, among them engendering confidence in predictions, enabling bias and error detection, and respecting the dignity of people affected by prediction.[62] Indeed, the European Union's General Data Protection Regulation (GDPR) has established what some scholars have labeled a "right to an explanation," consisting of a right "not to be subject to a decision based solely on automated processing" and various rights to notice of data collection.[63] Though researchers are actively developing explainable AI that can identify features' specific importance to a prediction and generate counterfactual predictions if features change value,[64] the field has yet to converge on a single set of explainability practices, and commercial approaches vary widely.

60 Sean La Roque Doherty, *Not All Litigation Analytics Products Are Created Equal*, A.B.A. J. (Aug. 1, 2020), https://www.abajournal.com/magazine/article/analytics-products-offer-different-results-depending-on-data-sources-quality-and-the-types-of-analytics-and-reports-they-provide.

61 Engstrom and Engstrom's contribution to this volume identifies yet another data limitation: the absence of reliable data on cases and claims that are settled, where the contents of the settlement are unavailable. *See* Chapter 6 in this volume.

62 Margot E. Kaminski, *The Right to Explanation, Explained*, 34 Berkeley Tech. L.J. 189 (2019).

63 *Id.*

64 *See, e.g.*, Scott M. Lundberg et al., *From Local Explanations to Global Understanding with Explainable AI for Trees*, 2 Nature Mach. Intelligence 56 (2020); *What Is Explainability?* Alibi, https://docs.seldon.io/projects/alibi/en/stable/overview/high_level.html#what-is-explainability.

Second, outcome prediction is limited by machine and deep learning algorithms' inability to reason by analogy. Legal reasoning depends on analogical thinking: the ability to align one set of facts to another and guess at the likely application of the law, given the factual divergences. However, teaching AI to reason by analogy is a cutting-edge area of computer science research, and it is far from well established. As computer scientist Melanie Mitchell explains, "'Today's state-of-the-art neural networks are very good at certain tasks . . . but they're very bad at taking what they've learned in one kind of situation and transferring it to another' – the essence of analogy."[65] There is a famous analogical example in text analytics, where a natural language processing technique known as word embedding, when trained on an enormous corpus of real-world text, is able to produce the answer "queen" when presented with the formula "king minus man plus woman."[66] The jump from this parlor trick to full-blown legal reasoning, though, is substantial.

In short, scaling up computationally driven litigation outcome prediction tools in a way that would fill the civil justice gap would require access to more and better data and methodological advances. Making bulk federal and state court and administrative agency data and records freely and easily accessible would be a very good step.[67] Marshaling resources to support methods and tool development would be another. Foundation funding is already a common ingredient in efforts to fill the civil justice gap. I propose that large law firms pitch in as well. All firms on the AmLaw 100 could pledge a portion of their pro bono budgets toward the development of litigation outcome prediction tools to be used in pro bono and low bono settings. The ABA Foundation might play a coordinating and convening role, as it is already committed to access-to-justice initiatives. Such an effort could have a much broader impact than firms' existing pro bono activities, which tend to focus on representation in single cases. It might also jump-start additional interest from the Big Three and other commercial competitors, who might invest more money in improving algorithms' predictive performance and spin off free or low-cost versions of their existing suites of tools.

7.5 UNINTENDED CONSEQUENCES

Time will tell whether, when, and how the data and methodological problems identified in Section 7.4 will be solved. Assuming that they are, and litigation

65 John Pavlus, *The Computer Scientist Training AI to Think with Analogies*, Quanta Mag. (July 14, 2021), https://www.quantamagazine.org/melanie-mitchell-trains-ai-to-think-with-analogies-20210714/; *see also* Katie Atkinson & Trevor Bench-Capon, *Reasoning with Legal Cases: Analogy or Rule Application?* 17 Proc. Int'l Conf. on Artificial Intelligence & L. 12 (June 2019).

66 Emerging Technology from the arXiv, *King – Man + Woman = Queen: The Marvelous Mathematics of Computational Linguistics*, MIT Tech. Review (Sept. 17, 2015), https://www.technologyreview.com/2015/09/17/166211/king-man-woman-queen-the-marvelous-mathematics-of-computational-linguistics/.

67 Adam R. Pah et al., *How to Build a More Open Justice System*, 369(6500) Science (2020).

outcome prediction tools can reliably generate highly reliable forecasts, there still may be reason for caution.

This Section identifies two possible unintended consequences of outcome prediction tools, which could develop alongside the salutatory access to justice effects described in Section 7.2: harm to would-be litigants denied representation whose claims are novel or less viable according to predictive tools, and harm to the common law system as a whole.

Here, the assumption is that such tools have access to ample data, account for all relevant variables, and are transparent and explainable – in other words, the tools work as intended to learn from existing patterns in civil litigation outcomes and reproduce those patterns as outcome predictions. Yet it is this very reproductive nature that is cause for concern.

7.5.1 *Harms to Would-Be Litigants*

Consider the facts of *Elisa B. v. Superior Court*,[68] a case decided by the California Supreme Court in 2005. Emily B. sought child support from her estranged partner, Elisa B., for twins whom Emily had conceived via artificial insemination of her eggs during her relationship with Elisa. If Emily walked into a lawyer's office seeking help with her child support action, the lawyer might be interested in the case's viability: How often have similar fact patterns come before California courts, and what was their outcome? The answers might inform the lawyer's decision about whether to offer representation.

In real life, this case was one of first impression in California. The governing law, the Uniform Parentage Act, referred to "mother" and "father" as the potential parents.[69] Searching for relevant precedent, the *Elisa B.* court reasoned by analogy from previous cases that involved, variously, three potential parents (one man and two women), non-biological fathers, non-biological mothers, and a woman who raised her half-brother as her son.[70] From this and other precedent, the court cobbled together a new legal rule that required Elisa B. to pay child support for her and Emily B.'s children.

I am doubtful that an outcome prediction tool would have reached this same conclusion. The number of analogical jumps that the court made would seem to be outside the capabilities of machine and deep learning, even assuming methodological advancement.[71] Further, judges' decisions about what prior caselaw to draw upon and how many analogical leaps to make may be influenced by factors like

68 Elisa B. v. Sup. Ct., 117 P.3d 660 (Cal. 2005).

69 *Id.* at 664 ("The UPA defines the '[p]arent and child relationship' as 'the legal relationship existing between a child and the child's natural or adoptive parents' .... The term includes the mother and child relationship and the father and child relationship.").

70 *Id.* at 667.

71 Atkinson & Bench-Capon, *Reasoning with Legal Cases.*

ideology and public opinion, which could be difficult to model well. Emily B.'s claim would likely receive a very low viability score.[72]

A similar cautionary tale comes from my own previous work with Camille Gear Rich and Zev Eigen on attorneys' non-computational assessments of claim viability. We documented plaintiffs' employment attorneys' dim view of the likelihood of success for employment discrimination claims and their shifting of case selection decisions away from discrimination and toward easier-to-prove wage-and-hour claims.[73] One result of this shift, we observed, was that even litigants with meritorious discrimination claims were unable to find legal representation. That work happened in 2014 and 2015, before litigation outcome prediction tools were widely available, and I am not aware of subsequent empirical studies on the effect of such tools on lawyers' intake decisions. Yet if lawyers were already using their intuition to learn from past cases and predict future outcomes, pre-AI, machine and deep learning tools could just cement these same patterns in place.

Thus, in this view, as civil litigation outcomes become more predictable, claims become commoditized. Outlier claims and clients like Emily B. may become less representable, much like high-loss risks become less insurable. While access to justice on the whole may increase, the courthouse doors may be effectively closed to some classes of potential clients who seek representation for novel or disfavored legal claims or defenses.[74]

Further, to the extent that representation is denied to would-be litigants because of their own negative personal histories, ingested by a model as data points, litigation outcome prediction tools can reduce people to their worst past acts and prevent them from changing course. Take as an example a tenant with an old criminal record trying to fight an eviction, whose past conviction reduces her chance of winning according to an algorithmic viability assessment. This may be factually accurate – her criminal record may *actually* make eviction defense more challenging – but a creative lawyer might see other aspects of her case that an algorithmic assessment might miss. By reducing people to feature sets and exploiting the features that are most predictive of outcomes, but perhaps least representative of people's full selves, computational tools enact dignitary harm. In the context of low-income

72 Prediction tools become like Oliver Wendell Holmes' Vermont justice: "There is a story of a Vermont justice of the peace before whom a suit was brought by one farmer against another for breaking a churn. The justice took time to consider, and then said that he has looked through the statutes and could find nothing about churns, and gave judgment for the defendant." Oliver Wendell Holmes, Jr., *The Path of the Law*, 10 Harv. L. Rev. 457 (1897).

73 Charlotte S. Alexander, Zev Eigen & Camille Gear Rich, *Post-Racial Hydraulics: The Hidden Dangers of the Universal Turn*, 91 N.Y.U. L. Rev. 1 (2016).

74 A future of "legal singularity," in which all outcomes are perfectly predictable, is not necessary for my argument here. Benjamin Alarie, *The Path of the Law: Towards Legal Singularity*, 66 U. Toronto L.J. 443 (2016). Even prediction that works well for some subclass of cases will change lawyers' preferences for those cases over other, less certain cases. This has consequences for those clients' civil legal needs.

litigants facing serious and potentially destabilizing court proceedings, and who are algorithmically denied legal representation, such tools can also cause substantial economic and social harm, reducing social mobility and locking people into place.

Indeed, machine and deep learning methods are inherently prone to what some researchers have called "value lock-in."[75] All data is historical in the sense that it captures points in time that have passed; all machine and deep learning algorithms find patterns in historical data as a way to predict the future. This methodological design reifies past practices and locks in past patterns. As machine learning researcher Abeba Birhane and her collaborators point out, then, machine learning is not "value-neutral."[76] And as AI pioneer Joseph Weizenbaum observed, "the computer has from the beginning been a fundamentally conservative force which solidified existing power: in place of fundamental social changes . . . the computer renders technical solutions that allow existing power hierarchies to remain intact."[77] It is no accident that the anecdotes above involve a lesbian couple, employment discrimination claimants, and a tenant with a criminal record: the fear is that would-be litigants like these with the least power historically become further disempowered at the hands of computational methods.

Yet as Section 7.2 suggested, a different story might also be possible: More accurate predictions might enable lawyers to fill their case portfolios with low-risk sure winners as hedges when taking on riskier cases like *Elisa B.*, or might help them discover and invest in previously under-resourced practice areas. At this stage, whether predictive tools would increase or decrease representation for outlier claims and clients is an open empirical question, which researchers and policy makers should work to answer as data and methods improve and outcome prediction tools become more widely used.

7.5.2 *Harms to the System*

I turn now to the second potential harm caused by computationally driven litigation outcome prediction: harm to the common law system itself.[78] As Charles Barzun explains, common-law reasoning "contains seeds of radicalism [in that] the case-by-case process by which the law develops means it is always open to revision. And even though its official position is one of incremental change . . . doctrine [is] constantly

[75] *See, e.g.*, Laura Weidinger et al., *Ethical and Social Risks of Harm from Language Models*, ARXIV (2021), https://arxiv.org/abs/2112.04359.

[76] Abeba Birhane et al., *The Values Encoded in Machine Learning Research*, ARXIV (2021), https://arxiv.org/abs/2106.15590.

[77] *Id.* (citing JOSEPH WEIZENBAUM, COMPUTER POWER AND HUMAN REASON: FROM JUDGMENT TO CALCULATION (1976)).

[78] David Freeman Engstrom, *Private Litigation's Pathways: Lessons from Qui Tam Enforcement*, 114 COLUM. L. REV. 1913, 1934 (2014) ("[P]rivate enforcers will tend to push into statutory and regulatory interstices.").

vulnerable to being upended."[79] Barzun points to Catharine MacKinnon's invention of sexual harassment doctrine out of Title VII's cloth as an example of a "two-way process of interaction" between litigants, representing their real-world experience, and the courts, interpreting the law, in a shared creative process "in which the meaning and scope of application of the statute changes over time."[80]

If lawyers rely too heavily on litigation outcome prediction tools, which reproduce past patterns, the stream of new fact presentations and legal arguments flowing into the courts dries up. Litigation outcome prediction tools may produce a sort of super stare decisis by narrowing lawyers' case selection preferences to only those case, claim, and client types that have previously appeared and been successful in court. Yet stare decisis is only one aspect of our common law system. Another competing characteristic is flexibility: A regular influx of new cases with new fact patterns and legal arguments enables the law to innovate and adapt. In other words, noise – as differentiated from signal – is a feature of the common law, not a bug. Outcome prediction tools that are too good at picking up signals and ignoring noise eliminate the structural benefits of the noise, and privilege stare decisis over flexibility by shaping the flow of cases that make their way to court.

Others, particularly Engstrom and Gelbach, have made this point, suggesting that prediction

> comes at a steep cost, draining the law of its capacity to adapt to new developments or to ventilate legal rules in formal, public interpretive exercises .... The system also loses its legitimacy as a way to manage social conflict when the process of enforcing collective value judgments plays out in server farms rather than a messy deliberative and adjudicatory process, even where machine predictions prove perfectly accurate.[81]

The danger is that law becomes endogenous and ossified. "Endogenous," to repurpose a concept introduced by Lauren Edelman, means that the law's inputs become the same as its outputs and "the content and meaning of law is determined within the social field that it is designed to regulate."[82] "Ossified," to borrow from Cynthia Estlund, means that the law becomes "essentially sealed off ... both from democratic revision and renewal from local experimentation and innovation."[83]

[79] Charles L. Barzun, *The Common Law and Critical Theory*, 92 Colo. L. Rev. 1, 13 (2021).
[80] *Id.* at 8.
[81] Engstrom & Gelbach, *Legal Tech*, at 1036–37.
[82] Lauren B. Edelman, Christopher Uggen & Howard S. Erlanger, *The Endogeneity of Legal Regulation: Grievance Procedures as Rational Myth*, 105 Am. J. Socio. 406 (1999).
[83] Cynthia L. Estlund, *The Ossification of American Labor Law*, 102 Colum. L. Rev. 1527, 1530 (2002). The same points have been made in connection with grant funding for scientific research, where the fear is that innovation is stifled because researchers hew too closely to the example of previous successfully funded proposals. *See, e.g.*, Scott O. Lilienfeld, *Psychology's*

7.6 NEXT STEPS

As noted above, whether any of the unintended consequences outlined above will come to pass – and, indeed, whether access to justice improvements will come to pass as well – turns on empirical questions. Given the problems and limitations identified in Section 7.4, will litigation outcome prediction tools actually work well enough to achieve either their potential benefits or cause their potential harms? My assessment of the present state of the field suggests there is a long way to go before we reach either set of outcomes. But as the field matures, we can build in safeguards against the endogeneity risks and harms I identify above through technical, organizational, and policy interventions.

First, on the technical side, computer and data scientists, and the funders who make their work possible, should invest heavily in improving algorithmic analogical reasoning. Without the ability to reason by analogy, outcome predictors not only will miss an array of possible positive predictions, but they will also be systematically biased against fact patterns like Emily B.'s, which present issues of first impression.

Further on the technical front, developers could purposefully over-train predictive algorithms on novel, but successful, fact patterns and legal arguments in order to nudge the system off its path and make positive predictions possible even for cases that fall outside the norm. This idea is adapted from OpenAI's work in nudging its state-of-the-art language model, GPT-3, away from its "harmful biases, such as outputting discriminatory racial text" learned from its training corpus, by over-exposing it to counter texts.[84]

Technical fixes focus on outcome prediction tools' production side. Organizational fixes target the tools' consumers: the lawyers, law firms, and other legal organizations that might use them to influence case selection. I propose here that no decision should be made exclusively on the basis of algorithmic output. This guards against the dignitary and other real harms described above, as would-be litigants are treated as full people rather than feature sets. This also parallels the GDPR's explanation mandate, though I suggest it here as an organizational practice that is baked into legal organizations' decision-making processes.[85]

Finally, I turn to policy. The story above assumes a profit-driven lawyer as the user of outcome prediction tools. Of course, there are other possible motivations for a lawyer's case selection decisions, such as seeking affirmatively to establish a new interpretation of the law or right a historic wrong. These cause lawyers, from all points on the ideological spectrum, may be particularly likely to take on seemingly

Replication Crisis and the Grant Culture: Righting the Ship, 12 PERSPECTIVES ON PSYCH. SCI. 660 (2017).

84 Irene Solaiman & Christy Dennison, *Process for Adapting Language Models to Society (PALMS) with Values-Targeted Datasets*, ARXIV (2021), https://arxiv.org/abs/2106.10328.

85 Kaminski, *The Right to Explanation, Explained*; *see also* CATHY O'NEILL, WEAPONS OF MATH DESTRUCTION 205 (2016) (proposing a Hippocratic Oath for data scientists).

high-risk claim or party types, which receive low computationally determined viability scores. Government lawyers, too, may function as cause lawyers, pushing legal arguments, in accordance with administration position, that diverge from courts' past practices. Government agencies should study trends in private attorneys' use of litigation outcome prediction tools in the areas in which they regulate, and should make their own case selection decisions to fill gaps in representation.[86]

7.7 CONCLUSION

This chapter has explored the consequences of computationally driven litigation outcome prediction tools for the civil justice system, with a focus on increasing access to justice. It has mapped the current state of the outcome prediction field in academic work and commercial applications, as well as in pro bono and low bono practice settings. It has also raised concerns about unintended consequences for litigants and for our legal system as a whole.

I conclude that there is plenty of reason for "techno-optimism," to use Tanina Rostain's term, about the potential for computationally driven litigation outcome prediction tools to close the civil justice gap.[87] However, reaching that optimistic future, while also guarding against potential harms, will require substantially more money and data, continued methodological improvement, careful organizational implementation, and strategic deployment of government resources.

86 For an analogous use of government resources to fill private enforcement gaps, see David Weil, *Improving Workplace Conditions through Strategic Enforcement*, Russell Sage Found. (2010), https://www.russellsage.org/research/report/strategic-enforcement.

87 Tanina Rostain, *Techno-Optimism and Access to the Legal System*, 148 Daedalus 93 (2019).

8

Toward the Participatory MDL

A Low-Tech Step to Promote Litigant Autonomy

Todd Venook and Nora Freeman Engstrom

Debate about legal tech and the future of civil litigation typically focuses on high-technology innovations. This volume is no exception, and with good reason. Advanced technologies are spreading (or seem poised to spread) throughout the legal landscape, from discovery to online dispute resolution (ODR) to trials, and from individual lawsuits to aggregate litigation. These tools' practical utility and social value are rightly contested.[1]

But in some contexts, straightforward, *low-tech* solutions hold tremendous promise – and also demand attention. Here, we zero in on a modest tool that bears upon the management of multidistrict litigation, or MDL. In particular, we explore how improved online communication could enhance litigant autonomy, usher in a more "participatory" MDL, and supply a platform for further innovation.[2]

The MDL statute – 28 U.S.C. §1407 – is a procedural vehicle through which filed federal cases involving common questions of fact, such as a mass tort involving asbestos or defective pharmaceuticals, are swept together into a single "transferee" court, ostensibly for pretrial proceedings (though very often, in reality, for pretrial

Both authors are grateful to Catherina Yue Xu for excellent research assistance.

[1] A growing discourse centers on the use of cutting-edge technology in aggregate litigation. *See, e.g.*, Peter N. Salib, *Artificially Intelligent Class Actions*, 100 Tex. L. Rev. 519, 544 (2022) (suggesting that machine learning algorithms could resolve individual questions and help satisfy the predominance requirement of Rule 23); Alexander W. Aiken, *Class Action Notice in the Digital Age*, 165 U. Pa. L. Rev. 967, 997 (2017) (urging courts and parties to consider using machine learning to identify and notify otherwise-unknown class members).

[2] Here, we play off Elizabeth J. Cabraser & Samuel Issacharoff, *The Participatory Class Action*, 92 N.Y.U. L. Rev. 846 (2017). In that piece, Cabraser and Issacharoff argue that technological and jurisprudential change have diminished the "absence" of class members because (inter alia) members are kept informed by social media, case-specific websites, and, sometimes, their individual attorneys. The insight is important, but class actions are today largely a dead letter (at least in the mass tort sphere). Recognizing that reality, we apply some of their insights to where mass tort cases are more frequently litigated: the MDL.

adjudication or settlement).[3] Thirty years ago, MDLs were barely a blip on our collective radar. As of 1991, these actions made up only about 1 percent of pending civil cases.[4] Now, by contrast, MDLs make up fully half of all new federal civil filings.[5] This means that *one out of every two litigants* who files a claim in federal court might not really be fully represented by the lawyer she chose, get the venue she chose, or remain before the judge to whom her suit was initially assigned. Instead, her case will be fed into the MDL system and processed elsewhere, in a long, labyrinthian scheme that is often far afield and out of her sight.[6]

Given these statistics, there's no real question that the MDL has risen – and that its rise is significantly altering the American system of civil justice. There is little consensus, however, as to whether the MDL's ascent is a good or bad thing. Some celebrate the MDL for promoting judicial efficiency, addressing harms that are national in scope, channeling claims to particularly able and expert advocates, creating economies of scale, and increasing access to justice – giving *some* judicial process to those who, without MDL, would have no ability to vindicate their essential rights.[7]

Others, meanwhile, find much to dislike. Critics frequently seize on MDLs' relatively slow speed,[8] their heavy reliance on repeat play,[9] and the free-wheeling judicial "ad hocery" that has become the device's calling card.[10] Beyond that, critics worry that the device distorts the traditional attorney-client relationship and subverts

[3] For an overview of the MDL process, see Eldon E. Fallon et al., *Bellwether Trials in Multidistrict Litigation*, 82 TUL. L. REV. 2323, 2327 (2008). For the infrequency of remands, see Abbe R. Gluck & Elizabeth Chamblee Burch, *MDL Revolution*, 96 N.Y.U. L. REV. 1, 16 (2021) (noting that more than 97 percent of cases centralized via MDL are resolved without remand).

[4] Nora Freeman Engstrom, *The Lessons of* Lone Pine, 129 YALE L.J. 2, 7 (2019).

[5] Elizabeth Chamblee Burch & Margaret S. Williams, *Perceptions of Justice in Multidistrict Litigation: Voices from the Crowd*, CORNELL L. REV. (forthcoming 2022) (manuscript at 2) ("[O]ne out of every two civil cases filed in federal court in 2020 was part of an MDL.").

[6] As Beth Burch puts it: "[Litigants] select a lawyer and a forum, but like Dorothy in the Wizard of Oz, they may quickly find themselves on unfamiliar turf." ELIZABETH CHAMBLEE BURCH, MASS TORT DEALS: BACKROOM BARGAINING IN MULTIDISTRICT LITIGATION 124 (2019).

[7] For certain advantages, see Andrew D. Bradt, *The Long Arm of Multidistrict Litigation*, 59 WM. & MARY L. REV. 1165, 1234–35 (2018); Abbe R. Gluck, *Unorthodox Civil Procedure: Modern Multidistrict Litigation's Place in the Textbook Understandings of Procedure*, 165 U. PA. L. REV. 1669, 1676, 1696 (2017).

[8] MDLs "last almost four times as long as the average civil case." Burch & Williams, *Perceptions of Justice in Multidistrict Litigation*, at 6; *see also* Fallon et al., *Bellwether Trials in Multidistrict Litigation*, at 2330 (arguing that the "excessive delay . . . sometimes associated with traditional MDL practice . . . cannot be defended").

[9] For criticism of repeat play, see Elizabeth Chamblee Burch & Margaret S. Williams, *Repeat Players in Multidistrict Litigation: The Social Network*, 102 CORNELL L. REV. 1445, 1453 (2017). For a defense, see generally Andrew D. Bradt & D. Theodore Rave, *It's Good to Have the "Haves" on Your Side: A Defense of Repeat Players in Multidistrict Litigation*, 108 GEO. L.J. 73 (2019).

[10] For a compilation of scholarly critiques, see Engstrom, *Lone Pine*, at 9 n.21.

litigant autonomy.[11] Critics fear that aggregation alters traditional screening patterns, which can unleash a "vacuum cleaner effect" and ultimately lead to the inclusion of claims of dubious merit.[12] And critics note that the device has seemingly deviated from its intended design: The MDL was supposed to aggregate cases for *pretrial* proceedings. So, the status quo – where trials are rare and transfer of a case back to a plaintiff's home judicial district is exceptional – means, some say, that the MDL has strayed off script.[13]

Stepping back, one can see: The MDL has certain advantages and disadvantages. Furthermore, and critically, *many MDL drawbacks are baked in*. There are certain compromises we *must make* if we want the efficiencies and access benefits MDLs supply. Aggregation (and, with it, *some* loss of litigant autonomy) is an essential and defining feature of the MDL paradigm. The same may be said for judicial innovation, the need to adapt the traditional attorney-client relationship, or the fact that some lawyers are tapped to lead MDLs in a selection process that will, inevitably, consign some able and eager advocates to the sidelines.

Recognizing these unavoidable trade-offs, in our own assessment, we ask subtly different and more targeted questions. We don't hazard to assess whether MDLs, on balance, are good or bad. Nor do we even assess whether particular MDL features (such as procedural improvisation) are good or bad. Instead, we ask two more modest questions: (1) Do contemporary MDLs have *avoidable* drawbacks and (2) if so, can *those* be addressed? In this analysis, we zero in on just one MDL drawback that is both practically and doctrinally consequential: MDL's restriction of litigant autonomy. And we further observe: Though *some* loss of litigant autonomy is an inevitable and inescapable by-product of aggregation and is therefore entirely understandable (the yin to aggregation's yang), the *present*-day MDL may be *more* alienating and involve a larger loss of autonomy than is actually necessary. As explained in Section 8.1, that is a potentially large problem. But, we also argue, it is a problem that, with a little ingenuity, courts, policymakers, scholars, and litigators can practically mitigate.

The remainder of this chapter proceeds in three Parts. Section 8.1 sets the scene by focusing on individual autonomy. In particular, Section 8.1.1 explains why autonomy matters, while Section 8.1.2 draws on MDL plaintiff survey data recently compiled by Elizabeth Burch and Margaret Williams to query whether MDL procedures might compromise litigant autonomy more than is strictly necessary.

[11] *E.g.*, Judith Resnik, *Procedural Innovations, Sloshing Over: A Comment on Deborah Hensler, "A Glass Half Full, A Glass Half Empty: The Use of Alternative Dispute Resolution in Mass Personal Injury Litigation,"* 73 Tex. L. Rev. 1627, 1641 (1995) ("In a large-scale mass tort, the act of consolidating the individual cases into a jumbo lawsuit risks breaking individual attorney-client relationships.").

[12] Engstrom, *Lone Pine*, at 24–25.

[13] As noted at *supra* note 3, more than 97 percent of cases centralized via MDL are resolved without remand. For criticism of that fact, see, e.g., Fallon et al., *Bellwether Trials in Multidistrict Litigation*, at 2330.

Then, to assess whether transferee courts are currently doing what they practically can to promote autonomy by keeping litigants up-to-date and well-informed, Section 8.2 offers the results of our own systematic study of current court-run MDL websites. This analysis reveals that websites exist but are deficient in important respects. In particular, court websites are hard to find and often outdated. They lack digested, litigant-focused content and are laden with legalese. And they rarely offer litigants opportunities to attend hearings and status conferences remotely (from their home states). In light of these deficiencies, Section 8.3 proposes a modest set of changes that might practically improve matters. These tweaks will not revolutionize MDL processes. But they could further litigants' legitimate interests in information, with little risk and at modest cost. In so doing, they seem poised to increase litigant autonomy – "low-tech tech," to be sure, but with high potential reach.

8.1 INDIVIDUAL AUTONOMY, EVEN IN THE AGGREGATE: WHY IT MATTERS AND WHAT WE KNOW

8.1.1 *Why Individual Autonomy Matters*

Litigant autonomy is a central and much-discussed concern of any adjudicatory design, be it individualized or aggregate. And, when assessing MDLs, individual autonomy is especially critical; indeed, its existence (or, conversely, its absence) goes to the heart of MDL's legitimacy. That's so because, if litigants swept into MDLs truly retain their individual autonomy – and preserve their ability meaningfully to participate in judicial processes – then the source of the MDL's legitimacy is clear. On the other hand, to the extent consolidation into an MDL means that individual litigants necessarily and inevitably sacrifice their individual autonomy and forfeit their ability meaningfully to participate in judicial processes (and offer, or withhold, authentic consent to a settlement agreement), the MDL mechanism sits on much shakier ground.[14]

On paper, that is not a problem: MDLs, as *formally* conceived, do little to undercut the autonomy of individual litigants. In theory, at least, MDLs serve only to streamline and expedite pretrial processes; they (again, in theory) interfere little, if at all, with lawyer-client communication, the allocation of authority within the lawyer-client relationship, or the client's ability to accept or reject the defendant's offer of settlement. That formal framework makes it acceptable to furnish MDL plaintiffs (unlike absent class members, say) with few special procedural

[14] *See* Andrew D. Bradt & D. Theodore Rave, *The Information-Forcing Role of the Judge in Multidistrict Litigation*, 105 CAL. L. REV. 1259, 1264 (2017) (explaining that MDLs derive their legitimacy, in large part, from the notion that the individual retains "ultimate control over her claim," and further observing that the MDL "is ultimately grounded on premises of individual claimant autonomy").

protections.[15] It is thought that, even in an MDL, our old workhorses – Model Rules of Professional Conduct 1.4 (demanding candid attorney-client communication), 1.7 (policing conflicts), 1.2(a) (clarifying the allocation of authority and specifying "that a lawyer shall abide by a client's decisions concerning the objectives of representation"), 1.16 (limiting attorneys' ability to withdraw), and 1.8(g) (regulating aggregate settlements) – can ensure the adequate protection of clients.

In contemporary practice, however, MDLs are much more than a pretrial aggregation device.[16] And, it is not necessarily clear that in *this* system – characterized by infrequent remand to the transferor court, prescribed and cookie-cutter settlement advice, and heavy-handed attorney withdrawal provisions – our traditional ethics rules continue to cut it.[17] Indeed, some suggest that the status quo so thoroughly compromises litigant autonomy that it represents a denial of due process, as litigants are conscripted into a system "in which their substantive rights will be significantly affected, if not effectively resolved, by means of a shockingly sloppy, informal, and often secretive process in which they have little or no right to participate, and in which they have very little say."[18]

Individual autonomy is thus the hinge. To the extent it mostly endures, and to the extent individual litigants really can participate in judicial proceedings, authentically consent to settlement agreements, and control the resolution of their own claims, MDL's legality and legitimacy is clearer. To the extent individual autonomy is a fiction, MDL's legality and legitimacy is more doubtful.

The upshot? If judges, policymakers, scholars, and practitioners are concerned about – and want to shore up – MDL legitimacy, client autonomy should be fortified, at least where doing so is possible without major sacrifice.

8.1.2 *Litigant Autonomy: What We Know*

The above discussion underscores that in MDLs, litigant autonomy really matters. That insight tees up a clear – albeit hard-to-answer – real-world question: How much autonomy do contemporary MDL litigants *actually have*?

Context and caveats. That is the question to which we now turn, but before we do, a bit of context is necessary. The context is that, ideally, to gauge the autonomy of MDL litigants, we would know exactly how much autonomy is optimal and also how much

15 For the many procedural protections afforded class action litigants, *see* Fed. R. Civ. P. 23.

16 *See* Bradt & Rave, *The Information-Forcing Role of the Judge*, at 1271 (explaining that, in contemporary MDLs, "actual individual control of the litigation by claimants is limited"); Gluck & Burch, *Bellwether Trials in Multidistrict Litigation*, at 67, 72 (calling the notion that an individual plaintiff controls her case a "fiction" and insisting that, in an MDL, a litigant "does not control her own lawsuit in any meaningful way").

17 *E.g.*, Elizabeth Chamblee Burch, *Monopolies in Multidistrict Litigation*, 70 Vand. L. Rev. 67, 99–100 (2017) (describing the coercive mechanisms in certain MDL settlement agreements).

18 Martin H. Redish & Julie M. Karaba, *One Size Doesn't Fit All: Multidistrict Litigation, Due Process, and the Dangers of Procedural Collectivism*, 95 B.U. L. Rev. 109, 114 (2015).

is minimally sufficient – and how to measure it. Or, short of that, we could perhaps compare rigorous data that captures the experiences of MDL plaintiffs as against those of one-off "traditional" plaintiffs to understand whether, or to what extent, the former outperform or underperform the latter along relevant metrics.

Yet neither is remotely possible. Though litigant autonomy is an oft-cited ideal, we don't know exactly what it would look like and mean, if fully realized, *to litigants*. Worse, decades into the empirical legal studies revolution, we continue to know shockingly little about litigants' preferences, priorities, or lived experiences, whether in MDLs or otherwise.[19]

These uncertainties prevent most sweeping claims about litigant autonomy. Nevertheless, one can, at least tentatively, identify several ingredients that are necessary, if not sufficient, to safeguard the autonomy interests of litigants. That list, we think, includes: Litigants can access case information and monitor judicial proceedings if they so choose; litigants can communicate with their attorneys and understand the signals of the court; litigants have a sense of where things stand, including with regard to the strength of their claim, their claim's likelihood of success, and where the case is in the litigation life cycle; and litigants are empowered to accept or reject the defendant's offer of settlement.[20] A system with these ingredients would seem to be fairly protective of individual autonomy. A system without seems the opposite.

Findings from the Burch-Williams study. How do MDL litigants fare on the above metrics? A survey, recently conducted by Elizabeth Burch and Margaret Williams, offers a partial answer.[21] The two scholars surveyed participants in recent MDLs,

[19] For the empirical revolution, see Daniel E. Ho & Larry Kramer, *Introduction: The Empirical Revolution in Law*, 65 Stan. L. Rev. 1195, 1196 (2013). As Deborah Hensler has powerfully reflected, we (still) don't know much about what claimants want, and we don't know much – of anything – about litigants' lived experience in, or satisfaction with, the judicial process. Deborah R. Hensler, *A Glass Half Full, a Glass Half Empty: The Use of Alternative Dispute Resolution in Mass Personal Injury Litigation*, 73 Tex. L. Rev. 1587, 1626 (1995).

[20] Alexandra Lahav boils it down even further, observing: "Autonomy requires that each individual plaintiff have a right to participate in the proceeding that determines his entitlements." Alexandra D. Lahav, *Bellwether Trials*, 76 Geo. Wash. L. Rev. 576, 610 (2008). Others see it slightly differently, describing litigant autonomy as including "process rights to supervise or manage one's own litigation; to engage in a meaningful relationship with an attorney of the litigant's choosing; to have an opportunity to develop the litigation and evidence related to the litigation; and to appear and give testimony before a jury." Linda S. Mullenix, *Competing Values: Preserving Litigant Autonomy in an Age of Collective Redress*, 64 DePaul L. Rev. 601, 613–14 (2015) (compiling perspectives). Similar to our summary of necessary elements, Bradt and Rave have observed that, "for individual consent to work as a governance mechanism, claimants need information – about things like how the settlement will work, the strength of their claims, and their likelihood of success." Bradt & Rave, *The Information-Forcing Role of the Judge*, at 1265.

[21] The study's findings should be viewed with caution. One issue is the survey's exceedingly low response rate. The survey ultimately cataloged the views of more than 200 respondents, but those respondents were drawn from claimants in more than 200,000 actions. A low response rate is widely understood to limit a survey's generalizability. *See, e.g.*, Nicholas D. Lawson, "*To*

gathering confidential responses over multiple years.[22] In the end, 217 litigants (mostly women who had participated in the pelvic mesh litigation) weighed in, represented by 295 separate lawyers from 145 law firms.[23]

The survey captures claimants' perspectives on a wide range of subjects, including their reasons for initiating suit and their ultimate satisfaction with case outcomes. As relevant to litigant autonomy, information, and participation, the scholars found the following:

- When asked if their lawyer "kept [them] informed about the status of [their] case," 59 percent of respondents strongly or somewhat disagreed.[24]
- When offered the prompt: "While my case was pending, I felt like I understood what was happening," 67.9 percent of respondents strongly or somewhat disagreed. Only 13.7 percent somewhat or strongly agreed.
- When asked how their lawyers kept them informed and invited to list multiple options, more than a quarter of respondents – 26 percent – reported that their attorney did not update them at all.
- Of the 111 respondents who reported on their attorneys' methods of communication, only two indicated that their lawyer(s) utilized a website to communicate with them; only one indicated that her lawyer utilized social media for that purpose.
- 34 percent of respondents were unable or unwilling to identify their lawyer's name.

Caveats apply: Respondents to the opt-in survey might not be representative, which stunts both reliability and generalizability.[25] The numbers, even if reliable, supply

Be a Good Lawyer, One Has to Be a Healthy Lawyer": Lawyer Well-Being, Discrimination, and Discretionary Systems of Discipline, 34 Geo. J. Legal Ethics 65, 75 (2021). Meanwhile, more than 85 percent of respondents were pelvic mesh plaintiffs – and it's not clear that issues that plague mesh litigation plague the MDL system more generally. *See* Alison Frankel, *First-Ever Survey of MDL Plaintiffs Suggests Deep Flaws in Mass Tort System*, Reuters (Aug. 9, 2021), https://www.reuters.com/legal/litigation/first-ever-survey-mdl-plaintiffs-suggests-deep-flaws-mass-tort-system-2021-08-09/ (discussing this issue). Beyond that, as Burch and Williams acknowledge (*Perceptions of Justice in Multidistrict Litigation*, at 4–5 n.16), the paper's methodology (an opt-in survey, which was available online but was not actually sent to claimants) leaves it open to significant response bias, as opt-in surveys may draw respondents with extreme views. *See, e.g.*, Nan Hu et al., *Overcoming the J-Shaped Distribution of Product Reviews*, 52 Comm. ACM. 144, 145 (2009). It is possible, then, that respondents were substantially more dissatisfied than the average MDL litigant, or that sample bias otherwise skews the survey's results. *Cf.* Lindsay M. Harris & Hillary Mellinger, *Asylum Attorney Burnout and Secondary Trauma*, 56 Wake Forest L. Rev. 733, 821 n. 173 (2021) (discussing sampling biases). Just as importantly, as the text points out, most surveyed MDL litigants expressed confusion—but *compared to what baseline? See infra* notes 28 and 29 and accompanying text.

22 Burch & Williams, *Perceptions of Justice in Multidistrict Litigation*, at 14.

23 *Id.* at 15.

24 *Id.* at 26.

25 For discussion of this and other methodological concerns, see *supra* note 21.

just one snapshot. And, with one data set, we can't say whether litigant understanding is higher or lower than it would be if the litigants had never been swept into the MDL system and instead had their case litigated via traditional means. (Nor can we, alternatively, say whether, but for the MDL's efficiencies, these litigants might have been shut out of the civil justice system entirely.[26]) Nor can we even say whether MDL clients are communicated with more, or less, than those whose claims are "conventionally" litigated.[27]

Even recognizing the study's major caveats, however, five larger points seem clear. First, when surveyed, MDL litigants, represented by a broad range of lawyers (not just a few "bad apples"), reported infrequent attorney communication and persistent confusion.[28] Second, knowledgeable and independent experts echo litigants' concerns, suggesting, for example, that "[p]laintiffs [within MDLs] have insufficient information and understanding to monitor effectively the course of the litigation and insufficient knowledge to assess independently the outcomes that are proposed for their approval if and when a time for settlement arrives."[29] Third, plaintiffs' lawyers in MDLs frequently have very large client inventories – of hundreds or thousands of clients.[30] When a lawyer has so many clients, real

[26] *See* Samuel Issacharoff & Robert H. Klonoff, *The Public Value of Settlement*, 78 Fordham L. Rev. 1177, 1184 (2009) (observing that if it weren't for "aggregation many cases could not credibly be pursued"). Currently, many who want a personal injury lawyer are unable to get one, and those who cannot find qualified counsel hardly ever prevail. *See generally* Stephen Daniels & Joanne Martin, Tort Reform, Plaintiffs' Lawyers, and Access to Justice 231 (2015).

[27] Even in the absence of aggregation, the attorney-client relationship sometimes bears little resemblance to a "traditional" model. *See* Nora Freeman Engstrom, *Run-of-the-Mill Justice*, 22 Geo. J. Legal Ethics 1485, 1500 (2009) (documenting how settlement mill lawyers who represent individuals pursuing one-off claims very rarely meet, or communicate with, clients); Deborah R. Hensler, *Resolving Mass Toxic Torts: Myths and Realities*, 1989 U. Ill. L. Rev. 89, 92 (1989) (reporting that, even in non-aggregate tort litigation, the lawyer-client relationship is frequently attenuated, "perfunctory," and "superficial").

[28] Notably, per Model Rule of Professional Conduct 1.4, lawyers – and even lawyers who practice law at scale – are duty-bound to communicate with clients. Model Rules of Pro. Conduct r. 1.4 (Am. Bar Ass'n 2020); *id.* r. 1.3 cmt. 2 ("A lawyer's work load must be controlled so that each matter can be handled competently."); *see also* Restatement (Third) of the Law Governing Lawyers § 20 (Am. L. Inst. 2000) (compelling lawyers to "explain a matter to the extent reasonably necessary to permit the client to make informed decisions regarding the representation," with no exception for lawyers with large client inventories).

[29] Deborah R. Hensler, *No Need to Panic: The Multi-District Litigation Process Needs Improvement Not Demolition* 4 (2017) (unpublished manuscript), https://www.law.gwu.edu/sites/g/files/zaxdzs2351/f/downloads/Deborah-Hensler-MDL-Paper.pdf.

[30] *See* Alison Frankel, *Medical Device Defendant Probes Origin of Mesh Claims*, Reuters, Mar. 10, 2016 (noting that, in the vaginal mesh litigation, one firm – AlphaLaw – had more than 10,000 claims); Letter from Shanin Specter to Comm. on Rules Prac. & Proc 3 (Dec. 18, 2020), https://www.uscourts.gov/sites/default/files/20-cv-hh_suggestion_from_shanin_specter_-_mdls_0.pdf (reporting that, in the transvaginal mesh litigation, "several attorneys represented in excess of 5,000 clients"); Nathan Koppel, *Vioxx Plaintiffs' Choice: Settle or Lose Their Lawyer*, Wall St. J. (Nov. 16, 2007), https://www.wsj.com/articles/SB119517263199795016 (reporting that, in the Vioxx litigation, one lawyer had "more than 1,000 Vioxx cases," while another firm

attorney-client communication and meaningful litigant participation is bound to suffer.[31] Fourth, when it comes to the promotion and protection of litigant autonomy, effective communication – and the provision of vital information – is not sufficient, but it is certainly necessary. Even well-informed litigants can be excluded from vital decision-making processes, but litigants, logically, cannot call the shots while operating in the dark.[32] And fifth, per Section 8.1, to the extent that individuals swept into MDLs unnecessarily forfeit their autonomy, that's a real problem when it comes to MDL legitimacy and legality.[33]

These five points paint a worrying portrait. Fortunately, however, alongside those five points, there is one further reality: Straightforward measures are available to promote litigants' access to case information, their ability to monitor judicial proceedings, and their understanding of the litigation's current path and likely trajectory. And, as we will argue in Section 8.3, these measures can be implemented by courts now, with little difficulty, and at reasonable cost.

8.2 CURRENT COURT COMMUNICATION: MDL WEBSITES AND THEIR DEFICIENCIES

Section 8.1 reviewed survey findings that indicate litigants within MDLs report substantial confusion and limited understanding. As noted, when given the prompt: "While my case was pending, I felt like I understood what was happening," only 13.7 percent somewhat or strongly agreed.[34] These perceived communication failures are surprising. It's 2023. MDL websites are common, and emails are easy; "the marginal cost of additional communication [is] approaching zero."[35] What explains these reported gaps?

had "about 4,000" such cases); Jack B. Weinstein, *Ethical Dilemmas in Mass Tort Litigation*, 88 Nw. U. L. Rev. 469, 494 (1994) ("In asbestos litigation, for example, some lawyers represent more than ten thousand plaintiffs. In other mass torts, such as DES, Dalkon Shield, or toxic dump pollution, lawyers routinely have carried many hundreds of clients at a time.").

31 Weinstein, *Ethical Dilemmas in Mass Tort Litigation*, at 497 (explaining that, when lawyers simultaneously represent hundreds or thousands of clients, lawyers frequently "do not maintain meaningful one-to-one contact with their clients" and instead, too often, "[t]he client becomes no more than an unembodied cause of action").

32 Recognizing this, Rule 1.4(b) demands that "[a] lawyer shall explain a matter to the extent reasonably necessary to permit the client to make informed decisions regarding the representation." Model Rules of Pro. Conduct r. 1.4 (Am. Bar Ass'n 2020). For the decisions reserved exclusively for the clients, see Restatement (Third) of the Law Governing Lawyers § 22 (Am. L. Inst. 2000).

33 Public confidence in our courts may also suffer. *See* Weinstein, *Ethical Dilemmas in Mass Tort Litigation*, at 497 (drawing a connection between adequate communication, litigant satisfaction, and public confidence).

34 Burch & Williams, *Perceptions of Justice in Multidistrict Litigation*, at 25.

35 Cabraser & Issacharoff, *The Participatory Class Action*, at 854.

To gain analytic leverage on that question, we rolled up our sleeves and looked at where some MDL-relevant communication takes place.[36] In particular, we trained our gaze on MDL websites – resources that, per the Judicial Panel on Multidistrict Litigation (JPML) and Federal Judicial Center, "can be ... invaluable tool[s] to keep parties ... informed of the progress of the litigation."[37] These sites are often described as key components of case management.[38] Scholars suggest that they facilitate litigants' "due process rights to participate meaningfully in the proceedings."[39] And, perhaps most notably, judges themselves have described these websites as key conduits of court-client communication.[40]

Do MDL websites fulfill their promise of keeping "parties ... informed of the progress of the litigation" by furnishing well-curated, up-to-date, user-friendly information? To answer that question, we reviewed each page of available websites for the twenty-five largest currently pending MDLs. Each of these MDLs contained at least 500 pending actions; together, they accounted for nearly 415,000 pending actions, encompassing the claims of hundreds of thousands of individual litigants, and constituted 98 percent of actions in *all* MDLs nationwide.[41] Thus, if judges are using court websites to engage in clear and frequent communication with individual litigants, we would have seen it.

36 Of course, MDL websites are not – and should not be – the only site of communication. Lawyers, as noted above, are duty-bound to communicate with clients, *see supra* note 32, and many lawyers take this responsibility seriously, *cf. In re* Shell Oil Refinery, 155 F.R.D. 552, 573 (E.D. La. 1993) (commending class counsel for excellent and patient communication with class members).

37 Jud. Panel on Multidistrict Litig. & Fed. Jud. Ctr., Managing Multidistrict Litigation in Products Liability Cases: A Pocket Guide for Transferee Judges 8 (2011).

38 *E.g.*, Bolch Jud. Inst., Guidelines and Best Practices for Large and Mass-Tort MDLs 88 (2nd ed. 2018) (offering "Best Practice 13 F").

39 Bradt, *The Long Arm of Multidistrict Litigation*, at 1235.

40 Abbe Gluck reports that, in her interviews with transferee judges, judges viewed MDL websites as an indispensable tool to help litigants "follow" the litigation. Gluck, *Unorthodox Civil Procedure*, at 1689–90. Likewise, Judge Eduardo C. Robreno, the transferee judge in MDL-875, has explained that that MDL's dedicated website facilitated the court's "communication with thousands of litigants." Eduardo C. Robreno, *The Federal Asbestos Product Liability Multidistrict Litigation (MDL-875): Black Hole or New Paradigm?* 23 Widener L.J. 97, 131 (2013); *accord In re* Asbestos Prod. Liab. Litig. (No. VI), 614 F. Supp. 2d 550, 551 (E.D. Pa. 2009) ("The Court has established an MDL 875 website .... The website ... is a helpful tool for the Court and the litigants.").

41 We arrived at this figure by calculating the number of actions pending in the twenty-five largest MDLs and then comparing that figure to the total number of pending actions. *See* Jud. Panel on Multidistrict Litig., MDL Statistics Report: Distribution of Pending MDL Dockets by Actions Pending (Jan. 19, 2020), https://www.jpml.uscourts.gov/sites/jpml/files/Pending_MDL_Dockets_By_Actions_Pending-January-19-2022.pdf.

We didn't. Websites did exist. Of the twenty-five largest MDLs, all except one had a website that we could locate.[42] But, many of these sites were surprisingly limited and difficult to navigate. Indeed, the sites provided scant information, were not consistently updated, and often lacked straightforward content (like Zoom information or "plain English" summaries).

8.2.1 An Initial Example: The *Zantac* MDL

Take, as an initial example, the website that accompanies the *Zantac* MDL, pending in the Southern District of Florida.[43] We zero in on this website because it was one of the best, most user-friendly sites we analyzed. But even it contained serious deficiencies.

For starters, finding the website was challenging. A preliminary search – "Zantac lawsuit" – yielded over 1 million hits, and the official court website did not appear on the first several pages of Google results; rather, the first handful of results were attorney advertisements (mostly paid) or attorney and law firm websites.[44] A more targeted effort – "Zantac court website" – bumped the desired result to the first page, albeit below four paid advertisements.

Once we located the site, we were greeted with a description of the suit: "This matter concerns the heartburn medication Zantac. More specifically, this matter concerns the ranitidine molecule – the active ingredient of Zantac. The Judicial Panel for Multidistrict Litigation formed this MDL (number 2924) on February 6, 2020."[45] We also were shown six links (Media Information, MDL Transfer Order, Docket Report, Operative Pleadings, Transcripts, and Calendar) and a curated list of PDF files (see Figure 8.1).

The "Calendar" led to a plain site listing basic information about an upcoming hearing, but with few details. The hearing in question was described only as "Status

[42] To confirm the existence of official websites, we searched on Google for combinations of the MDL number, names of judges affiliated with the MDL, and topical search terms (e.g., "3M hearing loss MDL"). As the text explains, of the twenty-five largest MDLs, as measured by number of actions currently pending, only one (MDL-2848) lacked a website that we were able to locate. Interestingly, the twenty-four sites we reviewed were court-run, though some sites in MDLs are attorney-run. These twenty-four websites represented websites from seventeen different judicial districts. We trained our gaze on the twenty-five largest MDLs in part because research indicates that "large MDLs are significantly more likely to have public websites than small ones." Gluck, *Unorthodox Civil Procedure*, at 1690.

[43] MDL Statistics Report.

[44] In an effort to minimize "personalized search effects," we performed searches in "incognito mode." *See* Lisa Larrimore Ouellette, *The Google Shortcut to Trademark Law*, 102 Cal. L. Rev. 351, 374, 401 & n. 270 (2014) (noting that incognito mode "reduces personalization concerns").

[45] *In re* Zantac (Ranitidine) Prods. Liab. Litig., No. 20-MD-2924, https://perma.cc/A9AB-FCM7.

20-MD-2924-Rosenberg - In Re: Zantac (Ranitidine) Products Liability Litigation

This matter concerns the heartburn medication Zantac. More specifically, this matter concerns the ranitidine molecule—the active ingredient of Zantac. The Judicial Panel for Multidistrict Litigation formed this MDL (number 2924) on February 6, 2020.

Media Information »

MDL Transfer Order

Docket Report (PACER)

Operative Pleadings »

Transcripts »

The following calendar lists all scheduled hearings in this MDL. Calendar activity pertaining to other cases before Judge Rosenberg is omitted from display, but all web-based calendar information is subject to change. The most accurate source for scheduled hearings is PACER.

Calendar

Selected case documents of special interest

Search

Title	Docket No.	Filing Date
MDL Pretrial Order # 78 - Order Setting Deadline to Unilaterally Dismiss Individual Cases and Deadline to Amend Short Form Complaints	5580	05/13/2022
MDL Pretrial Order # 77 - Order Setting Daubert and Summary Judgment Briefing Schedule	5579	05/12/2022
MDL Pretrial Order # 76 - Exhibit A	5505	04/21/2022
MDL Pretrial Order # 76 - Order on Review of Defendants' Leadership Structure and Additional Appointments	5504	04/21/2022
MDL Pretrial Order # 75 - Order Amending the Duties of the Special Master	5452	04/04/2022
MDL Pretrial Order # 74 - Order Extending the Deadline in Paragraph 17 of Pretrial Order # 72 for Unrepresented Registry Participants	5417	03/18/2022
MDL Pretrial Order # 73 - Order on Review of Plaintiffs' Leadership Structure and Additional Appointments	5383	03/08/2022
MDL Pretrial Order # 72 - Order Requiring Finalization of Registry Information and Certain Short-Form Complaints	5348	02/28/2022
MDL Pretrial Order # 71 - Deposition Protocol for Depositions in Class Action Cases	5093	01/19/2022
MDL Pretrial Order # 70 - Order Relating to Deceased Claimants in the Initial Discovery Pool	4922	12/23/2021

FIGURE 8.1 Zantac MDL docket

THIS PAGE WAS LAST UPDATED 03/13/2022 at 22:00.

UNITED STATES DISTRICT COURT
Southern District of Florida
The Honorable Robin L. Rosenberg

Case 9:20-md-02924 - Hearings Calendar

March 14, 2022 - May 6, 2022

Date	Time	DE #	Hearing Type	Interpreter/Court Reporter	Duration	Court Room
04/01/2022	02:30		Status Conference - Case Mgt			West Palm Beach Division

FIGURE 8.2 Zantac MDL hearing notice

Conference – Case Mgt," and it did not specify whether litigants could attend, either in person or remotely (see Figure 8.2).[46]

[46] *Id.*, *Hearings Calendar*, https://perma.cc/QK3N-C3JF. Virtual hearing information could plausibly have been added after our March 2022 review, though the calendar lacked a heading for Zoom credentials or teleconference information.

20-MD-2924-Rosenberg - Operative Pleadings

The following list contains pleadings of special interest, but the most accurate source for orders is PACER.

Class Economic Loss Complaint

Medical Monitoring Complaint

Second Amended Personal Injury Complaint

Boehringer Ingelheim Pharmaceuticals, Inc. Answer

GlaxoSmithKline, LLC Answer

Pfizer, Inc. Answer

Sanofi US Services, Inc. Answer

FIGURE 8.3 Zantac operative pleadings

A litigant who clicked on the "Operative Pleadings" tab was taken to seven PDF documents (Pfizer, Inc. Answer; Class Economic Loss Complaint; etc.) described as those "of special interest," plus a note that "the most accurate source for orders is PACER."[47] (The site did not include information regarding what PACER is, though it did include a link; see Figure 8.3.)

Finally, a search box allowed for a search of the case's orders, again available as PDFs.

8.2.2 *The Rest: Deficits along Five Key Dimensions*

Within our broader sample, usability deficits were pervasive and very often worse than the *Zantac* MDL site. In the course of our inquiry, we reviewed websites along the following five dimensions: (1) searchability and identifiability; (2) plaintiff-focused content; (3) use of plain language; (4) whether the site supplied information to facilitate remote participation in, or attendance at, proceedings; and (5) timeliness. We found deficits along each.

Searchability and identifiability. A website is only useful if it can be located. As such, our first inquiry was whether MDL websites were easy, or alternatively difficult, to find. Here, we found that, as in *Zantac*, court sites were often buried under a thicket of advertisements for lawyers or lead generators (see Figure 8.4).[48] Commonsense search terms for the three largest MDLs yielded results on pages 13, 4, and 8, respectively.[49]

[47] *Id., Operative Pleadings*, https://perma.cc/EM7U-YA69.

[48] Burch and Williams found much the same, reporting that, in one major case, an MDL page did not appear in the first twelve pages of Google results. Burch & Williams, *Perceptions of Justice in Multidistrict Litigation*, at 57.

[49] More specifically, we searched (on incognito mode in the Google Chrome browser): "3M earplug lawsuit"; "j&j talcum powder lawsuit"; and "hernia mesh lawsuit". Given Google's

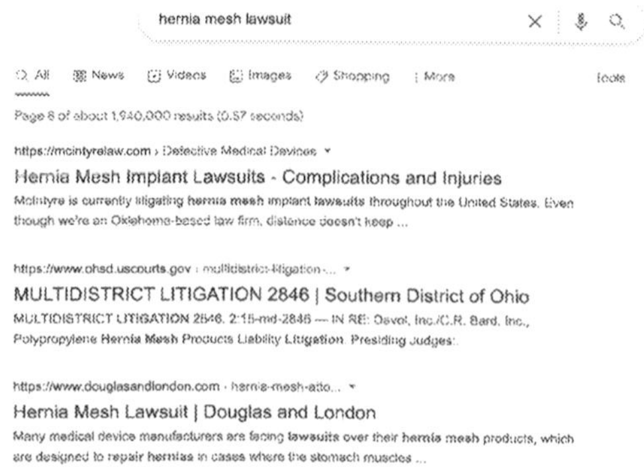

FIGURE 8.4 Hernia mesh Google search

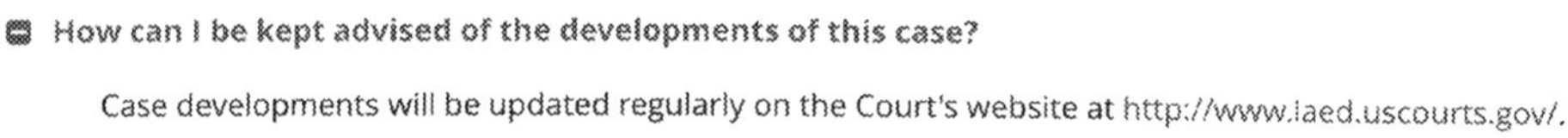

FIGURE 8.5 Eastern District of Louisiana website link

Litigant-focused content. Next, we evaluated whether websites featured custom content that was seemingly geared to orient individual litigants. Most didn't. In particular, of the twenty-four sites we reviewed, only eleven contained any meaningful introductory content at all. Even then, those introductions focused primarily on the transfer process (including the relevant JPML proceeding) and a statement of the case's overall topic – not its current status or its anticipated timeline. Meanwhile, only six of the twenty-four offered MDL-focused Frequently Asked Questions. And of those, most offered (and answered) questions at a general level ("What is multidistrict litigation?") or that were clearly attorney-focused (regarding, for instance, motions to appear *pro hac vice*). Some others, while well intentioned, supplied limited help (see Figure 8.5).[50]

Similarly, more than half of sites identified members of the cases' leadership structure (e.g., by listing leadership or liaison counsel) and provided contact information for outreach. But none directed plaintiffs with questions to a *specific* point of contact among those attorneys.

Finally, materials that were presented – typically, a partial set of key documents, such as court orders or hearing transcripts – were often unadorned. For instance,

targeted results, the precise page results will likely vary by user. For more on incognito mode, see *supra* note 44.

50 *MDL Frequently Asked Questions, In re* Xarelto Prods. Liab. Litig., No. 14-MD-2592, https://perma.cc/35FA-T3R5.

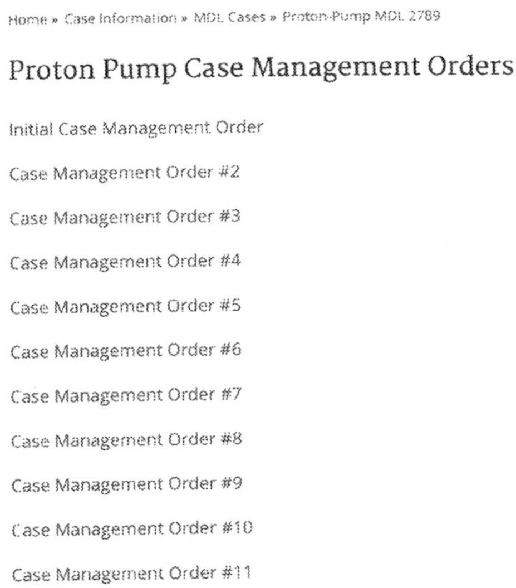

FIGURE 8.6 Proton Pump case management orders

seven of the twenty-four reviewed sites linked to orders, as PDFs, with essentially no description of what those documents contain (see Figure 8.6).[51]

Better: Sixteen of the sites offered some descriptions of posted PDFs. But only *two* included status updates that went much beyond one-line order summaries (see Figure 8.7).[52]

To a litigant, therefore, the average MDL site is best understood as a free, and often partial, PACER stand-in – not a source of curated, distilled, or intelligible information.

Jargon and legalese. We next assessed whether the websites were written in plain language – or at least translated legalese. Here, we found that the majority of sites relied on legal jargon when they described key developments.[53] For example, our review found websites touting privilege log protocols, an ESI order, and census implementation orders. Even case-specific Frequently Asked Questions – where one might most reasonably expect clear, litigant-friendly language – stopped short of "translating" key legal terms.[54] Put simply, site content was predominantly written in the language of lawyers, not litigants.

[51] *See, e.g., Proton Pump Case Management Orders, In re* Proton-Pump Inhibitor Prods. Liab. Litig. (No. II), No. 17-MD-2789, https://perma.cc/HL2C-CPKP.

[52] *See, e.g., Current Developments, In re* Aqueous Film-Forming Foams Prods. Liab. Litig., 18-MN-2873, https://perma.cc/62RU-FNH3.

[53] This problem has been discussed extensively in the context of class action notice. *See, e.g.*, Deborah L. Rhode, *Class Conflicts in Class Actions*, 34 STAN. L. REV. 1183, 1235 (1982).

[54] *See, e.g., MDL Frequently Asked Questions, In re* Xarelto Prods. Liab. Litig. (noting that cases in MDL "may be transferred by the Judicial Panel on Multidistrict Litigation (The Panel) to any federal court for coordinated and consolidated pretrial proceedings," but offering no

Current developments

May 1, 2020

The Court conducted the regular status conference, at which Plaintiffs and Defendants, including the United States of America, provided updates on the status of discovery.

April 3, 2020

The Court conducted the regular status conference, at which Plaintiffs and Defendants, as well as the United States of America, provided updates on the status of discovery including document production, noticed depositions and the United States of America's review of historical documents. Prior to the status conference, the Court issued Case Mangement Orders No. 10 and No. 10.A, which reappointed and appointed additional counsel to the Plaintiffs' Executive Committee and Defendants' Coordination Committee for the March 2020 through March 2021 term. The Court also previously issued Case Management Order No. 9, governing the procedure for exchange of third-party subpoena documents.

February 7, 2020

The Court conducted the regular status conference, at which Plaintiffs and Defendants, as well as the United States of America, provided updates on the status of discovery, including the United States of America's review of historical documents. The Court then conducted an in-Chambers conference with certain Defendants relating to management among the Defendants' Executive Committee. The Court then issued Case Mangement Order No. 5.B, governing the procedure for Defendants to share costs associated with Plaintiffs' Fact Sheets processing, review and storage. The Court indicated that it will not conduct a status conference in March, 2020, but remains available to resolve discovery disputes as required.

FIGURE 8.7 "Current developments" listing

Information to facilitate remote attendance. We also gauged whether the websites offered teleconference or Zoom hearing information. This information is important because consolidated cases – and the geographic distance they entail – leave many litigants unable to attend judicial proceedings in person, which puts a premium on litigants' ability to attend key proceedings remotely, via video or telephone.

Did the websites supply the logistical information a litigant needs in order to "attend" remotely? Not particularly. Of the twenty-four sites we reviewed, thirteen did not offer any case calendar that alerted litigants of upcoming hearings or conferences. Of the eleven that did:

- Five listed events on their calendar (though some of the listed events had already occurred) without any Zoom or telephone information;
- Two included Zoom or telephone information for some, but not all, past events;
- Two included Zoom or telephone information for *all* events listed on the case calendar; and
- Two included dedicated calendar pages but had no scheduled events.

discussion of remand or definition of "pretrial proceedings"); *Frequently Asked Questions, In re* Davol, Inc./C.R. Bard, Inc., Polypropylene Hernia Mesh Prods. Liab. Litig., 18-MD-2846, https://perma.cc/RP8H-JVCB (using the same language).

Put another way, most sites did not include case calendars; of those that did, more than half lacked Zoom or other remote dial-in information for some or all listed hearings. That absence was particularly striking given that, in the wake of the COVID-19 pandemic, nearly all courts embraced remote proceedings.[55]

Unsurprisingly, the sites' presentation of upcoming hearings also varied widely. In some instances (as on the MDL-2775, MDL-3004, and MDL-2846 sites shown in Figure 8.8 a–c), virtual hearings were listed, but no dial-in information was provided.[56] In contrast, some MDL sites (like MDL-2741[57]) linked to Zoom information (Figure 8.9).

Timeliness. Lastly, recognizing that cases can move fast – and stale information is of limited utility – we evaluated the websites to see whether information was timely. Again, results were dispiriting. Of the sites that offered time-sensitive updates (e.g., calendars of upcoming events), several were not updated, meaning that a litigant or even an individually retained plaintiffs' attorney who relied on the website for information was apt to be misinformed.[58] For instance, MDL-2913, involving Juul, was transferred to the Northern District of California on October 2, 2019. Its website included a calendar section and several "documents of special interest."[59] The latest document upload involved a conditional transfer order from January 2020[60] – even though several major rulings had been issued more recently.[61] (The website's source code indicates that it was last modified in May 2020.) Whether by conscious choice or oversight, the case's online presence did not reflect its current status. Other sites, meanwhile, listed "upcoming" proceedings that had, in fact, occurred long before.[62] And, when we accessed archived, time-stamped versions of sites, we

55 *See, e.g.*, David Freeman Engstrom, *Post-Covid Courts*, 68 UCLA L. Rev. Discourse 246, 250 (2020) (noting that, during the pandemic, courts "embraced remote proceedings and trials, whether by telephone or video connection").

56 *Upcoming MDL Events, In re* Smith & Nephew Birmingham Hip Resurfacing (BHR) Hip Implant Prods. Liab. Litig., 17-MD-2775, https://perma.cc/GX6W-8ZMC; *Multidistrict Litigation, In re* Paraquat Prods. Liab. Litig., 21-MD-3004, https://perma.cc/7XLQ-H6KX; *Upcoming Court Proceedings, In re* Davol, at https://perma.cc/65QA-SDFZ.

57 *In re* Roundup Prods. Liab. Litig., 16-MD-2741, https://perma.cc/4HL4–5AUF.

58 *Cf. In re* Nineteen Appeals Arising Out of San Juan Dupont Plaza Hotel Fire Litig., 982 F.2d 603, 605 (1st Cir. 1992) ("The IRPAs [individually retained plaintiffs' attorneys] handled individual client communication . . . . ").

59 *In re* Juul Labs, Inc. Mktg., Sales Pracs. & Prods. Liab. Litig., 19-MD-2913, https://perma.cc/2VGD-SKBU (last accessed Mar. 15, 2022).

60 As of March 15, 2022, the latest document posted was filed on January 21, 2020. *See id.*

61 *See, e.g., In re* Juul Labs, Inc., Mktg., Sales Pracs., & Prod. Liab. Litig., 497 F. Supp. 3d 552 (N.D. Cal. 2020) (ruling on substantive motions to dismiss in October 2020).

62 For instance, March 2022 searches revealed the following: MDL-2846, *see Upcoming Court Proceedings, In re* Davol (providing, on the site's "Upcoming Proceedings" page, a status conference scheduled for July 20, 2020), and MDL-2775, *see Upcoming MDL Events, In re* Smith & Nephew Birmingham (listing, on the site's "Upcoming MDL Events" page, events up to June 2021).

Upcoming MDL Events

Date	Event
June 23, 2021	A virtual status conference will take place at 9:00 a.m.
June 30, 2021	A pretrial conference and motions hearing in Redick v. Smith & Nephew, Inc., 1:17-cv-00944 will take place in Courtroom 7D at 9:30 a.m.
July 26, 2021	Trial begins in Paula and Jace Redick v. Smith & Nephew, No. 1:17-cv-00944
July 28, 2021	A virtual status conference will take place at 9:45 a.m.
August 25, 2021	A virtual status conference will take place at 9:45 a.m.
September 22, 2021	A virtual status conference will take place at 9:45 a.m.
October 27, 2021	A virtual status conference will take place at 9:45 a.m.
November 24, 2021	A virtual status conference will take place at 9:45 a.m.
December 22, 2021	A virtual status conference will take place at 9:45 a.m.

Upcoming Court Proceedings

Date & Time	Description	Location
4/01/2022 10:00 AM	Status Conference	Video Conference
5/13/2022 10:00 AM	Status Conference	Video Conference
6/10/2022 10:00 AM	Status Conference	Video Conference
11/15/2022 09:00 AM	Jury Trial	TBD

Home

Upcoming Court Proceedings

July 20, 2020 Status Conference will be held by telephone at 10:00am EST before Judge Edmund A. Sargus, Jr. and Magistrate Judge Kimberly A. Jolson.

FIGURE 8.8 A–C Link-less "Upcoming MDL Events" examples

Upcoming Proceedings & Deadlines:

Date	Proceeding or Deadline	Courtroom (If Applicable)
4/14/2022	Motion for Preliminary Approval of Class Action Settlement	via Zoom

FIGURE 8.9 Link-provided "Upcoming Proceedings" example

found several orders that were *eventually* posted – but not until months after they were handed down.[63]

Nor were the sites set up to keep interested visitors *repeatedly* informed, as most of the sites did not themselves offer a direct "push" or sign-up feature, so that visitors could be notified via text or email when new material became available.[64]

8.2.3 *Explanations for the Above Deficits: Unspecified Audience and Insufficient Existing Guidance*

What explains the above deficits? One possibility is that these websites were never *intended* to speak to, or otherwise benefit, actual litigants – and our analysis, then, is basically underscoring that websites, never meant to edify litigants, in fact, fail to edify them.[65] To some judges and attorney leaders, in other words, these sites may serve merely as internal or specialized resources, whether for state court judges involved in overlapping litigation, individually retained plaintiffs' counsel, or even scholars and journalists.[66] Or, it could be that the "audience" question has never been carefully considered or seriously addressed. As a result, the websites may be trying to be all things to all people but actually serve none, as content is too general for members of the plaintiffs' steering committee, too specialized and technical for litigants, and too partial or outdated for individually retained plaintiffs' counsel or judges handling parallel state litigation.

63 *See, e.g.*, MDL-2775, *In re* Smith & Nephew Birmingham (per our search on the Internet Archive, not publicly posting orders for more than two months after the orders were issued). For discussion of the Internet Archive, which allows users to view older versions of websites, see Deborah R. Eltgroth, *Best Evidence and the Wayback Machine: Toward a Workable Authentication Standard for Archived Internet Evidence*, 78 Fordham L. Rev. 181, 185 (2009).

64 The majority of sites did link to electronic filing systems (i.e., ECF and/or PACER), which offer a "push" feature that alerts the user when a new document is filed. But ECF and PACER require the creation of separate accounts, and PACER is not free. *See, e.g.*, *In re* Roundup ("To sign up for email alerts when a new document is filed, you may open an account with this Court's ECF system, then sign up for notices of electronic filing.").

65 There is some variability, and perhaps confusion, on this point. *Compare supra* note 40 (compiling judges' views that the sites exist, at least in part, to facilitate communication with litigants), *with* 1 Charles S. Zimmerman, Pharmaceutical and Medical Device Litigation § 10:3 (rev. vol. 2021) (explaining that MDL websites are "designed primarily for lawyers, judges, and other professionals who have interests in the litigation"); *and* Fed. Jud. Ctr. & Jud. Panel on Multidistrict Litig., Bellwether Trials in MDL Proceedings: A Guide for Transferee Judges 38 (2019) (indicating that transferee courts can use MDL websites to "apprise state courts of MDL developments"); *and* Bolch Jud. Inst., Guidelines and Best Practices, at 82, 87–88 (highlighting court websites as an efficient way to "coordinate with state courts handling parallel state actions"), *and In re* McKinsey & Co., Nat'l Prescription Opiate Consultant Litig., 21-MD-2996, https://perma.cc/WH7C-LTUR (explaining that the site is designed to assist "journalists and interested members of the public").

66 For the fact that different experts seem to view the "audience" question differently, see *supra* note 65 (compiling inconsistent authority).

A second culprit, in contrast, is crystal clear: Higher authorities have furnished transferee judges and court administrators with only limited public guidance.[67] In particular, current guidance tends to suggest categories for site content. But beyond that, it furnishes transferee judges only limited help. Illustrating this deficiency, the JPML and Federal Judicial Center's *Ten Steps to Better Case Management: A Guide for Multidistrict Litigation Transferee Court Clerks* includes a discussion of recommended webpage content, but its relevant section provides only that:

> The following information should be included on a multidistrict litigation webpage:
>
> - Case name and master docket sheet case number
> - Brief description of the subject of the case
> - Name of the judge presiding over the case
> - List of court staff, along with their contact information
> - Names of liaison counsel, along with their contact information
>
> In addition, it is useful to include the following types of orders in PDF:
>
> - Case management orders
> - Transfer orders from the Panel
> - Orders applicable to more than one case
> - Individual case orders affecting one case, but potentially pertinent to others
> - Suggestion of remand orders.[68]

Several other pertinent resources are similarly circumscribed.[69] These publications have likely helped to spur websites' creation, but they have stunted their meaningful evolution.

* * *

[67] There may be additional, nonpublic guidance on these subjects. *See* Jaime Dodge, *Facilitative Judging: Organizational Design in Mass-Multidistrict Litigation*, 64 Emory L.J. 329, 382 n.9 (2014) (describing FJC materials available only to judges and their staffs).

[68] Jud. Panel on Multidistrict Litig. & Fed. Jud. Ctr., Ten Steps to Better Case Management: A Guide for Multidistrict Litigation Transferee Court Clerks 12, app. D (2nd ed. 2014).

[69] For instance, the *Manual for Complex Litigation* also offers a model order for judges to use in creating a case website. It urges that a created site "contain sections through which the parties, counsel, and the public may access court orders, court opinions, court minutes, court calendars, frequently asked questions, court transcripts, court docket, current developments, information about plaintiffs' and defendants' lead and liaison counsel, and other information to be identified by the parties or the court and its staff." Fed. Jud. Ctr., Manual for Complex Litigation § 40.3, 762 (4th ed. 2004). It also recommends that judges order counsel to confer to "identify other information that might be included on the Web site," including case announcements or important documents. *Id.* Another (seemingly defunct) FJC site offers a sample order – covering, again, only the bare minimum. *See Technology – Examples*, Fed. Jud. Ctr., https://perma.cc/VL7E-XTTM. We state that the FJC site is "seemingly defunct" because, inter alia, the site lists six "Sample MDL Websites," but, as of March 2022, none of the links were operational. *See Sample MDL Websites*, Fed. Jud. Ctr., https://perma.cc/32YG-TYSM.

Whatever the reasons for the above deficiencies, the facts are these: Among the websites we reviewed, most suffered from basic deficits that could very well inhibit litigants' access and engagement. And the deficits we identify could easily be addressed.

8.3. A SIMPLE PATH FORWARD: A "LOW-TECH" MECHANISM TO KEEP LITIGANTS BETTER INFORMED

As noted in Section 8.1, MDLs rely, for legitimacy, on litigant autonomy, and while communication is not sufficient for litigant autonomy, it is necessary. Even well-informed litigants can be deprived of the capacity to make crucial decisions – but litigants, logically, cannot make crucial decisions if they are not reasonably well-informed. Meanwhile, while no one can currently *prove* that MDL litigants are underinformed, Section 8.2 compiled some evidence indicating information deficits are deep and pervasive. The Burch-Williams study paints a worrying portrait; knowledgeable scholars have long raised concerns; and our painstaking review of MDL websites reveals that one tool, theoretically poised to promote litigant understanding, is, in fact, poorly positioned to do so.

What can be done? Over the long run, the Federal Judicial Center (FJC), or another similar body, should furnish formal guidance to judges, court administrators, and lawyers on how to build effective and legible websites. This guidance would ideally be supplemented by a set of best practices around search engine optimization and language access. There is good reason to believe that such guidance would be effective. Noticeable similarities across existing websites suggest that transferee judges borrow heavily from one another. An implication of that cross-pollination is that better guidance from the FJC (or elsewhere) would (likely) rapidly spread.

In the meantime, we close with four concrete (though modest and partial) suggestions for transferee judges.

First, judges need to decide whom these sites are really for – and then need to ensure that the sites well-serve their intended audience. We suggest that MDL websites ought to be embraced as (among other things) a litigant-facing tool, and, as discussed below, they should be improved with that purpose in mind.[70] But, even if courts are not persuaded, they *still* need to do a better job tailoring sites to *some*

[70] *Accord* Alvin K. Hellerstein, *Democratization of Mass Tort Litigation: Presiding over Mass Tort Litigation to Enhance Participation and Control by the People Whose Claims Are Being Asserted*, 45 COLUM. J.L. & SOC. PROBS. 473, 478 (2012) ("It is important to provide full and fair information at all stages of a mass tort litigation, in a systematic and regular manner, to the plaintiffs who are the real parties in interest."); Weinstein, *Ethical Dilemmas in Mass Tort Litigation*, at 502 (calling for the use of innovative communication mechanisms and noting that, even in aggregate proceedings, judges "must insist on maintaining the essential aspects of our fundamentally individual system of justice, including communication and participation").

particular audience. As long as the specific audience remains undetermined, courts are less likely to serve any particular audience adequately.

If courts agree that websites should speak directly to litigants, then a second recommendation follows: At least some clearly delineated website content should be *customized for litigants*. Courts should, as noted, avoid legalese and offer more digested (rather than just raw) material. For instance, judges might ask attorneys to supply monthly or quarterly updates; these updates, which should be approved by both parties and the court, should summarize the progress made in the preceding month and highlight what is on tap in the MDL in the immediate future. Here, the website should capture both in-court activity and noteworthy activity scheduled outside of the court's four walls (e.g., depositions).

Third, irrespective of chosen audience, judges should take steps to ensure that MDL websites are visible and up-to-date. Regardless of whom the websites are meant to serve, websites cannot serve that audience if they cannot be quickly located.[71] And, because stale information is of limited utility, judges should ensure that the websites offer an accurate, timely snapshot of the case's progress. The first steps are uncontroversial and straightforward; they include reliably adding hearings to the online calendar, removing them after they occur, and posting key documents within a reasonable time frame. Judges should also consider an opt-in sign-up that automatically emails or texts interested individuals when new content is added.

Fourth and finally, judges should ensure that websites clearly publicize hearings and status conferences, and, recognizing that MDLs necessarily and inescapably create distance between client and court, judges should facilitate remote participation whenever feasible. As noted above, many MDL judges have embraced remote hearings out of COVID-generated necessity; judges overseeing large MDLs should consider how the switching costs they have already paid can be invested to promote meaningful litigant access, even from afar.[72] Indeed, judges might cautiously pilot tools for *two-way* client-court communication, or even client-to-client communication – though, in so doing, judges must be attuned to various risks.[73]

[71] "Of course, judges are not search engine optimization experts." Burch and Williams, *Perceptions of Justice in Multidistrict Litigation*, at 57. But others are, and an initial investment in developing and circulating best practices could yield meaningful improvement.

[72] *See* Bradt, *The Long Arm of Multidistrict Litigation*, at 1235 (advising that "all MDL hearings, depositions, and trials should be web-cast, with the recordings made available on the case website" – and, more generally, that "[c]ourts ... should take advantage of the benefits of modern communications technology" in order to promote litigants' "due process rights to participate meaningfully in the proceedings").

[73] Notably, any plaintiff-to-court or plaintiff-to-plaintiff communication platform would need to protect privileged information. *Cf.* Judith Resnik et al., *Individuals Within the Aggregate: Relationships, Representation, and Fees*, 71 N.Y.U. L. Rev. 296, 391–92 (1996). (proposing a "clients' committee" to "facilitate client-attorney communication and to ensure client knowledge about the litigation"); Weinstein, *Ethical Dilemmas in Mass Tort Litigation*, at 501–2 (calling for judges to explore ways to promote litigant participation and fortify court-client "[c]ommunication").

8.4. CONCLUSION: ZOOMING OUT

We harbor no illusions about the role that better MDL websites can play. They're no panacea, and vigorous debates about the merits and demerits of MDL will (and should) continue. But even so: Improved, refocused websites can keep litigants a bit more engaged; they can help litigants stay a bit better informed; and they can promote litigant participation in even distant MDL processes. More than that, improved websites can, however incrementally, promote litigant autonomy and, by extension, shore up the legitimacy of the MDL system. The day may come when some as-yet-unidentified high-tech innovation revolutionizes the MDL. Until then, low-tech changes can modestly improve the system, and just might serve as platforms for further reform.

PART III

Legal Tech and Access to Justice

9

The Supply and Demand of Legal Help on the Internet

Margaret Hagan

Millions of Americans have civil justice problems every month, and most of these go unmet. A recent survey of low-income Americans found that over 70 percent of households had at least one civil legal problem in a year, including around health care, housing, disability benefits, veterans' issues, and domestic violence.[1] But of these needs, 86 percent of the problems received inadequate or no legal help.[2] Without legal assistance, a person may lose their home to an eviction or foreclosure, suffer physical abuse without protection, go into debt or bankruptcy, lose custody of their children, or be denied medical care.[3]

Why is there such a large justice gap between the high volume of justice problems and the small percentage that receive legal assistance? This may be due to the increasing costs of providing legal services, with lawyers having to follow burdensome procedures and licensing requirements that make it difficult to sustain a business model serving low- or moderate-income households.[4] Or another commonly cited reason is the undersupply of public interest lawyers to assist people with civil justice problems. The underfunding results from decades of congressional restrictions on legal aid funding, which both limits the supply of free lawyers and restricts whom these free lawyers can serve.[5] Without widely available free or

[1] Legal Servs. Corp., The Justice Gap: Measuring the Unmet Civil Legal Needs of Low-Income Americans (2017), https://www.lsc.gov/justicegap2017.

[2] *Id.*

[3] See more individual stories of experiences with and without legal assistance for their civil justice problems at the All Rise for Civil Justice platform. *Stories from the Civil Justice Crisis*, *All Rise for Civ. J.*, https://allriseforciviljustice.org/stories/.

[4] Gillian Hadfield, *Legal Markets*, 60 J. Econ. Lit. (forthcoming 2022).

[5] *See* Rebekah Diller & Emily Savner, *Restoring Legal Aid for the Poor: A Call to End Draconian and Wasteful Restrictions*, 36 Fordham Urb. L. J. 687 (2009). For a more recent news report on the underfunding see Adiel Kaplan, *More People Than Ever Need Legal Aid Services, but the Pandemic Has Hit Legal Aid Funding Hard*, NBC News (Apr. 25, 2021), https://www.nbcnews.com/business/personal-finance/more-people-ever-need-legal-aid-services-pandemic-has-hit-n1264989.

affordable legal services, millions of people are turned away when they seek assistance.[6]

But what about those people that never seek legal aid assistance in the first place? This is the problem of awareness and capability. As Sandefur's research has highlighted, many Americans do not conceive of justice problems as ones that are "legal" or that legal assistance could help with.[7] Instead, they often attribute them to happenstance, bad luck, or other reasons – all of which make it more likely that they do not seek out legal or social services to have their rights protected and experts assist them. Here the problem is not a limited supply of affordable or free legal services. Instead, the problem is people's lack of consciousness of their legal rights and how legal professionals can help them,[8] and a lack of confidence, capability, or trust that they want to engage with legal assistance to deal with their problems.[9]

Recent decades have seen a variety of interventions aimed at closing the justice gap by increasing legal awareness among those with civil justice problems and their capability to use available assistance. In the early 1970s, consumer-facing legal clinics arose in storefronts with transparently priced menus of legal services, making legal help more approachable, demystifying the process of engaging a lawyer, and advertising how and why people should make use of legal services.[10] At the end of the 1970s, bans on attorney advertising were invalidated, and legal groups began to release audio, video, and print outreach to the public to drive up people's awareness about when and how they could use a lawyer to help them.[11] By the 1990s, however,

[6] Rebecca Buckwalter-Poza, *Making Justice Equal*, Ctr. for Am. Progress (Dec. 8, 2016), https://www.americanprogress.org/issues/criminal-justice/reports/2016/12/08/294479/making-justice-equal/.

[7] Rebecca L. Sandefur, Accessing Justice in the Contemporary USA: Findings from the Community Needs and Services Study (2014), https://www.americanbarfoundation.org/uploads/cms/documents/sandefur_accessing_justice_in_the_contemporary_usa._aug._2014.pdf.

[8] For more about social-legal studies of legal consciousness and for more exploration of how people think about and interact with the legal system, *see* Susan Sibley, *Legal Consciousness*, *in* New Oxford Companion to Law (2008).

[9] There is a growing literature framed around "legal capability" and "legal empowerment" that focuses on why people do not take action on justice problems, based on lack of knowledge, skills, or trust in the system. See Nigel J. Balmer et al., Knowledge, Capability and the Experience of Rights Problems (2010), https://lawforlife.org.uk/wp-content/uploads/2010/05/knowledge-capability-and-the-experience-of-rights-problems-lsrc-may-2010-255.pdf; Hugh M. McDonald & Julie People, *Legal Capability and Inaction for Legal Problems: Knowledge, Stress, and Cost*, Updating J., June 2014; Lisa Wintersteiger, Law for Life: Legal Needs, Legal Capability and the Role of Public Legal Education (2015); Kristina Brousalis, CLEO Connect, Building an Understanding of Legal Capability: An Online Scan of Legal Capability Research (2016), https://cleoconnect.ca/wp-content/uploads/2019/06/online-scan-legal-capability.September-2016.final_.pdf; Margaret Hagan & Kursat Ozenc, A Design Space for Legal and Systems Capability: Interfaces for Self-Help in Complex Systems, *Design Issues*, Summer 2020, at 61.

[10] Nora Freeman Engstrom, *Attorney Advertising and the Contingency Fee Cost Paradox*, 65 Stan. L. Rev. 633, 649 (2013).

[11] *Id.* at 653–54.

the use of lawyer advertising had shifted to focus primarily on personal injury needs rather than routine legal services (like divorces, debt, and estate planning). By the mid-1990s, the storefront legal clinic movement was extinct.[12]

More recently, awareness and capability efforts have centered on use of technology. Websites like LegalZoom and Rocket Lawyer emerged to serve the needs that storefront legal clinics had decades earlier, and these sites began to spend heavily in traditional and online advertising to build people's legal awareness.[13] More public interest organizations also began to build websites and apps, to make it easier for people to find and use legal help.[14] These sites have features intended to improve people's capability to engage with legal services, like referral engines to make it easier to engage a lawyer, self-help guides to understand the law, chat functions to get basic questions answered, and dispute resolution tools to generate agreements with the other party.[15] In recent years, new awareness-focused applications have begun to use artificial intelligence to automatically spot justice problems in their online posts, to diagnose what legal issue they might have.[16]

While justice problem-solving on the Internet remains a work in progress, all signs are that improving internet-based tools will be a central component of any successful effort to close the justice gap. This chapter presents a new approach to evaluating legal help websites as one of these internet-based tools. It posits that the mere existence of court and legal aid websites is not enough to close the justice gap. Rather, there must be accountability and research as to whether people are able to find and use these sites to build legal capability. This chapter presents one method to assess the impact of legal help websites: measuring the supply of sites, the demand for them, and the factors that may be impeding better matching of people with online resources.

9.1 THE NEED FOR RESEARCH ON LEGAL HELP ON THE INTERNET

As more service providers attempt to use the Internet to close the justice gap by increasing legal awareness and capability of people, more people are going onto the

[12] *Id.* at 657–59.

[13] Debra Cassens Weiss, *This Law Firm Will Spend More Than $25M in Legal Advertising This Year, Report Says*, A.B.A. J. (Oct. 28, 2015), https://www.abajournal.com/news/article/this_law_firm_will_spend_more_than_25m_in_legal_advertising_this_year_repor; Sarah Knapp, *Can LegalZoom be the Answer to the Justice Gap?* 26 Geo. J. Legal Ethics 821 (2013).

[14] See case studies of many such efforts in the special volume of Colloquium, *Using Technology to Enhance Access to Justice*, 26 Harv. J. L. Tech. 243 (2012).

[15] See an inventory of technology tools for civil justice problems at Rebecca Love Kourlis & Riyaz Samnani, Institute for Advancement Am. Legal Sys., Court Compass: Mapping the Future of User Access through Technology (2017), https://iaals.du.edu/sites/default/files/documents/publications/court_compass_mapping_the_future.pdf.

[16] Bob Ambrogi, *Stanford and Suffolk Create Game to Help Drive Access to Justice*, LawSites (Oct. 16, 2018), https://www.lawsitesblog.com/2018/10/stanford-suffolk-create-game-help-drive-access-justice.html.

Internet to find help for all kinds of problems (legal or not) that happen to them.[17] Many of these "life problems" that people search about (for example, getting calls from a debt collector, wondering if a past criminal record could be masked, dealing with a landlord threatening eviction, worrying about medical bills, or trying to get school services for a child with learning difficulties) are "justice problems."[18] In the past, people might have turned first to family, neighbors, librarians, or professionals to seek assistance for such life problems. People still might reach out through social connections, but increasingly the Internet figures prominently in this search for help.[19]

Yet little is known about the role of the Internet in people's problem-solving around legal life events. Do online sites and tools increase people's awareness and capabilities around their legal rights? Do they empower people to take action to resolve their justice problems? A handful of studies have surveyed people about whether and how they see legal assistance online.[20] This preliminary research, most of it done as small surveys and lab experiments, has established some useful insights and metrics as to how various internet intermediaries and resources may better serve individuals seeking out help on their problems. Among the insights are what kinds of search results, websites, and apps best improve people's understanding of the law, and which may best encourage people to take action on resolving their problem. Even so, we still lack knowledge about how many people are seeking help for justice problems on the Internet and how they behave when they do seek help online.

The limits of existing studies on justice problem-solving on the Internet stand in stark contrast with the medical field. Public health researchers and medical practitioners have developed data-driven techniques to understand people's health assistance–seeking behavior online, and what this means for how to better deliver services, predict needs, and communicate with the public.[21] Researchers gather data on what people are searching for, what kinds of websites they are visiting, what stories they are sharing about their health, and what actions they take in response to what they find online. This

[17] *Information Searches That Solve Problems*, Pew Rsch. Ctr. (Dec. 30, 2007), https://www.pewresearch.org/internet/2007/12/30/information-searches-that-solve-problems/.

[18] Sandefur, Accessing Justice in the Contemporary USA. There is a distinction between the "justice problem" (sometimes called the "justiciable problem") and legal need. A justice problem may cross over into being a legal need if the legal system is the best way

[19] Erica Turner & Lee Rainie, *Most Rely on Their Own Research in Making Big Life Decisions, and It's Often Online*, Pew Rsch. Ctr. (Mar. 5, 2020), https://www.pewresearch.org/fact-tank/2020/03/05/most-americans-rely-on-their-own-research-to-make-big-decisions-and-that-often-means-online-searches/.

[20] Margaret Hagan, *The User Experience of the Internet as a Legal Help Service: Defining Standards for the Next Generation of User-Friendly Online Legal Services*, 20 Va. J.L. Tech. 395 (2016); Catrina Denvir, *Online and in the Know? Public Legal Education, Young People and the Internet*, 92–93 Computs. & Educ. 204 (2016); Ginnifer L. Mastarone & Susan Feinberg, *Access to Legal Services: Organizing Better Self-Help Systems*, 2007 Inst. Elec. & Elecs. Engineers Int'l Pro. Commc'n Conf. 1.

[21] Gunther Eysenbach, *Infodemiology and Infoveillance: Tracking Online Health Information and Cyberbehavior for Public Health*, 40 Am. J. Preventive Med. 154 (2011).

research helps public health officials improve outreach and education, predict new outbreaks of disease, and develop better services to engage people.

The justice sector can leverage what the health sector has already developed: research protocols, data exchanges, and artificial intelligence aimed at improving people's access to the legal system via the Internet. The public health work on digital epidemiology and infoveillance can guide those working on access to justice to new knowledge on the volume and type of legal needs, people's preferences and needs for services, and opportunities for innovative technology that can improve people's knowledge that they can use the justice system to resolve their life problems, and that can improve their capabilities to participate meaningfully in it.

To develop this research and practice around the Internet for legal help, there is a need for dedicated, ongoing work on an ordinary person's online legal help landscape. This overarching work can spotlight where new directions for justice system outreach, services, and reform could be targeted.

1. What is the demand and supply for justice problem-solving on the Internet?[22]
2. Who are the key intermediaries that are receiving people's help requests and matching them with resources?
3. And what are the datasets and research protocols that we can use to make sense of internet activity, for use in access to justice services and policy making?

The remainder of this chapter tackles one part of this needed research – namely, the first question, on the supply and demand of legal help in the US on the Internet as of 2021. It does so, first, by canvassing past research on how people use the Internet to deal with legal problems. Then it lays out three understudied research questions about the supply-and-demand theme: What is the quantity of the supply and the demand, what is the quality of the supply, and what harms do people experience because of low quantity or low quality? Finally, it offers preliminary answers to these questions by surveying hundreds of commercial and public interest websites that aim to serve people with civil justice problems, calculating initial estimates of how many people are visiting them, and then comparing these visit estimates with the estimates of people's justice problems, based on legal needs surveys.

By way of preview, this analysis shows that that millions of people each month are coming to websites to seek out help for their problems, with many more visitors going to commercial sites than public interest ones. The ecosystem of public interest online resources is scattered among the states, rather than concentrated on national

[22] See an earlier survey of the supply and demand of legal help for ordinary citizens at Gillian K. Hadfield, *Higher Demand, Lower Supply? A Comparative Assessment of the Legal Resource Landscape for Ordinary Americans*, 1 Fordham Urb. L.J. 129 (2010). Hadfield's work was not focused solely on internet-based help, but her work on assessing the legal market is useful for this research.

hubs. Some states' public interest legal help portals are attracting a much higher relative number of visitors than others, indicating that there are substantial opportunities to improve how they offer help to the millions of people coming online for legal help each month.

This, of course, is only a start. Ideally, more researchers and practitioners will tackle the larger research agenda laid out above to build our store of knowledge about how courts, government agencies, legal aid groups, and justice technologists can engage with the public to improve their access and capabilities. In particular, there are many more data sources from internet intermediaries like search engines and social media that can provide insights about where people are going to seek help, whom they trust to help them, and what kinds of behavior they engage in to deal with their problems. Legal policy makers, service providers, and researchers can benefit from greater knowledge of what people are doing on the Internet, and how to increase people's access to the justice system online.

9.2 PRIOR RESEARCH ON LEGAL HELP ON THE INTERNET

Many legal practitioners and scholars in the 2000s highlighted the potential for new websites and internet-based tools to increase access to justice.[23] These proposals detailed how websites could increase the number of people who could find assistance, lower the burdens of time and cost to access help, and improve people's legal capabilities.[24] That "techno-optimism" about whether internet-based technology can increase most people's access to the civil justice system has been challenged in recent years, as website and application development have hit hurdles in accomplishing their goals around user engagement and outcomes.[25]

A small number of researchers have begun investigating if and how the Internet is improving access to justice. This research, primarily by Sandefur, Denvir, and Hagan, examines how people seek out legal assistance on the Internet and what kinds of tools are available for them to use.

9.2.1 *A Growing Supply of Online Help, but Not Always User-Centered*

Sandefur recently surveyed what digital legal help tools exist, and what forms of assistance they offer to users trying to use technology for self-help.[26] Her survey found 322 digital legal tools specifically for nonlawyer users. This included legal

[23] Ronald W. Staudt, *All the Wild Possibilities: Technology That Attacks Barriers to Access to Justice*, 42 Loy. L.A. L. Rev. 1117 (2008).

[24] Engine Room, https://theengineroom.org.

[25] Tanina Rostain, *Techno-Optimism & Access to the Legal System*, 148 Daedalus 93 (2019).

[26] Rebecca L. Sandefur, Legal Tech for Non-Lawyers: Report of the Survey of US Legal Technologies (2019), http://www.americanbarfoundation.org/uploads/cms/documents/report_us_digital_legal_tech_for_nonlawyers.pdf.

help websites with guides and forms, legal dictionaries to clarify jargon, lawyer referral service platforms, and then tools that provide almost end-to-end support for a specific problem (including diagnosis of an issue, evidence gathering, process guides, form assembly, filing, and follow-up). Sandefur observed a mismatch between what the tools offer and the apparent justice needs desired by the public, as well as the issue areas served.[27] Many of the digital legal tools were focused on providing information rather than facilitating user action. They also did not necessarily match the most common user needs reported by people: household finances, health and insurance, consumer problems, family problems, housing, and immigration. This study points to the need for more evaluation of the supply of online legal help, and the development of measures that can encourage more supply that matches the demands and preferences of people in need.

9.2.2 *People Finding Inappropriate Resources on the Internet*

Catrina Denvir has researched how different demographic groups, including young adults and senior citizens in the UK, attempt to use online search to deal with life and legal problems. Her research includes both simulation labs to analyze how people search for help and website assessments to measure the quality of the help people receive.[28] Denvir's work found some common patterns in people's behavior online. Many start with a search engine, type in short questions, and try to find pages that could help them. She observed that young people tended to find and use information with little regard to the importance of jurisdiction. Even as digital natives, they often were unable to use the Internet to get correct information on their problem. In some cases, the young people got distracted by irrelevant information, trying to apply it to their situation, even if it was not legally correct to do so. These lab studies confirm that more people are trying to use the Internet to find help but raise concerns about people (including digital natives) finding "help" that in fact has incorrect, out-of-jurisdiction, or anecdotal information that may lead them astray.

9.2.3 *Preferences for Clear, Authoritative, Open Access, Comprehensive Resources*

My own earlier research performed lab simulations, in which US adults were asked how they might respond to a legal problem using the Internet.[29] This study found that respondents, as in Denvir's studies, preferred to start with a search engine like

27 *Id.* at 10–11.

28 *See* Catrina Denvir, What Is the Net Worth? Young People, Civil Justice and the Internet 245–90 (May 2014) (PhD dissertation, University College London), https://pdfs.semanticscholar.org/b584/c82bbc1baebd435a36ac1aa25001930344fa.pdf (providing website assessment tools).

29 Hagan, *The User Experience of the Internet*.

Google to find help for their civil justice problem. And as with Denvir's respondents, they often ignored the importance of jurisdiction, and they sought out peer-to-peer anecdotes on forums. The study also had respondents evaluate different commercial and public interest legal help websites and express their reasons and preferences for the ideal online assistance. Most all respondents wanted a tool that met the following criteria:[30]

- *Authoritative,* if not directly from the government, then closely affiliated with it;
- *Open Access,* without paywalls, advertisements, or upselling – ideally being offered by a public interest actor rather than a commercial one;
- *Modern Design and Technical Capabilities,* that offer mobile-friendly, intuitive, and interactive resources, and that are accessible to people with disabilities;
- *Comprehensive,* with resources not just for initial understanding of a problem area, but also for taking action to respond to a problem.

These preferences echo Sandefur's concerns that current digital tools are not comprehensive enough (providing only information rather than tools to take action). The user preferences also suggest categories for a standard evaluation metric, which researchers could use to measure if sites are sufficiently meeting people's needs for usability, accessibility, and trustworthiness.

9.2.4 *Open Questions for Further Research*

Research studies so far on the Internet's role in access to justice have been relatively small, with surveys, simulation tasks, and user interviews of small groups of people. What is missing is a broader examination of how people use the Internet to seek help for justice problems. The early research has laid the groundwork: More people are going online to seek help, and there are more sites, tools, and apps being built to serve them. But what do we actually know about the supply and demand of legal help online?

Public health data-driven research can provide legal researchers with models for evaluating the Internet's use for access to a public good. The rise of digital epidemiology, infoveillance, and infodemiology[31] in the public health field offers lessons for legal researchers exploring how people are seeking and finding help for justice problems, on a population level. Digital epidemiology and infoveillance involve drawing upon digital sources of data where people share information about

[30] Denvir, *What Is the Net Worth?*

[31] These three terms are used by various research groups, but often connote the same essential type of research: harnessing digital datasets, internet behavior, and other online resources to track diseases, spot health assistance-seeking, and identifying other trends of interest to public health practitioners.

themselves, like on search engines, social media sites, and other platforms. This data can then be analyzed through techniques like natural language processing to identify patterns, intents, and possible problems. Digital epidemiology has been used to analyze internet datasets to identify possible influenza outbreaks based on patterns of user searches, mental health risks based on online forum posts, and risk of being infected with HIV based on tweets.[32] These techniques have identified patterns of people's medical needs, their preferences for assistance, and the coming outbreak of a crisis – though they may be problematic if relied upon as the sole evidence for where to deploy resources or make policy.[33]

Legal researchers might employ techniques akin to digital epidemiology in order to establish broader, population-level understandings of access to justice on the Internet. Returning to the core research questions introduced previously, but with a richer sense of the state of the field, new research might ask:

1. *What is the quantity of demand and supply for legal help on the Internet?* What is the volume of assistance being sought out? Does the supply match the demand? Are there "online legal help deserts," with minimal resources for certain issue areas? These can help make better agendas of where resources should be spent in creating more online help.
2. *What is the quality of the supply of legal help, and the matching of people to this help?* Are the websites and tools online providing resources that people want to use, are able to use, and that get them to good outcomes? And are intermediary platforms directing people to higher-quality help, or to lower-quality help? Research around quality of supply and quality of intermediary's matching can help set better policy about what kinds of online tools should be funded, and what internet platforms like search engines and social media ought to prioritize in their algorithms.
3. *Are there harms occurring when people seek help on the Internet?* Are people finding malicious or unintentional misinformation about their legal options, processes, and outcomes online? This may be because of their own misunderstanding of jurisdiction, their reliance on anecdotal advice, frauds and scams, or intentional misinformation campaigns. As with public health concerns over misinformation and over harms of

[32] *See, e.g.*, Han Chin Shing et al., *Expert, Crowdsourced, and Machine Assessment of Suicide Risk via Online Postings*, 5 Proc. Workshop on Computational Linguistics & Clinical Psych.: From Keyboard to Clinic 25 (2018).

[33] Google Trends data indices on common searches was trumpeted as an effective way to identify flu outbreaks; in 2013 studies revealed that its ability to track the flu did not correspond to the official public health agency's (the CDC) data – in part because of news reports about the flu leading the search engine to overestimate people actually experiencing symptoms. See Declan Butler, *When Google Got Flu Wrong*, 494 Nature 155 (2013). Researchers acknowledge that internet-based surveillance techniques (based on Google Search query data, Twitter posts, or self-reporting on crowd intelligence sites) had substantial limits and should not be the main source of policy making around services or resources for health.

medical advice being given over the Internet, legal practitioners and policy makers could benefit from more research on whether and how people are finding misinformation about their justice problems online, and what harms these may cause. This could lead to more intentional strategies by service providers, policy makers, and internet platforms to address misinformation and support quality sources of assistance.

This chapter, as already noted, tackles the first of these questions, about the quantity of supply and demand for legal help online. It provides initial data sources, techniques, and findings that can offer some insight into how the Internet is functioning in people's access to justice.

9.3 WHAT IS THE QUANTITY OF SUPPLY AND DEMAND FOR LEGAL HELP ONLINE?

How many people are coming to the Internet to find help for their justice problems? And how many resources are there to assist them with these problems? There is no perfect source of data on the demand or the supply for legal help on the Internet. But there are surveys and proxy data sources that can help us to estimate what is happening online. This section presents the data sources and methods to quantify the supply and demand of legal help online: the sites that are supplying help (either as intermediaries or as providers of legal help) and the numbers of people that are seeking help.

The Internet has billions of websites.[34] How many of these count as "supplying" legal help for people seeking help for justice problems? First, we must distinguish between two types of help websites: intermediaries and providers. Intermediary sites let people express their problem or story, and then discover links, people, or answers to their problem. Some of the primary legal help intermediary platforms in the US are search engines, social media platforms, and forums. Providers' sites, on the other hand, provide content for a person to deal with their justice problem (rather than just referrals to other sites).

9.3.1 *Intermediary Platforms Used for Justice Problem-Solving*

The main intermediaries for justice problems are likely to be the same as general problem-solving intermediaries: search engines, voice assistants, and social media platforms.

Search engines are platforms in which people present words, phrases, or sentences for the intermediary to then interpret and respond with sites (or direct

[34] Martin Armstrong, *How Many Websites Are There?* STATISTA (Aug. 6, 2021), www-statista-com.stanford.idm.oclc.org/chart/19058/number-of-websites-online/.

answers). Google Search is by far the most widely used search engine. For search engines from US desktop computers in 2021, Google received 86.64 percent of search queries, Microsoft's Bing search engine had 6.79 percent, and Yahoo, 2.75.[35] For mobile searches, the companies are in a similar order – but with Google with an even higher share. Of mobile searches in the US in 2021, Google has 93.4 percent market share, Yahoo has 2.02, Bing has 1.87, and DuckDuckGo has 2.3.[36]

Voice assistants, in the form of mobile phone–smart device assistant or voice-enabled speakers, are another rising type of intermediary. Voice assistants are increasingly used, in particular on one's smartphone, car, tablet, television, or computer. Over 63 percent of Americans used a voice assistant as of 2020, and 51 percent use a voice assistant on their smartphone.[37] In 2020, an estimated 128 million US residents used a voice assistant at least once a month.[38] Searching the Internet is the most frequent use cases for voice assistants.[39] For voice assistants specifically in home speakers, Amazon's Alexa brand (as of 2021, relying primarily on the Bing search engine) is the leading voice-enabled speaker with 69.7 percent of US market share in 2020, with Google's Home devices (using Google Search) at 31.7 percent, and others at 18.4 percent.[40]

Social media platforms are another key intermediary. The most popular platforms among US adults as of 2021 were YouTube (81 percent use it), Facebook (69 percent), Instagram (40 percent), Pinterest (31 percent), LinkedIn (28 percent), Snapchat (25 percent), Twitter (23 percent), WhatsApp (23 percent), TikTok (21 percent), Reddit (18 percent), and Nextdoor (13 percent).[41]

35 Joseph Johnson, *Worldwide Desktop Market Share of Leading Search Engines from January 2010 to September 2021*, STATISTA (Mar. 1, 2022), https://www-statista-com.stanford.idm.oclc.org/statistics/216573/worldwide-market-share-of-search-engines/.

36 Joseph Johnson, *U.S. Mobile Search Share 2021*, STATISTA (Mar. 1, 2022), https://www-statista-com.stanford.idm.oclc.org/statistics/511358/market-share-mobile-search-usa/.

37 Lionel Sujay Vailshery, *Share of Voice Assistant Users in the U.S. 2020 by Device*, STATISTA (Mar. 15, 2022), https://www-statista-com.stanford.idm.oclc.org/statistics/1171363/share-of-voice-assistant-users-in-the-us-by-device/; NAT'L PUB. MEDIA, THE SMART AUDIO REPORT (2020), https://www.nationalpublicmedia.com/insights/reports/smart-audio-report/#download.

38 Shanhong Liu, *Number of Voice Assistant Users in the United States, 2017–2022*, STATISTA (Mar. 18, 2022), www-statista-com.stanford.idm.oclc.org/statistics/1029573/us-voice-assistant-users/.

39 Alexander Kunst, *Usage of Google Assistant's Functions in the U.S. 2019*, STATISTA (Nov. 26, 2019), www-statista-com.stanford.idm.oclc.org/forecasts/1038131/usage-of-google-assistant-s-functions-in-the-us; Nicolas Loose, *Virtual Assistants in the U.S., 2019*, STATISTA (Feb. 2019), https://www-statista-com.stanford.idm.oclc.org/study/60113/virtual-assistants-in-the-us/.

40 Federica Laricchia, *Voice-Enabled Speaker User Share by Brand in the United States, 2017–2021*, STATISTA (Feb. 14, 2022), https://www-statista-com.stanford.idm.oclc.org/statistics/720066/us-voice-enabled-speaker-user-share/.

41 Brooke Auxier & Monica Anderson, *Social Media Use in 2021*, PEW RSCH. CTR. (Apr. 7, 2021), https://www.pewresearch.org/internet/2021/04/07/social-media-use-in-2021/.

We can assume that the general popularity of these search engines, voice assistants, and social media sites carries over to justice problem help-seeking. These intermediaries provide opportunities for research on internet problem solving. Just like in public health research, we can use them to observe what people are searching for, how they frame their problems, what they click on, and how they behave. That said, research using these intermediaries is difficult, because they do not make their data about users' searches, clicks, and other behavior open to researchers.

9.3.2 *Provider Websites That Offer Legal Help*

Apart from these intermediaries of online legal help, there are the provider websites, which offer assistance to people seeking help on a justice problem. Within the provider group, there is another division, between commercial providers and public interest providers. Commercial providers have a for-profit business model and are giving help, information, and tools in order to either upsell the user to other services or to get advertisement or referral fees from them. Public interest providers have a nonprofit business model and are trying to get assistance to the user in order to improve their outcomes. Some may aim to generate revenue through paid services, but most public interest sites are funded through grants or government funds.

9.3.3 *Commercial Legal Help Supply*

I surveyed the Internet for commercial websites that offered legal assistance for civil justice problems and identified over seventy sites that have over approximately 5,000 visitors per month. Some of the most prominent general commercial legal help websites are Nolo.com, Avvo.com, Findlaw.com, Legalmatch.com, AllLaw.com, and LawShelf.com. These sites offer resources for a wide variety of legal issue areas.

There is another layer down of commercial legal help suppliers: those that focus on particular areas of legal needs. Some focus on creating legal documents for estate planning, businesses, and contracts.[42] Other providers aim exclusively at business formation legal needs.[43] Another cluster of commercial providers focuses on family law needs, like divorce and child custody.[44] There is another cluster around bankruptcy, debt, and credit repair problems,[45] another around disability benefits

[42] See examples of these sites at the full list of commercial legal help websites compiled at Stanford Legal Design Lab, *Commercial Legal Help Websites*, Legal Help Dashboard, https://legalhelpdashboard.org/websites/commercial-legal-help-websites/.

[43] *Id.* (such as ZenBusiness and Northwest Registered Agent within the business category).

[44] *Id.* (such as Its Over Easy or Custody Xchange in the family category).

[45] *Id.* (such as Debt.org, Debt.com, or Consolidatedcredit.org).

claims and navigating resources for people with special needs,[46] and another around personal injuries and torts.[47]

In addition to sites whose mission is exclusively around providing legal help, there are also commercial sites in other, nonlegal domains that try to attract users with justice problems. In this parallel commercial group, there are sites that offer financial literacy and other professional services, such as Nerdwallet.com, Credit.com, Creditcards.com, Consumerhelpcentral.com, Studentloanhero.com, or Angieslist.com. These sites' resources often overlap with legal help resources, especially for life problems that have both legal and financial dimensions, like debt collection, homeownership, and landlord-tenant scenarios. The other parallel commercial group are news outlets. Sites like Usnews.com, Wusa9.com, WashingtonPost.com, and Cnbc.org offer articles that provide basic overviews of legal situations, with short articles aimed at giving general discussions of various life, legal, and financial problems.

I compiled a list of the most popular commercial legal websites, using search engine optimization (SEO) tools Ahrefs and Similarweb, which list the most popular websites for common keywords. By searching for sites that appear frequently for keywords around law, legal help, legal aid, legal answers, and related issues, I identified approximately seventy commercial legal help sites. This research focused on civil justice problems (so excluding criminal and immigration law keywords). Also excluded were commercial provider websites that appear to have fewer than 5,000 visits per month.

9.3.4 *Public Interest Legal Help Websites*

Apart from the commercial providers, there is a robust ecosystem of public interest legal help websites. They provide similar kinds of content as the commercial ones do articles, step-by-step guides, frequently asked questions, and form-filling tools. They also tend to have contact information for legal aid attorneys, free chat with law librarians, and other on-ramps to free services.

Unlike the commercial provider sites, public interest legal help websites are almost all at the state or local region level. It is notable that there is not a single national legal aid or public interest legal help portal that gives national guidance on civil justice problems. Rather, it has been state or local actors that have created legal help portals for their region, giving guides and contacts for people looking to address their justice problems.[48]

There are some national public interest websites around specific issue areas or demographic groups. For example, there are national public interest sites for sexual

46 *Id.* (such as Disabilitysecrets.com or Specialneedsanswers.com).
47 *Id.* (such as Forthepeople.com, Injuryclaimcoach.com, or EnJuris.com).
48 For a full list of these statewide legal help portals, see Law Help Interactive, https://lawhelpinteractive.org/.

assault and domestic violence,[49] women's law issues,[50] landlord-tenant issues,[51] immigration issues,[52] and bankruptcy and debt issues.[53] There are also some national legal help websites that provide specific tools or resources, like a legal dictionaries and reference materials.[54]

I identified approximately 340 civil help websites that provided free information and tools to people in the fifty states, as well as DC and Puerto Rico. I did not include local bar associations, law library, or county court websites, because the majority of them do not have substantial self-help material (though this may change in the future, and these sites might be added into future research).

Most public interest legal websites operate at the state or regional level. Within each state, frequently there is a local ecosystem of four kinds of public interest legal help websites:

1. A *statewide legal help portal,* which provides an overview of civil justice guides, contacts, FAQs, and tools.
2. A *legal aid organizational website (or sites),* which provides contact information, hotline numbers, clinic details, and a limited number of articles or guides on legal issues. (Some states have many regional legal aid groups, each with its own website, while others have a single main legal aid group serving the entire state.)
3. A *court self-help website,* which offers court-focused guides, tools, forms, and service hours to self-represented litigants who have an issue in civil, family, or traffic court. (Some local county courts may have their own self-help, but typically this is run by the statewide judicial council or administrative office of the courts.)
4. A *free online brief advice clinic* for low-income people, run through the ABA Free Legal Answers project. Not every state has a Free Legal Answers clinic, but more than thirty do.[55]

Some states, like California, Florida, and New Jersey, have many legal aid organizations and so have a large number of public interest websites. Other states, like Wyoming, North Dakota, Georgia, Wisconsin, or New Hampshire, do not have

49 See examples like Rainn.org and TheHotlineorg at the master list of public interest legal help websites, Stanford Legal Design Lab, *Public Interest Legal Help Websites,* Legal Help Dashboard, https://legalhelpdashboard.org/websites/public-sites/.

50 *Id.* (providing examples such as the National Women's Law Center and the Women's Law Project).

51 *Id.* (providing examples such as Legal Help FAQ).

52 *Id.* (providing examples such as Immigration Law Help and Immi).

53 *Id.* (providing examples such as Upsolve.org, Incharge.org, and ConsumerFinance.gov's national resources).

54 *Id.* (providing examples such as Cornell's Legal Information Institute and LegalDictionary).

55 See the full list at American Bar Association Standing Committee on Pro Bono & Public Service, ABA *Free Legal Answers,* https://www.americanbar.org/groups/probono_public_service/projects_awards/free-legal-answers/.

statewide legal help portals and may only have one or two public interest legal help sites.

9.4 WHAT IS THE DEMAND FOR LEGAL HELP ONLINE?

There is no public data source that represents exactly how many people are searching for justice problems. Google and other search engines do not release their data on exact numbers of search volumes for different queries. But there are other proxies that make possible some estimates of how many people are seeking legal help online.

9.4.1 *Estimates of Demand from Legal Needs Surveys*

One way to estimate how many people might be coming online to find help is to look at estimations of how many people experience justice problems in the US. Legal needs surveys ask adults about how often they have experienced justice problems, like situations of wage theft, eviction, debt collection, bankruptcy, domestic violence, foreclosure, access to medical treatment, and the care and custody of children and dependent adults.[56] Sandefur's study of a representative sample of US adults in 2013 found that two-thirds of them experienced at least one civil justice problem in the past eighteen months, with the average number of justice problems being 2.1 problems in eighteen months. Of the two-thirds of adults who reported having a problem, they averaged 3.3 needs in eighteen months.[57]

These rates of justice problems allow us to estimate how much demand there might be for legal help. By using this estimated rate of each adult experiencing 2.1 problems in eighteen months, we can use states' adult populations to estimate how many people are experiencing justice problems in a month. This estimation is likely to overestimate the number of people coming to the Internet to seek help for a justice problem. Surveys have found that 16 percent of US adults take no action (including reaching out for assistance or searching for help) when they experience a justice problem.[58] Accordingly, we can assume that a significant proportion of adults with a justice problem, akin to this 16 percent figure, may not come online to find help. There are not yet surveys that document the rate at which people experiencing a justice problem go onto the Internet to seek help.

56 Rebecca L. Sandefur, *Access to What?* 148 DAEDALUS 49 (2019).
57 SANDEFUR, ACCESSING JUSTICE IN THE CONTEMPORARY USA.
58 See the discussion about inaction after experiencing a justice problem at Rebecca L. Sandefur, *What We Know and Need to Know about the Legal Needs of the Public*, 67 S.C. LAW REV. 443, 448 (2016). Studies of torts and claim-making further explore why so few people are able to "name" their situation as legal, or why they decide against making a claim. DAVID M. ENGEL, THE MYTH OF THE LITIGIOUS SOCIETY (1st ed. 2016); Nora Freeman Engstrom, *ISO the Missing Plaintiff*, TORTS JOTWELL (Apr. 12, 2017), https://torts.jotwell.com/iso-the-missing-plaintiff/.

I calculated each state's expected number of justice problems per month, and the expected number of problems for which people seek help.[59] For example, we might assume that each month in California there are around 3,572,000 justice problems, and that people might take action on approximately 3 million of them. Or in Alabama, there may be around 445,000 problems per month, and people will seek help for around 374,000 problems. In total, we can assume that the whole US population has around 25 million acted-upon justice problems per month (with acted-upon meaning that the adult takes action to try to address it). These estimates provide a rough expectation of how many adults might be seeking help online.

Using these estimates of acted-upon justice problems per state, we can approximate if supply is matching demand. Are people in a state visiting legal aid, court, and public interest websites at the rate we may expect them to? Are there 3 million visits to California legal help websites each month – or is the number substantially higher or lower? How well is the supply of public interest websites matching the demand for legal help?

9.4.2 *Tracking Demand through Analytics and SEO Traffic Estimators*

Aside from estimates based on surveys, another strategy to measure demand is to count the visitors to legal help websites. There is a clear gap in this strategy: Not all people searching for help with a justice problem online will in fact find their way to a legal help website. Website visit counts will not capture demand from people who might have framed their online queries in terms that may have led them to other sites – or who looked at search results and decided not to click anything. Still, the visitor counts can help us see if the expected demand matches the actual demand, and if that matches the number of people using public interest sites.

Site analytics. Sites that have an analytics tool installed can track the numbers of people who come to visit, what search terms or other sites have referred them to this site, and what pages on the site they visit. These analytics numbers are useful because they are closest to being exact counts of visitors. They are not completely accurate. Often they will undercount visitors, because of the use of ad blockers, cookie blockers, and JavaScript disablers by visitors. When a person has these blockers in place on their browser, they can prevent Google Analytics from tracking their behavior – and thus stop the site from registering their visit. Researchers can use Analytics, from websites' administrators that have given them access or reports to their sites. These numbers will likely underestimate actual visits.

SEO platforms have developed tools to estimate the traffic to websites, even without access to websites' administrative backends. These SEO research platforms do not offer exact numbers of how many visitors come to a specific website in a

[59] Stanford Legal Design Lab, *Justice Problem Estimates per State*, Legal Help Dashboard, https://legalhelpdashboard.org/rank/#need.

month. But they provide useful estimations of how many visitors are coming from search engines to a site.[60]

SEO traffic estimator by search keywords. One type of SEO traffic estimation tool, like that from provider Ahrefs, makes these estimates by tracking billions of keywords that people tend to search for, and then seeing how many people are searching for them each month, which sites appear for them, and which sites people click on.[61] This permits estimates of the average monthly visitors coming from search engines to a given site. The SEO traffic estimation tools will most often underestimate actual visitors to a website because of several inbuilt constraints. First, some SEO tools (like Ahrefs) track only visitors who are coming from search engines, and not from other pathways (like those directly typing in the website URL or coming from another non-search website). Second, they do not track every single keyword (or search query) that a person might type into a search engine. Though a tool like Ahrefs Traffic Estimator follows over 6.1 billion keywords, visitors might use "long-tail" searches (like, "show me a legal aid group that can help me with an eviction notice please Google") that it does not track.

SEO traffic estimator by behavior tracking. Another SEO estimation tool, Similarweb, takes a different approach. It gathers data about users' online activities from internet service providers, a panel of monitored devices, and shared web analytics accounts.[62] They use their behavioral tracking data, analytics access, and other public data sources to estimate how many people are visiting a given website. Other SEO tools have found Similarweb to provide the most accurate estimates of total visitors to a site, though they tend to overestimate visitors.[63]

To assess which estimation tool might be useful, I used a website that I maintain with my team at Stanford Legal Design Lab. In May 2020, our team launched a national non-profit website for housing law information, Legal Help FAQ. We have Google Analytics tracking visitors to the website and keeping counts of users and visits. According to Google Analytics, in the month of January 2021, the site had 13,520 users and 30,623 page views. Similarweb estimated that the site had 18,126 users and 31,877 visits. They overestimated visitors by 34 percent (4,606 users), and visits by 4 percent (1,254 visits). Ahref estimated total traffic from Google Search to LegalHelpFAQ to be 42 visitors in January 2021. Google Analytics indicated that we had 4,385 visitors from Google Search in January 2021. This was a substantial

60 See an overview of these SEO research tools for website traffic estimation at Tyler Horvath, *8 Most Accurate Website Traffic Estimators*, Ninja Reps., https://www.ninjareports.com/website-traffic-estimators/.

61 See a full explanation of how Ahrefs' search traffic estimation works at *What Is Organic Traffic in Ahrefs and How Do We Calculate It?* Ahrefs Help Ctr., https://help.ahrefs.com/en/articles/1863206-what-is-organic-traffic-in-ahrefs-and-how-do-we-calculate-it.

62 See Similarweb's data strategy for estimating web traffic at *How We Measure the Digital World*, SimilarWeb, https://www.Similarweb.com/corp/ourdata/.

63 Joshua Hardwick, *Find Out How Much Traffic a Website Gets: 3 Ways Compared*, Ahrefs Blog (Aug. 16, 2018), https://ahrefs.com/blog/website-traffic/.

TABLE 9.1 *Comparison of different estimations of visitors to legal help websites*

Site	Google Analytics reported visitors per month (likely to underestimate)	Similarweb estimation of visits per month (likely to overestimate)	Difference between site Analytics and Similarweb's estimate
Legalhelpfaq.org	13,520	18,126	34 percent over, by 4,606
Wisconsin State Law Library	30,100	36,461	21 percent over, by 6,361
Michigan Legal Help	180,049	166,689	7 percent under, by 13,360
Texas Law Help	318,232	378,050	18 percent over by 59,818

underestimation of search traffic to our site, with a difference of 4,343 visitors. I then proceeded to measure Similarweb's estimates against other sites, whose administrators shared their Google Analytics reports with me (see Table 9.1).

Google Analytics tends to underestimate the number of visitors, though it is not clear by how much. Similarweb seems to overestimate the number of users visiting the site, differing from the Analytics by as much as 34 percent. Similarweb's numbers are substantially closer to the Analytics' numbers than the Ahrefs tool.

With those caveats on the tools' limitations to produce exact numbers, Similarweb does provide us with rough estimates of most legal help websites' traffic. Its ballpark estimates should not be relied upon for exact measures, but they can be approximate counts to help service providers and policy makers compare how different kinds of sites are performing and how they change over time.

9.4.3 *Legal Help Site Visits as Proxy for Demand*

By looking at rough estimates of visits to various types of legal help websites, we can see what kinds of justice problem-solving behavior is happening online. These numbers are estimates from Similarweb, so they may overestimate actual visitors. They are also for a single month, January 2021, which occurred during the COVID-19 pandemic, and so may be different than a typical month (without a public health emergency) (see Table 9.2).

These monthly estimates of visits to commercial legal help websites indicate that tens of millions of people come online to seek assistance and information about the law each month. Compared to our earlier estimate from legal need surveys that the US adult population has approximately 25 million justice problems per month, the visits to commercial websites almost double this estimate. This high number of visits may include "multiple visit" scenarios, in which a person with a single justice

TABLE 9.2 *Estimated visitors to commercial legal help websites in a month*

Type of commercial legal help website	Estimated monthly number of visits to this site in Jan. 2021, from Similarweb
All types of commercial legal help sites	50,909,394
General legal help websites	31,539,004
Legal forms sites	7,702,137
Immigration	3,312,554
Public benefits sites	2,050,050
Family law websites	1,857,023
Small business sites	1,765,107
Debt, credit, and bankruptcy sites	1,439,497
Personal injury sites	1,244,022

problem visits more than one website in order to find assistance. These website visits may also include visits from people outside the US, who found the resource online. Some visits may also come from legal professionals or researchers, using these websites in their own work. We cannot take each visit to a website as indication of a unique justice problem; these numbers of website visits are not direct proxies for legal need counts.

These caveats aside, this estimated traffic of over 50 million visits to US commercial legal help sites in one month strongly suggests that there is a substantial demand for legal information and assistance online. This survey also shows that there are active ecosystems of websites supplying assistance for certain legal issue areas, including immigration, public benefits and disabilities, family law, small business, bankruptcy, and personal injury.

9.4.4 *Visits to Public Interest Legal Help Websites*

As mentioned earlier, most public interest sites are local rather than national. There are approximately twenty public interest national sites, most of which focus on particular legal issues or provide national coverage with legal dictionaries or sets of forms.[64] The total estimated number of visitors in January 2021 to only the national public interest websites was around 6,290,000 visitors.

This 6.2 million visitor count must be adjusted downward, though 4.49 million of those visitors were to Cornell's Legal Information Institute (LII), which provides a legal dictionary and open access to legislation and other laws. Many users of LII are

64 See this the full list of US public interest legal help websites at Stanford Legal Design Lab, *Public Interest Legal Help Websites*, LEGAL HELP DASHBOARD, https://legalhelpdashboard.org/websites/#public.

TABLE 9.3 *Estimated visitors to national public interest legal help websites in a month*

Type of national public interest legal help website	Estimated monthly number of visits to this site in Jan. 2021, from Similarweb
All types of national public interest legal help sites	6,291,274 (or 1,798,274 without LII)
General legal help websites	4,800,403 (of which, 4,493,000 to LII)
Debt and bankruptcy	569,366
Domestic violence	444,591
Women's law	388,478
Immigration	56,559
Housing	31,877

legal professionals and students using its legal reference resources. It's impossible to discern how many of LII's 4.49 million visitors are legal professionals versus people seeking help on their justice problem. The monthly number of laypersons seeking help on the national public interest legal sites likely lies between 1.79 and 6.29 million (see Table 9.3).

The estimated traffic to national public interest sites is substantially lower than that to national commercial help sites, by at least 44 million visits per month. The coverage of issues is also quite different. National public interest websites focus more on debt, domestic violence, and women's law issues, and less so on family law, small business, immigration, public benefits, or housing. In some cases, such as family, benefits, and housing, the shortfall is likely because regional public interest sites are expected to serve this need. But the lack of a national public interest hub for these issues is noticeable, particularly given apparent high demand for these issues.

How do local public interest legal help websites (for instance, those of a local legal aid group or court self-help center) fare, in terms of estimated monthly traffic? Unfortunately, it is difficult to measure most courts' self-help sites, because of the nature of their websites. Most court help pages are located as a subpage of the main court website (like https://www.azcourts.gov/selfservicecenter or https://mdcourts.gov/legalhelp). This prevents estimation of their traffic, because the Similarweb estimation tool works on only the main domain and not the subpages. I was also unable to estimate many legal aid sites' visitors, because they apparently have fewer than 5,000 visits per month, and the Similarweb estimation tool could not reliably predict their visit count.

These limits result in a restricted measure of local public interest site visits. I ran visitor estimations for each state's statewide legal help portal. Not every state has a dedicated "Law Help" portal. In some cases, such as Delaware or Wisconsin, it is a legal aid group's site that functions as a de facto statewide resource. But most of the states do have something akin to Alaska Law Help, Law Help Hawaii, or

TABLE 9.4 *Estimated visitors to statewide legal help portals, including most highly visited sites*

Statewide legal help portal	Estimated monthly number of visits to this site in Jan. 2021, from Similarweb
All statewide legal help portals	3,453,921
Texas Law Help	578,563
Massachusetts Legal Help	424,324
Illinois Legal Aid Online	369,715
Connecticut Law Help	312,095
Michigan Legal Help	248,960
Washington Law Help	218,663
LSNJLaw	174,994
The People's Law Library of Maryland	152,816
Pennsylvania Law Help	100,665
Law Help New York	80,832
Legal Aid Oklahoma	77,806
Arizona Law Help	71,560

Massachusetts Legal Help. The estimated visitor counts to these statewide law-help portals is a first attempt to measure people's visits to local public interest sites.

The total estimated visitors to the statewide legal help portals were approximately 3,454,000 per month. Nine of the portals had over 100,000 estimated visitors per month, mostly from high-population states like Texas, Massachusetts, and Illinois. But the numbers of visitors did not necessarily correspond to population numbers or projected levels of justice problems (see Table 9.4).

9.5 DISCUSSION OF ONLINE LEGAL HELP TRENDS

When we compare the expected number of justice problems in each state to the visits to the statewide legal help portal, some sites have visitor numbers that are a much higher proportion of the estimated demand than others. For example, Connecticut's portal visitor estimates reach almost 95 percent of the estimated justice problems occurring in its adult population. For Massachusetts, this percentage is around 65 percent, Illinois is around 32 percent, and Washington at 31 percent. At the other end of the spectrum, the statewide legal help portals of California, Florida, and North Carolina seem to be getting visits for only around 2 percent of estimated problems in the state (see Table 9.5).[65]

The high proportion of visits to portals in Connecticut and Massachusetts may not mean that nearly every person in these states who experiences a justice problem

65 See the full list of portals' estimated traffic and percentages of expected problems to visits at Stanford Legal Design Lab, *Rankings of Legal Help Websites*, LEGAL HELP DASHBOARD, https://legalhelpdashboard.org/rank/.

TABLE 9.5 *Proportion of estimated acted-upon justice problems to statewide portal visits*

Jurisdiction	Expected number of acted-upon justice problems per month	Estimated visits on state legal help portal for this jurisdiction per month	Difference between estimated problems + web visits	Proportion of expected problems showing up as portal visits
Connecticut	331,082	312,095	−18,987	0.9426516694
Massachusetts	646,299	424,324	−221,975	0.6565444167
Illinois	1,149,627	369,715	−779,912	0.3215956132
Washington	694,380	218,663	−475,717	0.3149039431
Maryland	549,616	152,816	−396,800	0.2780413962
Michigan	915,008	248,960	−666,048	0.2720850528

is coming online and finding their statewide public interest resource. These portal websites may have content and technical strategies that attract visitors from outside their jurisdiction. Their relatively high number of visits does indicate that these states are effective at making public legal help accessible and discoverable online.

9.5.1 *State Portals as an Underdeveloped Resource*

For those states whose portals get relatively few visits, this may be because there is another public interest site in their jurisdiction that has a high-traffic site. For example, in California the statewide legal help portal gets far fewer visitors than the court's statewide Self-Help center website. In this state (unlike most others), the state court is the leader in online legal help.

Still, the estimates of monthly visitors to public interest legal help websites show that there is a broad section of the public that is not finding these free, non-profit resources when they are searching for their justice problems online. The estimated visitors to commercial websites indicate that there are tens of millions of people seeking information on legal topics on the Internet each month. A handful of public interest websites have been able to attract relatively high proportions of their potential audience. But most state portals seem to be getting visits from fewer than 20 percent of people in their state experiencing justice problems.

These findings indicate a gap that policy makers and service providers must prioritize. The supply of public interest legal help sites might be improved with more content, improved technical and design updates, and outreach strategies. The sites may be able to reach more of the people seeking legal help online if they improve their performance so that more people can find them, and more internet intermediaries are likely to place them high on search results.

How does a site improve its offerings and placement by intermediaries? One answer is investment in better content that matches what people are searching for and websites that engage visitors so that they do not click away quickly. It also involves improving the technical and design performance of the sites, so that search engines favor them. More work needs to be done with public interest sites to master these SEO techniques and content development work that many of the commercial sites have done, in order to engage the millions of people coming onto the Internet in search of help.

9.5.2 *Technology Companies' Role in Directing People to Commercial or Public Interest Sites*

Another area of policy concern is the dominance of commercial legal help websites in visitor patterns over public interest websites. To be sure, commercial legal help websites are not inherently bad. For-profit entities have high-powered incentives to offer user-friendly designs, responsive technology, and content and services that match the needs of the public. Their business models, however, tend to steer people away from free legal assistance and give only basic beginning information about a legal issue rather than a full protocol of steps and process.

A standard approach is to offer short descriptive articles about a problem like eviction or debt collection, rather than a full step-by-step guide like those that might be found at public interest websites.[66] One type of commercial model relies on attracting people to click on the site, in order to show them advertisements. These sites present short, generic articles framed around FAQs like "How Do I Stop an Eviction?" which give people descriptions about the law and options of what they can do while showing multiple advertisements for nonlegal content. These generic articles do not provide information about jurisdiction, defenses, laws, or free services a person can use.[67] Another for-profit model provides short summaries of substantial, local legal information for free, but then with a paywall around actionable help. For example, on Nolo's website about non-payment of rent and eviction, the site provides a summary of local legal requirements and defenses. If a visitor wants to understand how to make use of these laws, the site advertises that they should buy the website's books, forms, and templates, or that they should hire a lawyer affiliated

66 See for example the public interest court site on evictions in California, *The Eviction Process for Tenants*, Cal. Ct. Self-Help Guide, https://www.courts.ca.gov/27798.htm, which provides all the details, forms, timelines, and rules for tenants to defend themselves, versus the commercial Nolo site, *How Evictions Work: What Renters Need to Know*, Nolo, https://www.nolo.com/legal-encyclopedia/evictions-renters-tenants-rights-29824.html, which provides a short summary before recommending the purchase of a book or hiring of a lawyer through a referral service.

67 For example, see the SFGate article "How to Catch Up on Rent So You're Not Evicted" that provides a five-step set of advice, but without mention of legal aid, mediators, emergency rent programs, or other laws or services that can help people. Jenna Marie, *How to Catch Up on Rent So You're Not Evicted*, SFGate, https://homeguides.sfgate.com/catch-up-rent-not-evicted-42577.html.

with the site.[68] By contrast, public interest sites tend to give visitors a menu of free assistance, including do-it-yourself guides, form-filling tools, free legal navigators, legal aid representation, and holistic social services assistance.

Commercial websites may be getting so much traffic vis-à-vis public interest ones because they have deployed more search engine optimization strategies: producing more content that matches people's search keywords, creating sites that people stay on for longer amounts of times, having technically capable websites, and taking other actions that make it more likely for Google and other search engines to place them higher on search results pages. Public interest organizations may, as mentioned before, improve the content and technical performance of their sites to be more competitive.

Still another factor that shapes comparative use rates is the search engine companies' policies themselves. As with other sectors, the search engine companies could alter their ranking algorithm to prioritize court, legal aid, and other public interest legal help providers above commercial providers. Google, for example, has altered how it responds to its users' searches around health problems or voting and elections to provide information that is sourced from vetted public interest actors rather than commercial websites. In 2015, Google partnered with the Mayo Clinic and medical doctors hired by their company to curate medical knowledge panels to show in response to people's health searches.[69] In 2016, Google worked with a university and foundation-supported Voting Information Project to present knowledge panels on where to vote, requirements to vote, and who is on the ballot in local elections.[70] Could such an initiative be possible for users' queries around evictions, foreclosures, wage theft, divorce, custody, debt collections, and domestic violence protection? Technology companies play a substantial intermediary role, directing people to resources that can answer their questions and conferring authority to those that place high in their search results. Public interest organizations may partner with these search engine intermediaries to create knowledge panels and search rank algorithms that convey key local legal help information to people searching online that would appear before the normal search results from a mix of commercial and public interest providers.

More thinking remains to be done on how best to harness the capacities, resources, and profit-seeking motivation of the commercial sector alongside the

[68] An example is a California eviction help page from Nolo. Beth Dillman, *Eviction Notices for Nonpayment of Rent in California*, NOLO, https://www.nolo.com/legal-encyclopedia/eviction-notices-nonpayment-rent-california.html.

[69] *See* Prem Ramaswami, *A Remedy for Your Health-Related Questions: Health Info in the Knowledge Graph*, GOOGLE: KEYWORD BLOG (Feb. 10, 2015), https://blog.google/products/search/health-info-knowledge-graph/.

[70] *E.g.*, *VIP Projects*, *VOTING INFO. PROJECT*, https://www.votinginfoproject.org/projects; Shashi Thakur, *Google and YouTube Can Help Keep You Informed on Election Day*, GOOGLE: THE KEYWORD BLOG (Nov. 7, 2016), https://blog.google/products/search/google-and-youtube-can-help-keep-you-informed-election-day/.

public-interest orientation and ethical approach of non-profit and legal aid groups, whether public or private. The empirical analysis presented above aims to spur some of that thinking.

9.6 CONCLUSION

This chapter raises many questions for future research about the role of the Internet in access to justice. Is it an effective on-ramp into the justice system for people who come online to find help? Or is it confusing, misleading, or harmful – possibly directing people to incorrect or unhelpful resources, or overwhelming them so that they disengage, or offering them too-limited resources that don't empower them to take action to resolve a problem?

Future research can build off the initial data collection, methods, and analysis in this chapter. The documentation of the legal supply – the intermediaries, commercial providers, and non-profit providers – can be built upon, with greater evaluation of their traffic, their quality, and people's outcomes when using different kinds of online sites. The initial estimates of demand for online legal help might be refined in future work, with better information about the rates at which people go online for justice problems and the rate of different kinds of legal issues.

This chapter was not able to tackle many other important questions about the Internet's role in access to justice. In particular, *what is the quality of the supply of legal help online?* Are people able to discover the highest quality help, or are they being directed toward lower-quality or incorrect help by intermediaries? This type of quality evaluation can be done through a standardized scorecard of legal help sites, building off of earlier research on user preferences and effectiveness of legal technology. Building off of Sandefur, Hagan, and Denvir's earlier assessments of legal help tools' quality, some key measurements of quality are: (1) *content quality* (accuracy, relevancy, and actionability); (2) *human-centered design* (accessibility, amount of administrative burden, and engagement of user); (3) *technical performance* (speed, lack of bugs, responsiveness); and (4) *discoverability* (search engine placement, social media referrals, backlinks to trustworthy sources).

In addition, legal researchers can build from public health researchers' digital epidemiology and infoveillance techniques *to track legal needs through search engines and social media data sources.* Researchers could pool legal aid groups' Google Analytics, or use SEO traffic estimators, along with Google Trends and other intermediaries' APIs in order to track people's online expressions of justice problems and legal needs longitudinally. This research on legal needs can provide useful population-level knowledge about what kinds of justice problems people are experiencing, what seasonal patterns exist, and what outbreaks of needs may necessitate new emergency services or outreach.

The final priority area going forward should be *documenting and measuring harms* people may be experiencing when seeking assistance online. Are there situations akin to antivaccine misinformation in law? How often are search engines directing people to legal help resources from the wrong jurisdiction, leading people to rely on incorrect law, file incorrect forms, or use a defense they don't actually have?

Finally, in addition to more research-focused work, policy makers and justice stakeholders should focus on online strategies to address the justice gap. There are two main avenues. First are efforts to increase the prominence of public interest legal help online. This work could aim to reform existing state help portals, legal aid websites, and free tools, to have content that better matches people's searches, design that is more user-friendly, and technology that is more responsive and fast-loading. All of these factors can increase public interest websites' prominence in search results and numbers of visitors. The second reform avenue is for court and legal aid leaders to engage technology companies to change how search algorithms treat people's searches for justice problems. There is the potential for a public-private partnership, to develop more reliable, quality content for Google, Siri, and other search engines to feature when someone goes online to search "help I'm being evicted" or "how do I get a restraining order?" The Internet holds great promise in developing people's awareness of their rights and their capability to take action on justice problems, but there is still substantial work to be done to deliver on this potential.

10

Digital Inequalities and Access to Justice

Dialing into Zoom Court Unrepresented

Victor D. Quintanilla, Kurt Hugenberg, Margaret Hagan, Amy Gonzales, Ryan Hutchings, and Nedim Yel

The gravest public health challenge in a century has disrupted and transformed our civil justice system. In the span of weeks, courts across the country were forced to make countless, rapid, and difficult decisions. Many courts suspended in-person hearings and moved proceedings to online platforms, such as Zoom. While a shift to virtual courts has been lauded by technological enthusiasts and reformers for decades, little research has examined how this technological change may affect vulnerable unrepresented persons and low-income people in the United States on the "have-not" side of the digital divide.

In this chapter, we seek to cast light on how virtual proceedings unfold for these low-income unrepresented persons in the everyday. It is important to do so. To date, much of the conversation has lauded Zoom court proceedings as the future of civil justice, centering this praise on idealized forms of online proceedings and their conveniences, without interrogating the impact of the precarity that low-income people contend with or persistent digital divides.

In marked departure, we examine how these new technologies affect the experiences of low-income unrepresented persons who encounter, and contend with, adversities within virtual court proceedings. We examine how these new technologies reconfigure the features, affordances, and barriers present within the civil justice system, and the impact of these new technologies on the psychology of judges, lawyers, and unrepresented persons, as well as the impact of these new technologies on the meaning of the judicial role and on a person's unrepresented status. As political theorist of science and technology Langdon Winner observes, "[i]f the

We are incredibly grateful to Nora Al Haider and Rachel Wang for their help designing and administering this study, and to the research assistants who helped by observing the virtual hearings involved in this preliminary study, including Crystal Chidume, Annie Garau, Sabina Neagu, Roda Nour, Jocelyn Porter, Natalia Rivera, and RJ Vogel, and finally to Abby Akrong and Ingrid Radulescu for their research assistance with this manuscript. All credit belongs to this band of collaborators, and any errors are my own.

experience of modern society shows us anything ... it is that technologies are not merely aids to human activity, but also powerful forces acting to reshape that activity and its meaning."[1] In fact, we must "pay attention not only to the making of physical instruments and processes ... but also, to the production of psychological, social, and political conditions as part of any significant technological change."[2]

Here we adopt Winner's perspective by focusing not on an idealized future for virtual courts under techno-optimistic conditions, but on the actual practice and experience of low-income unrepresented persons in virtual courtrooms today. We do so to allow a forthright consideration of policies and reforms needed to improve access to justice. Unlike debating the costs and benefits of in-person versus virtual proceedings under idealized conditions, looking to the bottom casts light on the actual needs, experiences, and outcomes of real people in virtual proceedings. Moreover, we believe that examining how virtual proceedings unfold in the everyday will contribute to the development and refinement of accurate and useful theories about our dynamic civil justice system and best practices for enhancing access to justice in virtual proceedings. Finally, we center our analysis not just on the experiences of those on the "have" side of the digital divide or those who are the most powerful in these settings – judges and lawyers – but also on those on the "have-not" side of the digital divide: low-income people who contend with adversities and confront challenges when seeking justice in virtual courtrooms.

Past research on videoconference hearings is mixed on whether the use of videoconferencing negatively impacts assessments and outcomes.[3] Research does suggest that defendants appearing in videoconferences may be disadvantaged.[4] Indeed, one widely cited study revealed that video bail hearings resulted in bail amounts that were 51 percent higher for those who appeared virtually as opposed to those who had their hearings in person.[5] Yet these studies are dated, and the technologies employed in virtual courts during the global pandemic have vastly

[1] Langdon Winner, *Technologies as Forms of Life*, *in* Ethics and Emerging Technologies 48 (Ronald L. Sandler ed., 2014).

[2] *Id.*

[3] *See* Chapter 4 in this volume; Lily Trimboli & Judy Cashmore, *Child Sexual Assault Trials: A Survey of Juror Perceptions*, Crime & J. Bull., Sept. 2006; Louise Ellison & Vanessa E. Munro, *A Special Delivery: Exploring the Impact of Screens, Live-Links and Video-Recorded Evidence on Mock Juror Deliberation in Rape Trials*, 23 Soc. & Legal Stud. 3 (2014); Bradley D. McAuliff & Margaret Bull Kovera, *The Status of Evidentiary and Procedural Innovations in Child Abuse Proceedings*, *in* Children and the Law: Social Science and Policy 412 (Bette L. Bottoms et al. eds., 2002); Fredric I. Lederer, *The Road to the Virtual Courtroom? A Consideration of Today' s – and Tomorrow's – High Technology Courtrooms*, 50 S.C. L. Rev. 799 (1999); Natalie Taylor & Jacqueline Joudo Larsen, The Impact of Pre-Recorded Video and Closed Circuit Television Testimony by Adult Sexual Assault Complainants on Jury Decision-Making: An Experimental Study (2005), https://evawintl.org/wp-content/uploads/rpp068.pdf.

[4] *See* Shari Seidman Diamond et al., *Efficiency and Cost: The Impact of Videoconferenced Hearings on Bail Decisions*, 100 J. Crim. L & Criminology 869 (2010); Carolyn McKay, *Video Links from Prison: Court "Appearance" within Carceral Space*, 14 L. Culture & Humans. 242 (2018).

[5] *See* Diamond et al., *Efficiency and Cost*.

improved. Moreover, little attention has been paid, to date, to the implications of video conferencing for unrepresented persons, let alone cases involving asymmetries of representation involving low-income persons. In short, there is pressing need for a new and thorough look at the access-to-justice implications of virtual hearings.

In this chapter, we report the first phase of a multiphase research program made possible with funding from the Pew Charitable Trusts. In this preliminary phase, our research team engaged in observations of over 500 live-streamed Zoom/Webex proceedings in small claims courts in Indiana, most of which were eviction and debt collection cases. Our research revealed that the vast majority of low-income persons in these cases are unrepresented (98.6 percent), and a majority are dialing into virtual court (e.g., Zoom/Webex hearings) on their cell phones (64.4 percent) without access to the virtual capabilities of these remote proceedings, including cameras. In the main, these cases involve representational asymmetries, in which repeat-player plaintiff lawyers litigate against low-income persons who are unrepresented. Troublingly, these cases entail an additional layer of technological asymmetry, in which repeat-player lawyers regularly employ the full range of virtual interaction and videoconferencing capabilities of Zoom/Webex, while the low-income unrepresented persons whom they sue, because they dial into these proceedings, are limited to the audio-only capabilities of their cell phones.

The chapter proceeds as follows. Section 10.1 introduces the theory of "doing" unrepresented status, with an emphasis on the social production of unrepresented persons and the social construction of pro se status, orienting the reader toward the social-cognitive processes of judges, lawyers, and unrepresented persons. Section 10.2 describes persistent digital divides in the US. Section 10.3 reports results from empirical observations in virtual civil courts, including the surprising (to us) finding that low-income unrepresented persons are overwhelmingly using cell phones to dial into Zoom/Webex-based virtual hearings, limited to audio-only capabilities. Section 10.4 discusses our observations, considering the asymmetries in affordances, barriers, and constraints created by technological asymmetries and the impact of these asymmetries on the social cognition of judges, lawyers, and unrepresented persons.

10.1 DOING UNREPRESENTED STATUS: THE SOCIAL PRODUCTION OF UNREPRESENTED PERSONS AND THE SOCIAL CONSTRUCTION OF PRO SE STATUS

Over 15 million cases filed each year in our state civil justice systems involve one or more unrepresented persons,[6] and the percentage of unrepresented people has risen

6 *See* Colleen F. Shanahan & Anna E. Carpenter, *Simplified Courts Can't Solve Inequality*, 148 Daedalus 128 (2019); Paula L. Hannaford-Agor et al., Nat'l Ctr. for State Cts.: The Landscape of Civil Litigation in State Courts (2015), https://www.ncsc.org/__data/assets/pdf_file/0020/13376/civiljusticereport-2015.pdf.

rapidly in case categories where basic human needs are at stake, including evictions, family law, and debt collection cases.[7] Many unrepresented persons are members of racially and socially disadvantaged groups.[8] They encounter our civil justice system without legal representation to defend their basic civil legal rights.

The theory of doing unrepresented status[9] posits the social production of unrepresented persons. That is, the very presence, and the vast percentage, of unrepresented persons within our civil justice system is not a fixed, natural, or inherent quality of that system.[10] Rather, society produces unrepresented persons and the manner in which they appear, participate, and engage with our civil justice system through societal decisions and public policy choices – including public policy choices about the technologies that we employ to organize the civil justice system. These policy choices shape how unrepresented persons access and appear in the civil justice system, how they are perceived and socially constructed by court officials and other actors, and in turn, how they interact with others as a result.[11] These social dynamics create feedback loops, recursive processes, or self-fulfilling prophecies, in which expectations and social roles affect everyday interactions between persons within the civil justice system.

Second, the theory of doing unrepresented status posits the social construction of pro se persons.[12] That is, an unrepresented person's pro se status is an active process, involving social cognitive processes (how we think and feel about others), social identity processes (how we think and feel about social identities), and behavioral processes (how we speak and act toward others) that people do and ascribe onto unrepresented persons. Legal officials impute and apply mental schemas, expectations, stereotypes, and beliefs about the characteristics of pro se parties onto people navigating the civil justice system without lawyers.[13] This aspect of doing unrepresented status centers on the cognition, affect, and behavior of judges and lawyers toward these persons, and the intergroup interactions that unfold as a result within the civil justice system.[14] Everyone with whom an unrepresented person comes into contact within the civil justice system makes

7 *See* Stephan Landsman, *The Growing Challenge of Pro Se Litigation*, 13 Lewis & Clark L. Rev. 439 (2009).

8 *See* Matthew Desmond, Evicted (2016); Amy Myrick et al., *Race and Representation: Racial Disparities in Legal Representation for Employment Civil Rights Plaintiffs*, 15 N.Y.U. J. Legis. & Pub. Pol'y 705 (2012).

9 Victor D. Quintanilla, *Doing Unrepresented Status: The Social Construction and Production of Pro Se Persons*, 69 DePaul L. Rev. 543 (2019).

10 *See* Robert H. Frank, *How Rising Income Inequality Threatens Access to the Legal System*, 148 Daedalus 10 (2019).

11 Quintanilla, *Doing Unrepresented Status*.

12 *Id.*

13 *See* Kathryn Kroeper et al., *Underestimating the Unrepresented: Cognitive Biases Disadvantage Pro Se Litigants in Family Law Cases*, 26 Psych. Pub. Pol'y & L. 198 (2020); Victor D. Quintanilla et al., *The Signaling Effect of Pro Se Status*, 42 L. & Soc. Inquiry 1091 (2017).

14 Quintanilla, *Doing Unrepresented Status*.

use of shared meanings and mental representations about what it means for people, in general, to be pro se within the civil justice system and why they are unrepresented. These shared meanings invariably shape how unrepresented persons are perceived and the interactions that unfold between unrepresented persons and others within the civil justice system. Many judges, lawyers, and court officials hold subtle (and sometimes overt) negative attitudes about unrepresented persons. Moreover, merely being unrepresented can serve as a justification for treating unrepresented persons poorly, particularly those who are racial/ethnic minorities or who belong to socially disadvantaged groups.

Finally, the theory of doing unrepresented status also posits that different classes and groups of unrepresented persons will experience pro se status somewhat differently.[15] For example, these structural and psychological processes may unfold differently for persons who belong to advantaged societal groups who are on the "have" side of the digital divide than for low-income persons who belong to racially or socially disadvantaged groups on the "have-not" side of the digital divide.[16]

10.2 DOING PRO SE STATUS IN ONLINE COURT: PERSISTENT DIGITAL DIVIDES

How the digital divide impacts virtual court proceedings, especially given the technological asymmetries among represented and unrepresented parties, is a critical but unanswered question.[17] The digital divide and differential access to modern information technology (e.g., internet communication technology, computing technology, high-speed internet) impinges on the ability of low-income Americans to participate in important dimensions of modern social-political life online, including: learning, seeking out employment, working, identifying and obtaining social services, and participating in democratic institutions.[18] Americans find themselves increasingly separated into "digital haves," with easy and fluent access to information technology, high-speed internet, and technical savvy, and "digital have-nots," who rely primarily on smartphones for internet access, or the "smartphone dependent," often with interrupted and low-quality connections.[19]

[15] *Id.*

[16] *See* Rachel Kahn Best et al., *Multiple Disadvantages: An Empirical Test of Intersectionality Theory in EEO*, 45 LITIG. L. & SOC'Y REV. 991 (2011); Rebecca Sandefur, *Access to Civil Justice and Race, Class, and Gender Inequality*, 34 ANN. REV. SOCIO. 339 (2008).

[17] *See* Alicia L. Bannon & Douglas Keith, *Remote Court: Principles for Virtual Proceedings during the COVID-19 Pandemic and Beyond*, 115 NW. L. REV. 1875 (2021).

[18] *See* Amy L. Gonzales, *The Contemporary US Digital Divide: From Initial Access to Technology Maintenance*, 19 INFO. COMMC'N & SOC'Y 234 (2015).

[19] *See* Amy L. Gonzales, *Health Benefits and Barriers to Cell Phone Use in Low-Income Urban U.S. Neighborhoods: Indications of Technology Maintenance*, 2 MOBILE MEDIA & COMMC'N

Troublingly, given these existing digital divides, the shift from in-person to virtual proceedings may exacerbate societal inequalities in the courtroom. In other words, if many courtrooms are using Zoom/Webex videoconferencing technologies, many low-income unrepresented persons may not have the stable access to internet communication technologies necessary to fully participate in hearings that affect their life outcomes.[20] Consistent with the theory of doing unrepresented status – and the social production of unrepresented persons in particular – we posit that these first-order digital divides lead many low-income unrepresented persons to use cell phones to dial into Zoom/Webex hearings with audio-only capabilities, rather than videoconferencing capabilities. These unrepresented persons who access Zoom hearings in audio-only form would visually appear to judges and lawyers in these Zoom hearings as depersonalized black Zoom tiles.[21]

10.2.1 *First-Order Digital Divide(s): Access to Technology and Stable Internet Connection*

Many unrepresented persons – indeed, those facing the most economic precarity – do not have reliable access to the Internet or the videoconferencing technologies to fully participate in virtual hearings. According to the Pew Research Center, many low-income Americans rely on their cellphones to access the Internet and are "smartphone-dependent" internet users, meaning that they access the Internet on their cellphones and do not have broadband internet at home. About one-in-three do not have a cell phone at all. Moreover, there are substantial disparities in access to internet broadband and computers at home,[22] with Black, Hispanic,[23] and rural[24] households residing on the "have-not" side of the digital divide.

233 (2014); Amy L. Gonzales et al., *Cell Phone Disconnection Disrupts Access to Healthcare and Health Resources: A Technology Maintenance Perspective*, 18 New Media & Soc'y 1422 (2016).

20 *See* Paul DiMaggio et al., *Digital Inequality: From Unequal Access to Differentiated Use*, *in* Social Inequality 355 (Kathryn Neckerman ed., 2004); Kathryn Zickuhr & Aaron Smith, *Digital Differences*, Pew Rsch. Ctr. (Apr. 13, 2012), https://www.pewresearch.org/internet/2012/04/13/digital-differences/.

21 *See* Chapter 4 in this volume.

22 *See* Emily A. Vogels, *Some Digital Divides Persist between Rural, Urban, and Suburban America*, Pew Rsch. Ctr. (Aug. 19, 2021), https://www.pewresearch.org/fact-tank/2021/08/19/some-digital-divides-persist-between-rural-urban-and-suburban-america/; Jason Tashea, *Nothing Is Off-Limits for This California Bar Task Force*, A.B.A. J., (Feb. 1, 2020, 3:00 AM), https://www.abajournal.com/legalrebels/article/nothing-is-off-limits-for-the-calif-bars-task-force-on-access-through-innovation-in-legal-services.

23 *See* Vogels, *Some Digital Divides Persist*; Monica Anderson & Madhumitha Kumar, *Digital Divide Persists Even as Lower Income Americans Make Gains in Tech Adoption*, Benton (May 7, 2019), https://www.benton.org/headlines/digital-divide-persists-even-lower-income-americans-make-gains-tech-adoption-0; Zickuhr & Smith, *Digital Differences*.

24 *See* Anderson & Kumar, *Digital Divide Persists*; Andrew Perrin & Sara Artske, *Home Broadband Adoption, Computer Ownership Vary by Race, Ethnicity in the U.S.*, Pew Rsch.

Troublingly, bridging these first-order digital divides by providing initial access may not be enough to ensure true, reliable, material access or meaningful participation. Material access is a multidimensional construct,[25] and the ongoing struggle to ensure material access may be better understood through a lens of technology maintenance.[26] Technology maintenance refers to the burdens of time, energy, and money required to maintain digital access even after ownership of a cell phone.[27] Technology maintenance practices that limit functionality include: counting cell phone minutes to avoid "going over"; switching between cell phones depending on minutes; or "beeping" (calling and hanging up) to communicate without minutes.[28] Moreover, users share cell phones with family members, which requires maintenance of personal relationships.[29]

While most low-income Americans have intermittent access to the Internet, this access is often unstable and characterized by frequent periods of disconnection and cycles of reliable unreliability.[30] Low-income Americans contend with temporarily disconnected service, broken hardware, and barriers on public access. These disruptions diminish access to unemployment, healthcare, education, and social support.[31]

CTR. (July 16, 2021), https://www.pewresearch.org/fact-tank/2021/07/16/home-broadband-adoption-computer-ownership-vary-by-race-ethnicity-in-the-u-s/.

25 *See* JAN A. G. M. VAN DIJK, THE DEEPENING DIVIDE: INEQUALITY IN THE INFORMATION SOCIETY (2005).

26 *See* Gonzales, *Indications of Technology Maintenance*; Gonzales et al., *A Technology Maintenance Perspective*.

27 *See* Gonzales, *Indications of Technology Maintenance*; Gonzales et al., *A Technology Maintenance Perspective*.

28 *See* Jonathan Donner, *The Rules of Beeping: Exchanging Messages via Intentional "Missed Calls" on Mobile Phones*, 13 J. COMPUTER-MEDIATED COMMC'N 1 (2008); Gonzales, *Indications of Technology Maintenance*; Gonzales et al., *A Technology Maintenance Perspective*; HEATHER A. HORST & DANIEL MILLER, THE CELL PHONE: AN ANTHROPOLOGY OF COMMUNICATION (2006); Sebastian Ureta, *Mobilizing Poverty? Mobile Phone Use and Everyday Spatial Mobility among Low Income Families in Santiago, Chile*, 24 INFO. SOC'Y 83 (2008).

29 *See* Arul Chib & Vivian Hsueh-Hua Chen, *Midwives with Mobiles: A Dialectical Perspective on Gender Arising from Technology Introduction in Rural Indonesia*, 13 NEW MEDIA & SOC'Y 486 (2011); Arul Chib et al., *Midwives and Mobiles: Using ICTs to Improve Healthcare in Aceh Besar, Indonesia*, 18 ASIAN J. COMMC'N 348 (2008); Gonzales et al., *A Technology Maintenance Perspective*.

30 *See* Gonzales et al., *A Technology Maintenance Perspective*.

31 *See* Gonzales et al., *Indications of Technology Maintenance*; Gonzales et al., *A Technology Maintenance Perspective*; Amy L. Gonzales et al., *Technology Problems and Student Achievement Gaps: A Validation and Extension of the Technology Maintenance Construct*, 47 COMMC'N RSCH. 750 (2020); Ilana Gershon & Amy Gonzales, *You Got a Hole in Your Belly and a Phone in Your Hand: How US Government Phone Subsidies Shape the Search for Employment*, 23 NEW MEDIA & SOC'Y 853 (2021).

10.2.2 *Second-Order Digital Divide(s): Inequalities in Technological Capabilities and Efficacy*

The persistence of a second-level digital divide[32] refers to the fact that differences in digital proficiencies produce inequality, often revealed by limited digital literacy or efficacy in navigating the web.[33] Barriers to first-order access and the frictions of technological maintenance compound to produce negative attitudes toward, and perceived lack of utility of, the Internet.[34] Relatedly, low-income Americans who lack a computer at home experience higher emotional costs than others when using computing technology. That is, barriers on home computers engender psychological friction toward computing technology.[35] Undoubtedly, first-order structural inequalities contribute to a vicious cycle: Structural inequalities produce second-order digital divides by reducing technological efficacy, creating psychological friction, and affecting the type and quality of online activity,[36] ultimately conditioning the benefits of being online.

10.3 OBSERVATIONS IN VIRTUAL COURT

In spring 2020, we engaged in over 500 structured observations of virtual proceedings in Indiana in small claims courts among 20 Indiana judges who handle high volumes of small claims cases, debt-collection cases, and evictions online. Within these observations, our research team observed that the vast majority of low-income unrepresented persons are dialing into Zoom virtual hearings with their cell phones. The vast majority of these cases involve representational asymmetries in which opposing counsel has the full video capabilities of Zoom, while these unrepresented persons are limited to audio capabilities. In many instances, these unrepresented persons are members of racial and ethnic minorities, as judged by their paralinguistic intonations on the phone. These preliminary findings suggest that the effects of moving to virtual proceedings, both benefits and costs, are not evenly distributed

32 *See* Eszter Hargittai, *Second-Level Digital Divide: Differences in People's Online Skills*, 7(4) First Monday (2002).

33 *See* Massimo Ragnedda & Glenn W. Muschert, The Digital Divide: The Internet and Social Inequality in International Perspective (2013).

34 *See* Gonzales et al., *A Technology Maintenance Perspective*; Alison Powell et al., *The Essential Internet: Digital Exclusion in Low-Income American Communities*, 2 Pol'y & Internet 159 (2010); Constance Elise Porter & Naveen Donthu, *Using the Technology Acceptance Model to Explain How Attitudes Determine Internet Usage: The Role of Perceived Access Barriers and Demographics*, 59 J. Bus. Rsch. 999 (2006); Pieter Verdegem & Pascal Verhoest, *Profiling the Non-User: Rethinking Policy Initiatives Stimulating ICT Acceptance*, 33 Telecomms. Pol'y 642 (2009).

35 *See* Kuo-Ting Huang et al., *Access Is Not Enough: The Impact of Emotional Costs and Self-Efficacy on the Changes in African-American Students' ICT Use Patterns*, 20 Info. Commc'n & Soc'y 637 (2017).

36 *See* Dijk, The Deepening Divide.

between the "have" and "have-not" sides of the digital divide or between lawyers and low-income unrepresented persons. We now turn to the preliminary findings of this first phase of our multi-phase research program.

10.3.1 *Study Overview*

Method. A team of six law student observers at the Indiana University Maurer School of Law and Stanford Law School engaged in structured observations of over 500 live-streamed virtual proceedings among twenty Indiana judges who handle high volumes of small claims cases (e.g., evictions, debt collection, small claims) online. These observations were conducted between March 1 and April 23, 2021 (a seven-week window). These observers accessed the virtual hearings via the Indiana Office of Court Service's live-streaming website. To ensure that these observations focused on small claims, debt-collection, and eviction cases, these observers accessed the courts' public daily hearing calendars and private weekly hearing calendars provided by the Indiana Office of Court Services. A detailed coding scheme was developed, and these law students were trained over the course of two weeks on how to implement this coding scheme. The observation data was inputted via a Qualtrics survey.

Measures. For purposes of this chapter, which reports preliminary results, we report three coded measures: (1) Represented by an attorney? (2) Dialed in by phone to virtual hearing (e.g., Phone number on Zoom tile or only voice heard)? and (3) Camera on? The observers coded these features of each of the over 500 live-streamed hearings, indicating in categorical terms whether these features occurred: yes, no, unsure, NA.

Data preparation. Data was entered in Qualtrics, and analyses were performed in R version 4.0.2. The full dataset of live, virtual proceeding observations included n = 503 observations, and included hearings without a subject matter indicator. These miscellaneous hearings were removed from the dataset, and the dataset was narrowed to n = 455, which included observations of small claims cases, debt-collection cases, and evictions. Next, n =106 of these 455 cases were observed by multiple law students. Accordingly, we developed an inter-rater coding analysis strategy in which data in the above-mentioned measures were retained for purposes of analysis when a majority of these multiple observers agreed when resting whether (1) a party was represented or not at the virtual hearing, (2) a party dialed into the hearing on their phone or not, or (3) a party's camera was on or not. In the vast majority of instances, coders agreed about these aspects of a party's appearance at the hearing. After removing the duplicate observations from the dataset, n = 349 unique observations remained. Regarding the subject matter of these cases, these n = 349 cases entailed eviction cases (n = 150), debt-collection cases (n = 103), small claims cases (n = 90), and other cases (n = 6) appearing on these high-volume dockets.

10.3.2 *Preliminary Results*

Representational asymmetries. We first analyzed representational asymmetries (n = 349), and in doing so, we categorized parties as represented if a lawyer appeared in their case and classified cases in which defendants/respondents defaulted as cases in which they did not have counsel. As anticipated and consistent with the literature (Figure 10.1), a majority of hearings involved representation asymmetries in which plaintiffs/claimants were represented and defendants/respondents were not (n = 209, 59.9 percent). Defendants/respondents were rarely represented (n = 5, 1.4 percent). Both parties were unrepresented in nearly 40 percent of cases (n = 135, 38.7 percent).

Technological asymmetries. We first analyzed technological symmetries in a manner that included defaults by defendant/respondents and no-shows by plaintiffs/claimants (n = 338). As revealed in Figure 10.2, the most notable observation when including defaults and no-shows is that, despite the apparent conveniences provided by remote proceedings, defendants/respondents nevertheless default in approximately 55 percent of cases (n = 186, 55.0 percent), whereas plaintiffs/claimants rarely no-show (n = 6, 1.8 percent).

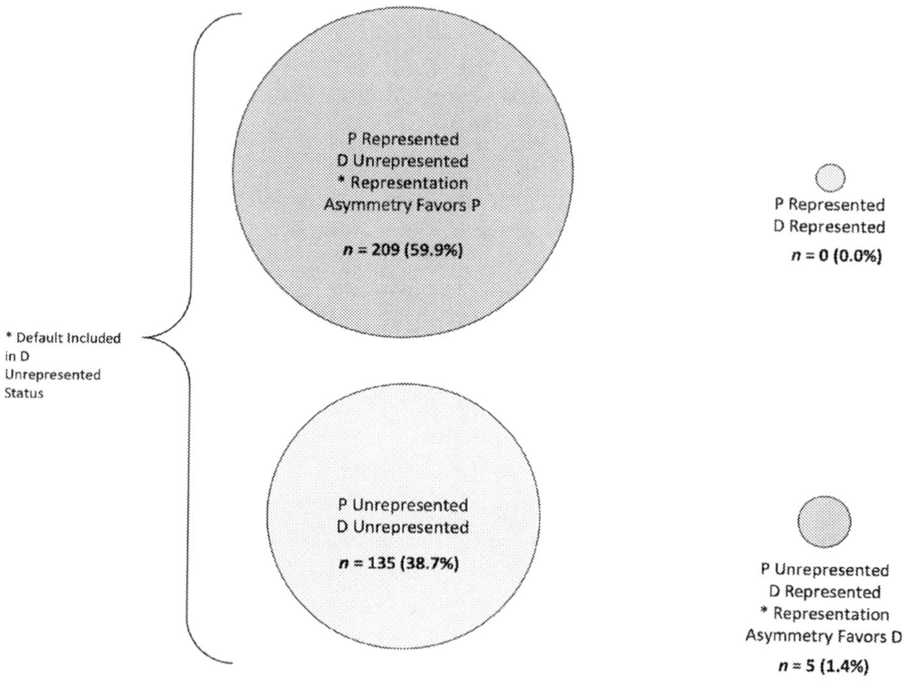

FIGURE 10.1 Virtual proceedings represented status

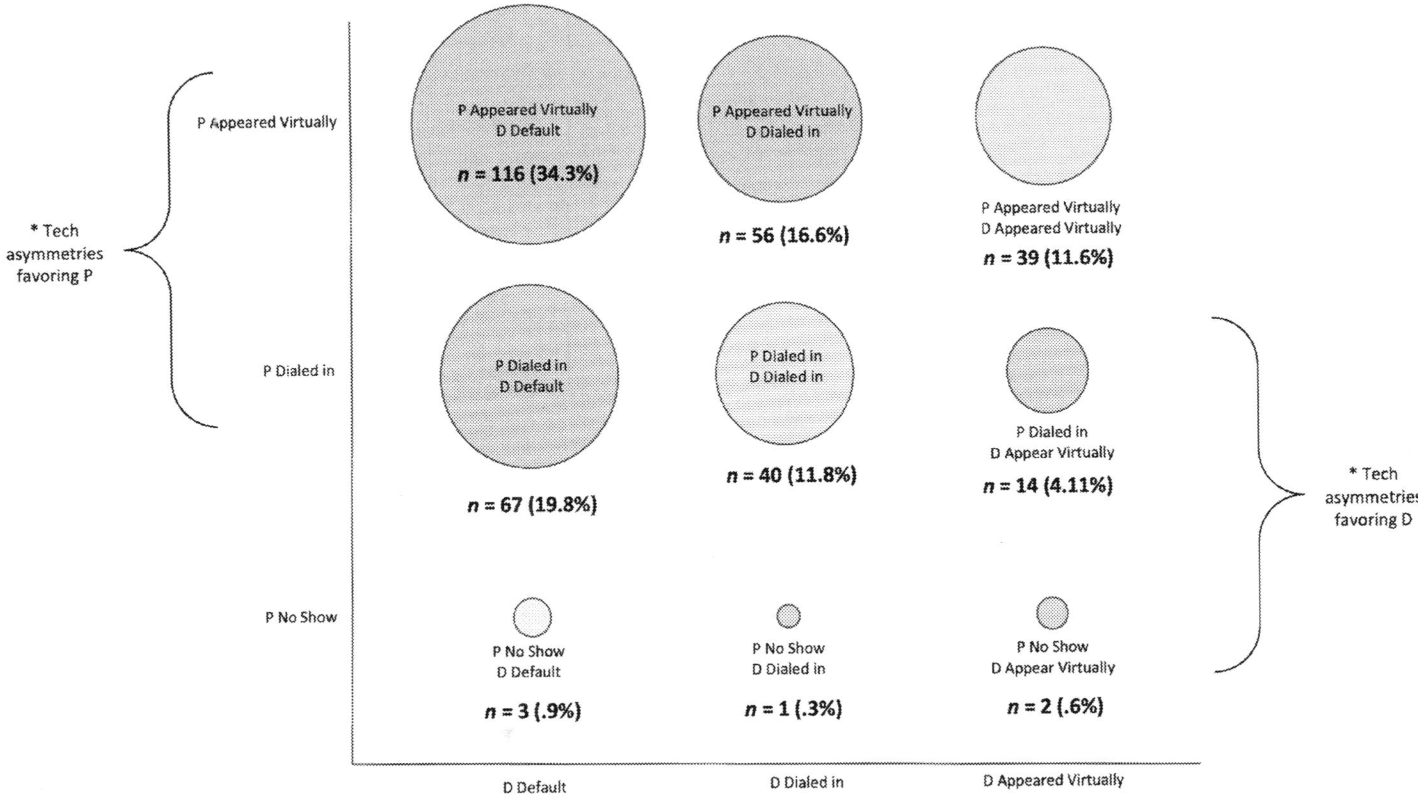

FIGURE 10.2 Virtual proceedings matrix of tech asymmetries (including defaults)

While this apparently reflects a decrease in the default rate, the conveniences provided by remote hearings are not a panacea for addressing the challenge of defaults in these cases. Over half of defendants/respondents still default in these cases; as such, the conveniences of remote proceedings may need to be coupled with other interventions that discern and more effectively address the underlying reasons why many defendants do not to attend court hearings.

Turning now to Figure 10.3, which describes virtual proceedings where both plaintiffs/claimants and defendants/respondents actually attend (i.e., excluding defaults) (n = 149), we found that a majority of these hearings involved scenarios in which defendants/respondents dialed into these Zoom/Webex hearings on their cell phones (n = 96, 64.4 percent). Many of these instances involved technological asymmetries in which the plaintiff had full Zoom virtual capabilities and the defendant/respondent dialed into the hearing (n = 56, 37.6 percent). Rarely did the technological asymmetry favor the defendant/respondent (n = 14, 9.4 percent). In many instances, the parties both dialed into these hearings, despite the possibility of appearing virtually on Zoom (n = 40, 26.8 percent). Both parties appeared virtually in a minority of cases (n = 36, 24.2 percent). Finally, we also revealed instances in which a party appeared via Zoom with their camera off, which is distinct from dialing in per se. In these scenarios, for example, a person would be able to see others on Zoom, but their camera would be turned off and they would not be able to be seen. This occurred in an extremely small fraction of cases (n = 3, 2.0 percent). In these cases, the defendant/respondent had turned their camera off, whereas the plaintiff/claimant had their camera on, another technological asymmetry.

Representational asymmetries × technological asymmetries. We then focused specifically on cases in which lawyers appeared for the plaintiff and unrepresented defendants appeared in these remote hearings (n = 96). This analysis (Figure 10.4) reveals ways in which representational asymmetries compound with technological asymmetries. In other words, the technological asymmetries are even more pronounced when plaintiffs with lawyers face unrepresented defendants.

As reflected in Figure 10.4, we found that a majority of these hearings involved scenarios in which *unrepresented* defendants/respondents dialed into these Zoom/Webex hearings on their cell phones (n = 68, 70.8 percent). Nearly half of these cases involved technological asymmetries in which plaintiff *lawyers* had full Zoom virtual capabilities while unrepresented defendants/respondents dialed into the hearing (n = 45, 46.9 percent). Rarely did the technological asymmetry favor unrepresented defendants/respondents (n = 6, 6.2 percent). In many instances, both a lawyer and an unrepresented defendant dialed into these hearings (n = 23, 24.0 percent). Both parties appeared virtually in a minority of cases (n = 20, 20.8 percent).

Again, we also revealed instances in which either the lawyer or unrepresented defendant appeared via Zoom with their camera off, which is distinct from dialing in. Although this rarely occurred (n = 2, 2.1 percent) and, when it did, it was the

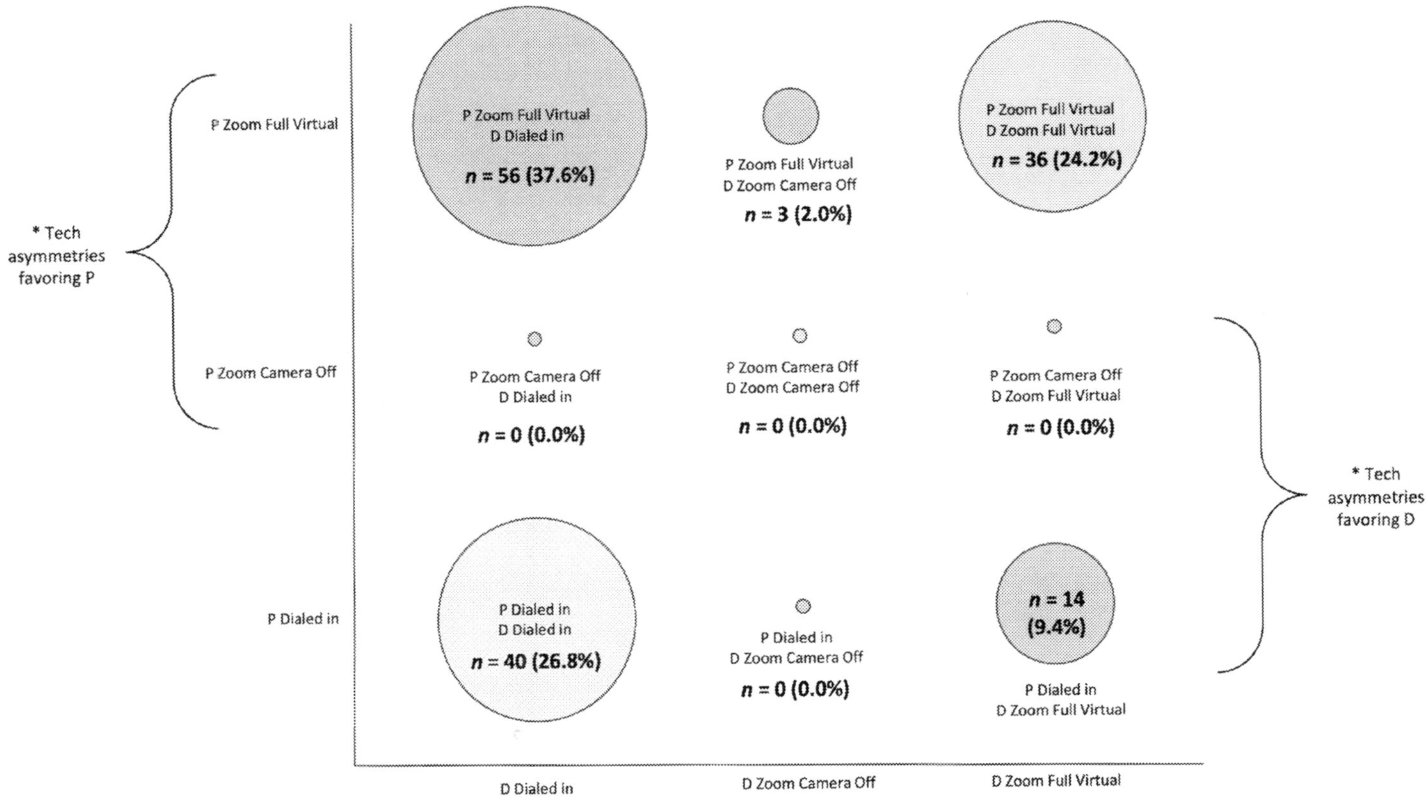

FIGURE 10.3 Virtual proceedings matrix of tech asymmetries (excluding defaults)

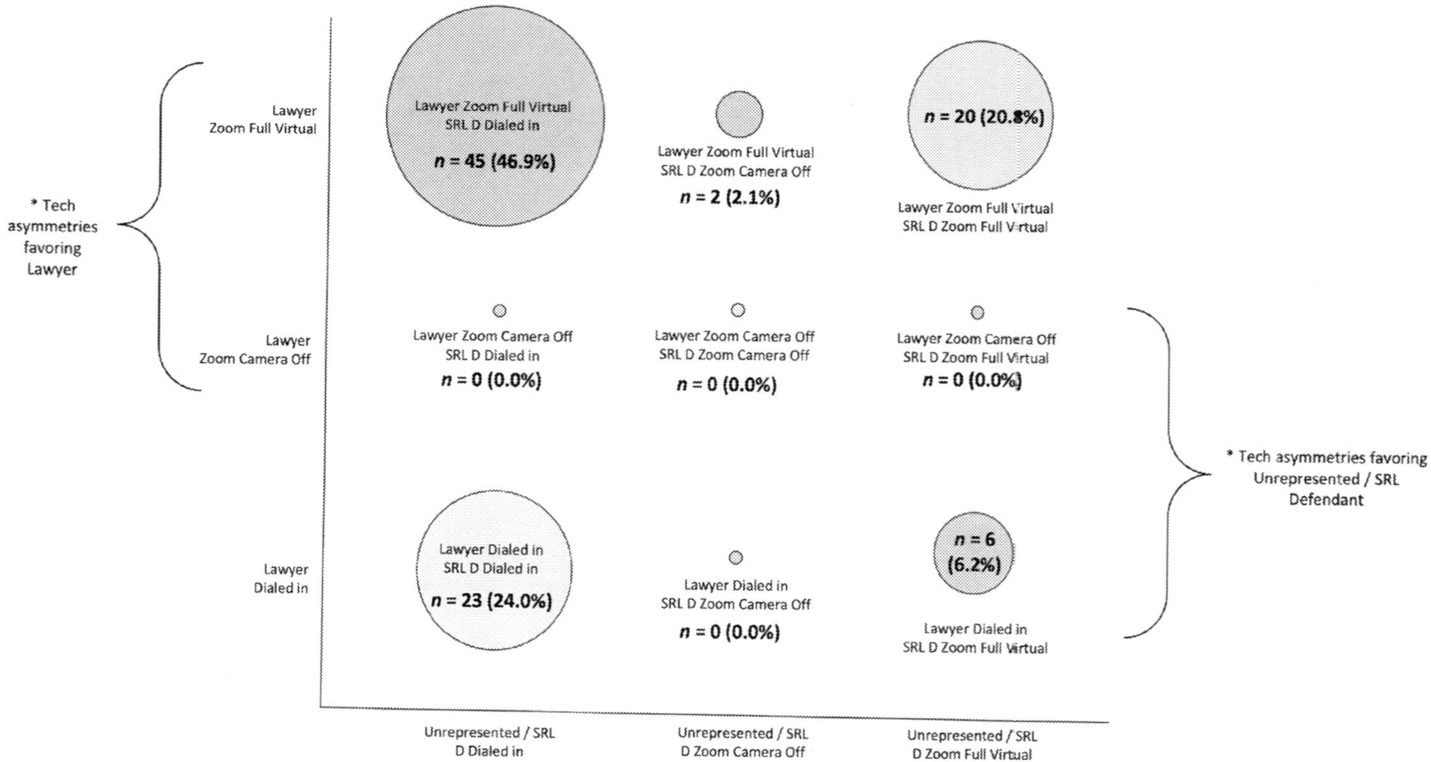

FIGURE 10.4 Virtual proceedings matrix of tech asymmetries lawyers versus unrepresented/SRL defendants

unrepresented defendant/respondent whose camera was off, and the plaintiff *lawyer* whose camera was on, compounding the technological asymmetries.

10.3.3 *Discussion*

In summary, we found that a majority of low-income defendants/respondents in these virtual hearings are unrepresented and most are dialing into virtual court (e.g., Zoom/Webex hearings) on their cell phones. These cases involve representational asymmetries, in which repeat-player plaintiff lawyers litigate against low-income defendants who are unrepresented. Troublingly, these cases also involve technological asymmetries, in which repeat-player plaintiff lawyers regularly employ the full range of virtual interaction and videoconferencing capabilities of Zoom/Webex, while low-income unrepresented defendants whom they sue are often limited to the audio-only capabilities of their cell phones.

10.4 UNREPRESENTED IN VIRTUAL COURT: THE SOCIAL PRODUCTION OF UNREPRESENTED PERSONS

Drawing on these findings, we now return to our framework, organized around Winner's core insight that "the complex interaction between law, technology and human institutions ... may lead to unanticipated and adverse social policy outcomes."[37] In this section, we turn first to the social production of unrepresented persons in virtual hearings and discuss the situational affordances and barriers, and technological features and constraints, entailed by virtual hearings and how they may differentially affect lawyers and unrepresented individuals in virtual courtrooms. Then we turn to the social construction of unrepresented persons in these virtual hearings and discuss ways in which the social cognitive processes of judges, lawyers, and unrepresented persons are likely influenced by these asymmetries.

By way of background, our civil justice system presents persons navigating within the system with situational affordances and barriers, that is, conditions that prompt or permit some actions and conditions that conceal or foreclose others.[38] Often people are not consciously aware of the influence of these situational affordances and barriers; nevertheless, these conditions powerfully guide and constrain behavior, and influence how this behavior is understood by oneself and others. These conditioning factors include the use of technology in virtual hearings. In this regard, theories of mediated communication explain the relationship between features of these technologies, affordances, and the communication that ultimately results from

[37] Winner, *Technologies as Forms of Life*.

[38] *See* James J. Gibson, *The Theory of Affordances*, *in* THE PEOPLE, PLACE, AND SPACE READER (Jen Jack Gleseking et al. eds., 1979); DONALD A. NORMAN, THE PSYCHOLOGY OF EVERYDAY THINGS (1988).

using those technologies.[39] These mediated communication theories reveal that videoconferencing technologies (e.g., Zoom/Webex) and audio-only technologies (e.g., speaking over the telephone) entail qualitatively different features, affordances, and constraints. For example, these different modalities alter the range of communication possible – including whether facial expressions, head nods, gestures, gaze, and visual perception can occur – in turn, altering the process, content, and outcome of communication possible.[40]

We focus first on the asymmetric affordances and constraints that shape how lawyers and low-income persons access and appear in virtual courts – that is, how technology *produces* unrepresented persons. Following that, we turn to how unrepresented persons are perceived by judges and other courtroom actors – that is, how technology *constructs* unrepresented status in the eyes of others. To raise just one possibility, might a judge's motivations, perception, and empathy be shaped by an asymmetry in which a lawyer appears in a hyper-personalized visual form, while a low-income unrepresented person is depersonalized into a black Zoom tile in the virtual hearing?

10.4.1 *Overview: Social Production of Unrepresented Persons*

The civil justice system presents courts, lawyers, and unrepresented persons with a set of situational affordances and barriers.[41] In this section, we will examine the ways in which virtual courts asymmetrically allocate situational affordances and barriers, and technological features and constraints, to lawyers and unrepresented persons. For example, lawyers can engage in fully virtual interactions, where they are able to hyper-personalize and can also Zoom in from staged law offices with reliable high-speed internet connections. Lawyers can also gaze directly into the camera – simulating eye contact with the court – while also using and perceiving nonverbal behavior to persuade. In contrast, low-income unrepresented persons who dial into Zoom court on their cell phones can only speak and hear from a distance, are often depersonalized into a black tile on the screen, cannot use or perceive nonverbal behavior, and are unable to use or perceive documents in Zoom hearings. These conditions and constraints are highly skewed and appear to exacerbate asymmetries between lawyers and unrepresented persons in virtual courts.

10.4.2 *Lawyers*

Situational affordances and technological features. Virtual courts provide lawyers a variety of situational affordances and technological features that may enhance their efficiency and effectiveness.

[39] *See* Steve Whittaker, *Theories and Methods in Mediated Communication*, *in* The Handbook of Discourse Processes (Arthur C. Graesser ed., 2003).
[40] *See* Chapters 4 and 12 in this volume.
[41] *See* Gibson, *The Theory of Affordances*; Norman, The Psychology of Everyday Things.

Virtual courts reduce the time and cost borne by lawyers who would otherwise have to travel to court and wait in courtrooms to attend in-person proceedings.[42] As a result, lawyers can reallocate this time to prepare for other cases and multitask while waiting for their virtual hearings to be called, which we observed. Moreover, lawyers often have stable, reliable internet access in their law offices and homes, and these home and law offices often contain legal resources, equipment, and staff – for instance, case files on computers, phones, fax machines, scanners, access to online legal databases, and administrative support – not available to lawyers physically present in courtrooms. We observed an instance, for example, in which a judge asked a lawyer for information specific to a case, which the lawyer did not have in hand but was able to obtain after a brief pause from a colleague in an adjacent room during the hearing.

Second, research has revealed that the inclusion of gaze awareness and upper-body nonverbal cues in a video frame may engender empathy.[43] High-quality videoconferencing systems that preserve gaze and upper-body cues have been found to be as effective as face-to-face meetings in preserving empathic concern. However, when systems do not preserve these cues, empathy and rapport are degraded.[44] The challenge, again, is the asymmetry: lawyers are more likely to have this high-quality videoconferencing technology than low-income unrepresented persons who dial into these hearings.

Finally, Zoom virtual hearings allow lawyers and others with the most technological capital, capabilities, and expertise to enhance their self-presentation above and beyond what may have been possible in an in-person hearing. This phenomenon is referred to as *hyper-personalization*.[45] Lawyers can carefully curate their online impression in Zoom hearings, using filters to soften and touch up their images, placing their names on Zoom tiles, and by staging their background (whether actual or virtual).

Barriers and constraints. As many lawyers have stable, reliable high-speed internet access and the technologies necessary to participate in Zoom proceedings effectively from their home or law offices, the shift from in-person to Zoom hearings appears to impose few situational barriers. Furthermore, lawyers who Zoom into virtual hearings face few technological constraints as compared to low-income unrepresented persons who dial into Zoom hearings. These lawyers will often have access to

[42] *See Resolution 2 In Support of Remote and Virtual Hearings*, CONF. CHIEF JS., CONF. STATE CT. ADM'RS 2 (July 28, 2021), https://ccj.ncsc.org/__data/assets/pdf_file/0016/67012/Resolution-2_Remote-and-Virtual-Hearings.pdf.

[43] *See* Chapter 4 in this volume.

[44] *See* David T. Nguyen & John Canny, *More Than Face-to-Face: Empathy Effects of Video Framing*, 2009 PROC. SIGCHI CONF. ON HUM. FACTORS COMPUTING SYS. 423.

[45] *See* Amy L. Gonzales, *Disadvantaged Minorities Use of the Internet to Expand Their Social Networks*, 44 COMMC'N RSCH. 467 (2015).

videoconferencing equipment that preserves their gaze awareness and nonverbal behavior and have the ability to hyper-personalize their self-presentation.

10.4.3 *Unrepresented Persons*

Situational affordances and technological features. Like lawyers, unrepresented persons may gain conveniences, including reduced travel and child-care burdens.[46] They may also enjoy the comfort of attending Zoom hearings from home or work (rather than attending court in person). Indeed, the Self-Represented Litigation Network has noted that virtual court proceedings may reduce the time and expenses associated with traveling, transportation, childcare, and other day-to-day costs that litigants incur when going to court.[47]

Relatedly, we observed instances where at least some unrepresented persons who attended these virtual hearings behaved quite confidently, perhaps more confidently than would be the case within an in-person hearing. This may be because, for some unrepresented persons, the convenience and lack of formality may decrease the sense of intimidation that may be present in an in-person hearing, an avenue for future research.

These conveniences may be translating to higher appearance rates, as suggested by the National Center for State Courts.[48] Yet caution is warranted before celebrating these court statistics.

For example, when a low-income person dials into a Zoom courtroom on a cell phone, this audio-only entry is counted as an "appearance." However, these low-income persons can neither see nor be seen by other court participants, unlike the lawyers who Zoom into these virtual courts. They are unable to perceive the facial expressions and nonverbal behaviors of other courtroom actors or to review documents used by lawyers and judges in these virtual hearings. In short, not all "appearances" are *appearances* in the conventional sense of what it means for something to appear to someone as an object of sight perception. In the future, we should consider the utility of moving beyond a strict dichotomy of whether a party "appeared" or not, and consider a construct that considers a continuum of the qualities of what it means for a person to *appear* in court. Certainly, this continuum will lend itself to many important questions that go beyond mere access, centering on equity and the experience of attending court whether online or in person.

[46] *See* Chapter 12 in this volume.

[47] *See* John Greacen, Executive Summary of the Resource Guide on Serving Self-Represented Litigants Remotely (2016), https://www.srln.org/system/files/attachments/Remote%20Guide%20Executive%20Summary%208-16-16_0.pdf.

[48] *See Will Remote Hearings Improve Appearance Rates?* NCSC (May 13, 2021), https://www.ncsc.org/newsroom/at-the-center/2020/may-13.

Barriers and constraints. Unlike lawyers, the shift from in-person to Zoom hearings imposes notable situational barriers and technological constraints on low-income persons.

First, unrepresented persons must prepare exhibits and documents in advance of hearings. While these documents are filed before Zoom proceedings, courts use these documents within the proceedings themselves. When low-income persons dial into Zoom proceedings, they are unable to see the court or documents shared by or with the court during the hearing. We observed that this led to miscommunication about documents (and negative outcomes) during Zoom hearings.

Second, the shift to Zoom removes situational affordances available to low-income people who attend court in person: mainly, access to in-court self-help ecosystems. This shift may impair the ability of navigators, self-help professionals, and legal-aid providers to help unrepresented persons. Relatedly, in immigration and criminal proceedings, lawyers have experienced difficulty meeting and privately conferring with their clients before virtual hearings.[49] Moreover, when low-income persons dial in to Zoom proceedings, they lose the ability to observe others and learn how the full complexity of the courtroom unfolds. While this may be of little value to lawyers, unrepresented persons often learn by watching. Without this opportunity to learn by watching, many unrepresented persons may not understand the process or the expectations of the court, which may decrease the effectiveness of their self-representation.[50]

Third, most low-income unrepresented persons access the Internet via cell phones that are, themselves, reliably unreliable.[51] Relatedly, many low-income Americans who have cell phones are on pay-as-you-go data plans and cannot afford to pay for the data required to attend. When these low-income Americans dial in to these hearings, they are *depersonalized* into black Zoom tiles in the hearing, set against a black Zoom backdrop, often with a case number (or phone number) attached to the Zoom tile. Many other low-income persons do not appear on the screen at all; rather, these Zoom tiles are hidden from the screen, and judges and lawyers merely hear their voice. For these persons, aside from this auditory presence, there is no sign that these unrepresented persons appeared at hearings at all.

10.5 SOCIAL CONSTRUCTION OF PRO SE PERSONS

This section turns to the way in which the asymmetric affordances, barriers, and constraints present in these virtual proceedings may influence the social cognitive

[49] *See* Eric T. Bellone, *Private Attorney-Client Communications and the Effect of Videoconferencing in the Courtroom*, 8 J. INT'L COM. L. & TECH. 24 (2013); Diamond et al., *Efficiency and Cost*; Anne Bowin Poulin, *Criminal Justice and Videoconferencing Technology: The Remote Defendant*, 78 TUL. L. REV. 1089 (2004); Ingrid V. Eagly, *Remote Adjudication in Immigration*, 109 NW. U. L. REV. 933 (2015).

[50] *See* Bannon & Keith, *Remote Court: Principles for Virtual Proceedings.*

[51] *See* Gonzales, *The Contemporary US Digital Divide.*

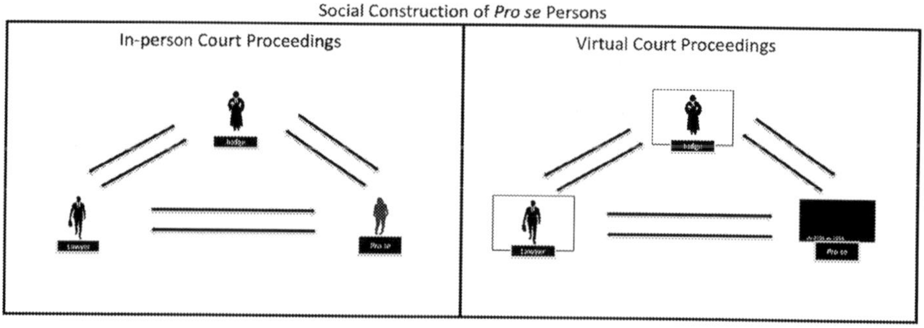

FIGURE 10.5 Model of civil justice interactions and social cognitive processes between judges, lawyers, and unrepresented persons in in-person and virtual court proceedings

processes and social perception of judges, lawyers, and unrepresented persons. We present a model of these social cognitive processes and the ensuing civil justice interactions, with an emphasis on the contrast between in-person and virtual court proceedings in Figure 10.5. In this section, we outline the possible implications of our findings to date for unrepresented persons exhibiting digital disparities in court proceedings and underscore areas that we will seek to address in future stages of this research.

10.5.1 *Judge's Perspective*

From the judge's perspective, judges can only see and be seen by the lawyer. From the judge's vantage point, low-income unrepresented persons who dial into Zoom hearings appear as a black Zoom tile with a case ID or phone number appended to the black tile. As such, the asymmetries created by this technology may, despite the well-meaning of judges, subtly affect their impressions, empathy, and motivations. These affordances and barriers will alter the judicial role.

Motivation. The shift from in-person proceedings to Zoom virtual hearings may affect the motivation and goals of judges and court personnel who operate under severe resource constraints. While courts have shifted to a therapeutic or problem-solving orientation when addressing in-person cases, including evictions,[52] the shift to Zoom court may affect this orientation. When low-income unrepresented persons dial into a Zoom virtual hearing, they appear as black Zoom tiles with a phone number (or merely a case ID), and this may hinder the empathic concern necessary for a therapeutic or problem-solving orientation.

52 *See* Jessica K. Steinberg, *Demand Side Reform in the Poor People's Court*, 47 CONN. L. REV. 741 (2015).

Perception and impressions. Video-mediated communication alters the way people are perceived and the impressions formed.[53] In this context, unrepresented persons who appear in Zoom virtual hearings via video, rather than in person, may be perceived as less warm and competent than those who appear in person, especially relative to the lawyers who appear virtually in court.[54]

Cognitive depletion. "Zoom fatigue" is depleting because video conferences are cognitively demanding, requiring one to "focus more intently on conversations in order to absorb information," as opposed to the nonverbal cues we usually rely upon.[55] Relatedly, Zoom participants have the ability to watch oneself during these video conversations. Yet seeing one's own video generates a state of objective self-awareness, which may increase the cognitive load of engaging in these technologies, and may impact a person's interactions in a videoconference.

Empathy. These technologies also affect the empathy expressed and experienced. Facial expressions, gaze awareness, and nonverbal behaviors build trust and empathy between people, and they affect person-perception as well. When these technologies interrupt or conceal these nonverbal behaviors, empathy may be reduced. For example, the video framing of cell phones (if video is available at all) and a stable mounted computer will have different effects on the inducement of empathy[56] because the video framing of stable mounted computers may capture these nonverbal features of the upper body and correct for gaze error. Moreover, empathy is more easily generated between people who have ongoing relationships or frequent conversations; thus, strangers are at a distinct disadvantage when presenting over video.[57]

Digital inequalities between lawyers and many low-income unrepresented persons may translate into disparities in the ability to gaze at the judge during these virtual hearings. Gaze awareness is an important factor that affects whether people are perceived as generally interested, trustful or approving, or attentive.[58] Gazing is an important expression of interpersonal attitude or affect. Indeed, lawyers are taught

53 *See* Chris Fullwood, *The Effect of Mediation on Impression Formation: A Comparison of Face-to-Face and Video Mediated Conditions*, 38 APPLIED ERGONOMICS 267 (2007); Gail S. Goodman et al., *Face-to-Face Confrontation: Effects of Closed-Circuit Technology on Children's Eyewitness Testimony and Jurors' Decisions*, 22 L. & HUM. BEHAV. 165 (1998); Molly Treadway Johnson & Elizabeth C. Wiggins, *Videoconferencing in Criminal Proceedings: Legal and Empirical Issues and Directions for Research*, 28 L. & POL'Y 211 (2006).

54 *See* Holly K. Orcutt et al., *Detecting Deception in Children's Testimony: Factfinders' Abilities to Reach the Truth in Open Court and Closed Circuit Trials*, 25 L. & HUM. BEHAV. 339 (2001).

55 *See* Susan A. Bandes & Neal Feigenson, *Virtual Trials: Necessity, Invention, and the Evolution of the Courtroom*, 68 BUFFALO L. REV. 1275 (2020).

56 *See* Nguyen & Canny, *More Than Face-to-Face*.

57 *See* Philip A. Powell & Jennifer Roberts, *Situational Determinants of Cognitive, Affective, and Compassionate Empathy in Naturalistic Digital Interactions*, 68 COMPUTS. HUM. BEHAV. 137 (2016).

58 *See* Jim Gemmell et al., *Gaze Awareness for Video-Conferencing: A Software Approach*, IEEE MULTIMEDIA, Oct.–Dec. 2000, at 26.

to gaze in order to enhance their persuasion,[59] ingratiate themselves to the judge and jury,[60] or assert dominance over opposing witnesses and parties.[61] Because those who dial into these Zoom proceedings are unable to gaze at the judge or opposing lawyer, they may be construed as being "defensive" or "evasive."[62] Moreover, eye contact is an important ingredient to social interactions and may prompt recursive processes of trust and rapport, whereas an inability to gaze may generate distrust and harm rapport in intergroup encounters.

The increased psychological distances that these technologies create may lead to depersonalization or, in the worst scenario, dehumanization.[63] This may be in part because these technologies may shape the way others are construed: whether they are construed more abstractly or individuated, whether they are experienced as close or far,[64] which may impact depersonalization. The risk in the scenario at hand is that low-income unrepresented persons who dial into these Zoom virtual hearings may be depersonalized, that their appearance in a Zoom tile with a number and a disconnected voice may subtly dehumanize them in the eyes of the court officials and lawyers.

Behavior. At least two studies suggest that Zoom virtual hearings may elicit faster interactions and decisions than in-person hearings. That is, that the discrete hearing time is faster than would otherwise be the case *because* of the social-cognitive dynamics produced by the technology employed. This was observed, for example, in the impact of videoconferencing in judicial decision-making about deporting immigrants[65] and is documented in research on the effect of videoconferencing on team performance.[66]

Contingent nature of the judicial role. Interactions between judges, lawyers, and unrepresented persons and their performances in the courtroom are contingent on the technologies employed within the civil justice system.[67] These court

59 *See* Albert Mehrabian & Martin Williams, *Nonverbal Concomitants of Perceived and Intended Persuasiveness*, 13 J. Personality & Soc. Psych. 37 (1969).

60 *See* Robert J. Pellegrini et al., *The Effects of an Approval-Seeking Induction on Eye-Contact in Dyads*, 9 British J. Soc. & Clinical Psych. 323 (1970).

61 *See* Ralph V. Exline, *Visual Interaction: The Glances of Power and Preference*, 19 Neb. Symp. Motivation 163 (1971); Phoebe C. Ellsworth, *Direct Gaze as Social Stimulus: The Example of Aggression*, 2 Nonverbal Commc'n Aggression 53 (1975).

62 *See* Robert E. Kleck & William Nuessle, *Congruence between the Indicative and Communicative Functions of Eye-Contact in Interpersonal Relations*, 7 British J. Soc. & Clinical Psych. 241 (1968).

63 *See* Chapter 4 in this volume.

64 *See* Min Kyung Lee, *Making Decisions from a Distance: The Impact of Technological Mediation on Riskiness and Dehumanization*, 18 Proc. ACM Conf. on Comput. Supported Cooperative Work & Soc. Computing 1576 (2015).

65 *See* Eagly, *Remote Adjudication in Immigration*.

66 *See* Demetrios Karis et al., *Improving Remote Collaboration with Video Conferencing and Video Portals*, 31 Human-Computer Interaction 1 (2016).

67 *See* Jose Bellido, *Forensic Technologies in Music Copyright*, 25 Soc. & Legal Stud. 441 (2016).

performances are shaped, in part, by the technological capital of these various actors.[68] For example, Rowden and Wallace, in studying the introduction of videoconferencing in Australia, found that the introduction of this technology had "a profound impact on the production, management and consumption of judicial images, [which] has implications for the judge's in-court role both as traditionally conceived and in practicing new types of therapeutic jurisprudence that require increased emphasis on engagement with other court participants."[69] In general, virtual hearings are associated with more distant or impersonal communication. Yet the introduction of these technologies has occurred at a time when there has also been a strong move toward more engaged styles of judging.[70]

10.5.2 *Lawyer's Perspective*

Like the judge, but unlike low-income persons who dial into these Zoom hearings, a lawyer will be able to see and be seen by the judge. This will affect their adversarial orientation and potentially exacerbate asymmetries against unrepresented people. These asymmetries may affect opposing lawyers, who are in an adversarial orientation, making it more likely for them to use nonverbal behaviors and documents that unrepresented people are unable to see. It may also lead them to dehumanize these unrepresented persons.

Initial face-to-face interactions and preexisting relationships. Initial face-to-face meetings are crucial for enhancing later virtual interactions.[71] Research on distributed teams in the business context reveals that conflict is mitigated by in-person meetings followed by regular video conferences, which can help to maintain a cohesive team and a sense of shared identity. One leading study noted that people who met in person before video-mediated meetings were better at establishing trust with other group members than those who had not met beforehand.[72] Another likewise found evidence that initial in-person contact could benefit later virtual conferences.[73] This research suggests that video conferences may be more effective for lawyers who are already acquainted with judges and have preexisting relationships with them.

68 *See* Pierre Bourdieu, Distinction: A Social Critique of the Judgement of Taste (Richard Nice trans., Harvard University Press 1987) (1984); Emma Rowden & Anne Wallace, *Remote Judging: The Impact of Video Links on the Image and the Role of the Judge*, 14 Int'l J.L. Context 504 (2018).

69 *See* Rowden & Wallace, *Remote Judging*.

70 *Id.*

71 *See* Guido Hertel & Susanne Geister, *Managing Virtual Teams: A Review of Current Empirical Research*, 15 Hum. Res. Mgmt. Rev. 69 (2005); Karis et al., *Improving Remote Collaboration*.

72 Elena Rocco, *Trust Breaks Down in Electronic Contexts but Can Be Repaired by Some Initial Face-to-Face Contact*, 1998 Proc. SIGCHI Conf. on Hum. Factors Computing Sys. 496.

73 *See* Rocco, *Trust Breaks Down in Electronic Contexts*; Nicola Derrer-Rendell & Chris Fullwood, *An Initial Face-to-Face Meeting Improves Person-Perceptions of Interviewees across VMC*, *in* Contemporary Ergonomics 296 (2006).

10.5.3 *Unrepresented Person's Perspective*

Finally, unlike judges and lawyers, an unrepresented person who dials into a Zoom hearing cannot see or be seen, and they appear as a black Zoom tile on the judge's and lawyer's computer screens. This may affect their participation, experience of justice, and the outcomes obtained.

Construal and meaning-making. When low-income unrepresented persons dial into Zoom virtual hearings, they have access to audio-conferencing capabilities only and are unable to see a courtroom at all. This will undoubtedly affect the sense of realism, solemnity, and gravity of the proceedings, when compared to in-person or videoconferencing enabled proceedings. This may leave them apathetic or confused, experiencing the process as less "real." Moreover, friction and barriers accessing these Zoom virtual courtrooms may lead unrepresented persons to infer that these virtual court proceedings are not truly designed for people like them.

Experiences of procedural justice. Research suggests that in-person participation may be perceived as more procedurally just than technologically mediated participation.[74] For example, research in organizational justice has concluded that applicants were less attracted to organizations that used video interviews compared to in-person interviews.[75] Other studies have noted that in-person interviews were regarded as fairer than video-mediated interviews, resulting in higher levels of job acceptance.[76] In still another study, interviewees rated their interviewers as less friendly during the video-mediated interviews (in comparison to in-person and telephone interviews).[77] This research suggests that some unrepresented persons may experience videoconference proceedings as less procedurally just than in-person proceedings. Extrapolating this research a step further, one can infer that unrepresented persons may find it procedurally unjust to be limited to audio-only capabilities when their adversaries have access to the full range of video-conference capabilities.

Relational feedback, turns, interruptions. Physical proximity supports the interaction and cohesion of groups.[78] This is, in part, because of bandwidth and network cost limitations that reduce the rate, clarity, and frequency of communicative

[74] *See* Fullwood, *The Effect of Mediation on Impression Formation.*

[75] *See* Derek S. Chapman & Patricia Rowe, *The Influence of Videoconference Technology and Interview Structure on the Recruiting Function of the Employment Interview: A Field Experiment*, 10 INT'L J. SELECTION & ASSESSMENT 185 (2003).

[76] *See* Derek S. Chapman et al., *Applicant Reactions to Face-to-Face and Technology-Mediated Interviews: A Field Investigation*, 88 J. APPLIED PSYCH. 944 (2003).

[77] *See* Susan G. Straus et al., *The Effects of Videoconference, Telephone, and Face-to-Face Media on Interviewer and Applicant Judgments in Employment Interviews*, 27 J. MGMT. 363 (2001).

[78] *See* Sara Kiesler & Jonathan N. Cummings, *What Do We Know about Proximity and Distance in Work Groups? A Legacy of Research*, *in* DISTRIBUTED WORK 57 (Pamela Hinds & Sara B. Kiesler eds., 2002).

turns.[79] Because low-income unrepresented persons are unable to observe or communicate with nonverbal behavior, this may exacerbate miscommunication, while at the same time making judges, lawyers, and unrepresented persons slower to correct these misunderstandings.[80] Indeed, we observed several instances in which this kind of miscommunication occurred for unrepresented persons who were not proficient in English. Unfortunately, these unrepresented tenants dialed into Zoom court and were not able to overcome the language barrier. Similar issues may occur for persons with disabilities, though virtual proceedings may also increase access for persons with mobility-impairing disabilities as well.[81]

One challenge is that these faster hearing times may be coupled with more problematic intergroup interactions. The asymmetries in these interactions may harm intergroup interactions in virtual environments. For example, many judges and lawyers are majority group members, while many low-income members are racial or ethnic minorities or belong to vulnerable groups. Past research has found that an audiovisual lag in an interaction may incite tension in intergroup interactions, particularly when persons are not well acquainted.[82]

Participation. If unrepresented persons experience the process as procedurally unjust, their participation and engagement may be dampened. Indeed, researchers have suggested that videoconferencing technologies may have prompted declines in participation, which may have explained adverse outcomes in research involving bail decisions[83] and immigration removal decisions.[84]

Contingent nature of unrepresented persons. Finally, these technologies and the digital inequalities engendered reveal the contingent nature of being a self-represented litigant in the civil justice system. As has been described, the very act of appearing in court is altered and dependent on the technologies employed within these proceedings. At the same time, this technology may benefit the most advantaged unrepresented persons who have technological capital, capacity, and wherewithal. Technological capital is a subset of, and an addition to, Pierre Bourdieu's cultural, economic, and social forms of capital in the information age,[85] marked by

79 *See* Souren Paul et al., *Impact of Heterogeneity and Collaborative Conflict Management Style on the Performance of Synchronous Global Virtual Teams*, 41 Info. & Mgmt. 303 (2004).

80 *See* Lori Foster Thompson & Michael D. Coovert, *Understanding and Developing Virtual Computer-Supported Cooperative Work Teams*, *in* Creating High-Tech Teams: Practical Guidance on Work Performance and Technology 213 (Clint Bowers et al. eds., 2006).

81 *See* Bannon & Keith, *Remote Court: Principles for Virtual Proceedings*

82 *See* Adam R. Pearson et al., *The Fragility of Intergroup Relations: Divergent Effects of Delayed Audiovisual Feedback in Intergroup and Intragroup Interactions*, 19 Psych. Sci. 1272 (2008).

83 Diamond et al., *Efficiency and Cost.*

84 *See* Eagly, *Remote Adjudication in Immigration.*

85 *See* Anthony J. Hesketh & Neil Selwyn, *Surfing to School: The Electronic Reconstruction of Institutional Identities*, 25 Oxford Rev. Educ. 501 (2019); Pierre Bourdieu, *The Force of Law: Toward a Sociology of the Juridical Field*, 38 Hastings L.J. 805, 807 (1987); Gonzales, *The Contemporary US Digital Divide.*

first-order and second-order digital divides in internet access, skill, and experience.[86] These societal patterns may, in part, explain why so many unrepresented persons dial into Zoom virtual hearings from their cell phones without videoconferencing capabilities.

10.6 CONCLUSION

In this chapter, we sought to illuminate how virtual proceedings unfold for low-income persons in the everyday by examining how these new technologies affect the experiences of low-income persons who encounter, and contend with, adversities within virtual court proceedings. Our preliminary findings revealed troubling phenomena in many small claims cases, including eviction and debt-collection cases, winding through virtual court proceedings in Indiana. We found that a majority of low-income persons in these cases are unrepresented, and most are dialing into virtual court (e.g., Zoom/Webex hearings) on their cell phones. The vast majority of these cases involve representational asymmetries, in which repeat-player lawyers litigate against low-income persons who are unrepresented. Of concern, many of these cases also involve technological asymmetries, in which repeat-player lawyers regularly employ the full range of virtual interaction and videoconferencing capabilities of Zoom/Webex, while the low-income unrepresented persons whom they sue are often limited to the audio-only capabilities of their cell phones.

We believe that examining how virtual proceedings unfold in the everyday contributes to the development and refinement of accurate and useful theories about our dynamic civil justice system and best practices for enhancing access to justice in virtual proceedings.

86 *See* Eszter Hargittai, *The Digital Reproduction of Inequality*, *in* Social Stratification (David Grusky et al. eds., 2008); Ellen Johanna Helsper, *A Corresponding Fields Model for the Links between Social and Digital Exclusion*, 22 Commc'n Theory 403 (2012); Neil Selwyn, *Reconsidering Political and Popular Understandings of the Digital Divide*, New Media & Soc'y 341 (2004); Nicole Zillien & Mirko Marr, *The Digital Divide in Europe*, *in* The Digital Divide: The Internet and Social Inequality in International Perspective 55 (Massimo Ragnedda & Glenn W. Muschert eds., 2013).

11

Online Dispute Resolution and the End of Adversarial Justice?

Norman W. Spaulding

There was a moment in the late-nineteenth and early-twentieth centuries when automobiles were being made with steam, electric, and internal combustion engines. As early as the 1840s, inventors had created "[r]echargeable batteries that provided a viable means for storing electricity onboard a vehicle."[1] Porsche's first car was an all-wheel-drive electric car that "set several records" in time and distance competitions, and by 1897 a fleet of taxis built by the Electric Carriage and Wagon Company of Philadelphia was running in New York City.

The internal combustion engine won out because of a conjunction of factors. Henry Ford figured out how to produce and sell the Model T at a price half that of standard electric vehicles. Charles Kettering made crankshaft starters obsolete. And the discovery of large petroleum reserves in Texas dramatically reduced the price of gasoline. The steam engine, on the other hand, took far too long to warm up – no one wanted to wait forty-five minutes before hitting the road. And although electric cars were cleaner, quieter, and initially easier to start than cars with internal combustion engines, they "disappeared by 1935," as did the kind of investment and research that would have improved their performance and affordability. They disappeared even though scientists knew, as early as the 1850s, that pumping CO_2 into the atmosphere would affect the earth's temperature.[2]

Knowing what we now know about the devastating effects of climate change and other negative externalities of crude oil extraction, one can't help but wonder about what the counterfactual world of a century powered by electric vehicles would have looked like. The question is for the most part unanswerable – perhaps we would have had a century of lithium wars rather than oil wars. But it is hard to escape the

1 C. C. Chan, *The Rise and Fall of Electric Vehicles in 1828–1930: Lessons Learned*, 101 Proc. IEEE 206, 207 (2013).

2 Clive Thompson, *How 19th Century Scientists Predicted Global Warming*, JSTOR Daily (Dec. 17, 2019), https://daily.jstor.org/how-19th-century-scientists-predicted-global-warming/.

feeling that almost any outcome would be preferable to the world of irreversible climate change in which we now live.

I raise the forgotten story of electric vehicles because it draws into relief an important feature of transformative innovation that is all too often obscured once path dependence and the leverage of market dominance set in. In the moment, there are often *many* design options, not just one obviously superior alternative, and the *full* cost (including negative externalities) of any one option can be difficult to calculate. But it is gravely irresponsible not to inquire what that cost might be when design options are still open and policy affecting incentives is being determined. Whatever one might have thought about this responsibility in a time before our own – eras preceding climate change, nuclear holocaust, and other apocalyptic consequences of technological innovation – we do not have the luxury of failing to inquire now.

The tech evangelism that reigns in Silicon Valley inhibits precisely this inquiry.[3] Uber's proponents spoke with religious fervor about the corrupt monopoly of cab companies and how that arbitrarily hindered both the mobility of customers and the autonomy of cab drivers. Very little was said about whether disrupting the industry would, on balance, be socially beneficial. But as it turns out, one of the negative externalities is likely diminished use of public transportation,[4] with attendant effects on climate change and declining resources for innovation in public transportation. Moreover, Uber increasingly behaves toward consumers and drivers like the very monopoly it "disrupted."[5] In other ways, the company's conduct is even more ominous. As one commentator has observed, "if you are one of its regular customers, Uber knows more about you than your own mother does."[6] And there are grounds to worry that the company's use of these data is not entirely benign.[7] Remarkably, despite its market valuation, the company has yet to prove it can turn a profit. It is far more convenient to hail a ride, and in this sense "access" to a form of transportation has increased. But the cost side of the ledger, as with other forms of "surveillance capitalism,"[8] is daunting.

[3] *Cf.* Clayton M. Christensen, Michael E. Raynor & Rory McDonald, *What Is Disruptive Innovation?* Harv. Bus. Rev., Dec. 2015 (questioning whether Uber is a disruptive innovation).

[4] Emily Badger, *Is Uber Helping or Hurting Mass Transit?* N.Y. Times: The Upshot (Oct. 16, 2017), https://www.nytimes.com/2017/10/16/upshot/is-uber-helping-or-hurting-mass-transit.html.

[5] Evgeny Morozov, *Cheap Cab Ride? You Must Have Missed Uber's True Cost*, Guardian (Jan. 30, 2016, 7:03 PM EST), https://www.theguardian.com/commentisfree/2016/jan/31/cheap-cab-ride-uber-true-cost-google-wealth-taxation.

[6] Prableen Bajpai, *How Uber Uses Your Ride Data*, Investopedia (Jan. 12, 2020), https://www.investopedia.com/articles/investing/030916/how-uber-uses-its-data-bank.asp. No matter how confessional a trip in a traditional cab ever becomes, neither the driver nor the taxi company ever learns anything close to this.

[7] *Uber Settles FTC Allegations That It Made Deceptive Privacy and Data Security Claims*, Fed. Trade Comm'n (Aug. 15, 2017), https://www.ftc.gov/news-events/press-releases/2017/08/uber-settles-ftc-allegations-it-made-deceptive-privacy-data.

[8] Shoshana Zuboff, The Age of Surveillance Capitalism (2019).

A third cautionary tale closer to the innovations in legal automation and access to justice I address in this chapter is TurboTax, software that has arguably revolutionized tax filing. As with taxi drivers and Uber, many accountants have either been displaced by Intuit's product or incorporated it into the services they provide. For consumers, a process fraught with uncertainty has been made more accessible and efficient. On the other hand, Intuit has repeatedly used its market leverage and lobbying power to prevent states and the federal government from adopting legislation that would make *free* "prefilled" tax forms automatically available to taxpayers.[9] The so-called disruptive innovator has become yet another monopoly rent seeker, blocking innovations that would be even more accessible, transparent, and consistent with the public good.

The three examples are commonsense reminders that some forms of innovation are transformative in ways we may (predictably) regret, that the rhetoric and fervor surrounding disruptive innovation can obscure sober assessment of the cost side of the ledger, that some transformations saturated with negative externalities become irreversible, and that the power reallocated by innovation – even innovation that increases access to a good or service – can be used to obstruct both broader public access and regulation.

Other examples could of course be given, enough to make the Panglossian enthusiasm surrounding artificial intelligence, legal tech, and online dispute resolution (ODR) smack of dangerously irrational exuberance.[10] ODR's moment, we are told, has arrived, "offer[ing] the promise of robust yet radically less expensive dispute resolution."[11] Dispute resolution, we are assured, is no different from other sectors in which digital, online systems optimize information processing:

[9] Jessica Huseman, *Filing Taxes Could Be Free and Simple but H&R Block and Intuit Are Still Lobbying Against It*, ProPublica (Mar. 20, 2017, 1:22 pm EDT), https://www.propublica.org/article/filing-taxes-could-be-free-simple-hr-block-intuit-lobbying-against-it.

[10] I focus for the most part in this chapter on "public ODR" systems developed and marketed to courts and administrators, not "private ODR" systems used within corporations to resolve C2C, B2B, and C2B disputes.

[11] Richard Susskind, Online Courts and the Future of Justice 1, 8 (2019) ("Online courts offer the most promising way of radically increasing access to justice around the world."); see also COSCA, Joint Technology Committee, Case Studies in ODR for Courts: A View from the Front Lines 19 (2017), https://www.ncsc.org/__data/assets/pdf_file/0023/18707/2017-12-18-odr-case-studies-revised.pdf (surveying various public ODR systems in operation in courts around the world and characterizing ODR as a "game changer for courts that are willing to innovate"). For an overview of the burgeoning ODR literature, see Robert J. Condlin's summary in *Online Dispute Resolution: Stinky, Repugnant, or Drab*, 18 Cardozo J. Conflict Res. 717, 717–22 (2017). I share some of Condlin's concerns, though his focus is on fully automated ODR systems (*id.* at 721 n.16), whereas the following analysis takes up systems that are automated and those involving third-party neutrals in ordinary/"simple" cases. See note 27. *See also* Scott Shackelford & Anjanette Raymond, *Building the Virtual Courthouse: Ethical Considerations for Design, Implementation and Regulation in the World of ODR*, 2014 Wis. L. Rev. 615, n.9 (offering a comprehensive survey of issues of transparency, efficiency, conflicts of interests, and trust in ODR systems and advocating a "polycentric governance" approach to these concerns).

> All forms of dispute resolution revolve around communication and information processing. For the Internet to be adapted to serve the needs of dispute resolution is no different conceptually from adapting the Internet to serve the needs of any other information intensive process, such as online banking, online auctions, online education, etc. Indeed, [these industries] often provide links on their home pages to dispute resolution systems.[12]

The excessive cost, delay, complexity, and confrontational culture of the adversary system, we are told, will be displaced by apps that resolve formal legal disputes as efficiently as eBay resolves auction disputes. In the most ambitious forms of ODR, there will be no more third-party mediators, arbitrators, or judges, and therefore no more conference rooms or courthouses.[13]

Justice will roll down in strings of code. Disputes suitable for ODR will not only be resolved cheaply and quickly; the conjunction of data mining, predictive analytics, and dispute systems design will help prevent disputes from arising in the first place.[14] Academic conferences populated by scholars who are funded by or work in the very industry they write about are conducted with all the sobriety of an Elmer Gentry revival meeting. Skeptics are dismissed as unrepentant sinners – elitists too attached to the ancien regime to appreciate the miracles of the "internet society," heartlessly indifferent to the crisis in access to justice, captive to self-serving, anachronistic ideas about the administration of justice. The capital offenders are judges and lawyers whose skepticism is dismissed as rationalization covering the prestige and monopoly rents they derive from the status quo. Fundamentally, law is not thought to be different from transportation or any other target of disruptive innovation: If you want to improve access, deregulate, disregard regulation that can't be set aside, and expand competition by letting the information economy and disruptive innovation work their magic.

Anyone familiar with the history of professions knows that power struggles between professionals often involve characterizing an entrenched group of experts as corrupt and the newcomers (here, software engineers) as avenging angels whose primary care and concern is the welfare of others.[15] New assertions of power are in

[12] Daniel Rainey & Ethan Katsh, *ODR and Government*, *in* ONLINE DISPUTE RESOLUTION: THEORY AND PRACTICE 249, 249 (Mohamed S. Abdel Wahab, Ethan Katsh & Daniel Rainey eds., 2012).

[13] *See, e.g.*, SUSSKIND, ONLINE COURTS.

[14] *See, e.g.*, Shackelford & Raymond, *Building the Virtual Courthouse*; Stephanie Smith & Janet Martinez, *An Analytic Framework for Dispute Systems Design*, 14 HARV. NEGOT. L. REV. 123 (2009); Lisa Blomgren Bingham, *Designing Justice: Legal Institutions and Other Systems for Managing Conflict*, 24 OHIO STATE J. DISP. RESOL. 1 (2008); Ethan Katsh & Leah Wing, *Ten Years of Online Dispute Resolution (ODR): Looking at the Past and Constructing the Future*, 38 U. TOL. L. REV. 19 (2006); Robert C. Bordone, *Electronic Online Dispute Resolution: A Systems Approach – Potential, Problems, and a Proposal*, 3 HARV. NEGOT. L. REV. 175 (1998).

[15] *See generally* BURTON J. BLEDSTEIN, THE CULTURE OF PROFESSIONALISM: THE MIDDLE CLASS AND THE DEVELOPMENT OF HIGHER EDUCATION IN AMERICA (1976).

this way masked by the discourses of progress and reform. At the same time, anyone familiar with the history of the Anglo-American legal tradition knows that legal elites have commonly and, it must be said, deservedly been targeted for many of the perceived flaws of the adversary system. The first movement to reduce law to code in America occurred in the early-nineteenth century, when Jacksonian populists launched an all-out assault on the complexity of common law pleading and the power of judges and lawyers.[16] Drawing on the Napoleonic Code and the famous anti-lawyer tracts of Jeremy Bentham, they sought to replace the common law with a democratically enacted code. They simultaneously sought to expand access to the practice of law by eliminating standards for entry to the bar. Finally, they sought to make judges democratically accountable through popular election and recall – procedures that endure to this day in many states. This was the most pronounced anti-lawyer movement in American history, animated by a desire to make the law simple and more affordable. But it is scarcely the only one. Shays' Rebellion pitted agrarian debtors against lawyers and judges who enforced the claims of elite creditors. The New Deal pitted progressive reformers and proponents of administrative agencies against conservative courts and the adversary system.[17]

What the anti-lawyer and anti-adversary system rhetoric of the current movement obscures is that the bar's protectionist arsenal is *weaker* than it has been at any point since the Jacksonian populist threat more than a century ago. Indeed, both practically and doctrinally, the bar's defenses have been decimated over the last fifty years. The network of price controls, minimum fee schedules, and restrictions on advertising and other rules that limited internal competition and "external" lay-lawyer combinations were dismantled by a series of landmark Supreme Court cases in the 1970s.[18] Competitors in banking, accounting, and other fields renounced the "treaties" that kept them from offering competing services at the same time. The legal-form business expanded under the protection of First Amendment decisions insulating it from unauthorized practice rules.[19] Mediators and especially private arbitrators now operate with the blessing of the Supreme Court, allowing corporations to use contracts of adhesion to displace millions of disputes from courts to alternative dispute resolution forums every year.[20]

In fact, the status quo in access to justice is as much if not more the product of neoliberal defunding and restriction of legal services for the poor and defunding of

[16] Norman W. Spaulding, *The Luxury of the Law: The Codification Movement and the Right to Counsel*, 73 FORDHAM L. REV. 983, 989–90 (2004).

[17] Norman W. Spaulding, *Due Process without Judicial Process? Antiadversarialism in American Legal Culture*, 85 FORDHAM L. REV. 2249, 2251–53 (2017).

[18] *See* Shapero v. Kentucky Bar Assn., 486 U.S. 466 (1988); Zauderer v. Office of Disc. Counsel, 471 U.S. 626 (1985); Bates v. State Bar of Ariz., 433 U.S. 350 (1977); Goldfarb v. Va. State Bar, 421 U.S. 773 (1975); Blhd. R.R. Trainmen v. Virginia, 377 U.S. 1, 5 (1964); NAACP v. Button, 371 U.S. 415, 439–45 (1963).

[19] *See, e.g.*, Florida Bar v. Brumbaugh, 355 So. 2d 1186 (Fla. 1978).

[20] *See* AT&T v. Concepcion, 563 U.S. 333 (2011).

state courts.[21] Tellingly, some of the same players who never lifted a finger to help low-income Americans obtain meaningful access to the adversary system or support funding of the court system are now enthusiastically supporting ODR as a substitute.[22] They are joined by liberal ethicists, lawyers, judges, and scholars who never much liked the adversary system to begin with – believing that ADR was the way of the future, that the New Deal vision of centralized, rational technocratic agency adjudication is more efficient and suitable to mass-processing of claims, or that, whatever the alternatives, adversary adjudication is morally flawed.[23] These are strange bedfellows, united by a shared desire to replace the adversary system – at least for people who cannot already afford it.

Once we understand the neoliberal aspects of the status quo, and liberals' gradual abandonment of the goal of providing lawyers to poor people and funding courts, there is reason to question why ODR travels under the banner of access to justice and whether it will serve the people its advocates claim they care so much about. After all, if the interests of poor people were truly motivating these reforms, the law already recognizes the right of non-lawyers to create organizations that fund and coordinate not-for-profit legal services.[24] The failure to innovate in this space suggests that rent-seeking packaged in Silicon Valley "solutionism,"[25] not access to justice and the needs of ordinary people who stand before the law, is paramount in the current movement.

In the pages that follow I set the debate about AI and ODR on a different plane by granting that access to some form of "law" will be expanded. AI, data mining, predictive analytics, and the widespread use of mobile computing devices are generally superb tools for reducing the cost of large-scale bureaucratic and logistical tasks. They are already proving genuinely transformative in other sectors of the economy and society. There remain, however, questions about how the architecture of these information systems fits with basic ideas about the structure of due process and the rule of law in a pluralistic, democratic society. Ultimately, these are questions about what version of "law" ODR will increase access to and what kind of justice and what kind of legal subject are produced by these systems.

To begin with, ODR advocates and designers tell us there are many "simple" cases that don't require adversary resolution, but when we look more closely, what we see is

[21] *See generally* David Luban, *Taking Out the Adversary: The Assault on Progressive Public Interest Lawyers*, 91 Cal. L. Rev. 209 (2003); Norman W. Spaulding, *The Ideal and the Actual in Procedural Due Process*, 2021 Hastings Const. L.Q. 48.

[22] On market-based solutions to access to justice that have been mobilized in support of legal tech, see Neil Gorsuch, A Republic, If You Can Keep It (2019).

[23] *See* Spaulding, *Due Process without Judicial Process*.

[24] *See, e.g.*, *Button*, 371 U.S. at 439–45 (affirming NAACP's First Amendment right to coordinate legal services); *Bhd. of R.R. Trainmen*, 377 U.S. at 5 (upholding union's coordination of legal services).

[25] Evgeny Morozov, To Save Everything, Click Here: The Folly of Technological Solutionism (2013).

that simplicity is assumed from and defined by the monetary value of the case, not the simplicity of the issues involved or the social, moral, and economic stakes for the litigants and the public. Given that small value cases make up the *vast* majority of American litigation, ODR actually poses a direct challenge to the courts as sites of adversary adjudication for ordinary people. I take up the "simplicity" hypothesis in Section 11.1.

Section 11.2 describes the architecture of ODR that enables efficient mass processing and resolution of legal claims. Although ODR designers and promoters tell us that it is cheaper and faster than litigation and that it helps ordinary people with "simple" disputes, current ODR systems are cheaper and faster mainly because they replace decision on the merits with easier-to-code "interest-based" negotiated resolutions. Equally situated parties may reach mutually advantageous resolution on such platforms, but where the state or powerful creditors are pitted against unrepresented individuals, as is true in most small value claims, "interest-based" resolution may simply enhance collection compliance with respect to debts and other legal claims that the defendant has a right to resist. Far from expanding access to justice, ODR may rather ominously accelerate unwarranted compliance and legal subordination. When the government itself is a creditor, and court systems therefore profit from collection, the risk of conflicts of interest in adoption of ODR systems that the public cannot evaluate is especially acute. In other cases, even though ODR may be cheaper than litigation, fee-for-service structures appear designed to induce early resolution rather than merits resolution for people of limited means.

Finally, the conjunction of AI's predictive analytic power and big data allows both public and private ODR system to achieve something dispute systems designers have long dreamed of: using data about existing disputes to *prevent* conflict in the future. As alluring as dispute prevention may seem in a conflict-ridden society, I argue in Section 11.3 that embedding dispute prevention and compliance into the architecture of the administration of justice through an automated system of surveillance and information control is inconsistent with human freedom. Asimov's second "law of robotics" states that "a robot must obey the orders given to it by human beings," not that humans must obey the orders of robots. Compliance-oriented and preventive ODR reverse this law, turning right holders into cogs in a machinery of compliance. I discuss alternative paths of ODR development and associated regulatory reforms to protect the due process rights of litigants, basic rule of law values, and the integrity of the administration of justice.

11.1 THE DOMAIN OF ODR: "SIMPLE" CASES?

> They have no lawyers among them, for they consider them as a sort of people whose "profession it is to disguise matters; and therefore they think it much better that every man" should plead his own cause .... [T]he plainest meaning of which words are capable is always the sense of their laws. And they argue thus.
>
> – Thomas More, *Utopia*

A foundational premise of current ODR systems is that there is a class of "simple" cases for which adversarial resolution is inappropriate, not least of which because the costs of the process exceed the value of these cases as measured by the size of the claim or judgment. The simplicity hypothesis has deep intuitive appeal. There are indeed many cases in which the costs of adversarial process exceed case value.[26] If these cases can be disposed of through an ODR system that does not require physical appearance in court, or even a judge, we are told, costs of adjudication are reduced for the state and perhaps for the parties. Resolution is faster and cheaper, giving the parties peace of mind sooner and the ability to move on with their lives. More complicated disputes might require the formalities of adversary procedure but due process can sometimes be provided without full judicial process. Finally, ODR will promote access to justice because it is precisely these simple cases in which ordinary people do not have access to counsel or avoid litigation altogether, believing that the game isn't worth the candle. Ordinary people will thus be better off as ODR expands.[27]

This simplicity/access nexus is pervasive in the ODR literature, the promotional materials of ODR vendors, and the webpages of court systems that have adopted ODR systems. One commentator observes that "the use of ODR to settle small claims and therefore free up judges and courtrooms for more complex cases is a given: 'Small claims courts, with smaller dollar amounts and less complex issues, are ideally situated to transition their operations online.'"[28] ODR, the author continues, "has proven to significantly reduce the delays and costs normally associated with a court case by eliminating the need for travel and synchronous communications."[29] Until the development of ODR, another advocate writes, "the average experience of a litigant 'going to court' amounts to . . . waiting in long lines" – if and when "a hearing actually begins, it is over almost at once. The outcome is generally predictable . . . as the decision is determined by standard pieces of information

[26] Paula L. Hannaford-Agor et al., Nat'l Ctr. for State Cts.: The Landscape of Civil Litigation in State Courts (2015), https://www.ncsc.org/__data/assets/pdf_file/0020/13376/civiljusticereport-2015.pdf.

[27] J. J. Prescott, *Improving Access to Justice in State Courts with Platform Technology*, 70 Vand. L. Rev. 1993, 2050 (2017); Susskind, Online Courts. Even critics of ODR accept the simplicity/access gospel, reserving their fire for the use of ODR for "complicated" disputes. Condlin, *Online Dispute Resolution*, at 217 ("It is not difficult to understand how routine, standardized, and uncomplicated disputes could be reduced to single issues and resolved acceptably by algorithms, or how parties to disputes could choose software-driven systems over human ones when the stakes are small, the issues routine, and cost and convenience are the overriding concerns.").

[28] Nicolas W. Vermeys & Karim Benyekhlef, *ODR and the Courts*, *in* Online Dispute Resolution: Theory and Practice 307, 318 (Mohamed S. Abdel Wahab, Ethan Katsh & Daniel Rainey eds., 2012). Matterhorn's website emphasizes that its "ODR brings the public, government staff, and others together to handle relatively minor and routine proceedings . . . streamlin[ing] the parts of processes that don't need to take place in person. And the efficiencies gained means your personnel can focus on the cases that can and should require more attention." *ODR Solutions*, Matterhorn, https://getmatterhorn.com/odr-solutions/.

[29] Vermeys & Benyekhlef, *ODR and the Courts*, at 313.

contained in the case file or provided by answers the litigant supplies."[30] This is not only hugely inefficient, "access to justice is subverted by the fact that courts continue to operate on the age-old model."[31] The adversary system

> makes much more sense for complex litigation in which credibility determinations ... and diverse forms of evidence are standard fare. For disputes of this character, the costs of physically using a courthouse (even day in and day out) are relatively modest, if not negligible, given the stakes of the lawsuit .... But for minor disputes in state court, in which the stakes are at least initially fairly low and decisions can be made on the basis of papers and are usually straightforward, the tradeoff cuts deeply the other way.[32]

Supposedly "[m]inor legal disputes" account for the majority of state trial court caseloads in the United States.[33] These include not only small claims cases between private litigants and landlord/tenant disputes, but "lesser misdemeanors and civil infractions" where the state is involved as the complainant or prosecutor.[34]

The first problem with the simplicity/access nexus is the assumption that low value cases are in fact simple. They can be made to seem simple by comparison to more sophisticated causes of action, but for the parties involved in "simple" cases, this is an irrelevant comparator. For parties to a case, the judgment whether their case is simple rests on factors such as

- whether they have dealt with similar disputes before and are familiar with the applicable law and procedure,
- the relative value of the case as compared to *their* other assets and debts,
- dignitary considerations linked to the harm they have suffered or are accused of causing as compared to other wrongs and emotionally charged problems they have dealt with,
- dignitary considerations linked to the degree of participation and understanding litigants have about the process that results in resolution of a dispute
- the capacity of designers of ODR systems to capture the interests of the parties, and
- the actual merits.

30 Prescott, *Improving Access to Justice in State Courts*, at 1997–98.

31 *Id.* at 1996.

32 *Id.*

33 *Id.* at 2000.

34 *Id.* at 2001–2002. Proponents also frequently compare ODR systems to the absence of access to *any* dispute resolution process, pointing to the same evidence that litigants with small money value claims cannot afford counsel and cannot afford to lose time from work to appear in court pro se. See *id.* Of course, almost anything looks good in comparison to nothing – indeed, the problem takes on real urgency when cast in this light. But against such a benchmark any solution that even modestly improves on the status quo might be considered worth pursuing even if it is flawed in other ways. I take this up in Section 11.3.

With respect to the first consideration, an experienced landlord likely has dealt with tenant disputes in the past and can therefore navigate legal issues in a new dispute with some degree of comfort even if the matter is not free of frustration. By contrast, a tenant who has never had an abusive landlord will not likely regard even a small money value dispute about a repair, return of a deposit, or penalty for late rent as "simple." With respect to relative value, the second consideration, even a seemingly "minor" fine or civil liability can loom large for a person of modest means, forcing painful choices about whether to put food on the table or pay up to avoid mounting fines and fees and continuing intervention on the part of the state. The stakes won't seem "minor" to such a party.[35]

Dignitary considerations are indeterminate and subjective, but an extensive, well-established body of social scientific and cognitive research makes clear that these considerations are *central* to the perceived legitimacy of dispute resolution systems. Quick resolution of emotionally charged cases in which people do not feel heard can have enduring negative repercussions not only for the parties, but for the administration of justice. As Alan Lind and Tom Tyler summarize, "people usually feel more fairly treated when they have had an opportunity to express their point of view about their situation."[36] This is just as true, they note, in "simple" cases as it is for "complex" ones: "In small claims cases . . . all parties to a case would like to have an opportunity to tell their story, taking as much time as they feel they need to articulate the issues that matter to them."[37] Unlimited participation obviously is not possible in any dispute resolution system. Finality matters to fairness. Judges are obliged to impose other limits as well, including legal relevance and consideration for the time that must be spent on other cases.[38] Nevertheless, Lind and Tyler emphasize, the tension between "objective justice and legal efficiency," on the one hand, and "the experience of subjective justice on the part of the litigant," on the other, doesn't evaporate just because a case is a relatively "simple" one from the perspective of judges and other dispute systems designers.[39]

They offer, as example, proceedings in a traffic court in Chicago:

> Judges in that court often take the view that showing up for court and losing a day's pay at work is punishment enough for a traffic offense. As a result, those who arrive

[35] The point is not that social costs should be ignored in favor of relative value concerns of the parties (see Prescott, *Improving Access to Justice*, at 2003 n.46), but that the relative value concerns of the parties affect perceptions of the stakes of even small money value cases. Further, it is reductive to equate social costs with the budget outlays of court systems. As the discussion *infra* demonstrates, social costs include perceptions of fairness and the cost of powerful repeat players such as creditors and the government gaining systemic advantages from court systems.

[36] Edgar Allan Lind & Tom R. Tyler, The Social Psychology of Procedural Justice 4–5 (1988).

[37] *Id.* at 5.

[38] *Id.*

[39] *Id.*

> in court often have their case dismissed without any hearing .... However, interviews with traffic court defendants suggest that *despite these favorable outcomes they often leave the court dissatisfied*. For example, one woman showed up for court with photographs that she felt showed that a sign warning her not to make an illegal turn was not clearly visible. After her case was dismissed (a victory!) she was angry and expressed considerable dissatisfaction with the court. ... Outcome-based models might find the woman's dissatisfaction difficult to explain, but process-based models would have little trouble in accounting for her reaction.[40]

The feeling of not being given the time of day, of not being heard, can ramify in other forms of civic engagement, and in other dealings with the state. If they are tied to deeper mistreatment at the hands of the state, the consequences can be grave.[41]

Even a simple case can also prove quite complex to code in an ODR system. Complexity in coding arises not only from the costs of good ODR design but from limits in natural language processing capacities in even the most advanced AI systems and other algorithms.[42] These systems are still capable of fairly comical errors in the interpretation of human language.[43] In some settings these errors present mere inconveniences – your Uber driver arrives late or drives to the wrong location. In law, the consequences can be catastrophic – including erroneous arrest and separation from one's family, destroyed credit, even the use of deadly force in executing a bad warrant. Natural language processing capacities will improve gradually. However, as with any symbolic system that attempts to reproduce, measure, and operationalize content from another symbolic system (here, human language), there will always be gaps. All symbolic systems err, and all are to one degree or another ineluctably "leaky."[44] This derives from the nature of representation itself – the fact that representation depends upon reduction of signified content to signs. Automated systems that displace human judgment offer advantages, but they also remove the possibility of real-time commonsense reconsideration.

This raises the question whether even truly "simple" cases are simple enough for ODR systems to handle.[45] The answer to that question cannot be found by

40 *Id.* at 2.

41 Monica Bell, *Police Reform and the Dismantling of Legal Estrangement*, 126 YALE L.J. 2054 (2017) (discussing legal estrangement as the result of procedural injustice, vicarious marginalization, and structural exclusion).

42 *See* Norm Spaulding, *Is Human Judgment Necessary? Artificial Intelligence, Algorithmic Governance, and the Law*, *in* OXFORD HANDBOOK OF ETHICS AND AI 375 (Markus D. Dubber, Frank Pasquale & Sunit Das eds., 2020); *See also* Chapter 3 in this volume.

43 Spaulding, *Is Human Judgment Necessary?*

44 *Id.* at 378 n.13 (quote re "leakiness" of all AI) (citing Carlos E. Perez, *AI Safety, Leaking Abstractions and Boeing's 737 Max 8*, MEDIUM (March 14, 2019), https://medium.com/intuitionmachine/ai-safety-leaking-abstractions-and-boeings-737-max-8-5d4b3b9bf0c3).

45 There is also open debate among ODR advocates, people who work in communications theory, and experts in conflict resolution about the parameters and conditions for establishing

comparing ODR to the cost of adversary resolution or to cases assumed to be more complex and therefore more suitable to adversary resolution. It can only be answered by taking stock of the merits.

Much of the adversary system is designed not only to maximize participation and party control (albeit for those who can afford it), but to avoid the problem of prejudging the merits – the temptation to decide a case based on reductive first impressions. This temptation is strong, reinforced by powerful cognitive biases (including confirmation bias, halo effects, etc.). A prominent nineteenth-century lawyer and judge famously admonished in defense of the adversary system that "the affairs of mankind are not so nicely adjusted as that one party in a law-suit should be entirely right and the other entirely wrong .... [T]ruth cannot be elicited and justice awarded unless both sides of a case are fairly represented."[46] This is so not only because of the "intricacies" of "commercial relations," the moral complexity of human action subject to legal regulation, or the "nice distinctions to be made in determining the degree of criminality," but because long experience shows that "[m]any cases which at first seemed to be bad have on examination proved to be good."[47] The adversary system thus rests on what one might call procedural skepticism – rules of procedure that reduce the risk of prejudgment.

The idea that there is a general category of "simple" cases and that the merits of these cases reveal themselves on first impression or on the initial pleadings is, from this perspective, a seductive fiction. It rests on a self-serving value judgment about small-dollar-figure claims – that they matter less and contain less complexity – and the triage imperatives of mass-processing.

As importantly, evidence from the last decade provides sobering proof that supposedly simple cases (small claims, landlord/tenant, and traffic and other misdemeanors) are not actually simple and that they have *profound* ramifications for the administration of justice. Firstly, we know that these cases dominate state trial court dockets, and that, in the vast majority, the individuals involved do not have counsel. So ODR is staking a claim to displace *most* state court adjudication, not experiment with a small subset of claims. We also know that, regardless of specific subject matter, these are mainly debt collection proceedings in which the plaintiff is either the state seeking to recover "legal financial obligations" (fines, fees, and other penalties imposed by the court) or a creditor (a lender, collection agency, or landlord) represented by counsel. There is thus a powerful repeat player (the state or a private creditor) on one side, and an individual defendant/debtor on the other.

trust in dispute resolution. *See generally* Mohamed S. Abdel Wahab, Ethan Katsh & Daniel Rainey EDS., ONLINE DISPUTE RESOLUTION: THEORY AND PRACTICE (2012).

[46] Norman W. Spaulding, *The Myth of Civic Republicanism: Interrogating the Ideology of Antebellum Legal Ethics*, 71 FORDHAM L. REV. 1397, 1436–37 (2003) (quoting Justice Jackson).

[47] *Id.*

This contrasts *sharply* with the image of the facilitation of cooperative resolution between individuals painted by the ODR literature.[48]

11.1.1 *Public Enforcement in "Simple" Cases*

With respect to public debts, the Department of Justice Investigation of the Ferguson Police Department and follow-on litigation against municipal courts around the country show that there has been widespread abuse of legal financial obligations as cash-strapped municipalities deprived of general funds by their states have converted courts into fee-for-service systems parasitic on the most financially vulnerable populations within their jurisdictions. In Ferguson, excessive fines and fees were imposed disproportionately on the African American population of the city. The Report's section on the court system found that enforcement actions involved shocking deviations from basic principles of procedural due process, including failure to make the constitutionally required inquiry into litigants' ability to pay before using imprisonment as a penalty or inducement for nonpayment.[49] Litigation in dozens of other jurisdictions reveals that the problems with setting and collecting legal financial obligations are widespread.[50] One report revealed that the

> courts in St. Louis city and the county collected over $60 million in revenue in 2013 . . . with some cities depending on such fines for more than 40 percent of their general fund. The report found that the cities most dependent on such revenue were majority African-American with large impoverished populations .... In Jennings, which has a population of roughly 14,750, [a] lawsuit found that the city had issued about twice as many warrants as there were households, "mostly in cases

[48] *Cf.* Noam Ebner & Elayne E. Greenberg, *Strengthening Online Dispute Resolution Justice*, 63 Wash. U. J.L. & P. 65 (2020) (arguing from a dispute systems design perspective that "ODR systems should no longer be touted as lawyerless .... [W]hile ODR programs may resolve discrete presenting issues without lawyers, clients may still need lawyers to help assess the appropriateness of a discrete ODR program and to help the clients consider the broader justice issues that may be implicated."); *see also* Noam Ebner & Elayne E. Greenberg, *Where Have All the Lawyers Gone? The Empty Chair at the ODR Justice Table*, 6 J. Online Disp. Res. 154 (2019). I concur, especially when the other side already has the benefit of counsel.

[49] U.S. Dept. Just., C.R. Div., Investigation of the Ferguson Police Department 52–54 (2015), https://www.justice.gov/sites/default/files/opa/press-releases/attachments/2015/03/04/ferguson_police_department_report.pdf.

[50] Arthur Liman Center, Yale L. Sch., *Fees, Fines, and the Funding of Public Services* (See Aug. 2020); ABA Comm. on Ethics & Pro. Responsibility, Formal Op. 490 (2020) (gathering cases and discussing ethical obligations of judges in setting and collecting legal financial obligations); *As Court Fees Rise, the Poor Are Paying the Price, NPR* (May 19, 2014), https://www.npr.org/2014/05/19/312158516/increasing-court-fees-punish-the-poor (discussing examples from court systems around the country; "What we found again and again, is that the costs of the justice system in the United States are paid increasingly by the defendants themselves," and "20 different fees charged to people who go to court in Michigan. In 2012, these raised $345 million. The state court system keeps track and sends judges spread sheets showing how much they collect.").

> involving unpaid debts for [traffic] tickets." In 2013, a 24-year-old inmate in the Jennings jail who was imprisoned for unpaid tickets hanged himself.[51]

"Tragic incidents such as these draw into vivid relief the human cost of ignoring the connection between procedural due process and human dignity".

As local courts have faced funding crises and failed to address racial bias, advocates of ODR have been marketing their platforms to court systems around the country and in the pages of law reviews by packaging enhanced efficiency in collecting public debts in the language of "access to justice." ODR advocates insist that in traffic cases faster, cheaper resolution benefits individual defendants because they get closure and avoid the additional fees associated with failure to appear and default.[52] But when one examines the use of the platforms marketed to court systems, one finds things like the Fort Collins, Colorado, municipal court's ODR system for "camera radar/red light tickets."[53] The ODR system provides for resolution of traffic camera tickets.[54] The sophisticated cameras cost $10,000 a month each to operate. Tickets are $75.[55] The city claims that the cameras are making a "huge difference" in driver education and safety, and it points to data showing reductions in accidents at one of the intersections where the cameras are used.[56] But the program also reportedly nets the city about $200,000 a year over operating costs, including payments to the private contractor who services the cameras.[57] Camera citations well exceed officer written traffic tickets in the city, and in other jurisdictions there is evidence that this enforcement tool invites politically corrupt outsourcing to private contractors and generates revenue without improving traffic safety at all.[58]

[51] Campbell Robertson, *Missouri City to Pay $4.7 Million to Settle Suit over Jailing Practices*, N.Y. Times (July 15, 2016), https://www.nytimes.com/2016/07/16/us/missouri-city-to-pay-4-7-million-to-settle-suit-over-jailing-practices.html.

[52] *See generally* Prescott, *Improving Access to Justice*.

[53] *Regulations regarding Radar/Red Light Tickets*, City Fort Collins, https://www.fcgov.com/municipalcourt/camera.php/title-vi.

[54] Dunrie Greiling, *Fort Collins Municipal Court Now Offers Red-Light Camera Citation Resolution Online*, Matterhorn (May 7, 2020), https://getmatterhorn.com/fort-collins-municipal-court-now-offers-red-light-camera-citation-resolution-online/.

[55] Katie Ruedebusch, Legislative Council Staff, Issue Brief: Automated Vehicle Identification Systems (2018), https://leg.colorado.gov/sites/default/files/18-13_red_light_cameras.pdf.

[56] Sarah Kyle, *Veto Gives Fort Collins Green Light on Red-Light Cameras*, Coloradoan (June 7, 2016), https://www.coloradoan.com/story/news/2016/06/06/how-fort-collins-police-use-red-light-traffic-cameras/85511892/.

[57] *Id.*

[58] *Id.* In other jurisdictions, the companies that run the cameras take the bulk of the funds generated, and the evidence on reduction of accidents is mixed – accidents fall at varying rates at the intersections that have cameras but increase at other intersections in the same jurisdiction, raising questions about the behavioral benefits. Mark Hemsky, *Are Red Light Cameras Life Savers or Revenue Generators?* Fox40 (Aug. 2, 2017, 7:00 PM PDT), https://fox40.com/news/are-red-light-cameras-life-savers-or-revenue-generators/. Other research shows political corruption in the awarding of red-light camera contracts to private vendors and even less

The Fort Collins ODR system does not appear to follow a pure bargaining model where the resolution results from negotiating what will be paid irrespective of the merits. Nor, however, does it appear to be designed to fully and faithfully ascertain the merits in each case, including educating defendants about how to explore and assert standard defenses. The defendant is assured there is a *prosecutor* who will review the case and the website's "About Online Case Review" page indicates that a defendant could "potentially have . . . fines and fees reduced or in some cases, dismissed altogether."[59] The FAQ page, however, characterizes ODR as a process to *enter a guilty plea* through an "Online Plea" process.[60] The page indicates that "You can plead guilty, be sentenced, and pay your fines/costs without going to court in person."[61]

If the system is mainly designed to enter guilty pleas and collect the fines and fees – if, that is, the private "review" conducted by prosecutors and the court is perfunctory, designed to "improve compliance" on the same terms as the designer's platforms sold to other jurisdictions[62] – then the efficiency gains accrue mainly to the city.[63] In cases where guilt is unclear or revenue generation dominates public safety priorities, defendants are saddled with unwarranted debts and the public with rent-seeking law enforcement. Indeed, a compliance-oriented ODR system that primarily increases the speed of collection for traffic camera fines raises the specter of fully automated law enforcement in derogation of every procedural value other than reduced cost to the state.[64] Nor does such an ODR enforcement process

convincing evidence regarding driver safety, including increases in rear-end accidents at intersections with cameras. See Austin Berg & Ben Szalinski, *Illinois Red-Light Cameras Have Collected More Than $11B from Drivers since 2008*, Ill. Pol'y Inst., https://www.illinoispolicy.org/reports/illinois-red-light-cameras-have-collected-more-than-1b-from-drivers-since-2008/.

59 *About Online Case Review*, City of Fort Collins, https://cii2.courtinnovations.com/COFCMC/about.

60 *Frequently Asked Questions*, City of Fort Collins, https://cii2.courtinnovations.com/COFCMC/faq.

61 *Id.*

62 Prescott, *Improving Access to Justice*, at 2036; *see also id.* at 2035 (noting that courts can "improve" their "revenue situation" through systems that "*encourage better legal compliance with existing fine and fee structures*" (emphasis added)); *id.* at 2038 (presenting data on compliance measured in terms of payment timing for Matterhorn); *id.* at 2038 (touting compliance data as showing that Matterhorn can "reduce the waste that comes from delay and the cat and mouse games that are common in today's justice system"); *id.* at 2045 (arguing that user satisfaction can be inferred when they "open their wallets – and doing so sooner rather than later"). When addressing courts, the company's ODR system is even more frank about the speed of fee collection: "Increase access to justice, decrease time to case closure, hasten fee collection, and decrease defaults with Matterhorn." *Get Results*, Matterhorn, https://getmatterhorn.com/get-results/.

63 For another example, note CyberSettle's cross marketing of ODR technology and technology to accelerate collection. CyberSettle, www.cybersettle.com/. I discuss the relationship between ODR design and merits determination in greater detail in Section 11.2, *infra*.

64 Michael L. Rich, *Machine Learning, Automated Suspicion Algorithms, and the Fourth Amendment*, 164 U. Pa. L. Rev. 871 (2016).

provide a public forum, as court proceedings do, for airing systemic concerns about whether revenue generation dominates legitimate public safety concerns. Public and media scrutiny of enforcement is literally short-circuited.[65]

Remarkably, ODR advocates commonly ignore or suspend the merits question altogether – either not seeking to measure it, excluding it from the design of ODR systems, or both.[66] Traffic cases are indeed minor relative to felony cases, but the lesson of Ferguson and broader litigation about excessive fines and fees is that incursions on civil liberty and civil rights in the design of dispute resolution systems for these offenses can be substantial. Recent scholarship on criminal law and procedure reinforces this conclusion, showing that twenty-first-century misdemeanor enforcement has been used to criminalize poverty, to impose onerous systems of regulation and continuing supervision on marginal populations, to feed mass incarceration, and to subordinate racial minorities through biased forms of "order maintenance," policing, and punishment.[67] To submerge these distortions in the administration of justice in automatic collection-compliance processes would obviously be inconsistent with the mission of enhancing access to justice for ordinary people.

11.1.2 *Private Enforcement in "Simple" Cases*

Even when the state is not a party to supposedly "simple" cases, recent empirical studies show that the simplicity hypothesis is untethered from the realities of the administration of justice. As ODR advocates describe small claims, it would be easy to assume not only that private individuals are on both sides of the litigation, but that in many "simple" cases people gin up "highly emotional conflicts over matters with relatively low monetary value."[68] This happens, to be sure, but the data show that far more often an individual unrepresented defendant is sued in small claims court by a powerful creditor or landlord represented by counsel. The greater leverage of these plaintiffs is mobilized not to force costly merits adjudication, but rather to accelerate reduction of a claim to a final judgment and proceed with enforcement.

65 Users have to have a docket number to enter the system, so it is not like an open court where the public can investigate or observe the process. *Record Search*, Fort Collins Municipal Court, www.ncourt.com/x-press/x-onlinepayments.aspx?juris=F311FB07-16CD-4525-B782-E681F830C1A6 (last visited Apr. 8, 2022). More broadly, see Julie E. Cohen, Configuring the Networked Self: Law, Code, and the Play of Everyday Practice (2012).

66 Prescott, *Improving Access to Justice*, at 2001; *see also* CyberSettle.

67 *See generally* Issa Kholer-Hausmann, Misdemeanorland: Criminal Courts and Social Control in an Age of Broken Windows Policing (2019); Alexandra Natapoff, Punishment without Crime: How Our Massive Misdemeanours System Traps the Innocent and Makes America More Unequal (2018).

68 Hannaford-Agor et al., NCSC Landscape Study, at 35; Shannon Salter, *Online Dispute Resolution and Justice System Integration: British Columbia's Civil Resolution Tribunal*, 34 Windsor Yearbook Access to J. 112, 119 (2017).

The National Center for State Courts Landscape of Civil Litigation study in 2015 found that three-quarters of all judgments in the state courts were less than $5,200.[69] Even among non–small claims cases that went to trial, "[t]hree quarters of judgments entered in contract cases following a bench trial were less than half of those in small claims cases ($1,785 versus $3,900). This contradicts assertions that most bench trials involve adjudication over complex, high-stakes cases."[70] Whatever the nature of modern trial, most civil cases, the study emphasizes, were "disposed of through an administrative process," and for cases that reached judgment, *the most common resolution was a default judgment*.[71] In these cases, then, there is no meaningful deliberation on the merits, often no hearing whatsoever preceding the entry of judgment.

Most revealingly, the Landscape Study found that

> [t]he vast majority of civil cases that remain in state courts are debt collection, landlord/tenant, foreclosure, and small claims cases. State courts are the preferred forum for plaintiffs in these cases for the simple reason that in most jurisdictions state courts hold a monopoly on procedures to enforce judgments. *Securing a judgment . . . is the mandatory first step to being able to initiate garnishment or asset seizure proceedings*. The majority of defendants in these cases, however, are self-represented.[72]

The conjunction of self-representation and default judgments in small value debtor-creditor disputes suggests that some state courts are operating as accelerated debt collection forums. In the forty-four states where judges, clerks, magistrates, and justices of the peace are allowed to issue capias warrants for failure to appear at post-judgment asset examination hearings, defendants in civil cases face arrest and incarceration with bond often set equals to the debt owed.[73] As with misdemeanor criminal cases then, civil litigation for people in financially precarious situations can result in restraints on liberty in order to force payment.

On this evidence, as with the use of ODR for misdemeanor cases and legal financial obligations to courts, the simplicity/access nexus looks quite ominous. The access-to-justice problem is not how to speed things up and substitute automated bargaining over settlement value (or private deliberation on facts adduced through strictly circumscribed online submissions) in place of public inquiry into

69 Hannaford-Agor et al., NCSC Landscape Study, at iv.

70 *Id.*

71 *Id.*

72 *Id.* at v (emphasis added).

73 *The Criminalization of Private Debt*, ACLU, https://www.aclu.org/issues/smart-justice/mass-incarceration/criminalization-private-debt (noting that an "estimated 77 Americans have a debt that has been turned over to a private collection agency," that "millions" are "threatened with jail" for failure to pay, and citing over a thousand specific cases in twenty-six states in which judges issued warrants for people collection companies claimed owed civil debts; describing capias warrant process).

the merits in small value cases. It is (1) how to slow creditors and other repeat players down in order to ensure attention to the merits and (2) how to address the systemic disparities in power that shape both the debts being collected (click-wrap and other contracts of adhesion; payday lending schemes, etc.) and enforcement procedures (default judgment, capias, etc.). ODR systems oriented toward speed and automated online resolution may be quite attractive to plaintiff creditors and other repeat players, but for individual defendant debtors, the risk is great that ODR systems will not include adequate exploration of defenses available under the relevant contract, lease, or state and federal consumer protection and fair debt collection practices laws.[74] These defenses are *not* generally regarded as "simple" by experts. A 2010 FTC report found that even basic affirmative defenses such as state statutes of limitations "on filing actions to recover debt are sometimes variable and complex, and generally not understood by consumers."[75] An allegation of identity theft raised by a debtor can "increase the complexity and time required" to resolve a matter.[76] The Truth in Lending Act's enforcement structure – which contemplates use of the statute as a counterclaim in a debt collection proceeding – is famously "confusing."[77]

Enough has been said, I hope, to make clear that small values cases are by no means simple or low stakes either for the parties concerned or the administration of justice. Nor are these cases small in number – they compose a substantial part of court dockets and therefore of the cases handled by the adversary system. The simplicity hypothesis is false. If there is a class of truly simple claims suitable for ODR, the hard question is how to define standards for accurately identifying them without having to adjudicate the merits along the way – the very task the avoidance of which makes ODR so affordable. As matters currently stand, then, the principal effect of using low money-value claims as a proxy for simplicity will be to produce a bifurcated system of justice – one in which low- and middle-income people already priced out of meaningful participation in the adversary system[78] will have no alternative but to avail themselves of ODR systems. This bifurcation in the

[74] *See* Condlin, *Online Dispute Resolution*, at 722 (warning that "[w]hen not based on normative standards, dispute resolution is just another form of bureaucratic processing . . . according to a set of tacit, often biased, intra-organizational, administrative norms . . . that are defined by repeat players who 'capture' the system and use it for their private ends").

[75] Fed. Trade Comm'n, Repairing a Broken System: Protecting Consumers in Debt Collection Litigation and Arbitration 2 (2010), https://www.ftc.gov/sites/default/files/documents/reports/federal-trade-commission-bureau-consumer-protection-staff-report-repairing-broken-system-protecting/debtcollectionreport.pdf.

[76] *Id.* at 47.

[77] *Class Actions Under the Truth in Lending Act*, 83 Yale L.J. 1410, 1411 (1974); *see* Coxson v. Commonwealth Mortg. Co. of Am., 43 F.3d 189, 194 (5th Cir. 1995) (TILA counterclaim allowed despite the fact that the loan origination was originated fifteen years prior to the proof of claim being filed); *In re* Wentz, 393 B.R. 545 (Bankr. S.D. Ohio 2008) (TILA counterclaim allowed approximately three years after origination).

[78] On the price of adjudication as compared to the value of judgments and the effects on access to justice, see Marc Galanter, Why the Haves Come Out Ahead (2014).

administration of justice will merely formalize, encode and multiply, not mitigate, problems of access to justice.

In the most ambitious ODR systems – those that remove the third party neutral human decision-maker altogether – low- and middle-income people will receive justice defined by software engineers unregulated by standards of judicial ethics except to the extent that courts supervise their outsourcing contracts. And we know that supervision will be limited by the fact that the best AI systems to date are opaque in their operation even to their designers.[79] So, for instance, a deep learning system used to generate "reasonable" settlement values might not be explainable – even by the engineers who program it. Systems that are more transparent because they rely on expert design rather than deep learning, on the other hand, remain highly reductive.[80] Absent regulation, this bifurcated system for the administration of justice will flourish on terms that limit assessment and accountability.

11.2 THE ARCHITECTURE OF ODR: ACCESS TO JUSTICE, HARMONY, OR "JUST HARMONY"?

The last section focused on the pervasive assumption that ODR will enhance access to justice because it is suitable for so-called simple cases as measured by money value. In this Section, I shift from the nature of the cases ODR systems regularly handle to the design of the systems themselves in order to examine exactly how the architecture of ODR promotes efficient resolution.

11.2.1 *ODR's Design Features*

Although the overall ecosystem is heterogenous and evolving rapidly, most current ODR platforms function by breaking dispute resolution into its component phases, reducing legal forms and rules to plain language questions, instructions, and guidance, and then using asynchronous electronic communication, document storage, retrieval, and review to facilitate the flow of information needed to define and resolve the dispute, as shown in Table 11.1.

In the first phase there is typically a webpage with plain language text, videos, and graphical information describing the specific ODR process. In some instances, general information on the law is provided (at varying levels of detail). In others, there is little or no information about the underlying rights and defenses that apply to the dispute or resources for ascertaining what the law is. The emphasis is instead on identifying the parties' interests. Rechtwijzer, the Dutch online ODR system

79 M. Ethan Katsh & Orna Rabinovich-Einy, Digital Justice: Technology and the Internet of Disputes 161 (2017).

80 Orna Rabinovich-Einy & Ethan Katsh, *Lessons from Online Dispute Resolution for Dispute Systems Design*, *in* Online Dispute Resolution: Theory and Practice 51, 61 (Mohamed S. Abdel Wahab, Ethan Katsh & Daniel Rainey eds., 2012).

TABLE 11.1 *Five phases of ODR*

Phase	I Opt In Phase	II Diagnosis/Intake	III Negotiation	IV Third Party Neutral/ Algorithm	V Closure / Opt Out
Process	Information to users about process and applicable substantive rules	Information gathered from users	– Open – Structured – Algorithm or AI System	– Review and approve – Facilitate to reach agreement – AI System	– Approval of enforceable order – Online adjudication by third party neutral – Referral to courts/ arbitration

that, until its demise in 2017, handled divorce, family law, debt, and neighbor disputes, explicitly encouraged the parties to approach the process through the framework of interest-based resolution.[81] Divorcing parties were initially informed of "rules such as those for dividing property, child support and standard arrangements for visiting rights so that they could agree on the basis of informed consent," but the software's negotiation framework prioritized interests, not rights.[82]

British Columbia's vaunted Civil Resolution Tribunal (CRT) includes a statute-of-limitations information page that defines what a statute of limitations is and advises parties that it is not tolled during the first phases of the CRT process. But it does not answer the question of what statute of limitations applies to the dispute the party has, how to determine either when it started to run, or when it will expire. The page ends with the statement: "We can't answer these questions for you. You may want to get legal advice. The CRT can't provide legal advice."[83] Indeed, CRT's detailed downloadable forms to help parties prepare for negotiation generally ignore rights and defenses, instead prompting the parties to identify and articulate their interests.[84]

To generate enthusiasm and induce users to opt in, introductory pages of ODR websites also include substantial promotional content highlighting perceived advantages of ODR relative to adjudication in court. The CRT home page begins: "Save time, money, and stress! The CRT lets you resolve your dispute when and where it's convenient for you .... The CRT helps you resolve your dispute quickly and affordably."[85] Rechtwijzer, the online divorce settlement platform, billed itself as providing a chance to "separate together" without the adversity and acrimony of divorce in court.[86] ODR websites generally do not counterbalance their self-promotion regarding the advantages of online resolution with sober assessment of potential downsides, clear notice about rights waived, or alternatives.

In Phase II, once users have opted in, questions are directed to the users through a range of graphical interfaces in order to gather basic information about the dispute, classify it, populate relevant forms, and upload relevant documentary evidence. Advanced systems use chatbots or other interfaces modeled off of apps people use daily on their smartphones and other devices. Matterhorn, the ODR system behind the Colorado traffic camera enforcement discussed in Section 11.1 has an online process for "the uploading of statements by parties, law enforcement and court

[81] Roger Smith, *Rechtwijzer: Why Online Supported Dispute Resolution Is Hard to Implement*, Law, Tech. & Access to Justice (June 20, 2017), https://law-tech-a2j.org/odr/rechtwijzer-why-online-supported-dispute-resolution-is-hard-to-implement/.

[82] *Id.*

[83] *Limitations Periods*, Civ. Resol. Tribunal (Apr. 28, 2021), https://civilresolutionbc.ca/wp-content/uploads/2021/04/Limitation-Periods.pdf.

[84] *Tips for Successful Negotiation*, Civil Resol. Tribunal (Dec. 16, 2021), https://civilresolutionbc.ca/wp-content/uploads/2017/07/Tips-for-successful-negotiation.pdf.

[85] Civil Resol. Tribunal.

[86] Katsh & Rabinovich-Einy, Digital Justice, at 161.

personnel from afar and in lieu of court hearings."[87] In this phase, assuming the design for information sharing is not reductive, there are obvious efficiency gains in cost, time, and convenience associated with "asynchronous processes" for fact gathering relative to filing papers in court.[88]

In the negotiation phase, Phase III, there is a wide range of approaches. Some, such as CRT's, simply provide online portals for direct, unmediated negotiation between parties with some basic ground rules about abusive communication and guidance about how to prepare and conduct a successful interest-based negotiation. Others introduce a human third-party neutral to guide negotiation. Still others are automated and more rigidly structured, channeling the parties into online negotiation in the form of blind bidding with an algorithm that is designed to identify an optimal settlement from the highest one party is willing to offer and the least the other is willing to accept.[89] This ostensibly allows parties to "overcome tactics often employed in face-to-face negotiations that hinder reaching an agreement despite the existence of a 'zone of possible agreement.'"[90] Smartsettle's software forces parties to "list their interests and assign numerical values to them, thereby creating a weighted spectrum of issues" from which an algorithm "generated various 'packages' or combinations of issues that might satisfy both parties" along with "a graph as a visual display of the level of satisfaction each package of issues represented for the parties."[91] Overall, both public and private ODR platforms share some of the following algorithmically automated features at varying levels of sophistication: "identifying dispute types; exposing parties' interests; asking questions about positions; reframing demands; suggesting options for solutions allowing; allowing some venting; matching solutions to problems; and drafting agreements."[92]

In the phase IV, a third-party neutral human expert may be brought in online to review and approve a deal reached between the parties. This was the case with Rechtwijzer. If online negotiations resulted in an agreement, an independent lawyer would be brought in to review the deal "to ensure that it meets legal requirements and is fair to both parties."[93] If no agreement was reached, a mediator or arbitrator would be brought in online to help facilitate resolution. Costs were a fraction of traditional costs for counsel in divorce proceedings in court, and "[e]ven at the higher end," costs were "lower than the costs to the Legal Aid Board for representing

87 *Id.* at 162.
88 *Id.*
89 *Id.* at 35 (discussing CyberSettle)
90 *Id.* at 36.
91 *Id.*
92 *Id.* at 34. For example, Modria's ODR system for courts was developed out of the eBay and PayPal model that is asserted to have resolved 90 percent of the 60 million cases per year it managed "through automation." Modria, Online Dispute Resolution 2 (2017), https://www.tylertech.com/Portals/0/OpenContent/Files/4080/Modria-Brochure.pdf.
93 Katsh & Rabinovich-Einy, Digital Justice, at 161.

both parties to divorce proceedings in court."[94] In the near future algorithms may not only structure negotiation and suggest solutions but displace the third-party neutral altogether by using artificial intelligence to review and validate negotiated solutions.[95]

In the fifth and final phase, an agreement reached online is reduced to an enforceable contract or court order. Generally, ODR negotiations cannot be introduced in court, but there are many exceptions. CRT participants, for instance, lose confidentiality if they use what the system designers determine is "abusive" language in settlement negotiations. ODR websites also vary widely in the promises they make regarding the use of user data (information such as identity, location, negotiation documents and communications, history of participation in ODR or other litigation, etc.), sale of such data to third-party data brokers, and how and on what terms such information is shared with court systems with whom they contract and other government entities. Generally, there is no public access to the ODR process in real time, no public ODR docket, and unlike codes of procedure and evidence in courts and the decisional law interpreting them, the lines of code in ODR systems are proprietary, insulated from public review, and treated as trade secrets by ODR companies.

11.2.2 *ODR as Interest-Based Dispute Resolution*

What can be inferred from this structure about ODR as a form of dispute resolution? What theory of justice does its architecture embody? The most important thing to notice is that the overwhelming emphasis in the structure of ODR systems is on "integrative negotiation" or interest-based, win-win bargaining, rather than the merits.[96] The "archetypical ODR approach is to provide an online forum and tools to facilitate the full settlement of claims without any human intervention."[97] However, users unfamiliar with law are not in a position to recognize that ODR is oriented toward integrative resolution rather than resolution based on their legal rights and defenses.[98]

94 *Id.* at 161–62.

95 Other formal automated adjudication systems may also be developed on the model of those currently used to predict outcomes in litigation for purposes of litigation funding decisions. On the use of AI in litigation funding, see *Using AI to Help Litigation Finance Pick the Winning Case*, Artificial Law. (May 29, 2019), https://www.artificiallawyer.com/2019/05/29/is-ai-the-future-of-litigation-finance-apex-courtquant-hope-so/.

96 Smith, *Rechtwijzer*.

97 Prescott, *Improving Access to Justice*, at 2016 n.117.

98 Some ODR systems deliberately blur the line, as in the title of British Columbia's Civil Resolution Tribunal, which blends interest-based bargaining in early phases with ex post tribunal adjudication should bargaining fall through. *The CRT Process*, Civ. Resol. Tribunal, https://civilresolutionbc.ca/tribunal-process/#5-get-a-crt-decision. See also Section 11.1 (discussing the confusing signals sent to users about whether the traffic camera enforcement ODR process is to enter a plea, adjudicate the merits, or both).

Although even the earliest theories of interest-based negotiation insisted that interests must be "legitimate" to warrant consideration, and that "community concerns" are relevant to bilateral negotiation,[99] some ODR systems eliminate these factors entirely. Blind bidding and other mathematical representations of interests have this effect – resolution arises from overlapping settlement values defined by the parties irrespective of any independent assessment of how the merits relate to the parties' quantification of their interests. In other ODR systems, such as CRT and Rechtwijzer, attention to the legal merits and third-party effects is backloaded into the review phase (phase IV) when a third-party neutral steps in. But at that stage, rejection of a settlement entails losing the efficiency gains accumulated through the ODR negotiation process. Delayed intervention of the third-party neutral thus virtually guarantees the subordination of concerns about the merits and negative externalities imposed on third parties and the community. The prize of agreement, once reached, is exceedingly difficult to refuse. As importantly, fact development to that point may not illuminate defects even for a third-party neutral deeply comitted exercising independent judgment and disposed to resist the allure of the prize.[100]

Even systems that bring a third-party neutral in earlier may not improve attention to the legal merits. As the orientation of many third-party neutrals is toward efficiency, "harmony and overcoming conflict," not the legal merits,[101] their disposition, training, and docket pressure may lead the them to "'trade justice for harmony.'"[102] This has long been a criticism of the alternative dispute resolution movement, sharpened by evidence that by privileging "harmony" in pluralistic societies (where there are competing conceptions of the good and systematic marginalization of minority groups), interest-based resolution can "suppress ... or silence ... the voices of those without political power."[103] In cases involving public debts to courts, revenue generated from these cases may diminish impartiality, attention to the merits, and community concerns. Some ODR systems are marketed

99 Roger Fisher, William Ury & Bruce Patton, Getting to Yes (3rd ed. 2011) (In addition to being efficient, "[a] wise agreement can be defined as one which meets the legitimate interests of each side to the extent possible, resolves conflicting interests fairly, is durable, and takes community concerns into account.").

100 The contrast between the relatively superficial role of third-party neutrals in these ODR systems and, for instance, the deep engagement contemplated in theories of live mediation such as Gary Friedman's is stark. *See* Gary Friedman, Challenging Conflict: Mediation Through Understanding (2008) (emphasizing interactions designed to increase mutual understanding as a foundation to finding acceptable resolutions: "We support each party in gaining as full an understanding as possible of what is important to him or her in the dispute, as well as what is important to the other party.").

101 "Orientation" may understate the point. In the alternative dispute resolution community, belief that interest-based negotiation can produce harmony and skepticism about rights talk are close to gospel.

102 Katherine R. Kruse, *Learning from Practice: What ADR Needs from a Theory of Justice*, 5 Nev. L.J. 389, 392–93 (2005).

103 *Id.* at 393.

to courts on precisely these terms, touting increased collection rates, decreased defaults, and reduced time to collection. For example, Matterhorn's contract with the court in Washtenaw County, Michigan, for traffic violations helped the company expand ODR to dozens of other counties on the back of reports that it produced a more than 40 percent increase in fines paid within thirty days.[104]

Although facts can generally be elicited efficiently online relative to live hearings and paper filings, important information can be lost in shifting from a hearing/forms combination to text-only,[105] writing skill is a built-in advantage for high-literacy litigants,[106] and without tailored advice about how the law applies to the facts of their case, litigants may omit relevant evidence. Everything hinges on how questions posed to elicit the facts are framed by the ODR platform. On the other hand, the more detailed the questions and guidance, the more expensive the code. Even the most advanced current AI systems thrive in bound environments, not open-ended, indeterminate ones.[107] The temptation, therefore, is ever to manufacture a bounded environment in coding for dispute resolution – reducing complexity in order to code efficiently.

Modria's brochure for courts considering adoption of its ODR software, proudly declares that it "helps courts resolve all manner of case types faster *without sacrificing accuracy*," but if we take the architecture of ODR systems seriously, the truth is that it is quite difficult to assess the accuracy of ODR systems.[108] Indeed, the earlier cases settle and the more interest-based bargaining drives resolution, the less certain we can be that any given settlement is a just reflection of the relevant rights and defenses of the parties.[109]

[104] Hannaford-Agor et al., NCSC Landscape Study, at 4.

[105] ODR systems can incorporate videoconferencing at costs lower than live hearings, but there is lively debate about the difference between live and video hearings and trials. *See, e.g.*, Alicia Bannon & Janna Adelstein, *The Impact of Video Proceedings on Fairness and Access to Justice in Court*, Brennan Ctr. for J. (Sept. 10, 2020), https://www.brennancenter.org/our-work/research-reports/impact-video-proceedings-fairness-and-access-justice-court.

[106] *See* Condlin, *Online Dispute Resolution*, at 743 n.103.

[107] See Kevin Roose, FuturеProof: 9 Rules for Humans in the Age of Automation (2021).

[108] Modria, Online Dispute Resolution, at 5 (emphasis added); *see also* Prescott, *Improving Access to Justice in State Courts*, at 2001 (conceding that Matterhorn data does not provide foundation "to observe outcomes" regarding "whether the resolution of the dispute is accurate or satisfactory" but insisting nonetheless that "the outcomes I can analyze are valuable proxies for pivotal dimensions of access to justice (not to mention court efficiency)"); Condlin, *Online Dispute Resolution*, at 745 (noting that the assumption that "Big Data" and predictive analytics will produce "just results ... isn't grounded in any well-known political or jurisprudential theory of procedural fairness or substantive justice"); Legal Educ. Found., Developing the Detail: Evaluating the Impact of Court Reform in England and Wales on Access to Justice 5, 14 (emphasizing that a core component of access to justice is "access to a decision in accordance with substantive law"; "constitutional legitimacy of Courts is inextricably linked to their ability to demonstrate correct application of the substantive law to the facts of individual cases").

[109] References to user satisfaction, which abound in ODR promotional materials – *see, e.g.*, Matterhorn, https://getmatterhorn.com/; Modria, Online Dispute Resolution: Civ.

11.2.3 *ODR Funding*

Funding remains one of the greatest barriers to the development of ODR and, ironically, one of the weakest pillars in its claim to expand access to justice. Many systems have failed because they have not produced a durable financial model despite receiving public subsidies and favorable user reviews.[110] The systems are costly to develop, and both the law and technology change in ways that make it costly to keep the systems up-to-date. One prominent provider, CRT, therefore relies heavily on a fee-for-service model. The parties using CRT pay not only initial filing fees, but fees for every subsequent phase of the process, making the process more expensive as it unfolds if no negotiated solution is reached.[111] CRT also charges a substantial fee ($200) to file a notice of objection in a small claims dispute.[112] This means that for a small claims dispute involving $1,000, challenging a settlement would cost 20 percent of the value of the dispute (on top of $75 to file the complaint, $75 to add a claim against a third party, $10 per records request, and $50 to switch from negotiation to an adjudicator).[113] Fee structures like this induce people who have financial constraints to resolve disputes quickly and accept a resolution that may be unjust. People of means, on the other hand, can afford to take advantage of every avenue of relief.[114]

Other ODR systems are free to users[115] and presumably paid for by courts. Contract terms between courts and private vendors of ODR software are not generally available to the public.[116] This makes any comparison with the costs of alternatives to ODR such as civil *Gideon*[117] difficult to assess. It also contrasts sharply

RESOL. TRIBUNAL, https://civilresolutionbc.ca/ – are no substitute when there is no indication the user knows what outcomes might have been reached with better information about their rights and defenses.

[110] KATSH & RABINOVICH-EINY, DIGITAL JUSTICE, at 35–36; Smith, *Rechtwijzer*; Roger Smith, *Goodbye, Rechtwijzer: Hello, Justice*, 42 LAW, TECH. & ACCESS TO J. (Mar. 31, 2017), https://law-tech-a2j.org/advice/goodbye-rechtwijzer-hello-justice42/.

[111] *Fees*, CIV. RESOL. TRIBUNAL, https://civilresolutionbc.ca/resources/crt-fees/#motor-vehicle-injury-disputes.

[112] *Id.*

[113] *Id.* There is a fee waiver process for low-income users. *Fee Waiver Request Form*, CIV. REVOL. TRIBUNAL (Mar. 22, 2019), https://civilresolutionbc.ca/wp-content/uploads/2019/03/FORM-Fee-Waiver-Request-April-2019.pdf.

[114] Modria's ODR system for courts appears by contrast to rely on a $25 user fee, though there may be other fees paid by courts to the software company. *Online Dispute Resolution*, YOLO CNTY. SUPERIOR CT. OF CAL., https://www.yolo.courts.ca.gov/divisions/small-claims/modria-faqs; *cf.* FAM. RESOL. CTR., SUPERIOR CT. OF CAL. CNTY. OF L.A., https://losangelescafam.modria.com/.

[115] JOINT TECH. COMM., NCSC, CASE STUDIES IN ODR FOR COURTS: A VIEW FROM THE FRONT LINES 4 (2017), https://www.srln.org/system/files/attachments/Case%20Studies%20in%20ODR%20for%20Courts.pdf (Franklin County, Ohio mediation study).

[116] *See, e.g.*, *Pricing*, MATTERHORN, https://getmatterhorn.com/pricing/.

[117] "Civil *Gideon*" refers to the idea of providing lawyers as a matter of right and at public expense to low-income persons in civil legal proceedings where core human needs are at stake. It is the

with the public budget process of funding courts as well as rules of judicial ethics that strictly regulate financial conflicts of interest in the judiciary.

11.2.4 *ODR Party Structure*

Although the ODR literature focuses on small value civil law disputes between roughly equally situated, unrepresented private parties, ODR is currently being used for disputes that involve parties of radically unequal status. These include criminal disputes between the government and individuals, where ordinary people are negotiating with prosecutors and judges regarding fines and fees the nonpayment of which could lead to incarceration, disputes between landlords and tenants, property associations and owners, creditors and debtors, contractors, subcontractors and home owners, nonunion employees and employers, insurers and parties harmed in an accident,[118] and couples who brought vastly different resources into the marriage and are unequally situated.[119] Some ODR systems permit parties to be represented if they can afford to do so, introducing potentially vast disparities in the level of expertise that one side brings to negotiations. Experience with other ADR systems such as arbitration is sobering on this front, indicating that powerful repeat-players not only fare better but are able over time to shape ADR procedures to maximize their interests.[120] Nor do the opt-in pages of ODR systems adequately disclose information to support knowing and informed waivers of due process rights and other rights a party would have in court.

In sum, democratically enacted and public rules of procedure and evidence are displaced by the proprietary technology of ODR systems.[121] Lawyers who work in principal-agent relationships for clients, and who have expertise in the rules of procedure and evidence, are replaced by software engineers whose highest loyalty

civil equivalent to Gideon v. Wainwright, 372 U.S. 335 (1963), in which the U.S. Supreme Court held that the Sixth and Fourteenth Amendments established a right to counsel for criminal defendants who cannot afford a lawyer. There is some evidence that expanding access to counsel in civil matters can save states money. *See* Permanent Commission on Access to Justice, *Report to the Chief Judge of the State of New York* (Nov. 2018) (reporting a return of $10 to the state for every $1 spent on access to free legal services from federal award benefits secured, civil awards, and indirect benefits such as shelter avoidance, foreclosure property value decline avoidance, domestic violence avoidance, increased wages due to work authorization, etc.).

118 *Cf.* Meera Jain, *Civil Resolution Tribunal Jurisdiction Declared Unconstitutional*, Clark Wilson (Mar. 22, 2021), https://www.cwilson.com/civil-resolution-tribunal-jurisdiction-declared-unconstitutional/ (discussing expansion and judicial contraction of jurisdiction of the CRT over certain subject matters).

119 *See generally Explore and Apply*, Civ. Resol. Tribunal, https://civilresolutionbc.ca/how-the-crt-works/getting-started/; Laura Kistemaker, *Rechtwijzer and Uitelkaar.nl. Dutch Experiences with ODR for Divorce*, 59 Fam. Ct. Rev. 232 (2021).

120 *See generally* Myriam Gilles, *The Day Doctrine Died: Private Arbitration and the End of Law*, 2016 U. Ill. L. Rev. 371 (2016).

121 *See* Condlin, *Online Dispute Resolution*, at 745–49.

is to investors and, secondarily, to the courts who retain them to help reduce costs. There is no malpractice cause of action for users against ODR providers, and no enforceable ethical code requiring fiduciary duty, competence, diligence, loyalty, communication, or confidentiality. Users of ODR platforms, who are constitutional right holders in the adversary system, become mere tertiary beneficiaries of contracts entered between courts and ODR providers. And as with other forms of alternative dispute resolution, ODR replaces the public appearance and reason-giving function of the judge either entirely (in systems that displace these decision makers with AI) or partially by changing the scene of adjudication from a public courtroom to a private online forum where third-party neutrals facilitate or impose resolution behind encrypted walls of code. We know that the reasons for conducting adjudication publicly in adversarial space are not exclusively performative.[122] Doing so helps prevent corruption, bias, and arbitrary decision. Justice, the saying goes, must not only be done, but must be "seen to be done."[123]

No one should therefore be surprised to see ODR systems that serve principally to induce settlement and improve compliance with judgments on behalf of the state, powerful creditors, and other well-resourced, represented parties, while failing either to establish the rights and defenses of unrepresented parties or make transparent potentially systemic abuses of the laws being enforced.

11.3 ODR AND PREVENTIVE JUSTICE

This chapter has so far focused on pragmatic concerns about current ODR systems. In closing I want to raise a more fundamental challenge: ODR systems rest on a theory of justice at odds with liberal democratic principles of the rule of law. For decades the dream of alternative dispute resolution advocates has been to design systems that not only resolve disputes when they arise, but to use information about such disputes to detect patterns of conflict and prevent them from occurring in the first place.[124] The ultimate goal is preventive justice, a culture of seamless compliance. ODR offers the means to realize this goal because it relies on the technology of algorithmic governance – coding that relies on big data to predict and steer human decision-making.[125] Whatever the appeal of preventive justice *within* a corporation for its ability to induce compliance with internal corporate norms and external regulations, or in other domains such as public health, as a general theory for the administration of justice it is destructive of human freedom.

[122] *See generally* Norman W. Spaulding, *The Enclosure of Justice: Courthouse Architecture, Due Process, and the Dead Metaphor of Trial*, 24 Yale J. L. & Hum. 311 (2012).

[123] Stuart Hampshire, Justice Is Conflict 9 (1999).

[124] On the history of "dispute systems design" and its commitment to preventive justice, see Katsh & Rabinovich-Einy, Digital Justice, at 44.

[125] On the broader implications of this technology, see Spaulding, *Is Human Judgment Necessary?*

Outside authoritarian regimes, the default rule for the administration of justice is that the law intervenes in the lives of ordinary people (1) after wrongdoing, not before, and (2) in response to specific instances of wrongdoing, not the broader collective conditions giving rise to them. Strict standards of substantive liability generally apply to inchoate offenses. Ex ante intervention and regulation are possible, as is structural relief addressed to conditions that repeatedly cause serious harm, but they are both exceptional – higher standards have to be met to authorize these remedies – and they are generally reserved for misconduct on the part of the state and regulated entities, not ordinary people.

These default rules can be found in the law of procedural due process, remedies, the prohibition on prior restraints against free speech, and so forth. Their purpose is to protect the sphere of social action from domination by the state and others who have the means to maximize enforcement of their interests and bend the law to their will. The adversary system embodies these default rules. It grounds the administration of justice not in a substantive concept of justice but in decentralized, participatory, public, ex post adjudication.[126]

ODR systems are oriented toward a very different theory of justice. Their proponents are quite frank about this, drawing on the work of earlier analog dispute systems designers. Ury, Brett, and Goldberg famously argued from the study of wildcat strikes that employee-employer conflict and ex post resolution costs could be avoided by studying patterns in those labor disputes and altering institutional structures to reduce conflict. For dispute system designers, conflicts are unfortunate and avoidable events; rights assertion and adjudication are disfavored, costly projects that amplify adversity. With the correct information, well-calibrated interest-balancing, and appropriate ex ante interventions, both social conflict and conflict in court can be avoided.[127] The true promise of the ODR is thus not merely to streamline dispute resolution, it is to develop products that realize the potential of dispute systems' design to *prevent conflicts from arising in the first place* – to instantiate a culture of compliance. As one commentator puts it, just as the value of Uber is the relevance of its data to a

[126] *See* Spaulding, *Due Process without Judicial Process?* Even in administrative regulation, which contemplates ex ante disclosure and reporting, as well as regulatory compliance monitoring, these default rules structure the APA's rule-making process, which is a predicate to valid regulation, and preventive enforcement proceedings. *See* 5 U.S.C. §§ 551–59.

[127] Leah Wing & Daniel Rainey, *Online Dispute Resolution and the Development of Theory*, *in* Online Dispute Resolution: Theory and Practice 35, 44–46 (Mohamed S. Abdel Wahab, Ethan Katsh & Daniel Rainey eds., 2012). This theory of preventive justice thus extends well beyond the traditional concept of the "preventive state" and its emphasis on national security, crime, disorderly conduct, and civil commitment. *See* Andrew Ashworth & Lucia Zedner, Preventive Justice 8 (2014) (associating preventive justice with "the state's primary task and indeed its very raison d'etre . . . to secure for its citizens the conditions of order and security that are prerequisites of freedom").

future market of automated cars, "the seeds of an effort to prevent disputes may lie in the technology employed to resolve disputes."[128] How? "[T]he use of technology provides ODR with more opportunities to identify systemic contribution to conflict and systemic opportunities to reduce conflict."[129] These opportunities arise from the capacity of ODR systems to exploit the information they gather about pending disputes to provide "automatic detection of problems, obviating the need to passively wait for complaints to arrive and allowing proactive remedying of the problem even before a potential complainant has been made aware of its existence."[130]

If this sounds futuristic, it is not. Private ODR systems are already valued by corporations for their capacity to prevent customer, user, and employee disputes.[131] It is now "commonplace" for private ODR systems to "captur[e] data and analyz[e] it for insight into the disputing environment of a particular institution to help prevent future disputes."[132] The objective is to identify patterns and sources of conflict, anticipate new ones, and snuff them out in advance. It's one thing of course when the lens is directed inward, to identify policies and practices of a corporation that are producing conflict or misconduct.[133] But it is quite another to direct the lens outward, combining the information saturation of digital interaction and predictive analytics to continuously monitor and manipulate the preferences, choices, and norms of users.

Private ODR already involves both – internal and external preventive surveillance, intervention, and restructuring of code to optimize compliance.[134] For companies like Airbnb, the

> effortless recording of large amounts of data relating to anyone operating on the site creates a huge database that can be cross-checked with information on problems and resolutions, generating unique insights on how to structure more satisfactory transactions, what problematic patterns need to be dealt with, what rules and practices require clarification or amendment, and which participants require mentoring or instruction.[135]

[128] Rabinovich-Einy & Katsh, *Lessons from Online Dispute Resolution for Dispute Systems Design*, at 45, 69 ("Where patterns can be identified, the dispute resolution system can move beyond the resolution of individual disputes and enhance prevention on a system-wide basis.").

[129] *Id.*

[130] *Id.* at 56.

[131] *Id.* (citing Wikipedia dispute resolution example); *id.* at 42 (citing eBay and its use of its ODR system); *id.* at 142, 245.

[132] Katsh & Rabinovich-Einy, Digital Justice, at 36.

[133] On the broader role of internal assessment and behavioral change, see Charles F. Sabel & William H. Simon, *Minimalism and Experimentalism in the Administrative State*, 100 Geo. L.J. 53 (2010).

[134] *Id.*

[135] Katsh & Rabinovich-Einy, Digital Justice, at 72.

In order to promote transactions that "are less likely to generate problems," the company may alter things like "which listing to display first" to a particular user.[136] There are plenty of nondigital examples of decisions like this inviting or reflecting bias – for example, one renter gets access to "A list" properties from an agency or landlord based on race, ethnicity, or assumptions about credit or past experience with the renter; another does not. The difference in an online platform is that the user may have no idea she is not seeing all the available properties in a location – code presents a smooth surface relative to live interaction that can obscure not only the fact that the user's information is siloed, but also the basis for the decision to do so, and thus, crucially, the opportunity to challenge it in court or any other forum.

Conflict prevention grounded in unjustified restriction of users rights *which cannot be detected and challenged by the user* thus creates a double silo – limiting choices as well as information about the limitation that might subject it to legal scrutiny. Conflict may be reduced, but in the manner of a falconry hood. In some settings the stakes may be relatively trivial, but errors in other settings can have significant life consequences.

Preventive justice is actively used in other areas of private ODR such as automated content moderation of speech on social media platforms, employment, and preventive medicine. Automated prescreening systems have become a significant form of content moderation.[137] They have the capacity to significantly reduce online disputes, but they can easily err by failing to incorporate important "contextual information" such as language and cultural differences that affect semantic meaning.[138] There is evidence that these preventive systems have overenforced copyright law to the detriment of fair use, and they "raise concerns about the limits of public speech, cultural sensitivities, and individual rights."[139] In the domain of medical prevention, genetic data can save lives, but it has also been incorrectly used to exclude children from school to prevent the spread of disease.[140] In the workplace, dispute prevention efforts can improve safety and performance, but they can also amplify the power of employers, undercut the rights of workers, and inhibit worker mobilization and unionization.[141]

In *public* ODR systems, the lines between dispute resolution and prevention are already "increasingly being blurred."[142] The data gathering and processing technology underlying ODR provides means previously unavailable to extend preventive intervention beyond the boundaries of individual organizations to the

[136] *Id.*
[137] *Id.* at 128.
[138] *Id.* at 127.
[139] *Id.* at 128.
[140] *Id.* at 106–107.
[141] *Id.* at 131.
[142] Rabinovich-Einy & Katsh, *Lessons from Online Dispute Resolution for Dispute Systems Design*, at 66.

administration of justice.[143] Commentators emphasize that data produced by ODR systems "will enable . . . the identification of large-scale trends and patterns we have never seen before, often through automated means instead of human analysis . . .. Those in control of these large data sets will be able to analyze the data and . . . prevent the occurrence of a dispute."[144] Indeed, "[b]y overcoming the need to rely on the aggrieved party's ability to recognize and pursue a remedy, *a larger portion of society's problems can be addressed and prevented regardless of the aggrieved party's awareness of his or her injury*."[145] For example, the data gathered by ODR systems and data being aggregated to inform predictive policing may prove lucrative for tech companies to combine and market, and tempting for prosecutors and law enforcement to exploit.[146] Or someone who loses the confidentiality protections of CRT's online mediation process because she uses what the system unilaterally defines as "abusive" language may find herself classified by any number of databases relying on predictive analytics as mentally unfit, a safety threat, a credit risk, unsuitable for hiring or admission into a training or credential program, and so forth. These cross-referencing effects are possible in analog record-keeping, but with big data and the power of the algorithms driving predictive analytics they can disseminate pervasively, instantaneously, and without public transparency.

The "politics of the preventive has a strong element of irresistibility built into it, since it generally appears perverse to argue against a preventive measure. Who could be against the prevention of harm? . . . [C]ritics . . . can be portrayed as courting insecurity and jeopardizing public safety" and harmony.[147]

[143] On Matterhorn's warrant data program, see *Warrant Prevention*, MATTERHORN, https://getmatterhorn.com/odr-solutions/warrants-pleas/warrant-prevention/. In a YouTube promotional, Michigan court staff emphasize that the Warrant Prevention program gives users a way to "follow through with their obligations that were already set." Court Innovations, *Warrant Prevention at the 61st District Court with Matterhorn*, Facebook (May 1, 2018), https://www.facebook.com/courtinnovate/videos/warrant-prevention-at-the-61st-district-court-with-matterhorn/1710129025743952/; *ODR Metrics*, MATTERHORN, https://getmatterhorn.com/odr-metrics-measure-access-by-geography-and-device/ (Apr. 8, 2022). The company also markets a tool for making ability-to-pay determinations under Bearden v. Georgia online, but these inquiries do not go to the merits of the legal financial obligation, only to the question whether the defendant has the current means to pay.

[144] KATSH & RABINOVICH-EINY, DIGITAL JUSTICE, at 166–67; RICHARD SUSSKIND, THE FUTURE OF LAW 3 (1996) ("The focus of these services will be dispute pre-emption . . . rather than dispute resolution in the courts; and on legal risk management instead of legal problem solving."); *id.* at 26 (analogizing to "preventive medicine").

[145] KATSH & RABINOVICH-EINY, DIGITAL JUSTICE, at 52.

[146] Tim Lau, *Predictive Policing Explained*, BRENNAN CTR. FOR JUSTICE (Apr. 1, 2020), https://www.brennancenter.org/our-work/research-reports/predictive-policing-explained. Law enforcement agencies already use information such as welfare records, renter and homeowner data, census records, and so-called dirty data (data unlawfully acquired). *See* Rashida Richardson, Jason M. Schultz & Kate Crawford, *Dirty Data, Bad Predictions: How Civil Rights Violations Impact Police Data, Predictive Policing Systems, and Justice*, 94 N.Y.U. L. REV. 192 (2019).

[147] ASHWORTH & ZEDNER, PREVENTIVE JUSTICE, at 13.

The problem is that the same class of elite software engineers who delight in disruptive innovation and flagrantly disregard regulation is developing ODR systems that would embed *compliance* in the architecture for the administration of justice for ordinary people. Doing so in the name of access to justice is not just ironic or hypocritical, it masks a potentially transformative struggle over the nature of the rule of law. Preventive compliance by code might be welcome if dispute system designers were right that legal conflict is usually a sign of social malaise, and if software engineers were uniquely adept at distinguishing legitimate from illegitimate conflict and resistance to law.

But neither proposition is true.

Not all resistance to law and noncompliance is a sign of delinquency or a threat to the body politic; in fact, noncompliance can be one of the very *highest* forms of civic engagement. Our most important progress in racial justice is the product of nonviolent civil disobedience. Indeed, on some accounts of liberal democratic theory under conditions of value pluralism, "justice *is* conflict."[148] Law without resistance is not law – it is domination, simpliciter, a panoptic prison of code. And software engineers have no particular expertise (or incentive) to correctly draw lines between socially desirable and undesirable rights assertion or defiance. *No one does*. That is precisely why the adversary system vests decisional authority in decentralized, democratically accountable jurors, judges, and regulators subject to appellate review, and, for the latter two, establishes legally enforceable standards of impartiality and professional conduct.[149]

ODR systems alter this structure – placing a single, professionally, and democratically unaccountable group of elites in control of the procedures for dispute resolution. Using these proprietary systems to *prevent*, not merely *resolve*, disputes would subvert the structure altogether. What has traditionally been understood as an exceptional form of the administration of justice would become the rule, at least for those priced out of the adversary system.

I hold no crystal ball, but we don't have to guess about the ominous authoritarian implications of big data in the hands of tech companies and the state.[150] ODR firms are currently modest in market capitalization. This gives courts and bar regulators some leverage in negotiating terms. Reliance on AI is nascent, reducing some of the problems for court administrators and the public of opacity in assessing how these systems run. But we know from other sectors of innovation that it doesn't take long for market concentration to emerge, and AI is evolving rapidly in ways that may amplify opacity. We also know that when tech companies consolidate a market, they

[148] Hampshire, Justice Is Conflict.

[149] On latent conflicts of interest in ODR systems, see Scott J. Shackelford & Anjanette Raymond, *Building the Virtual Courthouse: Ethical Considerations for Design, Implementation, and Regulation in the World of ODR*, 2014 Wis. L. Rev. 615.

[150] *See* Spaulding, *Is Human Judgment Necessary?*

not only exclude competitors in anticompetitive ways;[151] they use their position to exclude inexpensive public alternatives. This is precisely what TurboTax has done.

But these are not inevitable outcomes. ODR systems can be improved in a variety of ways if judges, court administrators, and state bar regulators recognize that we have arrived at the legal equivalent of the combustion engine–electric car design decision. On one path, unwarranted faith in innovation will lead to deregulation or lax regulation. Rent-seeking in the administration of justice will masquerade as innovation. By the time the costs of this path become clear, ODR providers may be too powerful to control. Alternatively, ODR could support and preserve human judgment on the part of all participants by exploiting the technology's efficient information gathering capacity while providing greater transparency. To achieve this ODR systems have to:

- be opt-in;
- include strict disclosure and consent requirements to validate opt-in decisions;
- protects the privacy of user data and require publication of ODR rules and system design;
- develop more precise heuristics for separating cases appropriately eligible for ODR from those that are not;
- elevate procedural values in ODR system design other than compliance and efficiency, especially merits assessment;
- strictly distinguish interest-based negotiation platforms from adjudication platforms;
- require that mediators, judges, and prosecutors document their reasons on record for resolutions they reach in ODR systems;
- gather and report performance data to promote assessment of biases and other distortions in relation to established standards of impartiality;
- reduce the costs of appeal;
- publicly disclose court/ODR firm contracts.

A third path would permit ODR systems to resolve disputes without human mediators or adjudicators subject to heightened scrutiny under the above regulatory standards. A fourth would refocus courts' access-to-justice initiatives on some combinations of paths two or three and increasing direct funding for access to counsel. Whatever the path, ODR's costs and benefits must be placed in relation to a tangible innovation baseline. All too often ODR's proponents compare it to "no justice" – the position of a party who cannot afford to appear in court or cannot afford a lawyer. But just as new medical interventions and drugs are assessed in relation to an

[151] Daisuke Wkabayashi, *The Antitrust Case against Big Tech, Propelled by Tech Industry Exiles*, N.Y. Times (Dec. 20, 2020), www.nytimes.com/2020/12/20/technology/antitrust-case-google-facebook.html.

evidence-based standard of safety and efficacy, not the condition of the untreated, ODR should be judged by comparison to standards of procedural fairness and the costs of alternatives such as expanding access to counsel.

In sum, innovation worthy of the name should *improve* the administration of justice for ordinary people, not just impose different and potentially more tragic trade-offs than the adversary system and traditional forms of alternative dispute resolution. ODR proponents contend that without the freedom to experiment, the best designs may never be developed. But just as any automobile must have more than an efficient engine, ODR must do more than end disputes for ordinary people quickly and cheaply.

The promise of ODR has prompted courts and bar associations to rush to deregulate under the banner of exemptions that promote experimentation.[152] Solemn language about the importance of consumer and public protection and risk assessment can be found in these materials, but all too often without reducing these lofty principles to concrete design parameters. ODR is no longer on the salt flats. It seeks to transform the rule of law. The brave new world will not be a form of code as law in the conventional sense – the way code architecture structures online behavior. It will be a (re)codification *of* law, of the administration of justice itself. We leave design parameters to unregulated engineers at our peril.

152 *See* State Bar of Cal. Task Force on Access through Innovation of Legal Servs., Final Report and Recommendations (2020), www.calbar.ca.gov/Portals/0/documents/publicComment/ATILS-Final-Report.pdf; Utah Work Grp. On Regul. Reform, Narrowing the Access-to-Justice Gap by Reimagining Regulation (2019), www.utahbar.org/wp-content/uploads/2019/08/FINAL-Task-Force-Report.pdf.

12

Using ODR Platforms to Level the Playing Field

Improving Pro Se Litigation through ODR Design

J.J. Prescott

A sea change is under way in how we talk and think about court technology.[1] For decades, court officials – judges and staff – have relied on computers for word processing and internal scheduling, case management systems to store and organize digital records, the internet for research, and email to communicate. Like many organizations, courts have long conceived of technology exclusively as a way to improve their operational efficiency, reducing the time and effort it takes for them to do what they have always done:[2] provide neutral, real-time, face-to-face proceedings to resolve disputes, with a judge or a magistrate overseeing safe and purportedly transparent hearings in a physical, courthouse setting.[3]

This perspective is changing. The advent of online dispute resolution (ODR) platforms has reminded courts that providing in-person, real-time proceedings in a physical courtroom is just a means to an end; courts exist first and foremost to resolve disputes, at least in state courts handling everyday matters.[4] Presumably, there is no

I am grateful to David Freeman Engstrom and Orna Rabinovich-Einy for comments on this chapter and to Daniel Byrne, William Ellis, German Marquez Alcala, and Abigail Ulcej for excellent research assistance. Disclosure: Prescott founded Court Innovations Inc., which developed Matterhorn, an ODR platform that operates in many states. Prescott no longer has an equity interest in Court Innovations or its parent company, but he may benefit from a licensing arrangement the companies have with the University of Michigan.

1 *See generally* Richard Susskind, Online Courts and the Future of Justice 33–45 (2019); Orna Rabinovich-Einy & Ethan Katsh, *The New New Courts*, 67 Am. U. L. Rev. 165 (2017).

2 *See* Ethan Katsh & Orna Rabinovich-Einy, Digital Justice: Technology and the Internet of Disputes 155–56 (2017).

3 Avital Mentovich, J.J. Prescott & Orna Rabinovich-Einy, *Are Litigation Outcome Disparities Inevitable? Courts, Technology, and the Future of Impartiality*, 71 Ala. L. Rev. 893, 925 (2020).

4 *See* Warren E. Burger, *Annual Report on the State of the Judiciary*, 62 A.B.A. J. 443, 445 (1976). In resolving disputes, courts also announce, reaffirm, and refine the law. Some consider this aspect of dispute resolution to be central to the function and purpose of courts. *See, e.g.*, Erwin Chemerinsky, Closing the Courthouse Door: How Your Constitutional Rights Became Unenforceable 1–19 (2017).

single best way to resolve disputes,[5] and courts are beginning to recognize that ODR – with its potential to improve accessibility while maintaining the integrity and values of traditional judicial process – can improve on conventional face-to-face courtroom proceedings for a significant fraction of cases.[6] But precisely how far such technology can take courts remains an open question – one with huge implications for the future of formal adjudication in our society.

In this chapter, I argue that court-based ODR platforms can do far more to improve dispute resolution than simply puncture the barriers inherent to accessing physical courthouses, as important as this achievement is in its own right. In particular, I show that ODR systems also have the capacity to reduce the pro se representation gap in adjudication by incorporating tools that mimic many of the essential functions of legal counsel. In the years ahead, courts should grasp the opportunity to design and deploy technology with this goal in mind to advance their core function of successfully resolving disputes, even when the prospect of doing so may push them out of their comfort zone and blur or even redraw traditional boundaries regarding court neutrality and concerns over "helping" litigants.

The first step in this argument is recognizing that effective dispute resolution depends on robust access to justice. While the defining virtue of ODR technology to date is its capacity to improve the accessibility of courts for litigants, the phrase "access to justice" hinges on what it means to achieve justice,[7] and any useful access-to-justice criterion must ask whether laws and institutions resolve disputes appropriately – that is, accurately and fairly.

One important class of access-to-justice issues relates to the sheer difficulty of using courts to resolve disputes.[8] If individuals cannot make meritorious claims or defend themselves against improper allegations because doing so is too costly or difficult, the system implicitly "resolves" disputes inappropriately – for instance, through default, coerced settlement, uninformed verdicts, or other outcomes that are more a function of litigation and court-imposed costs than underlying substance.[9] For this reason, some

5 *See* Lisa Blomgren Amsler et al., Dispute System Design: Preventing, Managing, and Resolving Conflict 111–31 (2020); Orna Rabinovich-Einy & Ethan Katsh, *Technology and the Future of Dispute System Design*, 17 Harv. Negot. L. Rev. 151, 155–64 (2012).

6 Richard Susskind, *The Future of Courts*, The Practice, July–Aug. 2020, https://thepractice.law.harvard.edu/article/the-future-of-courts.

7 *What Is Access to Justice?* Nat'l Ctr. for Access to Just., https://ncaj.org/what-access-justice; *Human Rights and Access to Justice*, A.B.A., https://www.americanbar.org/advocacy/rule_of_law/what-we-do/human-rights-access-to-justice/.

8 Maximilian A. Bulinski & J.J. Prescott, *Online Case Resolution Systems: Enhancing Access, Fairness, Accuracy, and Efficiency*, 21 Mich. J. Race & L. 205, 217–31 (2016).

9 J.J. Prescott & Alexander Sanchez, *Platform Procedure: Using Technology to Facilitate (Efficient) Civil Settlement*, *in* Selection and Decision in Judicial Process around the World 30, 30–34 (Yun-chien Chang ed., 2020); *see also, e.g.*, Pew Charitable Trs., How Debt Collectors Are Transforming the Business of State Courts (2020), https://www.pewtrusts.org/en/research-and-analysis/reports/2020/05/how-debt-collectors-are-transforming-the-business-of-state-courts.

access-to-justice advocates have criticized the justice system's reliance on physical courthouses that are few and far between, open only during business hours, difficult to navigate, and intimidating to use.[10] Especially in relatively low-stakes legal cases (a large majority of cases, in fact), like traffic or small claims matters, these hurdles leave large swaths of people out in the cold, unable to seek protection under the law.

First-generation court-connected ODR (or ODR 1.0)[11] has already shown technology's potential to overcome this particular class of access-to-justice barriers. First-gen ODR has opened up courts by leaving courthouses behind. In many states, and across a variety of dispute types,[12] ODR platforms allow people to interface with their cases using mobile phones from their homes at any hour of the day. Software design and "smart" forms simplify processes.[13] Notifications and error checks keep litigants in the know, allowing them to engage more quickly.[14] All in all, ODR platforms make accessing courts much easier.[15] Moreover, while today's ODR platforms are available for minor legal disputes, they also show potential for certain aspects of more significant litigation matters. The recent success of online voir dire proceedings, and even trials, intimates that the need for in-person hearings to resolve disputes with accuracy and fairness may be limited.

But existing court ODR systems do not go far enough. Even if these platforms were capable of allowing everyone to resolve their disputes from a place and at a time of their choosing, a meaningful access-to-justice gap would remain. In a society with significant socioeconomic disparities, the mere power to invoke the law, even at near-zero cost, hardly levels the playing field. Wielding the law *effectively* requires experience and expertise.[16] While some litigants can accrue experience and build expertise through repeated play, other parties to a legal dispute – usually, the "haves" – typically acquire these assets by hiring a lawyer.[17] Lawyers provide many services to their clients, but perhaps first among them is assessing likely outcomes in any matter. Lawyers also explain the nuts and bolts of the law and the range of

[10] *See, e.g.*, Sara Sternberg Greene, *Race, Class, and Access to Civil Justice*, 101 Iowa L. Rev. 1263, 1267, 1288–89 (2016).

[11] David Freeman Engstrom, *Digital Civil Procedure*, 169 U. Pa. L. Rev. 2243, 2273–83 (2021).

[12] *See, e.g.*, A.B.A. Ctr. Innov., *Online Dispute Resolution in the United States: Data Visualizations* (2020), https://www.americanbar.org/content/dam/aba/administrative/center-for-innovation/odrvisualizationreport.pdf (documenting the spread of ODR tools in the United States).

[13] Maximilian A. Bulinski & J.J. Prescott, *Designing Legal Experiences: Online Communication and Resolution in Courts, in* Legal Informatics 430, 433–36 (Daniel Martin Katz et al. eds., 2021).

[14] J.J. Prescott, *Improving Access to Justice in State Courts with Platform Technology*, 70 Vand. L. Rev. 1993, 2030–34 (2017).

[15] Alex Sanchez & Paul Embley, *Access Empowers: How ODR Increased Participation and Positive Outcomes in Ohio, in* Trends in State Courts 14, 17 (Nat'l Ctr. St. Cts. ed. 2020).

[16] Emily S. Taylor Poppe & Jeffrey J. Rachlinski, *Do Lawyers Matter? The Effect of Legal Representation in Civil Disputes*, 43 Pepp. L. Rev. 881, 885 (2016).

[17] *See* Jerome E. Carlin & Jan Howard, *Legal Representation and Class Justice*, 12 UCLA L. Rev. 381, 382–85 (1965).

options available to their clients, including the option to do nothing. Lawyers physically represent their clients in courtrooms as well, muting or obscuring demographic and/or educational differences between litigants when appearing before court (at least if we assume lawyers are likely to be more alike in background and training than any particular set of litigants).

Therefore, simply easing access to a courtroom through technology can only do so much to move us toward ideal dispute resolution. Indeed, access-to-justice advocates devote the lion's share of their attention to ensuring adequate legal representation in courtrooms, lambasting any system rife with pro se litigants as likely to get it wrong far too often.[18] For this reason, as first-gen ODR platforms proliferate, disparities in outcomes that are attributable to disparities in representation are unlikely to shrink and will probably increase. After all, as those long shut out of courthouses newly turn to ODR to pursue their legal interests, the significance of the representation chasm will become even more stark. A lot more "have-nots" will be seeking justice without a fair shot.[19]

Looking forward, a key goal for second-generation ODR platforms must be using data science techniques, design opportunities, and the treasure trove of data ODR platforms and court systems collect every day to bridge the legal representation gap.[20] Court-connected ODR platforms, if designed appropriately, can offer – for free – many of the same "services" that lawyers currently deliver to those fortunate enough to have a lawyer. The idea is not for courts to provide all litigants with a robot lawyer.[21] Instead, the idea is to recognize that much of what lawyers do to help their clients involves providing them with information (e.g., options, predictions) about how their case "stacks up" and helping them to put their best foot forward (e.g., presentation, representation). If courts enhance ODR platforms so that they may offer some of these same functions in the right way, the future of dispute resolution will not only be low cost and easy to access but will also disadvantage pro se litigants much less than traditional court processes.

18 *See* Kathryn M. Kroeper et al., *Underestimating the Unrepresented: Cognitive Biases Disadvantage Pro Se Litigants in Family Law Cases*, 26 Psychol. Pub. Pol'y & L. 198, 210–11 (2020).

19 Katsh & Rabinovich-Einy, Digital Justice, at 156–58.

20 Courts have always collected case and litigant data, and making this information public in a way that is consistent with current court practices is a good starting point. Engstrom, *Digital Civil Procedure*, at 2273–83 (describing a future in which ODR designers leverage these tools and data).

21 The notion of a robot lawyer connotes technology making decisions for people. By contrast, appropriately designed ODR would function as "decision support." This is not to say that decision support cannot nudge people toward certain choices – all environmental features do this, including how courts, procedures, and law are currently architected. *See* Ayelet Sela, *e-Nudging Justice: The Role of Digital Choice Architecture in Online Courts*, 2019 J. Disp. Resol. 127, 137; Mentovich et al., *Are Litigation Outcome Disparities Inevitable?* at 924–27.

12.1 THE CURRENT STATE OF THE ART: FIRST-GENERATION, COURT-CONNECTED ODR

As a concept, ODR emerged from the commercial consumer sector, as companies like eBay sought a means of resolving disputes (usually involving small-dollar values) that arose online between physically separated individuals. Many state court cases resemble small-stakes commercial disputes, and while litigants are often geographically proximate to each other, going to court to resolve a small-stakes case (say, under $500) still makes little sense to many. Even proceeding pro se routinely requires missing work, finding transportation, navigating the courthouse, and facing an intimidating judge. Add to this the fact that court is always a gamble – the prospect of improving one's chances, from 0 percent (default) to even a modest 50 percent, is uncertain, but a litigant pays the cost of accessing the law at a courthouse with certainty – and it is unsurprising that many individuals in small-stakes disputes simply default, wrongly admit fault, or decline to file a meritorious case.

12.1.1 *Where the Story Begins: Courts, ODR, and Access to Justice*

Less than ten years ago, state courts began implementing ODR platforms for high-volume, small-stakes cases, like alleged traffic violations and other cases where physical resolution of the matter could be very costly to one of the litigants (e.g., outstanding failure-to-pay warrants), making remote resolution particularly attractive. One of the very first ODR platforms, if not the first, to be widely adopted in US courts was Matterhorn, which Michigan adopted starting in 2014.[22]

The earliest Matterhorn ODR implementations sought to resolve disputes between individuals and the government: traffic, civil infractions, warrants, and a couple of misdemeanors. These ODR platforms were in many ways designed to "mimic" traditional proceedings, with a few key differences: ODR was made available at any time of day, information was exchanged asynchronously by text, and litigants could access the platform with any online remote device. But in most respects, litigants could expect to experience a process similar to going to court on their own. These systems inform the litigant of the charge or issue, "ask" the litigant whether they would like the court to review their case, and then ask the litigant to answer questions, including an open-ended invitation to "let the court know" anything else they felt was potentially relevant. These implementations are easy to use and make the process much easier to follow than what a litigant walking into a

[22] *See* A.B.A. Ctr. Innov., *Online Dispute Resolution in the United States: Data Visualizations* (2020), https://www.americanbar.org/content/dam/aba/administrative/center-for-innovation/odr visualizationreport.pdf (indicating Matterhorn as the first ODR system adopted by a state court); Lyle Moran, *Online Dispute Resolution Promises to Increase Access to Justice but Challenges Remain*, A.B.A. J. (Oct. 1, 2021), https://www.abajournal.com/magazine/article/online-dispute-resolution-promises-to-increase-access-to-justice-but-challenges-remain.

courthouse should expect to face, but at their core, they are an online version of a pro se courthouse experience.[23] The individual locates their case, makes a request for relief, and answers questions from the court.[24]

Matterhorn ODR soon grew to address disputes between private individuals. Early examples include ongoing family court cases, where parties negotiate in the online presence of a case manager without the need for in-person hearings,[25] and small claims disputes, where parties use an online text-based negotiating (chat) space (and perhaps online mediators) to engage in informal discovery or settle their case outright. These ODR implementations sought to reduce default by making it easier for everyone to come together outside of court in an informal way before being compelled to come together in court. Parties usually negotiate a resolution, and by making online negotiation and mediation free, easy to use, and court-sanctioned, courts were soon playing an important role via ODR in a significant fraction of cases. What's more, some tentative evidence hints that early engagement with court-connected ODR promotes traditional courtroom engagement later, which might have social benefits,[26] even if a case ultimately ends in face-to-face litigation.

Regardless, first-gen ODR works by moving courtroom or court hallway activity to a more amenable online venue that can be streamlined/individualized for the type of case. A pro se litigant may find it easier to negotiate with a counterparty or contest a civil infraction through an ODR platform, but such litigants are just as "pro se" during an online interaction as they would have been during an in-person tête-à-tête.[27] Whether first-gen ODR moves into asynchronous text-based exchanges or real-time video-based hearings (or any number of other ways parties can communicate, make offers and demands, share/present information, and work through outcome-determinative decisions), existing ODR platforms can make dispute resolution easier, faster, cheaper, and therefore more accessible, but the value of legal advice is likely to matter just as much as it does in traditional settings. True, more "have-nots" will be

[23] *See Family Court – Child Support Compliance*, MATTERHORN, https://getmatterhorn.com/odr-solutions/family-online-dispute-resolution/family-court/; Press Release, 20th Circuit Court Ottawa County, Michigan, Friend of the Court 20th Circuit Court Ottawa County Now Offering Online Dispute Resolution for Parenting Time Issues (Aug. 28, 2020), http://www.miottawa.org/courts/foc/pdf/MatterhornPressRelease.pdf.

[24] It is true that ODR-based interaction between judges and parties might not be as rich as it could be. For example, opportunities for back-and-forth exchanges are usually limited, at the request of the court. However, in traditional processes, judges also limit back-and-forth exchanges, *but judges do so at their arbitrary discretion*, and, in any event, such a limitation is simply an adjustable design feature – it is not inherent to ODR as an idea.

[25] *See, e.g.*, Amy J. Schmitz & Leah Wing, *Beneficial and Ethical ODR for Family Issues*, 59 FAM. CT. REV. 250, 258–60 (2021).

[26] Susan A. Bandes & Neal Feigenson, *Virtual Trials: Necessity, Invention, and the Evolution of the Courtroom*, 68 BUFF. L. REV. 1275, 1275 (2020); ALLAN GREENBERG, ARCHITECTURE OF DEMOCRACY 82 (2006).

[27] *See* Amy J. Schmitz, *Expanding Access to Remedies through E-Court Initiatives*, 67 BUFF. L. REV. 89, 104–25 (2019); *see generally* Bulinski & Prescott, *Online Case Resolution Systems*.

able to use courts and access the law. But the "haves" (with their lawyers, experience, and mastery of the rules of the game) will remain just as privileged (if not more so, given digital divide concerns) relative to their "have-not" counterparts as before.

Empirical evidence on ODR outcomes is consistent with this story. This expanding literature speaks to the improvements enjoyed by pro se litigants (as opposed to represented parties): Cases proceed more quickly, default rates plummet, and communication between parties, court staff, and judges increases.[28] This accessibility leads to more accurate outcomes (primarily by reducing default), giving more muscle to substantive law and reducing the role litigation costs play in determining legal outcomes.[29] In the case of Matterhorn, at least, litigants also report that they find ODR proceedings fair, the online process easy to understand, and the software straightforward to use.[30] On the whole, ODR-based improvements in pro se litigant outcomes (both quantitative and qualitative) appear significant, although these advances are relative to a pro se baseline where the relevant control groups of litigants are also unrepresented.

12.1.2 *From Courtrooms to ODR: Responding to Critics*

Moving from courtrooms to ODR is no panacea, of course. Critics raise a number of concerns, including the importance of the courtroom and human interaction in how litigants experience justice, the ability of efficiency-oriented designers to reduce choice and induce compliance, the lack of transparency in ODR hearings, the rigidity and inflexibility of procedures, and many others.[31] Most of these complaints, however, focus less on ODR's basic principles and more on the weaknesses critics observe in specific first-gen systems.[32] Like traditional procedures, ODR will only be

[28] *See* Meghan M. O'Neil & J.J. Prescott, *Targeting Poverty in the Courts: Improving the Measurement of Ability to Pay*, 82 LAW & CONTEMP. PROBS. 199, 221 (2019); Prescott & Sanchez, *Platform Procedure*, at 65; *see also* Darren Gingras & Joshua Morrison, *Artificial Intelligence and Family ODR*, 59 FAM. CT. REV. 227, 228 (2021).

[29] Shekhar Kumar, *Virtual Venues: Improving Online Dispute Resolution as an Alternative to Cost Intensive Litigation*, 27 J. MARSHALL J. COMPUT. & INFO. L. 81, 85 (2009); Prescott & Sanchez, *Platform Procedure*, at 70.

[30] Amy J. Schmitz, *Measuring "Access to Justice" in the Rush to Digitize*, 88 FORDHAM L. REV. 2381, 2383–84 (2020) (noting 92 percent of Michigan ODR users would recommend the system and 82 percent found it fair); Youyang Hou et al., *Factors in Fairness and Emotion in Online Case Resolution Systems*, 2017 PROC. CHI CONF. ON HUM. FACTORS COMP. SYS. 2511, 2518–19.

[31] *See, e.g.*, Norman W. Spaulding, *Online Dispute Resolution and the End of Adversarial Justice?* (Chapter 11 in this volume); Jean R. Sternlight, *Pouring a Little Psychological Cold Water on Online Dispute Resolution*, 2020 J. DISP. RESOL., 1, 2–4; Schmitz, *Measuring "Access to Justice" in the Rush to Digitize*, at 2384; Nancy A. Welsh, *Dispute Resolution Neutrals' Ethical Obligation to Support Measured Transparency*, 71 OKLA. L. REV. 823, 862–63 (2019); *see also* RICHARD SUSSKIND, TOMORROW'S LAWYERS: AN INTRODUCTION TO YOUR FUTURE 118–21 (2013).

[32] *See* Chapter 11 in this volume; Robert J. Condlin, *Online Dispute Resolution: Stinky, Repugnant, or Drab*, 18 CARDOZO J. CONFLICT RESOL. 717, 733–55 (2017).

as good as its design. Yet ODR's inherent flexibility gives courts the means to resolve many worries raised about existing systems, if they have the will: for example, all ODR-related policies, choices, and outcomes can be made public, and the workflow can be designed to maximize litigant voice, even if current instances of ODR score poorly on these measures. Furthermore, ODR is almost always an option, not a requirement, so those who object to ODR must defend disallowing low-cost access alternatives for litigants who retain more expensive "Cadillac" access to justice and yet prefer ODR when given a choice.[33]

More importantly, most criticisms fail to reckon with the very real problems of traditional adjudication, especially in low-stakes cases. Detractors compare ODR processes to a stylized and idealized version of traditional adjudication.[34] But this perspective ignores the existing brick-and-mortar system's huge access-to-justice issues – including regressive costs, biases, disparities, confusion, and intimidation – as well as the paper-thin procedures that many if not most litigants experience in courtrooms. These critics compare the best of courts to the worst of ODR.

Some criticisms rightly focus on ODR being peddled by the private sector and the implications of long-term profit motives.[35] But there is nothing inherent in ODR as a concept that requires deferring to a private vendor; courts can and do build their own ODR systems (albeit, often via work-for-hire, which is par for the course when it comes to government software adoption). There are potentially negative, more indirect consequences to making courts and the law easier to access, too. Once lawsuits are extremely easy to file, answer, and navigate, more disagreements will become lawsuits. While ODR can be designed to balance access costs for plaintiffs and defendants, for instance, it may actually increase litigation rates. But the argument that making courts more efficient and accessible in a party-neutral way might be socially problematic simply proves too much; a corollary would be that courts ought to move back to pen-and-paper orders and file cabinets.

12.1.3 *Auguries: First-Gen ODR and the Representation Gap*

With respect to pro se litigants and the "representation gap," at least some evidence suggests that ODR systems, even first-generation ones, can level the playing field just as retaining legal representation does. For instance, ODR proceedings in the traffic

33 Such arguments fall into two camps. The first presumes that litigants don't know what is good for them or make systematic mistakes and so must be forced to engage in traditional litigation for their own good. The second relates to negative externalities or third-party effects. The fact that ODR may be better for any particular litigant does not mean that it is best for society, which may suffer from less transparent ODR processes, for instance, or the stunted development of law. SUSSKIND, ONLINE COURTS AND THE FUTURE OF JUSTICE, at 107–109.

34 *See, e.g.*, Andrea Roth, *Trial by Machine*, 104 GEO. L.J. 1245, 1305 (2016) ("We should reject both a romanticized view of the virtues of unaided human justice and a fetishistic or statist view of the virtues of mechanical justice.").

35 *See* Chapter 11 in this volume.

context are associated with fewer race- and age-based disparities, either because switching to online proceedings (for example, text-based, asynchronous communication or at-home, video-based hearings) differentially benefits some groups over others or because ODR platforms reduce implicit bias by limiting decision-maker exposure to legally irrelevant identity traits.[36] The precise mechanism here is unclear, but this reversal is important and ties into questions about the benefits of corporeal representation in court. Lawyers "represent" their clients and so may disrupt implicit biases or other cognitive/behavioral distortions that attach to litigants who appear in person on their own. ODR may do this, too. At the same time, by offering litigants an alternative to a single, one-size-fits-all track, any single limitation a litigant might have in, say, communication (e.g., difficulty speaking in open court) is less likely to matter. In this sense, the addition of ODR makes our legal system more robust in its ability to accommodate pro se litigants.

Existing ODR platforms also implicitly provide guidance on the law and litigation process to litigants. For instance, ODR hearings are configured for the litigant and legal issue in question. All content is targeted and laid out in a single dashboard, and material that speaks to irrelevant contingencies can be omitted. Now consider a litigant's experience walking into a state courthouse, which is, by design or happenstance, an all-purpose space we use to resolve many types of legal matters. A courtroom is not hung with customized signs. The litigant must digest, sort, and navigate. This is costly and often confusing and scary. By contrast, ODR is akin to being met at the door by an usher who helps you to where you need to be, reminds you of your to-dos, and tsk-tsks when you cut a corner or appear distracted. ODR makes the experience less stressful and reduces error. Lawyers also play this role. Thus, even first-gen ODR mitigates the effect of pro se status, but ODR today is better analogized to an usher than to a counselor. A lawyer can help you decide whether going to your seat is a good idea; an usher can just tell you how to get there.

12.2 A NEW FRONTIER: NEXT-GENERATION COURT-CONNECTED ODR

In this section, I contend that legal representation – what lawyers *do* for clients – can be disaggregated into distinct functions and that many of these can be approximated, achieved, and perhaps even exceeded within a pro se architecture of next-gen ODR. The confluence of online technology, data collection and storage, and computational power in effect blurs the distinction between "mere" access to a forum like a courthouse and actively supplying pro se litigants with many of the benefits of legal representation. When designing and implementing ODR systems, courts that care about access to justice and successfully resolving society's disputes ought to set aside any historical reticence to offering robust litigant support – even when that support

[36] Mentovich et al., *Are Litigation Outcome Disparities Inevitable?* at 975.

overlaps with what lawyers do, such as providing objective information, even-handed guidance, and physical representation in court.

Thinking about next-gen ODR begins with a clear-eyed discussion of what (human) lawyers do and what they bring to the table – as well the drawbacks of legal representation (e.g., agency costs, limited communication). Lawyers serve many functions in a litigation context. Lawyers offer predictions,[37] counseling, representation, influence, and access,[38] and the option to litigate in ways that raise rivals' costs. Not surprisingly, represented parties often experience better litigation outcomes than pro se litigants.[39] But a better litigation outcome does not equate to a litigant being better off overall, and involving lawyers in dispute resolution is socially costly,[40] especially when attorney efforts on opposing sides are offsetting. From society's perspective, the relevant question is not how much a party's individual prospects improve with a lawyer, but how much net value a lawyer adds to the case in terms of outcome accuracy and its attendant benefits.

Even when a lawyer has critical skills and experience, a litigant's choice to hire that human being is always an imperfect strategy born of necessity. Lawyers as representatives suffer from agency issues,[41] at times second-guessing their client on the basis of "independent professional judgment."[42] Even when interests are roughly aligned, the frictions inherent to human communication limit the value of legal representation. Litigants hire people – not their expertise and experience. Litigants cannot download an attorney's judgment and know-how, nor can they upload the whole of their history and hopes. A client must communicate their preferences, constraints, and knowledge about the case to the attorney *without* knowing the law or what is possible and relevant. A lawyer has only limited time to prepare to "channel" their client when the moment of truth arrives. Far superior would be the ability to evaluate one's own case through the prism of a lawyer's training and

37 *See generally* Mark K. Osbeck, *Lawyer as Soothsayer: Exploring the Important Role of Outcome Prediction in the Practice of Law*, 123 Penn St. L. Rev. 41 (2018); *see also* Oliver Wendell Holmes, *The Path of the Law*, 10 Harv. L. Rev. 61, 61 (1897).

38 *E.g.*, Tianwang Liu & David Hao Zhang, *Do Judge-Lawyer Relationships Influence Case Outcomes?* 13 (Oct. 15, 2020), https://papers.ssrn.com/sol3/papers.cfm?abstract_id=3711873.

39 Mitchell Levy, *Empirical Patterns of Pro Se Litigation in Federal District Courts*, 85 U. Chi. L. Rev. 1819, 1844 (2018); Taylor Poppe & Rachlinski, *Do Lawyers Matter?* at 885. The picture is a complicated one, however. *Compare* D. James Greiner & Cassandra Wolos Pattanayak, *Randomized Evaluation in Legal Assistance: What Difference Does Representation (Offer and Actual Use) Make?* 121 Yale L.J. 2118, 2197–98 (2012), *with* D. James Greiner et al., *The Limits of Unbundled Legal Assistance: A Randomized Study in a Massachusetts District Court and Prospects for the Future*, 126 Harv. L. Rev. 901, 925–31 (2013).

40 *See* J.J. Prescott, *The Challenges of Calculating the Benefits of Providing Access to Legal Services*, 37 Fordham Urb. L.J. 303, 321–22 (2010).

41 *See generally* Lynn Mather, *What Do Clients Want? What Do Lawyers Do?* 52 Emory L.J. 1065 (2003).

42 *See id.* at 1068; Katherine R. Kruse, *Engaged Client-Centered Representation and the Moral Foundations of the Lawyer-Client Relationship*, 39 Hofstra L. Rev. 577, 585 (2011).

professional history (and perhaps objectivity). All of this is to say that legal representation, even at its best, is far from perfect.

In what follows, I identify three specific benefits of legal representation – outcome prediction, options guidance, and obfuscation/translation – and I argue that they can be approximated through court technology. When evaluating this claim, keep in mind that the relevant comparison is to a costly, limited, and sometimes selfish human agent. I do not claim that ODR platforms can or will render lawyers obsolete. But in weighing its relative merits, enhanced ODR may be able to deliver, implicitly or explicitly, many of the benefits of an expert counselor. I also do not claim that ODR systems have yet to push any of these frontiers.[43] Rather, I maintain only that adopting courts ought to think holistically about how ODR can support litigants in ways that reduce the pro se representation gap. By keeping in mind what lawyers do and how clients and society benefit from their involvement, future ODR systems may generate better outcomes and more satisfaction.

12.2.1 *Experience and Predicting Outcomes*

One of the most important services a lawyer provides a litigant is an informed, experienced perspective on the likely outcome of a case, with some overall take on whether the outlook is "good."[44] Typically, during intake, the prospective litigant describes the nature of the dispute, key aspects of the case, and the like, and the lawyer may even offer some preliminary advice. Once retained, however, the lawyer will engage in more intense prediction-oriented activity on behalf of the client, perhaps after researching the law, collecting more information, and weighing the necessary investment, probable venue, expected legal rulings, possible judges, and even likely jurors. These predictions are necessarily fuzzy; there is considerable uncertainty, but as time resolves many contingencies (e.g., the identity of the opposing attorney), predictions will become more accurate. Consequently, the lawyer is likely to revisit the prediction task repeatedly, presumably at each important decision point, when the litigant might seek advice on how to proceed. In a traditional litigation setting, the prediction problem is a complicated one; the environment is relatively unstructured, and the variables are nearly infinite. There are also conflicts of interest and cognitive biases tugging on a lawyer's predictions.

[43] For example, British Columbia's public legal aid system, MyLawBC, recently expanded from ODR to also offering "self-help" online legal aid in family law, including "guided pathways" for mediation. *See Tyler Technologies and Legal Aid BC Expand Partnership to Provide Full Service Online Dispute Resolution*, Bus. Wire (July 7, 2021), https://www.businesswire.com/news/home/20210707005171/en/Tyler-Technologies-and-Legal-Aid-BC-Expand-Partnership-to-Provide-Full-Service-Online-Dispute-Resolution.

[44] Osbeck, *Lawyer as Soothsayer*, at 43; Daniel Martin Katz, *Quantitative Legal Prediction – Or – How I Learned to Stop Worrying and Start Preparing for the Data-Driven Future of the Legal Services Industry*, 62 Emory L.J. 909, 912 (2013).

A lawyer's ability to "predict" a dispute's outcome builds on the human equivalent of supervised learning.[45] In most cases, the client defines a "good" outcome for the lawyer.[46] But even if the target is unclear or moving, the client and the lawyer are normally decided on the type of outcome that matters (e.g., damages, liability, share of custody, opportunity to be heard, etc.). The lawyer's task is to take the client's account, the law, the client's set of plausible "moves," the presiding judge, and anything else observable to the lawyer and then predict an outcome using the agreed-upon metric of success. This prediction may come in the form of an expected outcome alone and possibly with some measure of uncertainty that implicitly conveys the expected accuracy of the prediction (e.g., "I think you'll get $75K, give or take $10K"). If the client defines a minimally acceptable outcome, the lawyer will review the likely consequences for each set of potential moves and either report that this outcome is unrealistic or that taking a particular set of actions will be necessary (under current circumstances).

How does a lawyer do this? The lawyer effectively cognitively "models" prior cases to understand the complicated relationships between facts, choices, and outcomes. Put another way, lawyers detect patterns between predictors and outcomes.[47] The greater the number and variety of cases and types of predictors that lawyers incorporate into their modeling, the more flexible, unbiased, and accurate their predictions can be. A mental model is what we mean when we talk about the value of experience. An expert lawyer has witnessed many cases with many different characteristics proceed under many different circumstances. Delivering accurate predictions is helpful because they can guide a litigant's behavior toward their preferred outcome, whatever it happens to be. If the litigant's goal is to maximize their net "return" from a dispute, a schedule of litigation strategies (including their costs) and their likely outcomes (and uncertainties) produced by a lawyer is what a litigant needs to succeed.

ODR platforms can perform this task. In fact, under the circumstances, they may be able to do a better job.[48] First-gen ODR platforms already access an individual litigant's case, drawing information from the court's case management system. Once a case resolves, the platform archives the record and moves onto the next case. But there is no reason an enhanced platform cannot build models from *all* prior cases and even from data outside the court's case management system. Models can

45 Trevor Hastie et al., The Elements of Statistical Learning: Data Mining, Inference, and Prediction 1–2 (2nd ed. 2009). Lawyers build mental models using their experience with prior disputes or transactions. *See also Supervised Learning*, IBM Cloud Learn Hub (Aug. 19, 2020), https://www.ibm.com/cloud/learn/supervised-learning.

46 *But see generally* Kruse, *Engaged Client-Centered Representation*; Mather, *What Do Clients Want?*

47 Hanspeter Pfister et al., *Exploring the Gap between Informal Mental and Formal Statistical Models*, 3 Harv. Data Sci. Rev. (Jul. 30, 2021), https://doi.org/10.1162/99608f92.ba00865a.

48 *See* Jon Kleinberg et al., *Human Decisions and Machine Predictions*, 133 Q.J. Econ. 237, 240–41 (2018).

incorporate any plausible predictor, including judge identity, hearing timing, and docket backlog. By contrast, lawyers build models only from their own cases or those about which they hear or read (inevitably with error and uncertainty), and only with what they can observe about those cases and their circumstances. In effect, an enhanced ODR platform could display a distribution of how similar past cases – or, with enough data, only identical ones – fared using the litigant's preferred measure of success. These "predictions" (tendered as descriptions of what happened in prior cases – not as promises or legal advice!) can be presented at decision points and can be joined with statistics to impart precision.[49]

The challenges to operationalizing these ideas are manageable.[50] In many ways, litigation that occurs in an ODR environment may be more amenable to accurate prediction than litigation in a more traditional environment because the platform can easily capture the information about cases, choices, and outcomes needed for prediction. An ODR system may be more structured and less nuanced, either by necessity or design, which might also simplify the prediction problem. Consider an enhanced platform with asynchronous, text-based communication that requires parties to answer the same questions in the same order with the same answer options as part of an online hearing (versus open court with a judge asking different questions in different ways and expecting a narrative response on the spot) and where the system necessarily prevents or obscures certain actions (e.g., a litigant can't visibly sigh or roll their eyes at a judge).[51] The number of predictors would no longer be infinite *because* the environment eschews legally irrelevant details; in other words, the medium itself might simplify some of the prediction problems a lawyer would normally face in court.[52]

[49] Decision support of this sort has long been proposed for judges, just not for litigants, who are presumably assumed to have attorneys near at hand for such wisdom. Marc L. Miller, *A Map of Sentencing and a Compass for Judges: Sentencing Information Systems, Transparency, and the Next Generation of Reform*, 105 Colum. L. Rev. 1351 (2005). Again, the legal tech industry has already developed many successful such tools, so the push here is to incorporate these tools into ODR in an easy-to-digest format for pro se litigants.

[50] *But see* David Freeman Engstrom & Johan B. Gelbach, *Legal Tech, Civil Procedure, and the Future of Adversarialism*, 169 U. Pa. L. Rev. 1001, 1018–30 (2021).

[51] *See generally* Arthur Dyevre, *Text-Mining for Lawyers: How Machine Learning Techniques Can Advance Our Understanding of Legal Discourse*, 2021 Erasmus L. Rev. 7 (2021).

[52] Enhanced platforms would also need to contemplate, measure, and operationalize outcomes that litigants value. With a lawyer, a litigant might ask, "How angry do people get when you make this argument?" and litigants might *value* an outcome in which the other party emerges from a hearing angry at them. A lawyer can build a model on the spot, probably one that is at least marginally useful, *see* Kruse, *Engaged Client-Centered Representation*, and then share the likelihood of the outcome, allowing the litigant to decide whether the argument's worth trying. In the ODR context, many idiosyncratic outcomes would be practically unobservable (i.e., not recordable) – especially if observation must occur in person. To keep things simple, ODR systems might opt to forgo making predictions about many less idiosyncratic outcomes even when they might be easy to observe.

12.2.2 *Navigating, Counseling, and Identifying Options*

Lawyers often present options. They take raw facts and abstract law and suggest possible legal solutions. They also identify various strategies (or implement them directly), and they help clients weigh the upsides and downsides of those strategies. Lawyers do not necessarily perform this task well. The quality of counseling, when it occurs, is often suspect. Lawyers implicitly build models, but they also suffer from biases (e.g., availability), have limited observational and processing capacity, and must navigate their own conflicts (like economizing on time and avoiding high-risk innovations). In most contexts, lawyers are also busy. Identifying options, discussing them with clients – these activities take time. Consequently, lawyers work from scripts,[53] stocked with standard "moves" that usually do the trick in the vast majority of situations. Lawyers may deliver these options in rote fashion, with little thought paid to details that are individually unlikely to make a material difference in the long run (even if, collectively, such details can alter a legal dispute's trajectory).

This account is designed to present a human lawyer as a fairly simple algorithm. The lawyer asks intake questions, processes the answers, identifies the nature of the dispute and a set of typical solutions, explains the most common approaches to the client, and translates the client's reaction into a set of choices or next steps. Two tasks are occurring here. One is pattern recognition (the main point here). The second is prediction combined with an interpretation of what the client values. Put differently, lawyers determine the sort of dispute they face, collect relevant information for a dispute involving such features, identify an array of potential approaches or strategies, and assist the client in understanding and deciding between them.

This last step – helping a litigant understand and evaluate various options – falls squarely in the camp of outcome prediction. Enhanced ODR can define a large number of potential outcomes. Not all, true, but easily those outcomes that would matter to 99 percent of litigants. Counseling between options can be carried out simply by informing litigants of the likelihood that certain outcomes will manifest if the litigant pursues, say, track 1 or track 2.

With a real lawyer, counseling involves nuance.[54] But much of that nuance is the lawyer attempting simultaneously to ascertain a client's preferences. An enhanced ODR platform would do less "screening" and instead make much more information available to the client so they may digest with their own priorities in mind instead of relying on a black-box lawyer. There are challenges here: Litigants also face

53 Jack Chorowsky, *Thinking Like a Lawyer*, 80 U. DET. MERCY L. REV. 463, 464 (2003) ("Across ... different subjects, you'll start to see similar types and styles of questions and arguments. Look for patterns; try to understand the common 'moves' that lawyers make in certain situations.").

54 Heather Heavin & Michaela Keet, *Client-Centered Communication: How Effective Lawyering Requires Emotional Intelligence, Active Listening, and Client Choice*, 22 CARDOZO J. CONFLICT RESOL. 199, 206 (2021).

cognitive limits, and while they may have more time to immerse themselves in their own affairs, too much data can be worse than too little.[55] Just as an intimidating courthouse can paralyze, so too can an environment that dumps unstructured information on litigants and then asks them to sift it.[56] Thus, ODR platform structure and design must not only be accessible but also support effective decision-making.[57] We already use technology to help people make important choices about many things.[58] Even in the legal-aid and access-to-justice contexts, existing decision support tools streamline processes, minimize confusion, and improve decision-making.[59] Efforts are imperfect but improving,[60] and one must remember that the relevant benchmark is a pro se world with no support whatsoever.

To counsel, lawyers categorize a dispute and then compile the information necessary to identify options, avoid legal and factual pitfalls, and assemble plausible strategies (matched with predictions). This is complex, and early versions of enhanced ODR will likely be subject-matter specific. But precedents for algorithmic technology of this sort already exist, and courts should avoid letting the perfect be the enemy of the good. Legal aid groups already deploy triage and intake forms that are "smart."[61] An initial goal for next-gen ODR might be to determine a litigant's eligibility for digital or other assistance by collecting critical information about the litigant's situation.[62] The law's many branches can be incorporated directly into questions put to users.[63] Structure in the law and implicit groupings of fact patterns will lay bare most likely strategies.

55 Ron Friedman, *Why Too Much Data Disables Your Decision Making*, Fast Co. (Aug. 24, 2012), https://www.fastcompany.com/3000676/why-too-much-data-disables-your-decision-making.

56 *See* Timothy Van Zandt, *Information Overload in a Network of Targeted Communication*, 35 RAND J. Econ. 542, 542 (2004); *see also* Kathryn Hensiak, *Too Much of a Good Thing: Information Overload and Law Librarians*, 22 Legal Ref. Servs. Q. 85 (2003).

57 *See* Ayelet Sela, *Can Computers Be Fair? How Automated and Human-Powered Online Dispute Resolution Affect Procedural Justice in Mediation and Arbitration*, 33 Ohio St. J. Disp. Resol. 91, 139 (2018).

58 Consider Amazon's automated customer service chatbots. Jared Kramer, *Amazon.com Tests Customer Service Chatbots*, Amazon Sci. (Feb. 25, 2020), https://www.amazon.science/blog/amazon-com-tests-customer-service-chatbots.

59 *E.g.*, British Columbia's online legal aid service, MyLawBC, https://mylawbc.com/.

60 *See, e.g.*, Margaret Hagan, *Participatory Design for Innovation in Access to Justice*, 148 Daedalus 120 (2019); Daniel W. Bernal & Margaret D. Hagan, *Redesigning Justice Innovation: A Standardized Methodology*, 16 Stan. J.C.R. & C.L. 335 (2020).

61 *SLRN Brief: Examples of Legal Aid On-Line Intake and Triage Projects (SLRN 2016)*, Self-Represented Litig. Network (Mar. 22, 2022), https://www.srln.org/node/458/srln-brief-examples-legal-aid-line-intake-and-triage-projects-srln-2015; *Online Triage and Intake*, Legal Servs. Corp., https://www.lsc.gov/i-am-grantee/grantee-guidance/lsc-reporting-requirements/tig-reporting/online-intake-triage.

62 Algorithms can quickly and precisely identify eligibility given explicit criteria and high-quality records, helping legal-aid organizations and governments allocate scarce resources to the people they can help most. *See* Carla L. Reyes & Jeff Ward, *Digging into Algorithms: Legal Ethics and Legal Access*, 21 Nev. L.J. 325, 330–31 (2002).

63 *See Interactive Online Portals Offer Targeted Legal Resources on Demand*, Pew Charitable Tr. (Jan. 4, 2019), https://www.pewtrusts.org/en/research-and-analysis/fact-sheets/2019/01/inter

There is no limit to how complex any enhanced ODR data collection process might be. But this is *also* true when a litigant hires an attorney: The litigant explains their situation, and the attorney asks questions in response. The attorney may also look over papers, review video, or examine other evidence. This exchange might take a while, but lawyers ultimately triage and end their information gathering, and ODR software can too. As natural language processing improves, faster intake methods that ask open-ended questions instead of closed-ended questions can reduce the total number of questions.[64] Analysis of narrative answers can trigger relevant follow-up inquiries.[65] But there are reasons doctors don't only ask "so, what's bothering you?" at an appointment. Instead, you are first subjected to a long list of questions designed to prompt you to think about every system and part of your body.[66] Any natural language response to an open-ended question like "what's your legal problem?" may come from a person unfamiliar with the law whose take on what matters may be off-base.[67] Still, natural language responses, perhaps even voice submissions, might be a better, more accessible option for some litigants.[68]

A barrier to making data-collection functionality successful in next-gen ODR platforms is simply *how long* it might take a litigant to get in the front door. So much of what is good about ODR is that it is easy to use and minimally costly to try. Next-gen ODR might dissuade people from using courts all over again if it bogs down with seemingly countless questions and checklists. But consulting with a lawyer takes no small amount of time, and stacks of forms are not new to human institutions. Nevertheless, enhanced ODR platforms might be more attractive to more people if guidance and counseling functions were designated as optional.

12.2.3 *Replication/Obfuscation/Translation versus Representation*

Lawyers aren't just analytical input-output machines offering a litigant legal expertise in the background. Lawyers are corporeal and play a physical role on the stage of our justice system.[69] They actually "do" law by going to a courthouse to serve as

active-online-portals-offer-targeted-legal-resources-on-demand ("For example, . . . 'My landlord is kicking me out of my house' would be identified as an eviction issue.").

64 *See id.*

65 *See* Claudia King, 5 *Lawyer Bots You Can Try Now*, FIRMSY (Mar. 27, 2018), https://firmsy.com/blog/5-lawyer-bots-you-can-try-now.

66 *See* Lizzie O'Leary, *How IBM's Watson Went from the Future of Health Care to Sold Off for Parts*, SLATE (Jan. 31, 2022, 9:00 AM), https://slate.com/technology/2022/01/ibm-watson health-failure-artificial-intelligence.html.

67 *See generally* Jeena Cho, 5 *Mistakes to Avoid at Client Intake*, ABOVE THE LAW (Aug. 10, 2015, 1:00 PM), https://abovethelaw.com/2015/08/5-mistakes-to-avoid-at-client-intake/.

68 Margaret Hagan, *The Justice Is in the Details: Evaluating Different Self-Help Designs for Legal Capability in Traffic Court*, 7 J. OPEN ACCESS L. 1, 8 (2019).

69 For example, only a lawyer can represent someone in court. *E.g.*, STATE BAR OF MICHIGAN, UNAUTHORIZED PRACTICE OF LAW: FACTS AND INFORMATION (2009), https://www.michbar.org/file/professional/pdfs/uplfacts.pdf.

their client's mouthpiece. The corporeal representation function of lawyering matters in at least three ways in the context of court-connected ODR: lawyers replicate a litigant's ability to be physically present, lawyers obfuscate litigant traits, and lawyers translate and distill a litigant's lay arguments into an "expert's" legal arguments. Considering these roles separately demonstrates that enhanced ODR can advance these functions through text on a screen or other digital-information display even without a human body in a courtroom.

First, lawyers allow clients to be in two places at once. This function reduces the cost of litigation to clients, courts, and other parties, since schedule conflicts can slow litigation. Representation offers flexibility to meet competing obligations. Often, a client and their attorney come together in a courtroom at critical junctures, but there are many stages when a lawyer can physically "be" the client for purposes of advancing a case. Technically, ODR is unable to fulfill this function because, whatever it is, software does not stand in for a litigant before other parties or decision-makers. Yet, in an ODR environment, there is arguably no *need* for such a service in the typical case. Indeed, unlike hearings that take place at a particular time and place, ODR can be more flexible, accessible, and efficient, making the use of a lawyer to "cover" for someone less important.

Second, lawyers can "obfuscate" client traits. When judges walk into a courtroom and see a litigant's race, gender, age, or other identity traits, evidence suggests that unconscious implicit bias, if not explicit bias, affects subsequent decision-making.[70] Furthermore, the anticipation of such bias can alter a litigant's ability to communicate well in a courtroom. One strategy for a litigant facing the possibility of discrimination is to hire a lawyer with different – perhaps socially "preferred" – characteristics to block, blunt, or attenuate any such bias. Lawyers even advertise on this basis – for example, hinting at the advantages of a female lawyer defending a male defendant accused of sexually assaulting a female victim.[71] True, having a lawyer does not necessarily preclude a judge from ascertaining litigant identity traits, but outside of explicit, intentional discrimination, even sharing the stage with an in-group lawyer may disrupt the psychological processes that lead to bias.

For those unable to reduce their exposure to bias by using a lawyer,[72] ODR offers a substitute, perhaps superior solution. ODR can structure online communication to insulate judges and other decision-makers from legally irrelevant information that

70 Jeffrey J. Rachlinski et al., *Does Unconscious Racial Bias Affect Trial Judges?* 84 NOTRE DAME L. REV. 1195, 1209–11 (2009).

71 *E.g.*, *Hiring a Female Lawyer for a Criminal Sexual Conduct Case*, SHANNON SMITH LAW, PC, https://defendingabuse.com/blog-items/hiring-a-female-lawyer-for-a-criminal-sexual-conduct-case. Evidence suggests that an attorney's race and gender can influence a trial's outcome. *See* Alexis A. Robinson, *The Effects of Race and Gender of Attorneys on Trial Outcomes*, JURY EXPERT, May 2011, at 1, 4–5, https://www.thejuryexpert.com/wp-content/uploads/RobinsonTJEMay2011.pdf.

72 System-level or court-level debiasing strategies exist to address disparate treatment. Most begin by assuming decision-makers will come into personal contact with litigants, triggering bias. The

might trigger implicit biases (or allow purposeful discrimination). At least some first-gen ODR systems, for example, do not include a litigant's driver's license picture in the judge's dashboard. At least one court collects required picture ID information only *after* the judge decides the case but before the ruling is entered. First-gen ODR systems, by tracking traditional in-person processes, still tend to make a litigant's name visible (which may reveal gender and ethnicity) and, in some instances, date of birth (which, with some math, reveals a litigant's age).[73] ODR platforms can go further by thoughtfully, comprehensively obscuring litigant traits that are legally irrelevant (or even legally relevant when they are likely to bias or confuse decision-making),[74] whenever it is consistent with fair process.

Third, lawyers provide a "translation" function to clients. Lawyers distill what they learn from clients into core substantive facts, and then assemble and present those facts in the highly reticulated way that legal actors expect from legal professionals.[75] This professional repackaging may augment a litigant's story and substantive arguments by making them more palatable, reliable, and understandable to a judge.[76] Or it may just be a key into the club. If there are lawyers on both sides, any imprimatur may cancel out, yet the dynamics of the prisoner's dilemma apply, so all who can "lawyer up" still do so. Pro se litigants are left behind. Even if translation and delivery by an expert improves the litigant's prospects (relative to a counterparty), it remains an open question whether this function enhances the accuracy or efficiency of any adjudication. Regardless, if only one party has access to an attorney's stamp of approval or can speak "legalese," a pro se gap might develop.[77]

Enhanced ODR can diminish the role that legalese and professional status might play in litigation by reducing their use, making them ambiguous or less salient, or facilitating a pro se litigant's ability to employ them within the platform. ODR design can encourage (or require) litigants to use plain language, either via the structure of its data collection strategies (e.g., forms) or through ex post screening of user language. Alternatively, one can imagine a more involved ODR process that educates litigants about the meanings of legal words or legal communication norms or that offers something closer to a translation service, much the way smart form

goal is therefore to unwind or inhibit the effects of any such bias. Mentovich et al., *Are Litigation Outcome Disparities Inevitable?* at 903–12.

73 *See id.*

74 *Cf.* FED. R. EVID. 403.

75 *See* Robert W. Benson, *The End of Legalese: The Game Is Over*, 13 N.Y.U. REV. L. & SOC. CHANGE 519, 529–30 (1984–1985).

76 Importantly, critics of this portrayal argue that lawyerly translation can corrupt a client's story in a way that is harmful to clients, by shoehorning their views into poorly fitted legal categories or by substituting their own views for those of their client. *See generally* TAMARA RELIS, PERCEPTIONS IN LITIGATION AND MEDIATION: LAWYERS, DEFENDANTS, PLAINTIFFS, AND GENDERED PARTIES (2009).

77 This is not certain, however. *See* Scott L. Garland, *Avoiding Goliath's Fate: Defeating a Pro Se Litigant*, LITIGATION, Winter 1998, at 45, 45.

procedures operate today, by giving people choices. Either way, ODR platform "rigidity" in the allowable scope and style of communication can be a disparity-reducing positive;[78] such structure can ensure that parties speak the same language while also giving them equal opportunities to be heard.

Importantly, reducing "degrees of freedom" in ODR communications can also close a back-door source of implicit bias. An ODR system that scrubs case materials of identity-trait data after having encouraged a litigant to submit an open-ended statement may be closing the barn door after the horse has bolted. Intentionally or unintentionally, litigants reveal personal traits in their communications:[79] they explicitly indicate their race, gender, occupation, or age,[80] or they implicitly reveal these traits through language that correlates with demographic characteristics.[81] In any event, to the extent that legal representation liberates litigants from the need to speak legalese in the courtroom and insulates litigants from implicit bias by insulating judges from triggering face-to-face interactions, ODR systems have the potential to do much the same through careful design and creative solutions.

12.3 CONCLUSION

Courtrooms (spaces) and lawyers (people) complement each other in the resolution of disputes. Courts appear to be fixed, reactive, and generically available to all; lawyers, by contrast, seek justice by customizing how courts resolve disputes to align with client circumstances and preferences. A lawyer "configures" a court and the law it embodies by leveraging their experience, expertise, and corporeality to serve their client's interests. First-gen ODR makes courts more accessible, but platform technology, data science, and thoughtful design allow for so much more. In this chapter, I argue that courts should view ODR going forward not only as a potential opportunity for courtroom-like engagement in the traditional sense but as a substitute for many of the services historically provided by lawyers, which, in the end, are mostly about helping litigants understand how a court will perform and what it will produce in the specific instance of their case. Conceiving of ODR in this way – as the use of online communication technology and data science to make it easier for potential litigants to *use*, *understand*, and *benefit from* law in action – will get us much closer in the years ahead to "courts as a service."

[78] Mentovich et al., *Are Litigation Outcome Disparities Inevitable?* at 965.

[79] O'Neil & Prescott, *Targeting Poverty in the Courts*, at 223–24.

[80] For examples of unfiltered and revealing language, see some preliminary analysis from Matterhorn litigants at Stanford Law School, *Legal Tech and the Future of Civil Justice (Session 3)*, YouTube (Mar. 1, 2021), https://www.youtube.com/watch?v=X31czG4NbBc (beginning at approx. 49:05).

[81] *Id.* (beginning at approx. 49:40).

PART IV

Courts, Data, and Civil Justice

13

The Disruption We Needed

COVID-19, Court Technology, and Access to Justice

Bridget Mary McCormack

I think I bring good news. After decades of earnest efforts to address our growing access-to-justice crisis, we are weathering a storm that just might usher in the disruptive change we need. The COVID-19 pandemic has forced courts and lawyers to work differently, and we have learned that we *can* work differently. Innovation leapt into our courtrooms and our practices. Lawyers, judges, and court administrators were given the chance to rethink what they do and rebuild how they do it, and they seized the moment.

The pandemic has shown what many of us already knew, or at least suspected: There are many legal issues that can be effectively resolved without gathering in a physical space. In 2020 and 2021, "going to court" took on a whole new meaning. And as we look to 2022 and beyond, an opportunity remains for lasting, transformational change to our nation's civil justice system.

"Access to justice" can be abstract, but in busy state courts it isn't. For many Americans, and especially for those of limited financial means, our nation's courts have not been able to deliver. A 2017 report from the Legal Services Corporations found that seven out of ten low-income households experienced at least one civil legal problem each year, and most families received inadequate or no legal help to address them.[1] These numbers are now so familiar that we have grown used to them.

Many individuals simply never try to navigate our justice system; they leave home when they get an eviction notice, they accept a default judgment, or they go without disability accommodations or public benefits. Some try on their own. All too often, their experiences in the legal system leave them discouraged and frustrated.

Those impressions are often earned. By and large, today's courts are not structured to address the volume of modern legal problems. When COVID hit in February 2020, most courts looked a lot like they did during the 1918 flu pandemic. Legal

[1] Legal Servs. Corp., Justice Gap Report 6 (2017), https://www.lsc.gov/media-center/publications/2017-justice-gap-report.

proceedings played out in buildings constructed generations ago, governed by rules written by and for lawyers, at a time when dockets were small and most litigants were represented by lawyers.

Our profession has been focused on this problem for some time. Two decades ago, the Conference of Chief Justices resolved to support the promotion of equal justice by pledging to remove impediments to access, support public funding for civil legal aid, and expand the types of assistance available to self-represented litigants.[2] But the growth of self-represented and underserved individuals hasn't slowed. At the same time, legal technologists have urged us to rethink our courts as service-oriented institutions and to adopt tools that will expand access. Though state bars, court administrators, academics, public interest groups and other stakeholders have supported these calls to action, change has occurred only around the edges.

The COVID-19 pandemic can change all of that. It has required state courts to radically rethink almost everything we do. In the past year we have seen rapid adoption of videoconferencing technology.[3] State court leaders have been collaborating in new ways.[4] And while the pandemic has shown that courts have the ability to *replicate* many in-person systems and processes on web-based platforms, *reforming* those systems and processes is a further step yet.

I think the pandemic has proven the technologists right: For state courts, expanding access to justice will require courts to implement technology solutions that bring courts "to" the people they serve. Aside from the technical details, this presents a variety of administrative challenges for state courts: questions about what platforms to use, who will implement and maintain them, and how to measure outcomes to ensure that the constitutional promises of equal protection and due process aren't sacrificed in the name of efficiency. In this chapter, I will describe some of the remaining access-to-justice barriers as I see them, using my home state of Michigan, where I currently and proudly serve as Chief Justice, as an example.

But the challenges we face in Michigan are not unique. Rural communities without access to high-speed internet; large numbers of self-represented litigants; individuals who cannot afford or obtain adequate representation; disunified govern-

[2] Resolution 23, Conf. of Chief Justices (Jan. 25, 2001), https://ccj.ncsc.org/__data/assets/pdf_file/0023/23477/01252001-leadership-to-promote-equal-justice.pdf.

[3] *See* Chapters 4 and 10 in this volume.

[4] The National Center for State Courts has served as the primary convener for these collaborations, and it was well positioned to do so. In 2016, the Center published *Preparing for Pandemic*, a guidebook for state and local courts on developing a pandemic benchbook. Nat'l Ctr. for State Cts., Preparing for a Pandemic: An Emergency Response Benchbook and Operational Guidebook for State Court Judges and Administrators (2016), https://cdm16501.contentdm.oclc.org/digital/collection/facilities/id/194. And as the COVID-19 pandemic unfolded, the Center convened emergency workgroups and served as a digital warehouse for the hundreds of emergency orders issued by state courts.

ance and funding; outdated and often decentralized court management systems with a patchwork of technology vendors and conflicting data standards – these are all obstacles that most state court systems face in one form or another.[5] A growing literature has begun to lay bare these challenges as a central barrier to meaningfully expanding access to justice. This chapter will make these challenges concrete by describing the past, present, and future of A2J in Michigan.

I will begin by describing Michigan's state court structure, dockets, processes, and culture as of February 2020. I will include here the excellent work under way before the COVID-19 pandemic to address the civil justice gap and to accommodate the large number of people who had to access courts without lawyers. I hope to provide enough detail to illustrate clearly the significant barriers to disruptive change. I will then describe the transition that courts made beginning in March 2020, including the specific solutions courts in Michigan have adopted to keep justice accessible while also keeping people safe. Here I will also describe the lessons we (judges, lawyers, and administrators) are learning from this rapid forced transition. Finally, I will address the potential I see for change despite the challenges that remain.

13.1 MICHIGAN'S JUDICIARY – AND THE CHALLENGE OF DECENTRALIZED GOVERNANCE

Judicial administration in the United States is famously decentralized. A 2011 report from the Office of Justice Programs of the US Department of Justice indicated that, in many jurisdictions, the state court's central administrative office had only *partial* responsibility for providing information technology and technical assistance to trial courts.[6] The OJP report also indicated that many trial courts receive a sizable percentage of their funding from sources other than state government. These disjointed arrangements between state and local governance inevitably raise issues of administrative control and the discretion that goes with it, complicating change management.

This challenge features prominently in Michigan, which for many years has struggled to achieve a more unified court system. Our existing court architecture is a product of our most recent state constitution, which dates to 1963 and divides the state's courts into the Michigan Supreme Court, the Michigan Court of Appeals (an

[5] *See, e.g.*, Nat'l Center for State Cts., Justice for All: A Roadmap to 100% Civil Access to Justice 4–6, https://www.ncsc.org/__data/assets/pdf_file/0031/64975/5-year-report.pdf; Mary E. McClymont, Nonlawyer Navigators in State Courts: An Emerging Consensus 8–11 (2019)https://www.srln.org/system/files/attachments/Final%20Navigator%20report%20in%20word-6.11.hyperlinks.pdf.

[6] Ron Malega & Thomas H. Cohen, Bureau of J. Stat., No. NCJ 242850, State Court Organization, 2011 (2013), https://www.bjs.gov/content/pub/pdf/sco11.pdf.

intermediate appellate court that hears both civil and criminal appeals), and over 200 trial courts, most of which are circuit, district, or probate courts.[7]

The Michigan constitution vests the Michigan Supreme Court with administrative oversight authority over all the courts of the state, which it exercises through the State Court Administrative Office (SCAO).[8] Among other administrative functions, the SCAO develops statewide standards and guidelines, collects data, and provides technology solutions, assistance, and training for judges and court staff. The day-to-day operation of our trial courts, however, is managed by local administrators acting under the supervision of a local chief judge. Trial judges are selected in local, nonpartisan elections, and the chief judges are appointed by the Michigan Supreme Court. By law, the local county clerk (also an elected position) is designated as clerk of the circuit court but does not work for the court system. That means the clerk performs functions for the judicial branch and is subject to the circuit court's direction in such matters, but the office is not directly subject to the court's supervisory authority. (Seriously.)

The operations of our Supreme Court and Court of Appeals are funded by the state government. The funding of trial court operations is much more complex. Almost half of that funding comes directly from local governmental units. Court-generated revenue (including costs assessed on litigants and collected by the courts) represents about a quarter of all trial court revenue, as does funding from the state government. Federal funding represents less than 10 percent.[9]

This disunified trial court funding system creates problems that are well understood by the judges and court administrators. The problems are also familiar to lawmakers. In 2017, the Michigan Legislature tasked a commission to review trial-court funding. The commission found that, of the total operating budget for trial courts statewide, approximately 26 percent of that funding was generated by local courts in the form of assessments on criminal defendants. This excessive dependence on local funding led the commission to recommend a new approach: the creation of a statewide trial court fund that would receive all revenue generated by trial court assessments (as well as state funding), and then redistribute that money to trial courts based on specific operational requirements.[10]

7 Circuit courts have original jurisdiction over most civil suits and are the only trial court with the power to issue equitable remedies. MICH. COMP. LAWS § 600.601 (2022). District courts are courts of limited jurisdiction that hear misdemeanors, most traffic violations, and civil suits where the amount in controversy is less than $25,000. MICH. COMP. LAWS § 600.8301 (2022). Probate courts have exclusive jurisdiction over proceedings about estates, guardianships, and conservatorships, and adult protective proceedings. MICH. COMP. LAWS § 600.801 (2022). A comprehensive overview of Michigan court operations is available at STATE CT. ADMIN. OFF., MICHIGAN TRIAL COURT ADMINISTRATION: REFERENCE GUIDE (2021), https://www.courts.michigan.gov/490062/siteassets/publications/manuals/carg/carg.pdf.

8 MICH. CONST. art. VI, § 3.

9 STATE OF MICH., TRIAL COURT FUNDING COMMISSION (2019), https://www.michigan.gov/documents/treasury/TCFC_Final_Report_9-6-2019_665923_7.pdf.

10 *Id.*

One motivating concern was the conflict of interest that results when the assessing court keeps fees and costs to fund their own operations. But the commission also found that Michigan's reliance on local funding was a significant barrier to a unified information-technology system. In fact, the commission found that Michigan's trial courts used up to twenty different case management systems and an even greater number of computer systems. While historically localized funding may have allowed for "laboratories of innovation," this technological diversity has led to significant duplicated efforts and inefficiency. The commission recommended that the state provide for the technology needs of the courts (hardware, software, infrastructure, training, and ongoing technology support), which would then be operationalized by local administrators and court staff. Legislators were taking the first steps toward this system in early 2020, before COVID-19 upended the state legislative agenda (and Michigan's economy).

What does this mean for expanding access to justice? A unified approach, the commission thought, could save resources and improve the user experience. This view isn't exactly groundbreaking: standardization of local court rules and procedures was one of the driving concerns of the court unification movement of the 1970s and 1980s.[11] A similar challenge exists as state courts integrate technological advances into their courtrooms.

Another benefit of unified courts and technology systems is a centralized data architecture that allows for real-time review of both management and outcome-related case data. In 2012, President Obama issued a directive entitled "Building a 21st Century Digital Government,"[12] which called for federal agencies to establish specific, measurable goals for delivering better digital services, including the goal of transforming unstructured content into structured data. Our state courts face a similar challenge. Many state court systems struggle to collect data in a usable, digital format, which in turns limits their ability to leverage technology. Where data exists, it often exists in an unstructured format (like paper or PDFs). And without usable data, technological solutions have a limited ability to help automate court processes, assist self-represented litigants, or measure judicial outcomes across categories to track equity. Despite decades of efforts to unify courts and track their work, many states struggle to collect and publish statistics beyond filing numbers, case types, and clearance rates.

[11] *See* LARRY BERKSON & SUSAN CARBON, NAT'L INST. OF L. ENF'T & CRIM. J., COURT UNIFICATION: HISTORY, POLITICS AND IMPLEMENTATION (1978), https://www.ojp.gov/pdffiles1/Digitization/47168NCJRS.pdf.

[12] *Digital Government: Building a 21st Century Platform to Better Serve the American People*, THE WHITE HOUSE: PRESIDENT BARACK OBAMA, https://obamawhitehouse.archives.gov/sites/default/files/omb/egov/digital-government/digital-government.html.

To address our current piecemeal system, the SCAO created the Judicial Data Warehouse (JDW) in 2006 to provide a single repository for court data.[13] Given the complexity of the court system, creating the JDW involved monumental effort, highlighted by scores of data-sharing agreements that coaxed local trial courts to share data while not giving up local control. Moreover, each time a new initiative requires additional data, courts need to retool their data collection systems and the JDW needs reprogramming to receive the new information. It's clunky and inefficient.[14]

While JDW offers a workaround for nonunified systems, it is an example of how our decentralized funding structure requires the Supreme Court to exercise its constitutional administrative oversight duties by a mix of sticks and carrots. The sticks come in the form of rules and orders. The carrots come in the form of technology support and solutions, training, expertise, and some funding. Statewide access-to-justice improvements are thus extremely complicated; states with unified court systems have an enormous advantage in change management.

13.2 ACCESS-TO-JUSTICE EFFORTS IN MICHIGAN IN THE BEFORE TIMES

Each year, about 1.5 million people enter Michigan courts seeking resolution of some civil legal issue, and many do so without representation. In 2019, our trial courts handled about 105,000 domestic-relation cases, 35,000 adult personal-protective orders, 53,000 small-claims cases (up to $6,500), 209,000 landlord-tenant summary proceedings (including evictions), 6,000 housing and real estate matters (including foreclosures), 18,000 adult conservatorships and guardianships, and over a million civil infractions.[15] When we add in criminal cases, the number of cases trial courts are adjudicating annually is between 3 and 4 million.

While our trial courts do not measure the number of self-represented litigants, surveys and studies both in Michigan and nationwide show that self-representation is very common in all of these case types. For example, a survey of the 42,000 divorce cases filed in Michigan in 2013 found that 48 percent of complaints were filed by self-represented people, 68 percent of cases had one or more self-represented parties,

[13] *Michigan Judicial Data Warehouse Project*, COURTLAND CONSULTING (Aug. 6, 2012), https://court2018.devcourtland.com/project-management-and-training-delivered-for-michigan-supreme-court-for-jdw-project/.

[14] An early presentation by the team building the JDW that captures some of this complexity can be seen at Jewel Garrett, *Michigan's Judicial Data Warehouse (JDW)*, SLIDEPLAYER, https://slideplayer.com/slide/12237647/.

[15] Caseload report available at 2019 STATISTICAL SUPPLEMENTS, MICH. CTS., https://www.courts.michigan.gov/publications/statistics-and-reports/caseload-reports/statistical-supplements/2019-statistical-supplement/.

and 42 percent of cases had no attorneys involved at all, on either side.[16] In other case types, self-representation is asymmetrical. A recent analysis of eviction cases in Michigan from 2014 to 2018 found that only 4.8 percent of tenants were represented by an attorney. Landlords, on the other hand, were represented in 83.2 percent of cases.[17]

Before the pandemic there were significant ongoing efforts to address this civil justice gap, by the Bar, the Court, and traditional legal aid funders. The State Bar of Michigan helps connect attorneys with pro bono opportunities for persons with limited financial means,[18] and the Bar has several standing committees that focus on access-to-justice issues specifically.[19] A separate institution, the Michigan State Bar Foundation (MSBF), provides grants to legal aid programs around the state.[20] These include five regional legal programs that take on various cases, as well as several statewide programs that focus on serving specific populations such as migrant farmworkers, Native Americans, and older adults. And Michigan's five law schools have over forty-six clinical programs, many of which focus on serving clients who cannot afford an attorney.[21] Along with direct representation, these organizations and institutions have a robust record of promoting access to justice through policy advocacy, amicus briefs, and service as advisers to the courts and policy makers.

There have also been less-traditional efforts to better address the civil justice gap, and some of these efforts leverage technology.

13.2.1 *Michigan Legal Help*

In 2012 the Court partnered with the State Bar to launch "Michigan Legal Help," a website designed to provide practical, easy-to-follow information for people with civil legal problems who lack the resources to obtain an attorney (or who simply prefer to self-represent).[22] The foundational idea for Michigan Legal Help is that promoting access to justice means helping those with legal problems get the information they need to successfully navigate their problem, even if they don't need or cannot obtain an attorney. So many legal processes require a litigant to have a specific document, filed at the right time and in the proper place. Making sure

16 Kerry Sheldon, Bridgeport Consulting, LLC, Michigan Legal Help Evaluation Report 15–21 (2015), https://mplp.org/sites/default/files/2020-02/michigan-legal-help-evaluation-report-1-15.pdf.

17 Robert Goodspeed et al., Poverty Solutions University of Michigan, Michigan Evictions: Trends, Data Sources, and Neighborhood Determinants (2020), https://poverty.umich.edu/files/2020/06/Michigan-Eviction-Project-working-paper-1.pdf.

18 *Legal Resource and Referral Center*, *State Bar of Mich.*, https://lrs.michbar.org/.

19 *Committees*, *State Bar of Mich.*, https://www.michbar.org/generalinfo/committees.

20 Mich. State Bar Found., www.msbf.org/.

21 State Bar of Mich., Law School Clinics in Michigan (2020), https://www.michbar.org/file/programs/atj/pdfs/lawschoolclinics.pdf.

22 *Welcome*, *Mich. Legal Help*, https://michiganlegalhelp.org/.

people know what they need to do and giving them the tools to do it can go a long way.

By design, Michigan Legal Help does not provide legal "advice." Instead, it provides topical information, forms, and dozens of "do-it-yourself" tool kits for *specific* legal problems. For example, there are tool kits for obtaining a divorce if you have minor children, another tool kit if there are no children, and a tool kit on how to respond to a complaint for divorce. The materials are constantly updated to reflect changes in the law, court rules, and real-world trends. There is an article on "Zoom hearings" that includes information on what to expect and tips on how to connect. A legal triage system – the "Guide to Legal Help" – is built into the website and directs users to specific resources based on their responses to a series of short, easy-to-understand questions. On weekdays, a "live help" chat feature staffed by volunteer law students provides personal assistance to help people find what they need; on weekends and after hours, users can leave messages that an agent will respond to. Michigan Legal Help staff members train the student volunteers and review the chat conversations to ensure quality control for the hundred-plus live chat sessions and a similar number of overnight emails that the system sees each day. Michigan Legal Help is also affiliated with (physical) legal self-help centers located around the state, where users can get assistance navigating the site and completing and filing documents.[23]

Michigan Legal Help has enormous, unique benefits as one tool in a civil justice response system. In addition to the obvious, Michigan Legal Help (and similar web-based programs) generate data that provides a window into current trends and needs, which can then be used to inform other access-to-justice efforts. It is agile and iterative; the tool kits, forms, and processes are updated and improved based on user experience. And, of course, it is infinitely scalable. Indeed, Michigan Legal Help is maintained by a staff of only eight people, including four attorneys. In 2020, it had nearly 3.5 million sessions, 2.7 million users, and 6.6 million page views. Nearly 153,000 people used its resources to complete legal forms. Even accounting for the "pandemic spike" of users in spring of 2020, most of whom accessed information on unemployment benefits, the website has seen year-to-year increases since its rollout in 2012.

13.2.2 *ADR/ODR*

Michigan has promoted court-supported alternative dispute resolution as another solution for some legal problems and leveraged technology to support it. Beginning in 2014, a first-in-the-nation pilot program introduced online ticket resolution in two district courts. Using a system pioneered by University of Michigan Professor

[23] An early evaluation of Michigan Legal Help's resources is available at SHELDON, MICHIGAN LEGAL HELP EVALUATION REPORT.

(and fellow volume contributor) J.J. Prescott, the program empowers residents to contest traffic tickets online. It is now offered in more than thirty district courts around the state.[24] Traditionally, ticketed drivers wanting to seek a dismissal or negotiate a reduction in penalties had to show up to court in-person; the only "remote" option was to accept responsibility and pay the ticket as issued. Through the online system, users can request a review of their citation, submit a statement, and upload photos or other information. According to a study of outcomes in six Michigan courts, this online ticket-review system reduces court staff time by 80 percent, and cases are resolved in an average of two weeks instead of seven. Most importantly, 39 percent of users reported that they would not have been able to come to the court in person.[25] Courts nationwide are now using this platform, and the service has been a critical tool in helping courts respond to the pandemic.[26]

In 2019, the Michigan Supreme Court used this same platform to launch "MI-Resolve" in seventeen Michigan counties.[27] MI-Resolve is a fully online, asynchronous, dispute resolution program designed to resolve minor disputes, such as small claims, debt collection, noneviction landlord-tenant matters (like the return of a security deposit), and neighborhood disputes. Unlike traditional court-referred or party-selected mediation, which is usually done in-person and involves a mediator whose services are paid for by the parties, MI-Resolve is free for the participants and can be done with or without a mediator. The program is confidential and can be used regardless of whether there is active litigation. If the participants agree to a particular resolution, the system will produce a binding agreement and also generate any necessary forms for filing in court.

Michigan has led the way in online dispute resolution (ODR) programs like MI-Resolve, but experiences in other jurisdictions also show that ODR can provide an efficient and affordable way of resolving cases that do not involve complicated legal questions and where the amount at issue is modest. In 2020, the Joint Technology Committee of the Conference of State Court Administrators (COSCA), the National Association for Court Management (NACM), and the National Center for State Courts (NCSC) published case studies from ODR

[24] In Michigan, Washtenaw County's 14A District Court and Bay County's 74th District Court were the first in the nation to launch online ticket resolution in 2014.

[25] *Ticket and Minor Infraction Resolution Results: Multiple Courts*, MATTERHORN, https://getmatterhorn.com/get-results/traffic-court/ticket-minor-infraction-resolution-results/; J.J. Prescott, *Improving Access to Justice in State Courts with Platform Technology*, 70 VAND. L. REV. 30, 1993 (2017).

[26] That was the case in New York's Manhattan Civil Court, where all small claims cases less than $10,000 are referred to the program instead of to jam-packed courtrooms. Jane Wester, *Pilot Program Will Bring Online Resolution Option to Manhattan Small Claims Litigants, NY Court Leaders Say*, N.Y. L.J. (Jan. 27, 2021), https://www.law.com/newyorklawjournal/2021/01/27/pilot-program-will-bring-online-resolution-option-to-manhattan-small-claims-litigants-ny-court-leaders-say/.

[27] *Resolve a Dispute Online with MI-Resolve*, MICH. CTS., https://www.courts.michigan.gov/administration/offices/office-of-dispute-resolution/mi-resolve/.

programs across the nation.[28] In Franklin County, Ohio, use of ODR for city income tax cases led to fewer default judgments and a more even distribution of positive case dispositions regardless of socioeconomic factors and race.[29] Utah used ODR as part of a total restructuring of its court system's process for resolving small claims. The program has led to fewer hearings and faster dispositions in cases that do end up "in court."[30] In Connecticut, ODR has been used to create an online ticket review program for traffic court. Most ticket recipients chose to "opt into" the program, which has shortened the number of days from citation to adjudication.[31]

13.2.3 *SCAO's IT Solutions for Local Courts and Filers Depend on Agile Culture*

There have also been significant efforts in Michigan to transform the user experience of "traditional" court with technology solutions. Even without the benefit of a unified court system, the SCAO's technology division has partnered with private sector firms to speed up development and implementation of IT solutions that connect Michigan's courts with each other and with users, while improving the experience for both. If we could successfully provide excellent IT products and service to trial courts, we could make progress toward voluntary technological unification – carrots. But it means a fundamental transformation of our approach to IT. We are all familiar with government IT projects that promise to revolutionize process but fall short of expectations. Instead, we consulted private sector firms to bring agile culture to our public sector operation.

SCAO adopted Menlo Innovations' "high-tech anthropology."[32] Just as smartphone apps undergo continuous incremental updates that don't involve any inconvenience or loss of service, so too our court technology solutions improve as users provide feedback. We visit local courts and watch clerks, judges, and court users to see how they used our products and solicit their ideas to improve efficiency and service to the public. Agility is unusual in government IT and contrasts with the previous approach of taking down systems over a holiday weekend and launching a new platform on Monday morning. It limits risk, engages users, and steadily provides value-add, allowing for constant updates and changes with each iteration.

The agile process has been critical as we expand our case management product (MiCourt) to judges and court administrators who can be resistant to change.

28 Joint Tech. Comm., JTC Resource Bulletin: Case Studies in ODR for Courts (2020), https://www.ncsc.org/__data/assets/pdf_file/0033/39579/JTC-Resource-Bulletin-Case-Studies.pdf.

29 Prescott & Sanchez, *Platform Procedure*, at 30.

30 Deno Himonas, *Utah's Online Dispute Resolution Program*, 122 Dick. L. Rev. 875 (2018).

31 *Online Dispute Resolution, State of Conn. Judicial Branch*, https://www.jud.ct.gov/odr/.

32 *High-Tech Anthropology: Balancing User and Business Goals to Design Solutions, Menlo Innovations*, https://menloinnovations.com/services/high-tech-anthropology.

By engaging users for their input throughout the process, our developers benefit from on-the-ground knowledge and experience, and buy-in eases change. As a result, we have provided new features users asked for, including automatic calendaring, electronic docket boards, public dockets, case search, and text-message reminders of upcoming court dates and payments due. We are also using the agile approach to launch a new public website this spring that emphasizes mobile device use, which provides better and equal access to information for all users, as well as security, speed, and improved information architecture.[33]

The success of MiCOURT can be measured both by the satisfaction of court users, but also by the expansion of the case management system to courts throughout the state as they learn about the unique, value-added features not provided by their current systems. And, as the list of MiCOURT courts grows, system-wide change becomes easier and more efficient.[34] A single case management system – our ultimate goal – creates enormous potential for statewide improvement. It will allow for real-time access to comprehensive court data, statewide process updates, and a simpler system for court users. *That's* the holy grail.

To be sure, the picture is not all rosy. Michigan does not yet have statewide e-filing, and it will be another few years before that project is finished. Locally funded courts and locally selected IT systems mean that a statewide, online, case-filing system that aims to provide a consistent user experience for all filers in the state, regardless of jurisdiction and case type, is a heavy lift. Several counties had home-grown e-filing systems and electronic document management systems, while others continue to be limited to paper files. In other words, we are getting there, but it's a slog.

13.2.4 *Justice for All Taskforce*

The State Bar of Michigan (MSBF), the Bar's access-to-justice arm, and other access-to-justice oriented entities (like legal aid and law school clinics) traditionally collaborated through informal networks, not a formal structure. As a result, there had been no comprehensive assessment of the civil justice gaps and needs across the state, nor a measure of how the various programs and innovations were meeting the need.

33 Following agile precepts, the new One Court of Justice website will reflect interviews with both content users and content creators and is deliberately flexible and iterative to allow for constant improvement and additional features over time. MICH. CTS.: ONE CT. OF JUSTICE, https://www.courts.michigan.gov/.

34 While Michigan has 242 trial courts, there are 319 trial court locations, since some courts have more than one building. This fact adds further complexity to IT systems and the challenge of integrating them. Of the 319 locations, 65 of them (~20 percent) are not on the SCAO/JIS/MiCOURT system.

In May 2019, the Michigan Supreme Court formed a task force to change that by conducting a full assessment of the current state of our civil justice system. Partnering with the MSBF and Michigan Legal Help, and with funding from the National Center for State Courts (NCSC), the task force set out to do a comprehensive statewide inventory of resources for civil legal problems, as well as identify the gaps in those resources. The task force was charged with developing a strategic plan to address the legal needs of every Michigander.

* * *

Heading into 2020, the task force felt that access to justice was a priority in Michigan and that the community of lawyers, judges, administrators, and technologists working on it were looking for innovative solutions to civil justice problems. Despite structural barriers, progress was being made. We would not have declared the problem solved, but we were optimistic about what we might accomplish. We were working diligently on pockets of innovation, as well as an overall strategy. And yet, transformational change was not really on our radar.[35]

13.3 COVID-19: A ONCE-IN-A-LIFETIME DISRUPTION

Then came March 2020. All of a sudden, courts had to pivot on a dime to do things differently. And (maybe to our surprise) we did.

In Michigan we were fortunate to have a running start. In 2010 the SCAO began implementing a videoconferencing project to equip at least one circuit, probate, and district courtroom in every jurisdiction. A year before the pandemic, we had distributed Zoom licenses to every trial court judge. This was not because we were clairvoyant, but because we had identified the potential for increased accessibility and efficiency.

As a result, in March 2020 every Michigan trial judge was equipped to quickly move their proceedings to the Zoom platform. We followed up by acquiring licenses for magistrates and quasi-judicial officers. We partnered with clerks and county commissions to develop training material and best practices for judges and court staff.[36] We suspended rules and processes that were barriers to remote proceedings.

To maintain public access, virtual hearings were made available on YouTube, either live-streamed or uploaded right after. In May 2020 the Court built and

[35] I have thoughts about why that was in addition to the structural barriers I have already described, but it might be for a different essay. Here's the short version: resistance to change in law is unlike in other industries for cultural, normative, and even legal reasons. *See* Chapters 1 and 2 in this volume.

[36] Memorandum from Thomas P. Boyd, State Court Administrator, on Virtual Courtroom Task Force Documents (Aug. 7, 2020), https://www.courts.michigan.gov/4b000e/siteassets/covid/covid-19/08-07-20updatedresources.pdf.

launched an online Virtual Courtroom Directory.[37] Using the agile approach, a project that typically would have taken at least six months went from concept to launch in three weeks. At first, the functionality was a map with green dots showing where courts were livestreaming. The directory grew into a fully functional application that allows users to click on a county, search for a court or judge, and find out if live proceedings are ongoing. Using the directory, users can search by judge or by location (county). Search results include a link to the court's YouTube stream and show whether the court is "in session." If the "live" button is lit up, users can click and watch. Anyone with an internet connection can easily find and watch the proceedings in any trial court.

Very quickly, judges, court administrators, and litigants discovered what worked online and what didn't. The SCAO also organized more than fifty stakeholders in a work group to participate in a remote mock jury trial that generated detailed advice and guidance for courts.[38] Zoom proceedings work extremely well for some types of proceedings (motion hearings, status conferences, scheduling, civil trials, and so on) and less well for others (criminal jury trials). This aligned with our experience during the pandemic. For example, participants in guardianship and conservatorship hearings reported increased satisfaction with access and the ability to participate. There is preliminary evidence that online jury proceedings can increase jury participation and representation because those who do not have transportation or have to care for children or parents have more flexibility in serving.[39]

The results of this technology-driven push to keep courts open were dramatic. By the end of 2021, our trial courts had conducted nearly 5 million hours of online hearings. Michigan residents have used the Virtual Courtroom Directory to find a hearing on YouTube more than 450,000 times. Collectively, trial court YouTube channels have nearly 185,000 subscribers.

We also significantly sped up our efforts to move MI-Resolve to the remaining sixty-six counties in the state. By July it was available in every county, making Michigan the first to have a statewide ODR. To date, over 1,000 cases have been filed in the system, and nearly 100 are pending. Increasing numbers of judges are now including in their orders that mediation can be conducted on MI-Resolve.[40] Local mediation centers are promoting the service on kiosks, billboards, and by

37 MICH. VIRTUAL COURTROOM DIRECTORY, https://micourt.courts.michigan.gov/virtualcourtroomdirectory/.

38 STATE CT. ADMIN. OFF., MICHIGAN TRIAL COURTS REMOTE JURY TRIAL STANDARDS AND RECOMMENDATIONS (2020), https://www.courts.michigan.gov/4a11f3/siteassets/court-administration/standardsguidelines/operations/rjtrialstandardsrecommendations.pdf.

39 *See* RICHARD GABRIEL, ONLINE COURTROOM PROJECT: THE ONLINE COURTROOM AND THE FUTURE OF JURY TRIALS, https://www.courts.wa.gov/newsinfo/content/Reference%20Materials/Online%20Courtroom%20Project%20White%20Paper.pdf; *see also* Chapters 4 and 10 in this volume.

40 *Online Dispute Resolution, 27TH DIST. CT.*, http://www.wyandotte.net/departments/online_dispute_resolution.php.

highlighting the MI-Resolve web address on community partners' websites.[41] Promotional materials have also been distributed to local housing authorities, emergency service providers, and police agencies, so that they can provide the information to parties needing help resolving disputes.

Not only were we able to keep our courts operating; we could showcase the benefits that technology can provide to court users. Virtual hearings reduced or eliminated transportation and parking problems, as well as childcare and work conflicts. Recording the proceedings was seamless, and the number of people who could witness any hearing was endless; more than 7,300 people watched live a court hearing on a challenge to the governor's emergency powers.[42] And, frankly, the experience promoted digital literacy among judges and court staff.

Pandemic innovations were not only technology-based. For one example, we worked swiftly with the other government branches to establish a statewide eviction diversion program, funded by the American Rescue Plan Act and Michigan's COVID Emergency Rental Assistance program, which is anticipated to help over 50,000 families remain in their homes.[43] We even exported the model to other states: Texas and Indiana followed our model.

13.4 PROMISE OF SIGNIFICANT REFORM

The Justice for All Taskforce continued its work through the pandemic, adjusting to remote platforms. The task force held in-person and virtual meetings and focus groups with judges, court staff, attorneys, and community organization staff members. It participated in town hall–style gatherings in Michigan's two largest cities. It surveyed, interviewed, and focus-grouped members of the public about their experiences within the civil justice system.

[41] *See, e.g.*, *MI Resolve: A New Way to Resolve Disputes Online: Sponsored by the Michigan Supreme Court Administrative Office*, CMTY. MEDIATION SERVS., https://www.mimediation.com/mi-resolve; Jack Springgate, *New MI Resolve Kiosks Making Small Claims Disputes Easier for Berrien County Residents*, 16 NEWS NOW WNDU (Apr. 7, 2021), https://www.wndu.com/2021/04/07/new-mi-resolve-kiosks-making-small-claims-disputes-easier-for-berrien-county-residents/.

[42] The video has been viewed nearly 50,000 times. Michigan Court of Claims, *May 15, 2020, Court of Claims Hearing: Michigan Legislature vs. Governor #20-000079-MZ*, YOUTUBE (May 15, 2020), https://www.youtube.com/watch?v=ooIVrwU8kio.

[43] Priority Treatment and New Procedure for Landlord/Tenant Cases, Administrative Order No. 2020-17 (June 9, 2020); Amendment of Administrative Order 2020-17 (June 24, 2020); Amendment of Administrative Order 2020-17 (Oct. 22, 2020); Amendment of Administrative Order 2020-17 (Dec. 29, 2020); Amendment of Administrative Order 2020-17 (Jan. 30, 2021); Amendment of Administrative Order 2020-17 (Mar. 22, 2021); Amendment of Administrative Order 2020-17 (Apr. 9, 2021); Amendment of Administrative Order 2020-17 (July 2, 2021); Rescission of Administrative Orders Nos. 2020-1, 2020-6, 2020-9, 2020-13, 2020-14, 2020-19, and 2020-21 and Amendments of Rules 2.002, 2.107, 2.305, 2.407, 2.506, 2.621, 3.904, 6.006, 6.106, 6.425, 8.110, 9.112, 9.115, and 9.221 of the Michigan Court Rules and Administrative Order No. 2020-17 (July 26, 2021).

The Taskforce delivered its report in December 2020.[44] Following guidance materials developed by the NCSC,[45] the Taskforce prepared a comprehensive assessment of fifteen interrelated civil justice system components, such as the integration of Michigan courts within the broader community of services, provision of legal assistance without involving an attorney, education of private attorneys about fee-reducing business models like limited-scope representation, and training of judges and court staff on how to engage with self-represented litigants effectively. The assessment found that while Michigan had made substantial progress on some components (especially highlighting the extensive efforts of Michigan Legal Help across a wide range of topics), not one of the fifteen was more than partially accomplished. Several key areas showed minimal progress, including little progress on emerging practices and innovations and a lack of navigator services.

For each component, the Taskforce identified gaps and barriers in our existing system and made specific recommendations for improvement. These steps range from the easy, obvious, and nontechnical, such as simplifying the language in hundreds of court forms or transforming courthouses as service-oriented institutions by having multilingual signage and a "courthouse concierge" role distinct from the clerk's office. Many more of the recommendations, also highly achievable, rely on technology in one form or another: integrating self-help programs (physical and virtual) with a statewide e-filing program that is available to self-represented litigants and not just attorneys, revising court rules and procedures to maintain virtual hearings even after the pandemic, and providing publicly usable computers and printers in every courtroom (like the public library). Still others, both nontech and tech, are more difficult and potentially politically treacherous, like regulatory reform – that is, a relaxation of some of the rules that govern law practice – to give non-attorney "legal navigators" the ability to help clients handle simple legal problems.[46] Regulatory reform could extend to software-based service delivery models, too.

The Taskforce set an ambitious target of achieving 100 percent access to the civil justice system. Our goal isn't to provide a lawyer for each and every person; rather, we aim to ensure that, wherever possible, the civil justice system provides information, tools, and resources for those who self-represent.

Finally, the Taskforce identified that a key stumbling block to comprehensive change is the lack of a permanent infrastructure between and among access-to-justice stakeholders. A month later, in January 2021, the Michigan Supreme Court created the Michigan Justice for All Commission, a thirty-member commission of

[44] Mich. Justice for All Task Force, Strategic Plan and Inventory Report (2020), https://www.courts.michigan.gov/4af54d/siteassets/committees,-boards-special-initiatves/justiceforall/final-jfa-report-121420.pdf.

[45] Justice For All, NCSC Justice for All Initiative Guidance Materials (Nov. 2019), https://www.ncsc.org/__data/assets/pdf_file/0021/25464/pdf-jfa-guidance-materials.pdf.

[46] *See* Chapter 1 in this volume.

judges, court administrators, legislators, state executive officials, legal aid attorneys, and community and business leaders.

* * *

The changes that have taken place in courtrooms and across the state judiciary and access-to-justice community during the pandemic are more significant than any that had taken place over many decades. We learned that sometimes different is better. And all this has taken place while our hair was on fire. It has us convinced that a lot more is possible.

13.4 CHALLENGES THAT REMAIN

And yet significant barriers remain to growing access and making these changes permanent.

Some of these are cultural, maybe for judges most of all. While our judges and court staff responded admirably to the immediate challenge of the pandemic, I hear regularly from judges who "can't wait to get back to how we used to do it." I understand that sentiment: After all, judicial reasoning often depends on respecting decisions that have been made in the past, and many of our rituals are rooted in history and tradition. Being slow to change is a feature, not a bug.

Take one recent specific example. In 2019, the Michigan Supreme Court published for comment a proposed court rule that would allow non-attorneys to possess portable electronic devices (laptops, tablets, smartphones) inside a courtroom and use them to take notes, access the Internet, and make electronic copies of public records.[47] Previously, rules governing use of these devices varied widely based on locality. For self-represented litigants, restricting them to pen and paper was a barrier to access – one that was not imposed on attorneys (and therefore not on litigants who could afford attorneys). The push for change came from the public and the access-to-justice community. The resistance came from the bench. Some judges feared that allowing these devices into our buildings would lead to disrupted proceedings and diminish the "sanctity of the courtroom." Others argued that such decision-making should occur at the local level – that a one-size-fits-all approach was inappropriate. Despite this pushback, we adopted the rule change in January 2020 – a happy ending. It all seems unremarkable in hindsight. And it shows that state high courts can compel change in their administrative oversight role.

But the episode also suggests that more comprehensive reform will require trial court leaders – local judges and administrators – who see as their roles to drive change from the ground up. And not all judges view engaging with the community, gauging its needs and concerns, and proactively responding to them as part of the

[47] Mich. Comp. Laws § 8.115 (2022).

court's primary mission. While specialized dockets that emphasize problem-solving (like drug courts) have enjoyed support from local communities, many judges still take a hands-off approach to community engagement. In my experience, this judicial reluctance is driven, at least in part, by the idea that a disengaged court is also impartial, or at the very least appears so. There is also a concern that judicial leadership on issues of local concern will run into charges of "judicial activism." But courts aren't insulated from the realities of life, and judges who engage their communities are better able to understand the ways in which a justice system can respond to community needs.[48]

There are other barriers, too. Funding remains a significant hurdle to reform, especially as state and local governments continue to struggle with the financial consequences of the pandemic.[49] Persuading legislatures who control state judicial budgets means convincing skeptical policy makers that expanding access to justice can return economic benefits, as well as social ones. Sometimes the pitch is an easy one: New technologies such as virtual hearings promise efficiencies, for both courts and litigants alike. Other changes and programs require more nuance, and the economic benefits can be harder to quantify. Court leaders should consider engaging nontraditional stakeholders. For example, employers understand the benefits of an employee able to join a court hearing from the workplace, instead of needing a day off; the business community is a logical ally for court modernization.

New access issues unique to remote hearings and online processes will also need attention. Rural communities are already underserved when it comes to legal aid.[50] These same communities often have limited or unreliable internet access. The pandemic has made this plain. Implementing change will require unique efforts for the technologically challenged.

Finally, until state justice systems collect good data, comprehensive reform will be elusive. Measuring rates of self-represented litigants is challenging, as is defining and tracking the type of data outputs that are necessary for evaluating the performance of programs attempting to expand access to justice.[51] What is "fair" or "effective" can be highly contextual and is often (partially) subjective, and there is seldom adequate historical data to compare against. For states with disunified court systems, the challenge of developing data collection standards and mechanisms is even greater. Data collected through programs like Michigan Legal Help can help fill that void,

48 Bridget Mary McCormack, *Staying Off the Sidelines: Judges as Agents for Justice System Reform*, 131 Yale L.J.F., 175 (2021).

49 Legal Aid Interagency Roundtable, Access to Justice in the Age of COVID-19: A Roundtable Report 13 (2021), https://www.justice.gov/ag/page/file/1445356/download.

50 Michele Statz et al., *"They Had Access, but They Didn't Get Justice": Why Prevailing Access to Justice Initiatives Fail Rural Americans*, 18 Geo. J. Poverty L. & Pol'y 321 (2021); Michele Statz & Paula Termuhlen, *Rural Legal Deserts Are a Critical Health Determinant*, 110 Am. J. Pub. Health 1519 (2020); Robin Runge, *Addressing the Access to Justice Crisis in Rural America*, A.B.A. Hum. Rts. Mag., August 2014, at 15.

51 *See* Chapter 16 in this volume.

but that data is only as good as the number of people who know about the service. Similarly, data and resource-sharing between and among access-to-justice stakeholders can be limited. Each may not have the time, resources, or expertise to collect and analyze data, even when they recognize the many ways that better data can improve their services. Courts and state Bar leaders can play a role by creating or facilitating an infrastructure through which separate players can collaborate with one another.[52] Better data is critical to effective change.

13.5 SO NOW WHAT?

Despite the significant barriers that remain, there is reason to hope that we are at an inflection point for access to justice and that lasting, disruptive change is possible.

First, feedback to pandemic-driven changes has been overwhelmingly positive. Litigants and attorneys like remote proceedings not because they are technophiles, but because of the advantages that remote proceedings can provide. This new normal has beaten back inertia. Usually the cat doesn't get back in the bag; there will be no backtracking to the old way of doing business now that courts, lawyers, and the public have seen the advantages technology has brought to access and transparency. Many courts and legislatures are speaking openly about making permanent changes that were implemented as temporary, emergency measures.

Second, and perhaps more importantly, the pandemic forced us – judges, administrators, and lawyers – to think about our work differently. The pandemic has brought innovation to how we work. That skill, too, won't be unlearned. As COVID-19 subsides, the ability to use remote platforms will allow courts to prioritize in-person time to things that don't work remotely. This will help courts tackle backlogs: retired judges can preside in Zoom courtrooms from their homes, while local judges conduct jury trials in real courtrooms. The evidence that an entrepreneurial approach has taken root in the business of justice can be seen in many examples around the state. Consider these two.

In Washtenaw County, Michigan, a "mobile arraignment" program allowed a local magistrate to bring her courtroom to local community members who are homeless.[53] Partnering with a police officer with a smartphone, people in a local homeless shelter and even a local park were invited to clear up warrants with the officer's iPad tuning into the magistrate's courtroom. Legal documents were provided using a mobile printer. The roaming, tech-aided court operates weekly,

[52] *See* David Freeman Engstrom & R. J. Vogt, *The New Judicial Governance: Courts, Data, and the Future of Civil Justice*, 71 DePaul L. Rev. (forthcoming 2022).

[53] Meredith Bruckner, *Ann Arbor Police Offer Mobile Arraignment Program during COVID-19 Pandemic*, All About Ann Arbor (Nov. 10, 2020), https://www.clickondetroit.com/all-about-ann-arbor/2020/11/10/ann-arbor-police-offer-new-mobile-arraignment-program-during-covid-19-pandemic/.

serving members of the community most likely to have trouble navigating their justice system.

In East Lansing, Michigan, a local district court administrator who noticed how members of the public appreciated remote proceedings set up a virtual helpdesk. On the court's website, users can choose the virtual helpdesk and then enter into a Zoom room where a clerk is waiting to answer questions, look up documents, and give instructions. People can get information previously available only by visiting the courthouse during work hours.[54] The response has been overwhelmingly positive.

Third, there is recent agreement about the importance of data to reform, and resistance to sharing data has receded tremendously. In 2020, the Conference of State Court Administrators and the National Center for State Courts published the National Open Court Data Standards to support the creation, sharing, and integration of court data.[55] And, the National Center has convened a group of state court leaders and academics to share information and data to see what lessons we can learn from all of the change. It is hard to overstate how different this approach is. There is both better and more data, a groundswell of interest, and agreement about how important data is to better our systems.

Fourth, as much as infrastructure barriers remain, there is potential for significant funding for overhaul, as a result of policy makers' responses to the pandemic. Just as state and federal lawmakers quickly devoted funding to address the pandemic-caused eviction crisis, concerns about backlogs and realization that change is possible can spur funding to move state court systems beyond the clunky, data-poor, and ad hoc systems that have prevented large-scale reform.

Fifth, many states are exploring regulatory reforms that will allow testing of some of the bigger-picture solutions to our access-to-justice problem. Two major changes occurred just last year. Acting on recommendations from a task force on the delivery of legal services, the Arizona Supreme Court approved the creation of a new type of non-lawyer licensee that can provide (limited) legal services.[56] In neighboring Utah, the state supreme court established a new regulatory body (under the authority and oversight of the court) to license and oversee new types of legal providers and services through a so-called regulatory sandbox structure.[57] As noted previously, Michigan's Justice for All Taskforce report recommended the creation of nonlawyer "legal navigators," and the Commission has a working regulatory reform group. These experiments are perfectly timed, as we look for new ways of structuring the

[54] *54B District Court*, City of E. Lansing, https://www.cityofeastlansing.com/676/54B-District-Court.

[55] Nat'l Ctr. for State Cts., National Open Court Data Standards: User Guide (2020), https://www.ncsc.org/__data/assets/pdf_file/0014/34025/NODS-User-Guide.pdf.

[56] *Legal Paraprofessional Program*, *Ariz. Jud. Branch*, https://www.azcourts.gov/Licensing-Regulation/Legal-Paraprofessional-Program.

[57] *What We Do*, The Off. of Legal Servs. Innovation, https://utahinnovationoffice.org/about/what-we-do/.

service of justice by welcoming new providers into the system, whether non-lawyer humans of the "legal navigator" sort, software-based systems that have begun to show promise as a way to serve self-represented litigants, or new models yet to come.

Finally, there is a national conversation afoot about all of this that includes academics and practitioners, technologists, and designers, activists, and advocates. That much is plain from the collection of voices in this volume. We have been shaken loose in a way to think creatively, and we like it. We are working collaboratively. And while many voices out in the states calling for change can be powerful, a "champion" in Washington, DC, to advocate for continued transformation that builds trust in our nation's busiest courts is another important part of a national solution. The Department of Justice's renewed Access to Justice Office could well serve that role.[58]

As the pandemic (hopefully) recedes into something manageably endemic, the takeaway for our courts cannot be "the old way, but with Zoom." Technology is an important tool in building a civil justice system with access for all. But we have to think about what kind of civil justice system we would build if we could start over. The moment to do that is right now.

13.6 POSTSCRIPT

The COVID-19 vaccine rollout was still nascent when I drafted this essay in early 2021. Since then we have witnessed the vaccination of hundreds of millions of Americans, along with new coronavirus variants that have caused continued case surges and updated guidance from public health officials. Courthouses have begun the careful process of reopening their (physical) doors, even if sometimes temporarily closing them again. The roller-coaster continues, but there is unquestionably good news after an exhausting year.

During that time, I invited fellow state high court justices and their court administrators to participate in an informal survey. My goal was to capture their thoughts about technology changes spurred by the pandemic. The responses – from twenty-six of my colleagues from courts around the nation – have been illuminating.[59]

When I asked what they perceived as the main barriers to adoption of court technology prior to the pandemic, almost all respondents cited funding (no surprise there), with reluctance among judges and court administrators a close second (about 75 percent). Those rates dropped in half when I asked the same question, but this time since the pandemic began. As one court administrator put it, "oddly enough,

58 *Office for Access to Justice*, U.S. DEP'T OF JUSTICE, https://www.justice.gov/archives/atj.

59 The questions and responses can be viewed at the following link. *Court Structure and Technology Survey*, GOOGLE FORMS, https://docs.google.com/forms/d/e/1FAIpQLSe301axNkikpMGcQzy5ntYlh3UxGqXVK5iFjHq-taLg1yyrvg/viewanalytics.

our barriers weren't really barriers when we were forced with the need to do it." Hopefully, an instance where perception *is* reality.

I asked questions about the adoption of specific technological solutions. Self-help resources and ODR were widely used before the pandemic, with a slightly higher percentage (increases of ~10 percent) answering that their court systems put these technologies to use since the pandemic began. The biggest increase was in the use of automated text-message systems that remind litigants about their court dates. About half of respondents indicated that such services were used before the pandemic, while 70 percent of all respondents said that these services were used as of spring 2021. About two-thirds of respondents whose states had implemented this technology credited it as improving appearance rates among self-represented litigants. For jurisdictions that have yet to adopt text reminders, the off-the-shelf commercial availability makes it low-hanging fruit.

Unsurprisingly, many respondents indicated that little-to-no court business was conducted online prior to the pandemic (excluding purely voice communications, such as VoIP), and where videoconferencing was used, it was highly limited (for incarcerated litigants, involuntary civil commitment, etc.). Survey-takers reported higher participation with the change to remote access necessitated by the pandemic.

Very few respondents (about 10 percent) collected data from litigants about the litigants' personal satisfaction with court access and the perceived fairness of the proceedings. I note this in particular because the pandemic required many courts to either create or build out already-existing virtual platforms. I don't mean to suggest that "customer satisfaction" is the only measure by which courts should be graded, especially in an adversarial legal system. But for self-represented litigants especially, satisfaction with the process can be just as important as the outcome.[60] Questionnaires can help identify potential areas for improvement without compromising ex parte communication, and digital platforms adopted during the pandemic offer a seamless means of delivering them to litigants.

The survey was done on a short timeline, but I see reason for cautious optimism in the answers I received. As in-person proceedings resume, I'll end on this note for judges, court administrators, and lawyers: We can't allow the lessons learned and the skills developed over the pandemic to go to waste.

60 *See* Kevin S. Burke and Steve Leben, *Procedural Fairness in a Pandemic: It's Still Critical to Public Trust*, 68 DRAKE L. REV. 685 (2020) (discussing research on procedural fairness and its relation to litigant satisfaction and urging courts to adhere to procedural fairness principles during and after the COVID-19 pandemic).

14

Free PACER

Jonah B. Gelbach

Data can fuel innovation. The next generation of legal scholars will stand not just on the shoulders of their forbears, but – hopefully – on the structural foundation created by access to the electronic public record. When they "surf to the courthouse door," they should find it open.[1]

This is the worst of the best of times for federal court data. Docket reports are compiled electronically, and the overwhelming number of documents are filed electronically using the CM/ECF system. Litigants, attorneys, and members of the public can obtain case information using searches of the Judiciary's PACER system, which stands for Public Access to Court Electronic Records. Not so long ago, none of these things was possible; people had to travel to the courthouse and conduct or request laborious searches for case information. But access is so much less than it could be, and this sorry state of affairs is the result of deliberate policy choices. We should free PACER's data, making federal litigation data free to the same public whose judicial system creates and stores those data.

Much of my case is based on a general argument about the value of providing free public access, especially to the scholars and journalists whose analysis can help monitor and improve our justice system. But there's a tech-specific case, too. Freeing PACER would broaden access to data, possibly allowing the development of accessible, affordable legal technology for the "have-nots" as well as those without the budgets necessary to collect or purchase their own data.[2]

Still, my focus in this chapter is on two other aspects of access to justice. First, the public's access to the way the justice system operates: access for those who measure,

1 Proposed Brief Amicus Curiae for The American Association of Law Libraries, In Support of Plaintiffs' Motion for Summary Judgment at 13, Nat'l Veterans Legal Servs. Program, v. United States, 291 F. Supp. 3d 123 (D.D.C. 2018) (No. 1:16-CV-00745).

2 For consideration of the distributional effects of legal tech in general, *see* David Freeman Engstrom & Jonah B. Gelbach, *Legal Tech, Civil Procedure, and the Future of Adversarialism*, 169 U. Pa. L. Rev. 1001 (2021).

monitor, and evaluate the justice system as a whole. The second aspect is society's access to data-driven improvements in the justice system. Without access to large amounts of litigation data, society will forgo the gains from having scholars and journalists assess our judicial system's performance; anecdotes and surmise will rule the roost. I take as given that scholarship and journalism can help us evaluate and improve the justice we mete out. Thus, better data access gives us access to better justice by allowing us to better understand, better design, and better operate our justice system. For these reasons, this essay will focus on the case for freeing access to court data, especially for scholars.[3]

My argument is mercifully simple: The various policies and practices that have limited access to PACER for the past three decades have, as the Supreme Court once put it in an unrelated context, earned their retirement.[4] PACER began as an experimental dial-up system in 1988 before taking flight on the World Wide Web ten years later. It's been a long flight, actually. Though PACER has radically expanded public access compared to the status quo ante a third of a century ago, PACER searches cost too much for users and deliver too little. Its search functionality is roughly the same as it was back when. You can't search the text of docket entries, for example, much less the contents of filed documents. With some useful exceptions, PACER keeps our judicial system's public records behind a kludgy and unjustifiably high paywall.

PACER costs so much because in 1988, when Congress allowed the Judiciary to provide electronic public access, it directed the Judiciary to fund the initiative through user fees.[5] Happily, Congress could fix that problem with simple statutory text, and the fee revenues are so small relative to federal spending[6] that Congress needn't give a thought to whether it would break a sweat thinking about the question. Congress should mandate free PACER and cut the Judiciary a check large enough to replace the lost revenue. Problem solved.

* * *

3 This essay focuses on federal court data and on scholars' access because those are the data and the users' needs I know best. That said, I believe the case for open access to court data is no weaker with respect to state and local courts, or with respect to journalists' access.

4 *Cf.* Bell Atlantic Corp. v. Twombly, 550 U.S. 544, 563 (2007) (declaring that "after puzzling the profession for 50 years, [*Conley v. Gibson*'s] famous observation has earned its retirement").

5 *Frequently Asked Questions*, PUB. ACCESS TO CT. ELEC. RECS., https://pacer.uscourts.gov/help/faqs/why-does-pacer-charge-fee. The Judiciary's current obligations and discretion in this sphere are creatures of the E-Government Act of 2002; for background, *see, e.g.*, Stephen J. Schultze, *The Price of Ignorance: The Constitutional Cost of Fees for Access to Electronic Public Court Records*, 106 GEO. L.J. 1197 (2018). Whether PACER's fees fit within the scope of that statute is a matter of ongoing controversy, with litigation pending about whether PACER fees are unlawfully, or just indefensibly, high; various lawsuits have been filed related to this question. One case was recently remanded to the district court after the Court of Appeals affirmed the district court's denial of cross motions for summary judgment. National Veterans Legal Servs. Program v. United States, 968 F.3d 1340 (Fed. Cir. 2020).

6 *See* discussion in Section 14.3, *infra*.

Section 14.1 of this chapter provides a brief discussion of PACER's history and present. In Section 14.2 I argue that opening PACER up to the public, with a focus on scholarly access, would lead to a greater quantity of research on the federal courts while also allowing scholars to carry out higher-quality studies.[7] It is time to unlock the doors to the benefits of open research on our justice system. Section 14.3 offers a vision for the future, centered on free access to PACER and direct funding of Judiciary activities to replace lost fee revenues, as well as fostering an attitude of openness in the Judiciary.

It's time to take down the paywall that divides judicial records and the public.

14.1 DIAGNOSING SCHOLARSHIP'S PACER PREDICAMENT

Litigation in most federal courts is managed through the Case Management/ Electronic Case Files (CM/ECF) system operated by the Administrative Office of the US Courts (AO).[8] Parties file pleadings, motions, and other case documents through CM/ECF; the Court also uploads documents to this system, and textual information about case status, scheduling, and so on, exists as docket entry text. PACER is an online system that allows members of the public to get case information, including both docket reports that list case activity and case documents.[9]

[7] I have expressed some skepticism about quantitative empirical studies' ability to answer interesting questions related to litigation, due to the fact that litigant behavior is endogenous to legal rules; *see, e.g.*, Jonah B. Gelbach, *Can the Dark Arts of the Dismal Science Shed Light on the Empirical Reality of Civil Procedure?* 2 STAN. J. COMPLEX LITIG. 223 (2014), and also argued that with the right combination of data and analytical thinking we can learn about causal effects of legal rules; *see, e.g.*, Jonah B. Gelbach, *Material Facts in the Debate over* Twombly *and* Iqbal, 68 STAN. L. REV. 369 (2016). Moreover, there are areas where even solid descriptive work would advance our understanding of federal litigation. *See, e.g.*, Jonah B. Gelbach & Deborah R. Hensler, *What We Don't Know about Class Actions but Hope to Know Soon*, 87 FORDHAM L. REV. 65 (2018).

[8] The Administrative Office of the United States Courts provides links to the CM/ECF system for the United District Courts, Judicial Panel on Multidistrict Litigation, Courts of Appeals, Bankruptcy Courts, Court of Federal Claims, and International Trade at *Court CM/ECF Lookup*, PUB. ACCESS TO. CT. ELEC. RECS., https://pacer.uscourts.gov/file-case/court-cmecf-lookup. The US Supreme Court maintains its own case management system. *See* SUP. CT. OF THE U.S., https://www.supremecourt.gov/filingandrules/faq_electronicfiling.aspx (providing details).

[9] The AO's webpage describing PACER is PUB. ACCESS TO CT. ELEC. RECS., https://www.uscourts.gov/court-records/find-case-pacer. Information not uploaded via CM/ECF is not available. For example, federal courts implemented CM/ECF at different times. *See, e.g.*, Gelbach, *Material Facts in the Debate over* Twombly *and* Iqbal, at 396 n.71. Other documents may be unavailable if filed under seal or for privacy reasons. *See* PUB. ACCESS TO. CT. ELEC. RECS., https://pacer.uscourts.gov/help/faqs/are-full-social-security-numbers-displayed-court-documents?page=3).

14.1.1 PACER Basics

PACER[10] began as a dial-up-based experiment in 1988 by the Judicial Conference,[11] at a time when the public had to go to physical courthouses for case information.[12] Because PACER isn't free to operate, and Congress doesn't appropriate funds for it,[13] the Judicial Conference has long charged fees for PACER use. Since 1998, PACER has been accessible through World Wide Web connections; the per-page fee for downloaded information is now $0.10.[14]

Such fees make large case-info downloads costly. By policy choice, the Judicial Conference limits fees in some ways; today, charges are capped at $3.00 per document.[15] In addition, PACER waives fees for any quarter in which a user incurs under $30 in charges.[16] Parties and their attorneys receive a free copy of any electronically filed document "if receipt is required by law or directed by the filer."[17] Judicial opinions are supposedly free for anyone's download,[18] although that may not always be true in practice.[19]

Unfortunately, these policies do little for scholars who must download many documents for their work. The Judicial Conference does allow courts to exempt some persons from fees, including "individual researchers associated with educational institutions,"[20] and exemptions have facilitated important research, but much less than broader scholarly access would allow.

10 Much/all of this discussion comes from National Veterans Legal Services Program v. U.S., 968 F.3d 1340 (Fed. Cir. 2020). For more on PACER and CM/ECF, see Schultze, *The Price of Ignorance*; J. Michael Greenwood & Gary Bockweg, *Insights to Building a Successful E-Filing Case Management Service: U.S. Federal Court Experience*, INT'L J. FOR CT. ADMIN., June 2012, at 2; John Brinkema & J. Michael Greenwood, *E-Filing Case Management Services in the US Federal Courts: The Next Generation: A Case Study*, INT'L J. FOR CT. ADMIN., July 2015, at 3.

11 *Nat'l Veterans Legal Servs. Program* ("The Judicial Conference, in 1988, first authorized an 'experimental program of electronic access for the public to court information.'") (citing JUD. CONF. OF THE U.S., REP. ON THE PROC. OF THE JUD. CONF. OF THE U.S. (1988), https://www.uscourts.gov/sites/default/files/reports_of_the_proceedings_1988-09_0.pdf).

12 *Nat'l Veterans Legal Servs. Program.*

13 *Id.*

14 *Id.* (citing *Electronic Public Access Fee Schedule*, U.S. CTS. (Dec. 31, 2019), https://www.uscourts.gov/services-forms/fees/electronic-public-access-fee-schedule).

15 *Electronic Public Access Fee Schedule*, U.S. CTS. (Dec. 31, 2019), https://www.Uscourts.Gov/Services-Forms/Fees/Electronic-Public-Access-Fee-Schedule.

16 *Id.*

17 *Id.*

18 *Id.*

19 *See* Peter W. Martin, *District Court Opinions That Remain Hidden Despite a Long-Standing Congressional Mandate of Transparency – the Result of Judicial Autonomy and Systemic Indifference*, 110 L. LIBR. J. 305 (2018).

20 *See Electronic Public Access Fee Schedule*, U.S. CTS. (Dec. 31, 2019), https://www.uscourts.gov/services-forms/fees/electronic-public-access-fee-schedule. Other persons are also eligible for exemptions, e.g., indigent persons and pro bono attorneys. *Id.*

14.1.2 *PACER Serves Up Case Records in a Clunky Way*

What PACER allows users to access remains far too limited. Critically, as the Free Law Project notes: "There is no document-level search."[21] And although PACER users can search for litigants' names or retrieve a case using a known docket number, it is impossible to search, say, for some version of "all cases that have at least one docket entry with the string 'FAILURE TO STATE A CLAIM' or 'QUALIFIED IMMUNITY.'" The Free Law Project observes: "This makes the system utterly unusable for general purpose research."[22] Anyone seeking to obtain data from many cases of a type – those with a Rule 12(b)(6) motion, or involving qualified immunity – must pay for enormous numbers of documents. This drains research budgets for no good reason.

14.1.3 *Financial Facts for PACER*

The Judiciary receives no funding from Congress for PACER, and the CM/ECF backbone is supported entirely by PACER fees. Each year these fees bring in around $150 million.[23] To put it mildly, that greatly exceeds the costs to the Judiciary of operating PACER, which one source recently put at $3 million.[24]

Who uses PACER? The Judiciary emphasizes PACER's enormous user base – more than 3 million user accounts, by 2020.[25] As of 2015, 75 percent of PACER *usage* was unpaid due to fee waivers (perhaps principally the $30/quarter free-usage allotment), even as 75 percent of PACER *revenues* came from fees paid by just 1 percent of account holders.[26] Although I am aware of no precise data, it's easy to guess that the biggest paying users include the big three electronic legal data vendors – Westlaw, LexisNexis, and BLAW – and bankruptcy data providers that service claimants' data needs. As of 2015, 63 percent of PACER usage was

21 Brian Carver, *What Is the "PACER Problem"?* Free L. Project (Mar. 24, 2015), https://free.law/2015/03/20/what-is-the-pacer-problem/.

22 *Id.*

23 *See, e.g.*, Judiciary Info. Tech. Fund, U.S. Cts., https://www.uscourts.gov/sites/default/files/fy_2020_jitf_0.pdf (providing 2020 estimate of $147.7 million in "Estimated Receipts and Prior Year Recoveries" for the revenue on "EPA Program," which includes PACER, in Table 11.1 at page 11.2).

24 Matt Ford, *The Courts Are Making a Killing on Public Records*, New Republic (Jan. 31, 2019), https://newrepublic.com/article/153003/courts-making-killing-public-records-pacer-fees.

25 *See Members of PACER User Group Selected*, U.S. Cts. (Jan. 9, 2020), https://www.uscourts.gov/news/2020/01/09/members-pacer-user-group-selected.

26 These figures come from my notes taken at the Increasing Access to Federal Court Data Workshop held at Penn Law in Fall 2015, memorialized in Jonah B. Gelbach, Final Report and Summary of Workshop on Increasing Access to Federal Court Data (on file with author) (also noting that as of 2015 there were roughly 2 million PACER user accounts). Other information about the grant, including the required Project Outcomes Report, may be viewed at https://tinyurl.com/yxcnzgzd.

undertaken by law firms, 12 percent by litigants themselves, 10 percent by commercial users, and only 3 percent by academics.[27] That academics use PACER so little is likely a testament to the fact that the large data pulls we need to do serious quantitative research would cost so much that most scholars either never start or rapidly abandon plans to study federal litigation using PACER data; *see* discussion in Sections 14.1.4 and 14.2.2 for more.

These facts paint a simple picture. PACER's paywall brings some money to the Judiciary, allowing Congress to fund it a bit less. The wall doesn't stop the biggest legal data vendors from downloading a lot of data, which they make available to subscribers who pay for platform access. The wall likely doesn't stop litigants in most individual cases, at least not with respect to their own cases. Nor does it likely do much to keep interested small-hobbyists out.[28] But the PACER paywall sure *does* screen out scholars.

14.1.4 *PACER Is Prohibitively Expensive for Scholars*

To study litigation, the judicial system, and how they interact with social phenomena, scholars need large amounts of data. Because of PACER's high per-page download fees, even projects involving relatively modest data can be very expensive.[29] To wit, a recent PACER fee waiver request estimates that to download only the docket sheets for just two years' worth of FOIA cases would cost nearly $4,000.[30] And consider a commentary recently published in *Science*,[31] which presents information on thousands of cases in which a party sought *in forma pauperis* status and shows considerable variation within districts in the likelihood such a waiver would be granted. The authors downloaded every docket report for all cases filed in 2016, at a cost they describe as "more than $100,000."[32] That won't become a common research strategy.

Although some research is conducted with second-best data sources (*see* section14.2.2, *infra*), I've had numerous conversations over the years with scholars who abandoned research ideas they thought promising because PACER's prohibitive costs made it too costly to push forward.

27 *Id*

28 It is possible that free PACER would attract new hobbyists interested in bigger data corpora, though.

29 Discretionary fee waivers might make a difference, if they were reliably and liberally granted, but it appears they aren't. *See* Section 14.2.2.

30 *In re* Application for Multi-Court Exemption from the Jud. Conf.'s Elec. Pub. Access (EPA) Fees, No. 5:20-mc-00134 (D. Vt. Dec. 7, 2020) (estimating each docket report to cost an average of $2, with roughly 1,900 cases).

31 Adam R. Pay et al., *How to Build a More Open Justice System*, 369 Science 134 (2020).

32 *Id.*

14.2 THE CASE FOR ACCESS TO COURT DATA

As a general matter, PACER's paywall is unfortunate and out of place in a democracy, but it's especially irrational as applied to scholars. Under the status quo, scholars contribute very little in the way of fee revenues, so there is close to nothing to lose from granting us access. On the other hand, we'd contribute a lot of free research if we were allowed access. And privacy risks seem limited given that all documents in question already may be downloaded by anyone who knows to look for them. In sum, right now the Judiciary and the public are getting nothing for something.

14.2.1 *On Principle, Court Operations Should Be Presumptively Open to the Public*

Publicity is the very soul of justice. It is to publicity, more than to everything else put together, that the English system of procedure owes its being the least bad system as yet extant, instead of being the worst.

– Jeremy Bentham[33]

It's a basic principle of a democratic society that government's operations should be open to public scrutiny. Otherwise, the citizenry cannot tell whether government is operating justly, speedily, or inexpensively.[34] Even appropriate scrutiny of one governmental branch by another can be limited without sufficient openness.

Constitutional and federal common law bases for public rights to observe judicial proceedings are most developed in the context of criminal trials,[35] but these are of course only one spot in the landscape of judicial proceedings. Of the nearly 80,000 federal criminal cases filed in 2018, only about 2 percent went to trial,[36] a number that isn't much different for civil cases. With so few trials, pretrial proceedings delineate the fairness and future incentive effects of federal litigation. Accordingly, whatever interests of publicness inhere in open trial proceedings also extend to pretrial ones, too.

[33] Garth Nettheim, *The Principle of Open Justice*, 8 U. TASMANIA L. REV. 25 (1984).

[34] *Cf.* FED. R. CIV. P. 1 (the Federal Rules of Civil Procedure "should be construed, administered, and employed by the court and the parties to secure the just, speedy, and inexpensive determination of every action and proceeding.").

[35] Peter W. Martin, *Online Access to Court Records – from Documents to Data, Particulars to Patterns*, 53 VILL. L. REV. 855, 857 (2008) (citing Richmond Newspapers, 448 U.S. 555, 570 (1980)).

[36] *See* John Gramlich, *Only 2% of Federal Criminal Defendants Go to Trial, and Most Who Do Are Found Guilty*, PEW RSCH. (June 11, 2019), https://www.pewresearch.org/fact-tank/2019/06/11/only-2-of-federal-criminal-defendants-go-to-trial-and-most-who-do-are-found-guilty/.

Professor Peter W. Martin has described five purposes for public access to litigation-related documents: (1) assuring fairness – both actual and perceived – of proceedings, (2) ensuring that the public's ability to assess and criticize judicial performance can be done on an informed basis, (3) educating the public about how litigation works, and – hopefully – inspiring confidence as a result, (4) enabling the "check[ing]" of the judicial system by the public, and (5) "[p]-roviding an outlet for community 'concern, hostility, and emotion' in cases that are in the public eye".[37] At least the first four of these are implicated in the Judiciary's refusal to allow affordable public access to PACER for scholarly or journalistic research.[38]

In sum, as House Judiciary Committee Chairman Jerrold Nadler recently stated: "It is a disservice that in today's digital age, the public's access to public records in public proceedings is so resource-intensive and burdensome .... It is indefensible that the public must pay fees – and unjustifiably high fees, at that – to know what is happening in their own courts."[39]

14.2.2 *Important Research Could Be Done with Freer Access, and for Free to the Judicial System*

This section provides a brief, ad hoc review of quantitative empirical work that has been done using federal court data.[40]

The Limits of Non-PACER Data Sources. Even before PACER, there was much quantitative empirical research published using federal court litigation data. A chief alternate data source is the Federal Judicial Center's Integrated Database (IDB), "by far the most prominent" of data sources used for statistical research by legal scholars.[41]

37 Martin, *Online Access to Court Records*, at 856–57 & n.5.

38 For an excellent discussion, see Schultze, *The Price of Ignorance*.

39 Chairman Nadler Statement for the Markup of H.R. 8235, the Open Courts Act of 2020, House Comm. on the Judiciary (Sept. 15, 2020), https://judiciary.house.gov/news/documentsingle.aspx?DocumentID=3346.

40 To be sure, quantitative research varies in quality, and assessments can and should be done by those focused on relevant substantive questions. An example of a problematic study is Christian Michael Smith et al., *The Most Discriminatory Federal Judges Give Black and Hispanic Defendants At Least Double the Sentences of White Defendants* (July 27, 2021), https://osf.io/download/61006a1f0c4cba01ccbc7224/?version=1&displayName=Judge%20Discrim%20Manuscript-2021-07-27T20%3A18%3A39.619Z.pdf. After I and others pointed out methodological problems, the authors withdrew the paper's references to individual judges and retitled it. *See* Christian Michael Smith et al., *Racial Disparities in Criminal Sentencing Vary Considerably across Federal Judges*, SocArXiv (2021), https://osf.io/preprints/socarxiv/j2gbn/. Nevertheless, I take the view that added capacity to do research with administrative records from the civil justice system is a net plus.

41 Frank B. Cross, *Comparative Judicial Databases*, 83 Judicature 248, 248 (2000).

Scholarly work using the IDB has spanned the gamut of topic areas for years.[42] But the IDB has its flaws.[43]

So, when FJC researchers set out to study summary judgment practice at the request of the Advisory Committee on Civil Rules in the wake of the Supreme Court's 1986 summary judgment trilogy, these researchers analyzed docket sheets randomly selected in three district courts.[44] Subsequent FJC studies of summary judgment practice also used docket information.[45] This is particularly notable because summary judgment dispositions are the sort of issue of interest not just to scholars or elected officials, but also to the Judiciary. In fact, the sort of data the FJC, and Professor Burbank,[46] has used to study summary judgment is the primary source of information for judges doing rule-making. Yet as intensive as this work was, it typically involved studying few districts, or even just one at a time.

The CM/ECF system now contains all data necessary to enable nationwide studies, and by 2008 (if not sooner), the FJC was doing so in response to Advisory

[42] *See, e.g.*, Miguel F. P. de Figueiredo, Alexandra D. Lahav & Peter Siegelman, *The Six-Month List and the Unintended Consequences of Judicial Accountability*, 105 CORNELL L. REV. 363 (2020); William H. J. Hubbard, *Testing for Change in Procedural Standards, with Application to* Bell Atlantic v. Twombly, 42 J. LEGAL STUD. 35, 49–53, 60 (2013); Jason Scott Johnston & Joel Waldfogel, *Does Repeat Play Elicit Cooperation? Evidence from Federal Civil Litigation*, 31 J. LEGAL STUD. 39 (2002); Warren E. Agin, *Predicting Chapter 11 Bankruptcy Case Outcomes Using the Federal Judicial Center IDB and Ensemble Artificial Intelligence*, 35 GA. ST. U.L. REV. 1093 (2019); Erica J. Hashimoto, *Defending the Right to Self-Representation: An Empirical Look at the Pro Se Felony Defendant*, 85 N.C. L. REV. 423 (2007); Theodore Eisenberg & Margo Schlanger, *The Reliability of the Administrative Office of the U.S. Courts Database: An Initial Empirical Analysis*, 78 NOTRE DAME L. REV. 1455 (2003).

[43] For one, it contains only data of a certain snapshot type – what can be reported at case beginning and termination. It can't, for example, tell us anything about summary judgment motions that don't terminate an action. Stephen B. Burbank, *Vanishing Trials and Summary Judgment in Federal Civil Cases: Drifting toward Bethlehem or Gomorrah?* 1 J. EMPIRICAL L. STUD. 591, 606 (2004). And Professor Gillian Hadfield's influential study provides compelling evidence to doubt the accuracy of even the disposition coding that the IDB does contain. Gillian K. Hadfield, *Where Have All the Trials Gone? Settlements, Nontrial Adjudications, and Statistical Artifacts in the Changing Disposition of Federal Civil Cases*, 1 J. EMPIRICAL L. STUD. 705 (2004).

[44] JOE S. CECIL & C. R. DOUGLAS, FED. JUD. CTR., SUMMARY JUDGMENT PRACTICE IN THREE DISTRICT COURTS 1, 3 (1987).

[45] *See, e.g.*, JOE S. CECIL, REBECCA N. EYRE, DEAN MILETICH & DAVID RINDSKOPF, FED. JUD. CTR., TRENDS IN SUMMARY JUDGMENT PRACTICE, 1975–2000 (2007), https://www.uscourts.gov/sites/default/files/summary_judgment_1975-2000.pdf; JOE S. CECIL, DEAN P. MILETICH & GEORGE CORT, FED. JUD. CTR., TRENDS IN SUMMARY JUDGMENT PRACTICE: A PRELIMINARY ANALYSIS (2001), https://www.law.umich.edu/facultyhome/margoschlanger/Documents/Resources/Sources_Datasets_American_Trial_Trends/Trends_Summary_Judgment_Practice_Preliminary_Analysis.pdf); Joe S. Cecil, Rebecca N. Eyre, Dean Miletich & David Rindskopf, *A Quarter-Century of Summary Judgment Practice in Six Federal District Courts*, 4 J. EMPIRICAL L. STUD. 861 (2007).

[46] *See* Burbank, *Vanishing Trials and Summary Judgment*.

Committee requests.[47] Due to PACER's paywall, though, outside researchers cannot generally do likewise. That means the Judiciary, and society more widely, are partly subject to the limits of FJC's resources, however impressive its ingenuity, in addressing matters of interest to rule-making.

Another area of great interest in which the IDB is limited is the pleading standard, whose alteration in *Bell Atlantic Corp. v. Twombly*[48] and *Ashcroft v. Iqbal*[49] was arguably the top focus of procedure scholars for a period of several years. As Professor Burbank wrote even before those cases, the IDB's limitations make it difficult, at best, to determine anything specific about Rule 12(b)(6) and 12(c) motions decided under the Rule 8(a)(2) pleading standard, including even "the number of such motions filed or decided."[50]

There are still other data sources for scholars studying the federal legal system, all with key limitations. For example, the US Sentencing Commission posts defendant-level data on sentences in federal criminal cases.[51] Interesting research has been conducted using these data, for example, on racial disparities and the federal sentencing guidelines.[52] But they obviously concern only criminal sentences. Judicial opinion databases are another source of data; in some cases these can be useful,[53] though it is well known that for many others this approach often brings bias given that only some opinions are published.[54] Another alternative is the Court Listener RECAP archive,[55] hosted by the Free Law Project, which contains

47 *See* Memorandum from Joe Cecil and George Cort to Judge Michael Baylson (Aug. 13, 2008), https://www.fjc.gov/sites/default/files/2012/SuJuLRS2.pdf.

48 550 U.S. 544 (2007).

49 556 U.S. 662 (2009).

50 Burbank, *Vanishing Trials and Summary Judgment*. That said, there are some authors that have used the IDB in an attempt to learn about the effects of *Twombly* and *Iqbal*. *See* Hubbard, *Testing for Change in Procedural Standards* (using the IDB only); William H. J. Hubbard, *The Effects of* Twombly *and* Iqbal, 14 J. Empirical Legal Stud. 474 (2017) (using the IDB together with data coded based on PACER downloads); Kevin M. Clermont & Theodore Eisenberg, *Plaintiphobia in the Supreme Court*, 100 Cornell Law Rev. 193 (2014).

51 *See Individual Offender Datafiles*, *U.S. Sent'g Comm'n*, https://www.ussc.gov/research/datafiles/commission-datafiles#individual.

52 *See, e.g.*, Joshua B. Fischman & Max M. Schanzenbach, *Racial Disparities under the Federal Sentencing Guidelines: The Role of Judicial Discretion and Mandatory Minimums*, 9 J. Empirical Leg. Stud. 729 (2012); Sonja B. Starr & M. Amrit Rehavi, *Racial Disparity in Federal Criminal Sentences*, 122 J. Pol. Econ. 1320 (2014).

53 *E.g.*, Theodore Eisenberg & Geoffrey P. Miller, *Attorney Fees in Class Action Settlements: An Empirical Study*, 1 J. Empirical Leg. Stud. 27, 44 (2004) (using Westlaw and Lexis searches to generate a data set of cases with class action settlements); *see also* Eric Helland & Jonathan Klick, *The Effect of Judicial Expedience on Attorney Fees in Class Actions*, 36 J. Legal Stud. 171 (2007) (using the Eisenberg & Miller data as one source in studying whether judges with crowded dockets are more likely to approve settlements).

54 Burbank, *Vanishing Trials and Summary Judgment*.

55 *Advanced RECAP Search*, *Ct. Listener*, https://www.courtlistener.com/recap/. For a colorful history of the development of RECAP, see Stephen Schultze, *PACER, RECAP, and the Movement to Free American Case Law*, VoxPopuLII (Feb. 3, 2011), https://blog.law.cornell.edu/voxpop/2011/02/03/pacer-recap-and-the-movement-to-free-american-case-law.

"millions of PACER documents and dockets"[56] and grows over time as more users use RECAP, even as users are able to avoid paying for documents that RECAP already has.[57] As great a resource as RECAP is for documents that have been stored, there is no general way to measure how representative RECAP's sample of documents and docket reports is.[58]

PACER's Unrealized Potential. This brings me to work using all of PACER, or representative samples. Bankruptcy has been a prolific substantive area for empirical study, due in part to the enterprising efforts of Professors Teresa Sullivan, Elizabeth Warren, and Jay Westbrook. The challenges surmounted in this work are described engagingly by Professor Lynn LoPucki. In brief, the professors flew themselves and some photocopiers around the country, copied court files in the clerks' offices, and sent the copies to Austin, Texas, where they coded the information they would use – even though copy machines in the clerks' offices were unused after hours.[59] In 2001, after PACER's advent, the same researchers were able to secure judicial permission to hire "moonlighting assistant clerks to photocopy the files and ship the copies," because that allowed them to avoid PACER's per-page download fees.[60] As Professor LoPucki writes, "With the political constraints removed by judges, the 1981 technology – photocopying in the clerks' offices – was cheaper than the 2001 technology – internet PACER – with its one-page-at-a-time political restriction."[61] In sum, at enormous and duplicative cost, these researchers were able to obtain substantial data on bankruptcy cases. They used these data to publish numerous studies about an issue of great public policy concern.[62] Subsequent research on consumer bankruptcy reform was able to use both PACER fee waivers[63] – obviously a welcome development – and help from AACER, the Automated Access to Court Electronic Records, a service that collects bankruptcy court data on a daily basis and repackages

[56] *Advanced RECAP Search*, CT. LISTENER, https://www.courtlistener.com/recap/ (public landing page encouraging visitors to "Search our database of millions of PACER documents and dockets").

[57] RECAP has some additional, though limited, docket information provided by federal courts via RSS feeds. Rebecca Fordon, *RSS Feeds, PACER, and the Fight for Access to Federal Docket Information*, RIPS L. LIBR. BLOG (Sept. 16, 2020), https://ripslawlibrarian.wordpress.com/2020/09/16/rss-feeds-pacer-and-the-fight-for-access-to-federal-docket-information/.

[58] That has not stopped thoughtful researchers from using RECAP data for projects in which representativeness may not be critical. *See, e.g.*, Christina L. Boyd & David A. Hoffman, *The Use and Reliability of Federal Nature of Suit Codes*, 2017 MICH. ST. L. REV. 997.

[59] Lynn M. LoPucki, *The Politics of Research Access to Federal Court Data*, 80 TEX. L. REV. 2161, 2166–67 (2001).

[60] *Id.*

[61] *Id.*

[62] These include both books and scholarly articles. *See, e.g.*, TERESA A. SULLIVAN, ELIZABETH WARREN & JAY L. WESTBROOK, AS WE FORGIVE OUR DEBTORS (1989); Elizabeth Warren & Jay L. Westbrook, *Financial Characteristics of Businesses in Bankruptcy*, 73 AM. BANKR. L.J. 499 (1999).

[63] Robert M. Lawless et al., *Did Bankruptcy Reform Fail? An Empirical Study of Consumer Debtors*, 82 AM. BANKR. L.J. 349, 354 (2008).

it commercially.[64] AACER must itself pay the Judiciary to download data that are already in the PACER system, but the facts of the bankruptcy system evidently make it possible for market forces to sustain AACER's more rational approach to data distribution. There is little prospect for such a market solution to PACER's paywall for nonbankruptcy cases (and would-be users must still pay AACER).

Other scholarly work has been published using the fruits of PACER fee waivers. Examples include work by Professor David Engstrom,[65] Professor Gillian Hadfield,[66] and Professor Alexander Reinert.[67] But PACER fee waivers are at most a partial solution to the PACER paywall, and a highly imperfect one at that. Even though there is now a centralized process for requesting a fee waiver,[68] the decision over whether to grant requested waivers is up to individual district courts.[69] This can extend the time and uncertainty related to project feasibility. It results from the fact that the CM/ECF system underlying PACER is really an amalgamation of individual systems, each run by an individual court as it sees fit. It is hard to think of good reasons why one court would deny fee waivers for the same scholarly research another approves, yet that happens.[70] Further, my conversations with other scholars indicate the possibility of inconsistent treatment. For example, although Professor Lawless and his coauthors received fee waivers from all but the Southern District of Texas,[71] one scholar at a workshop on federal court data access that I organized in 2015[72] reported being unable to receive fee waivers from more than thirty-five of the ninety-four district courts.[73] Study of the Supreme Court's alteration of the pleading

64 *Id.*

65 *See* David F. Engstrom, *Public Regulation of Private Enforcement: Empirical Analysis of DOJ Oversight of* Qui Tam *Litigation under the False Claims Act*, 107 Nw. U. L. Rev. 1689 (2013). Professor Engstrom confirmed to me that he obtained such waivers for this paper and two companions.

66 Hadfield, *Where Have All the Trials Gone?*

67 Alexander A. Reinert, *Measuring the Impact of Plausibility Pleading*, 101 Va. L. Rev. 2117 (2015).

68 *Application for Multi-Court Exemption from the Judicial Conference's Electronic Public Access (EPA) Fees*, Jud. Conf. of U.S., https://pacer.uscourts.gov/sites/default/files/files/MultiCourt%20Exemption%20Request.pdf. Previously, exemptions had to be requested court by court. The multi-court exemption application mechanism is a recent development, perhaps the result of a constructive response by the AO to feedback from scholars. *See* Project Outcomes Report.

69 *See, e.g.*, Order Granting PACER Waiver, *In re* Application for Multi-Court Exemption from the Jud. Conf.'s Elec. Pub. Access (EPA) Fees, No. 5:20-mc-00134-gwc (D.Vt. Dec. 7, 2020), ECF No. 2.

70 David Freeman Engstrom, *The* Twiqbal *Puzzle and Empirical Study of Civil Procedure*, 65 Stan. L. Rev. 1203, 1248 (2013) (recounting one judge's statement that the relevant district court had a "long-standing policy not to grant exemptions to [PACER fees] for research" and characterizing such a "categorical unwillingness . . . to support empirical research designed to improve the administration of civil justice [a]s an embarrassment that calls out for correction by Congress or the Judicial Conference").

71 Lawless et al., *Did Bankruptcy Reform Fail?* at 354 n.23.

72 Increasing Access to Federal Court Data Workshop.

73 Gelbach, *Final Report and Summary of Workshop*.

standard in *Twombly* and *Iqbal* also shows PACER's potential, and the limitations of its alternatives.[74]

Another anecdote involves a July 2020 request by Plymouth State University Professors Chantalle Forgues and Daniel Lee for PACER fee waivers so they could download docket reports, complaints, and petitions for all New England district courts.[75] The scholars planned to use computer programs to target a subset of cases as classified using Nature of Suit codes.[76] All district courts petitioned granted the request except for the District of Massachusetts.[77] Events over several months culminated in a court order denying the professors' request,[78] because of the Chief Judge's belief that the researchers planned to use software that, "according to our IT security personnel, would present an unacceptable degree of risk to our system."[79] Professors Forgues and Lee explained that "the script that petitioners propose is used everyday, including on weekends, to download files from PACER. The script at issue is used by big law firms and larger universities on a regular basis, and has been used on the Court's system consistently for over seven (7) years."[80] A motion seeking reconsideration remains pending.[81]

The upshot of all of this is two-fold. First, bulk downloads are available, without limit, to users who can afford to pay PACER fees, even as federal courts create situations in which researchers who cannot afford PACER fees are out of luck. More generally, the PACER system, and judicial policies and practices around it, stymie what would otherwise be PACER's staggering research potential. PACER contains

74 *See* text accompanying note 50. See also reports including Joe S. Cecil et al., Fed. Jud. Ctr., Motions to Dismiss for Failure to State a Claim after *Iqbal* (2011), https://www.uscourts.gov/sites/default/files/motioniqbal_1.pdf; Joe S. Cecil et al., Fed. Jud. Ctr., Update on Resolution of Rule 12(B)(6) Motions Granted With Leave to Amend (2011), http://masonlec.org/site/rte_uploads/files/Gelbach_FJC%2012b6.pdf, which were based on access to PACER. These reports provoked considerable debate given the controversy related to the Supreme Court's actions in *Twombly* and *Iqbal*. Unfortunately, despite indications that it would release the underlying data, to my knowledge the FJC has never released even the docket numbers of the cases studied. That hamstrung other researchers and meant that further work would be delayed and costly in time and/or money. *See, e.g.*, Reinert, *Measuring the Impact of Plausibility Pleading* (performing an independent analysis of the issues and courts studied by the FJC, using PACER fee waivers to allow him to obtain data, but ultimately being able to obtain fee waivers for only fifteen of the twenty-three district courts the FJC included).

75 Petitioners' Memorandum in Support of Motion to Alter or Amend Judgment, or in the Alternative Motion for Relief from Judgment or Order at 1, *In re* Application for Exemption from Elec. Pub. Access Fees for Chantalle R. Forgues, Daniel Lee, and Plymouth State University, No. 20-mc-91510-FDS (D. Mass. Dec. 31, 2020), ECF No. 7.

76 *Id.*

77 *Id.* at 1–2.

78 *Id.*

79 *Id.* at 6 (quoting Letter from F. Dennis Saylor IV, Chief J. U.S. Dist. Ct. D. Mass. (Dec. 4, 2020)).

80 *Id.* at 7.

81 *Id.* at 10.

over a billion documents,[82] and that number grows daily. Many other federal agencies have made their data available, with privacy restrictions, allowing the public to benefit from enormous amounts of professional-quality research at no cost to the federal government.[83] The many examples of research noted above – from enterprising bankruptcy scholarship to illuminating work on summary judgment and pleading to work on trials – hint at the possibilities presented by piercing PACER's paywall. This research, much of it using inferior or limited sources of data, is a drop in the bucket compared to what we could have with free PACER.

14.2.3 *What about Privacy?*

A natural basis for concern about free PACER involves privacy of both litigants and witnesses. This essay is not the place to fully develop either the bases for such concerns, which are real, or the responses to them. But engaging these topics can allay certain aspects of these concerns while informing further inquiry as to others.

A first concern involves risks in the criminal justice system. Stephen Schultze chronicles one example:

> In 2006, the Department of Justice (DOJ) observed a disturbing new phenomenon: anonymous individuals had begun to use PACER to cull and republish witness information. DOJ stated in a letter to the Judicial Conference, "we are witnessing the rise of a new cottage industry engaged in republishing court filings about cooperators on websites such as www.whosarat.com for the clear purpose of witness intimidation, retaliation, and harassment." DOJ urged the Judiciary to suppress public access to all plea agreements.[84]

What DOJ wanted to preserve is what is sometimes called "practical obscurity" – "print-era barriers to access to sensitive criminal information."[85] After describing how federal judges engaged these questions, including at the level of the Judicial Conference's Court Administration and Case Management Committee, Schultze observes that "by the time whosarat.com appeared in newspaper headlines, the Judicial Conference had codified its approach to sensitive information in electronic court records," with the result that the Justice Department "could protect sensitive plea agreements by sealing or redacting the documents, but it could not rely on the Judiciary to recreate anachronistic approximations of practical obscurity."[86]

If this balance between privacy concerns and public access is good enough for those who might be at risk of physical violence, it is difficult to see why it should not

82 *See* Sup. Ct. of U.S., 2014 Year-End Report on the Federal Judiciary 6 (2014), https://www.supremecourt.gov/publicinfo/year-end/2014year-endreport.pdf.
83 Some of that research may be supported by public grant funding, but plenty of it is not.
84 Schultze, *The Price of Ignorance*, at 1206.
85 *Id.*
86 *Id.*

also be good enough for others in the justice system. This is especially true in the civil context, where concerns related to personal embarrassment or trade secret interests can be handled on a case-by-case basis. Just as the Freedom of Information Act contains exceptions for trade secrets and certain other delicate information,[87] so, too, may federal courts allow litigants to file documents under seal in appropriate circumstances.

The privacy case for limiting access to PACER records en masse seems especially weak given that the very same records are *already available electronically*. To the extent that practical obscurity exists now, it is thus limited only by PACER fees. The paywall does not protect anyone from PACER's large commercial buyers, including, for example, bankruptcy-related services such as AACER. But these fees are high enough to keep out scholars, most of whom have little to no interest in individual information – the point of much scholarly research being to generalize rather than investigate details of unknown persons. It also includes journalists, which places PACER in tension with the First Amendment values that animate the constitutional basis for open court records that the Supreme Court found in *Richmond Newspapers, Inc. v. Virginia*.[88]

14.3 A VISION FOR THE FUTURE

I'm hardly the first one to advocate dismantling PACER's paywall. More than a decade ago, Professor LoPucki argued that eliminating the paywall "would open a real-time window on court-system operation superior to any previously possible," with the happy result that "[n]ot only researchers, but parties, lawyers, the government, and the public could see every important aspect of how the courts operate."[89] The Free Law Project has long argued that there is a "PACER problem."[90] Other scholars are on the case, in both academic journals and popular media.[91] Litigation that could reduce the magnitude of PACER fees – shorten the paywall – has had

[87] 5 U.S.C. § 552(b)(4); *see also* Christopher S. Yoo, Protected Materials in Public Rulemaking Dockets 113 (2020), https://www.acus.gov/sites/default/files/documents/Christopher%20Yoo%20FINAL%20REPORT%2011%2023%202020.pdf (discussing balancing of public disclosure interests against privacy interests).

[88] Richmond Newspapers, Inc. v. Virginia, 448 U.S. 555 (1980). For more on *Richmond Newspapers*, and on privacy issues related to the case for freeing PACER, *see* Schultze, *The Price of Ignorance*.

[89] LoPucki, *Court-System Transparency*, at 537.

[90] Carver, *What Is the "PACER Problem"?*.

[91] *See, e.g.*, *Hearing before the U.S. House of Representatives Judiciary Committee Subcommittee on Courts, Intellectual Property, and the Internet*, 116th Cong. (2019) (statement of Michelle Cosby, President of the American Association of Law Libraries), https://www.aallnet.org/wp-content/uploads/2019/09/AALL-Statement-for-HJC-Hearing-Record-092619.pdf; Sarath Sanga & David Schwartz, *Tear Down This Judicial Paywall*, Wall Street J. (Dec. 13, 2020), https://www.wsj.com/articles/tear-down-this-judicial-paywall-11607900423.

some success and is ongoing.[92] And as I discuss momentarily, there is a real chance that Congress will finally act to free PACER.

But what should a freed PACER regime look like? My purpose in this Section is to provide some suggestions. If anything like the Open Courts Act makes it into law, then some of these suggestions will have been either taken or eclipsed. Others would still be up for consideration if, as seems likely, Congress left the AO with substantial discretion in choosing how to make court records publicly available. Some of the possibilities I raise are concrete. The last section, though, is a meditation on the need for the Judiciary to adopt a new institutional attitude favoring openness. That could go a long way.

14.3.1 *Free PACER and Replace Its Fees with General Revenue*

Encouragingly, in December 2021 the Open Courts Act of 2021 was reported out of the Senate Judiciary Committee with bipartisan support.[93] This bill would require all court documents to be presumptively freely accessible to the public within three years after enactment.[94] The bill also calls for modernization of PACER's feature set,[95] and a similar bill is pending in the US House as of this writing.[96] Although the costs of modernization might be offset partly by congressional appropriations,[97] future funding would need to come from fees paid by federal agencies for their PACER use, based on inflation-adjusted fees agencies paid in 2018,[98] and possibly also increases in filing fees on parties.[99]

I have doubts about this approach to funding. First, I have not been able to find a breakdown of PACER fees by source, but logic indicates that fees paid by federal agencies are only part of the revenue from PACER. Thus, without increasing filing fees, the Judiciary would absorb at least some revenue loss. My goal is to free PACER, not cut courts. Second, if the Judiciary exercised the authority the Open Courts Act provides to raise filing fees, that burden would fall on litigants. My goal is to free PACER, not raise additional financial barriers to courts.

The better course is for Congress to simply (1) eliminate the Judiciary's discretion to charge PACER fees and (2) increase general revenue funds for the Judiciary.

92 Nat'l Veterans Legal Servs. Program v. United States, 968 F.3d 1340 (Fed. Cir. 2020).

93 *See* Nate Raymond, *Free PACER? Bill to End Fees for Online Court Records Advances in Senate* (December 9, 2021), https://www.reuters.com/legal/legalindustry/free-pacer-bill-end-fees-online-court-records-advances-senate-2021-12-09/.

94 Open Courts Act of 2021, S. 2614, 117th Cong. § 3(a) (2021).

95 *Id.* § 2.

96 Open Courts Act of 2021, H.R. 5844, 117th Cong. (2021).

97 Raymond, *Free PACER?*

98 S. 2614, § 3(d)(1).

99 *Id.*

Congress could hold the Judiciary harmless, replacing all PACER paywall revenues, for just $150 million.[100]

Although $150 million would be a lot of money to have for yourself, it's a teeny-tiny little droplet in congressional terms. By way of comparison, Americans spend roughly twenty-five times as much on wild bird food as PACER fees brought in.[101] And overall congressional funding to the Judiciary in 2020 was fifty times what the PACER paywall brought in.[102]

A situation in which we have hamstrung public inquiry into the functioning of the federal litigation system over a literal rounding error may not be funny, but it really is silly. Let's stop it already. Congress should just cut an annual check to the Judiciary, allowing the public to better understand – and better inform Congress – how one of the three branches of our government functions.[103] It wouldn't even make a dent in the monthly auction of Treasury debt, and it would allow the Judiciary to free PACER and lose nothing.[104]

14.3.2 *Infrastructure Improvements*

As I discuss above, one of the real problems with PACER is that it provides very limited search capacity. The House bill introduced in the last Congress had modernization features directed at this problem,[105] and the Senate bill spoke

[100] *See, e.g.*, Judiciary Info. Tech. Fund (providing 2020 estimate of $147.7 million in "Estimated Receipts and Prior Year Recoveries" for the revenue on "EPA Program," which includes PACER, in Table 11.1 at page 11.2).

[101] U.S. Fish & Wildlife Serv., 2016 National Survey of Fishing, Hunting, and Wildlife-Associated Recreation 90 tbl.39 (2016), https://www.census.gov/content/dam/Census/library/publications/2018/demo/fhw16-nat.pdf (reporting $4 billion in such spending in 2016).

[102] *Federal Court Funding*, A.B.A. (Dec. 31, 2020), https://www.americanbar.org/advocacy/governmental_legislative_work/priorities_policy/independence_of_the_judiciary/federal-court-funding/.

[103] *See also* Sanga & Schwartz, *Tear Down This Judicial Paywall* (proposing abolition of PACER fees and advocating that "[t]o cover the shortfall, Congress should increase judicial appropriations accordingly").

[104] If Congress won't do that, the Judiciary should find other ways to increase access. It could, for example, eliminate fees for all documents and information docketed more than – say – a year earlier. That would probably preserve the Judiciary's ability to charge substantial download fees, assuming that the institutional customers that pay most of the fees need data quickly. And the operating cost to the Judiciary of ensuring that PACER's contents are available to the public for useful research is easy to approximate: zero dollars and zero cents. That's true because the Internet Archive has already offered to host the data for free; *see* Caitlin Olson, *Internet Archive Offers to Host PACER Data*, Internet Archive Blogs (Feb. 13, 2017), http://blog.archive.org/2017/02/13/internet-archive-offers-to-host-pacer-data/ (printing Feb. 10, 2017 letter from Brewster Kahle making this offer).

One can think of other smaller-loaf alternatives. For example, the Judiciary could release one or more random samples of documents, perhaps using case-level sampling to allow case-level study. Or it could provide restricted-use access with an approval process, as some other federal agencies do.

[105] H.R. 8235, 116th Cong. § 2(b) (2020).

generally of improvements in "data accessibility ... and performance."[106] Not knowing anything about PACER's back-end design and capabilities, I don't know whether its lack of a docket-entry or document text search function is a bug or is deliberate. But there are surely many nonprofit organizations that would and could host the data. As noted, the Internet Archive has already offered to do so for free, and to do so with considerably better functionality than PACER currently has.

There are other infrastructure improvements that the Judiciary could make. Some require more burden than others. Less demanding would be more refined docketing, for example, allowing docket coding for motions to dismiss according to the basis for the motion. On the high end would be redesigned forms such as the civil cover sheet, requiring more and/or better information from litigants.

A group of professors recently discussed many of the pathologies I have already described, in *Science* magazine.[107] They advocate a "collaborative research agenda to empower the public to access and analyze court records."[108] This agenda includes better organization of the data because of the fact that court records tend to include unstructured text. The professors advocate developing

> applications that not only support scholars and researchers who may want to analyze the data but also enable members of the judiciary, entrepreneurs, journalists, potential litigants, and concerned citizens to learn more about the functioning of the courts. To support inquiries made by the public, we should develop applications that can process natural language queries such as "What are the most recent data privacy cases?" or "How often do police officers invoke qualified immunity?"[109]

So there are surely a range of other infrastructure improvements worth considering. My purpose here is only to suggest that more about PACER than just the paywall can be improved.

14.3.3 *The Judiciary Should Adopt an Attitude of Openness*

Certainly there are many judges who embrace openness. Judges have approved many, perhaps even most, PACER fee waivers that scholars have actually submitted to the courts. An amicus brief by retired judges in the ongoing PACER class-action litigation indicates laudable support for public access to court data.[110] Over the years, I have had numerous conversations with professionals at the FJC and AO that indicate a range of support between partial and complete for providing more data access.

[106] S. 2064, 116th Cong. § 3(b)(1) (2019).
[107] Pah et al., *How to Build a More Open Justice System*.
[108] *Id.* at 135.
[109] *Id.* at 136.
[110] Brief of Retired Federal Judges as Amici Curiae in Support of Neither Party, Nat'l Veterans Legal Servs. Program v. United States, No. 19-1081 (Fed. Cir. Jan. 23, 2019), ECF No. 26.

At the same time, it is hard not to read a message of opposition from some of the Judiciary's choices, including setting PACER fees at an unnecessarily high level, opposition to legislation that would increase PACER access (including by circulating boilerplate "talking points" for federal judges to use in lobbying members of Congress),[111] and anecdotal evidence that some judges may reject openness as a categorical matter.[112]

My own experience is at least partially consistent with that picture, and it suggests that this rejection exists not only among particular judges, but also as an institutional fact. In 2015 I attended two workshops about access to federal court data. The first was one I organized at Penn Law, which was funded by the National Science Foundation,[113] and the second was the Federal Courts Civil Data Project Roundtable, which was held in Washington, DC, and hosted by the ABA Standing Committee on the American Judicial System and the Duke Law Center for Judicial Studies. Participants at one or both of these workshops included federal judges; academics who work with federal data; staff researchers and/or attorneys from federal agencies including the Federal Judicial Center, the AO, the Administrative Conference of the United States; a representative from the National Center for State Courts; and Michael Lissner, executive director of the Free Law Project. I have limited space to describe my impressions of the views of the Judiciary's representatives at these events. There were a variety of views, but it seems clear that AO representatives harbor skepticism about the economic, bureaucratic, and technological feasibility of opening up PACER (though the multi-court fee waiver exemption process that now exists occurred not too long after these events).[114]

In addition, at the ABA event, one Article III judge spoke forcefully against additional PACER access. This judge, whom I know from prior communications to be a devoted public servant, pointed to the example of a news story about a colleague that the judge thought was both unfair and professionally embarrassing. The judge at the conference expressed sincere and profound concern that the judiciary would be unduly pressured in this and other ways by the public availability of additional data that could be searched and filtered easily.

[111] *See* John Eggerton, *Fix the Court: Judges Are Lobbying against PACER Reform Bill*, MULTICHANNEL NEWS (Dec. 1, 2020), https://www.nexttv.com/news/fix-the-court-judges-are-lobbying-against-pacer-reform-bill.

[112] *See, e.g.*, Engstrom, *The* Twiqbal *Puzzle*; text accompanying note 75 (discussing *In re Application for Exemption from Electronic Public Access Fees for Chantalle R. Forgues, Daniel Lee, and Plymouth State University*).

[113] Increasing Access to Federal Court Data Workshop.

[114] For a somewhat longer discussion, see Jonah B. Gelbach, *Comments about Two 2015 Workshops on Federal Court Data*, JONAHGELBACH.COM (May 5, 2021, 5:00 PM EST), https://www.jonahgelbach.com/blog#h.6fappsisbbol. Interested readers may also find a discussion of the unfortunate judicial response to my attempts to obtain nationwide data about the demographic composition of jury pools. Jonah B. Gelbach, *Comments about Attempts to Obtain Data from District Court AO12 Forms*, JONAHGELBACH.COM (May 10, 2021, 2:39 PM EST), https://www.jonahgelbach.com/blog#h.1xufllwzpd24.

There is some evidence that the Civil Justice Reform Act distorts how judges approach their dockets, perhaps to avoid embarrassment.[115] I'm an economist who believes that people generally respond to incentives, so I'm not surprised. Even so, Article III judges have substantial constitutional protections precisely to allow them to buck public pressure and embarrassment in the service of judicial independence. Most obviously, they have life tenure, and their salaries cannot be reduced.[116] Their jobs carry considerable prestige, and no small amount of power; Chief Justice Stone once remarked, "the only protection against unwise decisions, and even judicial usurpation, is careful scrutiny of their action and fearless comment upon it."[117] I oppose unfair treatment of judges as much as anyone else, but it should go without saying that unfair treatment is not the same as informed public scrutiny. Citizens should have confidence that the federal judiciary will not be deterred from doing its job with integrity by the availability of such scrutiny, and for this reason the Judiciary should welcome rather than avoid it.[118]

Judges play an important and powerful role in our democracy, and citizens have a right to the fruits of studying how the courts do their, and thus our, business. Any defensible vision for the future of public access to court records should include a decision by the Judiciary to switch gears and foster an institutional attitude of openness toward the public.

14.4 CONCLUSION

There's a lot of federal court data. It sits on servers in district courts around the country, with a single access point through PACER. It's often inconvenient or impossible to use it to study the federal litigation system. Even where PACER use is technically feasible, it's often prohibitively costly in financial terms to acquire the magnitude of data that would allow scholars to do research that would then be available to the courts and the public for free. PACER has severely limited search functionality, and individual courts decide whether even that will be open to

115 *See* Miguel F. P. de Figueiredo, Alexandra D. Lahav & Peter Siegelman, *The Six-Month List and the Unintended Consequences of Judicial Accountability*, 105 Cornell L. Rev. 363, 364 (2020); Jonathan Petkun, Can (and Should) Judges Be Shamed? Evidence from the "Six-Month List" (Mar. 2020) (unpublished manuscript), https://jbpetkun.github.io/pages/working_papers/SixMonthList_WorkingDraft_20200327.pdf.

116 Bankruptcy judges do not have such protections. But the private service "AACER" – Automatic Access to Court Electronic Records – has already opened bankruptcy data to public bulk searches. *See Epiq* AACER, Eqiq Bankr., https://www.aacer.com/. AACER is not free to the public, however.

117 Schultze, *The Price of Ignorance* (quoting Alpheus Thomas Mason, *Harlan Fiske* Stone: Pillar of The Law 398 (1956)).

118 Things could be worse, to be sure. In 2019, France prohibited *all* data analytics using information about judges. *Understanding the French Ban on Judicial Analytics*, Gregory Bufithis (June 6, 2019), http://www.gregorybufithis.com/2019/06/09/understanding-the-french-ban-on-judicial-analytics/.

researchers without their paying ruinous fees to download documents that are owned by the public. All the while, the Internet Archive and who knows how many other nonprofits would gladly crawl, index, and host PACER's data for free public download.

This situation is an intolerable disgrace. It is unacceptable for a democracy to have but withhold such valuable information about the functioning of its courts. With only an imperceptible impact on the public fisc, Congress could both mandate free PACER and preserve the Judiciary's budget.

There do not seem to be large hurdles related to privacy or pressure on judges, because the data in question are already freely available for public download – just at a deliberately high price that renders useful research infeasible. Nor is there any real technical feasibility problem, as the offer by the Internet Archive to host the data for free forever shows. This is a problem of political and attitudinal will. Congress and the Judiciary should solve it, so we can use court data to increase access to better justice.

15

Technological Challenges Facing the Judiciary

Albert H. Yoon

James Branch Cabell wrote, "The optimist proclaims that we live in the best of all possible worlds, and the pessimist fears this is true." This witticism also applies to our present-day legal profession. Technological advances, having previously transformed labor markets that relied on physical labor, have in recent years influenced labor markets that rely on human thinking and judgment. During the 1980s, the legal profession underwent a dramatic shift from physical to electronic texts. Notwithstanding this change, the profession remained largely static for the next quarter century, with lawyers still required to process the texts, a time-consuming and costly process.

The advent of legal technology over the past decade has transformed the legal market. Companies – including many start-ups – have developed tools to help lawyers process information faster, assisting them in contract formation, discovery, and compliance, to name but a few.[1] More recent technologies use artificial intelligence (AI) to enable litigants to better understand their own case in light of existing legal precedent, predicting how a court would decide their case.

The optimist observes these developments and sees a world of potential. As in the past, new technologies will benefit consumers. The cost of legal services will decline, solving the paradoxical and seemingly intractable problem of a surfeit of both lawyers and litigants. The business model of the legal profession, long reliant on margin over volume, could reverse itself as legal technology enables lawyers to help more clients in less time.

The pessimist, observing the same developments, fears worsening inequalities that already hinder the legal profession. Thus far, legal technology has primarily catered

See James Branch Cabell, The Silver Stallion: A Comedy of Redemption (1926)

[1] For a helpful discussion of the legal tech landscape, see David Freeman Engstrom & Jonah B. Gelbach, *Legal Tech, Civil Procedure, and the Future of Adversarialism*, 169 U. Pa. L. Rev. 1001 (2021).

to wealthier litigants, beyond what most lawyers – for example, solo or small-firm practitioners – can afford. These technologies will, as Marc Galanter prophesized nearly half a century ago, allow the "haves" to yet again come out ahead of the "have-nots."[2]

This chapter identifies with both the optimist and the pessimist. The path toward a more efficient, democratized legal profession is within our reach. More to the point, the courts can help with this transition. Legal technology is expensive in part because judicial data is a barrier to entry. Legal technology centers around access to court documents – decisions and dockets – that are the foundation for data analytics. These documents are public, but often inaccessible and costly to access.[3] Courts could eliminate these barriers by making these documents freely and directly available to the public. While this data may subject them to heightened scrutiny, courts should embrace this trade-off. This scrutiny already occurs, albeit from the smaller subset of the lawyers who represent well-resourced clients. Second, this release of data will have a progressive effect on access to legal analytics, benefitting a wider range of litigants.

This chapter proceeds as follows. Section 15.1 discusses the evolution of legal practice, which until recently has remained unchanged for much of its history. The predicament facing the courts is set forth in Section 15.2: some financial, but much of it institutional and cultural. Section 15.3 describes a path forward, partially initiated by the COVID-19 pandemic, but also the change in the composition of judges over time. Section 15.4 concludes.

15.1 THE EVOLUTION OF LEGAL PRACTICE

Historically, the legal profession has undergone little change. Clients retain lawyers to solve their problems. Lawyers gather information from their clients and situate the client's case within the current law. Until recently, lawyers' task in effectively representing their clients has been a labor-intensive undertaking.[4] Lawyers are trouble-shooters, tasked with mapping their clients' problems into one or more legal issues. To do so, they must first determine the relevant legal authority, and then how this authority relates to the clients' situation.

15.1.1 *The Stubbornness of High Legal Fees*

The effort required to represent clients explains in large part why legal fees are expensive. Understanding their clients' circumstances requires effort and time; so

[2] Marc Galanter, *Why the "Haves" Come Out Ahead: Speculations on the Limits of Legal Change*," 9 LAW & SOC'Y REV. 95 (1974).

[3] *See* Simon Stern, *Copyright Originality and Judicial Originality*, 63 U. TORONTO L.J. 385 (2013).

[4] *See* RICHARD E. SUSSKIND, TOMORROW'S LAWYERS: AN INTRODUCTION TO YOUR FUTURE (2017).

too does understanding the relevant legal authority. And the economies of scale are limited, as each client is unique. As lawyers gain experience, they are able to work more efficiently, accomplishing more over the same unit of time than less-experienced lawyers. To reflect this experience, however, experienced lawyers often are more expensive.[5]

In *The Cost Disease*, William Baumol and William Bowen explain how certain jobs rise in compensation, even in the absence of an increase in labor productivity.[6] The authors characterize two types of jobs: (1) workers who become more productive over time, in large part due to technology and innovation and (2) workers largely immune to these advances. Auto workers provide an example of the former: because technology allows each worker to contribute more efficiently to the production of a car, her hourly wages have plateaued, even declined, as machines have come to perform more of the assembly process. For the latter, a string quartet: musicians devote the same amount of time to perform Beethoven today as did their predecessors. Compensation for workers in these technology-resistant fields rises if demand for these services remains constant and employers have to compete for these workers.

Until recently, lawyers were more akin to classical musicians than auto workers. The effort required to represent clients over time has remained stubbornly consistent. While digital libraries have enabled lawyers to identify relevant legal materials more efficiently, lawyers still have to process them.[7] Lawyers historically used leverage to contain legal fees: partners delegating the straightforward and labor-intensive work to less-expensive associates.[8] But the rate-limiting factor remains human effort, which – when unaffected by gains in productivity – becomes increasingly expensive.

The legal profession licensure requirements also create barriers to entry. The practice of law requires attending law school and passing the bar, reducing the supply of lawyers.[9] Over time, non-lawyers have engaged in certain legal work,

5 Sharon Miki, *Lawyer Statistics for Success in 2022*, Clio (Mar. 15, 2022), https://www.clio.com/blog/lawyer-statistics/. The highest was in DC, at $380, and the lowest was in West Virginia, at $166. But partners at some elite law firms charge over $1,000 per hour, and there is at least one documented case of a firm charging $1,795. *See* Samantha Stokes, *Will Billing Rates for Elite Firms Rise More in 2020?* The Am. Law. (July 30, 2020), https://www.law.com/americanlawyer/2020/07/30/will-billing-rates-for-elite-firms-rise-more-in-2020/.

6 *See* William J. Baumol, The Cost Disease: Why Computers Get Cheaper and Health Care Doesn't (2012).

7 *See* Emery G. Lee II, *Law without Lawyers: Access to Civil Justice and the Cost of Legal Services*, 69 U. Mia. L. Rev. 499 (2015).

8 See Albert H. Yoon, *The Post-Modern Lawyer: Technology and the Democratization of Legal Representation*, 66 U. Toronto L.J. 456 (2016).

9 Received wisdom seems to suggest that there are plenty of law graduates, yet they are underemployed. Emily A. Spieler, *The Paradox of Access to Civil Justice: The "Glut" of New Lawyers and the Persistence of Unmet Need*, 44 U. Toledo L. Rev. 365, 365–403 (2013).

under the authority of lawyers, and in some instances entirely on their own.[10] But even as non-lawyers reduce legal fees, human labor remains the rate-limiting factor.

15.1.2 *Three Stages of Lawyering*

For all these reasons, the legal profession has enjoyed an extended period operating as a well-paying guild.[11] Until recently, the fundamental nature of legal practice remained unchanged, even as the profession adopted new technologies. During that time, the profession has evolved across three stages: from *analog* to *digital* to *computational*.[12] It is only the third and latest transition that seems poised to force the legal profession to fundamentally change its approach, both conceptual and financial.[13] I briefly summarize these stages.

Analog. This stage represents the era where lawyers relied on hard copies of legal references – for example, case reporters, treatises, regulations, statutes, restatements – in their course of their legal work. This era's defining feature is that the lawyers themselves were the sole mechanism to process these references and to apply them to their clients' situation. Humans were the rate-limiting factor in the speed and efficacy of legal representation. Although varying in ability, lawyers performed tasks primarily as a linear function of the hours worked. Accordingly, larger law firms were able to take on more complex work because they could deploy larger numbers of lawyers onto a legal problem.

Digital. This stage coincided with the emergence of two technological developments during the 1980s: the personal computer and the creation of electronic legal libraries. The personal computer enabled greater efficiency. Lawyers who previously used typewriters found that an electronic format allowed them to write, edit, and share documents more easily. The advent of electronic legal libraries – notably Westlaw and LexisNexis – enabled lawyers to conduct their legal research through a dedicated terminal and, soon thereafter, on their personal computer. At a minimum, lawyers could access any decision, statute, or regulation by looking up its citation. Even more helpfully, lawyers could use keywords to identify the universe of relevant materials. The advent of electronic legal libraries untethered lawyers from physical reference materials, while simultaneously allowing them to digitally memorialize their work. These advances improved the rate of production, but, as with the analog stage, lawyer productivity remained a function of hours worked.

[10] For example, the Law Society of Ontario in 2007 began regulating paralegals to address concerns of inadequate access to legal services. *See* Access to Justice Act, 2006, S.O. 2006, c 21 (Can.).

[11] *See* Mark A. Cohen, *Goodbye Guild – Law's Changing Culture*, FORBES (July 3, 2017), https://www.forbes.com/sites/markcohen1/2017/07/03/goodbye-guild-laws-changing-culture/.

[12] Benjamin Alarie, Anthony Niblett & Albert Yoon, *How Artificial Intelligence Will Affect the Practice of Law*, 68 U. TORONTO L.J. 106, 112 (Supp. 2018).

[13] For a fuller discussion of these stages, see *id*.

Computational. This latest stage coincided with the emergence of AI and its application to law. Early developments during this stage are really extensions of the analog era, made possible because of the increased digitization of legal records. Discovery is one such example. During this pre-trial process, lawyers ask opposing counsel for materials – usually in the form of documents – that they believe could be legally relevant. The process historically required lawyers to read each document. Digitization expedites the process by allowing lawyers to electronically search for relevant words or phrases. A plethora of e-discovery start-ups exists to assist in this process.[14] What once required a small army of lawyers now requires a single lawyer and a few lines of code.

As its name suggests, the computational stage refers to the ability of machines (computers) to go beyond identifying relevant legal references, drawing upon these references, in conjunction with specific information about a client case, to generate legal analysis. It uses two methods of AI: machine learning (ML) and natural language processing (NLP), described briefly below.

ML statistically analyzes structured data to predict outcomes.[15] This process draws upon regression analysis, commonly used in both STEM and social sciences, as a means to test hypotheses by looking at data generated by observable phenomena. The difference lies in the objective: Rather than use regressions to *explain* outcomes, ML seeks to *predict* them. ML in legal technology involves digitizing legal information. Information from legal references – notably cases – can be expressed as pieces of data. These variables can be binomial in nature (is something X or Y); multinomial (is something A, B, C, D, etc.); or continuous (e.g., earnings, damages).

To illustrate: Whether a worker is an employee or independent contractor[16] frequently arises in tax and employment law, determining the rights and obligations of the worker. In most jurisdictions, courts weigh several factors – for example, the amount of training, who sets the hours, the right to delegate work – in making this determination. It is possible to code published decisions into a dataset that captures how courts weigh these factors in reaching their decisions. ML can predict, given a specific set of facts, how a court would decide this matter, given existing precedent. Transforming written text to bytes of data can be labor-intensive, particularly when done manually. Once transformed, however, scaling this data is trivially small: A million people can draw upon this data just as easily as a single person.

14 See Maura R. Grossman & Gordon V. Cormack, *Technology-Assisted Review in E-Discovery Can Be More Effective and More Efficient Than Exhaustive Manual Review*, 17 Rich. J. L. & Tech. 1 (2018).

15 Zoe Niesel, *Machine Learning and the New Civil Procedure*, 73 SMU L. Rev. 493 (2020)

16 This example is taken from Blue J Legal, a legal technology start-up for which I am a cofounder. Benjamin Alarie, *The Path of the Law: Towards Legal Singularity*, 66 U. Toronto L.J. 443 (2016).

NLP, which sits at the intersection of computer science and linguistics, is designed to understand and interpret human language, whether written or spoken. Whereas ML analyzes structured data – that is, that which could be captured in a spreadsheet – NLP is capable of working with unstructured data,[17] such as the text of a memo or an opinion. Both NLP and ML can identify patterns or relationships in data faster and more comprehensively than humans. The relationship can involve individual words, phrases, or even the proximity of words in relation to other words. NLP allows for interpretation beyond words qua words, extending to words in relation to other words, even when those words are not juxtaposed.

NLP already has applications in both the consumer and legal context. For example, firms can use NLP to more effectively evaluate customer feedback across multiple formats – for example, email, surveys, conversations from call centers – to identify recurring or common problems, even as customers express themselves in a myriad of ways.[18] Within law, firms can use NLP to evaluate and identify relevant provisions of a contract and their meaning.[19] This technology is helpful, given the human time, expense, and error that often results when done manually. Even with the promise of comprehending unstructured data, NLP performs better the more structured the text.

15.1.3 *Legal Ethics*

As the number of applications grows, the rate-limiting principle will not be technological, but ethical. It is helpful to distinguish between the ethical and the *legal* ethical considerations of AI. The two overlap but remain distinct. The general ethical debate speaks to the ethical dilemmas that technology poses, which can inform whether the technology should even be built, and if built, how to do it in accordance with ethical considerations. Legal ethics is arguably more restrictive, looking to how the profession uses technology in accordance with its own fiduciary and ethical obligations.

Legal technology raises several ethical concerns.[20] One is privacy, the blurring of boundaries of attorney-client privilege. Many of these technologies rest in the cloud,

17 See Paul D. Callister, *Law, Artificial Intelligence, and Natural Language Processing: A Funny Thing Happened on the Way to My Search Results*, 112 LAW LIBR. J. 161 (2020).

18 *See Natural Language Processing (NLP)*, SAS, https://www.sas.com/en_ca/insights/analytics/what-is-natural-language-processing-nlp.html.

19 For a helpful review of natural language processing applications within law, see Robert Dale, *Law and Word Order: NLP in Legal Tech*, 25 NAT. LANGUAGE ENG'G 211 (2018). For recent applications, *see, e.g.*, Fahud ul Hassand & Tuyen Le, *Automated Requirements Identification from Construction Contract Documents Using Natural Language Processing*, J. LEGAL AFFS. & DISP. RESOL. ENG'G & CONSTR. (May 2020).

20 *See* Axel Walz & Kay Firth-Butterfield, *Implementing Ethics into Artificial Intelligence: A Contribution, from a Legal Perspective, to the Development of an AI Governance Regime*, 18 DUKE L. & TECH. REV. 176 (2019).

and therefore potentially allow third parties illegal access to privileged information. The second is unlawful discrimination when algorithmic tools are used in criminal[21] and employment contexts. The third is the unauthorized practice of law, particularly as technologies advance and can perform tasks that draw closer to legal advice.[22] Finally, the evolution of legal technology raises issues of access to justice, because much of the technology is geared toward the elite private bar, not lawyers who serve regular people.[23] Most practicing lawyers lack these resources.[24]

15.2 CHALLENGES FOR THE COURTS

Courts face numerous obstacles with respect to technological change. Two obstacles are largely beyond the judiciary's control: caseloads and funding. The remaining three are within the judiciary's scope: judge Luddism, cybersecurity risks, and judicial aversion to public scrutiny. I discuss each in turn.

15.2.1 *Caseloads*

In a sense, courts perform a reactive role. They adjudicate disputes coming before them, but – save select courts, such as the US Supreme Court – do not control their docket. Nevertheless, the demand on courts continues to grow. Among US district courts, the caseload has grown over the years by 165 percent (from 127,280 cases in 1970 to 337,537 cases in 2017). The caseload demands are arguably even greater than the numbers suggest: Much of this growth involved civil disputes between private parties, which on average take more time to resolve than criminal cases (10.8 months versus 7.0 months in September 2019 in US District Courts, and there has been a

[21] *See* Loomis v. Wisconsin, 881 N.W.2d 749 (Wis. 2016), *cert. denied*, 137 S. Ct. 2290 (2017) (holding that judges' use of proprietary software to inform their own bail decisions does not violate a defendant's due process rights). For a discussion of the potential problems raised by proprietary software in the bail context, see Julia Angwin et al., *Machine Bias: There's Software Used across the Country to Predict Future Criminals. And It's Biased against Blacks*, ProPublica (May 23, 2016), https://www.propublica.org/article/machine-bias-risk-assessments-in-criminal-sentencing.

[22] *See, e.g.*, Drew Simsaw, *Ethical Issues in Robo-Lawyering: The Need for Guidance on Developing and Using Artificial Intelligence in the Practice of Law*, 70 Hastings L.J. 173 (2018).

[23] For example, there is a company called Closing Folders, https://www.closingfolders.com/ that provides a secure, centralized platform in which lawyers can keep track of.

[24] Over a third of lawyers are solo practitioners. *See* Clara N. Carson, Am. Bar Found., The Lawyers Statistical Report: The U.S Legal Profession in 2005 (2005), www.americanbarfoundation.org/uploads/cms/documents/2005_lawyer_statistical_report.pdf. A recent survey revealed that most lawyers, when conducting research, rely on free online resources. *See ABA Profile of the Legal Profession – Technology*, A.B.A., https://www.abalegalprofile.com/legal-technology/ (describing the ABA's 2020 Legal Technology Survey Report).

relatively consistent discrepancy of increased length for civil cases since at least 2000).[25]

The growth in caseload necessarily increases demands on the judiciary. The first is on the judges themselves. Among US district courts, the number of authorized judgeships from 1970 to 2017 grew by only 68 percent (from 394 judges to 663 judges).[26] Accordingly, judges are tasked with greater responsibilities, particularly after *Iqbal*[27] and *Twombly*,[28] whose heightened pleading requirements require judges to adjudicate matters earlier in the litigation process. Another is the litigants. Longer periods for a trial date, combined with costs of litigation, increase the likelihood that parties resolve their disputes through trial diminishes. It is a well-known and often repeated maxim that the vast majority of cases resolve prior to trial.[29]

15.2.2 *Funding*

As a branch of government, the judiciary is subject to the financial constraints that all public institutions face. In nominal dollars, judiciaries are often spared the budgetary cuts that befall other public services.[30] For example, Article III of the US Constitution authorizes Congress to create federal judgeships, but not diminish their salaries. Congress wields the authority to reduce the number of federal judges; it has yet to do so.

In most jurisdictions, salaries constitute the single largest expense of the judiciary budget. Drawing again from the US federal example, salaries (and benefits) from judges, clerks, and staff totalled 64 percent of the FY 2021 total budget request.[31]

[25] *See Caseload Statistics Data Tables*, U.S. CTS., https://www.uscourts.gov/statistics-reports/caseload-statistics-data-tables?tn=&pn=33&t=68&m%5Bvalue%5D%5Bmonth%5D=9&y%5Bvalue%5D%5Byear%5D=; CT. STAT. PROJECT, NAT'L CTR. FOR STATE COURTS, STATE COURT CASELOAD DIGEST: 2017 DATA 2 n.1 (2019) (providing state data, but apparently state civil courts do 99 percent of civil trials); Colleen F. Shanahan, Alyx Mark, Jessica K. Steinberg & Anna E. Carpenter, *COVID, Crisis and Courts*, 99 TEX. L. REV. ONLINE 10 (2020). But maybe all this can go as unrelated to federal courts.

[26] *See Caseloads: Criminal Cases, 1870–2017*, FED. JUDICIAL CTR., https://www.fjc.gov/history/courts/caseloads-criminal-cases-1870-2017.

[27] *See* Bell Atlantic Corp. v. Twombly, 550 U.S. 544 (2007).

[28] *See* Ashcroft v. Iqbal, 556 U.S. 662 (2009).

[29] The trial rate in federal courts declined from 11.5 percent in 1962 to 1.8 percent in 2002. *See* Marc Galanter, *The Vanishing Trial: An Examination of Trials and Related Matters in Federal and State Courts*, 1 J. EMPIRICAL LEGAL STUD. 459, 462 (2004); *see also* Marc Galanter & Mia Cahill, *"Most Cases Settle": Judicial Promotion and Regulation of Settlements*, 46 STAN. L. REV. 1339 (1994).

[30] *See* Robert J. Derocher, *Crisis in the Courts: Bars Take Steps to Stave off Judicial Funding Cuts*, BAR LEADER, May–June 2010.

[31] *See* ADMIN. OFF. OF THE U.S. CTS., THE JUDICIARY FISCAL YEAR 2021 CONGRESSIONAL BUDGET SUMMARY (2021), https://www.uscourts.gov/sites/default/files/fy_2021_congressional_budget_summary_0.pdf.

Given a total appropriation of nearly $6 billion for this year, the federal commitment to salaries is sizable.

At the same time, it is important to consider judicial salaries in a broader context. US district court judges, the most common form of Article III judge, in 2020 earn $216,400,[32] much higher than the US median income,[33] but much less than the elite private bar.[34] These pay differentials may deter high-skilled lawyers from joining the bench or, in some instances, encourage departure.[35] Moreover, this gap has only grown over time as judicial salaries lag behind the rate of inflation.[36] Concurrently, legislatures resist expanding the number of judgeships, resulting in the number of judgeships failing to keep pace with caseload increases.

15.2.3 *Judicial Reluctance toward Technology*

It is an understatement to say that courts and technology are not the best of friends. Judges, on average, constitute the higher end of the age distribution. Judges typically have distinguished themselves earlier in their career, whether it be in private practice, government, or academia. This process takes time, so it is perhaps no surprise that judges are often in their fifties by the time they join the bench. For example, the average age of an Article III judge at the time of their commission is fifty-one years old. However, given lifetime tenure, most judges remain on the bench well past the traditional retirement age of sixty-five. In 2020, the average age of a district judge was sixty-seven years old and sixty-nine years old for a court of appeals judge.[37]

Judges, like many older adults,[38] may be reluctant to adopt new technologies. Surveys show that among the general population, over 60 percent of Americans aged

[32] In 1972, Congress appropriated $1.2M for the federal judiciary. FED. JUD. CTR., ANNUAL REPORT 1971 (1971), https://www.fjc.gov/sites/default/files/2012/AnnRep71.pdf.

[33] The median earnings in 2019 were $52,000 for full-time, year-round workers. *See* U.S. CENSUS BUREAU, INCOME AND POVERTY IN THE UNITED STATES: 2019 (2021), https://www.census.gov/content/dam/Census/library/publications/2020/demo/p60-270.pdf.

[34] *See* James B. Stewart, *$11 Million a Year for a Law Partner? Bidding War Grows at Top-Tier Firms*, N.Y. TIMES (Apr. 26, 2018), https://www.nytimes.com/2018/04/26/business/cravath-kirkland-ellis-partner-poaching.html.

[35] For example, Judge J. Michael Luttig, a prominent federal appellate judge, resigned from the bench to become senior vice president and general counsel of Boeing, attributing the decision in part for an increase in salary. *See* Neil A. Lewis, *Judge Leaves Appeals Court for Boeing*, N.Y. TIMES (May 11, 2006), https://www.nytimes.com/2006/05/11/washington/11judge.html.

[36] For example, US district judges in 1970 earned $40,000 annually, which – adjusting for inflation – would be equal to $275,664. This amount exceeds the 2020 salary. Albert Yoon, *Love's Labor's Lost – Judicial Tenure among Federal Court Judges, 1945–2000*, 91 CAL. L. REV. 1029, 1032 (2003).

[37] *See Biographical Director of Article III Federal Judges, 1789–present*, FED. JUD. CTR., https://www.fjc.gov/node/7946 (author's analysis of statistics).

[38] *See* Kate Conger & Erin Griffith, *As Life Moves Online, an Older Generation Faces a Digital Divide*, N.Y. TIMES (Mar. 27, 2020), https://www.nytimes.com/2020/03/27/technology/virus-older-generation-digital-divide.html.

fifty to sixty-four and nearly 75 percent of those above age sixty-five identify as needing someone else to set up their new electronic devices.[39] Other academic studies show that older adults often possess a phobia about technology, particularly when it involves a technology that they did not develop familiarity with during their younger years.[40]

Judges likely share these experiences of the general public. Many judges are years removed from the type of legal work now reliant upon this technology. Either the nature of their work at the time did not demand it or they had junior lawyers who could perform these tasks. On the bench, technology has changed little since the 1980s inception of digital libraries such as Westlaw or LexisNexis. Newer technologies, however, differ categorically from traditional digital search technology by going beyond search to providing answers.

These technologies are in potential tension with an idealization of courts, and judges in particular. Judges, by institutional design, are deemed impartial arbiters of disputes. They are equal to the legislative and executive branches, and are protected against removal without cause. Judges confer with their clerks, or even other judges, but ultimately issue their own decisions, free from any outside influence. Newer technologies challenge the independent role of judges, allowing actors outside the judiciary to influence how judges make decisions. Under this view, judges may cede autonomy. It is one thing for judges to draw upon resources – from clerks, judges, the common law – to inform their view. It is something altogether different for judges to draw upon resources advising them what to do.

15.2.4 *Security of Judicial Documents*

Another concern for the courts is security of judicial documents. Increasingly, legal technology utilizes cloud computing, hosting applications on remote servers on the web rather than personal computers or local servers. These servers are vulnerable to access by unauthorized third parties. This risk is particularly concerning for the legal profession, where lawyers are ethically bound to maintain strict client confidentiality.[41] These ethics also apply to judges, who similarly must take affirmative steps to avoid disclosing case information outside of the judiciary.[42]

Client security is a long-standing issue for the legal profession, at the same time co-existent with technology. Before email, lawyers corresponded with clients

[39] *See* Monica Anderson & Andrew Perrin, *Barriers to Adoption and Attitudes towards Tech among Older Americans*, Pew Rsch. Ctr. (May 17, 2019), https://www.pewresearch.org/internet/2017/05/17/barriers-to-adoption-and-attitudes-towards-technology/.

[40] *See* Dina Di Giacomo et al., *Psychological Barriers to Digital Living in Older Adults: Computer Anxiety as Predictive Mechanism for Technophobia*, 9 Behav. Scis. (Basel) 96 (2019).

[41] *See* Model Rules of Pro. Conduct r. 1.6 (Am Bar Ass'n 2020).

[42] *See* Stephen G. A. Pitel & Liam Ledgerwood, *Judicial Confidentiality in Canada*, 43 Queens L.J. 123 (2017).

through traditional mail or fax. Both had the virtue of being secure, given their person-to-person formats. Email offered the lawyers the promise of instantaneous communication with their clients, while they risked the perils of breaches of client confidentiality, which in many instances could neither be easily remedied nor even traced. The legal profession initially responded by discouraging its use for client communication, but eventually recognized its advantages for facilitating communication between lawyers and clients.[43] Today, lawyers widely use email, cognizant of the inherent risks of electronic communication.[44] Contracts are now routinely finalized on the cloud.[45]

15.2.5 *Judicial Aversion to Public Scrutiny*

Judges, in contrast to legislators, are public servants who operate predominantly outside of public view.[46] Whereas trials and certain pre-trial proceedings are open to the public, much of what judges do occurs in private. In contrast to a legislature, judges do not reveal their deliberations, only their final decision in the form of a motion or an opinion. Adding to this opacity, while the disposition judges' decisions are of public record, they are not necessarily readily available. Moreover, judges elect whether to categorize their opinions as *published* or *unpublished*, which further limits their availability.[47]

The public's ability to access federal judicial opinions has historically required lawyers to have access to a physical volume of the federal reporter, or, alternatively, a subscription to an online legal database. In recent years, new media platforms (e.g., Justia) have made federal decisions and statutes publicly available and free of charge. Other public judicial documents, however, remain less accessible.[48]

43 *See* Catherine Sanders Reach, *10 Email Dos and Don'ts for Lawyers*, N.C. Bar Ass'n (Jan. 7, 2019), https://www.ncbar.org/2019/01/07/10-email-dos-and-donts-for-lawyers/.

44 *See* Martha Neil, *Hackers Are Stealing Closing Funds by Intercepting Lawyer-Client Email, Experts Say*, A.B.A. J. (Jan. 11, 2016), https://www.abajournal.com/news/article/hackers_are_stealing_closing_funds_by_intercepting_lawyer_client_email_expe.

45 *See* Sydney Franklin, *Real Estate Transactions Go Virtual*, N.Y. Times (Nov. 11, 2020), https://www.nytimes.com/2020/11/11/realestate/10virtual-deals.html (describing the emergence of Docusign as a means to finalize contracts).

46 *See* Arthur S. Miller & D. S. Sastri, *Secrecy and the Supreme Court: On the Need for Piercing the Red Velour Curtain*, 22 Buff. L. Rev. 799 (1973).

47 For a discussion of the impact of published versus unpublished opinions, see David C. Vladeck & Mitu Gulati, *Judicial Triage: Reflections on the Debate of Unpublished Opinions*, 62 Wash. & Lee L. Rev. 1667 (2005).

48 For example, federal docket sheets – which contain the procedural history of filed cases – are available through the Public Access to Court Electronic Records (PACER). This portal, however, imposes a fee of $0.10 a page, irrespective of whether the user prints or even reads the page, and generates costs even if a search fails to yield a result. *See PACER Pricing: How Fees Work*, Pub. Access to Ct. Elec. Recs., https://pacer.uscourts.gov/pacer-pricing-how-fees-work. In response, Court Listener, part of the Free Law Project, created CourtListener, which offers an Advanced RECAP – PACER spelled backward – search containing millions of

In addition, courts have been loath to link the identities of their judges to their decisions. For example, the Federal Judicial Center makes publicly available data on individual civil and criminal defendant filings and terminations filed in the federal district and appellate courts.[49] This data, however, omits the judges' identities for each record.[50] This omission prevents those analyzing the data to observe how differences in case outcomes vary by individual judge.[51]

From an academic and policy perspective, knowing which judges decide cases is essential for rigorous statistical analyses. For example, in a recent influential study on the bail decisions, researchers found that state court judges make two types of errors: (1) release defendants on bail who subsequently commit a crime while released and (2) deny bail to defendants who, based on observable characteristics, would have complied with bail conditions if released.[52] Given the random assignment of cases, researchers could identify when different judges were treating similarly situated defendants differently, and more broadly, the extent to which judges vary from one another.

Other countries worry about public scrutiny of judges. France has outlawed the publication of judge analytics, a crime punishable by up to five years of prison.[53] In accordance with the Act, any publication that is likely to undermine the security of any parties to a judicial decision, including judges, must be obscured.[54] In my own research, I sought to evaluate bail decisions of courts within a Canadian province. The province's judicial council – comprising judges – was willing to release individual-level data on bail proceedings but declined to reveal the identity of judges

PACER documents and dockets, free and open to the public. *Advanced RECAP Search*, Ct. Listener, https://www.courtlistener.com/recap/.

49 *See Integrated Database (IDB)*, Fed. Jud. Ctr., https://www.fjc.gov/research/idb.

50 The Judicial Conference in 1995 announced a policy "prohibiting the disclosure (except to the extent required by law) of judge-identifying information from statistical databases." This policy was subsequent reaffirmed by the conference in 1995 and 2003. *See* Fed. Jud. Ctr., The Integrated Database: A Research Guide 1 n.2 (2020), www.fjc.gov/sites/default/files/IDB-Research-Guide.pdf.

51 Notably, the judicial conference voted to increase transparency on federal civil proceedings: it rejected a proposal that would have allowed – upon consent of opposing parties to a civil dispute – to automatically seal court records. *See* Linda Greenhouse, *Judicial Conference Rejects More Secrecy in Civil Court*, N.Y. Times (Mar. 15, 1995), https://www.nytimes.com/1995/03/15/us/judicial-conference-rejects-more-secrecy-in-civil-court.html.

52 *See* Jon Kleinberg et al., *Human Decisions and Machine Predictions*, 133 Q.J. Econ. 238 (2018).

53 Article 33 of France's Justice Reform Act states, "No personally identifiable data concerning judges or court clerks may be subject to any reuse with the purpose or result of evaluating, analyzing, or predicting their actual or supposed professional practices." *See* Loi 2019-222 du 23 mars 2019 de programmation 2018–2022 et de réforme pour la justice [Law 2019-222 of March 23, 2019 on Justice Reform], Journal Officiel de la République Française [J.O.] [Official Gazette of France], Article 33.

54 *See* McCann FitzGerald LLP, *France Bans Analytics of Judges' Decisions*, Lexology (June 21, 2019), https://www.lexology.com/library/detail.aspx?g=ff53dfbe-ofe6-4dee-8a1d-990bf8459020#:~:text=France%20has%20banned%20certain%20types,or%20predicting%20their%20professional%20practices.

for each case, on the grounds that it could draw undue criticism of the provincial judges.

Arguments in support of judge anonymity range from distortion of the litigation process to the safety of judges. In 2019, the Constitutional Court of France upheld the constitutionality of the prohibition on revealing judges' identities, determining that court analytics based on individual judges could promote forum shopping, to the detriment of the administration of justice.[55] In 2020, an individual injured and killed family members of a US district judge, after having appeared before the judge in prior litigation and criticizing her handling of the case on social media.[56] This followed earlier instances – in 2005,[57] 1989,[58] 1988,[59] and 1979[60] – where federal judges were killed, all connected to litigants appearing before these judges. The Secretary of the Judicial Conference of the United States testified that identified threats and inappropriate communications directed at federal judges grew from under 1,000 in 2015 to nearly 4,500 in 2019.[61]

15.2.6 *Litigation as Arms Race*

Litigation has long favored those with resources. Litigants with the most resources tend to attract the highest-ability lawyers. At the same time, even sophisticated litigants prefer to trim unnecessary legal expenses. Many legal technology tools allow lawyers to perform legal tasks at a fraction of the time and cost that it took even a decade or two earlier. Thus, there is a segment of the practicing bar that

55 *See* Conseil constitutionnel [CC] [Constitutional Court] decision No. 2019-778DC, July 26, 2019, Rec. 80 (Fr.)

56 *See* Tracey Tully, *Judge Whose Son Was Killed by Misogynistic Lawyer Speaks Out*, N.Y. Times (Aug. 3, 2020), https://www.nytimes.com/2020/08/03/nyregion/esther-salas-roy-den-hollander.html.

57 An out-of-work electrician whose civil case was dismissed by Hon. Joan Humphrey Lefkow (ND-Ill) killed the judge's husband and mother. *See* Jodi Wilgoren, *Electrician Says in Suicide Note that He Killed Judge's Family*, N.Y. Times (Mar. 11, 2005), www.nytimes.com/2005/03/11/us/electrician-says-in-suicide-note-that-he-killed-judges-family.html.

58 A litigant with a case before the Eleventh Circuit Court of Appeals, sitting *en banc*, sent a pipe bomb to the residence of Hon. Robert S. Vance Sr., killing him and gravely injuring his wife. *See* Alan Blinder, *Alabama Executes Mail Bomber, 83, the Oldest Inmate Put to Death in Modern Era*, N.Y. Times (Apr. 19, 2018), https://www.nytimes.com/2018/04/19/us/alabama-execution-walter-leroy-moody.html.

59 The father of a litigant killed Hon. Richard J. Daronco (SD-NY) in the aftermath of the judge dismissing the litigant's case. *See* Robert D. McFadden, *Federal Judge Slain by a Gunman in Westchester*, N.Y. Times (May 22, 1988), https://www.nytimes.com/1988/05/22/nyregion/federal-judge-slain-by-a-gunman-in-westchester.html.

60 A defendant from an organized crime family arranged the assassination of Hon. John H. Wood, Jr. (WD-TX). *See* Wayne King, *3 Are Found Guilty in Assassination of Federal Judge*, N.Y. Times (Dec. 15, 1982), https://www.nytimes.com/1982/12/15/us/3-are-found-guilty-in-assassination-of-federal-judge.html.

61 *See Judiciary Steps Up Calls to Enact Security Measures*, U.S. Cts. (Sept. 22, 2020), https://www.uscourts.gov/news/2020/09/22/judiciary-steps-calls-enact-security-measures.

embraces legal technology to improve both the efficiency and quality of their practice. On the other end of the spectrum, many lawyers represent litigants of more modest means. Given the nature of their practice and their own limited resources, these lawyers are slower to incorporate these technologies.

Judges are not exempt from this competition. This asymmetry of legal sophistication threatens our civil and criminal justice system. This imbalance might be more palatable if litigation involved only parties of comparable means: that is, affluent litigants filing suit against affluent litigants; poor litigants filing suit against poor litigants. While this phenomenon occurs in certain situations – for example, intellectual property and corporate disputes typically involve well-financed litigants[62] – many instances reflect a more David-versus-Goliath disparity, such as personal injury, immigration, or civil rights. This imbalance may distort legal outcomes at trial, if lawyers financed by well-resourced litigants can generate outcomes that maximize chances of prevailing or, if that is not possible, ameliorating the terms of an unfavorable outcome. These decisions, in turn, affect both the manner and terms under which subsequent litigants resolve their disputes, irrespective of whether they proceed to trial.[63]

The courts' lack of technological sophistication also poses risks to our civil and criminal justice system. In terms of resources, courts fall somewhere between well-financed and modestly financed litigants. They certainly possess more resources – technological as well as labor – than the typical lawyer, but are increasingly falling behind the elite bar, typically those practicing at the largest law firms. Legal technology is transforming how the elite bar practices. In contrast, legal technology has had a modest effect on the judiciary. While existing developments are welcome – for example, judges increasingly allow litigants to electronically file their court documents – the courts' earlier adaptation to technology suggests a slow transition.

15.3 A PATH FORWARD

Legal technology presents both opportunities and challenges for the legal profession. It transforms the way that lawyers practice. For much of the profession's existence, all legal tasks, however mundane, were the exclusive domain of lawyers. Even as paralegals have taken on tasks, legal work remained the domain of humans. New technologies enable machines to assist lawyers in increasingly more of their legal tasks. As a result, for example, discovery can take a few hours of one lawyer's time rather than weeks requiring several lawyers. And finding answers to discrete legal questions can now take a few minutes rather than a few hours.

62 *See* Richard A. Posner & Albert H. Yoon, *What Judges Think of the Quality of Legal Representation*, 63 Stan. L. Rev. 317 (2010).

63 Robert H. Mnookin & Lewis Kornhauser, *Bargaining in the Shadow of the Law: The Case of Divorce*, 88 Yale L.J. (1978).

As with many new technologies, adoption of legal technology lags behind availability. Adoption among lawyers depends in large part on cost and value. Technologies that enable lawyers to improve both the quality and rate at which they work encourage broader adoption. Society is replete with examples of wide-scale technological adoption, both with respect to hardware (e.g., personal computers, smartphones) and software (Facebook; Twitter). Even when the costs of adoption are considerable, the costs of eschewing these technologies are arguably higher.[64]

While the legal profession is still in its early stages of adoption of legal technology, the profession recognizes the need for lawyers to develop and maintain a level of technical competence. The American Bar Association now includes technological competence in its model rules.[65] Courts have been slower than the profession to adopt technological change, for the aforementioned reasons. The path forward involves two parts, which I discuss in turn.

15.3.1 *Greater Technological Competence in the Judiciary*

At first blush, this competence may appear unnecessary. Very few cases result in a trial. Among civil cases filed in district court in the period 1970 through 2019, fewer than 3 percent of filed civil cases ended in a verdict.[66] Given this relatively low percentage, one can argue that judges have ample time to properly adjudicate the cases before them, without additional technology. Looking only at trial outcomes, however, provides an incomplete picture of the integral role that judges have in helping parties resolve their disputes. Based on civil filings in federal district court, parties resolved disputes on their own in roughly half the cases, without court adjudication. But in nearly a quarter of all cases, judges adjudicated the dispute, prior to trial, on procedural – for example, lack of jurisdiction – or substantive – for example, summary judgment, affirming findings of an arbitrator or magistrate judge – grounds.[67] This data provides evidence that, at a minimum, judges play an active role in helping many parties resolve

64 For example, in the United States in 2019, 96 percent of Americans owned a cell phone and 81 percent owned a smartphone. *Mobile Fact Sheet*, PEW RSCH. CTR. (June 12, 2019), www.pewresearch.org/internet/fact-sheet/mobile/.

65 *See* MODEL RULES OF PRO. CONDUCT r. 1.1 ¶ 8 (AM. BAR. ASS'N 2020) ("[T]o maintain the requisite knowledge and skill, a lawyer should keep abreast of changes in the law and its practice, including the benefits and risks associated with relevant technology.").

66 Data taken from analysis of Federal Judicial Center data of federal court decisions, as analyzed by the author. The data is available at *Integrated Database (IDB)*.

67 *See* Tracey E. George & Albert Yoon, Visible Trial: Judicial Assessment as Adjudication, forthcoming, 94 Colorado Law Review __ (2022).

their disputes. Even when parties do not proceed to trial, they take guidance from judges during the pre-trial phase.

The judiciary's response to the COVID-19 pandemic provides optimism that judges may be more open to technology than originally perceived. In the United States, every state has initiated online hearings in response to the pandemic.[68] In addition, a majority of states allow litigants to electronically file court documents.[69] In many respects, these transformations reflect the judiciary's adopting well-established processes within the practicing bar.

These changes also provide second-order changes that are just as beneficial, namely democratizing the litigation process by increasing its access. Online hearings and electronic filing allow litigants to advance their claims without having to miss time off from work or find childcare. Even as the pandemic brought about curfews and shelter-in-place ordinances, courts reported a dramatic drop in failure-to-appear rates for civil and criminal proceedings.[70]

It will be interesting to see how courts respond when governments – at all levels – lift restrictions as COVID-19 moves from a pandemic to an endemic state. Will courts revert to their traditional practices that rely heavily on in-person interaction, or will they make a permanent transition to using technology to reduce the transaction costs of litigating? While judicial adaption of technological has its bumps,[71] its benefits, on balance, outweigh the growing pains.

Judges can and should make greater use of legal technology. While some obstacles to adoption may be budgetary, judicial norms likely play a larger role. As with most matters, judges exercise considerable discretion as to how they use technology in their courtroom. As more judges become comfortable with technology, and advocate for its use, judicial norms will evolve toward using legal technology as yet another resource at their disposal. A New York Supreme Court justice in support of using technology recently commented, "Judges should have some knowledge of the technology .... If [judges] have the knowledge ... it makes the case more efficient."[72]

[68] *See* Eric Scigliano, *Zoom Court Is Changing How Justice Is Served*, THE ATLANTIC (Apr. 13, 2021), https://www.theatlantic.com/magazine/archive/2021/05/can-justice-be-served-on-zoom/618392.

[69] *See id.*

[70] *See How Courts Embraced Technology, Met the Pandemic Challenge, and Revolutionized Their Operations*, PEW TRS. (Dec. 1, 2021), https://www.pewtrusts.org/en/research-and-analysis/reports/2021/12/how-courts-embraced-technology-met-the-pandemic-challenge-and-revolutionized-their-operations.

[71] *See* David Horrigan, *COVID Technology Law Update: The Law of Virtual Court Proceedings*, LAW.COM (Feb. 8, 2022), https://www.law.com/legaltechnews/2022/02/08/covid-technology-law-update-the-law-of-virtual-court-proceedings/ (describing issues of virtual courtroom etiquette).

[72] *See* Ryhs Dipshan, *As Remote Proceedings Continue, Judges' Tech Knowledge Becomes Even More Critical*, LAW.COM (Mar. 10, 2022), https://www.law.com/legaltechnews/2022/03/10/as-remote-proceedings-continue-judges-tech-knowledge-become-even-more-critical/.

15.3.2 *Wide Availability of Judicial Data*

Using technology to increase access to justice is an important step, but only a partial solution. As discussed throughout the chapter, the available legal technologies go far beyond access and search. The next frontier of legal technology will be tools that assist lawyers in their tasks that involve discretion and judgment. Imagine a system where lawyers can, early on, have a comprehensive understanding of the client's legal issues, the factors most likely to determine success, and a probabilistic assessment of the litigation outcome. Of course, a good lawyer is capable of doing all of this, but it involves a fair amount of time. The emergence of legal technology allows the lawyer to achieve these objectives more efficiently, more accurately, and at less expense to their clients.

Development of this legal technology requires greater access to judicial materials. Most judicial documents – for example, opinions, orders, motions - are deemed public documents but are often difficult and costly to access. Courts can make these materials more readily available, most easily through their own webpages. Just as importantly, courts can encourage great use of these documents by the public, by making them available in electronic format (rather than as an image or pdf). Doing so saves third parties the time and expense of digitizing the documents and focuses on developing legal analytic tools.

Litigants, in turn, could use these analytic tools to make more informed choices about their legal disputes. Many litigants already do this: Sophisticated litigants – often through their lawyers – effectively evaluate the merits of their dispute, and choose the appropriate path. Less sophisticated litigants, however, often lack the resources to make this same determination. Analytic tools can help litigants more accurately evaluate their claim: for example, whether they have a legal claim, whether their legal claim is supported by statute or precedent, and even how a court might rule.

Litigants, by better understanding the legal dimensions of their disputes, could collectively change the distribution of case filings. In this reformulation, parties could resolve disputes where precedent points to a clear resolution, allowing courts to focus on disputes where either

(1) parties agree on the facts and for which the existing precedent fails to produce a clear result or
(2) parties disagree on the facts, such that they lead to divergent outcomes as a matter of law.

Academia and private sector researchers analyzing judicial data can have a symbiotic effect on one another to better understand the litigation, the judiciary, the legal profession, and the common law itself. Some research may be of interest primarily to academics or to the private sector. In many instances, however, research will generate interest among both groups, and push each other to develop tools that satisfy the rigor of their respective markets.

In addition to making judicial opinions widely accessible, courts can also release information about other judicial documents, such as motions and orders. As with opinions, orders are public in nature, but often difficult for the public to access, depending on the jurisdiction. This data is useful as a means of evaluating the courts' performance in both civil and criminal matters, both procedurally and potentially substantively. For example, judicial research has revealed that judges are most likely to deliver a favorable ruling to plaintiffs shortly after they had eaten.[73] A large-scale study revealed that judges routinely committed both Type 1 and Type 2 errors with respect to pretrial bail determinations.[74] These academic studies were made possible only because courts shared their data.[75]

While this chapter has focused on the promise of legal technology of judges, there are reasons to exercise caution. Judges, more than litigants, must be sensitive to constitutional considerations of technology as it relates to privacy, discrimination, and access to the courts. Not every technology will be applicable to the courts, and even those that are may prove problematic. In addition, logistical issues abound, in part because of the decentralized nature of courts, both across and within jurisdictions, which impedes data availability.[76] Lastly, judicial governance of technology is highly complex, for which scholars provide conceptual frameworks.[77] Ultimately, courts should neither delegate their authority to legal technology nor eschew it altogether. Rather, like much of the elite practicing bar today, courts can use this technology as a tool to inform their own independent decisions.[78]

15.4. CONCLUSION

This chapter embraces the potential virtue of legal technology to improve systemic access-to-justice challenges. The idea of using data to better understand the law is

[73] *See* Shai Danziger, Jonathan Levav & Liora Avnaim-Pesso, *Extraneous Factors in Judicial Decisions*, 108 Proc. Nat'l Acad. Scis. 6889 (2011).

[74] *See* Jon Kleinberg et al., *Human Decisions and Machine Predictions*, 133 Q. J. Econ. 237 (2017).

[75] *See* Sean Rehaag, *Judicial Review of Refugee Determinations: The Luck of the Draw?* (Compar. Rsch. in L. & Pol. Econ., Research Paper No. 9/2012, 2012), http://digitalcommons.osgoode.yorku.ca/clpe/7.

[76] For a description of these challenges, see Eleni Panagou & Manolis Vavalis, *Toward an Open and Decentralized Case Law Curation Ecosystem*, 15 PLoS ONE e0240041 (2020).

[77] *See, e.g.*, David F. Engstrom & R. J. Vogt, *The New Judicial Governance: Courts, Data, and the Future of Civil Justice*, 71 DePaul L. Rev. (forthcoming 2023).

[78] *See* State v. Loomis, 881 N.W.2d 749 (Wis. 2016) (stating that courts should use an algorithmic tool to determine bail risk only if they have the capacity for effectively evaluating the tool's efficacy).

itself well established. Back in 1897, Oliver Wendell Holmes famously wrote, "For the rational study of the law the black-letter man may be the man of the present, but the man of the future is the man of statistics and the master of economics."[79] In this respect, the recent developments in legal technology are simply fulfilling Holmes' prophesy. The judiciary can and should play an active role in this progression.

79 Oliver Wendell Holmes, *The Path of the Law*, 10 HARV. L. REV. 457, 469 (1897).

16

The Civil Justice Data Gap

Tanina Rostain and Amy O'Hara

Every year, millions of people living on the margins cycle through a civil justice system that exacts an enormous toll on their housing security and financial well-being. Eviction rates reached crisis levels before the coronavirus pandemic and are expected to continue to climb as emergency moratoria have been lifted.[1] Debt-collection cases have not received the same national attention as evictions, but may represent a quarter to a third of state civil cases according to recent statistics.[2] The pandemic has contributed to a rise in consumer debt, creating a looming threat of increased collection cases.[3] Civil courts have become eviction and collection mills, whose apparent function is issuing judgments to help landlords and debt collectors grind down tenants and creditors.[4] According to available evidence, the civil justice

Thanks to James Carey, Amy Olivero, Garrett Quenneville, Anna L. Stone, Stephanie Straus, and Eoin Whitney for their contributions to this chapter and to the Georgetown Civil Justice Data Commons project. This work is supported by grants from the National Science Foundation (AWD 1952067) and The Pew Charitable Trusts.

1 *See* Kathryn M. Leifheit et al., *Expiring Eviction Moratoriums and COVID-19 Incidence and Mortality*, 190 Am. J. Epidemiology 2503 (2021); Jacob Haas, Jasmine Rangel, Juan Pablo Garnham & Peter Hepburn, *Preliminary Analysis: Eviction Filing Trends after the CDC Moratorium Expiration*, Eviction Lab (Dec. 9, 2021), https://evictionlab.org/updates/research/eviction-filing-trends-after-cdc-moratorium/.

2 There is a lack of comprehensive data of debt-collection suits across state court systems. As of 2013, an estimated 24 percent of all state civil cases were debt collection. Of the twelve states that reported court data about debt claims past 2013, nine reported that debt claims were the most common type of civil case. In Texas, the number of debt-collection suits more than doubled and constituted about 30 percent of Texas' civil docket between 2014 and 2018. *See* Pew Trs., How Debt Collectors Are Transforming the Business of State Courts (2020), https://www.pewtrusts.org/en/research-and-analysis/reports/2020/05/how-debt-collectors-are-transforming-the-business-of-state-courts.

3 *See* Pamela Foohey, Dalié Jiménez & Christopher K. Odinet, *The Debt Collection Pandemic*, 11 Cal. L. Rev. Online 222 (2020).

4 *See* Paula L. Hannaford-Agor et al., Nat'l Ctr. for State Cts., The Landscape of Civil Litigation in State Courts (2015), https://www.ncsc.org/__data/assets/pdf_file/0020/13376/civiljusticereport-2015.pdf.

system is failing in its promise to protect the rights of poor people against powerful private interests and entrenching them further in poverty.

But "available evidence" is sparse. We know little about how courts dispense justice or how court entanglements affect peoples' lives. Our knowledge of how civil justice institutions function, despite the system's societal centrality, is piecemeal and relies on extrapolation from site-specific or out-of-date studies. In a system where all parties are meant to be treated equally, we don't know whether the race, ethnic origin, or gender of litigants affects case outcomes. We can't determine whether there are biases in the system or where they are concentrated. We don't know what events precipitate civil justice involvement, nor the consequences that flow from it. We don't know how unrepresented individuals fare against businesses with representation. We don't even have an exact number of how many unrepresented litigants there are or in which types of cases they are concentrated[5] or whether the scarce resources that *are* available are being allocated effectively and equitably.

As a recent report by the American Academy of Arts and Sciences emphasizes, many institutions and individuals have an interest in answering questions like these about the functioning of the justice system.[6] State, county, and municipal courts are a central feature in the lives of low-income people and, increasingly, the middle class. Courts have an obligation to the people who pass through their doors to administer justice equitably. Litigants are entitled to know whether courts are living up to this ideal. Courts and legal services providers have particular interests in gaining operational insights about how well they serve the people before them and how effectively they allocate their resources. And the public, which funds the civil justice system, has a stake in knowing how well the civil justice system functions and whether its outcomes are just.[7] Erosion of public trust puts the legitimacy of this system at risk.[8]

In other public spheres, large datasets are producing new and actionable knowledge about the performance of public and private institutions. Health care and health insurance datasets have been linked to show that more years of childhood Medicaid eligibility correlate with fewer adult hospitalizations for Black Americans.[9] In Cuyahoga County, Ohio, the Center on Urban Poverty and Community

5 *See SLRN Brief: How Many SRLs? (SRLN 2019)*, SELF-REPRESENTED LITIG. NETWORK (Mar. 22, 2022), https://www.srln.org/node/548/srln-brief-how-many-srls-srln-2015 (estimating more than 75 percent of civil court cases have at least one self-represented litigant); *see also* Jessica Steinberg, *Demand Side Reform in the Poor People's Court*, 47 CONN. L. REV. 741, 750–51 (2015) (in landlord tenant matters typically 90 percent of tenants appear unrepresented while 90 percent of landlords appear with counsel).

6 *See* AM. ACAD. OF ARTS & SCIS., MEASURING CIVIL JUSTICE FOR ALL: WHAT DO WE KNOW? WHAT DO WE NEED TO KNOW? HOW CAN WE KNOW IT? (2021), https://www.amacad.org/publication/measuring-civil-justice-all.

7 *See* GEOFFREY MCGOVERN & MICHAEL D. GREENBERG, WHO PAYS FOR JUSTICE? (2014).

8 *See* AM. ACAD. OF ARTS & SCIS., MEASURING CIVIL JUSTICE.

9 Laura R. Wherry, Sarah Miller, Robert Kaestner & Bruce D. Meyer, *Childhood Medicaid Coverage and Later-Life Health Care Utilization*, 100 REV. ECON. STAT. 287 (2018).

Development has used data from more than thirty-five different administrative programs to create two integrated data systems for research.[10] Linkages in these comprehensive data systems have shown increased shelter use by evicted families and identified downstream consequences such as childhood lead poisoning.[11]

As these projects show, big data are particularly powerful in the study of social institutions by delivering variety, volume, and velocity. Real-time data are captured for nearly all of our everyday whereabouts, purchases, searches, and interactions with private individuals and public institutions. Everyday interactions with other people and social institutions are chronicled by the terabyte through active or passive engagement with digital technologies. Data are created and available in near-real time.[12] These features produce broader knowledge than was possible with limited size and site-specific case studies, permitting both wide generalizations and highly granular views into the functioning of institutions and their effects on people's lives.

What explains the lack of data in civil justice? For one, not every court collects all case level information in electronic form. Some simply don't have the resources; others don't see value in doing so. Even where data exist, rules often restrict access. Courts are unwilling to share data, or uncomfortable doing so, for fear that vulnerable litigants will be harmed or that the data will be used to cast a critical eye on courts themselves.[13] Courts lack resources and incentives to improve their data, resulting in civil justice data that are incomplete, inaccurate, dirty, and disorganized. Despite the uniformity of needs among court administrators and a small handful of vendors providing case management systems, there are no widely used standards for data collection and harmonization. The absence of common standards makes it impossible to compare jurisdictions or even to study individual jurisdictions across different case types and subject matters.

The lack of high-quality, accessible data is a major deterrent to producing knowledge about civil justice. To obtain data, researchers must engage in a hunt-and-peck exercise that may or may not yield useful results. As a first step, they need to locate datasets that may be useful to them. Then, they determine whether there are legal limitations to obtaining the data. If the data are not publicly available but a

[10] *See CHILD Data System*, *The Ctr. on Urb. Poverty & Cmty. Dev.*, https://case.edu/socialwork/povertycenter/data-systems/child-data-system; *see also Harnessing Data for Social Good*, NEOCANDO, https://neocando.case.edu/.

[11] Francisca García-Cobián Richter et al., The Cleveland Eviction Study: Downstream Paths of Evictions into Homelessness and Loss of Human Capital (2019), https://lasclev.org/wp-content/uploads/Costs-of-Eviction_11052019.pdf; Claudia Coulton et al., Downstream Consequences of Childhood Lead Poisoning: A Longitudinal Study of Cleveland Children from Birth to Early Adulthood (2020), https://case.edu/socialwork/povertycenter/sites/case.edu.povertycenter/files/2020-07/Downstream_06182020_rev07082020.pdf.

[12] Rebecca A. Johnson & Tanina Rostain, *Tool for Surveillance or Spotlight on Inequality? Big Data and the Law*, 16 Ann. Rev. L. & Soc. Sci. 453 (2020).

[13] *See infra* Section 16.2.

court has discretion to share them, researchers must engage in protracted negotiations to obtain access. Once researchers have access, they must spend weeks cleaning the data. The process of finding and obtaining data and making them usable deters researchers from studying the civil justice system and impedes the development of evidence-based policies in the civil justice arena. Although data science is producing new insights about many social institutions, few data scientists are working in the civil justice field.

This chapter considers how improving data collection, sharing data, and ease of data analysis can make civil justice institutions more accountable to government institutions, their constituents, and the public at large, and create opportunities for civil justice reform.

Section 16.1 starts by identifying key questions that analysts are well positioned to address. These include problems of structural racism and bias against people of color, the advantages of being represented, and the antecedents and consequences of entanglement in the civil justice system. Section 16.2 considers the obstacles to increasing knowledge about civil justice problems. These obstacles include the lack of good (or any) data, legal barriers to obtaining data, and real and perceived institutional risks to sharing data.

Section 16.3 then describes a civil justice data commons as one promising avenue that the authors are prototyping to address current access-to-justice challenges[14] and free up the empirical opportunities offered by civil justice data.[15] This Civil Justice Data Commons (CJDC) functions as a trusted intermediary among data sharers and data users. The CJDC's technical infrastructure is automated to satisfy conditions for the supply of data and the demands of users. To facilitate access for researchers – speeding up the evidence-building process – the CJDC hosts documented, harmonized data, cleans and links files as needed, and provides tools and analytic software for research. The data commons allows for faster access to data for academic and policy research, as well as operational insights for courts and civil justice institutions to improve equity and service.

Several different tech trends examined in this volume – from ODR to online courts to e-filing to the growing menu of legal tech tools – will transform civil justice in the years to come. Each will increase both the amount of and focus on data. A key

[14] *See* Robert L. Grossman et al., *A Case for Data Commons: Toward Data Science as a Service*, 18 Computing Sci. Eng'g 10 (2016); *see also* Robert L. Grossman et al., *The Design of a Community Science Cloud: The Open Science Data Cloud Perspective*, 2012 High Performance Computing, Networking, Storage & Analysis 1051 (2012); Margaret Hagan, Jameson Dempsey & Jorge Gabriel Jiménez, *A Data Commons for Law*, Legal Design & Innovation (Apr. 1, 2019), https://medium.com/legal-design-and-innovation/a-data-commons-for-law-60e4c4ad9340.

[15] *See* Robert L. Grossman, *How Data Commons Can Support Open Science*, Sage Bionetworks (2019), https://sagebionetworks.org/in-the-news/how-data-commons-can-support-open-science/; *see also* Charles Q. Choi, *Migrating Big Astronomy Data to the Cloud*, 584 Nature 159 (2020).

question is whether the civil justice system – and the judges, lawyers, litigants, and justice partners who inhabit it – can harness data to promote the just, equitable, and efficient administration of justice. A civil justice data commons can help answer that question.

16.1 IMPORTANT QUESTIONS ABOUT THE FAIRNESS OF THE CIVIL JUSTICE SYSTEM

16.1.1 *Structural Racism and Bias*

In the criminal justice context, abundant high-quality policing and court data have allowed researchers to document the scope and depth of structural racism and other biases. This research underscores what smaller-scale observational and quantitative studies had previously shown: Black Americans are systematically treated worse than white Americans at every juncture of the criminal justice system. Policing data have shown that Black people are more likely to be subjected to roadside stops and are more likely to be the victims of lethal force.[16] Court datasets have allowed researchers to show that Black drivers are likely to pay higher traffic fines than white drivers[17] and that judicial mechanics and the peremptory challenge system adversely affect Black defendants.[18] If you are Black, you are more likely to receive a longer sentence than a white person in a plea deal.[19] These studies confirm the systemic pervasiveness of racism in criminal justice. Data access permits studies with sufficient granularity to pinpoint specific areas where race might have the strongest magnifying effect, which may suggest priorities for formulating and testing reforms.

Large-scale studies that investigate the impact of race, ethnic origin, and gender in the civil justice system are sparse but show promise.[20] One major foray comes from the Princeton Eviction Lab, which published the first study documenting the

[16] Emma Pierson et al., *A Large-Scale Analysis of Racial Disparities in Police Stops across the United States*, 4 NATURE HUM. BEH. 736 (2020); James W. Buehler, *Racial/Ethnic Disparities in the Use of Lethal Force by US Police, 2010–2014*, 107 AM. J. PUB. HEALTH 295 (2017); Cody T. Ross, *A Multi-Level Bayesian Analysis of Racial Bias in Police Shootings at the County-Level in the United States, 2011–2014*, 10 PLoS ONE e0141854 (2015).

[17] Felipe Goncalves & Steven Mello, *A Few Bad Apples? Racial Bias in Policing*, 111 AM. ECON. REV. 1406 (2020).

[18] Scott Kostyshak & Neel Sukhatme, *Down to the Last Strike: The Effect of the Jury Lottery on Criminal Convictions* (Geo. L. Fac. Publ'ns & Other Works, Working Paper No. 2156, 2020).

[19] *See* Angela J. Davis, *Racial Fairness in the Criminal Justice System: The Role of the Prosecutor*, 39 COLUM. HUM. RTS. L. REV. 202, 205–11 (2007).

[20] *See* Matthew Desmond, *Eviction and the Reproduction of Urban Poverty*, 118 AM. J. SOCIO. 88 (2012); Peter Hepburn, Renee Louis & Matthew Desmond, *Racial and Gender Disparities among Evicted Americans*, 7 SOCIO. SCI. 649 (2020); BRIAN J. MCCABE & EVA ROSEN, EVICTION IN WASHINGTON, DC: RACIAL AND GEOGRAPHIC DISPARITIES IN HOUSING INSTABILITY (2020), https://www.streetsensemedia.org/wp-content/uploads/2020/10/Georgetown-University-DC-Eviction-Report-2014-2018.pdf.

demographics of evicted renters on a national scale. Using a dataset containing 4.1 million records from public, private, and commercial sources, the study showed Black renters experienced the highest rate of eviction filings and judgments, and Black and Latin female renters faced higher eviction rates than their male counterparts.[21] Data-driven studies like those by the Eviction Lab can demonstrate the magnitude of inequity in the civil justice system. Their study is a significant step in understanding which demographic groups in the United States are suffering the brunt of the eviction crisis and raises new questions about how the civil legal system plays into this crisis. Do differing eviction rates among racial and gender groups mirror structural biases in society at large? Or does the civil justice system magnify these problems? Accessible civil justice data are needed not only to understand the system's role in replicating or worsening structural biases in eviction cases, but also its role in consumer debt and other areas that disproportionately affect poor people, people of color, and women. Population-level datasets contain large numbers of observations and variables to help pinpoint court contacts and processes that have the greatest impact.

16.1.2 *When Do Lawyers Make a Difference (and Why?)*

Civil justice data can also shed light on whether lawyers make a difference in outcomes and, if so, in what types of cases and why.[22] To date, studies comparing represented and non-represented parties have been site-specific and relied on observational data or randomized controlled trials. Consequently, their findings are not easily generalized to other subject matters and other settings. Large-scale court datasets will allow comparisons across courts, subject matter areas, types of representation, and jurisdictions, producing more nuanced knowledge with broader impact.

The few studies investigating whether being represented by a lawyer affects the outcome of a case tend to show that representation makes a difference, but how much difference it makes depends in large part on the type of service provided, case type, and procedural complexity of the case.[23] Some research suggests that, in select

[21] Hepburn, Louis & Desmond, *Racial and Gender Disparities among Evicted Americans.*

[22] *See generally* Rebecca Sandefur, *The Impact of Counsel: An Analysis of Empirical Evidence*, 9 SEATTLE J. FOR SOC. J. 51 (2010).

[23] *See* Ellen Degnan, Thomas Ferriss, D. James Greiner & Roseanna Sommers, Trapped in Marriage (Oct. 23, 2018) (unpublished manuscript), https://papers.ssrn.com/sol3/papers.cfm?abstract_idwww3277900 (suggesting that legal representation may have varied results based on setting and form of service offered); D. James Greiner, Cassandra W. Pattanayak & Jonathan P. Hennessy, *The Limits of Unbundled Legal Assistance: A Randomized Study in a Massachusetts District Court and Prospects for the Future*, 126 HARV. L. REV. 901 (2013) (finding full representation for eviction made a difference as compared to limited assistance); D. James Greiner & Cassandra Wolos Pattanayak, *Randomized Evaluation in Legal Assistance: What Difference Does Representation (Offer and Actual Use) Make?* 121 YALE L.J. 2118 (2012) (reporting that an offer of full representation by a law school clinic in unemployment benefits

settings, being represented by a non-lawyer advocate confers similar advantages to being represented by a lawyer. These studies raise important questions about how courts should deal with cases where one or both parties are not represented by a lawyer and how legal services providers should prioritize the provision of their resources.

Data-driven research confirming and extending these findings offers insights into how to "level the playing field" between represented and unrepresented parties. Some jurisdictions have changed their rules to allow judges a more active role in explaining the law or eliciting facts to a pro se party.[24] Courts might also focus on simplifying procedures or prohibiting lawyers in certain matters or fora altogether.[25]

Research showing whether and when being represented affects case outcomes can also be important for legal services providers allocating resources. In legal aid settings, eligible applicants may receive representation depending on the availability of a lawyer specializing in their type of case. Research on the differential effects of representation might persuade legal services providers, which turn away almost half of eligible applicants,[26] to shift their resource priorities. Some providers report that they have already begun targeting their resources to clients with income levels just below eligibility cut-offs after data-based research showed representation did not affect outcomes at lower income levels.[27] Large-scale data studies about the impact of lawyers would also provide evidence for or against various approaches being promoted to increase access to the civil justice system. With the eviction crisis

eligibility determination appeals delayed proceedings by two weeks; impact of actual use was unclear); Rebecca L. Sandefur, *Elements of Professional Expertise: Understanding Relational and Substantive Expertise through Lawyers' Impact*, 80 AM. SOCIO. REV. 909 (2015); Sandefur, *The Impact of Counsel*, at 73 (across forty-five studies, lawyers have significant impact on case outcome, but effect did not correlate with legal expertise; greatest effect was in procedurally complex cases); Anna E. Carpenter, Alyx Mark & Colleen F. Shanahan, *Trial and Error: Lawyers and Nonlawyer Advocates*, 42 LAW & SOC. INQUIRY 1023 (2017) (legal representation has benefits in unemployment cases, but non-lawyer advocates are less equipped to challenge judges or advance novel claims).

24 *See Self-Representation on Justice Index*, NAT'L CTR. FOR ACCESS TO JUSTICE, https://ncaj.org/state-rankings/2020/self-representation.

25 *See* Steinberg, *Demand Side Reform*, at 786–802; *see also An Overview of Small Claims Court*, MICH. LEGAL HELP, https://michiganlegalhelp.org/self-help-tools/money-and-debt/overview-of-small-claims-court (stating that no lawyers are allowed in small claims court in Michigan); *Basic Considerations and Questions*, STATE OF CAL. DEP'T OF CONSUMER AFFS., https://www.dca.ca.gov/publications/small_claims/basic_info.shtml (in California small claims court, rules are simplified, hearings are informal, and lawyers are typically not permitted).

26 LEGAL SERVS. CORP., THE JUSTICE GAP: MEASURING THE UNMET CIVIL LEGAL NEEDS OF LOW-INCOME AMERICANS 42–44 (2017), https://www.lsc.gov/justicegap2017.

27 Interview with Jim Sandman (Jan. 27, 2021); *see, e.g.*, Rachel Dissell, *Legal Aid "Securing Stability" for Low-Income Clients, Report Shows*, CLEVELAND.COM (June 16, 2019),https://www.cleveland.com/news/2019/06/legal-aid-securing-stability-for-low-income-clients-report-shows.html (Cleveland's Legal Aid turns away about half of qualifying low-income clients due to lack of resources).

worsening, the movement to fund lawyers to represent tenants at risk of eviction is gaining ground.[28]

Such studies might also be helpful in answering the question of which types of services make a difference. In the last ten years, limited scope representation has been promoted as an important means of increasing access to justice by allowing fewer lawyers to represent more people, an approach that many legal services providers are pursuing on the assumption that they can help more clients.[29] Despite the growth of brief advice services,[30] there is little evidence that these services have a positive effect on outcomes. One study found that while brief advice assisted clients in surmounting procedural barriers, it did not have significant effects on substantive outcomes.[31] However, this study, which focused on the evictions caseload of a legal aid provider in San Mateo County during the summer of 2009, may not be generalizable to other settings.

Improving short-term outcomes – helping a client win a specific case, stay in their home, or avoid wage garnishment – is one measure of effective representation. Others include helping clients understand the law, supporting them through the process, and empowering them to advocate for themselves.[32] An understanding of whether and when representation makes a difference is important knowledge to have in allocating scarce resources among eligible applicants who live in poverty and seek legal assistance.

16.1.3 *Civil Justice Involvement and Poverty*

The questions we have identified so far focus on whether civil justice institutions treat people fairly, allocate resources equitably, and achieve just results. Other research avenues focus on the people involved, not the court encounters themselves.

[28] Seven cities have enacted laws guaranteeing the right to counsel for low-income people in eviction cases: Cleveland, OH; New York City, NY; Boulder, CO; San Francisco, CA; Baltimore, MD; Newark, NJ; and Philadelphia, PA. *See* Sandra Park & John Pollock, *Tenants' Right to Counsel Is Critical to Fight Mass Evictions and Advance Race Equity during the Pandemic and Beyond*, ACLU NEWS & COMMENT. (Jan. 12, 2021), https://www.aclu.org/news/racial-justice/tenants-right-to-counsel-is-critical-to-fight-mass-evictions-and-advance-race-equity-during-the-pandemic-and-beyond; *see also* Beth Harrison, *District of Columbia Joins Right to Counsel Movement with New Eviction Defense Funding*, MGMT. INFO. EXCH. J. (Fall 2017), at 41, 41–42.

[29] *See* Jessica K. Steinberg, *In Pursuit of Justice? Case Outcomes and the Delivery of Unbundled Legal Services*, 18 GEO. J. POVERTY LAW & POL'Y 453, 453–56 (2011).

[30] *See* LEGAL SERVS. CORP., THE JUSTICE GAP, at 31–32 (citing that 40 percent of low-income people seeking professional legal help receive only legal advice; only 20 percent receive full representation in court); *see also* NPC RSCH., SARGENT SHRIVER CIVIL COUNSEL ACT EVALUATION 3 (2020), https://www.srln.org/node/1515/report-sargent-shriver-civil-counsel-act-report-legislature-judicial-council-california (stating that between 2012 to 2020, 39 percent of low-income litigants seeking civil legal help in California received "limited-scope legal assistance").

[31] *See* Steinberg, *In Pursuit of Justice?*

[32] *See* Catherine R. Albiston & Rebecca L. Sandefur, *Expanding the Empirical Study of Access to Justice*, 2013 WIS. L. REV. 101 (2013).

Getting a Fuller Picture from Big Data. More accurate and consistent data provide opportunities for deeper understanding about individuals' interactions with the civil justice system: who enters the system (and why), how they navigate the system, and what impacts this interaction has on them in the long term. Specifically, linked population-level datasets that consider the antecedents and consequences of court involvement can widen the lens of research, leading to inferences and interventions that can scale across sites. By linking information from before and after court involvement, it may be possible to understand mechanisms that help avoid entanglement in the justice system or to mitigate its negative effects. This research shifts the emphasis away from court processes and legal resources to understanding and addressing the conditions and events that lead up to court involvement to begin with. In doing so, it may help people avoid being evicted by landlords or sued by debt collectors altogether.[33]

This type of analysis is already being done at other intersections of poverty and policy. For example, researchers in Sonoma County, California, integrated four years of county and state records from health, mental health, substance abuse, housing, criminal justice, and human services systems.[34] This cross-domain dataset showed that 1 percent of the population accounted for one-quarter of jail time and behavioral health services and half of overnight homeless housing.[35] Another study linked administrative records from the Child Care and Development Fund, a federal subsidy program, with American Community Survey data to reveal that women who worked full-time but had less social support were more likely to receive the child care subsidy.[36] The study considered characteristics of the mother, such as education level, attainment of labor skills, and community ties, and found that relative to other low-income women, the women who received the child care subsidy tended to have higher educational attainment (high school diploma or higher).[37]

Understanding the long-term consequences of a government intervention has also been made possible with linked datasets. One recent study created more than 150 million parent-child links to analyze the downstream intergenerational effects

33 *See* Colleen F. Shanahan & Anna E. Carpenter, *Simplified Courts Can't Solve Inequality*, 148 Daedalus 128 (2019) (describing how court simplification reforms mitigate but do not solve the underlying problems of inequality and the failures of the legislative and executive branches to provide a social safety net).

34 Elsa Augustine & Evan White, Cal. Pol'y Lab, High Utilizers of Multiple Systems in Sonoma County (2020), https://www.capolicylab.org/wp-content/uploads/2020/07/High-Utilizers-of-Multiple-Systems-in-Sonoma-County.pdf.

35 Specifically, the 1 percent of the population accounted for 25 percent of jail time, 28 percent of annual behavioral health costs, 52 percent of overnight homeless housing. *Id.* at 6.

36 Rachel Shattuck, *High Labor Force Attachment, but Few Social Ties? Life-Course Predictors of Women's Receipt of Childcare Subsidies*, U.S. Census Bureau Ctr. for Econ. Stud., Working Paper No. CES-19-26, 2019, https://www.census.gov/library/working-papers/2019/adrm/ces-wp-19-26.html.

37 *Id.*

of the 1970 Clean Air Act Amendment and found that regulation-induced air quality improvements during pregnancy correlated with parental investment and higher college attendance in later generations.[38] This analysis was achieved through linking decennial census data, administrative records, and survey data and utilizing Protected Identification Keys (PIKs) in order to anonymize personal identifiers.[39] In another study, researchers linked national administrative data on the labor market and earnings with records on public housing to find that children who resided in public housing that was demolished later earned more than children who remained in non-demolished public housing, suggesting that job accessibility improved for children forced to relocate.[40]

The Interaction between Poverty and Entanglement with the Justice System. Just as these studies used linked data to understand the role of government policies in the lives of people living in poverty, research linking court datasets to datasets that are indicators of health, financial circumstances, and other measures of well-being can yield knowledge about the effect of court entanglement over the course of a person's life. Research is already under way. The Institute for Research on Poverty at the University of Wisconsin–Madison found women with an incarcerated family member have a higher risk of poor health, and Black women are, in turn, disproportionately likely to have an incarcerated family member.[41] Researchers looking at Connecticut evictions found persistent, largely untreated, mental health problems and continuing housing instability.[42] Other research, using mixed methods and blending administrative data with court data, shows correlations between eviction and criminal justice involvement,[43] how neighborhood disadvantage can exacerbate racial health disparities,[44] and how eviction in early childhood is associated with neighborhood poverty, food insecurity, and obesity in later childhood and adolescence.[45]

38 Jonathan Colmer & John Voorheis, *The Grandkids Aren't Alright: The Intergenerational Effects of Prenatal Pollution Exposure*, U.S. Census Bureau Ctr. for Econ. Stud., Working Paper No. CES-20-36, 2020, https://www.census.gov/library/working-papers/2020/adrm/CES-WP-20-36.html.

39 *Id.* at 11.

40 John C. Haltiwanger et al., *The Children of HOPE VI Demolitions: National Evidence on Labor Market Outcomes*, U.S. Census Bureau Ctr. for Econ. Stud., Working Paper No. CES-20-39, 2020, https://www.census.gov/library/working-papers/2020/adrm/CES-WP-20-39.html.

41 Hedwig Lee et al., *The Effects of Having an Incarcerated Family Member on Black Women's Health*, 36 FOCUS 22, 22–29 (2020).

42 Jack Tsai, Natalie Jones, Dorota Szymkowiak & Robert A. Rosenheck, *Longitudinal Study of the Housing and Mental Health Outcomes of Tenants Appearing in Eviction Court*, 56 SOC. PSYCHIATRY & PSYCHIATRIC EPIDEMIOLOGY 1679 (2020).

43 Aaron Gottlieb & Jessica W. Moose, *The Effect of Eviction on Maternal Criminal Justice Involvement*, 4 SOCIUS 1 (2018).

44 Douglas S. Massey et al., *Neighborhood Disadvantage and Telomere Length: Results from the Fragile Families Study*, RUSSELL SAGE FOUND. J. SOC. SCIS., Apr. 2018, at 28.

45 Kathryn M. Leifheit et al., *Eviction in Early Childhood and Neighborhood Poverty, Food Security, and Obesity in Later Childhood and Adolescence: Evidence from a Longitudinal Birth Cohort*, SSM – POPULATION HEALTH, August 2020, at 100575.

Studies that investigate correlations between involvement with the civil justice system and other public institutions are beginning to emerge. For example, a study linking bankruptcy filings to administrative tax and foreclosure data found that filers who received Chapter 13 bankruptcy protections experienced increased annual earnings and decreased foreclosure rates.[46] Several studies have also appeared that focus on the short- and long-term consequences of being evicted for poor families. Using New York City housing court records, researchers found that evictions correlated with an increased risk of homelessness, long-term residential instability, and emergency room use but did not significantly worsen longer-term financial circumstances.[47] A longitudinal comparison of Cook County court records to credit bureau and payday loans data illustrated how the effects of successful evictions were small relative to the financial strain experienced by both evicted and non-evicted tenants in the time leading up to eviction actions.[48] Taken together, these studies raise the possibility that the prevailing view (which assumes that preventing eviction will have long-term benefits on alleviating poverty) may be myopic and that the locus of policy should shift from court processes to poverty-reduction programs.

More and greatly accelerated research using large, linked datasets is needed to determine the consequences of court involvement for the life cycle of poverty across sites and population subgroups. Providing lawyers and legal assistance to poor litigants assumes that the best locus of intervention to alleviate the effects of poverty must be the civil justice system – and that more lawyers and more legal assistance is the best approach. More studies may tell us, however, that assistance and opportunities upstream may be the most effective way of addressing housing and financial insecurity to prevent eviction and consumer debt actions from being initiated in the first place. Studies may also show that the impact of representation varies across race, ethnic enclaves, age groups, and population density.

Easily accessible civil justice datasets are needed to undertake such studies. In Section 16.2, we describe current challenges to obtaining such data and explain how the development of a civil justice data commons may begin to overcome these barriers.

46 Will Dobbie, Paul Goldsmith-Pinkham & Crystal S. Yang, *Consumer Bankruptcy and Financial Health*, 99 R. Econ. & Stat. 853 (2017).

47 Robert Collinson & Davin Reed, The Effects of Evictions on Low-Income Households (Dec. 2018) (unpublished manuscript), https://www.law.nyu.edu/sites/default/files/upload_documents/evictions_collinson_reed.pdf (finding some evidence evictions modestly decrease earnings and little evidence evictions increase receipt of public assistance or significantly worsen employment comes, thus suggesting eviction prevention policies could provide consumption smoothing benefits for low-income households but are unlikely to significantly reduce poverty in isolation).

48 John Eric Humphries, Nicholas S. Mader, Daniel I. Tannenbaum & Winnie L. van Dijk, *Does Eviction Cause Poverty? Quasi-Experimental Evidence from Cook County, IL*, (Nat'l Bureau of Econ. Rsch., Working Paper No. 26139, 2019), https://doi.org/10.3386/w26139.

16.2 BARRIERS TO ACCESSING DATA

An overarching challenge with civil justice data is the disaggregation of authority over civil dockets among states, counties, and municipal jurisdictions. In some states, managerial authority over the court system, and therefore control over data collection and sharing practices, is centralized in the supreme court or chief court administrative office. This makes it possible for the court to dictate that the same data be collected under the same standards throughout the state's civil courts. As former Chief Justice Bridget McCormack notes in her chapter in this volume, Michigan has adopted a uniform system that is spreading to all its counties. Connecticut has also implemented a similar approach.[49] Other states have decentralized systems where each court has the power to dictate what data are collected. In some states, courts in different jurisdictions throughout the state have the option of maintaining their official records in either paper or electronic form.[50] This results in data that are siloed in multiple institutions and starkly unstandardized. Accessibility is governed by a huge and bewildering hodgepodge of laws and policies, rendering their availability for research limited. These barriers must be addressed if data-driven approaches are to produce knowledge about civil justice institutions.[51] This section describes five of the largest barriers to access.

16.2.1 *Data Disarray*

Although courts are moving to electronic case management systems, many are still managing case files the old-fashioned way: paper. Others are using case management systems, but case pleadings are handwritten hard copies scanned into the digital system and are not machine-readable.

The absence of machine-readable pleadings, which contain valuable information about the case and the litigants, is a major technical impediment to granular research on the civil justice system. To overcome this barrier, some researchers have resorted to hand-coding pleadings, an expensive and time-consuming process.[52]

49 *See* Chapter 13 in this volume; *About Connecticut Courts: Administration and Operation of the Courts*, State of Conn. Jud. Branch, https://www.jud.ct.gov/ystday/adminop.html.

50 *See Access to Electronic Court Records*, Cal. Cts.: The Jud. Branch of Cal., https://www.courts.ca.gov/12512.htm.

51 *See, e.g.*, Robert M. Goerge, *Data for the Public Good: Challenges and Barriers in the Context of Cities, in* Privacy, Big Data, and the Public Good: Frameworks for Engagement 153 (Julia Lane et al. eds., 2014) (discussing the opportunity for states to be data stewards, responsible for how data assets are used and transformed into public goods. Administrative data from government agencies in health, education, social services, criminal justice, and employment could be analyzed by social scientists and policy actors to improve delivery of services).

52 McCabe & Rosen, Eviction in Washington, DC, at 35 (explaining how McCabe and Rosen hand-coded PDFs because the other records didn't include "key pieces of information,

Over time, the adoption of e-filing that is integrated with case management systems may alleviate this problem (though many mandatory e-filing systems exempt unrepresented parties).[53] For now, it is necessary to hand-transcribe the information or develop optical character-recognition tools that can translate pleadings that are marked with stamps and often contain handwriting into machine-readable form.

Administrative case level data scraped from online court case search websites – which pull from case management system data originally entered by hand by a court clerk – can be messy and contain incorrect or inconsistent values, making them difficult to interpret. Addressing these issues often requires a manual comparison with the corresponding docket by a specialist who can align concepts properly. That is tedious when the dockets are available online and onerous when it is necessary to contact the clerk of the court to understand which dispositions numeric codes refer to. Improving data capture is critical to improving analyses and the function of courts.

16.2.2 *Barriers to a Common Taxonomy*

Another data challenge is the absence of a common taxonomy among courts. The lack of shared substantive and procedural classification systems results from the diverse sites of authority among state, county, and lower-level courts. Different definitions across courts, even for concepts as fundamental as indigency, hamper coding and comparisons. Court procedures with different terms for various pleadings, requirements, and judgments also complicate matters. A court may lump evictions and contract cases together under "contracts," or it may separate evictions and contracts but not distinguish among consumer debt cases (with some number of these classified separately under "small claims"). A rare few might use more granular categories that distinguish medical debt, consumer debt, and other debts, as an example. Coding these types of categories is necessary to study correlations between court involvement and life-course events. For instance, being able to identify medical debt is necessary to understand how much healthcare debt collection has grown since the pandemic.

In an attempt to tame some of this chaos, the National Center for State Courts (NCSC) developed the National Open Data System (NODS), intended to guide data collection in courts throughout the United States.[54] NCSC's exhaustive effort yielded standards for basic elements such as case type, representation by counsel,

including legal representation for landlords, subsidy status of tenants, or the amount of rent owed by the tenant").

[53] *See, e.g.*, *E-filing – Public*, Md. Cts., https://www.courts.state.md.us/mdec/efilingpublic ("E-filing is *not* mandatory if you do not have a lawyer."); Cal. R. Ct. 8.71 (self-represented litigants are *not required* to file documents electronically but may choose to do so).

[54] *National Open Court Data Standards*, Nat'l Ctr. for State Cts., https://www.ncsc.org/services-and-experts/areas-of-expertise/court-statistics/national-open-court-data-standards-nods.

case filing, disposition, and case closure date. NODS is an ambitious effort to transform the collection and classification of court data. Its adoption will be dictated by the cost of implementing or reconfiguring court case management systems and the extent to which courts believe that its implementation is consistent with the court's priorities.

While NODs is a forward-looking strategy, there may be other strategies to rationalize court records from different jurisdictions that have already been collected. One approach might be to use natural language processing to identify subcategories in court documents to generate classifications. These generated classifications could then be matched to NODS categories. For instance, an algorithm might be trained to recognize medical debt from other types of debt based on the language in pleadings. Whether such an approach could capture subcategories of case types or definitional and procedural variation – likely more challenging – remains to be seen.

16.2.3 *The Special Challenge of Assigning Demographic Characteristics*

A particular challenge involves obtaining demographic information for civil court participants – a prerequisite for understanding equity concerns within the civil justice system. Under NODS, civil courts are supposed to collect race, ethnicity, and other demographic data about litigants. Most courts do not currently capture these data, but even if they attempted to, they would face a fundamental difficulty: Many, if not most, defendants in certain types of civil actions do not appear in court. One recent study of debt-collection cases in state courts found that, for courts where there was available data, 70 percent of debt cases ended in default judgments.[55] With such high rates of default, it is impossible to collect information about the race, ethnic origin, or gender of the tenant or debtor using only court data.

One promising strategy to append demographic characteristics to court data is through data linkage to census or commercial data. Linking at the per-person level requires the court records to have complete, accurate name data or other unique identifiers to make a match. Previous linkages to census data have had match rates between 40 and 90 percent, depending on the completeness of the names and addresses available, with the higher match rates possible when additional fields such as age or date of birth are available. The sparse identifiers present on civil court records have led other researchers to incorporate additional data sources. For example, Case Western Reserve University's Center on Urban Poverty and Community Development matched Cleveland Housing Court data to Ohio

[55] *See* Pew Trs., How Debt Collectors Are Transforming the Business of State Courts (2020), https://www.pewtrusts.org/en/research-and-analysis/reports/2020/05/how-debt-collectors-are-transforming-the-business-of-state-courts.

Public Assistance records to obtain race information.[56] While this linkage allowed researchers to add otherwise absent demographic characteristics to eviction files, they were able to do so only for defendants who applied for and obtained public assistance.

16.2.4 *Legal Barriers*

While individual case files are available either online or in the clerk's office in every jurisdiction, legal rules may limit access to bulk electronic case records. Although all fifty states and the District of Columbia have enacted public records laws, more than a third exempt the judiciary from coverage.[57] Even when public record laws apply to the judiciary, it is unclear whether they entitle people to obtain electronic case files in bulk form.

Approximately thirty-two states have rules governing the availability in bulk form of electronic public case records. Some states like Arizona make case file records generally available for bulk download.[58] Even in states that do not bar access to case data, county courts may have rules that limit their accessibility.[59] Some states prohibit the dissemination of bulk court records in electronic form, except where explicitly provided by a court rule or order.[60] At least one state disseminates bulk court data only to commercial purchasers. Other states, in contrast, bar the bulk download of court files for commercial gain.[61] Finally, there are states like Hawaii, which will grant some requests for bulk data as long as the entity making the request is willing to pay for fees associated with the cost of providing the data.[62] Many states also charge a fee or have terms of service that prohibit the scraping of court websites or CAPTCHA intended to prevent it.[63] On top of this confusion,

56 García-Cobián Richter et al., The Cleveland Eviction Study.

57 *See State Freedom of Information Laws*, Nat'l Freedom of Info. Coal., https://www.nfoic.org/coalitions/state-foi-resources/state-freedom-of-information-laws.

58 Ariz. Code of Jud. Admin. § 1-605; Ariz. R. Sup. Ct. 123.

59 *See, e.g., Charleston County Public Index*, Charleston Cnty, S.C., https://jcmsweb.charlestoncounty.org/publicindex. For example, in Charleston and Greenville County, South Carolina, in order to access the court records, you have to accept a disclaimer that reads in part: "Access to the South Carolina Judicial Department Public Index web sites by a site data scraper or any similar software intended to discover and extract data from a website through automated, repetitive querying for the purpose of collecting such data is expressly prohibited." *Id.*

60 *See, e.g.*, Elec. Access Pol'y for Circuit Ct. Recs. of the Ill. Cts. § 4.40.

61 *See* Fla. Admin. Order No. AOSC14–19 (amended May 23, 2014); Mo. Ct. Operating Rule 2, Pub. Access to Record of the Jud. Dep't 2.10.

62 *See* Haw. Ct. Recs. Rules 2.5, 10.16, 10.17.

63 *See Just One Look: Alabama's ON-DEMAND Public Access to Trial Court Records*, Ala. Cts., https://pa.alacourt.com/default.aspx (illustrating that the state of Alabama charges $9.99 for a name search that includes one case detail; $9.99 for a case number search that includes one case detail; $5.00 for the first twenty pages of images and $0.50 per page thereafter; and $19.99 for case monitoring for the lifetime of the case if it is a district case and $29.99 if it is a circuit

states may have different privacy policies for court records with varying levels of restrictions.[64]

16.2.5 *Institutional Barriers*

Institutional barriers are arguably the most important to address to facilitate data sharing. In preliminary planning interviews for the CJDC, we found a wide spectrum of views among judges and court administrators about the value of collecting and sharing data. Some judges did not view the data as valuable for either research or operational purposes; others strongly believed that research on aspects of the civil justice system was important for determining how well the courts served their communities.

Courts also fear scope creep resulting in data misuse, where a project approved to study one topic veers to another and publishes a study that the data may not support. Safeguards and reviews of approved uses must keep pace with growing volumes of data. Courts may worry that errors in their data will come to light. The errors may result from hurried or flawed collection methods, or through poor data management, statistical analysis, logic, or communication. When errors arise, it is important to examine their origins and impacts.[65]

Even when court rules provide for public access to data, court personnel face administrative burdens to sharing them. They receive numerous requests for data and are pressed to develop internal custom-made approval processes on the fly. Most courts lack a data governance committee. Providing requested data is a time-consuming and mostly manual process fraught with risks of data misuse, errors in court data, and embarrassing findings.

16.3 WHAT A CIVIL JUSTICE DATA COMMONS OFFERS

A data commons provides institutions and policy makers a one-stop shop for both high-level and detailed information about civil justice problems, by giving institutions simple, secure methods to share their data with researchers, policy makers, and other civil justice stakeholders and researchers fast, frictionless, and facilitated

case); *New User Registration*, HARRIS CNTY. DIST. CLERK, https://www.hcdistrictclerk.com/eDocs/Secure/Registration.aspx; *Philadelphia Municipal Court Electronic Filing System*, PHILA. CTS. FIRST JUD. DIST. OF PA., https://fjdclaims.phila.gov/phmuni/login.do; *About This Site*, WASH. CTS., https://dw.courts.wa.gov/index.cfm; *Online Court Records Search*, BAKER CNTY. CLERK OF CT., www.civitekflorida.com/ocrs/app/search.xhtml; *Public Access to Court Information*, ARIZ. JUD. BRANCH, https://apps.supremecourt.az.gov/publicaccess/(X(1)S(ncwwtm45cm24di25fm5tozvl))/caselookup.aspx; *eAccess Terms and Conditions*, ARIZ. JUD. BRANCH, https://azcourtdocs.gov/arizona/publicTerms.admin.

64 *See, e.g.*, State of Me. Supreme Jud. Ct., Me. Rules of Elec. Ct. Sys. Rule 1(B)(2).

65 *See* Andrew W. Brown, Kathryn A. Kaiser & David B. Allison, *Issues with Data and Analyses: Errors, Underlying Themes, and Potential Solutions*, 115 PROC. NAT'L ACAD. SCIS. 2563 (2018).

data access. By centralizing data sharing and research functions, the commons can serve as a meeting place for analysts, and a space where participants can share subject matter expertise, technical tools, and research methods.

16.3.1 *What Is the CJDC?*

The civil justice data commons (CJDC) is built according to principles that underlie data commons in the health sciences, created to accelerate research on medicine and disease using large databases.[66] Like genomic and other health data commons, the CJDC is controlled by a governance regime negotiated between data sharers, data users, and the directors of the commons.[67] The terms of service reflect the data security needs and project scoping requirements of data contributors with access demands of researchers.[68] The governance model is "hardwired" into the commons' permissions infrastructure, ensuring that approved uses and users gain access efficiently.[69] Transparency is key: The commons makes clear what is the path to access, what requests have been granted, and what has been learned. Housed in an academic research center, the commons is able to act as an independent "trusted intermediary" for all parties.

The CJDC draws on the "Five Safes" framework to provide data access, balancing the terms and conditions of data providers and the needs of researchers.[70] Under this framework, the CJDC approves only "safe projects" intended to increase knowledge of the civil justice system. Researchers cannot use data for commercial purposes or for administrative purposes that have direct implications for affected individuals in the data. CJDC users are "safe people," who are affiliated with universities, courts, government agencies or non-profit institutions, such as policy institutes and community organizations. The CJDC is a "safe setting" for the data, which can be accessed only on the CJDC's platform. The data are "safe data": Data sharers certify

66 *See* Grossman, *How Data Commons Can Support Open Science.*

67 *See* Civ. J. Data Commons, CJDC Governance Model 9 (2021), https://georgetown.app.box.com/s/mj44l32ris28p7i237gci800kkrerf82.

68 The commons mitigates privacy concerns and promotes uses for the public good by ensuring a user of the CJDC must agree to certain terms, such as accepted and excluded uses of the data, in order to access the data at all. *See* Aziz Z. Huq, *The Public Trust in Data*, 110 Geo. L.J. (forthcoming 2022).

69 *See* Civ. J. Data Commons, CJDC Governance Model.

70 *See* Tanvi Desai, Felix Ritchie & Richard Welpton, *Five Safes: Designing Data Access for Research* (U. of the W. of Eng., Working Paper No. 1601, 2016), https://uwe-repository.worktribe.com/output/914745/five-safes-designing-data-access-for-research. The framework has also been adopted as a standard by institutions such as the UK Data Service, *What Is the Five Safes Framework?* UK Data Serv., https://ukdataservice.ac.uk/help/secure-lab/what-is-the-five-safes-framework/; the Australian Institute for Health and Welfare, *The Five Safes Framework*, Australian Inst. of Health & Welfare, https://www.aihw.gov.au/about-our-data/data-governance/the-five-safes-framework; and the Institute for Higher Education Policy, *Five Safes*, Inst. Higher Educ. Pol'y, https://www.ihep.org/wp-content/uploads/2021/02/ihep_fivesafes_onepager_web.pdf.

that the data they provide are legally and ethically sourced, and records in the commons are documented so the chain of their provenance is clear. Last, the commons follows the principle of "safe outputs." CJDC users must submit their analytic outputs to the CJDC team, who will ensure that the data were used for the study proposed and that statistical disclosure limitation methods have been applied to prevent re-identification of data subjects.

In essence, the data commons provides a regulated marketplace for data owners and data users. For data owners, the commons facilitates data provisioning and quality control and oversees researcher use of the data. For researchers, the commons provides an interface where researchers can conduct statistical analyses on requested data. The CJDC can enable data discovery across multiple sites and jurisdictions, allowing potential users to browse metadata documentation and propose projects. Project requests are reviewed and approved in accordance with terms of use dictated by the data contributors that govern such questions as who is allowed to use the data, the scope of the research, and the purpose for which the research is undertaken. When projects are approved, CJDC provisions data into a secure workspace with statistical applications that researchers need. By making this information more readily available, knowledge about the prevalence, incidence, and consequences of civil justice problems can be produced, reducing reliance on anecdotal, outdated, or qualitative data alone. CJDC provides a simple, responsive interface that permits researchers to determine what data are available and what research has already been done with various datasets. Users can receive updates about new or refreshed data sources, recommendations on new data topics, and findings from the community.

In its mature form, the CJDC will have a secure infrastructure to automate data provisioning and an interface for data contributors to facilitate data sharing. In addition, it will have separate interfaces for authorized researchers and civil justice institutions so that they have ready access to data for academic and policy research and operational insights. The CJDC will host only machine-readable and documented data, which will be encrypted and held according to industry standards for securely stored data. The CJDC will offer technical assistance or services to help with cleaning, harmonizing, data documentation, and linkages. Funding for the operations and expansion of the Commons might come from federal and state government and foundation grants. The prototype data commons integrates extracts of data from data contributors. A future version of the data commons may have a federated structure as well, enabling the controlled access of data from a data controller's servers. This may alleviate concerns about storage and control.[71]

[71] *See* Huq, *The Public Trust in Data* (proposing a data governance scheme for public trusts under which the data would be subject to the locality's regulation even if data is stored in a server located outside the locality).

16.3.2 *Addressing the Barriers*

Institutional Interests and Concerns. As noted above, the greatest barriers to making civil justice data more easily accessible are institutional. Courts are hesitant to share data out of concerns about data security, misuse, and errors, and findings that are embarrassing or ignite unwanted political controversy. The CJDC addresses these concerns by intermediating data sharing and access processes. Court administrators state their terms and conditions for data use, and CJDC screens requests and users, approving only requests that meet these conditions for data access. CJDC also takes over the monitoring role for approved data uses, ensuring scope and data security compliance. By using the well-established Five Safes framework for data access control, the CJDC ensures balance between the concerns of data providers and the needs of researchers. Institutions may also be sensitive to the optics of using these data. The CJDC provides greater privacy protection for data subjects than the open data portals already in place.[72] Finally, the CJDC helps courts avoid surprises by permitting output review. It is critical to have independent research and transparency but equally important for courts to be able to confirm that studies have interpreted local laws or policies soundly. Giving the courts this "heads up" can allow them to frame the findings as opportunities to address issues rather than being surprised by negative headlines.

The CJDC also provides valuable services for data sharers through the production of knowledge to increase their own transparency. We expect that CJDC documentation and data standardization will enable application developers to create tools that work across sites. CJDC data can inform institutions on where things are working well and where they are not, providing evidence to support resource reallocation.

Controlling the Data Disarray. Working with the commons is not an all-or-nothing proposal. Sites can contribute what they have and increase their data sharing over time. For example, a court may share their machine-readable docket information, knowing that key data elements are not yet digitized. Commons users may help the court address this gap, such as through character recognition software or clerical keying. This creates a win-win situation where both the court and researchers gain more usable data. Other courts may share data they know is

[72] One proposed model for how to balance promoting a data public good with protecting privacy is a "safe sharing site." In this governance model, only one party has full access to the raw data and PII. This party then controls what data others can access and analyze, restricting access to the raw data itself. *See* Lisa M. Austin & David Lie, *Safe Sharing Sites*, 94 N.Y.U. L. Rev. 581, 600–601 (2019).

discontinuous, perhaps because of a change in records management vendors, updates to laws or policies, or transitions from paper to electronic records. The CJDC staff will document the data, and CJDC users will enhance detail about the datasets and likely create code that bridges the discontinuity. By fostering a community of users, this knowledge will be shared back to the court and subsequent researchers.

A necessary step in building out the CJDC is the harmonization of court data across jurisdictions, with their disparate data collection policies and case management systems. The CJDC seeks alignment with and adoption of NODS. Important first steps are determining what court data are machine-readable across sites and documenting challenges to NODS standardization within and across datasets. CJDC also standardizes data elements across contributed files, for example, creating a common vocabulary for eviction and debt cases and geocoding location data to facilitate area-level analyses. This standardization can include both manual matching and algorithmic entity resolution, allowing an accurate picture of the *actual* cases despite typos or name changes in the data.

Much of this initial work will continue to be labor- and time-intensive until we understand paths to automate the process of aligning new sites and keeping information up-to-date from courts we have been working with. A key feature of the CJDC is user-friendly metadata (data about the data) noting the sources, time periods available, present or absent fields, and incompleteness rates. As this metadata conforms to NODS, both research and court users will benefit. This metadata goes hand-in-hand with tools to visualize the available data. This data cleaning and sorting is a significant benefit to data contributors, who likely do not have the resources or expertise to perform this work on their own, and provides a provides a clean foundation for research.

Appending Demographic Characteristics. Because court files cannot capture the demographic characteristics of litigants who do not appear in court, linkages to external data sets are necessary to produce this knowledge. The CJDC is pursuing linkages among civil justice, census, and administrative datasets to enable analyses of civil justice eviction and debt-collection cases to develop demographic information about court litigants. These data will be critically important for understanding systemic biases in the aftermath of the pandemic.

16.4 CONCLUSION

Data gaps are not filled overnight, nor by individuals or single institutions. The CJDC is as much a movement as a project. To succeed, it requires participation by courts, practitioners, researchers, policy makers, philanthropists, private industry, and the public. By making civil justice data findable, accessible, interoperable, reusable, and linked to other data, the CJDC will increase knowledge about biases that distort civil justice processes and outcomes. It can also reveal promising strategies to increase access to civil courts and deepen understanding of how civil justice involvement impacts people living in poverty. If successful, the CJDC can create the basis for evidence-based approaches to civil justice reform.

Index

Printed in the United States
by Baker & Taylor Publisher Services